Empowering the People

Empowering the People

Jesus, Healing, and Exorcism

RICHARD A. HORSLEY

CASCADE *Books* · Eugene, Oregon

EMPOWERING THE PEOPLE
Jesus, Healing, and Exorcism

Cascade Books
An Imprint of Wipf and Stock Publishers
199 W. 8th Ave., Suite 3
Eugene, OR 97401

www.wipfandstock.com

PAPERBACK ISBN: 978-1-6667-3071-5
HARDCOVER ISBN: 978-1-6667-2255-0
EBOOK ISBN: 978-1-6667-2256-7

Cataloguing-in-Publication data:

Names: Horsley, Richard A., author

Title: Empowering the people : Jesus, healing, and exorcism / Richard A. Horsley.

Description: Eugene, OR: Cascade Books, 2022. | Includes bibliographical references and index.

Identifiers: ISBN: 978-1-6667-3071-5 (paperback). | ISBN: 978-1-6667-2255-0 (hardcover). | ISBN: 978-1-6667-2256-7 (epub).

Subjects: LCSH: Jesus Christ—Healing. | Jesus Christ—Exorcism. | Healing in the Bible. | Bible—Gospels—Criticism, interpretation, etc. | Medical anthropology.

Classification: BS2555.6 H57 2022 (print). | BS2555.6 (epub).

Contents

Preface

THE COMPLETION OF THIS project has been a long time in coming.

In grad school in the NT field the agenda was narrowly focused word-studies and exegesis of carefully defined pericopes and considering how Jesus might have been fulfilling the Jewish expectation of the Messiah. Having been an undergraduate history major I had serious difficulty with the standard theological conceptual apparatus and approach in the NT field. Also I had earlier developed a habit of reading whole texts. I could not resist the temptation of reading through Josephus' *Jewish War* (reading or at least checking the Greek) and some of the newly discovered Dead Sea Scrolls that had been translated and the whole sequence of arguments in Paul's 1 Corinthians. The required seminar in the first term was a narrowly-focused word-study of the term *messiah* in late second-temple texts. In response to my carefully formulated suggestion that we broaden the focus to consider metaphors and the literary contexts of the occurrence of *messiah* or *christos* the professors' response was simply, "I think not." My reading outside of the field, including ancient history, recent (anti-)colonialism, and key books in anthropology and historical sociology was often more suggestive than the latest books and articles of mainline NT studies. From that period, for example, my copy of Frantz Fanon's *Wretched of the Earth,* its binding long since broken and the pages falling out, is heavily marked up in the margins with repeated "cf. Mark." The observations about Algerians' possession by the *djinn* from this Paris-trained psychiatrist (from Martinique) working in a mental hospital in Algiers in the early 1960s seemed to apply directly to the episodes of spirit possession in the Gospel of Mark.

During those tumultuous years in grad school (civil rights and anti-war movements), it became evident to me that the modern assumption of the separation of religion from political-economic life, the dominant

Western individualism, and the controlling synthetic constructs of the
NT field (such as "[early] Judaism," "[early] Christianity," "apocalypti-
cism") were blocking recognition of the complexities of life in ancient
Roman Palestine:

(a) the deep divide and conflict between the rulers and the people
    evident in the sources, including the division between elite attitudes
    and tradition and popular attitudes and tradition;

(b) forms of popular resistance short of outright revolt;

(c) that people did not live or act as individuals but lived in social forms
    and acted in movements

(d) that people did not think and communicate in separate sayings but
    in broader patterns;

(e) that there was diversity of both popular and scribal protests and
    movements;

(f) that Jesus was not just a teacher -- and not in separate sayings -- but
    engaged in political action and that his mission generated a move-
    ment in village communities that were the fundamental social form
    in Judean and Galilean society.

Administrative and parental responsibilities delayed publication
of articles and books that articulated these "revisionist" constructions
on the diversity of movements, on the social-political context of Jesus,
and on the mission of Jesus. In the reception of those articles and books,
the only one of those "recognitions" that was generally accepted was
the diversity of movements (see esp. Crossan, *The Historical Jesus*, Part
II). The sub-field of historical Jesus studies, like Anglo-American academic fields in general, however, seems to resist recognition especially
of the basic divide between the people and the wealthy and powerful.
And the burgeoning Jesus-books in the 1990s, still focused on Jesus as
an individual teacher in individual sayings, paid little attention to social-
political forms, and saw no connection between Jesus' teaching and the
emergence of a movement.

Neither the treatments of Jesus I consulted in preparation of *Jesus
and the Spiral of Violence* (1987), my first foray into a more complex
construction of Jesus' mission in a complex historical context—e.g.,
by Bultmann, Bornkamm, Perrin, Sanders—nor the surge of studies
that followed in the 1990s paid much attention to Jesus' healings and

exorcisms or to Jesus' conflict with the Pharisees. I resolved to address both as soon as possible. My tentative musings in classes led to insightful discussions about healing and exorcism with a most brilliant and insightful (undergraduate) student, Ana Ortiz. I regret that at the time I could not suspend other projects in order to develop our insights about Jesus' healing and exorcism. Colleagues in her anthropology major and I sent her over to pursue a PhD in medical anthropology with Arthur Kleinman at Harvard. Also in the 1980s I had intense regular discussions with Tony Saldarini about the Pharisees. The field suffered a serious loss when leukemia cut short his highly promising research on the Pharisees and their rabbinic successors.

In the late 1980s there seemed to be little interest in the field in further investigation of the complexities of life hidden by the standard controlling synthetic constructs in the field (e.g., "Judaism"), such as the differences in regional history between Galilee and Judea and the Roman conquest, reconquests, and imposition of client Herodian and high priestly rulers. Also working through available books and articles about the historical Jesus led to the conclusion that approaching Jesus primarily through his separate sayings, especially with the criteria of authenticity, was not defensible as historical method. It seemed necessary to reconsider what were the sources for the historical Jesus. Even before the surge of Jesus-books in the 1990s, interpreters of the Gospels had recognized that they were not mere collections of Jesus-traditions but stories, sustained narratives. Gospel interpreters' understandable borrowing from contemporary literary criticism, however, meant that they were reading the Gospel stories somewhat as modern narrative fiction. It seemed more appropriate to appreciate the Gospels as ancient stories on their own terms, before figuring out how they could be used as historical sources.

In the early 1990s therefore I laid out the steps of a complex research program that seemed necessary as a basis for further investigation of the mission of Jesus, steps that would take many years to pursue. It seemed necessary to investigate the historical political-economic-religious context, particularly the different regional histories of Galilee and Judea, much more precisely and comprehensively (the 1995 and 1996 books on Galilee). It was essential also, before considering how they might be used as sources for the historical Jesus, to investigate and appreciate the Gospels on their own terms as historical stories and speeches that fit well into the historical context as known from other sources (such as the Judean historian Josephus). I started with explorations of "Q" and the Markan Gospel story.

Meanwhile a few colleagues had begun to investigate the ancient cultural context more precisely and comprehensively and to explore how texts later included in the New Testament could be re-understood in that context. The field of biblical studies, of course, was embedded in modern Western print-culture. Recent research showing that literacy was extremely limited and communication predominantly oral-aural was (and continues to be) a challenge and a threat to the most fundamental assumptions, concepts, and procedures in the field(s). Learning from explorations in other fields (classics, folklore, ethnography), a few colleagues had begun to explore and appreciate how the Gospel of Mark could have been orally composed and performed. Having joined the group of scholars working on "Q" I challenged the basis of their hypothesis of different strata in the hypothetical document and I became convinced that "Q" was not a collection of separate sayings but a sequence of speeches. The poetic form of parallel lines and repetition of sounds and verb endings, moreover, strongly suggested that prior to their being incorporated in Matthew and Luke these were speeches that had been orally performed in communities of Jesus-loyalists. Such probing led to many articles and eventually the 1999 book (with Jonathan Draper) on Q as a series of speeches in historical context, followed by the 2001 book on Mark as a sustained story in historical context, probably in oral performance.

Meanwhile (again) the exploration of the Markan story and the series of speeches in "Q" as oral-derived texts were being reinforced by several related but largely separate lines of new and on-going research by scholars specializing in text criticism, scribal training and practice, oral performance, and exploration of the relation between the learning of texts from oral recitation and the inscription of those texts on scrolls (i.e., writing). These lines of research, moreover, were further challenging the standard (print-cultural) assumptions and concepts and procedures in the field. It has been a struggle to keep up with and, insofar as possible, to join in these researches and to attempt to bring together their implications for a new understanding of the Gospel stories and speeches in ways appropriate to the realities of ancient communication and communication media. All of this seems only appropriate and necessary in order to appreciate these "oral-derived texts" in their historical context (s), in order then to rethink how they can be used as the sources for Jesus in historical context.

Insofar as I am attempting to take seriously these lines of recent research and their the implications, as well as my own earlier historical and textual analyses, it is necessary to say that we no longer know what we thought we knew. The standard assumptions, concepts, and general-izations of the field are blocking fuller and deeper historical understand-ing. This is true even of the standard texts of the Gospels as "established" by previous generations of text critics. Upon careful examination of the earliest written fragments and manuscripts "revisionist" text critics have explained that there were apparently multiple versions of these texts, in-cluding considerable variation in key sayings of Jesus. The writing down of the Gospel texts did not mean stabilization of particular lines and say-ings. On the other hand, studies of long complex epics or sagas in oral performance in other fields suggest that while there is variation in the particular episodes or stanzas the overall story is consistent from perfor-mance to performance. Such lines of recent research are suggestive as we grope our way toward a more appropriate and comprehensive approach toward understanding how the Gospel stories and speeches might be used as the sources for understanding Jesus' mission in historical context.

If we take seriously the implications of the several lines of new re-search in ancient communication it seems most likely that what even-tually became the Gospel stories and speeches in the New Testament started as texts in oral performance in communities of Jesus-loyalists. The promise of this recognition has the advantage of forcing us to un-derstand the Gospel texts in their historical social contexts. Because training in biblical studies worked on the basis of print-culture and its assumptions we in New Testament studies were unprepared to deal with texts-in-performance. In the course of the 1980s and 1990s, John Miles Foley emerged as the foremost advocate of a multidisciplinary theory of the relation between oral communication and writing and of oral perfor-mance. He generously engaged biblical scholars in sessions of the Society of Biblical Literature and in a series of small conferences on the interface of oral communication and writing. As a participant in those conferences and sessions I became convinced that Foley's theory of oral performance could help develop our understanding of the Gospel texts in historical social context.

Pursuing this path, however, means moving well beyond the stan-dard assumptions, concepts, and procedures of New Testament studies.

In the chapters on Mark and the series of speeches parallel in Matthew and Luke I have been able to draw on my previous explorations of those "oral-derived" texts that are hopefully consistent with what we are learning from the lines of new research. Since there is not much by way of previous studies of the Matthean and Lukan stories to draw on, my exploration of those texts-in-performance will be even more experimental and provisional.

To investigate the healing and exorcism of Jesus, of course, it was necessary as a first step to free them from the standard concepts in the field that had overlaid and obscured them for generations. It was a bit of a surprise, after a year of research, to realize that the concept of miracle is not attested in ancient texts but, as part of the intellectual heritage of the European Enlightenment, is projected onto Gospel episodes. Similarly "magic" is a modern Western concept, rooted in colonialism, that lumps together and obscures several different kinds of ritual practices. It is difficult to discern any concrete practice of magic or any practitioners of magic in antiquity.

Several colleagues have also recently realized that the development of the new sub-field of medical anthropology offers a helpful alternative way of understanding and appreciating sickness and spirit possession and Jesus healings and exorcisms. Since medical anthropological theory and generalizations are based on studies of contemporary societies, situations, and practices, however, adaptation for exploration of historical texts and contexts must be careful and critical. The principal theorist in "cultural" medical anthropology has been Arthur Kleinman, a pioneer with joint appointments in medical schools as well as anthropology departments (at University of California Davis and then Harvard). I was privileged to have been included in a small five-member "study group" in which he was the dominant figure when he was pursuing post-doctoral studies at Harvard in the 1960s. In his magisterial book *Patients and Healings* (1980) the influence of Talcott Parsons, the towering theorist of structural-functional sociology at mid-twentieth century Harvard, is evident in the prominent concept of "the health-care system." Parson's and others' "systems" analysis was geared to systems-maintenance in complex contemporary Western industrial societies. The subsequent "critical" medical anthropology that, in effect, moved "underneath" systems-maintenance to discern "the social production of illness" is more suggestive for understanding the circumstances of Judeans and Galileans in early Roman Palestine and the mission of Jesus. As we enter the third year of the Covid-19 pandemic, which has more severely impacted historically marginalized and impoverished people, we are more fully aware of how significant political-economic factors are in illness and health care.

Interpretation of the healings and exorcisms of Jesus belongs properly in New Testament studies, more particularly in the subfield of study of the historical Jesus. Because of the diversification in the field of New Testament studies, the cumulative complexification of my own studies, and the exciting new lines of research into communications media in the ancient world, it has taken years, indeed decades to work toward an appropriate, more comprehensive approach. This has meant moving beyond what have been the standard assumptions, approaches, and the basic controlling concepts in New Testament studies. I only hope that pursing this highly complex approach will open toward new appreciation of the exorcisms and healings in the renewal of Israel that happened in Jesus' interaction and the resulting movements in historical context.

Because "miracle" and/or "magic" have been the modern constructs that have determined (and distorted) our understanding of the exorcisms and healings of Jesus and other phenomena and texts in the ancient world it seemed important to include this as a basic step in the exploration. Chap 2 is only somewhat of an abridgement of research previously presented in *Jesus and Magic*, parts I and II. Because they have been so deeply ingrained in biblical studies and related fields a critical review of how inapplicable these modern Western constructs are seemed important in order to clear the way for focus on accounts of healings and exorcisms as accounts of healings and exorcisms.

While working through the implications of recent new lines of research on ancient communications media for an approach to accounts of healings and exorcisms, I was also working through those implications for study of the historical Jesus more generally. While the purpose, framing, and functions of these somewhat parallel discussions are different, the substance of several of the steps in these reviews of researches and their implications are duplicated in chapter 6 here and in a long article in *Journal for the Study of the Historical Jesus* 19.1 (2021) 265–329.

There is a paucity of references in footnotes in chapters 7-10, particularly in those on the Matthean and Lukan Gospel stories. It seemed that calling attention to articles or commentaries focused on particular "miracle stories" separate from the ongoing story would distract from how episodes of healing and exorcism fit in the flow of the narrative and speeches of the Gospel texts.

In the chapters below, I sometimes seek what seem more appropriate translations of biblical passages. Otherwise, unless indicated, I follow the NSRV translation (with only minor adjustments). When citing passages from the Dead Sea Scrolls, unless otherwise indicated, I follow the translation by Geza Vermes, *The Complete Dead Sea Scrolls in English*.

Finally, I want to thank two of my mentors in particular and the friend who is an editor extraordinaire at Cascade Books. For more than twenty years my dear friend Werner Kelber has been my mentor on ancient communications media. Just how much and how importantly I have learned from him should be evident throughout chapter 6. In the last several years another dear friend, Walter Herbert, who had been a year ahead of me in college and then became an important interpreter of Herman Melville, made periodic visits to the Boston area. We began meeting for hours-long highly stimulating conversations about each others' work. He was generous enough to read early draft chapters and was instrumental in shaping the overall conclusions of this book. I also owe much to K. C. Hanson at Cascade Books. In many previous books he has made important suggestions and has diligently worked through my incompetence in writing. More than ever in this book he is to be thanked for its intelligibility and development of arguments. And he is a scholar in his own right. I am especially and exceedingly grateful to these friends and colleagues.

Abbreviations

Ancient Texts

1QapGen	Genesis Apocryphon from Qumran Cave 1
1QM	War Scroll from Qumran Cave 1 (1Q33)
1QS	Community Rule from Qumran Cave 1
1QSa	Rule of the Congregation from Qumran Cave 1 (1Q28a)
4Q444	Incantation from Qumran Cave 4
4Q510	Songs of the Sage[a] from Qumran Cave 4
4Q511	Songs of the Sage[b] from Qumran Cave 4
4Q521	Messianic Apocalypse from Qumran Cave 4
4Q560	Exorcism from Qumran Cave 4
11Q11	Apocryphal Psalms from Qumran Cave 11
Ant.	Josephus, *Antiquities of the Judeans*
Agr.	Cato, *De agricultura*
b.	Babylonian Talmud (Babli)
CD	Damascus Rule from Qumran Caves 5 and 6 (5Q12 + 6Q15)
Ep.	Pliny the Younger, *Episulae*
Ep. mor.	Seneca the Younger, *Epistulae morales*
Hist. eccl.	Eusebius, *Historia ecclesiastica*
Lyc.	Plutarch, *Lycurgus*
Med.	Aulus Cornelius Celsus, *De medicina*
Nat. hist.	Pliny, *Naturalis historia*

Resp.	Plato, *Respublica*
Rhet.	Dionysius of Halicarnassus, *Ars rhetorica*
Shab.	Shabbat (rabbinic tractate)
Sot.	Sota (rabbinic tractate)
t.	Tosefta
Theaet.	Plato, *Theaetetus*
Vit. Ap.	Philostratus, *Vita Apollonii*
Vit. Const.	Eusebius, *Vita Constantini*
War	Josephus, *Judean–Roman War*
y.	Jerusalem Talmud (Yerushalmi)

Modern Journals and Series

AB	Anchor Bible
ANRW	*Aufstieg und Niedergang der römischen Welt*
BibIntSer	Biblical Interpretation Series
BPCS	Biblical Performance Criticism Series
CPJ	*Corpus Papyrorum Judaicarum*
HTR	*Harvard Theological Review*
JBL	*Journal of Biblical Literature*
JJS	*Journal of Jewish Studies*
JSHJ	*Journal for the Study of the Historical Jesus*
LNTS	Library of New Testament Studies
NovT	*Novum Testamentum*
NovTSup	Novum Testamentum Supplements
NTS	*New Testament Studies*
RGRW	Religions in the Graeco-Roman World
SBIR	Studies of the Bible and Its Reception
SemeiaSt	Semeia Studies
WUNT	Wissenschaftliche Untersuchungen zum Neuen Testament

Introduction

JESUS FOCUSED HIS RENEWAL of Israel on healing the people of their sicknesses and casting out the invasive spirits that had taken possession of them. According to the Gospel sources, the principal activities of Jesus' mission in the villages of Galilee and beyond were healings and exorcisms.

Cross-cultural studies have found that illnesses of many kinds result from the debilitating effects of military conquest and the political-economic oppression of colonial rule. Such were the circumstances of the people's life in Galilee, Judea, and nearby areas that had recently been devastated by Roman conquest and further impoverished by the intensification of imperial rule. The upsurge of illnesses and spirit possession among the people corresponded to an unprecedented obsession with threatening spirits in educated scribal circles. At both the popular and scribal levels invasive and threatening spirits not attested in earlier Judean texts, suddenly appear in our textual sources for the life of the Judeans and Galileans under Hellenistic and Roman imperial rule.

The Gospel stories and speeches present Jesus' mission as a direct response to this crisis of spirit possession and debilitating illnesses. As the principal actions in his renewal of the people in the role of a prophet like Moses and Elijah, Jesus healed the illnesses and cast out the possessing spirits that had resulted from intensified imperial rule. The people responded with trust, as his reputation spread rapidly, and more and more people brought their suffering family members and neighbors to him for healing. In the Gospel sources, moreover, Jesus followed up his healing and exorcism with renewal of (Mosaic) covenantal community of mutual support and cooperation. This covenant renewal provided community support for people previously plagued by illness and/or spirit-possession in village communities that had been disintegrating under the trauma of imperial conquest and the draining demands for tribute, taxes and

1

tithes by multiple levels of rulers. His spreading fame and his renewal of cooperative covenantal community in the villages of Galilee and beyond led to the formation of a movement in which the healings and exorcisms continued.

In response to Jesus' principal activity of healing and exorcism that evoked the trust of the people, the scribes and Pharisees "came down from Jerusalem" to keep him under surveillance, according to the Gospel stories. His healings and exorcisms seemed so threatening to these representatives of the Roman client rulers in Jerusalem that they sought to destroy Jesus. In one of the exorcism episodes, the name of the possessing spirit that was causing extreme violence to the people is revealed to be "Legion," suggesting that at least some of the hostile spirits represented the Roman troops who had invaded and conquered the people in the countryside. After his mission of healing and exorcism and covenant renewal in the villages of Galilee and beyond, Jesus marched up into Jerusalem where he confronted the (Roman client) high priestly rulers in the temple. Not surprisingly this led the Jerusalem high priests to capture him surreptitiously and turn him over to the Romans, who crucified him as an insurrectionary leader ("king of the Judeans"). His confrontation of the client aristocracy and martyrdom at the hands of the Romans, however, became the breakthrough that energized the rapid expansion of the movement of his loyalists.

This book is entitled *Empowering the People* because the Gospel sources refer to the exorcisms and healings as (the effects of) *dynamis/eis,* power(s), working through Jesus, or rather Jesus-in-interaction. Galilean villagers identified Jesus as a prophet in the long line of Israelite prophets because *dynamis/eis* (power[s]) of healing and exorcism were flowing through him to the people. Insofar as it is awkward in English to say that Jesus was performing "powers" we may paraphrase with "acts of power," although it is not clear that the Gospels refer to particular exorcisms and healings as "acts of power." Because Jesus was casting out invasive spirits and healing illnesses and renewing covenantal community, the people acclaimed that he was "teaching with authority/power (*exousia*)" for/with the people, in contrast to the threatened high priestly rulers who had no authority/power with the people. The dominant conflict articulated in the Gospels was a power-struggle between Jesus and the movement he was generating, on the one hand, and the Roman-appointed high priestly rulers, on the other. Jesus was empowering the people, which was so threatening to the rulers that they eventually arrested and executed him.

The title *Empowering the People* in opposition to the rulers also fits the historical context of Roman-dominated Palestine. More precise recent historical investigations and a critical rereading of key Judean scribal texts have made it possible to move beyond the synthetic modern scholarly constructs of "Judaism" and "apocalypticism" that have blocked recognition of the complex constellation of conflicts in the historical context in which Jesus worked.

The historical visions of second-century BCE scribal circles in Daniel 7–12 and the Animal Vision in 1 Enoch 85–90 were previously taken as expressions of "Jewish apocalypticism," the "apocalyptic scenario" of the Great Tribulation, the Last Judgment, and the End of the World in cosmic catastrophe. Critical recent rereading of these texts produced by dissident scribes who had previously served the Jerusalem temple-state, however, has found that they are visionary interpretations of the historical crisis that condemn and resist imperial domination.[1] These texts explain the suddenly more invasive and exploitative imperial rule of the Hellenistic kings and the Romans as the effect and counterpart of a power-struggle between rebel heavenly forces and other heavenly forces who remained loyal to the Most High, the divine Power (heavenly King) who ultimately still ruled earthly affairs. In their rebellion against the divine governance of the world, the rebel heavenly forces had generated the violent invasions and economic exploitation of the imperial regimes. These Judean scribal circles understood their life as caught in the struggle between the rebel heavenly forces and the divine governance. But they were confident that God was ultimately in control and would bring violent imperial domination to an end and restore the people's independent life.

Evidently ordinary people understood the new situation of imperial conquest and invasive rule similarly to, although less systematically than the professional scribal circles. The Gospels, which are our only direct sources for what was happening among ordinary people, indicate that possession by various "unclean spirits" or *daimonia* had become a common experience. The people were also plagued by various illnesses, such as paralysis and blindness. In the Gospel stories, moreover, as in scribal texts, the invasive spirits and severe sicknesses are closely related to the conflict between the people and their rulers. This conflict in the Gospels matches the fundamental divide between the people and the Roman

---

1. Analysis of the scribal texts in Horsley, *Scribes, Visionaries*, chaps. 8–9; Portier-Young, *Apocalypse against Empire*.

rulers and their local clients portrayed in other sources, such as the Judean historian Josephus, as more precise recent historical investigation of the political-economic dynamics in Roman Palestine has shown.[2] While scribal circles were confident in divine restoration of the independence of the people, the people of Galilee and Judea mounted not only widespread revolts but also distinctively Israelite movements of resistance and renewal. This is the fuller context in which the mission of Jesus focused on healing and exorcism can be understood.

Rethinking Jesus' mission of renewal focused on healing and exorcism in terms of *power* and a *power-struggle* is also a way of avoiding projecting the modern separation of religion from political-economic life.[3] We can investigate how the Roman forces had centralized and consolidated their power in conquest and economic exploitation; how these forces were diminishing indebted and hungry families' ability to sustain personal and collective well-being and causing village communities to disintegrate so that they no longer had the power of cooperation and mutual support. This conceptualization in terms of a power-struggle enables us to understand how, primarily in his healings and his casting out of invasive spirits (and renewal of covenantal community), Jesus empowered the people, enabling families and village communities to resist the pressures that those who wielded destructive powers were bringing upon them.

Broadening Our Approach and Deepening Our Understanding

This picture of Jesus' mission portrayed in the Gospel sources is significantly different from presentations in many recent "Jesus-books." Whatever their theological perspective (neo-liberal, neo-Schweitzerian, evangelical, or other), these books construct Jesus primarily as a teacher, with a focus on his individual sayings. Indeed, the long "quest" for "the historical Jesus" has downplayed, obscured, or even ignored Jesus' healing and exorcism. This focus on the teaching of Jesus and general neglect of the exorcism and healing is rooted in assumptions, procedures, and

2. Goodman, *The Ruling Class of Judea*; Horsley, "High Priests and Politics"; Horsley, *Jesus and the Spiral of Violence*, chaps. 1–4; Horsley, *Galilee*, chaps. 1–5.

3. See my reconceptualization of the mission of Jesus in general in Horsley, *Jesus and the Powers*.

concepts that became standard in the study of "the historical Jesus" generations ago and have remained largely unquestioned. This has resulted in the limitations of this sub-field of New Testament studies that have kept it from conducting the investigations that would lead to recognition of how central healing and exorcism were to Jesus' mission and of their significance in the historical context. Some of these limitations are specific to historical Jesus studies and some are the limitations of the field of New Testament studies as it has developed in separation from other academic fields.

While the sub-field of Jesus-studies has focused on refining its procedures based on its long-standard assumptions and concepts, however, the wider field of New Testament studies has diversified considerably. In the last few decades several lines of investigation that are potentially closely related to Jesus-studies have been undermining its standard assumptions, particularly about its sources and how they can be used in historical investigation. These lines of research have remained largely separate, and historical Jesus studies have paid little attention to them and the challenges they pose. Meanwhile, there have been significant critical developments in other fields with which few New Testament scholars are familiar, particularly developments in medical anthropology that significantly broaden our understanding of sickness and its causes and different forms of healing in different cultures.

While these lines of research challenge the standard assumptions of historical Jesus studies, they also offer some new possibilities for understanding healing and exorcism. It may be possible to bring some of these lines of investigation together to develop a more comprehensive critical understanding of Jesus' healings and exorcisms in the Gospel stories and in historical context—the aim of this book. The project, however, is complex in its scope and procedure. It will involve critical examination of anachronistic assumptions and concepts, adaptation of concepts and comparisons from other fields, more comprehensive investigation of the historical context, and coming to grips with the implications of new researches into ancient communications media. It will thus be necessary to proceed cautiously and critically in a series of cumulative steps in four Parts and twelve chapters.

Beyond Modern Misunderstandings (Part I, chapters 1–3)

Gospel Portrayals versus Scholarly Interpretation (Chapter 1)

The first step is to appreciate how prominent the healings and exorcisms are in the Gospels. Even a brief survey of the Gospel stories shows that they present healing and exorcism as the principal actions in which Jesus was engaged. The Gospel stories in which the healings and exorcisms are so prominent, indeed Jesus' principal activity, stand in striking contrast with modern scholarly construction of "the historical Jesus" as an individual teacher focused on his individual sayings. When defensive theologically-trained scholars, under the impact of the Enlightenment, began examining the Gospels critically for evidence of the historical Jesus, stories and incidents that involved angels, spirits, and anything rationally inexplicable were suspect as "myth." Extraordinary happenings that apparently involved "supernatural" agency, including exorcisms and healings, were classified as "miracles." The meager results of the scholarly quest for particular elements in the miracle stories that might "go back" to Jesus himself reinforced the view that the healing and exorcism stories contained little reliable evidence about Jesus. Only the teaching of Jesus, mainly in individual sayings, appeared to provide credible evidence. This powerfully reinforced the understanding of Jesus as (primarily) a teacher, which continues in the recent resurgence of studies of the historical Jesus. By contrast, a brief survey shows dramatically just how prominent healing and exorcism are in all the Gospels.

Miracle and Magic: Modern Misunderstandings (Chapter 2)

In the minimal attention that recent Jesus-interpreters do give to exorcisms and healings, they continue to classify them as miracles. Because they appeared to involve supernatural causation that was by definition not knowable, healing and exorcism tended to be inadmissible as "data" for the historical Jesus. Rationalist modern scholars also defined many of the extraordinary phenomena mentioned in ancient texts and amulets as magic. Following the revival of interest in what appeared to be magic in the ancient world, some Jesus-interpreters found elements of magic in the miracle stories and some even interpreted Jesus as a magician. Jesus-scholars simply assumed that these terms refer to realities in the ancient world and that ancient texts were referring to particular incidents of miracle and/or magic. The classification of healings and exorcisms as miracles or magic thus blocked direct attention to the healing and exorcism of Jesus presented in the Gospel sources. It is difficult, however, to discern in ancient texts any terms or concepts that correspond to the modern scholarly constructs of miracle or magic. A critical review of the discrepancy between these constructs and ancient texts' references to healings and exorcisms suggests that these are inappropriate modern constructs. Abandoning these anachronistic constructs will make it possible to focus more directly on Jesus' healings and exorcisms in their historical context.

Understanding Exorcism and Healing in Historical Contexts (Chapter 3)

In yet another projection of modern concepts onto the ancient historical context, the NRSV translation that recently became standard in biblical studies, along with other recent translations, narrowed what ancient people were suffering from sicknesses to "diseases" and what Jesus was doing from healing to "curing." This followed the narrowing of focus in modern Western biomedicine to the "curing" of "diseases." Even historically critical Jesus-scholars followed the lead of translation committees in assuming that Jesus was "curing diseases."

Understanding sickness and healing is well beyond the competence of New Testament studies. In the last half-century, however, medical anthropologists have developed broader, cross-culturally appropriate understandings of sickness and healing as embedded in social and political-economic relations. Sickness cannot be reduced to a "disease," a physiological or psychological dysfunction, that can be "cured" by medical intervention. In most societies family and/or a local support network is often the most crucial factor in sickness and healing. Particularly relevant to sickness and spirit possession in Roman Palestine and the Gospels are recent studies by "critical" medical anthropologists. These studies show how, in various societies, political-economic power relations such as colonial invasion or poverty can be determining factors in sickness and healing. The impact of such factors often affect how sickness is understood and can shift in particular cultures. Critical medical-anthropological studies are particularly suggestive for what factors are important for understanding sickness, spirit possession, and healing and exorcism in the historical context of Roman Palestine in which Jesus lived and worked.

The Historical Context (Part II, Chapters 4–5)

Historical Jesus studies have been working on the modern Western cultural assumption that religion is separate from political-economic life and that the historical context in which Jesus worked was (early) Judaism. But this is a vague synthetic theological construct that blocks recognition of the conflictual political-economic-religious realities in Roman Palestine. In particular the construct of Judaism blocks recognition of the effects of the Roman conquest and the fundamental conflict between the people and their rulers that critical medical anthropological (and other) studies are demonstrating would have been significant factors in sickness and spirit possession and how people understood and dealt with them.

The Political-Economic-Social Context in Roman Palestine (Chapter 4)

In developing a more appropriate and comprehensive understanding of the historical context of Jesus' healings and exorcism we can draw upon more precise and comprehensive critical investigations. Since illness and healing depend on family and social networks, it is necessary to draw attention to the devastating effects on family and village life of repeated Roman conquests and the debilitating effects of the demands for revenues by multiple layers of rulers (Roman tribute, Herodian taxes, and tithes and offerings to the temple). This should provide a historical context for fuller investigation of the changing culture in which sickness and spirit possession occurred and were understood and for Jesus' response as portrayed in the Gospels.

Sickness and Healing, Spirit Possession and Exorcism in Judea and Galilee (Chapter 5)

Communication and meaning, like culture more generally, "happens" or is expressed and communicated in patterns and relationships and (social-political-) cultural institutions. Fuller appreciation of how sickness, spirit possession, and healing were understood in Israelite/Judean culture in particular will require attention to some of the fundamental cultural patterns, such as the Mosaic covenant. More critical probing of cultural patterns and meaning, moreover, will require moving beyond modern scholarly constructs such as "apocalypticism" in re-reading key Judean scribal texts that articulate significant shifts in understanding of what is happening in the heavenly governance of life and people's experiences in connection with the struggles they discern in that governance. Since there were cultural as well as political divisions in Roman Palestine, analysis must be prepared to recognize that the experiences and the understanding of villagers differed in significant ways from that of the literate elite who produced most of our written sources. Texts produced by the Judean scribal elite cannot be used as direct sources for the experience and attitudes of Judean and Galilean villagers. Yet insofar as the Judean scribal circles who produced (most written) texts and the non-literate ordinary people in hundreds of villages were rooted in parallel elite and popular Israelite traditions, and insofar as Hellenistic and Roman imperial conquest and domination affected both of them, the impact was similar. Texts produced in scribal circles can therefore be used cautiously and critically to project and to compare popular experiences and cultural understanding.

Rethinking and Hearing the Gospel Sources (Part III, Chapters 6–10)

The preceding steps (in chaps. 1–5) all prepare the way conceptually and explore the historical context for moving beyond the limitations (of the assumptions, concepts, and approaches) of previous studies of the historical Jesus in attempting to understanding the healings and exorcisms. The next major step is to examine the sources for the historical Jesus critically and carefully. It is in connection with the sources for the historical Jesus that recent lines of research and analysis have most undermined the standard assumptions and approaches of Jesus studies. These new lines of research have proceeded largely independent of one another. Yet they are closely related and, if brought together, are mutually reinforcing in dramatically changing our understanding of communication in the ancient world, in particular our understanding of the Gospels and investigation of the historical Jesus. By bringing together their implications it may be possible to develop a more (historically) appropriate, sensitive, and complex understanding of Jesus' exorcism and healing. These crucial steps in the investigation (Part III, chapters 6 through 10) will again mean moving well beyond the coverage and competence of standard New Testament studies and seeking help from other fields. The summary of the new lines of research and their implications for the Gospel stories and how they can be used as sources in chapter 6 lays out the new assumptions and approach that are then used in attempting to hear the Gospel sources in chapters 7–10.

The Gospel Sources: Stories, in Performance (Chapter 6)

Since before the recent revival of interest in the historical Jesus interpreters of the Gospels began to recognize that the Gospels are stories, sustained narratives in interrelated sequences of episodes and speeches. The Gospel stories (including speeches) are the sources for Jesus with which historical investigation must begin—that is with critical analysis of the sustained narratives of the stories.

The recognition that the sources for the historical Jesus are the Gospel stories, not separate text-fragments, is further complicated by more recent lines of research into ancient culture. These researches are challenging some of the most basic assumptions of biblical/New Testament studies that developed on the basis of modern print culture. Most fundamental in its implications is the ever-expanding evidence that oral communication was dominant in the ancient world. Literacy was limited mainly to ancient intellectuals and officials (in Palestine perhaps three percent of society). Other lines of investigation are finding that even literate Judean scribes learned and cultivated texts by oral recitation and that the Hellenistic cultural elite composed texts in their minds before "publishing" them in oral performance. Certainly, therefore, popular texts such as the Gospels, produced by non-literate ordinary people, were composed and developed as well as performed orally. The Gospel stories and speeches, the sources for the historical Jesus, are "oral-derived" texts that were orally performed in communities of Jesus movements. Insofar as the Gospels are stories developed and performed among ordinary people, moreover, special attention is necessary to appreciate how popular culture may have differed from the elite culture articulated in elite (scribal) texts from antiquity.

Since training in biblical studies leaves us unprepared to understand oral-derived texts, it is possible to adapt theory of oral performance developed in other fields to at least begin to appreciate the Gospels-in-performance and how to use them as sources. In particular the highly regarded interdisciplinary theory of John Miles Foley offers a suggestive approach to appreciating and understanding texts in performance, focusing on three inseparable aspects that are separable for analytical purposes: discerning the contours of the (oral derived) *text*, detecting the *context* of the hearing community from clues in the text, and appreciating how the text resonated with the audience by (metonymically) referencing the social-cultural *tradition* in which performer and audience are embedded. These aspects essential to appreciating texts in oral performance confirm the importance for modern interpreters of recognizing the Gospels as sustained stories, of knowing the historical context in its complications and conflicts, and of knowing the Israelite tradition, particularly the popular tradition, in which the performers and audiences of the Gospel stories would have been grounded.

Appreciating the Gospel Stories and Speeches in Performance in Context (Chapters 7–10)

The summary of these new lines of research and their implications and the outline of the highly regarded theory of oral performance in chapter 6 prepares the way for an exploratory investigation of how to appreciate the Gospels in oral performance, with a focus on exorcisms and healings, in chapters 7–10. These chapters are crucial steps to appreciate how each Gospel story and the series of speeches called Q portrayed the mission of Jesus, particularly the exorcisms and healings, as a basis for a more appropriate and comprehensive appreciation of the exorcisms and healings as central to the mission of Jesus-in-interaction-in-context. By far the most investigation of a Gospel as a sustained story and how it can be appreciated in oral performance has been done on the Markan story. The attempt to "hear" Mark in oral performance in a community of Jesus-loyalists as it resonates by referencing Israelite popular tradition in chapter 7 prepares the way for exploration of the series of speeches called Q in chapter 8 and of the Matthean and Lukan stories and speeches in chapters 9 and 10 respectively.

Exorcism and Healing in Jesus' Renewal of Israel
(Part IV, chapters 11–12)

The Effects of the Gospel Stories in Performance (Chapter 11)

Insofar as the Gospel stories in performance are the sources for understanding the interactive mission of Jesus we are aiming to discern not the "meaning" of the Gospel stories and speeches (the texts) abstracted from their contexts but the *effects* of the stories performed in those communities, the *work* the performed texts accomplished among the hearers. Then in a crucial step, a critical comparison of the Gospel stories and speeches helps ascertain what was the common collective memory of Jesus' mission focused on exorcism and healing and what may be subsequent developments distinctive to particular Gospels.

The Empowerment of Jesus' Exorcism and Healing (Chapter 12)

The final chapter will attempt to discern the interrelated aspects of Jesus' interactive healings and exorcisms, many of which appeared evident in the discussion of the particular Gospel stories and speeches, all informed by the steps of analysis taken in earlier chapters. Sicknesses and spirit possession as understood in the Gospel stories—far from being diseases. as in recent translations—evidently involved the effects of (outside) political-economic forces in what critical medical anthropologists refer to as the "social production of sickness" and the "manufacture of madness." The sicknesses and spirit possession of the people, and their closely related hunger and community disintegration were vivid manifestations of the crisis in the life of people who had experienced brutal violence from conquering armies that left collective trauma in its wake and of their exploitation by multiple layers of rulers. Sicknesses and spirit possession and Jesus' healings and exorcisms, moreover, involved not just individuals but also concerned parents, local support networks, and whole village communities. Jesus' healings and exorcisms, further, involved an interactive process. While Jesus, and not God or the Spirit, was the agent of healing, the people's trust was the enabling factor which is implicit if not explicit in nearly every episode. The people's trust, moreover, led to and then was reinforced and deepened by his spreading fame as a healer and exorcist. As his fame spread more and more people came in the expectation of healing. This, and other aspects of his renewal of the people, especially his renewal of covenantal community in the villages, resulted in a movement across many villages in Galilee and beyond, which continued and diversified into particular branches as it spread more widely. What held all this together was the interactive role in which Jesus acted and the people responded in trust, the role of a prophet of renewal of the people, as had been embodied in (the stories of) Elijah so prominent in Israelite popular tradition. In the dynamics of this interactive process recounted in the Gospel stories, Jesus' interactive mission generated power among the people, power of personal healing and of collective renewal, social-economic cohesion, and community well-being.

Part I

Beyond Modern Misunderstandings

1

Gospel Portrayals versus
Modern Interpretations

MODERN INTERPRETERS PRESENT JESUS mainly as a teacher, focusing mostly on the sayings of Jesus. They give little or no attention to his healings and exorcisms. If and when they do examine the Gospel portrayals of healing and exorcism they find little that is reliable as "data" for their construction of "the historical Jesus." This has been true for over a century, following the strong skepticism about the historical reliability of the Gospel sources that resulted from "the quest of the historical Jesus" that Albert Schweitzer surveyed at the end of the nineteenth century. The highly influential 1926 book on Jesus by Rudolf Bultmann, arguably the most significant New Testament scholar of the twentieth century, bore the significant title *Jesus and the Word*.[1] The focus on teachings and inattention to healings and exorcisms, moreover, has continued in the surge of books on the historical Jesus during the last three decades.[2]

1. Published in 1926, translated into English in 1934 and reissued in 1958, *Jesus and the Word* thus decisively influenced at least two generations of scholars. Bultmann included only a brief section on "Belief in Miracles." The most influential book produced by the German scholars who pursued "the new quest" in the 1950s, Günther Bornkamm, *Jesus of Nazareth*, barely mentioned any "miracles." Another highly influential treatment with a telling title, Norman Perrin, *Rediscovering the Teaching of Jesus*, simply ignored healing and exorcism stories.

2. For a sampling, Sanders, *Jesus and Judaism*, has a seventeen-page chapter on "Miracles"; Horsley, *Jesus and the Spiral of Violence*, has a ten-page section on healing and exorcism; Wright, *Jesus and the Victory of God*, devotes only ten pages out of six hundred to "miracles"; Fredriksen, *Jesus of Nazareth: King of the Jews*, gives a mere

Inattention to Healing and Exorcism
in Modern Scholarly Interpretation of Jesus

This overwhelming concentration on the teachings of Jesus and relative lack of attention to the healings and exorcisms can be explained from the modern European intellectual history in the midst of which study of the historical Jesus developed. The emergence of Enlightenment Reason placed biblical scholars on the defensive as they worked at interpreting the sacred Scripture in their branch of Christian theology. Whatever did not find a natural explanation, including many incidents and happenings portrayed in biblical stories, was defined as miracle, ascribed to a "supernatural" cause. Stories of Jesus' healings and exorcisms were included in the category of "miracles." As reality came more and more to be defined by the canons of Reason, Nature, and the modern scientific worldview, many biblical scholars found that they, as modern scientific people, could no longer "believe in" miracles. They could no longer place credence in miracle stories or in any narratives that seemingly involved the supernatural (angels, spirits, demons). As they sought to salvage parts of the Gospels as intelligible and acceptable, they retreated to the seemingly most rational parts. The only Jesus-traditions that could measure up to the canons of Reason as possible evidence for Jesus were his teachings, his parables and sayings. Unless a naturalistic "explanation" could be found, miracle stories were avoided as expressions of the "mythic" mentality of a by-gone era. They were hardly valid as evidence for the *historical* Jesus.

Critical biblical scholars also found other reasons to be suspicious of the Gospels and to move behind them to the sayings they still trusted as sources for the historical Jesus. They came to view the Gospels as products of "Easter faith," with generous overlays of theology and secondary embellishments of the teachings and deeds of Jesus. A highly influential reading of the Gospel Mark at the beginning of the twentieth century, for example, found it dominated by "the messianic secret" motif supposedly in many miracle stories, an explanation of why Jesus was not recognized and acclaimed as the Messiah before the crucifixion and resurrection.[3] In a development that illustrates the suspicion with which they viewed the "miracle stories," a number of twentieth-century interpreters, found a disturbing tendency among some "early Christians" to focus on Jesus'

---

seven pages out of two hundred ninety to "miracles"; Dunn, *Jesus Remembered*, gives thirty pages out of nine hundred.

3. Wrede, *Das Messiasgeheimnis in den Evangelien*; ET: *The Messianic Secret*.

miracles as evidence that he was a "divine man" (a charismatic miracle-doer). Some then interpreted the Gospel of Mark as having "blocked" that dangerous trend by affixing the passion narrative and empty tomb to the string of stories of Jesus' mighty deeds, so that it ended with a Christology of the cross that became the orthodox Christian interpretation of Jesus.[4]

Scholarly treatment of Jesus' healings and exorcisms in the recent surge of "historical Jesus" studies shows little change since Bultmann's work ninety-some years ago. Scholars view the Gospels basically as mere containers or collections of sayings and stories that had circulated separately. In typical scholarly practice, they sort the discrete items into categories such as individual sayings and various kinds of stories, the most extensive and important of which is "miracle stories." They then classify "miracle stories" more particularly into "healings," "exorcisms," "nature miracles," and stories of "raising the dead." But the controlling classification of episodes of healing and exorcism is "miracle stories."

Partly because the (supposedly historically reliable) sayings of Jesus also attest healings and exorcisms, many interpreters involved in the recent revival of interest in the historical Jesus repeat in some way Bultmann's conclusion in 1926: "Most of the wonder tales contained in the gospels are legendary, at least they have legendary embellishments. But there can be no doubt that Jesus did the kind of deeds which were miracles . . . to the minds of his contemporaries, that is, deeds which were attributed to a supernatural, divine cause; undoubtedly he healed the sick and cast out demons."[5] Yet the healings and exorcisms were not necessarily interpreted as something important in themselves. When included in the discussion, healings and exorcisms, like other "miracles," were interpreted merely as signs of the kingdom of God or as indicators of Jesus' authority or the means by which he attracted listeners to his teaching, rather than as actions central to his mission.[6]

The most telling illustrations of how unimportant healing and exorcism continue to be in reconstructions of the historical Jesus are some thoroughgoing recent investigations of the miracle stories. A mark of the rigor of their critical inquiry, these scholars simply ignored Bultmann's other conclusion of nearly ninety years ago, that there was "no great

4. Concise summary in Koester, "One Jesus and Four Primitive Gospels."

5. Bultmann, *Jesus and the Word,* 173.

6. See, for example, Sanders, *Jesus and Judaism,* chap. 5; and Dunn, *Jesus Remembered,* 671–95.

value in investigating more closely how much in the gospel miracle tales is historical."[7] They devoted huge amounts of time and energy to ferreting out fragmentary "historical facts" or elements that "have a chance of going back to some event in the life of . . . Jesus."[8] John Meier devoted twice as much space, 530 pages, to the miracle stories as to Jesus' message, and Robert Funk and the Jesus Seminar devoted 500 pages and five years of research, discussion, and voting (1991–1996) to analysis of "the deeds tradition."[9]

Viewing the Gospels as mere "collections" of aphorisms and stories assembled in arbitrary sequences, Funk and company purposely "dismantle the written gospels" into the words of Jesus and the stories about him that "once circulated as independent units."[10] Ostensibly recovering "the earliest version of individual stories," they test whether scenes are "historically plausible" and reflect a "core event," in order to "extract reliable historical information from the reconstructed tales."[11] Their basic stance is one of acute suspicion of these "folklore tales" that were invented for "marketing the messiah." Funk and company even break individual tales down into "status statements" and "action statements" so that they can "assess as fact or fiction each feature of the story."[12] Meier repeatedly reminds us that he remains strictly focused on one task throughout his extensive analysis of the miracle stories: "assessing the possible historical elements in individual cases" or, more broadly, "hints that the story either goes back to Jesus or was invented by the early church."[13] Throughout their extensive analyses these scholars assume that the individual stories are comprised of two kinds of elements, "fact" and "fiction," tidbits that have historicity or products of the early Christian imagination.

Both Meier and Funk et al. use the same criteria in their search for "bits and pieces of historical lore" in the miracle stories that they use to evaluate the "authenticity" of the sayings, despite their very different forms and much more limited number of independent documents in

7. Bultmann, *Jesus and the Word*, 174.
8. Meier, *Mentor, Message, and Miracles*, 648, 652, 726.
9. Meier, *Mentor, Message and Miracles*; Funk and Jesus Seminar, *Acts of Jesus*.
10. Funk, *Acts of Jesus*, 8–9.
11. Funk, *Acts of Jesus*, 24, 27.
12. Funk, *Acts of Jesus*, 30.
13. Meier, *Mentor, Message, Miracle*, 648.

which they might find "multiple attestation."[14] It is thus not surprising that they find far fewer historical elements in the miracle stories than in the sayings. Furthermore, assuming that "the parables and aphorisms form the bedrock of the tradition" and "represent the point of view of Jesus himself," Funk and company use them as one of the principal criteria against which they evaluate elements in the miracle stories for their historicity.[15] Of course they had already isolated individual sayings from their literary context, which would have been the principal guide to their historical configuration and context, and recontextualized them in modern scholarly concepts and constructs, such as "itinerant," "social deviant"—along with the modern Christian constructs of a monolithic essentialist "Judaism" (and its supposedly standard purity codes) and "intrusive Christian interests." They are thus using modern scholarly constructions to evaluate the supposedly independent healing and exorcism stories they have isolated.[16]

The results of all of this painstaking analysis of the miracle stories devoted narrowly to recovery of historical data, however, are meager. Of his inventory of fourteen healing stories in the Gospels, Meier finds that only half "have a good chance of going back to some event in the life of the historical Jesus": three cases of blind people (Mark 8:22–26; 10:46–50; John 5:1–9), two cases of paralyzed people (Mark 2:1–12; John 9:1–7); the deaf-mute (Mark 7:31–37); and the official's servant (Matt 8:5–15 par John 4:46–54). Funk et al. concluded that Jesus probably did heal the blind in the core of the two stories in Mark (8:22–23; 10:46–52; but not in John 5:1–9) and a paralytic in Mark (2:3–5; but not in 3:1–6). They also found historically credible that Jesus healed Simon's mother in law (Mark 1:29–31), the man with skin lesions (1:40–45), and the bleeding woman (Mark 5:25, 27, 29). But they dismissed the other stories in Mark and those in Matthew, Luke, John, and Q as having no historical elements.

From the seven exorcism stories, Meier finds the reliable data to be minimal. There is possibly some "historical core" behind the story of the possessed boy, the brief reference to Mary Magdalene's exorcism, and even the story of the Gerasene demoniac (which clearly offends Meier's sensibilities). The story of the demoniac in the Capernaum synagogue may be a "Christian creation," yet probably represents "the sort of

14. Meier, *Mentor, Message, Miracle*, 619–29; Funk, *Acts of Jesus*, 24–31.

15. Funk, *Acts of Jesus*, 9.

16. Funk, *Acts of Jesus*, 32–35.

thing" Jesus did. The story of the Syrophoenician woman is probably a
"Christian creation," and the story of the mute demoniac (Matt 9:32–33)
a Matthean creation, while the reference to the mute demoniac (Matt
12:24//Luke 11:14–15) may be a literary introduction to the Beelzebul
controversy. Funk and company, are far more skeptical of the exorcism
stories. They believe the lead-in to the Beelzebul controversy that some
people thought Jesus to be mad or demon-possessed, hence must have
performed exorcisms.[17] But they "could not identify a single report of an
exorcism that they believe to be an accurate report."[18]

More attention came to the healings and exorcisms of Jesus from
the recent revival of interest in ancient magic. By the second century CE,
Hellenistic and Jewish intellectuals alike were accusing Jesus of having
been a "magician." Ancient Christian intellectuals and again modern
Christian theologians defended Jesus against such charges.[19] In the wake
of revived interest in ancient magic as it had been constructed earlier
in the twentieth century, however, scholarly interpreters found magical
elements in the Gospel stories of healing and exorcism,[20] and some even
argued that Jesus was a magician. Morton Smith presented a bold and
wide-ranging argument that Jesus was a magician, based on loose comparisons of motifs in Gospel stories and passages in the so-called Magical
Papyri from Egypt in late antiquity.[21] Then, on the basis of the few stories
that he deemed trustworthy, John Dominic Crossan argued that Jesus
was practicing magic as a deviant private salvation of individuals.[22]

It appears from this review of modern study of the historical Jesus
that certain controlling assumptions account for the relative inattention
to and lack of appreciation of the healings and exorcisms of Jesus. Jesus-
scholars assume that the healings and exorcisms were (should be classified as) miracles, about which modern "scientific-minded" interpreters

---

17. Funk, *Acts of Jesus*, 50.

18. Funk, *Acts of Jesus*, 33. At the end of his discussion Meier (*Mentor, Message, Miracle*, 661) articulates the skepticism that most critical modern scholars have about the exorcism stories. Without elaboration he suggests that even theological moderates would see most instances of "possession" as mental or psychosomatic illnesses. In any case, the conclusion that "a true miracle has taken place" in any of the exorcisms goes beyond what can be established "on purely historical grounds."

19. For example, Origin, *Contra Celsum*; and Kee, *Medicine, Miracle, and Magic*.

20. E.g., see Aune, "Magic in Early Christianity."

21. M. Smith, *Jesus the Magician*.

22. Crossan, *Historical Jesus*, 303–32.

were deeply skeptical, and/or are (have elements of) magic, about which there is ongoing skepticism and debate. Jesus-scholars assumed that the sources for their "data" for the "deeds" of Jesus were the separate "miracle stories," just as the sources for their "data" for the teachings of Jesus were the separate sayings, isolated from the Gospels that they viewed merely as containers. They assumed, further, that the goal of the analysis was to establish which "elements" from the "miracle stories" might be credible, that is, might "go back to Jesus."

Having found so little by way of what they consider reliable "data" from their detailed examination of individual "miracle stories," recent interpreters give little or no attention to the historical social context of illness and healing or to the conditions of spirit possession and exorcism. Nor do they give attention to how the healings and exorcisms, some of which he must have performed, were related to the teachings or to what their significance may have been in Jesus' mission. Interpretation of healing and exorcism in studies of the historical Jesus appears to be stuck in the assumptions, concepts, and procedures that became standard generations ago.

The Prominence of Healing and Exorcism in the Gospels

The Gospels themselves, by contrast with scholarly interpretation, portray Jesus as performing extensive healing and exorcism. The Gospel of Mark presents him as engaged primarily in healing and exorcism, far more than in teaching. The Gospels of Matthew and Luke, which include extensive teaching of Jesus not in Mark's story, also present him as performing many healings and exorcisms as the principal actions of his mission. And although the gospel of John does not include any exorcisms, it has Jesus doing healings among the many "signs" he performs. A review of the Gospel stories of Jesus shows just how prominent healings and exorcisms are in their portrayals of Jesus' mission.

The Gospel of Mark

Mark is usually thought to have been the earliest and least sophisticated Gospel. The first half of the Gospel consists largely of one healing and exorcism after another, with repeated summary passages that Jesus healed many who were sick and cast out many "unclean spirits." Moreover, the disciples are appointed specifically to heal illnesses and to cast out demons, as well as to proclaim. Even the episodes of Jesus' conflicts with the scribes and Pharisees focus on or include healing and exorcism. Indeed early in the Gospel, the Pharisees are so threatened by his healings that they charge Jesus with capital crimes and begin conspiring to destroy him, and the scribes charge him with "having Beelzebul," and "casting out demons by the ruler of demons." A brief review of the Gospel can show just how prominent exorcisms and healings are in its portrayal of Jesus' mission.[23]

Almost all of the episodes in Mark prior to the parables speech (1:16–3:35) concern exorcism and healing (indicated in bold).

- Jesus called four disciples (1:16–20)

- Jesus **exorcized** an unclean spirit in the village assembly (synagogue) in Capernaum (1:21–28)

- Jesus **healed** Peter's mother-in-law (fever) (1:29–31)

- "They brought all . . . **he healed many with illness and cast out many *daimonia*"** (1:32–34)

- Jesus went **throughout Galilee** proclaiming in assemblies and **casting out *daimonia*** (1:35–39)

- Jesus **healed a leper**—and people came from everywhere (1:40–45)

- Jesus **healed a paralytic** = forgave sins, vs. scribes (2:1–12)

- Jesus called Levi & declared to scribes/Pharisees that it is **the sick who need healing** (2:13–17)

- Jesus spoke of celebrating, not fasting, because the new is here (2:18–22)

23. Ideally the following short surveys of the contents of the Gospels would serve merely as notes for each reader's own fresh rereading of each Gospel, preferably in a translation that does not have distracting indications of chapter and verse and often distorting subtitles for particular episodes. Recent scholarly translation committees (for example, of the NRSV) have chosen to use the terms "disease" and "cure" that became prominent in modern biomedicine. For reasons that will be explained later (chapter 3), however, the terms "illness/sickness" and "healing" would be less reductionist and more appropriate, since they include the broader psychological, social, and even political dimensions that may often be more important than biological factors. Similarly, in order to avoid what may be misleading demonic connotations of the term "demons" we can substitute the less ominous Greek term, *daimonia*, that is used in Mark, along with the term "unclean spirits."

- after Pharisees objected to disciples' plucking grain and eating on the Sabbath, Jesus declared that the Sabbath was made for people (2:23–28)

- Jesus **healed on the Sabbath** in village assembly, Pharisees plotted to destroy Jesus (3:1–6)

- **Crowds** from surrounding areas (Judea, etc.) **clamored for healings and exorcisms** (3:7–12)

- Jesus appointed **the twelve** to proclaim and to have **authority to cast out** *daimonia* (3:13–19)

- Scribes charged Jesus with casting out spirits by "Beelzebul," but Jesus declared **exorcisms** evidence of "strong man" bound (3:20–27, 28–29)

- Jesus declared that "Whoever does will of God is brother and sister and mother" (3:31–35)

In sum, prior to the parables Mark presents an exorcism and five healings, five summaries of how numerous they were, with three other episodes in the middle along with the two framing episodes. Two of the three episodes of calling the disciples are also about the healing or exorcism. And scribes and Pharisees appear mainly in opposition to healing and exorcism.

Again following the parables speech Mark (Mark 4:35—8:22/26) has mostly a succession of exorcisms and healings, summaries of healing and exorcism, and other episodes closely related to healing and exorcism.

- Sea-crossing (4:35–41)

- Jesus **exorcized** the Gerasene demoniac (5:1–20)

- Jesus **healed the twelve-year-old woman** (5:21–24a + 35–43)

- **healing of the hemorrhaging woman** through her own initiative/ trust (5:24b–34)

- reaction to Jesus' "acts of power" in the Nazareth assembly (6:1–6a)

- Jesus commissioned **the twelve, with authority/power over the unclean spirits** (6:6b–13)

- Herod (threatened by Jesus' as well as John's powers) killed John (6:14–29)

- Jesus' wilderness feeding of the 5000 (6:30–44)

- Jesus again crossed (walked on) the sea (6:47–52)

- **summary of healings in the whole region** (6:53–56)

- Jesus, accused, attacked scribes and Pharisees for economic exploitation of people (7:1–23)

- Jesus (reluctantly) **exorcized Syrophoenician woman's daughter** (7:24–30)

- Jesus **healed a deaf & dumb man** (7:31–37)

- Jesus' wilderness feeding of the 4000 (8:1–10)

- discussion of the feedings/bread (8:14–21)

- Jesus **healed a blind man** (8:22–26)

In sum, this stretch of the Gospel includes two exorcisms, four healings, two summaries of healings and exorcisms, the disciples' commissioning with power over the unclean spirits, and two episodes of the Pharisees' and Herod Antipas' reaction.

Striking in this narrative step is that twice a sequence of an exorcism and two healings are preceded by a sea-crossing and followed by a wilderness feeding. These two narrative sequences suggest that Jesus is a new Moses, the founding prophet of Israel, and (in his healings) a new Elijah, the prophet of renewal of Israel, associations confirmed by the appearance of Moses and Elijah on a mountain with Jesus several episodes later.

The other episodes that seem to have been inserted into these sequences include reference to Jesus as performing (acts of) *powers* (*dynameis*), but not many in his hometown because of the lack of trust there, and his commissioning the Twelve to extend his mission, with "authority/power over the unclean spirits" and the healing of the sick. Two other episodes refer to the Pharisees' and Herod Antipas' opposition, evidently because his "powers" are threatening to their authority.

The next series of episodes in Mark revolves around Jesus' three announcements that he must be arrested and executed (and rise), accompanied by the increasing inability of the disciples to understand the implications for Jesus' mission (8:27–33; 9:34; 10:35–37). This section of the Gospel, however, is framed by **two episodes of Jesus healing blind people** (8:22–26; 10:46–52). And **a healing or exorcism** follows each incident of the disciples' inability to understand Jesus' agenda (9:14–28). Over the objections of the disciples, **Jesus welcomes exorcism by a**

stranger (9:38–41). The **healing of the blind Bartimaeus,** contrasting with the "blindness" of the disciples, leads directly to the climactic events in Jerusalem.

Thus in the Markan Gospel's portrayal of Jesus mission, before his direct confrontation with the high priests and Roman rulers in Jerusalem, his principal action consists of exorcisms and healings. These are the principal ways that the direct rule (kingdom) of God he was proclaiming is manifested. And the exorcisms and healings are so threatening to the scribes and Pharisees who "had come down from Jerusalem" that they plot to destroy him.

The Gospel of Matthew

In five major speeches, the Gospel of Matthew presents a great deal of Jesus' teaching that is not in Mark, including much teaching that is paralleled in Luke. Yet *Matthew has no less healing and exorcism than Mark's story.* The Matthean summaries of Jesus' healings and exorcisms are, if anything, stronger and more elaborate than in Mark, as they set the stage for Jesus' first two major speeches. Matthew also highlights Jesus' healings and exorcisms as fulfillment of prophecies through Isaiah. A review of the Gospel will reveal that, as in Mark, the primary activities in which Jesus engaged were exorcism and healing. (The following observations are intended as "notes" to help consolidate the impression gained from a fresh reading of the Gospel.)

Following the "prologue" Matthew presents a summary that can only be described as remarkable in its emphasis on Jesus' healings, including of demoniacs. In connection with "teaching in their assemblies" he was also "healing every illness and every sickness among the people. So his fame spread throughout all Syria, and they brought to him all the sick, those who were afflicted with various illnesses and pains, demoniacs, epileptics, and paralytics, and he healed them" (Matt 4:23–25)! This is Matthew's summary of Jesus' new deliverance of the people that leads directly to his renewal of the Mosaic covenant, commonly known as the Sermon on the Mount.

In the sustained narrative in Matthew following the "sermon" (Matt 8–9), episodes of healing and exorcism dominate, just as they do most of Mark. In fact, nearly all of the episodes here parallel episodes in Mark. This narrative step includes seven episodes of healing, two of exorcism, two summaries of healings and exorcisms, and only four other episodes, including a related sea-crossing and debates with the Pharisees about eating vs. fasting. To the healings of the leper, Peter's mother-in-law, the paralytic, and the two women, Matthew adds that of the Centurion's servant and the healing of two blind people. While lacking the exorcism in the assembly in Capernaum, Matthew includes and condenses the exorcism of the Gadarene/Gerasene demoniac and adds the exorcism of a spirit that made a person mute.

This tour-de-force of healing and exorcism (summarized in 9:35), leads directly into Jesus' mission speech to the disciples (Matt 10). Significantly this begins not with instruction to preach, but with his giving the disciples "power over the unclean spirits, to cast them out, and to heal every illness and every sickness" (Matt 10:1), that is, to extend what Jesus himself has just been doing in the preceding narrative. The further instructions for mission, moreover, have the same emphasis, more than in either the parallel in Mark (6:7–13) or in Luke (10:2–16): "As you go, proclaim the good news, 'the kingdom of Heaven has come near.' Heal the sick, raise the dead, cleanse the lepers, cast out demons" (10:7–8). As in Mark's story, moreover, so in Matthew's, Jesus' and the disciples' healings and exorcisms appear to be manifestations of the kingdom.

The Matthean narrative between the mission speech and the parables speech (Matt 11–12), while having few healing episodes or summaries, is concerned with healing and exorcism throughout. Jesus' answer to John's question about whether he is "the one who is to come" points to what is happening in his mission: the healing of the blind, the lame, lepers, the deaf, and the preaching of good news to the poor (11:2–6). This healing and preaching are the manifestations of the kingdom, which is greater even than John, who was the greatest figure in history to that point (11:7–14). John and "the son of man" were attacked, but Wisdom is vindicated by her deeds. The next episode confirms that the Matthean narrative is referring to the deeds of Jesus, as he reproaches the towns "in which most of his (acts of) power(s) had been done . . ." (11:20–24). Matthew's Jesus still has his (acts of) power(s) in mind when he thanks the Father that while "these things" have been hidden from the cultural elite (learned scribes) they have been revealed to the ordinary people ("children;" 11:25–28). And it is evidently for just these (acts of) power(s) that Jesus invites those "who are weary and carrying heavy burdens" to come to him and "find rest" (11:28–30). The narrative then continues with parallels to the Markan episodes of eating on the Sabbath, healing on the Sabbath, and the summary of healing ("he healed them all"; Matt 12:1–8, 9–14, 15; cf. Mark 2:23–28; 3:1–6; 7–12). There follows one of the "formula quotations:" the healings were done in fulfillment of (one of the) servant-psalm(s) spoken through the prophet Isaiah.

The focus continues on Jesus' healings and exorcisms with his healing of a blind and mute demoniac that leads into Matthew's version of the Beelzebul charge and Jesus' response (12:22–29/32), which is more programmatic than in Mark. The key line ("since it is by the Spirit of God that I cast out *daimonia*, then the kingdom of God has come to you," 12:28) claims that the exorcisms of Jesus are not only indications that "the strong man" has been bound, but are manifestations of the kingdom come to the people. In Jesus' actions, something greater than (the preaching of) Jonah and something greater than Solomon is here! (12:38–42). The focus on exorcisms is confirmed in the next episode, about spirits that continue to possess "this kind/generation (of people)," those who resist the kingdom and its manifestations brought by Jesus—a virtual reversal of the charge of Beelzebul, with Jesus suggesting that those who accuse him are themselves possessed (12:43–45).

In the Matthean narrative following the parables speech (Matt 13), Jesus continues to perform healings and exorcisms, although the emphasis is no longer so heavily on them. That he has become widely known because of them, as well as his teaching, and that his performance of them depends on the trust of the people are dramatized in the episode in his "hometown" Nazareth (13:54–58, as in Mark 6:1–6). It is his (acts of) power(s) that have Herod Antipas wondering if he might be John the Baptist (whom he had beheaded) raised from the dead (14:1–12). As the Matthean narrative continues to parallel the Markan, he includes all of the same episodes of healing, exorcism, and summaries, with the exception of the strange exorcist (Mark 9:38–41). These include the summary in Matt 14:34–36, the exorcism of a Canaanite woman's daughter in 15:21–28, and that of the possessed "epileptic" in 17:14–21. Instead of the healing of the deaf-mute in Mark 7:31–37, Matthew 15:29–31 presents an elaborate summary of how "great crowds bring the lame, the maimed, the blind, the mute, and many others," and Jesus heals them.

He also seems to combine the two Markan episodes of healing of blind people into one episode in which Jesus heals two blind people (20:29–34). Finally, in a special touch not found in the other Gospels, Matthew has Jesus continue his healing, in the temple, after he marches up into Jerusalem and carries out his forcible demonstration dramatizing its divine condemnation (21:12–14). Thus the Matthean story, like the Markan, presents Jesus as engaged primarily in healings and exorcisms.

The Gospel of Luke

In the Gospel of Luke as well as in Matthew, *there is no less healing and exorcism* than in the Markan story of Jesus. Like Matthew, Luke includes extensive additional teaching, much of it evidently adapted from the same non-Markan "source" as in Matthew, and some distinctive to Luke. While evidently following the Markan narrative sequence, Luke "omits" a section of Mark (from the end of Mark 6 to the middle of Mark 8), and thus lacks the exorcism of the Syrophoenician woman's daughter and the healing of the blind man in Bethsaida. But Luke includes both the speech citing Jesus' healings and the Beelzebul debate from "Q" and includes an otherwise unknown exorcism episode and a healing episode.

From 4:31 to 6:19 Luke parallels (follows?) the Markan narrative of the exorcism in the Capernaum assembly and the healings in Mark 1–3. In Luke Jesus exorcizes with "power" as well as "authority." Luke 6:17–19 embellishes the summary in Mark 3:7–12 to set up the covenant renewal speech in Luke 6:20–49, much as Matthew does to set up the Sermon on the Mount. The great multitude from the areas surrounding Galilee had come not just to hear Jesus, but to be healed of their illnesses and their unclean spirits. "All were trying to touch him, for power came out from him and healed all of them." Following the covenant renewal speech come the healing of the centurion's servant (paralleled in Matthew) and Jesus' command to the son of the widow of Nain to "rise" (7:1–10, 11–17). Just before Jesus' answer to John's question as to whether he is the "coming one," Luke has Jesus "just then" heal many people of illnesses, plagues, evil spirits, and blindness (7:18–23). Clearly this episode in Luke is a summary, almost a catalogue of Jesus' healings and exorcisms, Jesus' actions that make the kingdom of God even greater than John, the greatest of the prophets up to the present of Jesus and the kingdom (7:24–29).

After Luke again parallels the Markan sequence of episodes following the parables of the kingdom, the narrative includes the exorcism of the violent spirit, "Legion," in Gerasa, and the healings of the two women. In the ensuing charge to the Twelve, Jesus "gave them power and authority over all *daimonia* and to heal illnesses, and sent them out to proclaim the kingdom of God and to heal." If anything, the emphasis is on healing and exorcism (more than preaching), in extension of Jesus' own mission (and power). After including Jesus' exorcism of the possessed "epileptic" and the strange exorcist episode, Luke has Jesus send out the seventy to extend his mission, again to heal those with illnesses and to say that the kingdom of God has come near (10:1–12). Distinctive to the Lukan story is the episode of the return of the seventy, who say that "in your name the *daimonia* submit to us," leading Jesus to the visionary exclamation, "I saw Satan fall from heaven" (10:17–20). In the ensuing episode, Jesus' thanking the Father, "these things" that are hidden from the cultural elite and revealed to the ordinary people are, as in the Matthean story as well, the exorcisms and healings. After the sending of the seventy, Luke has a lengthy section mainly of teaching before Jesus marches up into Jerusalem to confront the rulers. But included are Jesus' response to the charge of exorcizing by Beelzebul, programmatic in Luke as in Mark and Matthew, and an exorcism of a woman crippled by a spirit and the healing of ten lepers. As he is about to enter Jerusalem, finally, Jesus heals a blind beggar. As in both Mark and Matthew, the healings and exorcism constitute Jesus' principal actions, and as in Matthew, they are the subject of a good deal of his teaching and debate as well as the principal charge to the disciples to extend his own mission.

The "Source" of Teachings Used by Matthew and Luke

The preceding short surveys of the Gospels of Matthew and Luke suggest that, in addition to following or paralleling the Markan narrative, they share a common source for blocks of Jesus' teachings that are not in Mark. It has been striking to Gospel scholars that Matthew and Luke present these teachings in more or less the same order and that their wording is often the same or very similar. These teachings of Jesus are standardly referred to as "Q," short for *Quelle*, the German word meaning "source" (they are usually referred to in their Lukan order). The admittedly hypothetical "document" Q is thought to be earlier than the Gospel of Mark, hence the earliest source in the Gospel tradition. It will thus be important to investigate this (hypothetical) source for Jesus' teaching more fully (in chapter 8). Here it is significant to note that this collection of Jesus' teachings includes significant references to and discussions of healings and exorcisms.

"Q" has standardly been understood as merely a collection of individual "sayings." Recently some North American scholars have recognized that these teachings parallel in Matthew and Luke are rather a series of short speeches on various issues of concern to an early Jesus movement (to be discussed more fully in chap. 8). Readily discernible, for example, are the contours of speeches on covenant renewal (Q/Luke 6:20–49), mission (10:2–16), bold confession before courts (12:2–12), and anxiety about subsistence (12:22–31). The theme of the series of speeches is clearly the direct rule (kingdom) of God, which appears prominently in nearly all of the speeches.

With these speeches consisting almost entirely of Jesus' teachings (on various aspects of the direct rule of God), it is striking that two of the main speeches discuss the significance of his healings and exorcisms. The speech in Q/Luke 7:18–35 begins with Jesus' response to John the Baptist's question whether Jesus is "the one who is coming" (that John announced in the speech in Q/Luke 3:7–9, 16–17). Jesus points to what is happening in his mission: *all sorts of healings*. In the next step of the speech, moreover, Jesus declares that while John was the greatest prophet in history up to that point, the direct rule of God is greater, as manifested in the healings (Q/Luke 7:28). In Q/Luke 11:14–20 Jesus replies to the charge that he is casting out spirits by Beelzebul, the ruler of spirits. On the contrary, he declares, since he is casting out spirits by "the finger/ Spirit of God," the rule of God has come upon the people. His *exorcisms* are manifestations of the coming of God's direct rule. *In these two speeches in Q, Jesus declares that healings and exorcisms are not just integral to, but the fundamental actions in his mission of proclaiming and manifesting the direct rule of God in the life of the people.*

The Gospel of John

The Gospel of John seems very different from the Synoptic Gospels. It has been viewed as the more "theological" and "spiritual" Gospel. John's Gospel is different in style of presentation, with Jesus involved in long dialogues and monologues instead of a rapid sequence of shorter episodes.

Most significant for this survey of the Gospel stories' representation of Jesus' mission, John's Gospel includes no reference to exorcisms, and has only three episodes of healing. John has previously been thought to have drawn upon and elaborated a "signs gospel," a "chain of miracle stories" that is also detected behind the narrative in Mark 4:35—8:26. This has perhaps given the impression that John includes more healings than it does. Whereas the principal activity of Jesus' mission in the first half or two-thirds of the stories in Mark, Matthew, and Luke consists of healings and exorcisms, however, in John's story Jesus is primarily engaged in one confrontation after another with the high priests and Pharisees in Jerusalem at the "festivals of the Judeans" in the temple. Often correlated with those confrontations are "signs" that Jesus performs. But those are by no means all healings. The first is his changing water into wine (combined with his demonstration in the temple?) and the fourth is his feeding in the wilderness. John thus has Jesus performing only three "signs" that are healings: the recovery of the royal officer's son from a fever (4:46–54); the disabled man's becoming whole/healthy on the sabbath, which is linked with the forgiveness of sin (5:2–9); and Jesus' "opening the eyes" of a man blind from birth (9:1–7).

Nevertheless John repeatedly emphasizes that Jesus did numerous signs, and it seems clear that many of those involved healing people. The healing stories that John does include, moreover, parallel and reinforce the presentation in the other Gospels that Jesus healed paralyzed or disabled people and blind people, that he healed on the Sabbath and that his healing was linked with forgiveness of sins. Finally, John affirms that it was because of Jesus' performance of signs such as healing that so many people trusted in him and joined his movement, leading the Jerusalem rulers to arrest him and to turn him over to the Roman governor for crucifixion.

As indicated in these "notes" toward a fresh reading of the Gospel sources, the stories of Mark and Matthew and Luke, along with the series of speeches adapted in Matthew and Luke, present exorcisms and healings as the principal activities in Jesus' mission. They present these activities as the main manifestations of the direct rule/kingdom of God that he was proclaiming. And the healings and exorcisms appear in the Gospel stories as the actions that are so threatening to the rulers and their scribal and Pharisaic representatives that they scheme to destroy him.

Were we to take the Gospels themselves seriously as the sources for the historical Jesus, then it is clearly necessary to focus investigation directly on how the Gospels portray the healings and exorcisms. This will be the major step in the overall project of this book, in chapters 6–10. Meanwhile, it seems clear that the principal reason modern interpreters have not focused more attention on the healings and exorcisms is their classification as miracles and/or magic. The next step is to investigate critically these modern constructs, products of the Enlightenment that still dominate historical Jesus studies and are blocking focus on and critical understanding of Jesus' exorcisms and healings.

2

Miracles and Magic
Modern Misunderstandings

THE CLASSIFICATION OF JESUS' exorcisms and healings as miracles and/ or magic has made it virtually impossible to understand them in historical context. These distinctively modern Western concepts emerged as part of the post-Enlightenment "scientific" understanding of reality. They developed as poorly defined constructs into which scholars lumped a variety of ideas, ritual practices, and ostensibly odd beliefs or behaviors that seemed irrational to the "scientific" modern worldview.

Miracle(s) became deeply entrenched in New Testament studies as the fundamental concept for God's intervention in the regular workings of the natural world. Virtually all accounts of Jesus' actions in the Gospels were classified as "miracle stories" and the extraordinary deeds behind them understood as miracles. Healing and exorcism were lumped together with raisings from the dead and "nature miracles," the only explanation for such extraordinary occurrences being divine or supernatural causation. The recent spate of Jesus books has continued this categorization, raising little or no questions about whether the concept is appropriate.

Magic became an important area of study in New Testament studies a century ago, and "elements" of magic were discerned in the miracle stories. As it developed, the scholarly construct of magic was broad, synthetic, and vague. The recent revival of scholarly interest in ancient magic, however, did not include criticism of the construct and its applicability to ancient texts and ritual practices. It also failed to take note of the baggage it carries from its development in modern Western intellectual history. Ironically some significant interpreters of Jesus claimed that he was practicing magic, while expanding the concept still further. Since the modern scholarly construct of magic has also become entrenched in New Testament studies and closely related fields, it is important to examine critically its questionable basis in ancient texts and the way in which it distorts understanding of Jesus' exorcisms and healings.

A critical examination, indeed deconstruction of both of these modern concepts can clear the way for an appreciation of the healing and exorcism episodes as integral parts of the Gospel stories and for a more grounded sense of Jesus' healings and exorcisms in historical context.[1]

Miracle

The Modern Concept of Miracle

The concept of miracle is deeply embedded in modern biblical studies. Nearly all interpreters of Jesus and the Gospels simply assume that the healing and exorcism episodes are miracle stories and that the healings and exorcisms were miracles. They are thus applying to Jesus and the Gospels, and to Mediterranean antiquity generally, a concept developed in the European Enlightenment.[2] After centuries of discussion and debate in theological circles, interpreters of Jesus and the Gospels still have an understanding of miracle that closely resembles that of Enlightenment theologians.[3] While attempting to avoid distracting debate about "laws of nature," they still define miracle as having three aspects: "(1) an . . . extraordinary event . . . , (2) that finds no reasonable explanation in human abilities or in other known forces that operate in our world of time

---

1. This chapter is a condensation and revision of research presented in Horsley, *Jesus and Magic*, Parts I and II.

2. Perhaps articulated most influentially by David Hume. See Keener, *Miracles*, chap. 5, for extensive recent discussion of Hume's argument and epistemology, and chap. 6 for the effects of Hume and recent shifts.

3. Such as Jacob Vernet: "a striking work which is outside the ordinary course of Nature and which is done by God's all-mighty will, and such that witnesses thereof regard it as extraordinary and supernatural." See further Craig, "Problem of Miracles." For a recent survey of how the miracles in the Bible were understood in the Reformation and the Enlightenment, see Zachman, "The Meaning of Biblical Miracles."

and space [i.e., Nature], and (3) [hence is] . . . the result of a special act of God, doing what no human power can do."[4]

Belief in miracles or in spirits, moreover, seemed irrational to "scientific" modern scholars. Rudolf Bultmann articulated the view of critical theological scholars of the last century, that those acquainted with modern medical discoveries could not "believe in the New Testament world of spirits and miracles."[5] Although not always explicitly articulated, the concept of miracle continues to carry this baggage of irrational belief in scholarly interpretation of the healings and exorcisms of Jesus.[6]

Theologians and interpreters of Jesus have devoted endless discussion to whether Jesus performed miracles and how they should be understood, as Albert Schweitzer and others have discussed at length.[7] Yet even recent interpreters of Jesus have given little attention to whether the Gospel sources for Jesus, or contemporary Judean texts, or the Hellenistic culture into which Jesus movements expanded, had a concept of miracle, much less the same understanding of miracle as modern theologians and biblical scholars. John Meier, who devotes a lengthy chapter to "Miracles and Ancient Minds,"[8] simply assumes that "miracles were accepted as part of the religious landscape" and that the problem for the historian is . . . "the all-too-ready acceptance of them by ordinary people."[9] In New Testament studies more generally it is simply assumed that "miracle/

4. Meier, *Mentor, Message, and Miracles*, 512. Meier has devoted considerable critical review and reflection to the understanding of miracle. That this view is standard in the New Testament field is confirmed by Harold Remus' article on "Miracle" in the *Anchor Bible Dictionary*, 4:857.

5. Bultmann, "New Testament and Mythology, 4–5.

6. For example, Theissen, *Miracle Stories*, 231–32, 251, 269, 276 ; Trocmé, *La formation*, 37–44; Alkier, "Nothing Will Be Impossible," 7–8.

7. Albert Schweitzer was one of the few interpreters of Jesus in his generation to give serious attention to how problematic the miracle stories of Jesus had been for modern (theological) scholars. See also Meier's chapter on "Miracles and Modern Minds" in *Mentor*; Craig, "Problem of Miracles;" Zachman, "Biblical Miracles."

8. Meier, *Mentor, Message, and Miracles*, chap. 18, focuses instead on "Pagan and Jewish parallels to Gospel materials," and the relation of miracle and magic, both of which he simply assumes were realities in the ancient world.

9. Meier, *Mentor, Message, and Miracles*, 535. In yet another illustration of how scholarly assumptions are often rooted in modern western (rationalist) elite culture, Theissen, *Miracle Stories*, 231–32, 269, 276, viewed miracle stories as an expression of an irrational, childish state of humanity and that "belief in miracles and superstition" increasingly bubbled up from popular culture so that "even educated people" took up "irrational attitudes far removed from good common sense."

miracle stories" is the appropriate category under which a wide range of phenomena and/or stories, including Jesus' healings and exorcisms, can be classified and interpreted.[10]

Exploration of the Gospel accounts of Jesus' healing and exorcism, therefore, requires an investigation of whether there was something like the modern concept of miracle in Judean and/or Hellenistic culture at the time of Jesus, including the Gospel sources, and whether healings and exorcisms were included.[11] Since nearly all literary sources were produced by the cultural elite, they provide sources for elite culture, but are not direct sources for ordinary people, The Gospels, however, which were traditions and stories about ordinary people that emerged from ordinary people, provide sources at least for the villagers of Galilee and perhaps of nearby areas into which the early Jesus movements spread as well.

Elite Culture in Judea

Studies that examine "the concept of miracle" in one or more late second-temple Judean texts have simply assumed the concept and then looked for its equivalent.[12] The histories of Flavius Josephus are probably the most important texts to check for whether elite circles of Judeans had some equivalent to the modern concept of miracle. He interprets many episodes from Israelite tradition that modern scholars view as miracles, and his accounts are some of the principal sources for beliefs and practices around the time of Jesus. Studies of Josephus' view of miracles simply

10. For example, Cotter, *Miracles*; Labahn and Peerbolte, *Wonders*; Watson, *Miracle Discourse*. Even a recent collection of essays that probes the "concepts of reality" in the "miracle stories" and rejects the "rationalist hermeneutics" so prominent in New Testament studies nevertheless still works on the assumption that "miracle" is the appropriate classification, Alkier and Weissenrieder, *Miracles Revisited*.

11. As exemplified in the article by Remus on "Miracle" in *ABD* 4:857, it is standard in studies of miracle in the ancient world to start with the modern concept of miracle, on the assumption that it corresponds to a phenomenon in antiquity, and then to declare that "several [ancient] terms, variously translated, denote this phenomenon." Whether the modern term and concept of "miracle" is appropriate to ancient accounts that refer to *dynameis* or *terata* or *paradoxa* or *semeia*, however, is just the question that requires investigation.

12. The recent survey by Eric Eve, *The Jewish Context of Jesus' Miracles*, is particularly useful insofar as, while still claiming that most second-temple Judeans believed in miracles, he does not find evidence of a concept of miracle in most of the texts he examines. My own critical survey, summarized here, indicates that there is no concept in any Judean texts that corresponds to the modern construct of miracle.

assume that miracle was an operative concept in ancient culture.[13] They focus on the terms *semeia* ("signs"), *paradoxos* ("amazing/wondrous"), and *epiphaneia* ("manifestation") as his "vocabulary" or "language of miracle."[14] In Josephus' histories, however, these terms are not comparable to the modern concept of miracle.

Semeia. Josephus employs this term in reference to a variety of things, such as password, Roman military standards, signal, and symbol. He frequently uses *semeia* for an omen or portent of a future event, such as the Roman destruction of Jerusalem (*War* 1.23, 28; 3.404; 4.623; 6.296, 315).[15] These *semeia* include earlier occurrences mentioned in Israelite tradition as God-given omens or portents of key events in Israel's (and its heroes'/kings') deliverance. What makes them "signs," however, is not their occurrence beyond what is humanly or naturally possible, as in the modern concept of miracle, but their relation to those future events, and often a prophet's role in announcing and/or petitioning God for them. Josephus and other elite Judeans, like Tacitus and other ancient Romans, understood prophecy, dreams, omens, and portents as among the means by which God (the gods) governed the world and communicated with humans.[16] Such prophecy and portents, however, were "not regarded as miracles."[17] A derivative but more specialized usage is for the "signs" God provides (such as a sudden hailstorm, *Ant.* 10:24–29), to convince people that prophets are indeed delivering divine messages or carrying out divine commands. These "signs," however, do not include the event(s) of deliverance (2.237). The *semeia* in Josephus' accounts do not fit the concept of "miracle."

Paradoxos. Josephus uses this term mostly in the sense of "unexpected" or "amazing" or "wondrous" in reference to occurrences that

13. Delling, "Josephus und das Wunderbare"; MacRae, "Miracle in the Antiquities"; Betz, "Das Problem des Wunders."

14. Since Josephus does not use *dynamis* for unusual occurrences or events themselves, he provides no direct terminological comparison with the Gospels' representation of Jesus' "(acts of) powers." Similarly, Eve, *Jewish Context of Jesus' Miracles*, 33.

15. *Semeion* in Josephus' histories is often somewhat synonymous with *teras* (or *terastion*), another term for omen or portent, which he uses more frequently in the *War* than in the *Antiquities*. In suggesting that Josephus uses *teras* in the sense of miracle at *War* 1.331; 5.411, Eve, *Jewish Context of Jesus' Miracles*, 33, may be depending on Thackeray's questionable 1927 translation in the LCL.

16. Delling, "Josephus und das Wunderbare"; followed by MacRae, "Miracle in the Antiquities."

17. MacRae, "Miracle in the Antiquities," 132.

modern readers would not classify as miracles. For example, Moses was "amazingly" raised, including the "wonder" by which he was saved by being placed in a basket (*Ant.* 2:216, 221–223). Josephus does not seem to make much of a distinction between the "wonders" or the "signs" and other manifestations of God's power and providence, such as God's deliverance of the people in several "(divine and) wondrous" victorious battles (*Ant.* 5:28; 9:14, 58, 60).

Epiphaneia occurs in connection with certain of the wonders in Israel's history, "manifestations" of God such as the fire darting out of the air onto Solomon's altar and Isaac's marriage to Rebecca (*Ant.* 8.119; 1.255; cf. 3.310). The *epiphaneia* (of God) stands parallel to the power of God as what is revealed in such amazing events. But it does not correspond to the modern concept of miracle.

Josephus, finally, does not include healings and exorcisms among either the "signs" or the "wonders."[18] Elijah's raising of the widow's son to life is "beyond all expectation," but not called a sign or a wonder. In his account of Elisha's actions, Josephus is evidently focusing on political events and omits several of his actions mentioned in the scriptural narrative (2 Kgs 1–13), including his healings. The exorcism of a "demon" by Eleazar before the future emperor Vespasian and his entourage, often cited as evidence of Jewish magic and miracle, is neither a "sign" nor a "wonder," but a "healing" (*therapeia*; *Ant.* 8.46–48). For Josephus, healings and exorcisms were evidently *not* "signs" or "wonders," much less miracles.

The Judean historian understands prophecies accompanied by "signs" and events that were "amazing" portents—whether in the history of Israel or in contemporary affairs—within his overall "theology" of history as some of the ways that God governs the world. In contrast with the modern Enlightenment worldview, Josephus found omens, portentous events, and prophetic signs as compatible with the (rational) nature of the universe. As he says regarding his historiography in his introduction to the *Antiquities*, "nothing will appear unreasonable, nothing incongruous with the majesty of God and his love for humanity; everything, indeed, is here set forth in keeping with the nature of the universe (*tei ton holon physei*)" (*Ant.* 1.24).[19]

---

18. Cf. Eve, *Jewish Context of Jesus' Miracles*, 51.
19. MacRae, "Miracles in the Antiquities," 131.

The modern Enlightenment division between nature and the supernatural (and miraculous) worldview did not govern the thinking of ancient Judean sages such as Ben Sira or historians such as Josephus. God, "the Most High," was involved in earthly governance either directly or through one of the many heavenly forces ("messengers"/"angels"). They did not make dramatic distinctions between divine and human agency. Events of political-economic deliverance of the people and healings alike resulted from divine-human synergism (Sirach 38:1–15; 48:1–14; *Biblical Antiquities,* throughout; Josephus' accounts of events of deliverance).[20]

Josephus and other Judean elite contemporary with Jesus thus evidently had no concept corresponding to the modern western concept of miracle.[21]

Hellenistic-Roman Elite Culture

The Hellenistic-Roman cultural elite, like their Judean counterparts, had no concept that corresponds to the modern western concept of miracle. It is difficult to find terms in Greek or Latin that might correspond. There are several that refer to wonders, omens, portents, prodigies, or signs, often ominous events or strange occurrences that bode well or ill for city-states or public figures. Such extraordinary phenomena were sometimes attributed to divine agency and sometimes not. Developing usage of the Latin term *miraculum* in late antiquity provides the link to the later Christian and then modern concept of miracle. In early usage, *miraculum* usually meant merely something that aroused wonder (frequently in Livy: 1.47.9; 2.13.13; 4.35.9; 5.46.3). By the second century CE it could also be used for wondrous events attributed to a deity (Apuleius, *Met* 2.28). Unusual healings, however, were not usually thought of as wonders

20. Sirach 48:1–14 hardly provides a basis for suggesting that miracles "could come to be seen as the most important activity of the prophet." *vs.* Eve, *Jewish Context of Jesus' Miracles,* 113. The inappropriately titled "Messianic Apocalypse" (4Q521) does not refer to individual "miracles" of healing and raising the dead, but to the restoration of the whole people that had been languishing under imperial rule, vs. Eve, *Jewish Context of Jesus' Miracles,* 192, following others.

21. See further MacRae, "Miracle in the Antiquities," 139–40, and his broader explanation of Josephus' seemingly apologetic "rationalistic" statements regarding the events he narrates, 138–41, and, more generally, on Josephus' understanding of the history of the Judeans, see Attridge, *Interpretation of Biblical History.* On the relative unimportance of references to or tales of wondrous acts of deliverance in early rabbinic discussions, see Becker, *Wunder und Wundertaeter;* and Becker, "Miracle Traditions."

or portents. While *miraculum* had no such meaning at the time of Jesus himself, however, by late antiquity Christians came to use the term for the wonders Jesus worked, as well as for the acts of the martyrs.[22]

In contrast to modern "scientific" thinkers, ancient intellectuals did not make a sharp distinction between divine causation and reason or nature, between "supernatural" ("miraculous") and "natural." The divine was rational and natural, the gods an integral part of nature, the cosmos. The healings of Asclepios were understood as caused by the god, but also as in accord with human healing practices. The well-known second-century physician Galen believed that God and nature belonged to the same continuous reality in which universal laws prevailed. The significant dreams he sent were not miraculous in the sense of interrupting the natural order. They came not from a supernatural realm, but from a higher level in a continuum of reality.[23]

Reports of cases usually included by modern interpreters as miracles can be used instead to illustrate how, since there was no dichotomy in ancient culture between the natural and the supernatural, there was no need to resort to divine agency to explain extraordinary/wondrous healings.

Modern scholars have standardly classified as miracles the healings performed by the emperor-to-be Vespasian in Alexandria, of which the Roman historians Tacitus and Suetonius provide accounts.[24] After the death of Nero, when the Roman general who had been devastating Galilee and Judea was waiting to sail to Rome to consolidate his power, a blind man and a disabled man sought healing from the new Caesar. The Hellenistic-Egyptian god Serapis had advised that the emperor could heal the blind man by moistening his cheeks and eyeballs with his spittle and could heal the lame man by touching his leg or arm with his foot. Vespasian's hesitation, the advice he was given, and his decision to proceed may be particularly illustrative of the attitude of the Roman elite. The emperor-to-be was uneasy that he still lacked the numinous *auctoritas*

22. Remus, *Pagan/Christian Conflict*, 52 and n.16, 234.

23. Tieleman, "Natural Cause," 112. On ancient intellectuals such as Celsus and Galen, see more broadly Martin, *Inventing Superstition*, who emphasizes that they did not have a category of the supernatural in which divine forces were separated from nature (13–14).

24. Tacitus, *History* bk 4, ch. 81; Suetonius, *Vespasian* 7. See discussion in Morgan, *Year of Four Emperors*, 170–255; Luke, "A Healing Touch" (with a very broad concept of miracles); and Leppin, "Imperial Miracles."

(prestige/divinity) of an emperor or that he might exhibit a certain *vanitas* (the term can mean "vanity" or "failure"). Suetonius says that although he lacked faith/trust (*fides*) that he could succeed, his "friends" prevailed upon him. Tacitus has him asking the opinions of physicians whether such blindness and infirmity could be healed by human skill. Persuaded that he might be the chosen minister of the divine will and that all things were possible by his good fortune, he attempted both healings in public before a large crowd—successfully.

These are vivid accounts of how such healings happened in a network of relations between the person seeking healing, an agent in whom people believed healing power to be working/available, and the divine/gods (both Serapis and the gods of the Romans). The ancient Alexandrians and Romans, including the elite "friends" of Vespasian and the historians Tacitus and Suetonius as well as the ordinary people, believed that divine favor was involved in the healing of the blind and disabled who sought healing by the nascent emperor. But all looked to Vespasian himself as the agent of the healing. To abstract (the accounts of) such healings into the concept of miracle sweeps them up into a broad general modern category inapplicable to the accounts of Tacitus and Suetonius.

Another illustration comes from a raising from the dead by Apollonius of Tyana (*Vit. apol.* 4.45).[25] Contrary to the widely used Loeb Classical Library translation,[26] "a miracle which Apollonius worked," however, the episode begins rather less ominously: "And here is another of Apollonius' wonders" (*thauma*). Contrary to the modern concept of miracle, moreover, the unusual occurrence is not inexplicable (by nature), nor is it attributed to divine causation. It begins, "the girl seemed to have died;" then it continues, with his touch and whisper, Apollonius "woke the girl up (from sleep) from seeming death." The episode ends with two alternative (possible) explanations, neither of which involves the divine: he restored a dead girl by the warmth of his touch *or* he detected a spark of life in her, "for it was said that although it was raining at the time, a vapour went up from her face." Thus one of the stories from antiquity that interpreters have used as a prime example of a Hellenistic miracle story that helps explain (so to speak) the development of the miracle stories about Jesus simply does not fit the concept of miracle presupposed by modern interpreters.

25. Since at least the foundational form-critical work of Bultmann, *History of the Synoptic Tradition*.

26. Conybeare, *Apollonius of Tyana*.

Popular Culture: The Gospels

Recent scholars of Jesus and the Gospels, such as John Meier, find that "the all-too-ready acceptance of [miracles] by ordinary people" poses a problem for the historian (as noted just above).[27] Interpreters of Jesus working on the assumption that the modern concept of miracle is applicable to the Gospel accounts claim that the Gospels "have a number of words to designate Jesus' miracles: e.g., *dynamis, semeion, teras, paradoxon*."[28] But that is simply not the case.[29] That neither these terms nor any other designate miracles in the Gospels[30] indicates that the Gospels had no concept by which some actions of Jesus, including exorcisms and healings, were distinguished from other actions as miracles.

It is significant that Mark, Matthew, and Luke do not (explicitly) compare Jesus' exorcisms and healings to exodus events by referring to them as "signs and wonders."[31] The latter are what false messiahs and prophets will do in the future (Mark 13:22//Matt 24:24). Jesus insists that he will give no sign to satisfy his elite opponents (Mark 8:11–12//Matt 12:38–39; Luke/Q 11:(16,) 29–30; Matt 16:1–4; Luke 23:8)—except for "the sign of Jonah," which is presumably the warning in his prophetic

---

27. Meier, *Mentor, Message, and Miracles*, 535.

28. Meier, *Mentor, Message, and Miracles*, 600.

29. Alkier, "Nothing Will Be Impossible," 8, discerns clearly that "what we call miracle is not the same as what biblical texts call *dynameis, paradoxon, semeia kai terata*, and so on," yet continues to project the modern concept "miracles"/"miracle stories" onto Gospel stories and other ancient texts.

30. *Teras* does not occur at all; *paradoxon*, which appears only at Luke 5:26, is how all of what happens, evidently including the forgiveness of sins, in the episode in Luke 5:17–25 strike all of the amazed onlookers, evidently including the scribes and Pharisees who charged Jesus with blasphemy.

31. In contrast to the Gospels, however, early passages in the book of Acts do refer to healings and exorcisms as "signs and wonders," and these may have influenced the later Christian theological concept of miracle. The Jerusalem community of Jesus-loyalists evidently understand the healings and exorcisms performed by the apostles and/or by God and/or through the name of Jesus as "signs and wonders," that is as new acts of deliverance in continuation or resumption of the exodus-wilderness deliverance of old (4:27–30; 5:12; 6:8). Most striking is the passage in Peter's post-Pentecost speech in which he proclaims Jesus as "a man attested to you by God, with powers, wonders, and signs that God did through him among you" (Acts 2:22). To modern theological interpreters this might have seemed to attest their definition of miracles, that is as extraordinary happenings that are done by God. It is significant to note also that Peter's brief proclamation also emphasizes the centrality of the healings and exorcisms in Jesus' mission, just as do the Gospels of Mark, Matthew, and Luke.

declarations. "Signs" in these exchanges, moreover, evidently refer to some omen or portent, not to a healing or exorcism. Luke presents the child Jesus laid in the manger as a "sign" to the shepherds (Luke 2:12, 34). In such passages "sign" refers not to some action by itself, but to the great significance of an event in its context. This is the way the Gospel of John understands sign, as the text elaborates on the significance of key events that Jesus catalyzes at points and places in the story.

In some of Jesus' exorcism and healing episodes the onlookers or crowds are "amazed" or "astounded" (*thaumazo, ekstasis, existemi*), although no term of "wonder" is applied to the exorcism or healing. This motif, however, is less prominent in the healing and exorcism episodes than often imagined. In the Markan story it occurs only at the end of the episodes of the healing of the paralytic, of the exorcism of the spirit named "Legion," and of the resuscitation of the twelve-year-old woman (2:12; 5:20, 42; some parallels in Matthew and Luke). Amazement, moreover, is not confined to people's response to an exorcism and healings. In Mark Jesus himself is amazed at the lack of trust he encounters in his home town, and Pilate is amazed at Jesus (Mark 6:6; 15:5). Matthew has the disciples frequently amazed and the Pharisees amazed at how Jesus responds to their attempt to entrap him over the tribute to Caesar, and Luke has people amazed at what happened to Zechariah (Matt 8:27; 21:20; Luke 1:21, 63).

The term *dynameis* ("powers") is used in some summaries and discussions of Jesus' healings and exorcisms (and other incidents). The English translations of the term as "acts/deeds of power" or "mighty acts" may have been misleading in shifting the focus to actions of Jesus rather than the power that flows from or through him to others. The people of his hometown wonder, "What is this wisdom that has been given to him; what *powers* are being done by his hands!" and the narrator adds "he could do no *power* there, except that he laid his hands on a few sick people and healed them" (Mark 6:1–6 and parallel). In the introduction to Herod Antipas' beheading of John, some were speculating that "the reason why these powers are at work in [Jesus]" is that "John the Baptist had been raised from the dead" (6:14). Jesus admonished the disciples not to stop someone from casting out spirits in his name, that is, doing a power in his name (Mark 9:39). In the mission speech in Q (Luke/Q 10:2–16), Jesus pronounces woes on some villages because they had not responded positively to "the powers" that had been done (happened) among them. In these summary or discussion passages in Mark and

Matthew and Luke, *dynameis* evidently refers to the restorative healing power that is flowing from or through Jesus or the disciples or others in interaction with people. This is clear particularly in the episode of the hemorrhaging woman where Jesus feels power flow from him. The phrase "doing a (an act of) power" in the Nazareth episode and in the "strange exorcist" episode appears to refer more specifically to the performance of an exorcism. But the term "powers" is not used of particular healings and exorcisms and wilderness feedings as if it were an equivalent for the modern concept of miracles. *Dynameis* are not miracles that can be explained only by reference to supernatural causes.

Is the Modern Concept of Miracle Appropriate to Jesus' Healings and Exorcisms?

Finally, the applicability of the concept of miracle to the Gospel accounts of Jesus' healings and exorcisms can be tested against Meier's carefully considered general definition of miracle, cited above.

The sicknesses healed and spirit possession and its exorcism were not all that extraordinary in the historical context and elsewhere historically. The legends of Elijah and Elisha in Israelite tradition included healings. The healing of skin lesions was fairly well-known in antiquity.[32] Affliction by spirits was known in Israelite tradition and in the wider Hellenistic world. Spirit-possession, while unknown in earlier Israelite tradition, is presupposed as common in the Gospels. That others besides Jesus performed exorcisms is assumed in the rhetorical question ("by whom do your sons cast out spirits?") Jesus asks in the "Beelzebul" debate in Q/ Luke 11:19. Special kinds of healing and spirit possession and exorcism, moreover, are now well-known phenomena in many societies.

In contrast to modern rationalist interpretations, the Gospel accounts of Jesus' healings and exorcisms exhibit virtually no concern for "explanation." Jesus' healing or exorcism follows upon his speaking to or touching the sick person or commanding the possessing spirit. The power that Jesus felt go forth from himself in the healing of the hemorrhaging woman is clearly operative in the world of time and space, as are Jesus' words to the paralytic, "your sins are forgiven," as are his touch and words to the "leper" (Mark 5:25–34; 2:1–12; 1:40–45).

---

32. Weissenrieder, *Images of Illness*; Cotter, *Christ of the Miracle Stories*, 25–27.

Accordingly, the Gospel accounts of Jesus' healings do not ascribe them to God's or other superhuman agency, certainly not to supernatural agency. In virtually none of the Gospel accounts is anything but Jesus' touching, speaking, or command mentioned as the agency of the healing. Only in the more general discussion of exorcisms in the Beelzebul controversy is superhuman agency an issue: Jesus is charged with casting out spirits by the ruler of spirits. The extraordinary, bizarre, and often violent behavior of "demoniacs" was understood as the result of being possessed by superhuman spirits. Indeed there was a struggle going on in the world of spirits that mirrored and to a degree determined the struggle going on in the social-political world (to be discussed in chapters below). So the casting out of spirits involved superhuman agency, as in Jesus' declaration about "the finger/Spirit of God" (Luke/Q 11:20). But application of the modern construct of miracle bypasses or blocks the way toward understanding Jesus' exorcism in the historical context of the rise of spirit possession and the struggle between superhuman spirits and other heavenly forces that was relatively new among Israelite people and in Israelite culture (further discussion in chapter 5).

Finally, as will be discussed in later chapters, far from illuminating the stories of Jesus' healing and exorcism, the modern concept of miracle seems to obscure their relational character. In many of the episodes, the explanation or cause of the healing, whether implicit or stated explicitly, is the trust (inadequately translated "faith") that the suffering person and/or her/his support network have in (the powers working through) Jesus, of whom they have evidently heard reports (e.g., Matt 8:5–13; Mark 1:40–42; 2:1–12; 3:7–8; 5:21–43; 7:24–30; 8:22–26; 10:46–52; and in two cases of exorcism, Mark 9:14–29; Luke 17:11–19).

Ironically, the projection of the concept of miracle onto antiquity is one of the principal ways that scholars have been "modernizing Jesus." As Henry Cadbury warned eighty years ago, we forget how many of our thought categories are distinctively modern and fail to consider that ancient people had a different worldview. To scientific-minded unbelievers as well as to conservative modern believers, he suggested, "miracle has a meaning which it could never have to pre-scientific minds . . . The rise of the scientific viewpoint changed the meaning of a miraculous event even for those who believe in it . . . To the modern theist the miracles are . . . a special direct intervention in an otherwise largely automatic universe."[33]

33. Cadbury, *Peril of Modernizing Jesus*, 72, 81–82.

No more than the Judean and Hellenistic cultural elites in antiquity, however, did ordinary people think of the world as divided between the natural and the supernatural. To Jesus and his contemporaries, God and other spiritual forces were actively engaged with earthly life.

Magic

Both ancient and modern intellectuals accused Jesus of practicing magic. In reaction, twentieth-century Christian theologians, like their ancient Christian counterparts, Justin Martyr and Origin, have generally defended Jesus against the charge. They often argued that magic was something distinctively different from the miracles Jesus performed. It became almost standard, however, for twentieth-century interpreters of Jesus to admit that Jesus used magical elements in some of his healings and exorcisms. Influenced by the resurgence of interest in ancient magic in the 1970s and 1980s, moreover, some well-known scholars made the bold claim that Jesus was a magician.

It would seem impossible to argue that Jesus was a magician on the basis of the Gospels, the primary sources. In Matthew, Mark, and Luke (the "Synoptic Gospels"), Jesus is accused of casting out spirits by Beelzebul, the ruler of spirits, and he is crucified by Pontius Pilate as "the king of the Judeans," that is, as a rebel leader against the Roman imperial order. But he is not accused of practicing magic. Such accusations do not come until mid-second century. Discussion of whether Jesus was a magician or used elements of magic, however, has little to do with the Gospel accounts and everything to do with modern scholarship. Both those who denied and those who claimed that Jesus was practicing magic were assuming the same modern scholarly construction of ancient magic, without critically examining the sources that supposedly attest it.

In order to approach Jesus' healings and exorcisms free of their previous distortion as magic or having elements of magic, it may help to critically review several steps in the twentieth-century scholarly construction of ancient magic and its applications to stories about Jesus.

The Construction of Ancient Magic

The modern scholarly construct of "ancient magic" was a quagmire of conceptual confusion. Scholars applied the concept to a wide range of material and in diverse ways, and engaged in heated debates about how it related to miracle or religion or philosophy. Most declined to define it. They simply assumed that there was such a reality as magic in the ancient Mediterranean world and that they knew what it included. Since most of the sources came from late antiquity, however, it was utterly unclear what *mageia/magos* might have meant in the first century CE, that is, at the time of Jesus.

The Ambiguity of Mageia/Magos

The conceptual confusion about magic is partly rooted in the ambiguous connotations of the term *mageia/magos* and associated ritual practices as early as the fifth century BCE and continuing through late antiquity. As the eminent scholar Arthur Darby Nock laid out clearly and concisely over eighty years ago, *magoi* had two very different references and associations.[34]

The *Magoi* (a loanword from the Persian) referred to the Median priestly clan serving the Persian Empire (Strabo, *Geogr.*, 15.3.15; Herodotus, *Hist.* 1.101), They were highly revered by Greek and Hellenistic intellectuals for their sacred rites, divination, dream-interpretation, and knowledge of the divine powers of the cosmos, like other high-ranking priestly or scribal groups in "Oriental" kingdoms (Herodotus, *Hist.* 1.107–108, 120, 128, 132, 140; 7.19, 39, 43, 113–114; cf. Joseph in Genesis 41; and Daniel in Daniel 1). The legend of the Magi following the star in the Gospel of Matthew (2:1–12) builds on their reputation for astronomical knowledge. Nothing in these references to the *Magoi*, however, suggests that they were magicians. In Hellenistic culture they were rather examples of the few people in the world who are truly wise and just as well as virtuous, as in the first-century Jewish philosopher Philo's discussion of "the order of the Magi among the Persians." These are model philosophers who "search out the workings of the universe (*ta physeos erga*) to gain knowledge of the truth and, through visions clearer than speech, give and receive the revelations of the divine excellencies" (*Prob liber Sit* 73–74). They possess "the true wisdom" (*ten alethen magiken*),

---

34. The following discussion is dependent on the unrivaled knowledge of the ancient sources in Arthur Darby Nock, "Paul and the Magus"; Becker, "*Magoi*," repeats Nock's survey of the varied meaning and usage of *magoi*, with some additional references.

the scientific vision by which the workings of the universe are presented in a clearer light (*Spec. leg.* 3.100).

By the fifth century BCE, however, the terms *magos* and *mageia* had begun to appear in polemics and accusations against foreign or otherwise despised ritual practitioners as "quacks." In Plato's *Republic, magoi* are "clever deceivers" (*Rep.* 572E). This shift or ambivalence in the meaning and connotation of *magoi/mageia* was parallel to that in a number of other terms that were highly positive in the official city-state religion and approved healing practices but polemical and accusatory for foreigners and less reputable ritual practitioners. Thus *epoidai* (hymns/songs/chants; prayers) could be "spells" or "incantations," *thusiai* (sacrifices) could be suspect, and *pharmakeia* (medicine/herbs) could be "potions" or even "poisons."[35] The tone and meaning must always be determined by context. The same or similar ritual practices were part of the regular official religion in one instance but the subject of accusation or ridicule in another. Or a polemical passage might involve both. For example, *On the Sacred Disease* (1.4), an early treatise of the Hippocratics,[36] who have been taken as the pioneers of "scientific" medicine, criticizes the standard healing practices of sacrifices, ritual chants, and purification rituals. But the appearance of ambiguous terms such as *magoi* or *epoidai* or *pharmaka* can hardly be taken as evidence for the practice of magic by magicians.

As Nock pointed out, accusations of *mageia* or *goeteia* or *pharmakeia* were made primarily against private individuals' use of rites, recipes, or skills to damage others and against the religious practices of foreigners or people who were disapproved of.[37] As is well-known from the accusations of the "respectable" philosopher Celsus against Jesus and his followers to which Origen responds, elite intellectuals' accusations against popular and/or foreign practices as *mageia*, in distinction from the proper practices of official religion and respectable wisdom, played an important role in the Graeco-Roman response to new movements such as early "Christianity." Despite the negative accusations and polemics, however,

35. See further the references in Nock, "Paul and the Magus," 310.

36. Recent critical treatment of the Hippocratics and this treatise in Martin, *Inventing Superstition*, chap. 4.

37. Nock, "Paul and the Magus," 315; cf. 313, where he further specifies self-protection from harmful forces, which fits under the first two categories. The much more extensive discussion of Hopfner, *Griechisch-aegyptischer Offerbarungszauber*, 1.41–45, classifies ancient Greco-Roman magic into the four categories of protective and apotropaic, malevolent and harmful, manipulative for love and power, and divinatory.

some Graeco-Roman intellectuals continued to hold in high regard the learning of *magoi* that ranged over several branches of knowledge, such as astrology, divination, prayers and chants, the properties of roots and herbs and stones, and their use in healing. Modern intellectuals, however, often failed to note the two different uses of the key terms or even fused the two in their modern construction of ancient magic as deviant and manipulative dabbling in the supernatural. In the carry-over from the ancient Greek *magos/mageia* to the Latin *magus/magia*, the cognates in English, *magician/magic* became the deeply entrenched terms for both the modern concept and the scholarly construction of ancient magician/ magic based on polemical texts taken at face value.

The (So-called) Magical Papyri

The scholarly construction of ancient magic, however, became based primarily on an extensive set of papyri discovered in Egypt in the nineteenth century, mostly in Greek but also in Demotic, that were labeled the Magical Papyri.[38] While most of these texts date from the fourth and fifth centuries CE, much of the material they contain was thought to be earlier. The texts inscribed on these papyri from late antiquity were taken to confirm not only that ancient *magic* was a coherent set of language and ritual practices, but also that many terms, phrases, formulas, and hymnic elements were distinctively *magical* language—and they were labeled accordingly: "incantations," "spells," "potions/poisons," and "techniques." Scholars then further assumed that when such terms, phrases, and formulas are found in earlier texts, they are evidence of a magical worldview and the practice of magic. On the basis of these papyri, therefore, scholars projected certain language and practices they believed to be magical into the first century. Most of the references that scholars have cited to attest particular terms, formulas, and practices as magical are to texts inscribed on these papyri.

The eclectic mix of cultural forms and elements of different provenance in the Magical Papyri,[39] however, makes these assumptions and

38. Preisendanz edited two volumes of *Papyri Graecae Magicae: Die Griechischen Zauberpapyri* in 1928–1931; these were revised and republished by Heinrichs in 1973–1974. Most of these ritual texts are translated in H. D. Betz, ed., *The Greek Magical Papyri*.

39. For the following, see Betz, "Introduction," xlv; and Betz, "Formation of Authoritative Tradition in the Greek Magical Papyri."

projections quite unwarranted. As indicated particularly in the mix of Greek and Demotic (Coptic) languages, much of the material is derived from traditional Egyptian religion, but as transformed by generations of adaptation into Hellenistic culture. The cultural mix also includes material of Jewish derivation, particularly the names and epithets of god(s), and even some seemingly Christian elements, such as "Jesus the god of the Hebrews." That the texts were written on papyri indicates that they were cultivated in elite circles, not in popular culture. This general mix of cultural materials suggests that these texts of late antiquity derive from a more general earlier confluence of high cultural traditions rather than from some hypothetical enclaves of magicians. In an illustration of the ready availability of ancient traditions from the Persian Magi, Pliny the Elder incorporated extensive quotations or paraphrases ostensibly from Zoroaster in his *Natural History* (especially books 26, 29, 30, and 37). Included were a way to determine the time to sow seed (28.200), the beneficial features of puppies' brains and dog's gall (29.117 and 30:82), and a considerable amount of apotropaic and medicinal material. The works of Philo of Alexandria, of Plutarch (e.g., *de Iside et Osiride*), of the Neoplatonists Porphyry and Plotinus, and the Hermetic texts all illustrate the availability and previous mixing of Persian, Egyptian, and other "Oriental" cultural elements such as divination, dream- and omen-interpretation, and eclectic knowledge of plants and herbs, metals and stones, animals and birds. Astronomy/astrology was particularly important, with its special set of symbols such as the signs of the zodiac and other constellations that were used widely in various connections.

In an influential essay on "The Temple and the Magician," the highly regarded scholar Jonathan Z. Smith lent considerable credence to the concept of magic among scholars of Christian origins.[40] He presents the second-century CE astrobotanist Thessalos as an example of the entrepreneurial "creativity of magic" through which, supposedly, the magician gradually replaced the traditional sacrifices in a temple by transforming archaic practices of sacrifice into salvific events of divination.[41] According to the obscure primary text, the comparative materials, and the older scholarly studies that Smith cites, however, it is not appropriate to label Thessalos a magician. The book of Thessalos, prefaced with a brief

40. J. Z. Smith, "The Temple and the Magician."
41. J. Z. Smith, "The Temple and the Magician," 186–89.

autobiography, is an astrobotanical treatise.[42] It provides a telling illustration of how Greek intellectuals aspired to the powerful higher wisdom they might gain from Egyptian priests and other "Magi"—a quest for wisdom from the East, in the ancient predecessor of this aspect of modern European Orientalism.[43]

Having traveled to Alexandria from his home in Asia Minor to study "dialectical medicine," Thessalos discovered in a library an astrological treatise "by [the legendary] Nechepso, which described a way of treating the whole body and every illness according to the signs of the Zodiac, along with stones and plants."[44] Having failed in his attempts to heal by following the book, Thessalos prevailed upon a priest in Thebes (deeper into the mysterious culture of Egypt) to initiate him into a vision of Asclepios, "alone, face to face." In his vision with the great healer-god, he obtained the yet higher knowledge of "the times and places" to gather the herbs, that is of the effective affinities of plants and stones with the stars for purposes of healing. His quest for a mystical vision resembles those of other mystics of late antiquity. But neither he nor they were practicing magic. His treatise, with his preface, was rather a mystical combination of astrology and herbal medicine, the effective application of which he attributed to a visionary experience.

As with Thessalos and his mystical mix of astrology and botany, it is unclear what would justify scholars' classification of the terms, phrases, hymnic fragments, formulae, and rituals of the Magical Papyri as magic, supposedly derived from much earlier practice of magic. This is true even of the long sequences of seemingly nonsense syllables and names of strange gods and *daimones* (in other/foreign languages), the symbolic representations of certain transcendent powers, and the chanting of the sounds of the seven Greek vowels that have been so striking to scholars as features of many "incantations" in the papyri. These represent the special language(s) necessary in communication with superhuman powers.[45] According to the first-century CE rhetorician Demetrius (*On Style*, 71), when singing hymns in praise of the gods, Egyptian priests utter the seven

42. One of the two extant versions of the book names the author as "Thessalos the Astrologer," as Smith notes, 173–74. Earlier modern scholars published it in the *Catalogue codicum astrologorum graecorum*.

43. The highly influential first analysis was Said, *Orientalism*.

44. J. Z. Smith translation, "Temple and Magician," 175.

45. Gager, "Introduction," 9–10; Tambiah, "Magical Power of Words"; Wallis, "The Spiritual Importance of not Knowing," and P. C. Miller, "In Praise of Nonsense."

vowels in succession: "the sound of these letters is so euphonious that men listen to it in place of flute and lyre." Representative of the spiritual culture of late antiquity in general, Clement of Alexandria explained that transcending normal human language was necessary in addressing gods and other higher powers (*Stromata* 1.143.1). He appealed to Plato as the authority that the gods communicated in a special discourse (*dialektos*), as evident in the experience of oracles, dreams, and the language of those possessed by *daimones*.[46] The Valentinian Christian (Gnostic) Marcos had his followers recite the vowels to praise and evoke the Father of all (Irenaeus, *Adversus Haereses* 1.14.1ff.). Clearly the chanting of the vowel sounds was not distinctive to the Magical Papyri and is hardly evidence of magic.

What is distinctive to the ritual texts on the papyri (that have evidently been inappropriately labeled magical) are the practical purposes for which language, formulas, recipes, prayers, and hymns are deployed, often indicated at the outset of particular units of text. The papyri include more than seventy "charms/spells" to coerce the sexual submission of a woman; prayers and phylacteries for protection from *daimones* and fate; pleas to gods/*daimones* for divination, revelation, dreams and dream-interpretation; "spells" to interfere with rival charioteers and other ways of causing harm to enemies; and "charms" to attract business. Particularly prominent in the papyri are rituals and hymns ("incantations") for obtaining a spirit/*daimon*/god as an assistant who will perform myriad tasks or empower the petitioner to do so. These often lengthy texts include instructions for sacrifices and other rituals, hymns and prayers, and instructions for sacred writing and amulets. "The spell of Pnouthis, the sacred scribe" (*PGM* I.42–195) for example, gives instructions for sacrifices on the rooftop, followed by an elaborate description of the appearance of the spirit/angel (in a vision) who can be commanded to bring women, kill, destroy, bring gold, prepare a banquet, and, when you are dead, carry your spirit into the air, etc. Clearly these are references to visionary experiences—as the text itself comments, "partly real and partly just illusionary."

46. As will be discussed again, *daimones* does not mean "(evil) demons," but some sort of transcendent spirit. Depending on the context, the connotation might be a semi-divine spirit, or god. The Christian theologian Origen, who defended Jesus against charges of magic, observed that "a man who pronounces a hymn in its native language can bring about the effect that the hymn claimed to have. But the same hymn translated into any other language would be weak and ineffective" (*Contra Celsum* 1.25).

There was a revival of interest in ancient magic by scholars of Christian origins in the 1970s and 1980s. This revival, however, appears to have involved little critical review either of the construct or of the sources. Scholars simply assumed that there was a "system of magical belief" and that the "magic" expressed in the "magical papyri" was a coherent worldview.[47] Hans-Dieter Betz even argued that the syncretism in the "magical" papyri was more than a hodge-podge of heterogeneous items and, in effect, a new religion altogether, displaying unified religious attitudes and beliefs."[48] It is difficult to discern what that unity may have been, however. The seemingly ad hoc collection of hymns, prayers, rituals, and recipes appear rather to be private measures of individual protection and advantage taken in the face of an opaque, arbitrary world. As has often been observed about life in the Roman Empire, especially in late antiquity, established worldviews connected with the broader political-economic-religious order of ancient civilizations and empires had broken down. The gods of order, light, and life no longer held in check the powers of disorder, darkness, and death. Those at the mercy of myriad arbitrary forces and searching for sex, health, wealth, assurance about the future, or control over or harm to another person, etc., appealed to whatever forces they might contact through rituals or prayers. Gaining influence with forces that transcended the powers of the dominant order or came from outside it was especially appealing. Since the so-called magical papyri date from late antiquity, however, we have no idea whether such rites were practiced in the much earlier context of Jesus and the Gospels. Since the concept of magic/magician was derived from accusations and polemics, moreover, we cannot imagine that there were actual magicians practicing magic.

The Construction of Jewish Magic

The scholarly construction of ancient Jewish magic has paralleled and been influenced by the construction of Graeco-Roman magic. *Magic* became the standard term for knowledge and ritual practices that were disapproved or simply forbidden. Not just the classic surveys by Ludwig Blau and Joshua Trachtenberg,[49] but more recent studies and review essays as

47. Hull, *Hellenistic Magic and the Synoptic Tradition*, 37.
48. H. D. Betz, "Introduction," xlvi–xlvii.
49. Blau, *Zauberwesen*; Trachtenberg, *Jewish Magic*. Criticism in Schiffman and

well,[50] assumed that there were ancient Jewish magicians practicing Jewish magic. Scholars kept adding to the variety of texts, knowledge, and ritual practices that they lumped together under the concept of magic, leading to further conceptual confusion. The engagement of esoteric and mystical Jewish texts from late antiquity and medieval times with spirits and heavenly powers led scholars to classify them as magical.[51] The *Book of Mysteries* (*Sepher ha-Razim*) and other such texts were even discussed as "magical manuals of spells and incantations," the "stock-in-trade of working magicians."[52] Similarly, when amulets and bowls with Hebrew inscriptions were discovered, mainly in Syria, they too were classified as magic.[53]

That these texts and inscriptions had much in common with texts later included in the Hebrew Bible and rabbinic texts, however, led to their recognition as "genuinely Jewish expressions." The tendency among scholars of such material was to relax the distinction between genuine religion and deviant magic and to make magic a subdivision of religion.[54] This suggests, however, that the scholarly construct of Jewish magic is neither necessary for nor appropriate to these mystical texts and bowl-inscriptions that turn out to be genuine Jewish expressions after all.[55] The

---

Swartz, *Incantation Texts*.

50. For example, Veltri, *Magie und Halakha*; and the overview of research in Becker, *Wunder und Wundertaeter*. The review essay by Alexander, "Incantations and Books of Magic" in a standard handbook concluded that most Jews in the late second-temple period believed to some extent in the power of magic. A recent study is G. Bohak, *Ancient Jewish Magic*. For more critical recent treatments of various accusations, texts, and "magical piety," see the articles by Stephen D. Ricks, "The Magician as Outsider"; Seidel, "Charming Criminals"; and "Magical Piety in Ancient and Medieval Judaism."

51. Schiffman and Swartz, *Incantation Texts*; Margalioth, *Sepher Ha-Razim*; the latter book, which is a reconstruction of modern scholarship, is often referred to as a "magical handbook."

52. Alexander, "*Sepher Ha-Razim*," 170; and the wider speculative discussions in "Wrestling with Wickedness in High Places"; and "Contextualizing the Demonology of the Testament of Solomon."

53. Naveh and Shaked, *Amulets and Magical Bowls*.

54. Even the rabbis themselves evidently had knowledge of mysteries and delved into certain esoteric practices, according to the early research of Jacob Neusner. See *History of the Jews*, vols 4 and 5; several chapters are collected in Neusner, *Wonder Working Lawyers*.

55. Emphasis on the power of God's name and appeal to the intermediacy of heavenly forces (angels) is hardly distinctive to magical piety, *vs.* Swartz, "Magical Piety," 171.

inscriptions on bowls and amulets are mostly appeals for protection: in general, from hostile spirits, from named persons, and for healing of babies. They often include words, phrases, or longer "scriptural" passages, most of which came from weekly prayers and liturgies. So how are appeals to God for protection on bowls somehow "magical" while the same or similar language in weekly prayers are genuinely "religious"?[56]

Many late-second temple Judean texts or text-fragments focused on superhuman spirits or heavenly forces have also been classified as magical and some of those have been taken as evidence of exorcisms, which are also classified as magic.[57] Found among the Dead Sea Scrolls at Qumran were a number of psalms for protection, such as the Apocryphal Psalms (11Q11; and 4Q560). These were ritual acts of protection, warning off a hostile spiritual force in anticipation of God's action. They were evidently spoken over a person afflicted by a hostile spirit, but not a casting out or defeat of a spirit that had taken possession of the person, and were hardly magical.[58] In the Songs of the Maskil (4Q510, 4Q511), the teacher-leader "proclaims the majesty of (God's) beauty to frighten and ter[rify] all the spirits of the angels of destruction and the spirits of the bastards, demons, Lilith, 'howlers and yelpers,'" who might lead astray "the sons of light," to which the community responds by blessing God's name (4Q510 1:4–8). There is nothing magical about these psalmic prayers for protection.[59]

56. Naveh and Shaked, *Amulets and Magic Bowls,* are evidently aware that scholars are imposing a modern construct onto Jews of late antiquity, with "fanciful interpretations and unreasonable speculations" (23), that the ancient Jews would say that they were practicing healing and protection, in reliance "not on magical powers, but on the power of God and his angels" (36)—but they continue to use the construct.

57. Alexander, "Wrestling with Wickedness," 319, calls these "magical texts" that indicate the Qumran sect "had a deeply magical outlook on life." Lange, "Essene Position on Magic," holds that magic was an integral part of Jewish belief in the second-temple period. Schiffman, "Dead Sea Scrolls," 351, understands magic in Qumran texts and Judaism generally very broadly as "eliciting God's help in warding off the forces of evil." A critical review of protective psalms and other materials at Qumran that avoids the concept is Brooke, "Deuteronomy 18:9–14 in the Qumran Scrolls." Sorenson, *Possession and Exorcism,* 64–74, discusses most of these Qumran texts with an overly broad understanding of possession and exorcism.

58. Alexander, "Incantations," 326: "The absence of technical magical praxis is once again striking." Cf. the rather uncritical discussion of Penney and Wise, "Aramaic Incantation."

59. Alexander, "Wrestling with Wickedness," 323–24, admits that they are "conspicuous for the absence of *materia magica,* of technical magical rituals and formulae and of divine names" (and of *nomina barbara*)—although it is unclear how he knows what may have comprised *materia magica* and "technical magical rituals and

They simply presuppose the same worldview of a struggle between the two camps of spirits led by the Prince of Light and Belial in the Community Rule (1QS 3–4). Rather than simply label it as magical, it will be important to investigate the struggle between these two opposing camps of spirits in the context of Hellenistic and Roman rule of Judea (discussed in chap. 5).

The story of Tobias driving away the killer-spirit Asmodeus from the bridal chamber of Sarah (Tobit 6–8), frequently claimed as a case of both exorcism and magic, is neither. The killer-spirit is not exorcized, but rather flees the smell given off by the smoldering liver and heart of a fish that Raphael ("God has healed"), the divine messenger-in-disguise, instructed Tobias to burn in the bridal chamber. This was evidently the known healing effect of a fish's liver and heart, parallel to that of the fish's gall, whose application to the eyes could (help) heal blindness (cataracts?; 6:1–9).

Perhaps the exorcism story most widely discussed as "Jewish magic" is Josephus' claim to have witnessed how the Judean Eleazar, before the soon-to-be emperor Vespasian and his officers, drew a demon out of a man through his nostrils by placing a ring to his nose that had under its seal a root prescribed by King Solomon (Ant.8.45–49).[60] In contrast to the protective psalms recited to ward off spirit-affliction found among the Dead Sea Scrolls, Eleazar is drawing a spirit out of a man it had invaded. But Josephus is not presenting this as a case of magic. As noted above, the Greek and Roman cultural and political elite accused foreigners as well as people of lower rank of performing harmful rituals that were a danger to the established order. Augustus had ordered 2000 "magical" scrolls burned in 13 BCE. During and after the great revolt of 66–70 by Judeans and Galileans, in the aftermath of which Josephus composed the *Antiquities,* there was great suspicion of and hostility to "the Judeans," not a context in which to boast of great acts of *mageia* by the renowned Judean king.

Josephus is rather touting Eleazar's feat as an impressive illustration of the great wisdom (*sophia*) that God had granted to the philosopher-king Solomon (*Ant.* 8.21–49). He had not only composed many books of odes and songs, parables and similitudes, that displayed his wide general knowledge of trees, birds, animals, and fish, all of which he had studied

formulae."

60. Critical analysis of Josephus' account of Eleazar's exorcism in Duling, "Eleazar Miracle."

"philosophically." He had also gained knowledge of the art (*techne*) used against spirits (*daimonon*) for the benefit and healing (*therapeia*) of people. He also composed songs (*epoidas*) by which illnesses are relieved, and left behind forms of exorcisms in which spirits are driven out of those possessed.

There thus does appear to have been knowledge of exorcism and at least one case of its practice among the Judean scribal/intellectual elite. Strange as it may seem to modern readers, however, exorcism was evidently not understood as *mageia* among the Judean cultural elite any more than was the interpretation of dreams (Daniel 1–2). And the apologist-historian Josephus certainly does not seem to be worried lest his boast of Solomon's great wisdom and its efficacy in exorcism would result in Roman accusations that Jews were practicing magic.

Jesus and Magic

Considering that the ostensible sources for ancient magic are either very late or polemical and that they focus on such matters as coercing sex, harming an enemy, or enhancing one's business, it is puzzling that interpreters of Jesus could find elements of magic in Jesus' healings and exorcisms. Scholars of Christian origins, however, simply shifted the focus of ancient magic to healing and exorcism, evidently without critical investigation.[61]

Shifting the Focus of Magic to Healings and Exorcisms

Having been trained to concentrate on the meaning of particular words and phrases in text-fragments on the basis of their occurrence elsewhere, New Testament scholars focused narrowly on words and phrases (mainly) in the Magical Papyri rather than on complete texts of "spells" and other rituals. Not surprisingly, the threads by which New Testament scholars connected the stories of Jesus' exorcisms and healings to magic were thin indeed, consisting of a few terms and phrases that occur in a

61. E.g., see Aune, "Magic in Early Christianity." When Aune moves his discussion of ancient magic to Jesus (1523–24), he suddenly shifts to a list of Jesus' miracles. More telling may be his insertion of "healing" into his paraphrase of Hopfner's inventory of the goals of Graeco-Roman magical activities. Other discussions of Jesus and magic similarly focus on healing and exorcism.

few late ritual texts that had been labeled magical. Adolf Deissmann, for example, called attention to the "binding" in supposedly magic texts in connection with the healing of the deaf-mute in Mark 7:32–37 and the importance in magic of knowing the name of a *daimonion* in connection with Jesus' question to "Legion" in Mark 5:9.[62]

More recently it has been claimed that the command "come out" (*exelthe*) in some of the exorcism stories of Jesus is the standard form of address to demons in the Magical Papyri.[63] It is also claimed that the purpose of the formula "I adjure you (by . . .)" (*horkizo se [kata . . .]*) is "to harness supernatural powers in order to effect the exorcism."[64] None of the three passages cited, however, concerns exorcism.[65] Adjuration of superhuman powers does indeed appear in the papyri, but not for purposes of exorcism. Moreover, as with other terms, phrases, and names that appear in the Papyri, it is unwarranted to conclude that adjuration was distinctively magical.[66] Indeed, it seems likely that the Magical Papyri took over adjuration from its wider use in earlier syncretistic Hellenistic culture. With regard to healing, it is often claimed that Jesus' touching and his use of spittle are magical techniques. But neither touch nor spittle is mentioned much in the magical papyri or in any other sources for ancient magic. Again the use of touch in healing was common and hardly distinctively magical. And spittle, like other bodily fluids, was commonly believed to carry certain powers (helpful and/or harmful).

Far more problematic for Jesus scholars' assumption that healing and exorcism were included in the practice of magic, however, is the lack of sources that might suggest this. Not even the elite intellectuals' accusations of magic in the first century and before seem concerned about healing or exorcism. More telling is that, although terms and phrases in

62. Deissmann, *Light from the Ancient East.*

63. Hull, *Hellenistic Magic and the Synoptic Tradition*, 68; Aune, "Magic," 1531, points out that it occurs only four times in the papyri.

64. Aune, "Magic," 1531–32.

65. One of the three (III.1–164, esp. lines 11, 36, 70–80), for example, after the lengthy summoning of Helios/the (cat-faced) Chthonic One (which follows the ritual drowning of a cat), adjures the god to impair rival chariots, charioteers, and race-horses.

66. As Aune notes: "Jesus' use of the imperative mood in exorcisms is in fact a widely known and used form of adjuration in the ancient world' (citing Philostratus, Vit Apoll 4.20; Acts 16:18), "Magic in Early Christianity," 1532. It is puzzling that he then concludes that Jesus' authoritative commands to demons are "formulas of *magical* adjuration."

the Magical Papyri have been used as sources to argue that (some of) the language and techniques in the stories of Jesus' exorcisms and healings are magical, few of the ritual texts have anything to do with either exorcism or healing.

Texts in the Magical Papyri often have to do with *daimones/daimonia* and gods. The aim, however, is almost always to bring a superhuman power into the control of the practitioner to do his bidding (e.g., as in *PGM* V.96–172, esp. 165–170), not to expel the superhuman power from someone. Only a few ritual texts in the Papyri are concerned with protection against or driving out of *daimones*.[67] Exorcisms appear only in three long conjurations in which the language is clearly derived from earlier Jewish and/or Christian tradition. For example, an "excellent rite for driving out demons" (that uses an olive branch as a whip) has a formula in Coptic appealing to "God of Abraham . . . Jesus Chrestos, the Holy Spirit" and the command to "come out (*exelthe*), *daimon* . . . ," in Greek (IV.1227–1264). The background in "Hebrew" tradition and adjuration of the Jewish and/or Christian God to gain power over (superhuman) spirits is even more extensive in the other two (IV.3007–3086; V.96–172).[68] These texts so obviously dependent on Jewish and/or Christian tradition can thus hardly be used as evidence that exorcism was included in the supposed practice of magic in the early first century CE. That exorcism appears in only a few out of the hundreds of ritual texts in these extensive papyri suggests that even in late antiquity it was a rare practice in the repertoire of those who may have used them.

As for healing, several very short passages in the "magical papyri" have to do with "cure" of relatively simple "diseases." Some brief remedies or phylacteries, for scorpion sting, discharge of the eyes, migraine headache, coughs, hardening of the breasts, swollen testicles, and various fevers, appear in a sequence (from VII.193–96 through VII.218–21). Among the myriad tasks an angel assistant will perform, including killing and destroying, are finding wild herbs and empowerment to cure

67. Smith's statement that "spells and amulets for exorcism are frequent in the papyri" (*Jesus*, 107) is simply wrong.

68. "A tested charm of Pibechis for those possessed by daimons" includes a phylactery of secret names of superhuman powers, and the adjuration to "the god of the Hebrews, Jesus (followed by more secret names) . . . , by the God who appeared to Osrael [sic] in a shining pillar.... for this charm is Hebraic . . ." (IV.3007–3086). In "the stele of Jeu the hieroglyphist" the practitioner identifying himself as "Moses your prophet" summons the "Headless one, who created earth and heaven. . ." to "deliver NN from the daimon which restrains him" (V.96–172).

(I.42–195). Beyond those brief items and a one-line prayer, a brief charm, and a geometrically arranged set of secret names for various fevers (XVIIIa.1–4; XVIIIb.1–7; XX.13–19), it is difficult to find any healing rites among the hundreds of ritual texts. Healing, like exorcism, is simply not a major concern of the Magical Papyri."[69] The Papyri are concerned far more with causing bodily suffering and incapacitating illness and other forms of harm than with "curing" fevers and headaches and sexual dysfunction.

There is thus no more basis in the Magical Papyri than in earlier polemical sources for applying the scholarly construct of ancient magic to the exorcisms and healings of Jesus.

A Broad Argument that Jesus was a Magician

The most provocative initiative in the revival of interest in ancient magic in the 1970s and 1980s was Morton Smith's presentation of Jesus as a magician in the broadest terms, with extensive references to ancient sources, particularly the Magical Papyri.[70] He expanded the composite concept of magic constructed earlier in the century to include not only healing and exorcisms but also prophecy, revelation, and divination. Unusual among scholars of magic, Smith was quite candid about projecting the modern understanding of magic onto antiquity, as he scoured ancient sources to document everything "we now regard as 'magic'" whether or not they were regarded as *mageia* in antiquity.[71] However, although he adduced a plethora of supposed parallels, primarily in the Magical Papyri, for various "traits" of Jesus' life, they are not convincing and his broad claims are simply not credible.

Smith does not seem to notice the inconsistency of his own construction of ancient magic/magician. On the one hand, he insisted that magic is mainly "private dealings with supernatural beings," that is 'private religion.'[72] On the other hand, Smith significantly broadened the

69. Again, Smith seriously overstates the case: "cures are a major concern of magic . . . [and amount to] prescriptions or stories of cures for most afflictions cured by Jesus . . ." such that "the miracles with which Mark represents Jesus at the beginning of his career in Galilee are drawn entirely from the magician's repertory" (*Jesus*, 107).

70. M. Smith, *Jesus the Magician*.

71. M. Smith, *Jesus the Magician*, 76.

72. M. Smith, *Jesus the Magician*, 69. Smith rejects the argument that "the religious man petitions the gods while the magician tries to compel," a view restated by Kee,

category of magician to include a certain "social type"[73] that included: deified philosophers and wonder-workers, such as Apollonios of Tyana, whom Smith had previously labeled "divine men";[74] "prophets who introduced new religious observances unknown to reasonable men"; "madmen" who had been divinely possessed;[75] and the prophets who led popular movements mentioned by Josephus.[76] Smith's magicians were thus not just "social," but a mishmash of what appear in the sources as several different "social types."

With this greatly expanded composite picture of ancient magician in mind, Smith argued that many of "the traits in Jesus life" were those of a magician from what he saw as parallels between Gospel portrayals of Jesus and phrases and motifs mainly in the Magical Papyri. In two of his more far-fetched arguments he even found Jesus' "conversion" of the disciples to be magical (comparable to "love charms" such as *PGM* IV.327f; 2708–2784)[77] and the eucharist to be "the clearest evidence of Jesus' knowledge of magic," similar to the use of "enchanted food to cause love" in the Magical Papyri.[78]

He devoted most discussion to the "miracles," the exorcisms and "cures" that he took as the most fundamental marks of a magician. Jesus was empowered to perform these by the intimacy he had gained in his baptism with the divine spirit of the dead man, John the Baptist.[79] He claimed that the extensive list of the powers gained in several ritual texts in the Magical Papyri (*PGM* I.54–195; IV.1930–2005; 2006ff-2125)[80] "include most of those with which Jesus is credited."[81] In fact, the list includes none of them, and what it includes are far from what Jesus is credited with, such as bringing women or men for sex, killing, bringing

---

Miracle in the Early Christian World.

73. M. Smith, *Jesus the Magician*, 69.

74. Hadas and M. Smith, *Heroes and Gods.*

75. M. Smith, *Jesus the Magician*, 77; on the analogy of the synthetic construction of "shamanism," primarily on the basis of Siberian materials, by Eliade, *Shamanism.*

76. M. Smith, *Jesus the Magician*, 79, with no discussion.

77. M. Smith, *Jesus the Magician*, 106–7.

78. M. Smith, *Jesus the Magician*, 152, cf. 124, 146.

79. Toward the beginning of his discussion (*Jesus the Magician*, 97–98), Smith had admitted that the demons of dead men were most often employed for single assignments, usually to harm enemies or to bring women for sex.

80. M. Smith, *Jesus the Magician*, 96–104.

81. M. Smith, *Jesus the Magician*, 100.

gold, and breaking the teeth of savage serpents. Given that most such "parallels" he adduced are strained, even the center of his argument, that in his healings and exorcisms Jesus was practicing magic, still depends on the previously adduced thin philological threads connecting the stories about Jesus' "miracles" with phrases mainly from the Magical Papyri. Smith's wide-ranging argument that Jesus was a magician is thus a mix of supposedly parallel motifs taken out of context, gross exaggerations of questionably similar motifs, and idiosyncratic interpretations.

Magic/Magician as a Sociological Type

Little more than a decade after Morton Smith—and following his presentation in certain regards —John Dominic Crossan mounted an even broader argument that Jesus was a magician. While presupposing the composite scholarly concept of ancient magic,[82] however, he did not base his argument on similarities of terms and techniques attested in ancient sources for *mageia/magoi*.[83] Rather he dramatically broadened the concept of magic on the basis of an abstract typology from the sociology of religion.[84]

Toward the end of his career, Bryan Wilson had applied his typology of religious "sects" in modern western societies to "deviant religious responses to the world (or evil)" among "less developed" peoples.[85] Among the many types of "deviant" religious response he delineated, he saw as the most frequent the *millennial* or *revolutionist* and the *thaumaturgical*

---

82. As reviewed by Aune, "Magic," and (re-)defined as deviant religious practice.

83. The only particular item he mentions that New Testament scholars label as "magical techniques" is the spittle Jesus uses in the healing of a man's blindness (Mark 8:22–26; cf. John 9:1–7). Crossan here (*Historical Jesus*, 325) relies on Smith and Aune. But Smith's notes (*Jesus the Magician*, 204) rely for parallels on older secondary works and sources from late antiquity whose references to spittle do not necessarily have to do with techniques thought to have been magical. Aune bases his assertion that saliva and foreign words (etc.) are magical techniques" not on texts typically cited to attest magic, but on his own definition of what constitutes "magic," that is, "the deviant context" in which they were performed, and on Jesus' having made health available to an individual "by means which were thought guaranteed of success." (1537–38). Crossan's sole reference to the "magical papyri" is to a recipe/ritual-incantation in III.410–423, which has nothing to do with healing.

84. Crossan, *Historical Jesus*, 137–38, 303–4.

85. Wilson, *Magic and the Millennium*.

or *magical*, which he saw also as the pristine religious orientation.[86] Crossan made Wilson's "most profound" typology of religious responses to evil the controlling "strand" in his construction of Jesus.[87] Having adopted Wilson's *thaumaturgical/magical* response as determinative for his interpretation of Jesus, he had to add "magician" (as a fifth type) to the historical social forms of leaders of renewal-and-resistance movements he had discussed in Part II (based on what I had discerned through the accounts of Josephus).[88]

While Wilson used the term "thaumaturgical" to avoid the controversial "magical," Crossan wrote boldly of "magic/magical." With Aune (and others) he insisted that magic cannot be distinguished from religion in substantive terms of rites and beliefs, but only perspectivally or prescriptively. The key differences, in Crossan's discussion, are that the *magician* attempts "to change the sorry state of the individual rather than that of the group."[89] He repeatedly emphasized that magic focuses on "the private, personal, and individual" in contrast to the communal.[90] The *magician* can make divine power present *directly through personal miracle* rather than *indirectly through communal ritual*.[91] Magic is also unofficial, unapproved, and often lower-class religion, in opposition to the official, established rituals and institutions.[92]

With this broad yet individualistic definition of magic in mind, controlled by Wilson's *thaumaturgical* type of response to "evil," Crossan "presumes" (his term) that Jewish magicians were "widespread" on the popular level around the time of Jesus.[93] In order to present at least some examples, he claims that Honi the Circle-Drawer and Hanina ben Dosa, whom Geza Vermes had characterized as "charismatics" or "holy men"

---

86. But if magic is the pristine religious orientation, how can it be deviant?

87. Crossan, *Historical Jesus,* 303–4.

88. Crossan, *Historical Jesus,* part II and 137–58 (with numerous references to my earlier articles), and 421, where he admits that this is "a type barely discernible behind and despite later rabbinical prophylaxis."

89. Crossan, *Historical Jesus,* 137.

90. Crossan, *Historical Jesus,* 140–41.

91. Crossan, *Historical Jesus,* 138.

92. Crossan thus returned to Marcel Mauss's individualistic but broad definition of over a century ago, that magic is "any rite which does not play a part in organized cults, it is private, secret, mysterious . . . ," continuing to follow Aune, "Magic," 1514–15.

93. Crossan, *Historical Jesus,* 157.

who did miracles, were magicians.[94] Drawing on earlier studies of how the later rabbis had "rabbinized" these figures by attributing their deeds to prayer and proper piety,[95] he finds magical rain-making and healing in the earliest layer of their legends, individual magic underneath the communal concerns of the rabbis.[96] "Before the Second Temple's destruction it was magician against Temple, thereafter magician against rabbi."[97]

Unfortunately, not only does Crossan's discussion of ancient "magic" fail to subject the standard scholarly construct of ancient magic to critical examination, but his extension of the composite concept of magic to include Wilson's thaumaturgical type and the ancient holy men is problematic in several respects.

First, evidently accepting the earlier scholarly construction of ancient magic, Crossan continues to make what was polemical accusation into a definition of historical reality. In effect he is saying that Celsus had it right: Jesus was a magician.

Second, Crossan creates (supposedly) historical magicians out of legendary holy men. His claim that a magician was a type of popular figure current in first-century Palestine on the basis of Honi and Hanina is no more credible historically than Vermes' claim of a "holy man" tradition within what he posited as "charismatic Judaism."[98] Contrary to

94. Vermes, *Jesus the Jew,* had suggested that these were the figures most comparable to Jesus as healer and exorcist.

95. Green, "Palestinian Holy Men"; Bokser, "Wonder-Working and the Rabbinic Tradition."

96. Crossan, *Historical Jesus,* 142–56.

97. Crossan, *Historical Jesus,* 157. It would be difficult for Crossan to find any sources to attest this grand claim that "before the second Temple destruction it was magician against Temple." This assertion comes in striking contrast with much of his presentation in Part Two, a lengthy discussion (drawing on my earlier articles) of the different kinds of popular leaders and movements that opposed the rulers in the Jerusalem temple as well as the Romans. The image of "magician against Temple" surely derives from Jonathan Z. Smith's influential essay on "The Temple and the Magician" (discussed above). Smith, however, made his sweeping generalization about how the sophisticated and well-educated (not peasant) "holy man" or "magician" had come to rival the traditional "temple" *in late antiquity in the Roman empire as a whole,* which was a significant change from the situation in earlier centuries in areas such as Palestine. As noted above, moreover, Smith based this on one figure, whose self-characterization was not as a magician but as a learned Greek astrobotanist who obtained higher wisdom in a "face to face" vision of the god Asclepius.

98. Which Crossan deemed "profoundly correct" as a framework for discussion of Jesus, *Historical Jesus,* 157. Among the telling criticisms of Vermes' construction of the Palestinian "holy men," in addition to the critical analysis of the sources by Green and

Crossan's claims, critical analyses of Josephus' account of Honi and the legends of Honi and Hanina in rabbinic texts from later centuries find it impossible to establish anything about them other than their rough dating (to a century before and a few decades after Jesus, respectively).[99] The legends have Honi praying successfully to God to send rain (but not actually making rain) and Hanina knowing whether his prayers for healing will be answered (but not actually doing acts of healing). As noted above, however, although the Greek and Demotic Magical Papyri include prayers, prayer was hardly distinctively "magical." And although authorities might have objected to unauthorized practices, rites intended to influence the weather were common practice in the ancient world: in Greek city cults as well as in villages, not to mention Elijah's contest with the prophets of Lord Storm (Ba'al; 1 Kgs 18).

Third, by subsuming "magic/magician" under the "thaumaturgical" response to "evil" in Wilson's seven-fold typology of movements among "undeveloped" peoples Crossan makes the concept of magic even more incoherent and confusing. The focus of Wilson's "thaumaturgical" type on the individual's relief from specific ills is attractive to Crossan's own individualistic orientation. But Wilson understands thaumaturgy (magic) very broadly as including basic religious rituals that were central to traditional tribal culture and persisted in most religions (including what he calls the great "founded" religions) and even as a magical world-view or way of thinking. The working of wonders, while happening to individuals, is usually not private but public. Wilson's "thaumaturgical response" is far broader than the scholarly construct of ancient magic based on the Magical Papyri in which "magicians" obtained superhuman spirits as "assistants" through certain rites and then used them for private advantage.

The resulting conceptual incoherence is evident in the tension between Crossan's quotations from Wilson and his own editing and application of them. While Wilson was discussing numerous movements among underdeveloped peoples that exhibited somewhat the same "response" to evil or the world (abstractly conceived), Crossan is trying to create a

Bokser, see especially Meier, *Mentor, Message, and Miracle*, 581–88.

99. Especially Green, "Palestinian Holy Men," esp. 627; and Bokser, "Wonder-Working and the Rabbinic Tradition." At one point (147) Crossan unaccountably misuses a statement by Green about the function of a "rabbinized" legend of Honi (Green, 641) to insinuate that the historical Honi had practiced rain-making, hence was a "magician." Bokser (69–70) saw a concern about "a community in danger" in the earliest layer of the legend about Hanina protective action against the dangerous lizard's bite (cf. Crossan, *Historical Jesus*, 153).

"type" for Jesus as an unapproved individual worker of miracles for individuals, in opposition to the official rituals in the Jerusalem temple. In the discussion from which Crossan takes the epigraph to his chapter 8 Wilson was discussing "new thaumaturgical *movements*" that were "deviant" because of their "*organizational forms*."[100] Crossan immediately, in the first sentence of the chapter, shifts Wilson's typology of *movements* (e.g., "magical or millennial") to one of *individual figures*, in a discussion that drives toward establishing "the magician as type" of individual figure over against the temple.[101]

In one of the key statements in *The Historical Jesus*, Crossan claims that Jesus' individual practice of magic was pointed directly against the "patronage and clientage, honor and shame" at the heart of (urban) Mediterranean society.[102] Ironically he takes the quotation used to set up this declaration from Wilson's discussion of "Thaumaturgy and Organization."[103] Wilson had just explained that at an early stage in the development of some movements, "the thaumaturge may train acolytes" who establish themselves as operators of shrines, setting up the "need to claim superior powers in order to sustain patronage and to satisfy their clientele."[104] In the movements they headed Wilson's thaumaturges created networks of patronage in rural areas.

Finally, it is problematic to take from the modern Western *sociology of religion* the highly abstract sociological type of magic/magician as the controlling concept for a *historical* inquiry into a historical figure in an ancient historical context.[105] Wilson states at the outset precisely how he is

100. Wilson, *Magic and the Millenium*, 192, italics added.

101. The same tension with Wilson's discussion runs through much of Crossan's individualistic adaptation. Wilson (*Magic and the Millenium*, 170) observes that individuals' charisma must be validated in the community and, to a degree, manifested for corporate benefit; and that thaumaturgical movements become agencies of rationalization and socialization, enabling "underdeveloped peoples" to assimilate into the dominant order—not exactly what Crossan has in mind for Jesus as magician focused on the private individual.

102. Crossan, *Historical Jesus*, 303–4.

103. Wilson, *Magic and the Millenium*, 131.

104. Wilson, *Magic and the Millenium*, 129.

105. Wilson's typology is not anthropological, despite what Crossan suggests (p 303), although he draws on numerous anthropological studies of particular peoples from the 1950s and 1960s. In a sharply critical review of *Magic and the Millenium*, Kenelm Burridge calls Wilson's sociological framework "outmoded," resembling "the functionalism of the 1920s and 1930s" in its merely "epiphenomenal" analysis, fuzzy categories, and "little or no sense of history." Less severe but still critical is the more

proceeding. He begins with "an earlier taxonomy" that he had developed in dealing with "sects" primarily in Britain and America.[106] Claiming to have weeded out the specific Christian connotations, he "looked for continuities between sectarianism in Western countries and the new sectarianism of the third world."[107] Most of the questions and concepts thus unavoidably come from studies of Western religious movements in their reaction to the "founded" religions, as in the focus of the whole study and its typology on "the search for salvation." Ironically, while he criticizes some of the problematic theories and concepts of "structure-functional" sociology, he exemplifies them in subsuming particular movements into his general types by virtue of their similarities of "structure, function, and process." Wilson is remarkably candid that his approach means not just inattention to, but the sacrifice of history and historical context. "What the sociologist hopes to gain must be reluctantly paid for in the coin of the historian and the anthropologist."[108]

Magic: A Modern Western Concept that Distorts Historical Life

Crossan's adaptation of Wilson's "type" of thaumaturgy leads directly to the principal reason for simply dropping the term "magic" in consideration of Jesus' exorcism and healing: the "baggage" that the concept carries in Western culture of ("scientific") reason and imperial power-relations. Wilson's typology in *Magic and Millennium* provides a prime illustration of this baggage.

Under the influence of the Reformation and the "humanists'" emphasis on reason, religion came to be understood in elite Western culture increasingly in terms of true belief. In defining and defending official, established religion, intellectuals and Church authorities defined other, often popular, "beliefs" and practices as "magic." It was often closely associated with the practice of "witchcraft," with tragic implications for

---

extensive retrospective review by an Africanist thoroughly knowledgeable in the studies Wilson had used: Peel, "An Africanist Revisits *Magic and the Millennium.*"

106. Wilson, *Magic and the Millenium*, 18, referring to Wilson, *Sects and Society*; and Wilson, *Religious Sects*.

107. Wilson, *Magic and the Millenium*, 2.

108. Wilson, *Magic and the Millenium*, 18; cf. 133–34. See the fuller discussion of how the ghost of Weber's concept of "charisma" and its "routinization" lurks behind Wilson's discussion of "thaumaturgical" and other movements in Horsley, *Jesus and Magic*, 87.

midwives, herbalists and other folk healers, and local diviners.[109] While the dawning "Enlightenment" may have contributed to the demise of the officially sponsored witch-burnings, the rise of Reason further crystal-ized the differentiation of (true) *religion* as rational belief and *magic* as the dark realm of popular superstition, irrationality, and coercive ma-nipulation. Reason was understood in terms of Nature; what was natural was rational. With the rise of science, particularly empirical science, the rational came increasingly to be defined in terms of what was empirically valid, as judged by the senses.

Closely interrelated with the consolidation of the Enlightenment rational-natural worldview in elite Western culture was European intel-lectuals' emergent understanding of the "primitive" or "savage" peoples of the world whom Europeans were encountering and subjugating, from the voyages of "discovery" to the intensifying colonization of the late nineteenth century. It is impossible to separate the colonial encounter from European intellectuals' delineation of the evolutionary scheme of a development, in the increasing triumph of reason, from magic to religion to science.

Particularly influential in making this evolutionary scheme univer-sal by applying it to what was known of earlier cultures or "primitive" peoples were the works of E. B. Tylor and Sir James Frazer.[110] The scheme is an abstract one of the stages of thought as it perfects itself, without correlation with social structure or historical context. Frazer's highly in-fluential formulation came to dominate elite cultural views both of evolu-tion in Western civilization and of more "primitive peoples" to whom the Europeans had only recently brought the enlightenment of rational thought: "magic" is an early expression of science based on a deluded sense of cause and effect; "religion" advanced manipulation and coercion of forces to supplication and veneration of the gods; "science" returned to principles of cause and effect but now on the basis of true correlation known from observation of nature.

At least three full generations of anthropologists focused on "mag-ic" as one of their principal concerns.[111] The superiority of reason and

109. See further Horsley, "Who Were the Witches"; and Horsley, "Further Reflec-tions on Witchcraft."

110. Tylor, *Primitive Culture*, 1871; Frazer, esp. the one-volume edition of *The Golden Bough* in 1922.

111. From the evolutionists of the 1870s and after to the structural-functionalists in the first half of the twentieth century. As a mark of how important the concept

science in Western society over the "backward" peoples of the world had become an integral component of the West's "grand narrative." By the 1950s and 1960s the difference between "magic" and "religion" was no longer so clear, but "magico-religious thought" was still understood as an earlier or more primitive stage that had yielded or would yield to the spread of reason and science.[112] The social sciences were clearly backing away from this abstract, synthetic construct. As a significant review concluded, somewhat tentatively: "Magic is not a uniform class of practices and beliefs which can be immediately discerned in every society."[113]

Wilson's typological definition of thaumaturgy, however, which Crossan makes the controlling "type" of Jesus the magician, perpetuates the evolutionary scheme of magic, religion, and science/reason that had become part of the West's "grand narrative."[114] This can be seen both in his understanding of magic and in his assumption of the evolutionary perspective on magic among "less developed peoples" and in religion in general. Magic is by definition contrary to natural reason and science. "The thaumaturgical (= magical) response is a refusal to accept the testimony of the senses and natural causation as definitive."[115] Throughout his discussion, thaumaturgy "is belief in empirically unjustified practices and procedures which affect personal well-being."[116] Indeed, the evolutionary view of "magic-religion-(empirical-scientific) rationality" determines much of his agenda in the book, including how thaumaturgy gives way to rationalization. "Such belief in thaumaturgy has greatly declined in the nineteenth and twentieth centuries, as empirico-rational explanation has

---

was, the *Encyclopedia of Religion and Ethics* (published in 1917) devoted seventy-six double-column, small-print pages to magic. Malinowski, *Magic, Science, and Religion*, widely read in liberal arts programs in the 1950s, exhibits an interesting mix of evolutionary view of societies with an appreciation of the positive *social-cultural* function of magic (based on his field work in the Trobriand Islands) as ritual acts that bridged over people's dangerous gaps of knowledge in every important pursuit.

112. See earlier review articles such as Wax and Wax, "The Notion of Magic"; and Aberle, "Religio-Magical Phenomena."

113. Yalman, "Magic," 521; the article is only seven pages of large print.

114. Wilson, moreover, was relying on studies (largely by anthropologists) of African and American peoples carried out from the 1940s to the 1960s (some much earlier), many of which also still shared the evolutionary scheme.

115. Wilson, *Magic and the Millenium*, 70.

116. Wilson, *Magic and the Millenium*, 484.

expanded, and has declined perhaps even more sharply than specifically religious belief and practice have declined."[117]

Moreover, Wilson understands magic in religious movements among less-developed peoples as the beginning stage in "wide, evolutionary processes."[118] "Thaumaturgical practice is usually part of the tradition of primitive religion itself."[119] "Thaumaturgy is the primal stuff of primitive religion. Curing ceremonies, protective devices, and miracle-making are found very widely . . . in almost all preliterate societies."[120] The very starting point of his presentation, therefore, is that "thaumaturgical preoccupations are the fundamental orientation of new religious movements among simpler peoples—just as they were of their indigenous religion. Movements arising among indigenous peoples soon after cultural contact with white men are, understandably, fundamentally magical."[121] As the movements develop, accordingly, "Magical explanations give place to better-tested hypotheses . . . Thaumaturgical movements themselves embrace more rational procedures, and more systematic patterns of organization . . . Sometimes they come to accept the insights of science . . . and increased education and medical facilities . . ."[122]

In his "Conclusions" Wilson complains that the problem with "broad categories—such as *anomie, charisma, relative deprivation, nativism, and culture-shock* —is their tendency to become catch-all phrases, . . . summary solutions to intellectual problems, . . . [adding] to the problems of comparative sociology by reducing the rigour and the exact specification of abstract propositions."[123] Ironically the same can be said of "broad categories" such as "less-developed people," "thaumaturgical," and "rational." From the vantage point of critical retrospect such categories appear to be "summary solutions" to intellectual problems generated among modern Western academics. As some historians of religion are now saying, however, "magic does not exist; it is the product of scholars' minds."[124] Almost more important, the concept of magic carries Western

---

117. Wilson, *Magic and the Millenium*, 71.

118. Wilson, *Magic and the Millenium*, 4.

119. Wilson, *Magic and the Millenium*, 54.

120. Wilson, *Magic and the Millenium*, 70.

121. Wilson, *Magic and the Millenium*, 5.

122. Wilson, *Magic and the Millenium*, 8.

123. Wilson, *Magic and the Millenium*, 498.

124. Penner, "Rationality, Ritual, and Science," applies to magic what Levi-Strauss had said about totemism. That "magic," like "miracle," is an issue in modern scholars'

rationalist and imperial baggage that seems singularly inappropriate to antiquity in general and to Jesus' exorcism and healing in particular.

Significant Shifts in Recent Critical Discussion of Ritual Practices in Antiquity

The surge of scholarly interest in ancient "magic" had barely begun at the time of Smith's and Crossan's presentations of Jesus as a "magician." Investigations during the 1990s, like that of Nock eighty years ago, recognized not only that what ancients thought of as "magic" was different from the modern concept but also that polemical references and accusations are not good sources for historical practice. Investigators have also considered whether the modern concept may hinder understanding.[125] The more candid scholars, aware of the earlier critical reflection by social anthropologists in the 1960s, sense that there is no longer much point in "reification of transcultural categories at the expense of history, culture and social context."[126]

Yet even critical scholars, after issuing caveats about how problematic the concept is, continued to write as if, historically, there were

---

minds (that does not correspond to historical literary references and ritual practices) seems to be illustrated in every successive attempt by a theologian, biblical scholar, or sociologist to review and reconceptualize it. For example, sociologist Rodney Stark, "Reconceptualizing Religion, Magic, and Science," recognizes that "the term magic has been a conceptual mess," but remains imprisoned by the modernist "scientific" mentality and discourse in which science deals with the natural and religion and magic with the supernatural. Stark's own "reconceptualization," partly a "throwback" to Malinowski, is heavily indebted to Christian theological understanding of magic (and miracle).

125. Not only is the term "magic" "one of the most persistent problems in the study of so-called magic in the ancient Mediterranean," as noted by James Rives, "*Magus* and its Cognates in Classical Latin," 53; but also "there has been a loss of faith in the traditional underpinnings of the category magic itself," as noted by Richard Gordon, "Reporting the Marvellous," 65. In a seeming inconsistency, in the massive collection of essays in *Guide to the Study of Ancient Magic*, edited by David Frankfurter, the essays in parts 2 and 3 avoid the term "magic" (and stick to indigenous nomenclature, since ancient texts did not use "our term"), but suddenly in part 4 Frankfurter himself discusses magic as a certain quality (of language) in theorizing that draws heavily on Malinowski, whose anthropology was implicated in colonial conceptions. Several of the essays included appropriately and helpfully discuss their focal material in terms of ritual.

126. Gordon, "Reporting the Marvellous," 65, citing Tambiah, *Magic, Science, Religion and the Scope of Rationality*, 29.

magicians engaged in the practice of magic in the ancient world, not only in late antiquity, but also earlier in the Greek and Hellenistic-Roman world.[127] The continuing critical investigations and discussions have nevertheless resulted in important recognitions that should enable New Testament scholars finally to move beyond the problematic twentieth-century construction of ancient magic and to focus on discussion of Jesus' healings and exorcisms not as (having elements of) magic but as healings and exorcisms.

The Ancient Discourse of Magic

Increasing recognition that references to *magoi/mageia* and *magi/magia* and related terms were polemical and accusatory has led to critical discussion of such references as a *discourse of magic*, not evidence of the historical practice of magic. Well-known scholars produced major books that restated the modern scholarly construction of magic from Greek and Latin sources, insisting that "the practice of magic was omnipresent in classical antiquity."[128] Knowing that such sweeping statements were simply untrue, however, they repeatedly issued caveats that the sources in fact do not attest the practice of magic and that the concept is problematic. One even admitted: "the truth of the matter is that we are in no position to assert that belief in magic was the norm at any period in Classical Antiquity, let alone in the first centuries of our era."[129] The recent shift in the focus of discussion to the *discourse* of magic avoids the previous naïve use of literary references as if they were straightforward evidence of historical ritual practice. They are rather evidence of what some people (the elite, who produced literature) believed or feared about secret rituals, particularly divination and the social and political function

127. Given the surge of interest in "magic" in antiquity, leading scholars see themselves as creating a new (sub-)field of study (with academic conferences and expanding publication of papers, dissertations, and books): see, for example, Faraone and Obbink, "Preface," vii; and Gordon and Marco Simon, "Introduction," 1. It would presumably be academically impolitic to state too sharply that not only the modern concept of magic is hopelessly problematic but also the modern scholarly construct of magic is inappropriate to ritual practices in antiquity and unnecessary—suggesting that this surging field of study bears an inappropriate title.

128. Fritz Graf, *Magic in the Ancient World*, 1; Dickie, *Magic and Magicians*.

129. Dickie, "Magic in the Roman Historians," 85, although in the next sentence he writes as if somehow behind Tacitus' accounts of political accusations of dangerous divination were actual magicians.

of such beliefs or fears. The principal function of the belief was to discourage and control marginal ritual practices through belittlement, scary exaggeration (e.g., of necromancy), silencing, and even trials, executions, and lynchings.[130]

Nock had long since concisely laid out the evidence of the discourse of magic in Greek sources. Recent studies now supply the corresponding evidence for the discourse from Latin literature, with warning about how remote the concept of magic in the modern scientific world is from the ancient discourse—to which we should add how different the twentieth-century scholarly construction of ancient magic still presupposed in many studies is from the ancient discourse.[131] References to *magi/magia/magicus* from roughly 50 BCE to the mid-second century CE are relatively limited, with dramatic differences between prose and poetry. A minimally coherent discourse of "magic," including the first occurrence of the noun *magia* (in Apuleius' self-defense), did not develop until the second century CE, and even then was not particularly prominent. The discourse, moreover, made reference only to a few ritual practices about which some elites were anxious, such as divination, as well as fearsome mythic figures, such as Circe and Medea. The discourse consisted, variously, of poetic references to those mythic "witches" and their chants and spells, prose traditions of the venerable Persian Magi, with their divination and other rituals, and accounts in Tacitus (and other historians) of a handful of high-level trials, mainly of women, for unauthorized divination threatening to prominent imperial figures. Clearly there is no evidence in this discourse for assertions about practice of magic in the Roman empire at the time of Jesus.[132]

The Transformation of Egyptian Religion That Led to "the Magical Papyri"

Egyptologists have recently explained the transformation of traditional Egyptian religion under Roman imperial rule that led to its western misunderstanding as magic and the background from which the "magical

---

130. Gordon and Marco Simon, "Introduction," 6, referring to other studies such as Ogden, *Greek and Roman Necromancy*; and Rives, "Magic in Roman Law."

131. See especially Rives, "*Magus* and Its Cognates."

132. Critical studies of the ancient discourse of magic continue; see, for example, Janowicz, *Magic in the Roman World*; and Stratton, *Naming the Witch*.

papyri" emerged.[133] In archaic Egyptian culture the divine figure Heka ("One Who Consecrates Imagery") was the creative Word-Force that transformed performative speech-acts into tangible earthly form, becoming a real presence in every temple ritual. The scribal lector-priests, as extensions of Pharaoh, were responsible for composing, collecting, learning, and performing this ritual repertoire, and maintaining it in written collections (of hymns, prayers, ritual techniques, curses, healing rites, etc.) in the "houses of life" (temples). People could petition a god publicly during regular processions of statues or privately under priestly instruction (via lamps, bowls, and images). Such rituals led by lector-priests staffing local temples became the standard arbiters of justice.[134] Under Ptolemaic rule, Greek became, to a considerable extent, the language of the temples and lector-priests as well as elite culture generally, although Egyptian culture continued also in Demotic as well. Insofar as the divination, oracles, and other wisdom of the lector-priests was analogous to those of the Persian *magoi* outsiders understood them as practicing *mageia*. In the modern western (Orientalist) construction that continued in academic circles it became standard to refer to Egyptian divination, wisdom, and culture generally as "magic" and the priests as "magicians." But there were evidently no itinerant ritual experts in chanting or drugs or cursing or divination in Egypt that corresponded to the "charlatans" accused of harmful rituals in Greece. Rather the lector-priests of the local temples, keepers of all the traditional ritual texts, also served the needs and desires of the local population, private as well as public.[135] Second-century sources such as Plutarch and Clement of Alexandria suggest that Egyptian priests and the traditions they cultivated and rituals they practiced were still alive (Plutarch, *De Iside et Osiride*; Clement, *Stromateis* 6.4.35, 37; *Paedogogus* 3.2.4; *Protrepticus* 2.39).

The Romans, long suspicious of foreign religious practices, especially of Egyptian and other "oriental" religion, cut off state subsidy of the temples, leaving the lector-priests all the more dependent on the local population whose religious needs they had traditionally served. Eventually suspicious Roman officials moved to suppress the practices of the lector-priests that they saw as a threat to Roman morals, social control,

133. On the following, see e.g., Robert K. Ritner, *The Mechanics of Ancient Egyptian Magical Practice*; and "Religious... Parameters of Traditional Egyptian Magic."

134. Ritner, "Religious . . . Parameters of Traditional Egyptian Magic," 51–56.

135. Ritner, "Religious, Social, and Legal," 55–56; Frankfurter, ""Ritual Expertise," 120; and *Religion in Roman Egypt*, chap. 5.

and financial domination.[136] Q. Aemilius Saturninus, prefect of Egypt under the emperor Septimius Severus, in 199 CE, for example, decreed that "no one, through oracles, that is, by means of written documents supposedly granted in the presence of the deity, nor by means of the procession of cult images or suchlike charlatanry, pretend to have knowledge of the supernatural, or profess to know the obscurity of future events"—under threat of capital punishment.[137] "Much of what had constituted public religion was driven underground, becoming secretive and 'private' practice."[138] Performed in household "shrines" rather than in the temples, it seemed to match the discourse of magic.

For the way in which the Roman Egyptophobia may have led to the emergence of "magical" papyri, the parallel phenomenon of Egyptomania must also be taken into account, as exemplified by the Greek astrobotanist Thessalos (already discussed above), particularly in his collaboration with the priest in Diospolis who arranged his face-to-face encounter with Asclepius. While Roman officials were suspicious of the Egyptian lector-priests' divinations, Greek and Roman intellectuals were eager to obtain their higher wisdom, like what Philo had referred to as "the true wisdom" (*ten alethen magiken*) of the Magi. A recent study of Thessalos' self-serving preface argues that in "publishing" what he claimed surpassed even the knowledge of the legendary Egyptian astrologer Nechepso, he was creating a commodity to be consumed in the elite intellectual circles of the Roman empire, pandering to the burgeoning fascination with the "magical powers" of "the East."[139] As for the priest in Upper Egypt who had set up the vision of Asclepius for Thessalos, who had come to Egypt "with a large amount of money," his collaboration with Thessalos may have become his ticket to prestige and fortune, say, in the more cosmopolitan cultural milieu of Alexandria.[140] In the Egypt of late antiquity those who knew the ritual texts were hungry, and "western" (Greek and Roman) intellectuals hungry for the wisdom of the East provided an eager market for what they had to offer.

136. Ritner, "Religious, Social, and Legal," 57; Frankfurter, "Ritual Expertise," 125; see further Gordon, "Religion in the Roman Empire," 241–42.

137. Papyrus Yale Inv 299, translation adapted from John Rea, "A New Version of P. Yale Inv 299"; G. H. R. Horsley, *New Documents Illustrating Early Christianity*, 1.47–51. Naphtali Lewis calls this "A Ban on False Prophets."

138. Ritner, "Religious, Social, and Legal," 57.

139. Moyer, "Thessalos of Tralles and Cultural Exchange," 52–56.

140. See also Frankfurter, *Religion in Roman Egypt*, 225–33.

Not Magic, But Particular Types of Ritual Practice

A critical review of recent scholarship shows that what is labeled magic and the supposed evidence for it from texts and artifacts are in fact a number of different kinds of ritual practices that became lumped together under the synthetic scholarly construct. The late collections of texts in the "Magical Papyri," moreover, are texts of various types of rituals. It is surely significant, further, that the ancient Greek and Latin discourses of magic included anxiety and accusation about only a few of these different kinds of (secret/unofficial) rituals. Recent studies are focusing on some of these particular kinds of ritual practices or artifacts, sometimes without application of the concept of magic. These more focused studies are suggestive for how the problematic concept of magic could simply be dropped and focus shifted to the actual (attested) particular ritual practices in the ancient world. It is appropriate for historical investigation to consider such ritual practices according to type and the way they functioned, with appropriate attention also to their common features, overlap, and the relation between them.

The best attested, hence probably most common type of private (unofficial) ritual practice in antiquity, was *protective* in the broadest sense ("apotropaic" or "eudaemonic"). Most familiar are the (inscribed) amulets or phylacteries of small pieces of papyrus or metal or precious stones.[141] Recitation and/or inscription of a special text invested these amulets with special protective power. These are closely related to the extensive Greek and Roman Lapidaries, or "Books of Stones" that describe the marvelous powers (properties) of precious stones (most familiar through book 37 of Pliny the Elder's *Natural History*. In the lapidary tradition the properties/powers of stones were correlated with those of plants and animals, drawing on the earlier Babylonian lapidaries that were translated into Greek in the Seleucid period.[142] Even studies that still assumed that amulets were "magic" found that the chants and prayers inscribed on amulets are not

141. For a list of the published catalogues of these, see Gordon and Marco Simon, "Introduction," 31 nn91–93.

142. It has commonly been supposed that protective ritual practices were derived from and remained rooted in the nonliterate indigenous "wise-folk," herbalists, and diviners. This supposition may be rooted in the western elite attitude toward peasants (*pagani*). The role of writing in the evolution of the lapidaries and the herbalist tradition of classical Greece and the lapidary tradition from the "high" culture of the Near East, however, all suggest rather an elite cultural basis of such practice. Cf. Gordon and Marco Simon, "Introduction," 40–42.

appreciably different from chants and prayers that are not usually labeled magical by scholars.[143] There would appear to be no good reason why amulets inscribed with Homeric verses or "standard angelic and divine names" or well-known lines from Jewish (or Christian) scripture should continue to be classified as magic.

Katadesmoi and *defixiones* were another distinctive type of ritual practice. Because they were so aggressive, coercive, and self-serving— and appeared to rational, scientific moderns to be based in superstition—they attracted a great deal of attention and were labeled as "malign and aggressive magic" or "sorcery." But again there is no good reason to classify them as magic. Brief formulaic messages inscribed (or scratched) mainly on thin sheets of lead (or on ostraca, papyrus, gems, or bowls), pierced by a nail, and deposited in graves, springs, or other bodies of water, were surreptitiously deployed by individuals against some private or public rival or enemy such as a lawyer/orator or a chariot driver or to coerce a desired woman. These "binding spells" have now been analyzed, grouped into subtypes (such as "judicial") and suggestively interpreted without recourse to the modern construct of magic. That problematic concept would only obscure their interpersonal functions as they became articulated with the wider social and political dynamics of a given city.[144]

Other ritual practices included hymns/chants and prayers and the mixing and administering of drugs/medicines. These practices were very widespread, and only a fraction of them were attacked as harmful acts (*veneficia*) by those anxious, for example, that their crops were being "charmed away" or that they were being "poisoned."[145]

One of the most widespread and prominent kinds of ritual practice, especially in political circles, was *divination* by various means. Closely related or interrelated were astronomy/astrology, necromancy, "soothsaying," dream-interpretation, and interpretation of omens. Divination was of great importance in the royal courts of the ancient Near East. Imperial

143. Kotansky, "Incantations and Prayers," 107–8. The conceptual muddle continues as Kotansky (121–22) writes of "prayers for salvation that seem embedded in an indisputably magical context." See further Faraone, *Transformation of Greek Amulets*.

144. Review of older and more recent investigations in Gordon and Marco Simon, "Introduction," 14–30; Gager, ed., *Curse Tablets and Binding Spells*; Eidinow, *Oracles, Curses*.

145. Plato proposed a law against certain kinds of *pharmakeuein* (including chanting) that would be harmful, in which the perpetrator who was a skilled healer or herbalist would be punished more severely. But by no means were most chants, prayers, drugs, and other healing attacked or banned, much less attacked as "magic."

regimes and subordinate temple-states maintained staffs of highly trained scribes and/or priests who cultivated the traditional higher knowledge and rituals. The official civil religion in the Greek *poleis* and in Rome had well-developed standard rituals for divination. As discussed above, however, anxiety focused on dangerous private divination that might lead to subversive action.[146] Perhaps because scholars of ancient "magic" also know about the importance of divination to ancient regimes they have not labeled divination generally as magic.

These results of studies of ancient ritual practices in the last two decades further confirm the conclusions reached in the review of the discussion of Jesus as engaged in "magic." The shift of focus to the discourse of magic is the confirmation as well as the result of the recognition that Graeco-Roman references to "magic/magician" were polemical and accusatory, hence not evidence of historical ritual practice. The explanation of the transformation of Egyptian religion under Roman rule confirms that the "magical papyri" of late antiquity were hardly good sources for the general practice of "magic" by "magicians" at the time of Jesus. Recent analyses of particular kinds of ritual practice without reference to the scholarly construct of ancient magic not only illuminates these practices and their functions, but suggests that the synthetic concept only obscures social and political functions and contexts.

Since the scholarly construct of ancient magic is without evidentiary basis and since it is deeply problematic in various ways because of its roots in and continuing connotations of the Western concept of magic, it should simply be abandoned. The construct never did pertain much to healing and exorcism, except in adaptation by scholars of Christian

---

146. In the Christian intensification of attacks on what had become defined as magic the learned ancient Egyptian and Babylonian priests and scribes who cultivated divination and related practices became demonized in Biblical (mis-)translations that persist even in the (N)RSV. In the book of Exodus (7:11; 8:7), Moses is engaged in competition with "sorcerers and magicians" with "their secret arts" (and ironically Moses is portrayed as performing the same "magic" tricks, only better). The key term translated "magician" (*hartom*) is borrowed from the Egyptian *hr tp*, "lector-priest" (that was not earlier associated with the *magoi*, as noted by Stephen Ricks, "The Magician as Outsider," 135–36. In the book of Daniel, the Judean youth are trained, like all the other learned court functionaries, "in all the branches of wisdom, endowed with knowledge an insight," so as to be able to serve in the King's court (1:4). When the narrative focuses on dream-interpretation, however, the NRSV labels the other learned experts at court "magicians and enchanters" (Dan 1:20; 2:4; 4:7; 5:7, 11). By contrast, Josephus (*Ant.* 10.195–205) represents the highly-learned dream-interpreters at the king's court as *sophoi, magoi,* and *chaldaioi.*

origins and of ancient Jewish religious practice. Just as classical scholars now feel free to discuss protective rituals and divination without the baggage of the concept of magic, so New Testament scholars should now be free to discuss the healings and exorcisms of Jesus not as miracles or magic, but as healings and exorcisms.

3

Understanding Exorcism and Healing in Historical Contexts

RECENT STANDARD BIBLE TRANSLATIONS widely used in scholarly circles as well as church services have created further misunderstanding of Jesus' healing and exorcism. In earlier English language usage (reflected in standard dictionaries) the terms sickness, illness, and disease were often used interchangeably, as were the terms healing and curing. But healing had broader connotations, even of making whole, while curing pertained to particular ailments. Similarly, sickness was the broader term, with disease referring to particular ailments with certain symptoms. In the later decades of the twentieth century, standard Bible translations shifted from the broader concepts of sickness and healing to the narrower concepts of disease and cure. Standard dictionaries and lexica in New Testament studies and classical studies edited earlier in the twentieth century still listed "sickness/illness" along with "disease" as translations for terms such as *nosos* and "heal" for the term *therapeuein*. While rendering the terms *nosoi* and *mastigai* as "diseases," the Revised Standard Version, produced in mid-twentieth century, still had Jesus "healing" those who were "sick" (see, e.g., Mark 1:32, 34; 3:2, 10; 6:13). The New Revised Standard Version of the 1980s, however, narrowed the portrayal of Jesus' healing the sick to his "curing" of "diseases" (again see Mark 1:32, 34; 3:2, 10; 6:13; Luke 7:21).[1] The New Jerusalem Bible made a similar shift toward Jesus' "curing" of "diseases."

1. The picture of Jesus as a doctor who cures all sorts of diseases (biological disorders and malfunctioning) is suggested further in the translation of his response to the scribes that it is not the healthy but the sick who have need of a "physician."

One suspects that this shift in translations by scholarly committees reflects the increasing dominance of Western medicine in health care and in society generally. With its increasing effectiveness in finding cures for diseases, scientific Western biomedicine gradually consolidated its dominance in health care in the first half of the twentieth century, marginalizing other forms of healing. In the later twentieth-century medicine, based primarily in biological science, became ever more prestigious, as well as ever more prominent in the political-economy, first in Western countries and then world-wide. Both in the field of medicine and in (at least Western) culture more broadly, disease became the standard term for a biological disorder or malfunctioning in the organism of a human (diagnosed from particular symptoms) that is then cured by medical intervention that eliminates the disease and/or restores the proper biological functioning. The curing of diseases in biomedicine, moreover, was understood as science dealing with phenomena of nature. It is understandable perhaps that scholarly translators would shift toward what had become the dominant cultural discourse in their translation of the stories and summaries of Jesus' healings and exorcisms.

The irony of the representation of Jesus in these more recent translations (and scholarly discussion) somehow goes unnoticed. The portrayal of Jesus as curing diseases, with connotations of modern biomedicine, suggests that his healings were similar to those of a modern doctor. But medical practice that can diagnose and cure diseases is a development of modern Western science, which Jesus of Nazareth could not have known in ancient Galilee. So if he was curing diseases, it would indeed have been by magic or miracle.[2]

The portrayal of Jesus' healing as the curing of diseases in standard translations of the Gospel sources is thus problematic in two fundamental regards.

First, the translations distort the sense of the Gospel narratives. The translations narrow the meaning of the terms used for the sick people whom Jesus heals, terms that suggest a range of suffering broader than biologically defined "diseases." That Jesus heals *tous kakos echontas,* literally "those having (something that makes them feel or that affects them)

2. It was ironic that the effects of New Testament interpretation striving to become more "scientific" (*wissenschaftlich*) was to become more reductionist of Jesus' healings, forcing them into scientific-rationalist explanations while simultaneously finding the healing and exorcism stories to be miraculous. Here is another of the perils—and confusions—of modernizing Jesus that Henry Cadbury warned of nearly eighty years ago.

badly" (Mark 1:32; etc.), is broad and inclusive in reference to a range of malaise, suffering, distress, anguish, or torment. The various *nosoi* with which they are plagued (Mark 1:34; Luke 7:21) suggest sickness, anguish, distress, and even madness, not particular diseases that can be diagnosed and cured by a physician. The term *mastix*, used in the Gospels for what many people were suffering, derived from the flogging of horses, slaves, soldiers, prisoners, those being examined under torture, or those the Romans condemned to crucifixion (as in Mark 10:34; Matt 10:17; 23:34; Josephus, *War* 2.306). *Mastix* thus compares the torment of sickness to being beaten by the political authorities, suggesting extreme suffering under some plague or scourge (such as the woman who had been hemorrhaging for twelve years, Mark 5:29; cf. Mark 3:10; Luke 7:21).

The term *therapeuein*, often used for Jesus' healing, had broad connotations of caring or caring for, as in doing service to gods, cultivating plants, preparing food or drugs, maintaining temples, assuaging or remedying, hence suggests a broad range of healing with regard to sickness and suffering. The terms *iaomai* and *iatros* referred somewhat more particularly to caring for the sick or sickness. The verb referred to treating, remedying, or healing more generally. The noun referred to healers or care-givers such as a midwife, a physician, or a more general healer. In particular healing stories what Jesus does is not curing at all, but issuing commands or sensing that power has passed through him (e.g., Mark 1:40–45; 2:1–12; 3:1–5; 5:21–43; 10:46–52). What was happening in Jesus' healing was evidently broader than and different from the curing of diseases.

Second, in shifting to "disease" and "cure" the Bible translators were adopting language used for the practice of medicine that had narrowed its understanding of sickness and healing to what was scientifically manageable. According to the "scientism" that came to dominate Western medicine, biological processes alone constituted the "real world" of disease and treatment and became the central focus of research, diagnosis, and medical manipulation and "intervention."[3] Only those variables susceptible of reduction to biological analysis and "intervention" became acceptable as scientific.[4]

Even as the field of medicine expanded to include more and more aspects of life previously in the jurisdiction of other fields and institutions

3. Kleinman, *Patients and Healers*, 25.
4. Kleinman, *Patients and Healers*, 31–32.

(such as religion or education), moreover, scientific biomedicine continued to define disease and treatment as if it were independent of other aspects and processes of life. Particular diseases were definable entities virtually independent of the case histories of sick persons. Medical practitioners diagnosed and treated diseases, not sick people. Pressures of professionalism and productivity further enforced the reduction of the diagnosis and treatment to biological processes. Biomedical practice excluded consideration of both the social context and the meaning context of sickness, as well as alternative therapies.

Even though biblical studies, and particularly interpretation of Jesus, paid little attention to other academic and professional fields, biblical scholars (as patients themselves) would have been generally aware of the discourse of the increasingly dominant field of medicine. As their understanding of sickness and Jesus' healing in Gospel stories became narrowed to disease (bodily dysfunction) and yet they found no "ordinary" means comparable to the scientific means of medical curing in the stories, miracle became all the more important as the explanation of Jesus' healings and exorcisms. Since, like biomedical practice, interpreters of Jesus' healings and exorcisms had excluded consideration of both the social context and the meaning context of sickness (as disease), miracle was the only possible explanation left.

Just as the translators of the Gospels were narrowing the scope of Jesus' healing to curing under the influence of Western medical practice, however, Western medicine was coming under increasing criticism (including self-criticism) for its narrowness. Beginning at least in the 1960s western doctors became ever more cognizant of the "disconnect" between their practices of brief consultation, diagnosis, prescription, and other medical intervention and their patients' dissatisfactions and lack of compliance with "what the doctor ordered." This "disconnect" between medical practice and what patients were looking for was even more striking as Western biomedicine spread into non-Western and "developing" countries. It became a major factor that led to criticism of Western biomedicine and critical rethinking of its assumptions and practices, both within the field of medicine and in the closely related developing field of medical anthropology. As anthropologists and others became more acquainted with sickness and healing in other cultures, they recognized the reductionism as well as ethnocentrism of Western "scientific" medicine.[5]

5. The literature is now vast. See, for example, the analysis of Eisenberg, "Disease and Illness"; Kleinman, *Patients and Healers*, 18–32; and Good, *Medicine, Rationality,*

Medical anthropologists suggested that only by stepping outside of the biomedical paradigm and its rules could western investigations discern how sickness and healing are embedded in the social and cultural world and begin to move toward a more holistic view. Moving beyond the reductionist "scientism" of biomedicine is thus parallel to moving beyond the modern western "scientific" mentality that consigned healing that was not due to "natural" causation to the realm of "miracle" or "magic" that was due to the "supernatural" (as discussed in chapter 2).

Medical anthropology developed partly in encounters with other cultures with traditional indigenous forms of healing that led to criticism of "scientific" western medicine. Developments in medical anthropology may thus be helpful to the field of New Testament studies, still so embedded in the assumptions of modern Western culture, in becoming more sensitive to ancient cultures on their own terms. While medical anthropology is still a relatively young field of study, different perspectives have emerged. Particularly helpful for moving toward a more comprehensive approach to the healing and exorcism of Jesus may be work in both "meaning-centered" medical anthropology and "critical" medical anthropology that came to maturity in the 1970s and 1980s.[6] Insofar as medical anthropologists are working in the current situation dominated by Western biomedicine that did not exist in the ancient world, however, we can only learn from but not directly apply theory and schemes of medical anthropology in analysis of the healing and exorcism of Jesus in its ancient historical context.

Sickness and Healing as Culturally Constructed

Interpretive/Meaning-Centered Medical Anthropology

In moving toward a more comprehensive understanding of sickness and health-care in a world where biomedicine was reductionist yet increasingly powerful, "interpretive" or "meaning-centered" medical anthropologists made a theoretical distinction between the biological (or psychological) and the personal-social aspects of sickness (and healing). "A key axiom in medical anthropology is the dichotomy between

---

25–52, and references there.

6. The literature for both of these perspectives in medical anthropology became extensive. I will focus here on some of the key formative statements of each, with reference to review articles.

. . . disease and illness. *Disease* refers to a malfunctioning of biological and/or psychological processes, while *illness* refers to the psychosocial experience and meaning of perceived disease. Illness includes secondary personal and social responses to a primary malfunctioning (disease) in the individual's physiological or psychological status (or both)."[7] Illness involves affective valuation of and response to the disease and its symptoms and interpersonal communication and interaction, particularly in the family and social network. Illness includes responses to disease which attempt to provide it with a meaningful form and explanation as well as control. "At times we can talk securely about disease *qua* disease, but illness . . . can only be understood in a specific context of norms, symbolic meanings, and social interaction."[8] Correspondingly, in the "interpretive" theory of sickness and healing, "cure" was typically used with reference to the medical treatment of "disease," while the broader term "healing" was used with reference to the care or treatment of "illness."

Interpretive medical anthropologists were not always clear in making this "axiomatic" distinction, not always consistent in use of the corresponding terms, and understood that the distinction was incompletely worked out.[9] But their juxtaposition of the concept of illness and that of disease provided a way to take into consideration what "scientific" biomedicine had excluded, especially patient and lay perspectives on, and the meaning contexts of, sickness.[10] The concept of illness brought into focus the ways that the sick and their healers are embedded in particular configurations of social relationships and cultural meanings, not

---

7. Kleinman, *Patients and Healers*, 72. Similarly Eisenberg, "Disease and Illness," 11, but with the important caveat that illness and disease do not stand in a one-to-one relationship," that is, illness is not simply a response to disease.

8. Kleinman, *Patients and Healers*, 77. In a 1982 review essay, "The Anthropologies of Illness and Sickness," Allan Young suggested an expanded triple distinction between *disease* (organic pathologies and abnormalities), *illness* (individual consciousness), and *sickness* (process of giving socially recognized meanings).

9. Kleinman, "Concepts and a Model." See the sharp criticism of the distinction in Craffert, "Medical Anthropology as an Antidote," 2–8.

10. In an important early statement of the distinction, Eisenberg, "Disease and Illness," states it flatly: "Patients suffer 'illnesses'; physicians diagnose and treat 'diseases'" (11). In the unrelenting "medicalization" of society, however, as the distinction of disease and illness helped create a common language for clinicians and social scientists, the unanticipated effect has been that the medical establishment has moved to claim illness as well as disease for its domain, as pointed out by Scheper-Hughes and Lock, "The Mindful Body," 10.

only in patterns of interpersonal interaction, but even institutionalized power-relations.

The fundamental point made and stressed in "meaning-centered" medical anthropology is that both "disease" and "illness"—and correspondingly "cure" and "healing"—are *culturally constructed*. They are not entities in nature, but social constructions of reality (ways of explaining sickness and healing). This recognition is particularly important for historical investigations into healing (such as that of Jesus in ancient Palestine), just as it is for the understanding of healing in other societies as well as for the disconnect between medical practitioners and their patients who speak different "languages."

Symptoms and significance of sickness come to expression and communication in particular language, including expression of strong feeling, and including gestures and other "body language." Peoples have been socialized into particular language, different from society to society in significant ways, that forms the link between consciousness and action. Language is the essential medium in which beliefs about sickness, behavior of the sick and their supporters, their expectations of treatment, and the ways they are cared for are expressed.[11] Through language culture provides much of the specific content of sickness and healing.[12] The experience of sickness is thus embedded in specific configurations of cultural meanings and social relationships. Sickness and healing are thus culturally constructed as forms of social reality in the transactional world in which social roles are performed and people negotiate with each other in established relationships under a system of cultural rules.[13] And these vary significantly from society to society, even sub-culture to sub-culture.

Given the often intimidating claims of biomedicine to be "scientific" as the basis of its widely accepted authority and political-economic power in the modern "scientific" world, it may be especially important to recognize that disease (along with medical diagnosis and cure), as well as illness, is culturally constructed.[14] This can be seen in the training of doctors in medical school and internships. Although the idea that disease is fundamentally biological remains enormously powerful in the medical field, clinical medicine constitutes the body and disease in distinctive

11. Kleinman, *Patients and Healers*, 38.

12. Kleinman, *Patients and Healers*, 33.

13. Kleinman, *Patients and Healers*, 35–36.

14. See also Kleinman, "Medicine's Symbolic Reality"; and Good and Good, "The Semantics of Medical Discourse."

cultural forms.[15] In a central metaphor, medical training is likened to learning a foreign language—except that it is not learning a different set of terms for ordinary everyday reality, but rather learning to construct a whole different world. It involves new ways of "seeing" and defining a different reality and special ways of thinking, writing, and speaking within the practice of medicine. It involves learning a vast amount of knowledge from biological sciences, such as anatomy and radiology. But these have their own language and moral norms. In anatomy lab, for example, the skin is drawn back and the "interior" body is invaded, cutting across the natural layers of tissue in unnatural fashion to expose and identify tiny nerves, veins, glands, and tendons. The medical student unnaturally invades and deconstructs the body (the cadaver) and then constructs it in separable parts and dimensions in order to be able, as a doctor, to deconstruct patients' bodies in attempts to identify (label) a disorder or dysfunction.

Doctors-in-training then learn to formulate, write up, and present, in as concise a form as possible, a diagnosis of each case in clear logical fashion, adducing the ostensible "facts" that argue in favor of the diagnosis and discounting the counter-indicative "facts." Such write-ups and presentations (in later clinical practice perhaps internal and unspoken in the physician's mind) are creative, formative practices that shape as much or more than reflect a patient or a project. In order to work with the requisite efficiency, moreover, the doctor (-in-training) listens to patients selectively, with potential indicators, diagnoses, and "write-ups" already in mind. The doctor does not merely depict bodily reality, but constructs the diagnosis of a case of a disease that is recognizable because it has been similarly constructed many times before in this formative process. This cultural construction is then used to reshape the body with pharmacological agents and medical procedures. Disease(s), diagnosis(es), and cure(s), no less than illness(es), sickness, and healing, are cultural constructions. Diseases diagnosed and treated in medicine are the cultural construction of modern Western society. We who have been socialized in modern scientific culture may believe that certain diseases are/were universal. But their modern scientific cultural construction would not have been known in the ancient world

15. On the following see the probing discussion in Good, *Medicine, Rationality,* chap. 3.

Implications for Historical Investigation

The distinction between disease and illness and the recognition that both are culturally constructed are important steps toward dealing with sickness and health care more holistically in the contemporary multicultural and now globalized world. In learning from or adapting "meaning-centered" medical anthropology for historical investigation of Jesus' healing and exorcism, however, the distinction between disease and illness may be as problematic as the recognition of the cultural construction of sickness is crucially important. Kleinman's and others' distinction between disease and illness pertains to the modern life-situation in which biomedicine is either dominant, as in Western countries, or prominent, as in most other countries. In the latter, many people who depend primarily on traditional folk-healers as well as family and friends do go to practitioners of Western medicine and its medicines for certain symptoms. In modern society generally, including in Western countries, while western medical practitioners are oriented toward disease, the laity are oriented toward illness.[16] Indeed, illness can occur in the absence of disease.[17] Since illness behavior includes the perception, affective response to, cognizing, and valuation of the symptoms of disease, along with their (verbal and non verbal) communication, *all* symptoms are molded by the illness experience.[18] In patients' understanding of sickness, disease and illness are usually not distinguished.[19] Thus even in modern society the distinction between symptoms of disease and those of illness is not easily sustained.

Premodern societies, prior to the development of biomedicine and its construction of disease, therefore, had no knowledge of disease (as an explanation of sickness)—even if we believe that some of the diseases constructed by modern medicine are universal. To project the concept of disease onto ancient Mediterranean societies is not just a logical fallacy (disease is constructed by biomedicine; there was no biomedicine

---

16. Kleinman, *Patients and Healers*, 73. Kleinman comments, 355, that "Problems in clinical care seem to arise when the practitioner is concerned only with "curing" the *disease* and the patient is searching for "healing" the *illness*." It thus makes no sense for historical inquiries into the healing of Jesus to imagine that he was engaged in the (miraculous) curing of disease while oblivious to the culturally defined experience of sickness and healing.

17. Kleinman, *Patients and Healers*, 74.

18. Kleinman, *Patients and Healers*, 75.

19. Kleinman, *Patients and Healers*, 356.

in antiquity; therefore there was no disease in antiquity), but a histori-cal anachronism. In antiquity there was no one, including intellectuals in the Hippocratic tradition and sophisticated "natural scientists" such as the astrobotanist Thessalos, who would have constructed sickness as disease.[20] In the complex multicultural Roman Empire there were many different cultural constructions of sickness and healing, but the construc-tion as disease and curing developed in the modern West was not among them.[21] Nor would ancient societies have known the distinction (or even what appears to be a dichotomy in some formulations) between disease and illness. This distinction has been formulated in the attempt to gain some critical leverage on the biomedical reduction of sickness to disease.

For historical investigation into ancient sickness and healing, there-fore, it is only appropriate to drop the modern conceptions of disease and cure, along with the distinction of disease and illness, and shift to a broad-er conceptualization of sickness and healing, as indicated in whatever sources we have for particular cultures. The broader conceptualization of sickness and healing should include the personal and social aspects that interpretive medical anthropologists were attempting to consider in their concept of illness, but not in dichotomy with the (mal)functioning of bio-logical or psychological processes.[22] A broad construction of sickness and healing would be inclusive of the cultural and social aspects that may be distinctive in different cultures. As interpretive medical anthropologists have recognized, "cultural settings provide much of the specific content of sickness and healing."[23]

To deal with the diverse constructions of disease and illness and diverse forms of healing in the highly complex modern world, Kleinman

20. Ancient herbalism was the result of generations of villagers' experience of try-ing out and matching certain herbs/roots, etc., with certain symptoms; Hippocratic intellectuals developed a critique of what they considered irrational explanations, such as of "the sacred disease/illness"; and astrobotany developed a system of correlations between symptoms, plants, stones, and heavenly bodies. But none were the same em-pirical scientific investigation as in modern biology.

21. Scarborough, *Roman Medicine*, 11, warned that "very often modern termi-nologies superimpose themselves upon ancient definitions. For medicine as it existed among the Greeks and Romans, one of the basic problems is simply conceptualization."

22. This is a key component in a more general shift to a more comprehensive re-lational and contextual approach to the historical Jesus necessary once we recognize the reductionism and distortion of earlier approaches focused mainly on religion ab-stracted from political-economic life.

23. Kleinman, *Patients and Healers*, 33.

and other "interpretive" or "cultural" medical anthropologists analyze them according to different "sectors" in "the health-care system," a cultural system that overlaps with other cultural systems such as language or religion or kinship in a complex modern society.[24] To abstract a "health-care system" with the three sectors of "professional," "folk," and "popular," however, only obscures the way that sickness and healing were embedded in the fundamental social forms of family, village community, and their interaction with the indigenous rulers and outside forces in a relatively simple agrarian society. With the increasing medicalization of complex modern societies, "the professional sector" of "health care systems" becomes ever more dominant as medicine takes over functions formerly performed by other "cultural systems" such as religion. But even in complex multicultural modern societies, by far most sickness and healing happen in family and local social networks, what gets labeled as "the popular sector" of "the health care system." As Kleinman comments, however, "In societies lacking professionalization, the folk sector and popular sector constitute the entire health care system."[25] For such societies it is not clear how projecting a "system" brings clarification to sickness and healing, which are simply part of the flow of local life. Kleinman himself points out that previous treatment of folk healers has been problematic in not having taken into account their close relationship with local life. For historical investigations, therefore, to think in terms of a "popular sector" and/or a "folk sector" of an abstract "health care system" would simply obscure the fundamental social forms of family and village in understanding sickness and healing.

Further Implications of Rethinking Sickness and Healing

Moving beyond the reduction of sickness and healing to disease and cure also entails moving beyond the key dichotomies of modern scientific/Enlightenment culture (mind/body, individual/society, natural/supernatural), as often discussed by medical anthropologists. This is especially significant for historical investigation of pre-modern cultures such as that in which Jesus worked.

Contrary to the modern scientific assumptions of medicine, interpretive medical anthropologists insist that disease is not natural (in

24. Kleinman, *Patients and Healers*, chap. 2 (definition on 24).
25. Kleinman, *Patients and Healers*, 59.

nature), but cultural, as is illness or, more comprehensively, sickness. Modern Westerners and other peoples alike engage nature not directly but through their respective sociocultural systems. Correspondingly, the broad dualism of natural vs. supernatural, according to which New Testament scholars have interpreted Jesus' healings and exorcisms, is also a modern Western cultural construction (as discussed in chap. 2). If we want to understand how sickness and healing were understood in a premodern culture, then it is important not to impose the modern cultural dichotomy of natural vs. supernatural.

Some medical anthropologists noted explicitly that biomedicine is rooted in the modern western (Cartesian) separation of the mind from the body and identification of the self with the rational mind.[26] Scientific Western medicine developed highly sophisticated ways of diagnosing and treating diseases of the body, without attending to the mind or soul, that is, without attention to the self that was experiencing the disease. More significantly, perhaps, medicine expanded its scope, developing psychiatry to deal with problems of the mind—which then moved to dealing biologically with mental illness, by means of psychotropic drugs. Meanwhile, in close study of and interaction with other cultures, anthropologists recognized that most peoples of the world experience themselves as embodied. And medical anthropologists recognized that sickness and healing are embodied experiences (even when healing is accomplished by maneuvering in the world of spirits).

Because they were precursors of the modern Western separation of mind and body, the tiny intellectual elite in Hellenistic-Roman antiquity (philosophers) who had identified the self with the mind/soul/spirit garners a great deal of attention in modern academic fields. But the vast majority of people in the ancient Mediterranean world would have experienced sickness and healing, like life in general, as embodied. It is a significant indication of how entrapped we remain in the distorting discourse of modern Western culture that we must resort to hyphenated (Greek and medically derived) terms such as "psycho-somatic" to indicate an embodied personal experience such as sickness. In striving toward a broader, more holistic sense of sickness and healing it may be well to have in mind a reintegrated concept such as "biopsychosocial" or "socialpsychosomatic."

26. Eisenberg, "Disease and Illness," 9–10; Scheper-Hughes and Lock, "The Mindful Body," 6–10.

Closely related with and implicit in medical anthropologists' more holistic conception of sickness and healing is a move beyond another dichotomy fundamental to modern Western culture, the opposition of individual and society. Like those in many other academic fields deeply rooted in Western culture, even anthropological studies had often focused on the individual as an almost sacred, legal, moral, and psychological entity. As often encountered in much sociology and economics, even earlier ethnographical studies assumed that the individual was a rational decision-maker maximizing value in responding adaptively to disease, as if in the abstract economic market-place.[27] As anthropological theorist Clifford Geertz argued decades ago, however, this Western assumption of the individual "as a bounded, unique . . . integrated . . . dynamic center of awareness, emotion, judgment, and action . . . is a rather peculiar idea within the context of the world's cultures."[28] The "interpretive" medical anthropologists' understanding of illness as social as well as personal entails the recognition that the person and personal are embedded in fundamental social forms of family and community. In some cultures there is no sense of the individual as separate from familial position and social roles and relationships. Not only would sickness be handled almost completely in the family and community context; but in many cultures sickness would be understood as (and attributed to) the breaking of social codes or disharmony in the family or village or disruption of relations with ancestors or spirits. Similarly healing is sometimes also collective, as in the weekly therapeutic trance-dance ritual of the !Kung of Botswana that is both therapeutic and preventive.[29] As some anthropologists have emphasized, there are analogues and communications between the personal body and the social body.[30] These include symbolic associations or even equations between the sick body and the sick society and the healthy/healed person and the healthy social body. The socially embedded person is dependent on the attitudes, feelings, and actions of

27. Good, *Medicine, Rationality,* 44–47.

28. Geertz, "From the Native's Point of View, 126.

29. Lock and Scheper-Hughes, "A Critical-Interpretive Approach," 53.

30. Most influential among anthropologically aware New Testament interpreters was Mary Douglas, *Purity and Danger.* See now the suggestive discussion by Scheper-Hughes and Lock, "The Mindful Body"; and Lock and Scheper-Hughes, "A Critical-Interpretive Approach." They point out that although the body was invoked by Douglas and others, it was conceptualized as little more than a passive participant, in the domain of the natural sciences, while the lively mind to which it was attached used it to symbolize and "to think with."

others, including perhaps spirits. Social relations are a key factor in sickness and healing.

Moving beyond the modern Western separation of mind and body opens toward consideration also of pain and the emotions, both of which have been relatively neglected in medicine and previous medical anthropology, as well as in interpretation of Jesus' healing. It was a telling commentary on medicine and medicine-related fields that it was an interpreter of literature, Elaine Scarry, who drew wider (public) attention to the "psycho-somatic" reality as well as the cultural importance of pain in her ground-breaking book *Body in Pain* (1985). Pain entails suffering for embodied selves, and people in pain cry out for meaning as well as relief. Since pain is an inner experience, it cannot easily be expressed in language, certainly not objectified, so that even those closest to the sufferer cannot share in the suffering. The experience of pain thus defies language and confronts the limits of meanings given by cultural discourses and practices. Extreme pain, as in the effects of torture inflicted on ancient people and, more often than we know, on people today, deconstructs, disassembles, destroys the world of the victims. Given the dichotomization of mind and body in Western scientific culture, medicine reduces pain to disorder of nerves and psychology reduces pain to the somatization of mental disorders, neither offering relief. Meaning centered medical anthropologists, however, insist that the experience of pain is not only of the body but of the person and is even intersubjective, profoundly affecting the lives of family, friends, co-workers, and the care-giver, all of whom in turn help shape the experience of the sufferer.[31] The suffering of pain, therefore, can be approached and understood only in a broader historical and civilizational context, all the more so in pursuing historical inquiry into sickness such as that healed by Jesus of Nazareth.

Moving beyond the separation of mind and body and individual and society also opens toward fuller consideration not just of pain but of emotions more generally, which have often not been included in medical anthropology (and are often simply ignored in biomedicine).[32] While only some emotions are related to sickness and healing, it is difficult to

31. See further the discussion in Kleinman et al. "Pain as Human Experience: An Introduction," and the case studies in Kleinman et al., *Pain as Human Experience.*

32. Some earlier anthropologists had attended to emotions as formalized and distanced in ritual performances (e.g., Geertz on Balinese cockfights), while psychoanalysis treated them somewhat obliquely in terms of drives, instincts, and impulses, as pointed out by Scheper-Hughes and Lock, "The Mindful Body," 28.

imagine that the experience of sickness (and of healing) does not involve emotions such as sorrow, shame, the feeling of indignity, inadequacy, or despair, and resentment or anger. Interaction with family and a caring network might involve desire for and appreciation of gestures of comfort and caring. Many emotions are integrally related to familial and social relations. As with illness generally, so the expression and even the fundamental feeling of emotions are shaped by culture. Insofar as emotions entail both feelings and cognitive orientations, public morality and cultural ideology, they provide an important "missing link" capable of bridging mind and body, individual and society.[33] Emotions are the catalyst that transform experience into understanding and brings commitment and intensity to human action.[34]

Emotions may be particularly instrumental and effective in the experience and process of healing. In experiences such as those of sickness-and-healing (or intense encounters of lovers or of mother/parent and child), mind and body and self and other become one. In healing experiences, as in rituals involving music, movement, dance, or communal chant, "waves of fellow-feeling" can wash over and between mindful bodies (embodied selves). While this may happen without language, without semiotic symbols, such experiences involve "body language," rhythm and movement of bodies and collective spirit (which are also distinctively cultural). Indeed, such body language, in gesture or ritual or articulated in symptoms of emotion, is more overdetermined and powerfully ambiguous than speech. These are non-verbal but powerfully expressive ways to "feel" the sick person back to wellness and wholeness and remake the social body. It may be partly or largely in such bonding of person to person that the healing of the embodied and socially embedded person happens.

It may be that we should think of what is often termed "miraculous healing" or "magical death" as involved with intensely felt emotion as socially expressed or acted out. "Faith healing" and "culturogenic death," such as happens in the practice of voodoo, are familiar examples. In this

---

33. Scheper-Hughes and Lock, "The Mindful Body," 28–29. Three decades ago, along with certain other anthropologists, Michele Rosaldo urged anthropologists to attend more fully to the force and intensity of emotions in motivating human action, as in "Toward an Anthropology of Self and Feeling." See further, for example, Rosaldo, *Knowledge and Passion*; Lutz, "The Domain of Emotion Words"; and Kleinman, "Depression and the Translation of Emotional Worlds"; and other essays in Kleinman and Good, eds., *Culture and Depression*.

34. Blacking, *Anthropology of the Body*, 1–27.

connection it has recently been observed that the trust that has developed in certain circles in the cultural system of biomedicine, is somewhat analogous to faith in a religious system. In many studies placebos have proven as effective in curing diseases as the drugs being tested. In cases where surgery had technically failed or simply been faked, the patient's dysfunction healed anyhow, leading to the observation that "the laying on of steel" in medical (surgical/healing) rituals might be as effective as "the laying on of hands" in religious (healing) rituals.

In sum, the efforts of "meaning-centered" medical anthropology to establish a more holistic approach to sickness can thus be adapted for a more complex and comprehensive historical investigation of the sickness and spirit possession dealt with by the historical Jesus. Most helpful in the contemporary Western scientific context, in which biomedicine has reduced sickness to the "natural" biological dysfunctions of "disease," is that sickness involves intersubjective personal and social relations. Fundamental is the recognition that sickness is culturally defined. Insofar as there was no biomedicine in antiquity to reduce sickness to disease, however, the appropriate concept for historical inquiry is sickness, with no distinction much less dichotomy between "disease" and "illness." And insofar as there was no "differentiation" of "health care" from the fundamental social forms of family and village, moreover, to think in terms of a "health care system" would only obscure the familial and community context of sickness and healing. The sickness (and spirit possession) and healing (and exorcism) of Jesus can be appropriately understood only in the social-cultural context of ancient Galilee and Judea and nearby areas. Adapting the insights of meaning-centered medical anthropology, we can thus also move beyond the dichotomies of mind and body and the individual and society that have severely limited previous interpretation of Jesus' healing, and take into consideration the suffering of pain and key emotions involved in the people's experiences of sickness and in Jesus' healing.

Historical, Political, and Economic Factors in Sickness and Healing

There are still other key factors, however, to be taken into account in a more comprehensive approach to the sickness and spirit possession and Jesus' healings and exorcisms encountered in the Gospel sources, factors that many medical anthropologists have been investigating in the last several decades.

Critical Medical Anthropology

In dialogue with the "meaning-centered" medical anthropology, what was called "critical" or "political-economic" medical anthropology argued that not only sickness and healing but also the culture by which they were defined was embedded in particular historical, political-economic contexts.[35] Reacting to earlier decades of anthropologically assisted colonial 'practical activities' and their neocolonial variants, critical medical anthropologists were eager to broaden the focus to include the effects of political, economic, and historical factors on sickness and healing. Their efforts were part of a general interest among anthropologists in integrating analysis of historical forces, such as colonialism, political-economic structures, and "subaltern" studies of indigenous resistance movements into their ethnography. African anthropologist Omafume Onoge, for example, rejected the emphasis on cultural determinism of sickness and its localized microanalytic focus, which left unelaborated the global political-economic relations that were involved.[36] Soheir Morsy was concerned that narrow "sociocultural" attention to culture and perception led to the neglect of both local and global power relations.[37] John Janzen argued that sickness and health may be more determined by "external" macro-level structures of inequality than by people's cognitive cultural factors at the familial and community level.[38] In an influential review essay, Alan Young called for an alternative model of sickness "which gives primacy to the social relations which produce the forms and distributions of sickness in society."[39]

Critical medical anthropologists thus focused on attempting to understand "health issues in light of the larger political and economic forces

35. Cultural medical anthropologists such as Kleinman had suggested that factors "external" to the health care system, including social structures and economic circumstances could have important effects on illness and healing, but maintained a mainly clinical focus within the health care system of a given society.

36. Onoge, "Capitalism and Public Health."

37. Morsy, "Sex Roles, Power, and Illness"; and Morsy, "The Missing Link in Medical Anthropology."

38. Janzen, "Comparative Study of Medical Systems."

39. Young, "Anthropologies of Illness and Sickness," 268.

that pattern interpersonal relationships, shape social behavior, generate social meanings, and condition collective experience."[40] Such forces contribute to the "social production" of illness and the "manufacture" of madness.[41] A burgeoning number of complex studies focused on how wider social and political-economic influences, including colonial and now global economic forces, contribute to *the social production of illness* in given societies. In the 1970s a number of studies drew heavily on "dependency theory" (the "development of underdevelopment") focused on the capitalist world system as production for the market.[42] More complex multifactor analysis has subsequently developed, with emphasis on webs of power relations, including the interface of local and global political and economic forces, relations, and processes, and with a more holistic attention to history, including specific historical formations.[43] These studies discern that sickness and healing are social-cultural experiences constructed and reconstructed in the interface of the political-economic forces that shape personal and social life and the socially-constituted patterns of meaning/interpretation. To understand this interface, such studies (in various combinations) investigate both the historical political and economic (as well as more local social) factors that produce sickness and the historical political and economic forces that affect the cultural understanding of sickness. These are interrelated, but analytically distinguishable.

In the last few decades investigative reporters, newspaper columnists, and medical reports have raised awareness of the many ways in which political and economic forces have generated health crises. It is long since clear that conditions in coal mines generated "black-lung disease" among the miners. It is fairly well-known that automobile and tire manufacturers and oil companies campaigned against mass-transit, leading to higher consumption of fossil fuels, leading to air-pollution, thus exacerbating global warming, with many ill-effects on public health.

40. Singer, "Reinventing Medical Anthropology."

41. McKinlay, "The Case for Focusing Upstream."

42. See, for example, the discussion, criticism, and plethora of references in Navarro, *Medicine under Capitalism*; and Lynn Morgan, "Dependency Theory in the Political Economy of Health."

43. See, for example, Comaroff, *Body of Power, Spirit of Resistance*; articles in the special issues of *Medical Anthropology Quarterly* 17 (1986) and *Social Science and Medicine* 30, no. 2 1990); the overviews in Hans A. Baer, Merrill Singer, & Ida Susser, *Medical Anthropology and the World System*; and Soheir Morsy, "Political Economy in Medical Anthropology."

The high incidence of cancer in certain locations has been linked to toxic industrial wastes, as in the famous case of "Love Canal" in Niagara Falls, New York. Popular books on the food-supply have raised awareness of how subsidies of corn-farming by the United States government have fostered the production of corn and high levels of corn-syrup in high-caloried manufactured food and drink, leading to the burgeoning obesity and the type-two diabetes crises. Medical anthropological studies have investigated parallel relations between political-economic forces and sickness in many other areas of the world, cases historical as well as contemporary.

In agrarian societies ruled by states, for example, ruling classes dominated subordinate peoples through a mix of cultural-religious hegemony and a monopoly on coercive forces, such as the military, legal codes, and courts.[44] For such societies, particularly for imperial political-economic relations, anthropologists have borrowed historian William H. McNeill's suggestion in *Plagues and People* (1977) that invasive political-economic forces are "macroparasites" comparable in their effect on people to "microparasites" such as viruses, bacteria, and protozoa,[45] again with the obvious implications for traumatic effects on not just health but mortality. Critical medical anthropologists have recognized that historical and political-economic forces leave their "traces" in both the social and the individual mindful body.[46]

Correspondingly, critical medical anthropologists have recognized that political-economic and other power relations also impact the cultural understanding of sickness and healing as they condition collective experiences and shape social behavior. The sophisticated historical studies of Michel Foucault have provided a virtual revelation of the means developed in modern Western societies to regulate and control individual and social bodies for production and reproduction. Scheper-Hughes and Lock think these studies are suggestive for the ways in which pre-industrial regimes have controlled their populations, producing docile bodies and pliant minds in the service of some definition of collective stability, health, and social well-being (or perhaps rather in service of rulers and their regimes).[47] Meanwhile, when subordinated communi-

44. Baer et al., *Medical Anthropology*, 49.

45. McNeill, *Plagues and People*.

46. For example, among peasant women in southern Italy, as laid out in Mariella Pandolfi, "Boundaries Inside the Body."

47. Scheper-Hughes and Lock, "Mindful Body," 7–8.

ties are threatened by outside political-economic forces they will respond by expanding social controls regulating the group's boundaries, as Mary Douglas pointed out some time ago.[48] "At points where outside threats may infiltrate and pollute, the inside becomes the focus of particular regulation and surveillance."[49] Spirit possession was previously often interpreted as a "culture-bound" phenomenon. But it is surely more complex. A number of studies have suggested that there is a correlation between spirit possession and the impact of outside political-economic forces (as we will see more extensively below).[50]

Some critical medical anthropologists have also argued that cultures are not simply systems of meaning that orient humans to one another and their world. They are also often "webs of mystification" that disguise political and economic realities, including how they produce sickness and affect the possibility of healing.[51] Certain representations of illness may well be "misrepresentations" that serve the interests of the elites who control cultural as well as economic production.[52] The dominant cultural constructions may serve the interests of those in power, whether colonial powers, social-economic elites, or dominant economic arrangements. Cultural representations need to be probed for such influences. It should be added that a subject people's own cultural representation of their circumstances under seemingly unchallengeable power, far from being labeled as "unscientific" or "delusional" might well be understood as defensive, even self-protective: their "mystification" distracts attention from the concrete power-relations that it would be suicidal to oppose actively.

"Critical" medical anthropologists have also discerned that some forms of illness, such as nervous disorders or "hysteria" or "possession," are (also) *forms of resistance*. In this regard they build on the observation by Foucault that "where there is power, there is [also] resistance," who may have taken that insight from Frantz Fanon.[53] I. M. Lewis had earlier ar-

48. Douglas, *Purity and Danger*.

49. Scheper-Hughes and Lock, "Mindful Body," 24.

50. For example, Morsy, "Sex-Roles, Power, and Illness"; Ong, "Production of Possession," 28–42.

51. Keesing, "Models, 'Folk' and 'Cultural'"; and Keesing, "Anthropology as Interpretive Quest," 161–62.

52. Young, "Anthropologies of Illness and Sickness"; Taussig, "Reification and the Consciousness"; Lock and Scheper-Hughes, "Critical-Interpretive Approach."

53. Foucault, *The History of Sexuality*, 1:95–96. The insight is more poignantly and

gued that spirit possession was a form of protest, often by women, against their circumstances in family and community.[54] Far more complex investigations and analyses by several medical anthropologists showed how, in certain different situations, collective outbreaks of trance or spirit possession or forms of "nervous disorders" were forms of resistance against the circumstances imposed by political and economic forces.[55] Particularly in circumstances of closely controlled working and living conditions imposed by outside forces, trance or spirit possession or other form of sickness might be the only safe form of resistance, insofar as sufferers would not be held fully accountable for their behavior. Thus, for example, in outbreaks of spirit possession in factories of multinational corporations in Malaysia, the women workers only recently brought from indigenous village communities brought production to a halt as they resisted their working conditions and forced change of identity.[56] A considerable body of research has explained "nervous disorders" in various circumstances as culturally constituted expressions of malaise of political and economic origins and, sometimes, even a way of negotiating working and living conditions.

Implications for Historical Inquiry

The very range of historical and contemporary circumstances in which critical medical anthropologists have examined the effects of political and economic factors on health and (the possibility of) healing offers considerable opportunity for development of more comprehensive historical investigation of sickness and healing in a traditional agrarian society such as ancient Roman Palestine. Even the effects of industrialization and of the globalization of capitalism may be instructive, although only indirectly for pre-industrial societies. Anthropologists' attention to the interaction of local and colonial-imperial power relations, however, have more direct implications for what in many ways was an analogous set of relations between people in village communities and their local rulers

---

powerfully articulated by Fanon in books published in the 1960s, such as *The Wretched of the Earth*.

54. Lewis, *Ecstatic Religion*.

55. Comaroff, *Body of Power*; Boddy, *Wombs and Spirits*; Scheper-Hughes, "The Madness of Hunger"; Lock, "On Being Ethnic"; Lock and Scheper-Hughes, "A Critical-Interpretive Approach," 64–68.

56. Ong, *Spirits of Resistance and Capitalist Discipline*.

and the effects of Roman imperial rule. For historical investigation as well as study of current situations these power relations are analytically separable into effects on people's health and the corresponding effects on their cultural understanding of sickness and healing. As anthropological studies have demonstrated, moreover, it is important to maintain historical perspective on how relations may have changed and cultural understanding adapted.

As studies of the impact of political-economic forces on people in agrarian societies indicate, power relations, including the expropriation of the people's agricultural produce (food), become institutionalized. Even if those power relations were maintained more by cultural hegemony than by coercion, the effects could be a threat to the people's food supply. The effects of local rule, however, were compounded by colonization or, in ancient history, by imperial conquest and domination. As potentially key factors in "the production of sickness" among such historical peoples, it is important to take into account the effects of conquest and destruction as well as of economic exploitation and enforced malnutrition. As anthropologists have recognized, what might seem like separate incidents of sickness or small-scale local malaise have a much broader context in large-scale political-economic structures and historical events. History, particularly political-economic forces, left their "traces" in ancient bodies as well as in more recent ones. Anthropologists' attention to "the political-economy of brutality" in order to understand the impact on the personal and social body of conquered or colonized peoples has extended to consideration of the effects of torture as one of the more intense forms of personal suffering, with a debilitating effect on the social body.

Political-economic forces not only helped produce sickness but also affected how sickness was understood in many historical and contemporary situations. It is important in historical inquiry to investigate this aspect of sickness, as anthropologists have done mainly in contemporary cases. In traditional agrarian societies headed by states, political-economic-religious relations had become institutionalized in temple-states or monarchies that maintained hegemony through systems of time-honored sacrifices and law-codes that provided explanations of sickness and "therapeutic" rituals with legitimating sacred ideologies.

As anthropologists were slow to recognize and deal with more deliberately, however, "societies" are not self-contained entities or closed systems, but are impacted by other "societies," most significantly by military conquest, colonial invasion, and imperial rule. Religious ideologies, rituals, and law-codes do not remain static, as a conquered people (including its ruling elite) struggles to adapt to understand and respond to invasive outside forces In response to threats from outside forces, the "social body" can intensify its internal regulations. As critical anthropologists have argued, interpretation of key cultural symbols and other culturally meaningful constructs involves consideration of their historical political and economic context.[57]

To take a key example, as several recent anthropological studies have shown, the relatively sudden prominence of spirit-activity and spirit-possession cannot be explained (away) as a "culture-bound syndrome." Spirit-possession emerges in certain circumstances from the dynamics of the indigenous culture's response to the impact of outside forces.

What may seem especially difficult to explore in historical inquiry is the possibility that some forms of sickness are not just responses to impinging outside political-economic forces but protest or resistance to them. Often confined largely to extant textual sources, historians cannot do the kind of direct observation of situations, for example, in the factories of multinational corporations in Malaysia or the shanty-towns of Northeast Brazil.[58] Working critically from analogous circumstances in today's world would be particularly important. In this connection moving from the previously standard focus, both in biblical studies and in modern medicine, on isolated individual cases to a wider focus on communities or a whole people in the context of the broader political-economic circumstances is crucial. Recognition that sickness and healing are embedded and happening in families, networks, and communities is also a fundamental prerequisite. This leads to two implications that have not yet been recognized in much medical anthropological work.

One implication of their investigations medical anthropologists might have picked up by paying more attention to the earlier work of Frantz Fanon, the Martinique-born, Paris-trained psychiatrist who became director of a mental hospital in Algeria during the Algerian

57. Morsy, "Political Economy in Medical Anthropology," 22; Comaroff, *Body of Power.*

58. Scheper-Hughes, "The Madness of Hunger." Physicians and psychiatrists attempted to diagnose such sicknesses as symptoms of individualized pathologies such as exhaustion or PMS that may be susceptible of medical treatment. But it is reductionist to interpret such politically and economically-generated sicknesses as mere "somaticization."

resistance to severely violent repressive colonialism. Fanon found spirit possession rampant in French-dominated Algeria in the early 1960s. And he found that overwhelming power generated efforts among the dominated that were both self-defensively creative and debilitatingly mystifying.[59]

French-dominated Algeria, concluded Fanon, was "a Manichaean world," created by violent colonial military conquest and maintained by police violence. The French and their intermediaries brought violence even into the homes and the minds of the Algerians. The conquerors and occupiers "painted the native as a sort of quintessence of evil . . . [He was] "the depository of maleficent powers, the unconscious instrument of blind forces."[60] To the Algerians their situation seemed impervious to any action they might take. The hemmed-in natives quickly learned to stay in their place and not go beyond certain limits, even though they did dream of freedom. Colonial power kept alive in the natives an anger, a resentment to which it denied any outlet.

Fanon discerned that a particularly important means of social-polit-ical control in a colonial situation is a belief in maleficent spirits or fate as a way of avoiding direct confrontation with the colonial rulers. The *djinn* in Algerian culture were traditionally the spirits generally, sometimes benign and sometimes malign. Under French colonialism, however, they became "maleficent spirits which create[d] around a native a world of prohibitions, of barriers and of inhibitions far more terrifying than" the French military and police.[61] In social-psychological terms, Fanon suggested that this way of avoiding direct conflict with the French by living in fear of the *djinn* was at the same time a symptom and a solution. "The colonized chose the lesser evil in order to avoid catastrophe."[62] In a "regression in service of the self," the subjugated dealt with the colonial situation in a way that did not threaten the dominating colonial power. The *djinn* and possession by them were self-protective but were also a mystification of the situation.[63] This was the concrete manifestation of

59. Fanon, *Wretched of the Earth*.

60. Fanon, *Wretched of the Earth*, 41.

61. Fanon, *Wretched of the Earth*, 55–56.

62. Fanon, *Wretched of the Earth*, 290.

63. Among New Testament scholars, Paul Hollenbach (1981) pioneered the explo-ration of the social-psychological and ideological pertinence of Fanon's analysis for spirit possession and Jesus' exorcisms. It remained to explore the political-historical relevance of Fanon's, begun in Horsley, *Hearing the Whole Story*, chap. 6.

Fanon's insight that where there is power there is also resistance to power, as in the Algerian Revolution.

Much can be learned also from the anthropological and historical analysis of "everyday forms of resistance" by James C. Scott.[64] He explained that because of the coercive forces arrayed against them most subordinated peoples could not actively oppose the oppressive circumstances of their lives. But they often did engage in various "hidden" (or "disguised") forms of resistance, such as foot dragging, dissimulation, false compliance, pilfering, and sabotage. In his highly suggestive reflective study of "domination and the arts of resistance," Scott also found that where there is power there is often not only resistance but creative resistance short of widespread insurrection. People under domination, suffering various forms of indignity, often develop a discourse of dignity, including images of a revived or new social order of justice.[65] It seems highly likely that historical peoples suffering various forms of illness were capable of imagining and dreaming of healing and wholeness as part of a renewed society.

The second implication is that just as cultural construction of sickness and healing are embedded in and not differentiated from religious formations and practice, so sickness and healing as responses to how outside forces impinge on people's lives may be embedded in or part and parcel of emergent religious formations and practices. The case of Mr. Chen in Taiwan that Arthur Kleinman analyzes extensively offers an example.[66] While Kleinman is focused closely on clinical practice and the effects of folk healing, the symptoms he describes as having brought Mr. Chen to the *tang-ki* (Kleinman calls him a "shaman") were at least partly responses to the social dislocation and economic pressures of making a livelihood for his family in a Taiwan undergoing "rapid social-economic transformation." While it seemed difficult to determine whether and how his treatment by the *tang-ki* on his symptoms, the longer-term management of his symptom was embedded in his joining and gradually becoming prominent in the cult centered at the *tang-ki*'s shrine. The mitigation of his suffering was part and parcel of the alternative life he found in the cult that was, in effect, a therapeutic resistance to the emerging

64. Scott, *Weapons of the Weak*.

65. Scott, *Domination and the Arts of Resistance*; adapted in interpretations of Jesus and the Gospels in Horsley, ed., *Hidden Transcripts and the Arts of Resistance*; and Horsley, ed., *Oral Performance, Popular Tradition*.

66. Kleinman, *Patients and Healers*, 333–74.

social-political order rooted in traditional Taiwanese culture. In historical inquiry, the management of sickness and healing may appear embedded in religious cults or movements.

Bringing these two implications together may facilitate a more holistic investigation into Jesus' healing and exorcism. As Scott observes, leading spokespersons of subordinate people play a crucial role in the formulation and articulation of images of a new social order of justice. In some cultures that "discourse of dignity" included images of wholeness (the meaning of "salvation") and the traditional role of such a leader included healing. Healing of sickness could also be part and parcel of, integral to a *social-religious movement* as well as a religious cult.

Case Studies

The important implications of both "interpretive" and "critical" medical anthropological studies for investigation of the healing and exorcism of Jesus can be further illustrated and explored from some "case studies." These summaries of studies of spirit possession among young women in Malaysia and among various peoples in Africa illustrate how traditional indigenous cultures respond to the impact of outside political-economic-religious forces in their shifting understanding of sickness and spirit possession and their attempts at healing and exorcism.

Spirit Possession among Young Women Factory Workers in Malaysia

In the 1970s the government of Malaysia established free-trade zones (exempt from taxation and labor regulations) to encourage multinational corporations to set up manufacturing plants, which could cut their costs further by using young unmarried women as a cheap and easily controlled labor force.[67] Within the decade these corporations were using over 47,000 women mainly from *Kampong* society. Exposure to strong solvents, acids, and fumes induced headaches, nausea, dizziness, and skin irritation in the young women workers. Exposure to strong cleaning solvents, moreover, led more slowly to lead poisoning, kidney failure, and

67. A Malaysian investment brochure advertised "the oriental girl" as "qualified *by nature and inheritance* to contribute to the efficiency of a bench assembly production line" (Federal Industrial Development Authority, Malaysia, 1975, emphasis added).

breast cancer. What gained attention from both management and "the health care system," however, were the frequent outbreaks of spirit possession among the women on the production lines.

At one point anthropologists would have interpreted such outbreaks as culturally specific forms of conflict-management that disguise yet resolve social tensions within the indigenous society.[68] Aihwa Ong's careful investigation of the newly arrived political-economic forces that suddenly were determining the lives of these young women rooted in traditional Malay village life and culture, however, opens up a far more complex understanding of these outbreaks of spirit possession.[69]

Spirit beliefs in Malay village society were part of the mix of traditional religion with its overlays of Muslim and other influences. They reflected anxieties about the management of social relations in village communities, spirits (a *datuk* or a *hantu*) attacking people who unknowingly deviated from the social order, guarding against human transgressions. Women were believed more vulnerable to spirit possession because of their spiritual frailty, polluting bodies, and erotic nature that made them more likely to transgress moral space and thus become open to attack. They were more vulnerable at times of transition from one phase of life to another. Great care was taken with the disposal of women's exuviae and effluvia. Traditionally, mainly married women were possessed by spirits, young unmarried women being carefully protected by village customs (for example, about disposal of fallen hair and menstrual rags) that hedged them in by special vigilance. When spirit possession occurred, the *bomoh*, the local religious specialist and folk healer, performed rituals that restored the proper spirits' relations with the social order.

When young unmarried women went to work in the factories, spirit possession suddenly shifted to them. Traditionally expected to be shy, obedient, and deferential, they suddenly were speaking in other voices that refused to be silenced. Once the attacks subsided they did not remember and were not blamed. Outbreaks of spirit possession occurred in several factories.

Attacks involving 120 operators engaged in assembly work requiring the use of microscopes had an American factory shut down for three days. In a Japanese factory, twenty-one workers were taken

68. Lewis, *Ecstatic Religion*; and Crapanzo and Garrison, *Case Studies in Spirit Possession*.

69. The following is a summary of Ong, *Spirits of Resistance and Capitalist Discipline*; and Ong, "The Production of Possession."

to ambulances, some screaming "I will kill you! Let me go!" In another American factory fifteen women were possessed, sobbing and screaming in fury and struggling against restraining male supervisors, shouting "Go away!" They were dragged off the shop floor and injected with sedatives, and hundreds of frightened workers were sent home.

In traditional Malay culture, spirits dwelt in nonhuman places such as jungles, swamps, and other bodies of water. Customary codes kept women separated from these spirits. When the factories were constructed without regard for Malay concerns about moral space, the displaced spirits took up residence in toilet tanks. Young village women brought in to work on the production lines expressed a horror of the Western-style toilet, which they avoided, if possible, as a place where their customary discreet disposal of bodily waste was no longer possible. Factory workers complained that, while the production floor and canteen areas were "clean," the toilets were "filthy." They believed that toilets left unflushed and napkins carelessly dropped by frightened women in their hurry to leave offended the spirits all the more. And the offended *datuk*s that haunted the toilets would attack women who had become "unclean" by violating customary moral codes.

Spirit attacks also occurred to women at the work bench, usually during the "graveyard" shift. Upon seeing a ("were-tiger") spirit a worker began sobbing, shrieking, and flailing at the machine, fighting back as the foreman and technician pulled her away. A coworker said that the workplace was haunted by the *hantu* (spirit) dwelling under the factory, which had been built on an area that had previously been all jungle, including a burial ground. The microscopes, which became in effect instruments of torture after hours of work, sometimes disclosed spirits lurking within. Some workers said that the steady hum of the factory and its pollutants permanently disturbed graveyard spirits, who were threatening women for transgressing the zone between the human and nonhuman worlds as well as the modern spaces formerly the domain of men. Life on the shop floor also exposed the young women to the dangers of sexual harassment by male managers. In all, the young women workers were placed in a situation in which they were unintentionally violating customary codes that defined social and bodily boundaries, hence susceptible of attack by the spirits guarding those boundaries.

In professional journals psychological and medical experts explained the attacks that were causing serious disruptions as caused not by offended spirits but by interpersonal tensions, the low educational level, superstitious beliefs, and personal failings of the women workers. In Western psychological discourse such outbreaks of spirit possession were diagnosed as "epidemic hysteria" or "mass psychogenic illness." As the professionals recommended, the outbreak of spirit possession was handled like an epidemic of bacterial origin, with the use of sedatives, "isolation" of "infectious" cases, and "immunization" of those susceptible to the "disease." Disruptive workers were made into patients—and after three seizures by spirits were simply fired.

In addition to their use of sedation and isolation of the "hysterical" young women, factory managers coopted traditional Malay culture by hiring a *bomoh* to perform ritual acts that might defuse the situation and calm the workers' fear. In one factory a *bomoh* sacrificed a goat on the premises, in another he sprinkled holy water, thereby assuring the workers that the factory was rid of spirits, thus producing the illusion of exorcism. Management arranged regular *bomoh* visits and displayed photos of the *bomoh*. These devises both acknowledged and manipulated the workers' fear of spirits, but were only temporarily effective, as outbreaks resumed.

By contrast, Ong investigated the traditional Malay culture according to which spirit belief and spirit possession was culturally understood, and then investigated how the women's sudden subjection to the circumstances of work on the production lines in the multinationals' factories affected them as embedded in their indigenous culture. She was then able to interpret the episodes of spirit possession in the factories both as expressions of intensifying fear and as protest and resistance against the many unintentional violations of (Malay) moral boundaries to which work in the factories subjected them.

Sickness and Spirit Possession among Certain African Peoples

Numerous African peoples were profoundly impacted by European colonial invasion and before that many lived under Arab or Turkish rule. For at least the last century there has been a plethora of studies of peoples, regions, events, and movements in Africa, especially from the 1950s–1960s, then the 1980s into the 1990s. Since the 1980s information from earlier reports and ethnographies and new "field work" is being studied by medical anthropologists and ethnographers, including African scholars, who have moved well beyond the reductionism of modernist post-Enlightenment reason. Various African cultural constructions and responses to the steady and/or sudden impact of political-economic forces from outside should prove suggestive for the kinds of issues that might be considered in a more comprehensive investigation of Jesus' healing and exorcism. The cultural configurations of spirits in some African peoples led to spirit possession as a form of accommodation to and defense against the impact of impinging forces. The destructive effects of colonial invasion were so sudden and/or intense that the correspondingly more intense spirit possessions seem more of an adoption of toxic foreign forms, even in an attempt at self-defense.

A wide range of African peoples, both prior to and after European incursions, represented strangers (*saan*) as indigenous aspects of their own culture, expressed in various rites in which the strangers' spirits played a role.[70] The Shona, for example, a conglomeration of tribes in the area of present-day Zimbabwe, had (have) four kinds of spirits (*mwea* = air, breath, wind): heroes, ancestors, restless dead, and alien spirits, or *mashave*. The spirits of the heroes protect the well-being of the land and govern the political fortunes of the inhabitants. But the hierarchy in which the heroes are arranged reflects the political system of the conquerors. The *shave*, the ghosts of strangers, like foreigners themselves, are outside of the jural system guarded by the heroes. Conventicles of people possessed by these alien spirits carry out rituals in which the spirit hosts assume the characteristics of foreigners, whether a strange tribe or Europeans or traders from the coast. It is not difficult to discern the identity of the spirit Varungu, for example, who incites the people to meticulous cleanliness and whose hosts' clothes and food are those of Europeans. The hero cults and the *shave* conventicles represent a system of virtually frozen history of past decades, that part of Shona history relating to their encounters with the Portuguese, the Ndebele, and the people from the coast, while the ancestor and hero cults transmit an idealized past of the people's own indigenous social life. Both hero cults and *shave* cults involve spirit possession. But the one is constitutive of the social order as it appropriates outside influence, the other seemingly a defensive or

---

70. Kramer, *The Red Fez*, drawing on many previous studies, presents a analysis of spirits, spirit possession, and exorcism that ranged across several African peoples over several decades in the twentieth century. This paragraph draws upon his discussion in chapters 1–2, esp. 71–77.

self-protective measure by those in whom those outside influences happen to become manifest in possession by the spirits of strangers.[71]

Other African peoples had similar social-cultural ways of dealing with the succession of forces to which they had been subjected over several centuries, including Arab and Turkish rule, British military expeditions and colonial rule, and American missionary, medical, and development initiatives. Swahili peoples, for example, interpreted sickness and grief as signs that *pepo* or spirits of strangers wished to embody themselves in persons and to demand sacrifices and worship. They used the Arabic word *sheitani* (satans) to name the *pepo*, which misled Christian missionaries to believe the possession was demonic. The possessed persons, rather, were hosting the spirits of the people of Kilimanjaro (*Kilima*) or the spirits of Europeans (*Kizungu*), those of the Arabs, or those of the Nubians. In cases where the alien spirits were experienced as threatening the possession appears to have had a defensive or self-protective character. For example, early in the twentieth century among the Kamba people possession by *Kijesu* was an alternative to conversion to Christianity.[72] *Kijesu* was the spirit not just of Jesus, but of the whole invasive Christian mission, the whole alien culture that posed a serious threat to the traditional way of life, an impact by strangers not easily manageable in an already existing cult.

How a people, in its constituent local village communities, deals with the cumulative effect of domination by outside forces can be seen particularly in the *zar* cult in Sudan.[73] In this cult can be seen the enduring results of how an Africa people adjusted to the conversion of its males to Islam and influence by Arabic culture, the impact of foreign influences from Ethiopia, the relatively more recent incursion of the British military, and the recent influence of American medical and development initiatives. After Islam became dominant among the males of Sudanese villages, the women continued to cultivate traditional African culture, while also developing the *zar* cult in which they sought to identify and exorcise the alien spirits that had possessed them. The catalogue of the various identities of the *zayran* adumbrates aspects of the history of domination by various outside forces as it is met with resistance by the women in village communities, in the guise of accommodation, negotiation, and

---

71. Kramer, *Red Fez*, 85–92.

72. Kramer, *Red Fez*, 97–100.

73. See the very suggestive study by Boddy, *Wombs and Alien Spirits*.

mollification. "We look to women's bodies for villagers' statements on how the external world impinges on their own . . . The apparently powerless and subordinate gender represents the apparent powerlessness and subordination of the community in wider perspective" as the Sudanese villagers respond creatively "to the challenge of colonial capitalist encroachment."[74]

The inventory of *zayran* includes West Africans, servants, slaves, and Blacks from the South, as well as imposing and threatening outsiders. The *Bashawat* spirits represent the Pashas, Turks and other malevolent conquerors. The *Khawajat* are light-skinned spirits, clearly representing Europeans or Westerners (alternatively referred to as *nasarin,* i.e., "Nazarenes," Christians), among whom the British general Lord Cromer is the most prominent. They demand "clean" western foods associated with the power of the outside world: bottled beverages, expensive fruits, tinned goods, biscuits and white bread. They have considerable wealth, yet another aspect of power. Especially notable among the colorful western spirits is Dona Bey, an American doctor and big game hunter who drinks prodigous amounts of whisky and beer and carries an elephant gun. He clearly represents western technological overkill, destroying what he hunts, and the hegemony of masculine science situated within a display of unprincipled lascivious action.[75]

Sudanese village women, however, developed a thriving cult to deal with their possession by such spirits. In prolonged collective ceremonies with much drumming and dancing, they invited the spirits to manifest themselves in possession, so that an exorcist could first identify the spirit and then, with more drumming and dancing, perform the exorcism.[76] In the *zar* cult, under the guise of accommodation, negotiation, and mollification, we can also discern a personal freeing from possession by the alien spirits (and the corresponding collective social relief), although the spirits are not defeated or destroyed but remain at large.

The peoples discussed so far, with previously developed cults of possession, dealt with the intensified impact of European colonialism by enlarging their inventories of alien spirits and adapting their already existing self-protective ceremonies and exorcism cults.[77] For other, largely

74. Boddy, *Wombs and Spirits,* 269–70.

75. Boddy, *Wombs and Spirits,* 280–94.

76. Vivid descriptions in Boddy, *Wombs and Spirits.*

77. Kramer, *Red Fez,* 116–17.

homogeneous peoples in which alien spirit possession was less developed, however, the impact of European colonial invasion happened more suddenly and traumatically. They were more completely and exclusively possessed by the spirits of the invasive colonial forces. The Tonga along the Zambezi River were invaded by spirits with names such as *maregimenti* and *mapolis* (clearly representations of military regiments and the police) at the height of the invasion of the colonial state.[78] Interestingly, the defensive healing antidotes were also derived from invasive influences. In Tonga, women's possession dances spirit-hosts washed themselves compulsively with scented soaps and girls "drank soapy water in order to make the insides of their bodies clean and sweet-smelling."[79]

The sudden impact of European colonization and development was also felt by homogeneous peoples with centralized political authority, such as the Zulu. The rapid impact of mining operations, with the mixture of migrant workers from different peoples under the control of overwhelming European power exacerbated the disintegration of traditional social forms. A bewildering array of new alien spirits under the control of sorcerers suddenly attacked people who would become possessed, by Sothos, Indians, and Europeans. Spirit hosts would rage uncontrollably, sob uncontrollably, run back and forth in a daze, tear clothes off their bodies, or attempt to kill themselves. "There was no appeasing these raving hordes of spirits, let alone domesticating them as helpful spirits."[80] Such possessions manifest the people's estrangement from their own culture and their acute vulnerability to the foreign powers.

To mobilize their cultural resources against the invasion, the Zulus looked to exorcism by traditional healers and especially to their *izangoma*, the possessed mediums of their ancestors. When the *izangoma* exorcized the hordes of alien spirits they "inoculated" their subjects with "soldier" spirits, *amabutho*, to defend them against further attack.[81] When the "soldiers" spoke through their subjects they used foreign languages, such as English or railroad sounds, and the spirit hosts used symbols of alien origins, such as machine oil or white men's hair, to express their

---

78. Luig, "Constructing Local Worlds." That the referents of the spirit names changed with changing historical circumstances, *maregimenti* later coming to represent the opposing sides in the Zimbabwe civil war, only confirmed that the names of invasive spirits correspond with the forces that are impinging on the people's life.

79. Kramer, *Red Fez*, 118–22.

80. Kramer, *Red Fez*, 125.

81. Sundkler, *Bantu Prophets*, 247–49.

new, protected identity.[82] They made particular manifestations of alien powers their own in order to resist and ward off the greater alien powers that were destroying them.

While many of the more traditional possession cults that were increasingly concerned with the spirits of European colonial forces had little apparent political implication, the organization of dance ceremonies of the possessed appeared to be more of a direct response to an escalating colonial invasion. Among the most significant was the hybrid *beni ngoma* ("band-dance") that began in the 1890s, spread rapidly, and continued through the 1920s. These dance ceremonies placed great emphasis on imitative colonial attire. Possessed participants in the *hauka* cult that spread in West Africa in the 1920s imitated not only Islamic Arab authority figures and French and British colonial officers, but the flag, uniforms, and drill formations of the British army.[83]

Even more political in their implications and effects were the charismatic possession cults or movements led by prophets that countered the divisive effects of the colonial impact early last century. These movements, which included spirit possession and healing, formed wider communities of peoples against the effects of colonial invasion and repression, moving from local focus and diverging interests to more general common interests over against the colonizing forces. New in these charismatic movements led by prophets was their claim to exclusive and unlimited authority, which they appropriated from the corresponding claim by the colonizing powers and/or Christian missionaries. The African prophetic movements demanded self-less devotion to a broader cause and unity. It is not merely circumstantial that many of these prophetic movements prepared the way for and were the precursors of the anti-colonial movements that were more directly politically oriented.

The case of Dodo spirits and the healers and healing networks/movements they empowered in villages of Niger in the 1970s and 1980s provides a more recent case of spirit possession in response to intrusive political-economic forces, personal and social healing, and social accommodation and resistance.[84] In Niger, as elsewhere in Africa, the invasive outside powers shifted from (mainly French and British) colonial governments to expanding Westernizing capitalist economic development.

---

82. Kramer, *Red Fez*, 126.

83. Kramer, *Red Fez*, 134–35.

84. See the suggestive study by Adeline Masquelier, "Invention of Anti-Tradition."

Among the Hausa-speaking Mawri villagers in Niger the traditional *bori* force (through its mediating healers) was concerned with maintaining the symbiotic relationship between spirits and humans upon which the prosperity of individuals, households, and communities depend.[85] As an illustration of the continuing power of the traditional *bori* in the aftermath of colonial rule, even educated elite such as civil servants, who felt the sting of competition and experienced anxiety about unemployment, viewed *bori* as a source of healing power. When Qur'anic medicines and prayers did not have the desired effect, teachers and bureaucrats would seek the services of a *bori* healer to insure their protection and prosperity in a ruthless world.

In Niger, as elsewhere in Africa, colonial rule was succeeded by the even more complex and subtle invasive forces of "development" as the vanguard of capitalist social-economic relations in the 1970s and 1980s. With capitalist commercialism creeping into the society an increasing number of healers set up shop to sell medicines and services, so that *bori* began to seem like a religion of façade and pretence run by eager entrepreneurs who had little knowledge of medicinal plants, charged exorbitant prices, and showed no commitment to their patients.[86]

In this context Dodo spirits began possessing people, demanding commitment and integrity from their mediums. Villagers would become sick; conventional treatment was not effective. Only by agreeing to do the will of the superhuman force in offering healing to others did certain villagers become healed themselves. Eager to heal others, they held ceremonies twice or more a week, their reputation spread like wildfire, and people flocked to them from far and wide. To keep a Dodo spirit, a medium had to be honest and not demand a return "gift" of money (that is, charge a fee). They did not use and sell the *bori* medicines made from carefully gathered roots, barks, and leaves. The possessed healers were rather repositories of Dodo's condensed powers. Anything they touched, such as a handful of sand picked up from the ground, could become a channel for healing. This was an interesting contrast with the Muslim practice in Niger of removing sand from the grave of an exemplary Muslim so that his *Baraka* (blessing, power) could be transferred to others, by

---

85. Masquelier, "Invention of Anti-Tradition."

86. The *bori* practitioners thus display some similarities to the "charlatans" that both Celsus and Origen were complaining about and that Lucian satirized in late antiquity.

being carried in a pouch. Dodo mediums used sand only in the immediate healing, to be mixed in and drunk with water.

The Dodo mediums also avoided learning literacy as taught in school, riding in motorcars, and other mechanical things. Dodo mediums were reviving the ties that once united people and spirits, while rejecting literacy, which symbolized the power of outside forces such as the state, and refusing commodities that had become fetishized in the encroaching consumer culture. They were re-creating a safe network of socio-moral relations that insulated them from what they saw as dangerous invasive forms of power that had begun to de-stabilize their local communities. This was not a reactionary indiscriminate denunciation of modernism or capitalism. Their healing, combined with their rejection of cars and other fetishized commodities, became instruments of empowerment that enabled them and their people to retain or regain some coherent local power amidst a world run amok.

The case of the Dodo spirits, the healers they empowered, and their emergent social networks in the Mawri villages of Niger embody far more than sickness and healing of particular persons. The spirits and the mediums that they empower are clearly responses to the disintegrative effects of invasive superhuman outside political-economic forces. The Dodo empowerment of healing is explicitly interrelational, the empowerment of the healer for the healing of others freely available to an expanding network of sick people eagerly seeking healing—as the healer's reputation spreads and people come to the spirit-possessed healer. By his own refusal to acquiesce in the invasive forces, moreover, the healer becomes a model for a wider network of renewal of the traditional way of life over against those forces.

These case studies are suggestive for investigation the conflict between two camps of spirits in "apocalyptic" texts produced by circles of Judean scribes, evidently in response to the suddenly more invasive Hellenistic and particularly Roman rule. They are also suggestive for investigation of sickness and spirit possession and healing and exorcism as portrayed in the Gospel sources in their historical context.[87]

87. While most of the studies consulted above focus on spirit possession and illness, some more recent studies of traditional healing and healers among African peoples are also suggestive for the stories of Jesus' healings. In "Jesus, the African Healer," Owusu, drawing on medical anthropology, explains how, if we avoid reading the exorcisms and healings through the lens of western Christian theology and biomedicine, Jesus appears very similar in many respects (touch, speech, laying on of hands) to traditional African healers in interactive social contexts.

Part II

The Historical Context

4

The Political-Economic-Social Context in Roman Judea and Galilee

THE EXTENSIVE STUDIES OF sickness and healing by medical anthropologists and others in the last fifty years suggest that it is important to consider the political-economic-cultural situation of the people among whom Jesus was working and in which the Gospel portrayals of (sickness and) healing and (spirit possession and) exorcism were being cultivated. This investigation of the fundamental social forms, the local patterns of political-economic-religious domination-and-subordination, and the effects of increasingly invasive imperial domination—the historical context of Jesus' healings and exorcisms—will be a significant departure from standard study of the historical Jesus. Much interpretation of Jesus, deeply rooted in modern western individualism and based on his individual sayings, presents him as an individual teacher unencumbered by basic social forms and interaction. Standard interpretation of Jesus has him born into but then oppose "(early) Judaism," a synthetic theological abstraction that hides the historical political-economic-religious dynamics of early Roman Palestine. The social and political context of Jesus is beside the point, for example, for restatements of Schweitzer's interpretation of Jesus as an apocalyptic preacher who proclaimed the end of the world. The historical political-economic context also has little relevance for liberal interpreters who believe that Jesus called individual followers to abandon home and family to lead an itinerant lifestyle.

For investigation of the historical context of Jesus, the Jesus-movements, and the Gospels they produced, the factors that medical anthropologists have found important in the kinds and incidents of sickness and spirit possession (and in the cultural understandings of illness) can be discussed in four interrelated dimensions.[1]

First, cultural medical anthropology emphasized that sickness is always social as well as personal. Along with being defined in particular cultures, sickness almost always occurs and is treated in the family and immediate social network. Indeed, the experience of pain is not only of the individual body but of the whole person and is even intersubjective, profoundly affecting the lives of family, friends, and community. Thus also in the historical context of Jesus and the Gospels, the sick and the spirit possessed would have been embedded in particular social relationships such as family and friends (relationships that were also embedded in the particular configurations of cultural meaning). Understanding Jesus' healing of sickness in historical context thus also entails investigation of the fundamental social forms and patterns of social interaction.

Second, those basic social forms and interactions were situated in historically institutionalized power relations that determined people's social location and entailed conflict. In agrarian societies ruled by states, ruling classes dominated subordinate peoples through a mix of cultural-religious hegemony, including legal codes, and a monopoly on coercive forces, such as the military. As illustrated by the Judean temple-state (under overall imperial rule), this domination is often done in the service of institutions that symbolize collective productivity, stability, and social well-being. Correspondingly, critical medical anthropologists have recognized that political-economic-religious power relations also impact the cultural understanding of sickness and healing as they condition collective experiences and shape social behavior.

Third, the effects of local rule are compounded by colonization or, in ancient history, by imperial conquest and domination. Imperial demands of tribute on top of local rulers' demands for taxes, tithes, and offerings would have compounded pressures on historical peoples' food supply as a factor in "the production of sickness" among such peoples. Further, anthropologists have called attention to "the political-economy of brutality" in order to understand the impact on the personal and social body of conquered or colonized peoples. Contributing to the "social production

---

1. In the last few decades I have been attempting to develop a more multifaceted and comprehensive relational approach that includes these and other factors in order to understand the *historical* Jesus in *historical* context. See, for example, *Jesus and Empire*, chap. 3; *Jesus in Context*; and *Jesus and the Politics of Roman Palestine*.

of illness" (and "the manufacture of madness"), political-economic forc-es, what McNeill called "macroparasites," leave their traumatic "traces" on the social as well as individual mindful bodies. These critical studies suggest the importance of considering the effect of the more invasive im-perial rule of Judea that began with the Hellenistic imperial regimes and escalated further in the Roman conquest, reconquests, and imposition of client rulers of the Judeans and Galileans. As several recent anthropologi-cal studies have shown, moreover, the relatively sudden prominence of spirit-possession, far from being explained (away) as a "culture-bound syndrome," emerges in certain circumstances from the dynamics of the indigenous culture's response to the severe impact of outside forces.

Fourth, anthropological and other studies have also found that in-digenous resistance and renewal movements have grown out of healings or provide a supportive context for healing and figures who take on the role of a healer. Such movements and roles usually have roots in the cul-ture in which sickness and healing are constructed. These studies suggest attention to the many popular movements in Galilee and/or Judea more or less contemporary with Jesus, as well as to the Israelite tradition of the prophets Elijah and Elisha who performed healings as an integral part of their leadership of a popular movement of renewal and resistance.

These interrelated factors set the agenda for investigation of the historical context of the Gospels and Jesus in this chapter, which will pre-pare the way for investigation of the cultural understanding of sickness and healing in the historical context of Jesus and the Gospels in chap. 5. Chapters 4 and 5 can then inform a new approach to the Gospel sources for the healing of sickness and exorcism of spirit-possession that were at the center of Jesus' interactive mission in the historical context of Roman Palestine.

The Galilean and Judean People

At the time of Jesus' mission the vast majority of people(s) of Israelite heritage lived in village communities in the different regions of Palestine that had recently been conquered by the Romans, who then demanded tribute and installed client rulers. The wealthy Jerusalem priest and histo-rian Flavius Josephus mentions that there were 200 such villages in Gali-lee (*Life* 235), a number consistent with recent archaeological surveys. He also refers to villages in Samaria, in Judea, and in areas to the north and east of Galilee subject to Roman client rulers in Tyre, Sidon, Caesarea Philippi, or the cities of the Decapolis.

"Insider" sources for Roman-ruled Palestine at the time of Jesus refer to the people by the district in which they lived. In his historical accounts Josephus refers fairly consistently to the people living in Galilee in the north as "the Galileans," to the people living in Judea in the south as "the Judeans," and to the people living in the hill country in between as "the Samari(t)ans."[2] Josephus, the Gospels, and later rabbinic texts, refer to these people collectively as "Israel/Israelites." They shared a common tradition of their origins as a people, but had lived for centuries under different local rulers appointed by and/or subject to a succession of imperial regimes.

As in most agrarian societies, village communities consisted of a larger or smaller number of (multigenerational) families or households.[3] Households and villages were the fundamental social forms in which virtually all aspects of life took place. The small buildings in which families lived were clustered closely together, with two or three houses around a common courtyard in which they cooked and ate. A whole network of such houses and courtyards were connected by paths and alleyways. Villages were surrounded by or close to fields that were divided among and worked by the component households/families. In Israelite tradition, as in other agrarian societies, the fields were understood as the (ideally unalienable) ancestral inheritance of households/families, the basis of their subsistence livelihood—although the ideal was rarely sustainable, given the historical dynamics of political-economic power-relations.

With variations that depended on historical circumstances, villages were semi-independent self-governing communities.[4] The principal

2. "Outsider" Greek and Latin/Roman sources apply the term "Judeans" to Galileans and others in addition to those who lived in (the district of) Judea. In the generations before the Romans conquered Palestine, the high priestly rulers of the Judeans in Jerusalem had become rulers also of the Galileans as well as the Idumeans and the Samitans (discussed below). The Roman Senate appointed Herod as "King of the Judeans" with the implications that as ruler over the Judeans he was also ruler over Idumea, Samaria, and Galilee.

3. A summary of village life in Galilee, based on textual and archaeological information, in Horsley, *Galilee*, chaps. 8–9; *Archaeology, History, and Society*, chaps. 4–5. It is important not to project onto ancient and other societies the nuclear family living in one house, an idealization often presumed in modern western societies.

4. Fuller critical discussion in Horsley, *Galilee*, chap. 10; and Horsley, *Archaeology, History, Society*, chap. 6.

form of governance and community coherence was the village assembly, for which the Greek term in the Gospels is *synagoge* (the Hebrew/Aramaic term in rabbinic texts is *knesset*). The local assemblies were led by the village elders, with one or more prominent elders presiding (an *archisynagogos* was not a "ruler" but a leading elder of the assembly, as in Mark 5:21–43). Archaeologists who have dug diligently to find buildings in which village assemblies may have met have found that such buildings do not become frequent until late antiquity. In the Gospel portrayals, villages and village assemblies (*synagogai*) are the principal scenes of Jesus' healing and exorcism as well as of his proclamation of the rule of God. And in the "mission discourses," Jesus sends out his envoys to extend the healings and exorcisms into other village communities while they stay in particular households (living on whatever meager fare the family can provide; Mark 6:6–13; Luke 10:2–16).

The Judean and the Galilean People under the Jerusalem Temple-State

The ideal in the cultural traditions of the Mosaic covenant and related customs and practices from early Israel was that Israelite village communities would be directly under the rule of God (as their literal ruler/king) with no human ruler controlling them and taking a portion of their crops as taxes, tithes, and offerings (e.g., Exod 20; Josh 24; Judg 8:22–23; 1 Sam 8:4–8). But they were eventually forced to submit to the rule of kings in Jerusalem and Samaria and, after the Assyrian and Babylonian conquests, to one empire after another and the local rulers that the empires maintained in power. The two major factors in the subjection of the people were military conquest that often devastated people's lives and economic exploitation that often became outright oppression that disintegrated the fabric of family and village life. The Judean texts that were later included in the Hebrew Bible provide information both about the history of the people's subjection by conquest and exploitation and about the culture of subjugation that developed. Much of this literature that later became "biblical" (sacred scripture) is at least critical of the subjection, and some of it collects prophecies that pronounce God's condemnation of the rulers' violent conquest and the economic oppression. Also evident is that through the centuries of subjection, the people's memories of earlier liberation nourished a sustained longing and hope for future deliverance.

The standard scheme of the history of "(early/second-temple) Judaism," with its sequence of "the exile" followed by the "post-exilic" period in which "the Jews" returned to Jerusalem and rebuilt the temple, focuses on the political-economic-cultural elite and obscures the complexities of this history, including what was happening to the vast majority of people. A survey of some of the key events that affected the people's life-situation leading up to the circumstances in which Jesus worked can illuminate the relationship of the people to their rulers and the regional differences in the historical experience of the Galileans and Judeans.[5]

After the Babylonian armies conquered Judah they deported the ruling class in Jerusalem to Babylon. The Babylonian conquest and the Assyrian conquest of the kingdom in Samaria a century earlier was devastating. The rural population of Galilee, Samaria, and Judah was decimated, their houses and villages destroyed and fields ruined.[6] The trauma of conquest persisted for many generations. The surviving people were left struggling for subsistence and suffering from multiple maladies, the social-psycho-physical effects of military violence such as disabling injury, paralysis, blindness, and the sense of being prisoners on what had been their ancestral land. In the resulting culture of subjection, the people longed intensively for relief from their suffering, hoping that God would somehow bind up their wounds and heal their debilitating illnesses (e.g., Isa 29:18–19; 35:5–6; 61:1–2).

For the many centuries through the time of Jesus and beyond the three principal areas of Israelite heritage were ruled by a succession of empires, through different imperial jurisdictions or local extensions of the imperial administration.

In Judea, the Persian imperial regime sent descendants of elite Jerusalem families deported by the Babylonians back to Judea to rebuild

5. Some of the controlling concepts of New Testament studies, particularly the synthetic theological construct of "(early) Judaism" (with the related construct of its "spin-off" "early Christianity") simply block recognition of the fundamental complexity, diversity, and conflict of peoples' life in Palestine under increasingly invasive imperial rule and the rule of the Roman-client Herodian and high priestly rulers (as attested in Judean scribal texts as well as in Josephus' histories). The historical approach followed here will hopefully allow the complexity and conflict to appear as it developed over the course of several centuries of history under one empire after another, as the Judean temple-state consolidated and expanded its power and then squandered its authority.

6. Among the many studies, see the account of the devastated situation in Judea in Carter, *Emergence of Yehud*.

the temple.[7] Under this arrangement institutionalized in the Jerusalem temple-state the people in Judea would be continuing to serve their ancestral god ("the god who is in Jerusalem," Ezra 1:1–4). By yielding up tithes and offerings from their crops in support of the temple and priestly aristocracy the people would supposedly receive blessings of sufficient production from the land. In an indication of the ideology by which the temple and its priestly heads attempted to generate support of the people of the land, the prophet Haggai threatened that the productivity of the land depended on their support of the temple with their produce and labor (Hag 1:7–11). The political-economic reality is fairly clearly indicated in the "memoirs" of Ezra and Nehemiah. Under the oversight of Persian governors, such as Nehemiah, the emerging priestly aristocracy of the tiny Jerusalem temple-state served as the local representative of the imperial administration, responsible for maintaining order and rendering up tribute to the imperial court (as stated in the books of Nehemiah and Ezra). The temple and high priesthood eventually consolidated their power as controlling political-economic-religious institution of Judean society, demanding sacrifices, tithes, offerings, and the celebration of pilgrimage festivals in the temple, which consolidated economic centralization in Jerusalem. Even the elite lamented that they were living as slaves in the land that had been given to their ancestors, while its rich yield was taken by the imperial regimes that wielded power over their bodies and resources (Neh 9:36–37). But that did not stop them from wielding their own coercive power over the Judean villagers, further draining away the people's produce when they were still struggling to recover from the devastation by earlier imperial conquests (Neh 5:1–13).

The northern Israelites in Samaria and Galilee lived under separate rulers from the Judeans for many centuries. The Persian empire (and the successor Hellenistic imperial regimes) ruled the people who lived in Samaria through a client aristocracy with their own temple. In Galilee, under a separate imperial province, there is no evidence that a local aristocracy was ever imposed or developed. Although we have no direct information, it can be surmised that Israelite customs and traditions continued to be cultivated in the struggling village communities of Samaria and Galilee insofar as popular movements with distinctively

7. Some of the extensive recent critical analysis and discussion of the sparsely attested history of early second-temple Judea is summarized in Horsley, *Scribes, Visionaries*, chaps. 1–2.

Israelite forms later emerged in these areas as well as in Judea in response to Roman imperial domination.[8]

In the tiny district of Judea powerful figures used their wealth to manipulate peasants overburdened by the double layer of tax and tribute into debt and debt-slavery. The people complained to the Persian governor Nehemiah that "We are having to borrow on our fields and vineyards to pay the emperor's tax . . . [they] are forcing our sons and daughters to be slaves, and some of our daughters have been ravished; we are powerless and our fields and vineyards now belong to others" (Neh 5:1–5). To keep the wealthy Judeans from destroying the peasant producers on which the imperial economy of Judea depended, Nehemiah forced them to observe the (by then) time-honored covenantal customs of cancellation of debts and release of debt-slaves (Neh 5:6–13). But he did not reduce "the emperor's tax" that had forced them into debt to feed their families in the first place. Sources are scarce for the next few centuries, but it is highly likely that exploitation of peasants ("people of the land") and conditions of indebtedness, poverty, and malnutrition continued. In the proverbial wisdom of the scribes, "the poor are feeding grounds for the rich" (Sir 13:19). As studies by anthropologists have shown, this is the perpetual situation of subsistence peasants under multiple demands of local rulers, wealthy creditors, and imperial or colonial regimes for tribute as well as tithes and taxes.[9]

The priestly aristocracy that eventually consolidated its power in Jerusalem under imperial oversight was assisted in its governing and collection of revenues by a professional staff of scribal retainers, serving the temple-state as advisers and experts in the laws and cultural traditions.[10] These were the predecessors of "the scribes and Pharisees" of later centuries, known from the Gospels and the histories of Josephus. The scribes of the Jerusalem temple-state collected and edited Judean laws and historical legends into the precursors of what we know as the books of the Pentateuch that were later included in the Hebrew Bible. These

8. See the cautious discussion of the limited, fragmentary evidence for this period in Horsley, *Galilee*, chap. 1.

9. Wolf, *Peasants*.

10. Drawing on studies of the training of professional scribes in Mesopotamia and Egypt, David Carr has described the training of Judean scribes in *Writing on the Tablet of the Heart*. Analysis of the political-economic location and role of the scribes serving in the Judean temple-state, esp. in the early second century BCE in Horsley, *Scribes, Visionaries*, chaps. 3–6.

"constitutional" (written) texts, along with others such as the memoirs of Nehemiah and Ezra, served to authorize (and to provide regulations for the operations of?) the temple-state. The scribes' role in the temple-state was to learn and to be able to recite as needed these sacred laws and traditions in councils of state (Sir 38:24—39:4). The local regime in Samaria may have had a similar staff of professional scribes. But since there was apparently no local aristocracy in Galilee, it seems unlikely that there were any scribal circles cultivating Israelite traditions there.

It seems highly unlikely that Judean villagers, much less Galilean villagers, had direct knowledge of texts produced by scribes and laid up in the Jerusalem temple, since literacy was limited mainly to scribal circles (and the texts were in the archaic language of Hebrew, while people spoke dialects of Aramaic).[11] As with villagers in other agrarian societies, however, they would have cultivated their own (parallel) ancestral customs and traditions orally (discussed further in chapter 6). In the case of ancient Israel, extensive scholarly studies have concluded that much of the contents of texts of history and texts of torah that were later included in the Hebrew bible were stories/legends of earlier heroes and movements and popular customs, laws, and ceremonies that must have been cultivated in village communities.

The Passover celebrated the legend of the people's origins in an escape from bondage under the Pharaoh of Egypt led by the founding prophet Moses. This was originally a ceremony celebrated in the family setting. The rulers in Jerusalem, however, centralized the celebration in the temple, so that families were expected to bring the resources for the ceremony to Jerusalem to be expended there. The history books later included in the Hebrew Bible contain early Israelite songs that celebrated God's deliverance of the people, such as the Song of the Sea and the Song of (the prophet) Deborah (Exod 15; Judg 5), as well as the many summaries of the exodus story.

Included in the collections of "laws" adapted by the scribes that were incorporated into the texts of Exodus, Leviticus, and Deuteronomy were many customs pertaining to social-economic interaction among

11. On the severely limited literacy and predominant oral communication in Roman Palestine see the thoroughly documented study of Catherine Hezser, *Jewish Literacy*. For analysis of the implications of several lines of recent research into communications media in ancient Judea and Galilee, see Horsley, "Can Study of the Historical Jesus Escape," and chap. 6 below.

the people.[12] Many of these were practices that protected the economic viability of families in village communities, such as gleaning, liberal lending at no interest to needy neighbors, cancellation of debts and freeing of debt-slaves every seventh year. At the center of these customs were the commandments of (the Mosaic covenant), social-economic principles of interaction that protected people's economic rights by prohibiting coveting, stealing, false oaths, and even insisting on support of elderly parents.[13] The commandment to honor the sabbath became a sacred symbol of the importance of protecting people from the unlimited exploitation of their labor.

The Judean and Galilean people evidently also cultivated stories and other memories of heroes and prophets who had led the people in struggles against outside forces or their own kings who expropriated their produce so intensively as to drive them into hunger and social breakdown. These included legends of the liberator Gideon and of the young brigand-chieftan David whom the Israelites "messiahed" to lead them against the Philistine raiders. Stories of the exploits of the prophets Elijah and Elisha would have been particularly prominent in Israelite social memory in the north, including Galilee (1 Kgs 17–21; 2 Kgs 1–9). These covenantal principles of social-economic justice and the stories of the leaders of resistance remained alive among the people and decisively informed their later movements of resistance against Roman imperial rule (to be discussed below).

The Escalating Impact of Invasive Imperial Rule ("the Political-Economy of Brutality")

While sources for the fourth and third centuries BCE are few and fragmentary, it is clear that the military conquest of Alexander the Great and his army of "Greeks" and particularly the continuing military campaigns of the successor Hellenistic empires had a profound impact on people in Palestine. The rival imperial regimes of the Ptolemies, based in Egypt, and the Seleucids, based in Antioch (in Syria), fought a series of wars for control of Palestine. In the immediately surrounding areas both regimes established Hellenistic cities with Greek political forms, in which a combination of military officers and local elites, who eagerly adopted the new

---

12. See the thorough critical investigation by Knight, *Law, Power, and Justice.*

13. Fuller discussion in Horsley, *Covenant Economics*, chaps. 2–3.

political culture, dominated indigenous peoples. Galilee became virtually surrounded by Hellenistic cities, in the fertile Great Plain to the south, along the Mediterranean coast to the west, and in the territories across the Jordan to the east.

The Persian imperial regime had been content to maintain its empire by setting up client temple-states and other local regimes to control and tax the subject peoples in accord with indigenous laws and cultural traditions. Under Hellenistic imperial rule, the high priestly aristocracy in Jerusalem maintained the Judean temple-state set up under the Persians for over a century. But they became increasingly attracted to and under the pressure of the dominant Hellenistic imperial culture. Finally in 175 BCE the dominant faction of the aristocracy carried out a Hellenizing "reform" that abandoned the temple-state and set in its place a Hellenistic *polis* in which they themselves formed the elite corporation of "citizens." This touched off a series of events that became the great "watershed" of Judean history for the rest of the second-temple period. The *maskilim*, the scribal circle who produced the visionary history in Daniel 10–12 and another circle of scribes who produced the Animal Vision in 1 Enoch 85–90 mounted active resistance to the "reform." The emperor Antiochus Epiphanes invaded to enforce the reform militarily. In response the villagers of Judea mounted a widespread insurgency of guerrilla warfare. After a prolonged struggle in the Maccabean Revolt they fought the imperial army to a standoff.

In the modern Western separation of religion from political-economic life, the Hellenizing reform, the imperial military invasion to enforce it, and the forcible replacement of sacrifices to "the God who is in Jerusalem" (Ezra 1:2–4) with sacrifices to Hellenistic gods has been interpreted narrowly as an issue of worship. The extreme reaction of some Judean scribal circles as well as the villagers to the escalating violence of the Hellenistic imperial regimes, however, suggests that far more was at stake in the crisis in which their lives were caught.

Judean scribes had been trained to serve the Jerusalem temple-state, on which they were economically dependent. What would drive multiple circles of scribes to actively resist the priestly aristocracy they were trained to serve? Villagers in most agrarian societies were left to run their community life according to time-honored customs and traditions so long as they rendered up the usual taxes, tithes and tribute. Only rarely have peasants mounted active revolts. Why did Judean villagers mount sustained guerrilla warfare against the Hellenistic imperial army? Hellenistic imperial rule, enforced by military invasion, was not just an interference with temple sacrifices, but was a threat to the very social-economic existence of the Judean people in their traditional way of life. Indeed, part of the impact of invasive Hellenistic imperial rule was to effect a significant change in Judean (scribal) culture: the sudden appearance in Judean scribal texts of a whole range of hostile heavenly forces in the divine governance of history unprecedented in earlier Judean texts. The preoccupation of some scribal circles with these hostile spirits will require fuller discussion as the context of spirit-affliction and spirit-possession in chapter 5.

While the Maccabean Revolt was successful in holding off further invasion by the Seleucid armies, it had unintended consequences in the subsequent historical experience of the Samaritans and Galileans as well as the Judeans. The Hasmonean brothers of Judas the Maccabee (Hammer), who had led the revolt, consolidated their power in Judea and negotiated their own recognition as the new high priests of the temple-state. Launching their own imperial-style expansion of rule over the neighboring peoples, the second and third generations of the Hasmonean high priests conquered the Idumeans to the south and the Samaritans to the north, destroying their temple (Josephus, *Ant.* 13.257–258). In 104 BCE, just a hundred years before the birth of Jesus, they took over Galilee as well (*Ant.* 13.318–319). Thus for the first time in many centuries the Galileans came under Jerusalem rule.[14]

The high priests in Jerusalem required the Galileans, if they wanted to remain on their land, to submit to "the laws of the Judeans" (Josephus, *Ant.* 13.318–319). Far from suggesting a "forced conversion" to a conquering "religion" ("Judaism"), this probably meant submission to the revenues required in "the laws of the Judeans" in tithes and other taxes.[15] The Hasmonean regime, like Herod the Great after them, evidently established fortresses with garrisons of troops to control and gather revenues from the Galilean villagers (*Ant.* 14.413, 433). A certain number of Judeans may thus have become established in Galilee as local officials of the Hasmonean high priesthood in Jerusalem. Such would appear to have been the *dynatoi* (those holding power) whom the Galileans rebelled against and drowned in the Sea of Galilee when Herod was conquering Galilee in 39–37 BCE (*Ant.* 14.450).

14. Critical analysis of the limited evidence for Galilee under Jerusalem rule in Horsley, *Galilee*, chaps. 2 and 6.

15. Discussed more fully, with references, in Horsley, *Galilee*, 42–52.

While Judean villagers had been under the Jerusalem temple-state for centuries, Galilean villagers were ruled by Jerusalem for only about a century before the lifetime of Jesus. It is thus rather unclear what relationship may have developed between the Galileans and the Jerusalem temple and its high priestly rulers—probably at least an ambiguous one.[16] Insofar as the village-based peasantry would not have been literate, it seems doubtful that they had much direct contact with the scrolls on which the legitimating texts of the temple-state were inscribed (see chap. 6). Living at a considerable distance from Jerusalem, Galilean villagers would hardly have been eager to undertake the arduous travel to any of the pilgrimage festivals in Jerusalem, such as the Passover. For the Galileans, Jerusalem, the temple, and high priestly rulers represented the capital city that had taken over their territory and forced them to pay taxes and tithes.

The Roman conquest in 63 BCE again made the Jerusalem temple and high priesthood, which now ruled Palestine from Idumea in the south to Galilee in the north, into client rulers of the dominant empire. The people subject to the temple-state had already experienced the destructive effects of military violence due to the ongoing conflict between rival Hasmonean claimants to the high priesthood. The battles between rival Hasmoneans continued under the first decades of Roman rule, and the violence imposed on Galileans and Judeans was compounded by the Roman civil war that was carried out largely in conquered territories such as Palestine. The recurrent wars between rival Hasmoneans and the periodic Roman campaigns to "pacify" Palestine in repeated reconquests meant regular raids on villages to seize crops and animals. In certain areas, including lower Galilee, the frequent warfare brought severe destruction and slaughter. The recurrent violence and devastation of village communities in the middle decades of the first century BCE would have left collective trauma in their wake.

Until recent years Western scholars of ancient Rome, on whose work New Testament interpreters have been dependent, have downplayed the violence and brutality of the Roman conquest of other peoples. Indeed, ancient Roman historians themselves were more candid about Roman practices than modern scholars, as in Tacitus' repetition of a Caledonian chieftan's complaint:

16. See further the analysis of the limited evidence in Horsley, *Galilee*, esp. chaps. 1–2, and 6.

> [The Romans are] the plunderers of the world . . . If the enemy
> is rich, they are rapacious; if poor they lust for dominion. Not
> East, not West has sated them . . . They rob, butcher, plunder,
> and call it "empire"; and where they make a desolation, they call
> it "peace." (Tacitus, *Agricola*, 30)

Classical historians are finally providing much more critical accounts of
the brutality of Roman conquest and retaliatory reconquest, accounts
more in keeping with ancient Roman historians such as Tacitus.[17] These
more candid accounts suggest that interpreters of Jesus and the Gospels
take more seriously the portrayals of the Roman (re)conquests of Galilee
and Judea by the Judean historian Josephus, himself an eyewitness of the
decimating Roman reconquest in suppressing the great revolt of 66–70.
The standard Roman practice was to terrorize conquered peoples into
submission by devastating their villages, slaughtering or enslaving the
inhabitants, and publicly crucifying leaders of resistance.

Josephus' histories include several accounts of Roman violence that
would have left a considerable impact on the people in areas where Jesus and the Jesus movement(s) were active. In and/or around Magdala
along the Sea of Galilee in 52 BCE (several decades before the generation of Mary Magdalene), the Roman warlord Cassius carried out a mass
enslavement of people (although Josephus' number of 30,000, which
would have been at least one-tenth of the population of Galilee, must be
an exaggeration; *War* 180; *Ant.* 14.120). Shortly thereafter, when Cassius demanded a special levy of tribute, the brutal young Herod, recently
appointed military governor of Galilee, quickly strong-armed the quota
from Galilee. When some Judean towns such as Emmaus and Gophna
were slow to render up, Cassius simply enslaved the people. For Galileans
the devastation intensified after the Roman Senate appointed Herod as
King of the Judeans in 40 BCE. He proceeded to conquer his people with
the aid of Roman troops during the next three years. He mounted three
successive military expeditions into Galilee to suppress the persistent
resistance there. In sum, for the twenty-five years following the initial
Roman conquest (i.e., 63–37 BCE), the campaigns of Roman warlords to
control Palestine, including suppressing the rival Hasmonean factions,
wrought repeated slaughter of people, plunder and destruction of their
villages, and collective trauma for the survivors.

---

17. See, e.g., Mattern, *Rome and the Enemy*.

Herod's rule over Roman Palestine was tightly repressive. Then, after the countryside erupted in revolt following his death in 4 BCE, the Roman military campaign to put down the rebellion again visited devastation, slaughter, and enslavement upon the people. In particular, Josephus recounts how severe the Roman terrorization was in Sepphoris in Galilee, near the village of Nazareth, and in Judea at the large village of Emmaus. Those suspected of leading resistance to the reconquest were publicly crucified, to further intimidate the surviving villagers. The Roman warlord Varus ordered thousands publicly crucified in his reconquest. This form of excruciatingly painful slow torturous public execution that the Romans devised for rebellious slaves and provincials would have had a seriously debilitating effect on families, village communities, and the villagers in wider areas. The Roman conquest thus would have left collective trauma in its wake in lower Galilee and Judea right about the time Jesus and his followers were born. Coming upon the repeated slaughter, enslavement and devastation two generations earlier, the Roman reconquest in 4 BCE meant further death, injury, trauma and economic ruin for families and whole village communities. A family's loss of a member or two or the loss of half a village would have been a devastating blow to the ability to survive at a subsistence level, leading to debt, servitude, hunger, and malnutrition for the survivors.

It was previously standard in New Testament studies to pretend that Jesus and the Gospels belong in a sphere of religion, separate from politics and economics. More recently it has been debated whether Judea and Galilee were or were not "occupied" by the Romans at the time of Jesus. But that is a diversionary issue. What has not been taken seriously, although our main sources, the histories of Josephus, recount it at length, is the severe violence and devastation of the Roman conquest and reconquests and its effects on the people—what some medical anthropologists have called "the political-economy of brutality."

The Roman conquerors and the client rulers they set in place, moreover, exacerbated the villagers' plight by multiple demands for revenues. After conquering a people, the Romans laid them under tribute, which was (meant as) a humiliation as well as a source of imperial revenue. They demanded that the people render up a portion of their crops in addition to what they were already yielding up in tithes and offerings to the temple and priesthood. For "the Judeans" (who in the view of the Roman outsiders were all of those subject to the temple-state, including Galileans and others, as well as the Judeans proper) the Romans set the rate at 25% of the crop every (second?) year (except sabbatical years, when the land was supposedly left fallow; *Ant.* 14.202–203).[18] The Romans charged the high priesthood with collecting the tribute, and viewed failure to pay in timely fashion as tantamount to rebellion, which would be punished by military vengeance.

As illustrated by their keeping the high priesthood in power and charging it with collection of the tribute, the Romans ruled Palestine, like other areas in the East, through client rulers. The face of Roman rule in Judea and Galilee was thus the high priestly aristocracy and/or the client Herodian "kings." Like the Romans themselves, their client rulers pursued programs and practices that exploited and aggravated their Galilean and Judean subjects.

Most famous in legend and history was Herod. In order to establish tighter control after recurrent uprisings led by rivals to the Hasmonean high priesthood, the Roman Senate appointed the young military strongman as "the King of the Judeans" in 40 BCE. After conquering his own subjects with the help of Roman troops, as just noted, Herod became a model Roman client king. He built imperial temples and whole new cities in honor of the emperor Augustus, the seaport city of "Caesarea" and the military colony in Samaria, named "Sebaste" (that is "Augustus"; *War* 1.402–421; *Ant.* 15.331–341, 364). In Jerusalem he established alien Roman institutions such as a theater, amphitheater (hippodrome), and games in honor of Caesar (*War* 1.402; 2.44; *Ant.* 15.267–291; 318). Most significantly, surely, he massively rebuilt the temple and the temple-mount in grand Hellenistic-Roman style, with a golden Roman eagle mounted over one of the gates (*War* 1.401; *Ant.* 15.380–425; 17.151). Throughout his reign he maintained tight control, with several impregnable military fortresses around the country for "security." He also instituted repressive measures, required loyalty oaths to Rome and to his own rule, deployed informers, and mercilessly executed dissenters (*Ant.* 15.280–291, 292–298; 323–325; 365–372; 16.235–240; 17.42).[19]

Herod's grandiose building projects, in addition to his expansive royal court and his lavish gifts to the imperial court and to key cities of the empire (*War* 1.422–428; *Ant.* 15.326–330; 16.146–149), required rigorous taxation of his subjects (*Ant.* 15.365). The rigor of his political

18. On tribute and taxes in early Roman Palestine, see the study by Udoh, *To Caesar What Is Caesar's.*

19. Richardson, *Herod,* presents extensive discussion of most of these aspects of Herod's client kingship, which he views as relatively more benign.

rule made possible an intensified exploitation of villagers and his own extensive royal estates. Having pressed the people to the limits of economic viability, he was forced to back off, even to import food to keep his economic base from starving during a period of drought (*Ant.* 15.299–315). Reliable sources are scarce, but from parallel historical cases it is clear that intensive economic exploitation of peasant producers forced them to take loans from wealthy outsiders, at interest, in order to feed their families, after rendering up large portions of their crops in taxes, tithes, and tribute. Judean and Galilean villagers and even some scribal circles in Jerusalem were deeply discontented under Herod's tyrannical rule. Pharisees, whom he evidently deployed in some capacity in his regime, refused his loyalty oath (*Ant.* 15.370; 17:41–45). One scribal circle articulated their yearning for a legitimate king, one who was the anointed of God (instead of installed by the Romans; Psalm of Solomon 17). Finally, at Herod's death in 4 BCE, the popular resentment that had been building up burst forth in widespread revolts in Galilee and the TransJordan as well as in Judea (*War* 2.55–65; *Ant.* 17.271–285; discussed further below).

Once the Romans reconquered the country following the widespread popular revolt after Herod's death in 4 BCE, they installed his son Antipas, who had been raised at the imperial court in Rome, as ruler over Galilee and Perea.[20] The Galileans were thus no longer under Jerusalem rule during the life and mission of Jesus. After having been ruled from distant capitals for centuries, Galileans were now for the first time ruled by an administration located directly in Galilee. Antipas built two capital cities in lower Galilee during the first two decades of his rule, Sepphoris, only a few miles from Nazareth, and Tiberias, prominently in view across the Sea of Galilee from villages such as Capernaum and Chorazin. In a rare inclusion of such detail, Josephus mentions explicitly the disruption and dislocation of several villages involved in the construction of Tiberias (*Ant.* 18.36–38). Having most Galilean villages within sight of one or another of his capital cities, Antipas could be rigorously "efficient" in collection of revenues. And he would surely have needed extensive revenues

20. Fuller critical discussion in Horsley, *Galilee*, esp. chaps. 3, 5, 7. Jensen, "Antipas: Friend or Foe?"; and Jensen, *Herod Antipas*, reviews much of the plethora of recent research, particularly archaeological studies, on Galilee. Many of the findings would lead to different conclusions, however, if examined in the context of the political-economic-religious structure and conflicts evident though sources such as Josephus' histories—and not filtered through synthetic theological constructs such as 'Judaism'.

to support the construction of the two capital cities within twenty years, as well as to support his court and administration and even his own army.

It has been difficult to estimate just how severe the situation of the Galilean villagers may have been under Herod the Great and Herod Antipas.[21] In some areas, such as that around Magdala in the 50s BCE, western Galilee in the 40s BCE, and the area around Sepphoris in 4 BCE, villages had been destroyed, people killed or enslaved, and crops seized by one or more military attacks. Such brutal, terrorizing conquest and reconquest would have left collective trauma among the survivors in their wake, as noted above. Throughout early Roman rule, Galilean villagers faced demands for revenues from multiple layers of rulers: tithes and offerings to the Jerusalem temple-state, tribute to the Romans, taxes to Herod and then Antipas. The Gospels suggest that even after Galileans came under Antipas' jurisdiction and were presumably no longer under Jerusalem rule, the high priestly heads of the temple were devising new ways to extract revenues from Galilee, e.g., by persuading villagers to "devote" some of (the produce of) their land (Mark 7:1–13, thus leading to their inability to feed their families).

In 6 CE, ten years after Herod's death, the Romans placed Judea under the rule of the high priestly aristocracy of the four families that Herod had elevated to prominence, overseen by a Roman governor resident in Caesarea on the coast. The Roman governors had the power to appoint and depose high priests and usually held custody of the high priestly vestments. The frequent change of high priests, as each successive governor designated his own creature, indicates how vulnerable the high priesthood was to its Roman overlords. That Caiaphas lasted so long under Pontius Pilate suggests that he collaborated closely. Like Herod's kingship and Antipas' tetrarchy, the high priesthood based in the temple massively rebuilt by Herod was the face of Roman rule, responsible for maintaining order and for collection of the tribute to Caesar. The high priestly aristocracy always at least tacitly sided with their Roman patrons and never represented the people in their protest of provocative Roman actions.[22]

The high priestly aristocracy, which had long since lost its authority (i.e., legitimate power) among some scribal circles as well as among the

---

21. Again fuller discussion in Horsley, *Galilee,* chaps. 2–3, 6–7.

22. On this and the next paragraph, see the critical analysis in Horsley, "High Priests and Politics"; and Goodman, *Ruling Class of Judea.*

Judean people,[23] was increasingly unable to maintain social order. During the escalation of social turmoil, with popular protests, popular movements, and surges of social banditry, the high priestly families evidently engaged in increasing exploitation of Judean villagers. They continued to be the beneficiaries of the tithes and offerings and pilgrimage festival income of the temple, as surplus wealth piled up in the temple. Analysis by Jewish historians have concluded that the powerful wealthy Jerusalem high priestly families used the surplus wealth under their control to make loans at high rates of interest to desperate villagers who could no longer feed their families after yielding up tribute, taxes, and tithes.[24] There appears to have been a direct correlation between the centralization of wealth in the Jerusalem aristocracy and the increase, just at this time, of large estates in the hill country north of Jerusalem and the ever more luxurious mansions of the high priestly families in Jerusalem, unearthed by archaeological digs. The historian Josephus reports that the high priestly families became blatantly predatory on the people. Each family kept a gang of toughs whom they would send to the threshing floors to seize the tithes intended for the ordinary priests, with whatever violence was necessary (*Ant.* 20.181, 205–7). An illustration of how intolerable the situation had become by mid-first century, at least to a circle of dissident scribes, was the formation of a scribal group of "dagger-men" (*sicarioi,* named for the Latin term for curved daggers), who assassinated high priestly figures who were collaborating too closely with the Romans (*Ant.* 20.186–87; *War* 2.254–57).[25]

The result of the rulers' steady escalation of exploitation was the increasing impoverishment of the people. The ability of neighbors to come to the aid of struggling families was quickly exhausted as they felt the ever-tightening pinch of supporting themselves until the next harvest after rendering up tribute, tithes, and offerings. Villagers were forced to take loans at high rates of interest from the people who controlled surplus resources, that is, evidently the aristocratic families in whose hands wealth had become concentrated. Unable to repay their spiraling debts, the peasants were forced to yield up family members to debt-slavery and lost (control of) their land to their wealthy creditors. As families disintegrated so also did the village communities as a whole.

23. Most extant Judean texts include sharp criticism of the high priests. See further Horsley, *Galilee,* 132–37; *Jesus and the Politics,* 33–36.

24. Broshi, "Role of the Temple"; Goodman, "First Revolt."

25. See Horsley, "The Sicarii."

As with the Galileans among whom Jesus worked, as portrayed in the Gospels, the result for Judean villagers would have been poverty, hunger, and malnutrition.

Conditions would have been similar for villagers in the areas surrounding Galilee, into which the Jesus' movement(s) quickly spread, perhaps even beginning with the mission of Jesus himself (see on the Gospel of Mark below). After conquering these areas the Romans placed client rulers in control (such as Marion, "the tyrant of Tyre," placed in power by Cassius; Josephus, *War* 1.238). Syrian villagers were burdened with tribute to Rome and/or taxation by their local rulers, and suffered the effects of conflicts and skirmishes between local rulers. In these areas, the new Roman imperial order often meant disorder for subject peoples. It may not be surprising that a movement of the renewal of local village communities spread quickly into areas with conditions similar to those in Galilee and Judea. This appears to be what the Gospel stories are about, to be discussed in chaps. 6–10.

Movements of Resistance and Renewal

As noted above, standard studies of the historical Jesus generally focus on individual sayings and "miracle stories" separated from context. Studies by medical anthropologists and others indicate that illness and healing can be adequately understood only in context, including local social relations and broader political-economic forces. Frantz Fanon and James C. Scott observed that "where there is power, there is also resistance" and that resistance can take the form of movements of resistance and renewal, while medical anthropologists find that healing is often included in popular movements or leads to broader movements. The historical context in which Jesus carried out his mission involved a fundamental divide and conflict between the people and their rulers in Roman Palestine. That conflict notably produced considerable resistance to the Roman imperial order in Palestine, including popular movements with significant similarities to the developing Jesus-movement(s).

The Galilean and Judean people were unusual, one might even say distinctive, for how persistently they resisted Roman imperial rule. As noted briefly above, in Judea widespread resistance to more oppressive imperial rule had come to a head a century before the Roman conquest in the Maccabean revolt against the priestly aristocracy's transformation of the temple-state into a Hellenistic *polis* and Antiochus Epiphanes' military invasion to enforce it. Resistance became more frequent and persistent in response to Roman conquest and intensifying imperial rule.

The mission of Jesus was framed historically, both before and after, by widespread revolts against Roman rule. Judeans and Galileans resisted the initial Roman conquest led by Pompey in 63 BCE, then for three years resisted Herod's attempt to subdue them after the Romans appointed him "king of the Judeans." After his death forty years later, in 4 BCE (right about the time of Jesus' birth), the countryside erupted in revolt in Galilee, Judea, and the TransJordan. Protests and movements of resistance occurred through the lifetime of Jesus and during the ensuing decades among the Samaritans as well as the Galileans and especially the Judeans, and at the scribal level as well as among the villagers. Historically best known was the great revolt in Galilee as well as Judea a generation after Jesus' mission (66–70 CE). In vengeful retaliation the Romans devastated villages in the countryside, slaughtered and enslaved the people, and destroyed Jerusalem and its temple, then memorialized their Triumph on the Arch of (the emperor) Titus in the Roman forum. While the Markan Gospel may have been produced during the decades of social-political turmoil just before the great revolt, the Matthean and Lukan Gospels were evidently produced in the decades following the Roman devastation of Galilee and Judea in 70.

This stubborn resistance to Roman imperial rule was rooted in Israelite tradition, in which the yearning for freedom ran deep, yearning for an independent life as a people living directly under the rule of God. Josephus mentions repeatedly that the ideal of and drive for "freedom/ independence" (*eleutheria*) was what motivated resistance. At the very center of Israelite tradition, of course, were the origins of the people in the exodus from hard bondage under Pharaoh in Egypt and the Mosaic Covenant in which the people, guided by the "ten words," would live directly under the rule (kingdom) of God. Early Israelite tradition included many stories and songs of the people's struggles against attempted conquest by outside rulers, such as the Song of Deborah and the tales of Gideon. Much of the historical tradition of Israel consisted of resistance to the Philistines and persistent popular rebellion against the centralized rule of kings, including those of David and Solomon and Ahab and Jezebel. In those struggles the people were led by popularly acclaimed ("messiahed") kings such as the young David and/or by prophets from among the people such as Samuel and Ahijah. Most prominent among the prophets who led or catalyzed movements of renewal as well as resistance among the northern Israelites were Elijah & Elisha, whose acts of renewal included healings and multiplication of food in time of dearth. In the composition and development of books of torah and history scribes had incorporated and adapted popular traditions such as the stories of the prophets Elijah and Elisha, narratives of the exodus, and Mosaic covenantal commandments and customs. Israelite tradition was the basis of resistance by circles of dissident Jerusalem scribes as well as of popular protests and movements of resistance and renewal. That even circles of scribes mounted resistance may be a good indicator of just how intolerable, invasive, and oppressive imperial rule was for people rooted in Israelite tradition. And since we have relatively more information on them, it makes sense to begin with examination of their protests and, particularly significant, a scribal-priestly movement.

Protest, Resistance, and a Renewal Movement in Scribal Circles

Given that scribes served as advisors and representatives of the temple state and were economically dependent on the priestly aristocracy, it is remarkable that any dared offer resistance. As the professional cultivators and guardians of the official Judean tradition, however, they had developed a sense of their own authority that was independent of their high priestly patrons. Thus when the priestly aristocracy abandoned Israelite tradition for Hellenistic imperial forms in close collaboration with the imperial regime of Antiochus Epiphanes (as mentioned above), three different circles of scribes mounted resistance to the Hellenizing "reform" and its imperial enforcement. While we know very little about the *hasidim* who joined in the Maccabean Revolt, we know a great deal about the perspective and motivation of the *maskilim* and the "Enoch" scribes from the texts they produced.

In their struggle to understand what was happening under the increasingly invasive and violent Hellenistic imperial rule, these dissident circles of scribes produced a new form of political-religious texts. Daniel 7, 8, and 10–12, and the Animal Vision, 1 Enoch 85–90, are visionary reviews of Judean history under a series of increasingly oppressive imperial regimes.[26] By imposing the modern synthetic scholarly construct of

26. The following sketch depends on recent "revisionist" interpretation of "apocalyptic" texts in Horsley, *Scribes, Visionaries*; Horsley, *Revolt of the Scribes*; and

"apocalypticism," many biblical scholars have misunderstood these texts as scenarios of the End of the world. These visionary reviews of history are rather sharp rejections of imperial domination. Following a review of increasingly violent imperial domination they anticipate divine judgment of imperial rule and a renewal of the people, evidently without the temple-state. These texts articulate a dramatic change in the perspective and role of Judean scribes from their traditional service and support of the temple-state to active opposition to the imperial order of which it was the local representative. The crisis of the Hellenizing Reform enforced by the military intervention of the Seleucid regime led them to see the Hellenistic empires as violently invasive and oppressive and a threat to the traditional Judean way of life. Their visionary perspective on history, including their anticipation of a restoration of the people's independence, enabled them to actively resist imperial rule in anticipation of the renewal of the society. Their visionary perspective on history also marked a dramatic shift in Judean/Israelite cultural understanding of what was happening in their experience of the highly invasive and brutal new imperial rule by the Hellenistic and Roman imperial regimes that may help explain the sudden appearance of spirit- affliction and spirit-possession in the life of Judeans and Galileans (more fully discussed in chap. 5).

The discovery of the Dead Sea Scrolls brought to light the formation and remarkable two-hundred year persistence of a unique renewal movement of Judean scribes and priests centered in the community that had withdrawn to the wilderness at Qumran. The historical visions in Daniel 7, 10–12 and the Animal Vision in 1 Enoch 85–90, at the end of their reviews of oppressive imperial rule, envisioned a restoration of the Judean people (or "Israel") independent of imperial rule. Insofar as scribes and priests served and were economically dependent on the aristocracy, however, there was no basis in their own social location and experience for the formation of a community of renewal. This makes it all the more remarkable that a group of scribes and priests took their resistance to the point of establishing such a community.[27] The movement formed in reaction to the Hasmonean leaders of the Maccabean Revolt arrangement with the Seleucid regime to become the new high priests in Jerusalem. As articulated in the Community Rule (1QS) and the Damascus Rule (CD), they withdrew into the wilderness in a new exodus and there established

Portier-Young, *Apocalypse against Empire.*

27. This sketch is dependent on the fuller analysis in Horsley, *Revolt of the Scribes*, chap. 7; and much fuller examination in Collins, *Beyond the Qumran Community.*

a renewed Mosaic covenantal community. After the Roman conquest, the community evidently refocused its opposition on the Romans, for whom the "scriptural" code name was "the Kittim," against whom the community rehearsed ritual warfare (in the War Rule, 1QM). And indeed the end of the community may have come in battle with Roman troops at the very end of the great revolt of 66–70. The Qumran community has particular importance for our understanding of spirit-affliction and of Jesus' exorcisms because of its sense of close interaction with divine heavenly spirits (to be explored in the next chapter).

As illustrated by the Qumran community, significant scribal protests and resistance continued under Roman imperial rule. While the many popular movements of renewal of Israel and resistance to Roman rule are far more important for our understanding of Jesus' healings and exorcisms as aspects of his mission and movement, scribal protests are also illuminating. Josephus recounts two major actions of scribal resistance that happened a few decades prior to the mission of Jesus. Both actions insisted on adherence to the most fundamental principles of the Mosaic Covenant, the first two commandments: the declaration that God was the sole God and ruler of the people and the divine prohibition of bowing down and serving another god/ruler with tribute and offerings.

After the Romans installed Herod to maintain tighter control over the areas of Palestine, he massively reconstructed the temple in grand Hellenistic style—so that it became one of the wonders of the Roman imperial world (as noted above). He placed a golden Roman eagle, symbol of Roman sovereignty, over the gate and instituted sacrifices on behalf of Rome and Caesar, making it blatantly clear that the temple was an instrument of imperial rule. As Josephus notes, leading scribal figures had criticized Herod for his actions contrary to the law (*Ant.* 17.151), but Herod's tightly repressive rule effectively discouraged overt protests. As Herod lay dying, however, Judas ben Saripha and Matthias ben Margala, "the most learned of the Judeans and unrivalled expounders of the ancestral laws," inspired some of their students to cut down the Roman eagle from above the temple gate (*War* 1.648–655; *Ant.* 17.149–167).[28] Josephus' accounts suggest that the scholar-teachers and their students understood their resistance was commissioned by God and "the law of our fathers" (*Ant.* 17.158–159; *War* 1.653). In his characteristic brutality Herod ordered the scholars and their students burned alive (*Ant.* 17.161–167). When

28. The following paragraphs depend on, while shifting the perspective and emphasis in Horsley, *Jesus and the Spiral of Violence*, 71–77.

Herod died shortly afterwards, their brutal execution quickly became a rallying cry of the Jerusalem crowd in demanding a reduction of taxes, freeing of political prisoners, and ouster of oppressive Herodian officials (*War* 2.5–7). The protest intensified and spread into the countryside, and became one of the factors that inspired the widespread popular revolt in 4 BCE.

Another group of scribal teachers mounted a less dramatic but more politically ominous resistance to Roman rule ten years later, in 6 CE, after the Romans installed the priestly aristocracy as rulers over Judea under the oversight of a Roman governor. The Romans' new assessment of how much they could extract from the area evoked an organized refusal to pay the tribute led by what Josephus calls the "Fourth" Judean philosophy (*Ant.* 18.2–3).[29]

> A certain Judas, a Gaulanite from the city named Gamala,[30] in league with the Pharisee Saddok, pressed hard for resistance. They said that [the Roman] tax-assessment amounted to slavery, pure and simple, and urged the people to claim their freedom. They argued that . . . God would eagerly join in promoting the success of their plans, especially if they did not shrink from the slaughter that might come upon them . . . They agree with the views of the Pharisees in everything except their unconquerable passion for freedom, since they take God as their only leader and master. They shrug off submitting to unusual forms of death and stand firm in the face of torture of relatives and friends, all for refusing to call any man master. (*Ant.* 18.4–5, 23)[31]

29. This section builds on, but shifts the perspective of and makes corrections in my previous treatments of the "Fourth Philosophy" in *Bandits, Prophets, and Messiahs*, 190–99; and *Jesus and the Spiral*, 77–89. Keying on Josephus harangue that they "planted the seeds of those troubles which subsequently overtook [the people]" (*Ant.* 18.6, 9), some influential modern interpreters claimed that Judas and the "Fourth Philosophy" were the beginning of "the Zealots," a "nationalist" party that advocated armed insurrection against the Romans and eventually touched off the great revolt of 66–70. But Josephus does not say that they advocated armed revolt and, at the end of his account, says it was the governor Gessius Florus who provoked the revolt "by his overbearing and lawless actions" (18.25). I attempted to dismantle this synthetic scholarly construct in the series of articles on which *Bandits, Prophets, and Messiahs* was based.

30. Contrary to the synthetic scholarly construct of "the Zealot party," moreover, Josephus clearly distinguishes Judas the "teacher/scholar" (*sophistes*, *War* 2.118), who helped lead resistance to the Roman tribute in Judea in 6 CE, from Judas son of the bandit chieftan Hezekiah who, ten years earlier, was acclaimed "king" by his followers.

31. Translation adapted from that of John S. Hanson, in Horsley with Hanson,

The conviction that God was "their sole ruler and master" (*monon hegemona kai despoten*, 18.23) refers to the first commandment of the Mosaic Covenant, that demands exclusive loyalty to God in a social-political sense inseparable from the religious. Their application of it to the Roman tribute indicates that they also took seriously the economic demands of the second commandment, the prohibition of bowing down and serving another "ruler and master" with the produce of the people's labor (cf. *War* 2.118).

Although they did not advocate violent insurrection, they evidently understood that the Romans, who viewed failure to pay the tribute as tantamount to revolt, would take brutal military action. They were prepared to suffer martyrdom for insisting on the fundamental principles of Israelite tradition, that the people live under the exclusive, direct rule of God. Josephus' observations that Judas, Saddok, and their colleagues urged others to resist the tribute and "persuaded not a few Judeans" to refuse to enroll" (*War* 7.253; *Ant.* 18.6) indicate that they were organizing wider resistance among Judeans.

In both of these cases circles of scribal teachers and/or Pharisees risked their lives in steadfast resistance to Roman imperial rule. Their desperate actions suggest how much more intolerable Roman rule would have been for villagers, who bore the brunt of Roman conquest and the intensification of economic demands from the imperial order the Romans imposed in Palestine.

Popular Movements of Resistance and Renewal

Of particular importance in understanding the historical context of Jesus' mission are the movements of resistance and renewal among the Judean, Samaritan, and Galilean peasants. Popular movements and popular life in general are usually given only slight attention or simply ignored, partly because the sources are so limited and fragmentary and partly because historians and biblical scholars are usually oriented to elite culture. Modern western historians generally classify popular movements as (merely) "religious," having no particular significance for "real" political-economic affairs. Accordingly biblical scholars have more or less acquiesced in the marginalization of their subject matter and their own work as "religious," separate from politics. Among historians and political scientists,

Bandits, Prophets, and Messiahs, 191–92.

moreover, it has been generally understood that history is made by those who wield political and military power. Historian John Kautsky, for example, whose study of *The Politics of Aristocratic Empires* sheds considerable light on the Roman empire and its impact on Palestine, contends that subordinated peasantries do not participate in politics, at least the politics of those aristocratic empires.[32]

During the last generation, however, Indian historians of Indian history who produced the *subaltern studies* patiently explained that popular movements, dismissed by colonialist and Marxist historians (of India) alike as merely "religious," had far broader significance for history in general, and particularly for anticolonial struggles.[33] Popular movements were often the form in which subordinated peoples facing political-economic and cultural crisis were able to maintain some social cohesion by drawing upon and adapting their own cultural tradition.

Peasant movements of resistance and particularly widespread peasant revolts are rare. Their occurrence depends on certain circumstances. Displaced landless laborers or heavily dependent tenants are generally unable to mount collective resistance or movements. Peasants still on their land in their villages, but slipping into debt and hunger, are more likely to join movements or revolts. In the Great Plain just to the south of Galilee were large estates worked by tenants, and Galileans would have known about them. They could see what would happen to them as they were slipping into debt from the periodic Roman destruction and the economic pressures of multiple demands on their produce. The area of Judea northwest of Jerusalem was becoming consolidated into large estates by wealthy creditors, probably Herodians and high priestly families. And Judean peasants were, like their Galilean cousins, facing crises of subsistence (see the "slice of life" parables in Matthew 20:1–15 and Mark 12:1–9). This suggests that the fundamental social forms of family and village community were beginning to disintegrate. Yet while under considerable economic pressure, many Galileans and Judeans were evidently still in their villages and working the land. This gave them the requisite basis for mounting collective action in an agricultural strike and resistance movements.

Judging from the accounts of Josephus, our principal source for events in early Roman Palestine, peasants appear not just to have been

---

32. Kautsky, *Aristocratic Empires.*
33. Guha, *Subaltern Studies.*

participating in but even driving historical events. In reaction to the circumstances imposed by their rulers, they were taking the initiative in
making history. As noted at the outset of this chapter, Judean and Galilean
and Samaritan villagers mounted protests, sizeable movements, and even
temporarily successful revolts that regularly had their rulers reacting to
their initiatives. The movements were violently suppressed by the rulers
because they were generating the collective power of the people in resisting the rulers' control and revenues. In these popular protests and movements, moreover, religion and politics were inseparable. Deeply rooted
in Israelite tradition, these were movements of *renewal of the people* (of
Israel) as well as of resistance to the rulers. Of the many popular protests
and movements, we focus on the most historically significant, which also
happen to be those whose forms were most significant for understanding
the mission of Jesus and his movement(s).

Among the many popular *protests*, the most remarkable was surely
the widespread and highly-disciplined agrarian "strike" of Galilean peasants touched off by imperial armies marching through their land to forcibly install divine honors to the emperor Gaius' in the Jerusalem temple
(*Ant.* 18.261–288; *War* 2.184–203; Philo, *Legat.* 222–226).[34] Soon after
his accession to power, Gaius (Caligula) became the first Roman emperor
to actively seek divine honors. When Judeans living in Alexandria refused, Gaius retaliated by ordering Petronius, the new Legate of Syria,
to lead a large military expedition to set up his statue in the Jerusalem
temple. This of course was a blatant challenge to and violation of Judean
and Galilean Israelites' exclusive covenantal loyal to the God of Israel and
the commandment against bowing down and serving (the images/idols)
of other gods, service that Gaius was now demanding in divine honors as
well as the tribute.

As the Roman army came into western Galilee large numbers of
peasants ("many tens of thousands," according to Josephus) protested before Petronius, also refusing to plant their fields. "On no account would

---

34. Josephus' accounts and Philo's rhetorically more embellished treatment of the
events are heavily concerned with the diplomatic mediation in Rome by Agrippa I,
recently appointed ruler of Galilee, and high ranking Herodian officials in Tiberias,
and communication between Gaius and Petronius, the Legate of Syria. But there is
basic agreement in the sources regarding the motive of the popular protest, the wide
scope of resistance, how long the peasant strike was sustained, and that it was well
underway before the Herodian rulers and officials warned Petronius about the consequences (including for their own position and revenues). Earlier discussion in *Jesus
and the Spiral*, 108–16.

we fight," said the people, "but we would sooner die than violate our laws" (*Ant.* 18.269–272). Recognizing the ominous implications of the peasants' refusing to plant their fields, the nervous brother of King Agrippa I (the newly-appointed Herodian ruler of Galilee) and high-ranking advisers pointed out that, "since the land was unsown, there would be a harvest of banditry, because the requirements of the tribute could not be met" (18.273–274). Josephus' phrasing of the Herodians' warning seems to focus on the Roman reaction to the failure of subject people to pay the tribute. Viewing it as tantamount to rebellion, the Romans would have retaliated with military action, which would have forced villagers to "head for the hills" or be slaughtered. But the lack of a harvest would also have left the villagers themselves starving, and many would have resorted to banditry simply to stay alive.

Both Josephus and Philo frame their accounts from the perspective of the tense relations between the arrogant Gaius and the Judeans more generally, including diaspora Judeans and Agrippa I and other Herodians trying to maintain the Roman imperial order in Galilee. But Josephus' accounts make clear that this protest happened in Galilee and was carried out by Galilean peasants. Galilean villagers, not the Herodian officers, much less the priestly aristocracy from Jerusalem, were the ones protesting. The people took action. The rulers, the Herodian officers and others of power and position, like Petronius himself, were in a position of reaction, struggling to determine how to respond. It is not even clear, moreover, that the people's concern was primarily for the potential sacrilege to the temple. As suggested in Josephus' earlier account, their law prohibited an image of a god, and even more of a human claiming to be divine, being erected anywhere in the country(side), not just in the temple (*War* 2.195). More important probably, the people saw and made the connection with the tribute demanded by Caesar, son of god. This is clear in their remarkable collective use of the only leverage they had, as powerless, defenseless people subjected to Roman imperial rule: refusal to raise and render the tribute. This of course was also a huge risk, both of Roman military devastation in retaliation and of their own starvation, since they would have no food themselves.

This collective refusal to plant the fields, furthermore, illustrates the peasants' ability to organize across villages communities. Because of the difficulty of such organizing across villages, some of which were physically separated by ridges, the Galilean villagers' organization of this widespread agricultural "strike" is far more impressive than the scribal

"Fourth Philosophy's" urging others to resist the tribute. That the peasants were able to sustain the strike not just for days but for six weeks, finally, indicates their remarkable dedication to the covenantal commandments of exclusive loyalty to God and the prohibition of "bowing down and serving" any other purportedly divine force. It also indicates the collective discipline they were able to maintain—in the face of the extreme cost that it might well entail for themselves.

We can only speculate whether Petronius' continuing implementation of Gaius provocative order would have resulted in the Roman devastation of Galilee and Judea in 41 CE, a quarter-century before their vengeful destruction in retaliation for the great revolt in 66–70. But Petronius decided that the more prudent course of action was to back away from the confrontation, and further crisis was averted by the assassination of Gaius in Rome. This remarkable peasant "strike," however, indicates that the Galilean villagers were ready to take risks in insistence on their traditional Israelite way of life, and that they were capable of organizing collective action, even across the separate village communities.

In the many *movements of renewal and resistance* mounted by Judean, Galilean, and Samaritan peasants close to the time of Jesus large numbers of people were mobilized on the basis of the Israelite popular tradition cultivated in village communities. Most of them took one or another of two social-political forms distinctive to Israelite tradition. Both forms of movement, however, must be carefully separated from scholarly misunderstandings that have previously been projected onto the sources and the history they recount.

The revolts in Galilee, Judea, and the Transjordan in 4 BCE all took the form of what appear to have been popular *messianic movements* (*War* 2.55–79; *Ant.* 17.271–294). In his accounts of these movements, the historian Josephus says that groups of people from the country "acclaimed" one of their number "king," and that the leaders "aspired to the kingship" or "donned the diadem," or acted "like a king" (e.g., *War* 2.55, 61–62; *Ant.* 17.273–274, 278). In Galilee the people looked to Judas, son of the Hezekiah, who had been a prominent brigand-chief whose murder by Herod a generation earlier was long remembered. In the TransJordan they followed a former royal servant. And in the hill-country of Judea the peasants acclaimed a strapping shepherd named Athronges. Again seventy years later, in the middle of the great revolt of 66–70, moreover, the largest force of people from the countryside that fought against the

Roman armies took the same form, as Judean peasants acclaimed Simon bar Giora their king.[35]

That the people themselves acclaimed their leader as "king," who led them in resistance to foreign rulers, is almost certainly an indication that a particular social memory from Israelite popular tradition cultivated in village communities shaped the form of these movements (discussed further in chap. 6). The Galilean and Judean villagers remembered the stories of how the Israelites had "messiah-ed" the young David to lead them in resistance to the Philistines (2 Sam 2:1–4; 5:1–4) and that memory *informed* the movements they formed to resist Roman rule and to reestablish their own independence. It may be significant that Judas was the son of a brigand chief, just as the young David had been a brigand chief, that Athronges in Judea was a shepherd, as the young David had been, and that Simon bar Giora's movement was centered around Hebron as it gathered momentum, just as David had been anointed ("messiahed;" 2 Samuel 2:2–4; 5:1–4) by his followers initially in Hebron.

These *messianic movements*, however, should be carefully distinguished from the synthetic Christian theological construct of "Jewish expectations" of "the Messiah." Only about a generation ago did biblical scholars begin to recognize not only that no standard expectation of "the Messiah" was attested in late second-temple Judean texts, but also that references to an "anointed" figure were rare in such texts.[36] The key "prooftext," Psalms of Solomon 17, referred to a rather scribal "anointed son of David" who would defeat foreign rulers "with the word of his mouth," and not a sword. The few key passages in the newly discovered Dead Sea Scrolls, moreover, referred to multiple "messiahs," an "anointed son of Aaron" as well as "an anointed one of Israel," who were anticipated to have ceremonial functions at collective meals (1QSa 2.12–24).

---

35. Analysis and discussion of Josephus' accounts and the Israelite popular tradition in which these movements were rooted in Horsley, "Popular Messianic Movements"; and Horsley with J. S. Hanson, *Bandits, Prophets, and Messiahs*, chap. 3.

36. The article by de Jonge, "The Use of the Term 'Anointed' in the Time of Jesus," led to seminars and conferences in which scholars critically reviewed the very limited textual references to any sort of anointed figure. See the collections of articles in Neusner et al., eds., *Judaisms and Their Messiahs*; and Charlesworth, ed., *The Messiah*. Taken together these critical examination of texts effectively deconstruct the previously standard construct of "the Jewish expectation" of "the Messiah (son of David)" (in late second-temple times). For an attempt to put back together the pieces of "messianic" expectations that other scholars had distinguished and deconstructed, see Collins, *The Scepter and the Star*.

The priestly aristocracy and the scribes who articulated their interests would hardly have been looking for an "anointed" king who would defeat the imperial regime that maintained them in power. Even the dissident scribes who produced the anti-imperial historical visions (in Daniel 7–12 and 1 Enoch 85–90) had no interest in an "anointed one." Judean and Galilean villagers, on the other hand, had cultivated the memory of the young shepherd-warrior David whom their ancestors had "anointed" to lead them, and that memory influenced the form of their movements of resistance and renewal.

Although Josephus offers merely sketchy information on them, all of these "messianic movements" appear to have been movements of renewal of the people as well as of resistance to rulers. They not only took control of their immediate area, but managed to maintain their independence of Roman and Jerusalem rule and enabled village communities to run their own affairs for months or even years. In Galilee and the Jordan valley they attacked the royal fortresses and took back the goods that had been seized and stored there and attacked royal palaces and the mansions of the wealthy (*War* 2.56–58; *Ant.* 17.271–277). In Judea the movement led by Athronges attacked both Romans and Herodian officers, who had treated them with arrogance and violence. Despite the size and brutality of the Roman military forces, the movement managed to control parts of Judea for years. They held councils to discuss policies and plans. It took the Romans three years before they could take control of these areas that had established their effective independence. Nearly seventy years later, Simon bar Giora and his movement in central and southern Judea established covenantal "reforms," the cancellation of debts and the release of debt-slaves.

These several popular messianic movements that occurred a generation before and after Jesus' mission indicate that the social memory of the young David was very much alive among Galilean and Judean villagers as a pattern of interaction between leader and followers in wide-spread movements of renewal of the people's independent life in resistance to Roman rule. Clearly one of the roles or models of interaction of leader-and-followers alive in Israelite popular tradition was that of a popularly acclaimed king (messiah). Josephus's accounts offer no indication that healing or exorcism was included in the repertoire of any of these popularly acclaimed kings. But their agenda did include declaration of release of debt slaves and restoration of people's land, and restoration of the people's independent life in their village communities.

The second distinctively Israelite form in which large numbers of peasants were mobilized were the *popular prophetic movements* that arose in mid-first century CE.[37] Josephus presents accounts of two particular prophetic movements among the Judeans, one among the Samaritans, and makes general references to several such movements. As Josephus' accounts indicate, the Roman governors viewed these movements as serious "revolutionary actions" against which they sent out their military. But his accounts also indicate that, in contrast with the messianic movements, they were basically non-confrontational and nonviolent, with prophet and followers caught up in eager anticipation of an imminent act of deliverance.

Their anticipatory mentality has led some interpreters to characterize these prophets as "apocalyptic." But they have virtually nothing in common with the scribal circles and scribal texts that have been classified as "apocalyptic," other than a shared confidence in God's eventual deliverance. These prophets in Josephus' accounts, moreover, should not be classified or confused with the modern scholarly construct of "eschatological prophet." The latter is a scholarly composite and conceived with variations of emphasis, but seems to be imagined as a figure that appears at the end-time either to bring the message of the End or to bring about the End. Josephus' accounts of the prophets who led movements, however, do not suggest that the new acts of deliverance they anticipated were eschatological. Both "apocalyptic prophet" and "eschatological prophet" are modern scholarly concepts imposed on sources and not historical figures patterned after figures in Israelite tradition that are attested in sources.

Josephus' brief summary references to several prophets who led numbers of people out into the wilderness "where God would show them signs of imminent liberation" (*War* 2.259; cf. *Ant.* 20.168) have misled some scholars into labeling them as "sign prophets."[38] This may be an attractive label for those seeking a possible parallel to Jesus as portrayed in the Gospel of John as having performed "signs," which are also usually understood as "miracles." It is only in these brief references to these movements in general, however, that Josephus uses the term "signs." And whatever he meant by the term in the summary statements, in his accounts of particular prophetic movements he refers not to signs but to

---

37. References and critical discussion in Horsley, "Like One of the Prophets of Old"; and Horsley, "Popular Prophetic Movements."

38. Barnett, "Jewish Sign Prophets."

anticipated events of liberation and renewal. In the synoptic Gospels, of course, Jesus' healings and exorcisms are not referred to as "signs." In fact, when the scribes and Pharisees ask him for a sign, he refuses to give them one (except for "the sign of Jonah," which may be a reference to his proclamation of the kingdom of God, the message of deliverance itself and not a sign of something else to come).

The first prophetic movement Josephus recounts emerged among the Samaritans shortly after the mission of Jesus of Nazareth, when Pontius Pilate was still governor (of Judea and Samaria). The Samaritans, like the Judeans and Galileans, were deeply rooted in Israelite tradition, except that their tradition would have been focused more on the independence of early Israel and the Mosaic covenant of the twelve tribes with God and expectation of a prophet like Moses in renewal of the people. Samaritan tradition would probably have had negative attitudes toward the temple and high priesthood in Jerusalem. Less than two centuries before, the Hasmonean high priesthood had conquered the Samaritans and destroyed their temple on Mount Gerizim (as noted briefly above). This sacred mountain became the focus of the prophetic movement in Samaria (*Ant.* 18.85–87). The prophet led a crowd of his followers up the mountain where, he said, they would find the holy vessels buried where Moses had placed them, apparently anticipating the renewal of the people around the holy place and vessels. But Pilate sent out his cavalry and infantry which attacked the people assembled for the ascent, slaughtered some, routed others, and took many prisoner, and executed the "ringleaders."

In Judea, under the Roman governor Fadus (44–46 CE), the prophet Theudas persuaded a large crowd to take their possessions and follow him out to the Jordan River, where "at his command the water would be divided to allow them an easy crossing." Fadus, however, "sent out the cavalry, which killed many in a surprise attack, took many alive, then cut off Theudas' head and carried it off to Jerusalem." (*Ant.* 20.97–98) That Theudas' movement is remembered alongside the "Fourth Philosophy" led by Judas (of Gamala/Gaulanitis) in Acts 5:36 as one of the two most significant movements that in some way resembled the nascent Jesus movement in their challenge to the imperial order must mean that it had been a significant event in mid-first-century Judea.[39] Large numbers of people had left their lands, homes, and villages, taking their goods with

39. The implied dating before the Fourth Philosophy in Acts 5, however, is surely a confusion.

THE POLITICAL-ECONOMIC-SOCIAL CONTEXT 155

them. Josephus' account suggests an historical analogy with or memory of the Israelites' exodus into the wilderness, with the waters parting to liberate them from bondage. But the parting of the waters of the Jordan also suggests an analogy with or memory of Joshua's leadership of the entry into the land of promise, or even an analogy with or memory of Elijah and Elisha dividing the waters as a symbol of the renewal of Israel (2 Kgs 2:6–8).

A decade later, under the governor Felix (52–60 CE), a prophet, recently arrived in Judea "from Egypt," rallied thousands of people from the countryside to follow him in a route through the wilderness up to the Mount of Olives, opposite Jerusalem. He said that the walls of the city would fall so that they could make an entry into the city. Felix sent out heavily armed troops and cavalry, who killed or captured most of the people, while the prophet escaped with some of his followers (*War* 2.261–263; *Ant.* 20.169–171).[40] The action (apparently by God) promised by the prophet "from Egypt" was also conceived by analogy with or the social memory of a story from early Israel, "the battle of Jericho," in which the walls of the city fell down, making the people free of the ruling city.

Probably John the Baptist should be included in this brief survey of prophets who led movements of resistance to the rulers and renewal of the people. Judging from the accounts of John in Josephus as well as the brief accounts in the Gospels, he prophesied judgment against the rulers and their supporters in Jerusalem as well as against Herod Antipas in Galilee (*Ant.* 18.116–119; Mark 6:17–29; Luke 3:7–9). But unlike the later Jesus son of Hananiah, he was more than a prophet of judgment against the rulers.[41] His baptism of repentance was clearly a ritual of the renewal of the Mosaic covenant as the commitment and bond that held the people together. Unclear is whether he preached and practiced baptism as the definitive new divine act of deliverance, or as a ritual of renewal that sent people back to renewed community life in their villages.

40. The statement, in Acts 21:38, that "the Egyptian" had stirred up a revolt and led 4000 men of the Sicarii out into the wilderness can be explained simply as a confusion of two groups active at the same time. Note that they appear in successive accounts in Josephus' narrative. Josephus' accounts of Theudas also indicate that even an unarmed popular movement appeared to the authorities as a serious threat to the Roman imperial order.

41. John should be grouped with the popular prophets who led movements, *vs.* my earlier presentation in "Like One of the Prophets of Old"; see rather Webb, *John the Baptizer*, 333–46.

In these movements led by prophets we can discern yet another common and distinctively Israelite form deeply rooted in the tradition of the origins of the people. Each of these prophets led hundreds (perhaps even thousands) of people from Judean or Samaritan villages out to experience some new act of deliverance by God. The prophets and their followers believed that God was about to perform a new act of liberation similar to or patterned after one of the great acts of liberation in the origins of Israel, such as the exodus (or entry into the land) or the establishment of the tabernacle in the wilderness or the battle of Jericho. The participants were so caught up in their expectation of a new act of deliverance that they proceeded to act it out, to realize the new deliverance they were anticipating. Memory of the great events of deliverance of old informed the movements in which the people went out to experience new events of deliverance. When the people formed a movement led by a prophet, both people and prophet already knew the scenario for the renewal of Israel free of imperial domination. These movements were thus not simply of resistance, but of renewal of Israel patterned after an/the event(s) of the original formation of the people. Just as in their origins the people of Israel had to follow a prophet's leadership in withdrawing from the dominant order and to await God's initiative effecting an act of liberation (exodus or battle of Jericho), so again they were following a new prophet (like Moses or Joshua) in anticipation of a new divine act of deliverance.

The occurrence of these several popular prophetic movements right around the time of Jesus are of considerable significance for understanding the Gospel portrayals of the "role" of Jesus in interaction with villagers in Galilee and beyond and the form of the movement he generated. Because the accounts in Josephus are brief, we don't know many of the actions of these prophets or the features of their movements, for example whether healing was involved. Both Jesus and these other prophets generated followers from many villages. In a significant difference, the other prophets drew people out of their villages to experience God's new acts of deliverance, while Jesus worked in villages toward the renewal of local community. The principal significance of these prophets and their movements is that they indicate that the social memory of movements of renewal and resistance led by prophets like Moses, Joshua, and perhaps Elijah were very much alive among villagers of Israelite heritage.

The context of Jesus' mission and of the development of the Gospel stories in Roman Palestine was a severe historical crisis for the subjugated people. The Judean, Samaritan, and Galilean people had been conquered and subjected to imperial rule and the client rulers they set in place for centuries. The Hellenistic empires, however, became far more invasive militarily and economically. Then the Roman warlords conquered the Galileans and Judeans repeatedly with severely debilitating violence and, with the client rulers they placed in power, subjected the people to multiple economic demands that left many impoverished and hungry, with their previously supportive village communities disintegrating. Those who wielded power in the Roman imperial order were sapping the individual and collective strength out of the people. In response to the crisis the subjugated Galileans, Samaritans, and Judeans, drawing upon and adapting social forms from the Israelite cultural tradition, formed movements of resistance and renewal. The next step will be to investigate traditional Israelite cultural understanding of sickness and healing and cultural shifts in response to the impact of more invasive imperial forces as key aspects of the historical cultural context in which Jesus responded to forms of personal and social malaise, some of them unprecedented.

5

Sickness and Healing, Spirit Possession and Exorcism in Judea and Galilee

STANDARD TRANSLATIONS OF THE Gospels would have us believe that the people Jesus encountered were suffering from "diseases" and that Jesus "cured" them, as noted in chap. 3. Similarly under the dominant influence of modern medicine, scholarly investigations of sickness and healing in antiquity tend to focus narrowly on "medicine in the biblical world" or on "doctors and diseases in the Roman Empire." They look for the symptoms of diseases as defined in modern medicine and apply criteria of modern medicine, often ignoring the immediate context of the reference and the point of the story in the ancient sources. They tend to pay little or no attention to the historical cultural patterns or social contexts that may be implicit or even explicit in the sources, which often offer significant information about social relations and/or broader cultural patterns.[1]

Cultural medical anthropologists, attempting to move beyond the parochial conceptualization of modern Western bio-medicine, recognized not only that "illness" is more broadly personal and social, but is culturally defined. It is promising that at least a few scholars have recently

1. To take just one typical case, the article by Max Sussman on "Sickness and Disease," esp. 7–8, in a standard and widely used handbook in biblical studies, pointedly striving for medical diagnoses, takes stories in biblical texts credulously as accounts of "diseases" and ignores the cultural realities indicated in the texts and the functions of the stories in Israelite society. For example, the article diagnoses "food-poisoning" as the cause of death in the legend of the people dying while eating the quails (Num 11:31–33), when the overall story is clearly about the people, after having received the manna, complaining about the lack of meat to eat.

appropriated cultural medical anthropology for application to sickness and healing in the ancient world in general and Jesus' healing more particularly.[2] But this has not always been done with critical perspective on how the schemes of cultural medical anthropology may not be historically applicable and without much attention to critical medical anthropological studies. As discussed in chap. 3, to distinguish between "disease/cure" and "illness/healing" hardly makes sense prior to the rise of modern bio-medicine. And to project a "health-care system" consisting of "professional, folk, and popular segments" only adds a needless layer of abstraction in considering the lives of peoples subjected to the Roman Empire. There was little or no "professionalization" outside of the cities and royal courts, and sickness and healing were embedded in the fundamental social forms of family and village community, and their interaction with the indigenous rulers.[3]

The mission of Jesus and the Jesus movements(s) in which the Gospels were produced happened in Roman Palestine, among Galileans and Judeans and other, nearby peoples living in village communities. So sickness and healing would have been experienced in the particular historical context of Roman Palestine. Insofar as sickness and healing were culturally defined, then it is necessary to investigate the ways in which Galilean and Judean (Israelite) culture would have determined the forms, prevalence, and course of sickness and the healing process. This particular historical cultural situation would have provided much of the "content" ("meaning") of particular sicknesses and even determined the forms of healing. Of fundamental importance in the personal and social aspects of sickness and healing are interpersonal communication and interaction, particularly in the family/household and social network according to the fundamental social forms, patterns, and rules. But these, as critical medical anthropological studies make clear, were situated in historically institutionalized power relations that determined people's social location and condition. Also, the effects of the more invasive and violent imperial

2. Pilch, *Healing*; Avalos, *Health Care*; Crossan, *Historical Jesus*; Wainwright, *Women Healing/Healing Women*.

3. From available sources it would be difficult to discern anything in ancient Galilee and Judea that would correspond to what Kleinman covers in discussion of the professional and folk sectors, *Patients and Healers*, 53–60. For example, there is only passing mention of "physicians," among the elite (see below), and there is little evidence for "folk-healers" who could be fitted into the "folk-sector," and it is unclear where to slot the priests in the temple who handled the sacrifices prescribed for certain illnesses such as skin lesions in Leviticus.

rule of the Hellenistic and Roman Empires, including on the forms and incidence of sickness, may have led to significant shifts in the cultural understanding of sickness.

Partly because the Gospels, in Greek, were later appropriated by communities in Greek-speaking towns and cities more familiar with Hellenistic culture, it may also be pertinent to survey some of the forms of sickness and healing in the wider Hellenistic-Roman culture. This survey may provide some significant comparisons and contrasts with Israelite culture in Roman Palestine in which the sicknesses encountered in the Gospels were rooted. And it may in some cases suggest ways in which the Gospel portrayals may have been understood by later generations.

A growing number of studies by medical anthropologists and other cross-cultural studies have suggested several key, interrelated factors of sickness and healing. Chapter 4 examined the local social forms and interactions and the broader political-economic structures and forces that would have helped generate sickness and the conditions of healing among Galileans and Judeans under Roman rule. That examination prepared the way for exploration of the personal-social ways in which sickness and healing were understood among Galileans and Judeans (and nearby peoples) and for the particular construction of sickness and healing and spirit possession among these people rooted in Israelite cultural tradition. Again taking a cue from critical medical anthropological studies, chapter 4 also examined the effects of the more invasive and brutal conquest and intensification of exploitation by the Hellenistic imperial regimes and especially the Roman Empire on the subjected Galileans and Judeans. This is a basis for now examining how the impact these new outside political-economic forces may have had in the change of the Judean cultural understanding of sickness, in particular in the scribal speculation about the struggles between spiritual forces in the governance of the world and on the upsurge of spirit-affliction and spirit-possession.

In ancient Greek, Roman, and Judean societies, as among other traditional peoples, sickness and healing were not merely dysfunctions of individual bodies. They were understood and experienced in relational terms, in relation to family, community, and the whole people, and in relation to spirits and gods and other forces that impacted people's lives. Sickness and healing had social and political-economic as well as religious-cultural dimensions.

That most of our sources come from the cultural elite imposes significant limitations on historical inquiry. Many scholarly studies, moreover, project the perspective of the modern educated "rational" elite, labeling phenomena and attitudes articulated in ancient texts as "irrational" or "superstitious" or "magical." Only by critical examination of the sources can we, in certain cases, extrapolate information about ordinary people, the vast majority in any traditional agrarian society.

Whether in Galilee and Judea where Jesus worked and Jesus-traditions emerged or in the villages and towns of the eastern Roman Empire where Jesus-movements expanded, it seems clear from a variety of sources that the vast majority of people, who lived at the subsistence level, suffered mainly from hunger and malnutrition. Their lives generally involved a struggle for survival, and they were seriously at risk during times of food shortage.[4] The physician Galen tells of the urban elite in Asia Minor expropriating most of the food stored in villages, leaving the peasants to starve. "There was an obscene disparity between their humble fare and the gross over-indulgence of a few immensely wealthy families."[5] Slaves laboring on the large estates may have been better fed, but they were viewed as comparable to domestic animals. The wealthy Roman patrician Cato advised others to "sell worn-out oxen, blemished cattle, blemished sheep, . . . old tools, an old slave, a sickly slave, and whatever else is superfluous" (*Agr.* 2.7). Or wealthy slave-owners might simply abandon sick slaves at a temple.

On the basis of limited references in Greek, Roman, and Judean sources and more abundant evidence from other agrarian societies we can reasonably project that villagers generally in antiquity had a fairly extensive knowledge of herbal remedies and of the influence of heavenly bodies and weather patterns on sickness and healing. Precious few references to folk-healers survive, although we can reasonably imagine that such were active in ancient as well as in more recent peasantries.

There is considerable evidence for the elite culture of sickness and healing from classical Greece extending into the Roman Empire. The sources for Judean culture, also from elite circles, seem more concerned about circumstances and consequences for the whole society, although from the perspective of the elite. Of course it should be remembered that

---

4. In any traditional agrarian society, the peasants lived mainly on grain, with oil, nuts, figs and other fruit; meat, enjoyed more often by the wealthy, was far too costly for peasants and reserved for celebratory feasts. After the rulers and creditors seized portions of their harvest from the threshing floors and olive presses, peasants often did not have enough to sustain themselves.

5. Jackson, *Doctors and Diseases in the Roman Empire*, 39.

in their "civil religion," Greek and Roman city-states included ceremonies, dramas, and rituals for the welfare of the whole society and took extraordinary measures in times of health crises. It is important to keep in mind that Judean texts, some of which were later included in the Hebrew Bible, are not evidence for an essentialist culture known as "Judaism" which most or all people in Judea and Galilee supposedly shared. They offer rather the views mainly of the Judean scribal elite and the traditions they cultivated. We may reasonably project that Judean and Galilean villagers of Israelite heritage shared some of those traditions. But Judean texts are not direct evidence for non-literate villagers. For more direct evidence for villagers we are dependent on material in the Gospels, which evidently derives from popular movements, This will be the focus in later chapters.

Some Significant Modes of Healing in Greek and Roman Culture

Sickness, Health, and the Gods

In Greek and Roman cultures, as in most others, sickness and health depended on relations with the gods. Sickness and disability were understood as punishment by the gods. Zeus had inflicted infertility or blindness or Apollo had sent a plague for some known or unknown moral or ritual transgression. The early Spartans and Romans had killed deformed children (Plutarch, *Lyc.* 16:1–3; Dionysus of Halicarnassus, *Rhet.* 2.15.1–2) and Plato approved such a practice for his ideal society (*Theaet.* 160c; *Resp.* 460c). Just as people saw the gods as sending sickness in punishment, so they looked to the gods for healing. Ancient Greek and Latin texts are full of references to gods' healing people's sicknesses, and votive dedications express the same trust or hope that the gods will heal, in a kind of "if . . . then . . ." agreement.[6] The trust in the gods to heal continued at the official state level as well as in personal life, as attested by the practices of divination and augury in Rome. There were many [other] divine spirits (*daimones, daimonia*) involved in healing and other social relations, some of mainly local significance, and some of wider influence

---

6. Burkert, *Ancient Mystery Cults*, 14.

in the general mixing of the spirits and gods of the different peoples sub-ject to the Roman Empire.[7]

Peace and Security and Salvation under the Imperial Savior

African peoples were not the only ones to deal with the impact of over-whelming outside forces, particularly imperial domination, by incorpo-rating spiritual powers into their culture. It should not be imagined, in colonialist fashion, that supposedly "uncivilized" peoples were the only ones to experience "spirit-possession," while "advanced" civilizations were more fully "rational." Because modern Western political elites, both classical and biblical scholarship, and "liberal education" generally have idealized ancient Greek and Roman civilization, the historical realities of domination and subjugation have gone unattended or simply ignored. More recently ancient historians have been far more candid about how the Roman warlords completely destroyed Carthage and, more pertinent to New Testament studies, the classical city of Corinth, partly as a way of terrorizing subjected peoples into submission. Then those warlords sent to Greek sites such as Corinth and Philippi colonies of army veterans and the unwanted surplus of people who had flooded into the city of Rome or had been brought there as slaves. The response of the urban elite, after "Augustus" brought "Peace and Security" to the world by winning the battle of Actium, was to incorporate the overwhelming Roman power into the dominant images and rituals of their mythic and civil religion. Most striking, because ubiquitous, was that the elites of Greek cities im-planted the divinized emperor into their traditional temples, festivals, and pantheons.

In contrast to the relatively egalitarian African peoples with limited division of labor, the ancient Greek cities were sharply divided, with the vast majority of peasants and urban poor dominated by a tiny wealthy elite who controlled the land and headed the centralized political-eco-nomic structures and central cultural-religious institutions. The elites of Greek cities added the divinized emperor to the pantheon of the respec-tive institutions that symbolized and structured urban life. In traditional temples they erected statues of Caesar alongside the statues of the gods to

---

7. Since the English cognate "demons" has primarily negative connotations of malevolence or even maleficence, it seems best either to transliterate the Greek terms *daimones/daimonia*, etc. or to substitute the similarly ambivalent terms "gods" or "spirits" or "powers," as appropriate to the context.

whom the temples were dedicated. They installed shrines of the emperor in between the temples of the city gods that surrounded the public space of the city-centers (*agora* = central public "square" or "market place"). In some cases, such as Ephesus, the magnates rebuilt the center of their cities to focus on a temple specifically dedicated to the divine Caesar. Traditional festivals and games they dedicated to the emperor and renamed in his honor. As a result of all these steps the presence of the emperor came to *pervade public space*—although (until Hadrian?) the emperor never set foot in any of those cities. The magnates of the Greek cities also restructured the annual cultural calendar and set up inscriptions and monuments honoring Caesar as the Savior of who had established Peace and Security and *Salvation* (prosperity and well-being) for the world. One could say that the Greek cities, or at least their elites, were "possessed" by outside divine force(s) and accordingly served their Lord and Savior with lavish gifts to the emperor and imperial family as well as their munificence to build the new temples and shrines and fund the games.[8]

The visible and ritual presence of imperial power thus became pervasive in public space and even structured the annual rhythm of public life. Not only was imperial power incorporated into the traditional religion of Greek cities. Indeed, the cities' religion became focused on the imperial power that had become the most important among the many powers that impacted or determined the common life. On the other hand, since we have virtually no sources for ordinary people in the eastern Roman Empire, we have no idea of what they thought about the incorporation of imperial power into the traditional city religion. We have no idea if they, like their superiors, were possessed by the presence of the emperor, or whether they believed that rule by the divine Savior had brought Salvation (that is, personal and collective well-being) to them.[9]

Pharmaka and Physicians

That the gods were the agents of sickness and healing, however, in no way excluded trust in and use of healing substances, rituals, and practitioners. Over many generations villagers had learned to cut herbs and dig roots

8. Price, *Rituals and Power*; Zanker, *The Power of Images*; both abridged, with further discussion, in Horsley, ed., *Paul and Empire*.

9. The Greek term, *sozo*, verbal form related to *soteria*, is one of the key terms for the healing that Jesus brought to people in the Gospel stories.

for healing purposes and knew how to mix many medicines (*pharmaka*). Such popular lore continued for generations in villages, and was taken up into elite culture, where it continued into Roman imperial times. The wealthy Roman Cato's favorite "cure-all" was cabbage, sometimes taken internally, sometimes applied externally. City markets in the Roman Empire included root cutters and sellers of ointments, with the associated equipment of "mortar and pestle" and scales and weights. Pliny knew of nearly nine hundred such remedies, and the famous second-century physician Galen mentions six hundred substances.

"Physicians" were prevalent in the cities but not in villages. The imperial court and wealthy households had their own staff. They trained by practicing on patients, perhaps in apprenticeship to a mentor. The reputation of physicians was not high. As noted in discussion of accusations of "magic/magician" (chap. 2 above), the literary stereotype had become an adulterous swindler who might as easily poison someone as administer medicine. Pliny comments that doctors' experiments put people to death: "a physician is the only man who can kill a man with sovereign impunity," and refers to an inscription on monuments, "the gang of doctors killed me" (*Nat. hist.* 20.8.18–21; 29.5.11). Martial cites the epigram, "Lately was Diaulus a doctor, now he is an undertaker. What the undertaker now does the doctor, too, did before" (*Epigrams* 1.47). The physicians' most common practice was probably bloodletting, as suggested by the frequent finds of bleeding cups.

The Cult of Health

What can only be described as a cult of health and healing emerged and expanded rapidly in the elite culture of the "classical" Greek cities and on into the Roman Empire. The central figure was the great healing god (*daimon*) Asklepios, whose symbol was a staff with a coiled serpent and whose children are personified health and healing functions, exemplified in his daughter *Hygieia* ("Health").[10] Asklepios was not one of the Olympian gods of "classical" Greek culture, but came into such prominence as a legendary healer that he commanded far more attention and had far wider influence than they did. Rome imported Asklepios in the third century BCE to help deal with a plague. Temples of Asklepios multiplied

10. The standard examination of sources and interpretation is Edelstein and Edelstein, *Asclepios.*

to over three hundred in the Greek world. The most famous temple-complex, at Epidauros, became a pilgrimage destination (and still is today). It came to be rivaled by the Asklepeion on the island of Cos, which became a favorite center of healing, and the magnificent temple-complex at Pergamon became one of the "wonders of the world."

In these temples ceremonies were conducted morning and evening, with prayers and hymns and ritual washings at a sacred well. Next to the sanctuary was an *abaton*, a rectangular structure where devotees awaited a nocturnal visit of the god. Dreams played a particularly important role in the healings. In some cases they were sufficient to effect a healing, perhaps by the lick of a sacred snake or a god. Most often the dreams remained to be interpreted by priests, who might prescribe exercise, diet, bathing, or drugs. Numerous dedications at Epidauros and other temples mention the healing of paralysis, lameness, war wounds, tumors, irregular pregnancies, dropsy, consumption, tapeworm, lice, migraines, and baldness. Afflictions were attributed to punishment by the gods and healings to people's response in penance and expiation. Curiously lacking in these inscriptions, however, are expressions of wonder, joy, or celebration.

It is surely significant to take note of the multiple dimensions of healing at the temples of Asklepios. Insofar as they were pilgrimage destinations, people were coming with heightened hopes and expectations. In connection with their incubation in the *abaton* of the temple, many experienced a deep engagement with the god through dreams (visitations) and a priest who would interpret the dreams (the term "therapist" would seem apt). The incubation and dreams and their interpretation should point us to the significance of the performative aspect of the complex healing experience. Temple complexes included a theater (again the most famous one was at Epidauros), where plays and speeches testifying to healings by Asklepios were performed regularly, further intensifying the devotees' faithful anticipation that they too would be healed.[11] Many pilgrims would stay for several days or weeks, taking in performances while also incubated at night in the temple or *abaton*. While Asklepios may also have had devotees among the poor, most of those who came

---

11. See Hartigan, "Drama and Healing," esp. 172–75, who mentions (175) that Galen wrote about the role drama played in healing (*de Sanitate Tuenda* 1.8.19–21, in Edelstein and Edelstein, *Asclepios*, 413). Athenaios mentions several dramatic texts titled "Asklepios"; see *Deipnosophistae* 11.485b; 11.487a; 14.617b.

to temples for healing, staying there day after day, were clearly well-off, often wealthy.[12]

The cult of healing was personified in Hygieia, the daughter of Asklepios, who became ubiquitous in sanctuaries and inscriptions. It became the "ancestral custom" at Athens of physicians in the service of the state to sacrifice to her and her father twice a year on behalf of those they healed (*IG* 2. 2nd ed. 772.9–13, roughly 250 BCE).[13] Her cult was brought to Rome along with that of Asklepios in the early third century. As Lucian (second century CE) acclaimed, "If Health is the greatest of the gods, her work, the enjoyment of health, is likewise to be put before other goods" (*De lapsu* 6). The cult of health, of course, took more "secular" forms as well. Celsus, who denigrated the crass magic and miracles of Jesus among the riff-raff, recommended wealth, leisure, and self-discipline (in eating, drinking, and sexual intercourse) as a regimen for health: "A man in health . . . should be now in the country, now in town, and more often about the farm; he should sail, rest sometimes, but more often take exercise" (*Med.* 1.1.1). Under the Empire, the wealthy elite suffered a whole range of new "sicknesses of high living" (Plutarch, *Table Talk* 7.9) or "the tortures that resulted from high living" (Seneca, *Ep. mor.* 95.18). So the rural ambience of their country villas was ideal for the wealthy, who also attempted to create such an ambience in their city mansions. And the baths, the panacea of Roman physicians, were centers of treatment as well as socializing.

The "Sacred Discourses" (*hieroi logoi*) of the second-century orator Aelius Aristides, oddly underutilized as a source, offers richly illuminating information about the cult of health and the elite culture of sickness and healing in general under the Empire. This highly educated son of a wealthy family in Mysia (Asia Minor) was presented at the imperial court at age twenty-six. His oration in praise of Rome has become one of the principal sources for the ubiquitous honors to the emperor, the (religious-political-economic) images and rituals of power that held the Roman imperial order together at the top.[14] Within the year, how-

---

12. Vlahogiannis, "'Curing' Disability," 190–91, claims a "broad following among the poor" for Asklepios, but offers no evidence. Perhaps what leads to his claim is that he, like many other scholars, judge that the view that afflictions were divine punishments and that cure could be achieved through expiation (only) "reflect the popular mentality" or "the popular imagination."

13. Stafford, "Without You No One is Happy,"128.

14. On how these honors (rituals, monuments, inscriptions, games, etc.) held the

ever, he was stricken with severe sicknesses, including fever, respiratory difficulties, swollen stomach, deafness, and toothaches. Having received his first revelation from Asklepios at a resort near Smyrna and "converted," he became intensely devoted to the god, who guided his life in every aspect through a steady stream of dreams and visions—which he dutifully wrote down in his *Hieroi Logoi* . Soon he incubated at the magnificent sanctuary at Pergamon, where he moved in a circle of cultivated leisured devotees of Asklepios. With staffs of servants attending to their daily needs and indulgences, they were free to discuss their illnesses, share one another's dreams, and compare notes on their treatments. "We were sitting in the temple of Hygieia and asking one another, as we were accustomed, whether the god has prescribed anything new" (4.16). His regimen for the long process of therapy included riding horseback, walking barefoot, bloodletting, sweating under blankets, and cold baths. After two years he was not exactly healed, but had learned to live with his illnesses, and resumed his quest for fame as an orator.

Hippocratic "Scientific" Medicine

What is referred to as "rational" or "scientific medicine" in classical Greece arose not just simultaneously with, but in close interaction with the cult of Asklepios and other gods of healing, that is, *not* in conflict with what have been referred to as "irrational" beliefs, dreams, rituals, and "miraculous" cures sent by the gods.[15] A clear indication is the "Hippocratic Oath": "I swear by Apollo the healer, by Asklepios, by Hygieia, by Panakeia, and by all the powers of healing, and call to witness all the gods and goddesses, that I may keep this Oath and Promise to the best of my ability and judgment." In its origins, Hippocratic medicine was closely connected with philosophy, from which it evidently derived some of its theoretical framework. Hippocrates, from the family of healers called Asklepiads at Cos, which traced its origins to Asklepios and a fifth-century contemporary of Socrates, supposedly made the break of rational medicine from philosophy (Celsus, *Med.* 6–8). But Aristotle's interests included medicine, and his philosophy had a lasting influence on biology and anatomy. A generation or two after Aristotle, human cadavers

---

Empire together at the top, see further Horsley, ed., *Paul and Empire*, part I, esp. 10–24.

15. Cf. Jackson, *Doctors and Diseases*, 138; the material he cites shows close connections, not just "parallel development."

were being systematically dissected in Alexandria in order to establish anatomical information. The Hippocratic corpus in the library at Alexandria is thought to have resulted from a haphazard collection of many anonymous works, some as early as fifth or fourth century, not formed deliberately with a certain design.[16]

The second-century CE physician Galen was probably the most famous figure in "scientific" medicine in the Roman Empire. He was educated in rhetoric as well as philosophy, partly in Alexandria. But the decisive influence on his pursuit of medicine was an appearance of Asklepios in a dream, and he continued to value dreams as means of diagnosis and prognosis. He mastered all the medical and related learning he could muster, having scribes make copies of borrowed medical books, and himself dictated twenty-one volumes of his medical knowledge which today are a prime source for "scientific" medicine at the time.

A key principle in Hippocratic "science" was that sickness and health are universally definable conditions. There are no cultural variations in sicknesses; symptoms have the same meaning wherever they are found. The same biological structure is common to all humans. The very idea of "health," moreover, implies medical intervention in sickness. This was more important for women than for men because their bodies were (supposedly) constantly in flux between excess and evacuation insofar as the organ that maintains the balance, the womb, can close, open, tilt, or retreat up the body. Hippocratic knowledge also had pretenses of being authoritative, normative, and setting limits.

The aetiology of illnesses (the rationalization of their causes) among Hellenistic intellectuals in the early Roman Empire offers an interesting contrast with the prominence of afflicting or invasive spirits in Judean scribal texts and the Gospel stories. They attributed illness to an imbalance in the individual body's component elements rather than to the influence of external spirits.[17] Of course this theory of some of the intellectual elite hardly displaced the widespread understanding in the Hellenistic world that there was a plethora of spirits/powers (*daimonia/theoi*) that played an active role in fortune and misfortune, sickness and health.

16. Weissenrieder, *Images of Illness in the Gospel of Luke*, esp. chap. IV, presents a critical history and taxonomy of Hermetic "Scientific" medicine. See also Kee, *Medicine, Miracle, and Magic*.

17. Martin, *Corinthian Body*, 152–62.

Sickness and Healing in Israelite/Judean Culture

Judean texts that were developed and cultivated in scribal circles under the Persian, Hellenistic, and Roman Empires, some of which were later included in the Hebrew Bible, provide direct evidence for the literate elite. In some cases, however, they may provide indirect evidence for popular culture insofar as the scribes adapted stories, songs, customs, and prophecies that derived from earlier and/or popular culture, which presumably continued to be cultivated in village communities (to be discussed further in chap. 6). It is also possible, perhaps even likely, that as scribal circles came to experience more invasive imperial rule, including military invasion and conquest and the imposition of foreign political-religious forms, their response reflected and/or influenced the popular response to such experiences.

Given the persistent individualistic assumptions and lack of attention to fundamental social forms and interaction in New Testament studies, it is important to recognize that, in contrast with modern western culture (and the culture of modern medicine), ancient Israelite culture was not individualistic. As noted in chap. 4, people were embedded in household and village community, and more widely in their whole people. The actions of parents had implications for their children; actions of leaders and rulers for their followers and subjects; actions of earlier generations affected the lives of their descendants. It is important, therefore, to consider the collective or corporate dimension along with the personal and the collective transgenerational or historical dimension of the people. It should also be noted that in Israelite/Judean culture, in contrast with elite Greek and Hellenistic culture and modern scientific culture, there was no soul-body or mind-body dualism. People evidently experienced themselves as embodied, as well as socially embedded. Also in ancient Israelite society/culture there was no separation between what in modern Western life are often considered separate aspects of life, such as religion and politics or sickness/health and economic circumstances. As discussed in chap. 3, as "biblical" scholars learn from medical anthropology, it makes no sense to imagine that there was a "health care system" in ancient Judea or in the Israelite/Judean cultural tradition in which it was rooted, with different "sectors." There is little or no evidence for "physicians/doctors" among the elite (see below), much less for "folk-healers."[18] Also, as discussed in chap. 3, since biomedicine was unknown

18. There is no evidence from Roman Palestine even of the diverse specialists found in Greek and Hellenistic cities (such as itinerant herbalists or priests of the temples of

before modern times, the distinction that cultural medical anthropological theory makes between disease-cure and illness-healing is not applicable to the ancient world.

Sickness and healing are not prominent as issues in Judean (scribal) texts. References to sickness and particularly to its treatment are rare. Stories of healing are few in the texts that were later included in the Hebrew Bible, and virtually missing from (other) late second-temple Judean texts. It is clear, however, that in Judean culture (and perhaps in earlier Israelite culture) sickness was understood as punishment for sin, with God as the source or agent of both sickness and healing. Healing substances and healers are barely mentioned. The only humans portrayed positively as agents of healing are the prophets, principally Elijah and Elisha.

Sickness and Sin

Certainly in official Judean culture but fairly clearly also in popular Judean and Galilean culture, the dominant understanding of sickness as well as misfortune in general was as divine punishment for not having kept the covenantal commandments and rulings. Sickness was due to sin, collectively and transgenerationally as well as individually. This was deeply rooted in and implied in the very structure of the Mosaic covenant that had guided social-economic interaction in village communities for centuries and was the core of the extensive collection of customs, laws, and teachings that formed (the) *torah* (in its many written and apparently oral versions). That the Mosaic covenant was still operative as the guide to community life in scribal circles as well as in village communities in early Roman times is evident in the Community Rule (1QS) and the Damascus Rule (CD) that guided the Qumran community.[19]

The Mosaic covenant was not simply a set of commandments or several overlapping collections of laws, but was a structure of the relations between God and the people, God and the individual person/family, and persons and families with each other in the body-politic of the people.[20] God had done justice for the people in delivering them from

---

Asclepius, much less the intellectuals of the Hippocratic tradition). Similarly, there is little evidence of folk healers to be grouped in "the folk sector" comparable to the *tangkis*, indigenous pharmacists, and others that Kleinman studied in modern Taiwan.

19. See Balzer, *The Covenant Formulary*.

20. Mendenhall, "Covenant"; Hillers, *Covenant*; Horsley, *Covenant Economics*, 19–30.

domination by rulers. God therefore demanded that the people maintain exclusive loyalty to divine rule, particularly in observing the divine demands to maintain justice in their social-economic relations with one another. These were given not only in the ten "words" or principles of social-economic-political interaction, but in the many laws and ordinances that specified their implications. The sanctions on the people keeping or not keeping the commandments and laws included blessings and curses on the people, including their descendants. The most extensive collection of blessings and curses, toward the end of Deuteronomy, focuses on the fundamental aspects of production and reproduction of the people. Included explicitly among the anticipated results of observing or violating the covenant commandments were health and sickness. In one of the curses, for example, YHWH "will afflict you with consumption, fever, inflammation . . ." (Deut 28:21–22).[21] The blessings and curses were of course originally solemn rhetorical sanctions on covenant keeping. In social-religious practice, however, they became the basis on which sickness was understood as divine punishment for not keeping the covenantal laws.[22]

It is important to note that in this covenantal Israelite culture, particular illnesses were understood in the context of the broader agrarian community and society and its historical situation. In the series of covenantal curses in Deuteronomy 28, (the Hebrew terms translated) "consumption, fever, inflammation," are specifications of the curses on the basket and kneading bowl, the fruit of the ground, and the increase of the flock that result from failure to keep covenantal justice, and they are related to the cursed agricultural conditions of "fiery heat and drought" and "blight and mildew" (sickness of the crops). In the corresponding covenant curses of the Holiness Code in Leviticus 26, (the terms translated)

21. As illustrated in Sussman, "Sickness and Disease," 8, investigations of texts such as Deut 28:22 and Lev 26:16 in terms of modern medicine take them out of historical context. They attempt rather to draw connections of the Hebrew terms with particular "diseases" such as tuberculosis, acute intestinal infections, and different types of fever.

22. Sickness as God's punishment for sin could result not only from the sins of people's parents, but also from the sins of a ruler. According to Josephus, for example, as Herod's sickness at the end of his long and brutal reign became more and more severe, diviners and sages explained it was because God was inflicting justice for his actions that were against the law (*Ant.* 17.168–170). In Josephus' account of Herod's accusation and execution of his Hasmonean wife, Mariamme, moreover, people suspected that the epidemic sickness that killed large numbers of people and some of Herod's "friends" that he most honored was brought about by God in anger at Herod's violation of the law (*Ant.* 17.168–170).

"consumption and fever" stand in sequence with being conquered and ruled by enemies, who eat the crops the people planted as the punishments that result from failure to keep the commandments. In other texts as well sickness (mildew/rust) of the crops along with human sicknesses are the result of failure to keep covenantal justice (e.g., Amos 4:9; 1 Kgs 8:37; 2 Chr 6:28)[23]—and of course crop-failure would result in hunger and malnutrition. The prophet Haggai exploited the people's conviction of just this connection, using the threat of blight and mildew of the crops as God's punishment if they did not devote their labor to the reconstruction of the temple (Hag 2:17). In Israelite covenantal culture, particular illnesses were understood in the context of hunger-and-malnutrition as the general sickness that accompanies drought and/or conquest by foreign enemies as punishment for disobedience of the commandments.

God as the (Main) Agent of Healing

Just as sickness was divine punishment for sinning, health was the blessing of God for covenant keeping, often in the sense of the health or wellfaring of the whole people. In the narrative of the people's exodus from hard labor in Egypt, God declares that he will not bring upon them the illnesses and plagues that he brought upon Pharaoh, "for I am YHWH who heals you" (Exod 15:26). On the same covenantal basis, healing of sickness was understood as due to God, after and if a person or the people had repented and/or performed penitence. Psalm 38 is a prayer for healing that begins with the requisite penitence:

> There is no soundness in my flesh
> > because of your indignation;
> there is no health in my bones
> > because of my sin.
> For my iniquities have gone over my head; . . .
> I confess my iniquity;
> > I am sorry for my sin . . .
> Do not forsake me, O YHWH; . . .
> make haste to help me,
> > O YHWH, my salvation. (Ps 38:3–4, 18, 21–22)

23. Ironically the latter two references are parts of prayers of penitence (of the people) spoken by king Solomon, whose every major act, including the building of the temple by means of forced labor, was a gross violation of the Mosaic covenantal commandments.

In the parallel lines of a psalm, God's forgiveness of sin and healing of sickness become closely linked, virtually synonymous (Ps 103:2–3). Late additions to the prophetic tradition of Isaiah make explicit the obvious connection: God's forgiveness.

> And no inhabitant will say, "I am sick";
>> the people who live there will be forgiven their iniquity.
> (Isa 33:24)

The connection between repentance (forgiveness) and God's healing in response was the same for the whole people as for the individual. The prophet Isaiah could hope that the whole wounded and ailing people would make supplication to God, who would heal them (Isa 6:10; 19:22; 30:26). Jeremiah, on the other hand, senses that the kingdom of Judah's wound or sickness is beyond healing (Jer 8:15–22; 14:19).

This broad covenantal understanding of health and sickness probably originated with the early Israelites and may have been as cultivated in semi-independent village communities. Observance of the covenantal principles of social-economic justice and related covenantal practices of mutual aid, liberal lending, and cancellation of debts would have resulted in sufficient nourishment and well-faring of the community and its households. Violation of the covenantal commandments and customary practices would likely have resulted in sickness and hunger and made households and communities vulnerable to drought, famine, and further exploitation by local or foreign rulers. Similarly, the hope for God's healing that would result from penitence and prayer probably originated with the early Israelites.

That the covenantal understanding of the functioning of social-economic life, including sickness and healing as coming only from God, was operative among the people in general, however, meant that it could be an instrument for social control in the hands of the priests in the temple and scribes as experts in the law. As critical medical anthropologists point out, traditional agrarian societies headed by (temple-)states, could attempt to maintain hegemony through systems of time-honored sacrifices and law codes that provided explanations of sickness and "therapeutic" rituals with legitimating sacred ideologies. The Mosaic covenantal system, including the blessings and curses, became prominent in nearly every segment of the Judean cultural repertoire in texts produced by circles of scribes serving the temple-state: texts of torah (Deuteronomy and the Holiness Code [Lev 17–26]), historical narratives (Deuteronomistic

History and Chronicles), prophetic books (such as Jeremiah on the one hand and Haggai on the other), and instructional wisdom (esp. in the book of Sirach). The early second-century BCE scribe Ben Sira, loyal propagandist for the Oniad high priesthood (Sirach 50), made the connection with the temple (and the economic cost to the penitent) quite clear.

> My child, when you are ill, do not delay,
>> but pray to the Lord, and he will heal you . . .
> Offer a sweet-smelling sacrifice, and a memorial portion of choice flour,
>> and pour oil on your offering, as much as you can afford.
> (Sir 38:9, 11)

The book of Leviticus includes elaborate directions for particular sin-offerings. The Judean temple-state with its legitimating tradition, including law-codes that included prescribed rituals for key personal and social malaise, would presumably have affected how not just priests but even villagers understood sickness and the requirements for healing. That sickness was punishment for sin, could be healed only by God, and would happen in response to making proper sacrifices in the temple is presupposed in the Gospels, specifically in the scribes objections to Jesus' pronouncement that the paralytic's sins are forgiven. As anthropologists have pointed out, further, religious ideologies, rituals, and law-codes do not remain static, as a conquered people, or rather its ruling elite, struggles to understand and respond to invasive outside forces. In response to threats or invasion by outside forces, the self-appointed guardians of the "social body" might well intensify its internal regulations. Such efforts by the scribes and Pharisees may well underlie the charges against Jesus and his sharp rejoinders to these representatives of the temple-state.

References to Medicines and Physicians: Rare, and Mainly Negative

That sickness and health were an integral aspect of people's relation with God is so dominant in Judean culture is indicated by how seldom extant Judean texts, particularly those later included in the Hebrew Bible, mention either healing substances, techniques, or rituals or healers of any sort. The few references indicate that "medicines" for the healing of sicknesses and wounds were known and used (Jer 30:12–13; 46:11), but the valuation tends to be negative. Like most other societies, Israelites used certain herbs and roots for healing purposes (Jub 10:12, explaining how such knowledge had been revealed to Noah). As in ancient Greece and elsewhere, this lore would have been cultivated by villagers. Scribal circles had picked up such lore and correlated it, for example, with astrological knowledge (1 Enoch 7:1; 8:3). Some may have drawn upon this lore in their own healing practices. This is suggested in Josephus' portrayal of the Essenes, often associated with the Qumran community that left the Dead Sea Scrolls, who "conducted investigations into medicinal roots and the properties of stones for the healing of sicknesses" (*pros therapeian pathon*; *War* 2.136). In a positive reference that stands virtually alone in Judean texts later included in the Hebrew Bible, a poultice of figs is applied to a boil afflicting King Hezekiah, but it is prescribed by the prophet Isaiah, not by a physician (2 Kgs 20:1–11; Isa 38). Josephus mentions in passing that the asphalt or bitumen that floats on the Dead Sea was useful not only for caulking ships but for healing bodies, hence was used as an ingredient in many medicines (*War* 4.481). But drugs (*pharmaka*, in Greek) could also be used for nefarious purposes; Josephus lists a law unknown from earlier legal collections that forbids Judeans/Israelites from possessing drugs used to poison people (*Ant.* 4.279).

One of the only positive references to a healing substance and technique is included in one of the only tales of healing in ancient Judean texts, the book of Tobit.[24] The pious Tobit, who scrupulously practiced covenantal justice, developed white films on his eyes and physicians' treatment with ointments only made it worse until he became completely blind. After he prayed for God's forgiveness of his own and his ancestors sins, God sent the heavenly agent Raphael (disguised as Azariah = "God helps") to instruct his son Tobias to keep the gall, heart, and liver of a fish, which are "useful as medicine" (Tob 6:1–9). Instructed by Raphael, Tobias smeared the gall of the fish on his father's eyes, and peeled off the white films, as Tobit praised God for restoring his sight (11:1–14).[25]

Among healing techniques, as Josephus mentions about the encyclopedic knowledge of King Solomon, were chants (*epodas*) for the relief of sicknesses (*ta nosemata*; *Ant.* 8:45). Judean texts prohibit divination (of sickness and in general) by means such as consultation of (the spirits of) the dead or omens or astronomical or meteorological knowledge

24. This romance from the diaspora was evidently composed in Hebrew or Aramaic around 200 BCE and, insofar as copies were found among the Dead Sea Scrolls at Qumran, was known at least in scribal circles in Judea.

25. Use of a fish's gall as a remedy for ailment of the eyes is also known in Pliny, *Nat. hist.* 32.24.

(Lev 19:31; Deut 7:15–16; 1 Sam 28:7–8; 1 Enoch 7:1; 8:3)—suggesting, of course, that such divination rites were practiced. If there were healing rituals (other than chants and divination) in Israelite culture, whether at the popular level or in the temple, they do not appear in Judean texts. The sacrifices prescribed in Leviticus 14 and 15 were not for the healing of "leprosy" and the extraordinary discharges of bodily fluids, but the requisite offerings by people who were already healed, so that they might be pronounced "clean" by a priest and accepted back into normal social interaction.

The criticism of King Asa for consulting physicians about the affliction in his feet (2 Chr 16:12) suggests a negative attitude toward them. But the scribe Jesus Ben Sira manages to legitimate the consultation of physicians as well as use of medicines in Jerusalem aristocratic and scribal circles by incorporating them into broader (scribal) theological perspective (Sir 38:1–15).[26] God, of course, is the real healer. Thus, as noted above, when one is sick the requisite first steps are penitential prayer to God and sacrificial offering (as much as one can afford). Yet since both physicians and medicines mixed from herbs and roots of the earth are integral aspects of the creation of the Most High for healing, the alleviation of pain, and general human health (the meaning here of *eirene*, or *shalom*, in Hebrew), one can resort to physicians' services as a complement to penitential prayer and sacrifices. From Josephus' account of Herod's severe sickness at the end of his reign it is clear that there were then plenty of physicians at the court of the Roman client king with a repertoire of healing techniques (*Ant.* 17.171). The court physicians' knowledge of drugs (*pharmaka*), of course, could also be used to poison high ranking figures—which led to the suffering of the servants when Herod had them tortured for information (*War* 1.582–600; cf. 1.272).

Healers among the People

Stories of Women Healers

Later rabbinic texts contain references to healers, including women, suggesting that such would have been active in earlier centuries as well. In a discussion of permitted means of healing on the Sabbath in the Tosefta

26. For analysis of Ben Sira's instructional wisdom speeches see Horsley, *Scribes, Visionaries*, chap. 7; and Horsley, "Oral Composition-and-Performance of the Instructional Speeches of Ben Sira," in *Text and Tradition*, 73–98.

occurs the comment that these should not be done solely "according to women" (a man should also be consulted; t. Shab. 15:15). A later story about Rabbi Yohanan has a certain woman referred to as Bat-Domitianus treat his ailment with an ointment the recipe for which was known only to a certain guild (y. Shab. 14:4, 14d). Another story, about Rabbi Meir, who complained of a sore eye and asked for a woman healer to come and heal him indicates that the remedy required saliva of a woman healer who would spit into the eye (y. Sot. 1:4, 16d). Such women healers were evidently also midwives, and, like their latter-day successors among early modern European peasantries who were burned as witches by Christian demonologists, were called "wise women."[27]

Prophets as Healers

Most of the healing stories in Judean texts are told of the prophets Elijah and Elisha. Healing, along with provision of food during famine, is an integral activity of these prophets, who also pronounced God's judgment against exploitative rulers (he was commissioned by YHWH to "anoint" a new king) and, with other (sons of) prophets, generated renewal of the people of Israel. The Elijah-Elisha narratives appear to be representative legends of the actions of these "men of God" that had been cultivated in popular circles prior to their inclusion in the Deuteronomistic History.[28]

The Elijah narratives feature his leadership of the great ceremony of the renewal of the people Israel on Mount Carmel, symbolized by the twelve stones of the altar, his persecution by Ahab and Jezebel, his commission by YHWH, and his prophecy against Ahab's (and Jezebel's) expropriation of Naboth's family inheritance (1 Kgs 18–19; 21). In the stories leading up to his leadership of the ceremonial renewal (1 Kgs 17:8–16, 17–24), however, mediated by his prophecy, he ensures that a starving widow and her son, symbolic of those most vulnerable to the famine, (will) have sufficient grain and oil to make it through the drought. When the son becomes severely ill, the widow is afraid that the presence of "the man of God" has brought attention to her sin and caused the death of her son. Elijah appeals to God, stretches himself out upon the boy and, since YHWH listens to the prophet, life comes back into the boy. The prophet is the agent of sustenance and healing for the people as they

27. I owe these references to Ilan, "In the Footsteps of Jesus," 129. Cf. investigations of early modern European witchhunts in Horsley, "Who Were the Witches."

28. See Coote, ed., *Elijah and Elisha.*

struggle under famine and the exploitative rule of Ahab. While it was not a significant part of the repertoire of Moses, the founding prophet of Israel, healing was integral to the agenda of Elijah, the paradigmatic prophet who led the renewal of Israel in resistance to oppressive rulers. The memory of Elijah, including his "wondrous deeds," was very much alive, in scribal cultivation as well as among the people, and building on the legend that he had been taken up in a fiery chariot, he was expected to return "to restore the tribes of Jacob" (Sir 48:1–12).[29]

The legends of Elijah's protégé Elisha portray the repertoire of the prophet of resistance and renewal similarly. Besides prophesying to and against kings, Elisha is the agent of provision for the people during the drought and famine. He is instrumental in the multiplication of oil so that the widow of one of the company of the prophets can pay her debts and keep her children from being taken as debt-slaves (2 Kgs 4:1–7). He shares a gift of first fruits with a hundred people for whom it seems utterly insufficient, but all eat and have some left (4:42–44). He brings the Shunammite woman's son back to life (4:18–37). Having gained a reputation as a healer, he instructs the army commander of the king of Aram to wash seven times in the Jordan River and his leprosy will be healed so that he is clean (5:1–19). These stories preface those of Elisha's prophecies against the rulers of Israel and his finally fulfilling God's commission to Elijah to foment revolt by anointing a new king. In the stories about Elisha as well as the legends about Elijah, healing is pointedly referenced as a distinctive and defining action of "a man of God" (1 Kgs 17:24) or "a prophet in Israel" (2 Kgs 5:8). These prophets who are performing healings, moreover, are fomenting resistance to exploitative rulers and generating wider movements of renewal of the people under the rule of God.

Other prophets as well were known for their healing, if not in connection with the renewal of the people as a whole. An earlier "man of God," after King Jeroboam's hand withered when he intervened in the prophet's pronouncement of God's destruction of the altar at Bethel, appealed to God and the hand was restored (1 Kgs 13:1–10). While the later prophet Isaiah mainly delivered prophecies against oppressive kings and their officers (as represented in 2 Kgs 17–19 as well as in the early sections of the book of Isaiah), he also apparently engaged in healing.

---

29. This has been one of the key "prooftexts" for the Christian theological construction of the "eschatological" or "apocalyptic prophet." A future restoration of Israel and a returning Elijah, however, are not "eschatological" and Sirach is not usually categorized as an "apocalyptic" text.

When king Hezekiah contracted a serious sickness, Isaiah, as interpreter of the sickness in relation to God, announced that Hezekiah would die soon (2 Kgs 20; Isa 38; cf. Sir 48:23). Yet when Hezekiah, portrayed as the most just of the Davidic kings, pleaded to YHWH that he had been faithful and obedient, the word of YHWH suddenly came to Isaiah with the message for Hezekiah: "I have heard your prayer . . . and I will heal you." Whereupon the prophet Isaiah, and not a court physician, prescribed the means of healing (the poultice of figs mentioned above). Unusual, at the end of the story of Isaiah's role in God's healing of Hezekiah, is that the king asks for a "sign" that YHWH will heal him, which Isaiah announces will be a ten-interval reversal of the sun's shadow on the sundial. This element is more characteristic of scribal lore in royal and imperial courts of the ancient Near East where omens and astrological and other forms of divination played a major role in interpretation and treatment of the sickness of kings. There is no indication in Israelite/Judean tradition that healings themselves were prophetic "signs."[30]

No Expectation of "the Messiah" as Healer

In contrast with the prominent memory and longing in Israelite culture for a prophet (like Elijah) who would bring healing to the people, there was virtually no expectation of an anointed (messiah) king in second-temple scribal texts, much less of one who would have a healing role. There were earlier scribal-prophetic fantasies at the birth of a royal son of what a wonderful ruler he would be (e.g., Isa 11:2–9). Closer to the time of Jesus, there are only two texts of note that anticipated an anointed king, as noted in chap. 4: Psalm of Solomon 17 imagined an anointed king who would establish justice in Israel; and 1QSa 2:11–23 from Qumran that imagined that the priestly "messiah of Aaron" and the lay "messiah of Israel" would preside at the banquet of the community at the time of fulfillment. No healing role is imagined.

A fascination with Solomon, the son of David, as patron of wisdom, including lore of healing and techniques of exorcism, continued in elite (scribal) circles from the first century into late antiquity. Related to this,

30. As noted in chapter 4, a "sign prophet" is a modern scholarly construct based on Josephus' summaries about the many prophets leading movements in mid-first century CE. His reference to "signs and wonders," moreover, were a way of suggesting that those prophets were leading new acts of deliverance like the exodus led by Moses, and did not have to do with God's acts of healing.

some have claimed that a fragment found among the scrolls at Qumran (4Q521) attests "the Messiah" as a healer. The first extant line in the fragment proclaims that "[the hea]vens and the earth will listen to his anointed . . . ," hardly a clear reference to "the Davidic Messiah." In the rest of the fragment, "the Lord" (*Adonai,* i.e., God) is the agent of the people's deliverance, including at the end of the fragment, healing the wounded and bringing good news to the poor. This is simply not evidence that the repertoire of "the Messiah" was expected to include healing. In Israelite tradition, particularly in popular circles where the focus may have been on the figures of Elijah and Elisha, it was a/the prophet who was expected to bring healing as integral to the renewal of the people.[31]

Images of/Longing for Healing in Future Renewal of the People

As noted in chapter 4, the people of Israelite heritage in all areas of Palestine, Galilee, Samaria, and Judea, lived under the rule of one empire after another. The conquests by the Assyrian and Babylonian armies had killed many people and devastated their villages and their lands. This would have brought a collective trauma of death, hunger, paralysis, and other injuries and sicknesses that lasted for generations, and a certain culture of having been conquered and now living as captives in their own land. In the stories of the prophets Elijah and Elisha, God's healing and restoration of life are aspects of a broader renewal of the people suffering under oppressive rulers. So it is not surprising to find indications in several fragments of prophecies in the later sections of the book of Isaiah of the longing for and expectations of a restoration of the people focused on healing of the kinds of injuries and sicknesses that resulted from conquest.

Opening eyes that are blind and freeing prisoners are images of God's future deliverance of the people in one of the songs of "the servant of YHWH" imagined in the role of a prophet (Isa 42:7). In another prophecy, "the deaf shall hear the word" and "the eyes of the blind shall see" out of their darkness in the future restoration when "the neediest people shall exult," since there will be no more rulers that oppress and deny justice (Isa 29:17–21). In a sustained prophecy of the new exodus, the "holy way" through the wilderness (Isa 35:1–10),

---

31. Casey, *Jesus of Nazareth,* 271–73, also sees this clearly.

> The eyes of the blind shall be opened,
>> the ears of the deaf unstopped;
> the lame shall leap like a deer,
>> and the tongue of the speechless sing for joy. (Isa 35:5–6)

In another prophecy, this renewal of the people is attributed to a prophetic voice, whom YHWH has "anointed" and through whom "the spirit of YHWH" is acting,

> To bring good news to the oppressed,
>> to bind up the brokenhearted,
> to proclaim liberty to the captives, . . .
>> to comfort all who mourn. (Isa 61:1–2)

This evidently standard set of images appears in lines of (longer) prophecies that were collected and edited in the scribal circles that produced the book of Isaiah. These would appear to have been the descendants of some of those deported into exile by the Babylonians, either in anticipation of or following their restoration to Jerusalem/"Zion" (Isa 35:10; 61:3, 5–6). After the Babylonian armies destroyed Jerusalem and deported them, they too had come to share the despair of captivity and sickness. Now they too adopted the image of the exodus in their imagination of future restoration. One strongly suspects that prophetic images such as "the eyes of the blind being opened" and "the ears of the deaf unstopped" are reflections of a longing for deliverance among the people who were suffering under continuing imperial subjugation.

Spirits and Conflict of Spirits—but not Much Exorcism

Spirit possession and exorcism in the Gospels is closely connected with, indeed appears to overlap with sickness and healing. There is little or no evidence for possession or exorcism in (elite) Judean sources. It has long been noted, however, that there seems to be a dramatic shift in Judean culture indicated in texts classified as "apocalyptic," beginning in the second century CE.

In contrast with the prophets' speaking of God's more direct involvement in political events, a whole range of heavenly forces (often called "angels" and/or spirits) that directly or indirectly influenced the circumstances and welfare of the people, maleficently and/or beneficently, suddenly appeared in "apocalyptic" texts. This heavenly world of spirits in interaction with people seems especially prominent in some of the key texts found among the Dead Sea Scrolls that were produced by the Qumran community itself. Since these texts also offer indications that the conflict of heavenly spirits is related to the more direct impact of imperial rule (discussed in chap. 4), they may well signal a cultural shift relevant to spirit possession among ordinary people, as is evident in the Gospel sources for Jesus' mission.

The first step may be to recognize that much of the conceptual apparatus in scholarly discussion derives from or is heavily influenced by Christian theology and demonology. Not only is "apocalypticism" a modern scholarly construct projected onto ancient Judean texts. But terms such as "demons" and "evil (demons)" and concepts such as "cosmic dualism" do not appear to be attested in or are not good translations of terms in the texts. It may be best to avoid terms and concepts not evident in the sources, and to avoid cognate terms that have changed meaning or connotations over centuries of Christian theology and polemics. It seems only appropriate to avoid translating Greek terms such as *daimonia/ daimones* with "demons" since those terms usually ranged in meaning from gods to spirits and often had ambivalent connotations.[32] It would be less distorting to use the awkward alternative of transliteration. It will be important also to distinguish what was evidently spirit-affliction with pain or sickness from spirit-possession, in which outside/alien spirits invaded people and seized control of their behavior.

The Rare References to Spirit-Possession and Exorcism in Judean Elite Culture

Examples of spirit-possession in Judean sources are rare and cases of exorcism are even rarer. Some texts claimed as references to spirit possession and exorcism are more appropriately described as stories or concerns about spirit affliction and how it was or might be warded off. Such, for example, is the story of Abraham's treatment of Pharaoh in the Genesis Apocryphon discovered at Qumran (1QapGen 20.11–30). To keep Pharaoh from approaching Sarai, whom he had taken as a wife, the Most High God sent a spirit . . . to scourge him and his whole household. Abraham prayed for and laid hands on Pharaoh, and the scourge departed and

32. The terms *daimonia/daimones* in Greek and Hellenistic culture referred to a class of semi-divine beings that were trans-human and superhuman, and could exert benign and/or malign influence on people, depending on the context and circumstances.

the spirit was driven away. Josephus' account of David's charming away Saul's affliction caused by spirits (*daimonia*) by playing his harp and singing hymns (*Ant.* 6.166–169) draws a comparison with healing (*therapeia*) by a physician (*hiatros*).

The legend of "the wicked demon" that had killed the seven husbands of Sarah in Tobit is also a case of spirit-affliction rather than of possession and of driving away rather than casting out the spirit (Tobit 3:7–8). The legend portrays how she was healed by Raphael, after praying to God, parallel to how Tobit himself was healed of blindness. On the night of his wedding to Sarah, Tobias, following Raphael's instructions, burns the liver and heart of the fish and the odor causes the "demon" to flee (6:7–8; 8:1–3). While it does not include an exorcism, the tale of Tobit (third-century BCE) is an early attestation of a struggle between a spirit that afflicts the people (with blindness, etc.) and a spirit that helps heal them (named both "God heals" and "Yahweh is merciful," Azariah). The story of the ending of affliction and healing of blindness, moreover, is also about confidence in the restoration of the people of Israel.

All of these stories present cases of spirit-*affliction* rather than spirit-possession. But spirits there are, whether agents of God or independent or opposed to God, and sickness and death are attributed to affliction by spirits. The stories of the healing of Saul by David's playing and singing and that of Pharaoh by Abraham's prayer and hands do not seem closely connected with the welfare of the people more broadly. On the other hand, insofar as the overall story of Tobit appears to be an allegory of the situation of the people of Judah/Israel, the hostile spirit's affliction of Sarah may also represent the affliction of the whole people under imperial rule.

As often noted, the only extra-Gospel account of a particular case of spirit possession and exorcism is the story Josephus tells to illustrate the surpassing wisdom of Solomon (*Ant.* 8.42–49, discussed in chap. 2 as inappropriately classified as an example of Jewish magic). Along with the myriad psalms and chants composed by Solomon and his vast wisdom about heavenly and earthly matters, God granted him the knowledge of *the art* (*techne*) to be used against spirits in order to heal people. As an example of how this mode of healing was still strong among the Judeans in his own day, Josephus offered a story of a healing by which Eleazar freed a man possessed by a spirit.[33]

33. See the many-faceted analysis in Duling, "The Eleazar Miracle and Solomon's Magical Wisdom.

> He placed under the nose of the man possessed by the spirit
> (*tou daimonizoumenou*) a ring that had under its seal one of the
> roots that Solomon prescribed; then as (the man) was smell-
> ing (it), (Eleazar) drew out the spirit through his nostrils, and
> when the man immediately fell down, adjured the spirit never
> to come back into him, repeating Solomon's name and reciting
> the chants that he had composed. (8.47)

To convince the spectators that he had this power, Eleazar placed a basin
of water nearby and commanded the spirit, as it went out of the man, to
overturn it. This "demonstration" of the exorcism points to the common
"form" of exorcism stories that Josephus or his source appear to be following, which can be seen by comparing one of the stories Philostratus
told of Apollonios of Tyana over a century later (*Vit. Ap.* 4.20). As told by
Josephus, in what must have already become a typical story-pattern, this
exorcism story involves not only a performance but a "command performance" before the conquering general and future emperor, Vespasian.
While, in the fuller report, Josephus distinguishes forms of exorcism of
spirits from (other) healing of sicknesses by the recitation of chants in
the wisdom and art attributed to Solomon, this exorcism also involves
chants for healing as well as the use of "one of the roots" from the age-old
scribal knowledge of healing substances that, in Judean tradition, were
also attributed to Solomon.

In his account of the Roman army's "mopping up" after its reconquest of Judea after the great revolt Josephus recounts among sensational
features in the area of the Herodian fortress of Machaerus a special root
near the town of Baaras (*War* 7.178–189). "The so-called *daimonia*, the
spirits of wicked men that enter the living and kill them unless aid is
forthcoming, are promptly expelled by this root, if merely applied to the
sick." The only ways of capturing the elusive flame-colored root is to pour
menstral blood on it or to tie a dog to it that instantly dies when he runs
away and yanks it out of the ground. This sensationalist embellishment
of historiography is one of the few references to expulsion of possessing
spirits, although by means of *pharmaka*, and not exorcism by a human
agent. While not exorcism by a human or divine agent, this is a treatment
of spirit-possession known to Josephus and presumably others in Judea.

The Domination of Life by Spirits in Elite Judean Culture under Hellenistic-Roman Rule

While there are thus very few references or stories in Judean texts that attest spirit-affliction or spirit-possession and the driving away or casting out of spirits, there are significant indications that spirits, both benign and maleficent, suddenly became prominent in elite Judean culture in the third century BCE and after. Leading New Testament scholars, as noted in chap. 1, simply dismissed spirits and spirit-possession as something irrational that modern scientific people could not believe in, a world-view that biblical interpretation had to "demythologize." Anthropologists in general were slow to recognize that "societies" were not self-contained systems and that spirits and spirit possession were not "culture-bound" phenomena. Recent studies by critical medical anthropologists, however, have recognized that when seriously impacted by outside forces such as colonial invasion or military conquest, peoples struggle to understand and adapt (as discussed in chap. 3). More specifically, anthropological and other studies have suggested that there is a correlation between the relatively sudden prominence of spirit possession and the impact of outside political-economic forces.

Such studies suggest that it cannot be coincidental that the sudden obsession with a myriad of spirits in Judean texts appears more or less simultaneously with the change from the relatively low impact of Persian imperial rule to the more invasive Hellenistic and Roman conquests and ensuing domination. It is important to gain critical historical perspective in order to discern cultural changes in response to the impact of outside political-economic forces. Thus the suddenly intense concern with heavenly spirits in Judean texts can be investigated as part of the Judean cultural response to seemingly overwhelming outside forces. The obsession with spirits might appear as a "mystification" of those forces that, in retrospect, we can see were political-economic. As critical anthropologists—and before them Frantz Fanon—suggest, however, such mystification may also have been the threatened culture's self-preservative way of adjusting to the seemingly unchallengeable power of the invasive forces.[34]

A whole range of superhuman (*not* "supernatural") heavenly forces or spirits became prominent in Judean texts dated to the late third and mainly the second century BCE, such as Daniel 7–12 and sections

---

34. Horsley, *Jesus and the Spiral*, 133–37.

of 1 Enoch and Jubilees. Biblical scholars seem unable to explain how "Judaism" became obsessed with "angels" and "demons," in contrast with the earlier prophets' focus on God's will in earthly life. Rather, they took these texts as evidence for the "apocalypticism" that somehow became dominant in "(late second-temple) Judaism." "Jewish apocalypticism" has been constructed as an anticipation of the End of the world in a cosmic struggle between God and Evil or God and Satan. The stories of Jesus' exorcism—and indeed whole Gospel stories—have been interpreted mainly in that framework.

Some recent critical reexaminations of these texts recognizes that they do not attest the modern scholarly construction of Jewish apocalypticism. These Judean scribal texts can be read without imposing the modern theological construct of apocalypticism and its supposed determinism and cosmic dualism. A fresh critical reading may open the way to discerning indications in the texts of how they were reacting to the invasion of Judea and Judean culture by new imperial forces far more threatening politically and culturally than Persian rule had been.[35]

According to the foundational legend of the exodus and principal accounts of the Mosaic covenant, God was the exclusive ruler of the Israelite people. Other regimes and/or peoples served configurations of other gods (divinized superhuman forces that controlled the people's lives in their environment). The Canaanite kings, for example, served Lord Storm, Sea, and Death with produce extracted from their subjects. Indeed, YHWH the God of Israel had delivered Israel from serving other gods, and in the Covenant with Israel the first two commandments insisted that YHWH was literally their ruler and that they not bow down and serve other gods with portions of their produce (Exod 20:2–6; Deut 5:6–10). The stories about Elijah insist that YHWH was the sole divine power that determined the weather, the productivity of the land, and (hence) the welfare of the people (1 Kgs 17–18).

At points in the history of the monarchies in Jerusalem and Samaria, especially when required by imperial regimes, the gods of the controlling imperial regime were installed in the temple alongside YWHW to be served by Israelites (e.g., 2 Kgs 21:1–7). Albeit at the level of the ruling elite of Judah or Israel, this seems somewhat analogous to African peoples who incorporated into their own culture forces and rituals and symbols of other peoples with whom they were interacting (discussed in

35. Horsley, *Scribes, Visionaries,* chaps. 8–9; Portier-Young, *Apocalypse against Empire.*

chap. 3 above). Other strands of Israelite culture, however, demoted or disempowered the divine powers of the Canaanite kings and the imperial regimes that succeeded them in Palestine. In the texts of what became the dominant culture of the Judean temple-state and the more popular culture in which a prophet such as Micaiah ben Imlah was embedded, what were for royal and imperial regimes a whole "pantheon" of divine forces became "the children of the gods" (*bene-elohim;* 1 Kgs 22:19–23), a set of mere shadowy figures in the heavenly court of YHWH, the divine king. They had no function or role in the governing of earthly life other than serving as figures/attendants in the heavenly court and occasional voices that spoke out in the visions of prophets caught up into that court (1 Kgs 22:19–23; Isa 40:1–11). In stories of the crises of the people's life, moreover, the spirit of YHWH had a virtual monopoly on inspiring repentance, renewal, and resistance to subjection by foreign rulers (e.g., 1 Sam 10:9–13; 2 Kgs 2:9–18). Only rarely did another spirit, a bad spirit, play even a temporary role, as when Saul suddenly went from his seizure by the spirit of YHWH to his jealous brooding (1 Sam 18:10–11).

Professional scribes serving the temple-state were probably acquainted with much of the theological/astrological/meteorological "wisdom" cultivated at the Babylonian and Egyptian courts.[36] Yet none of this crops up explicitly in the few texts that originate in the Persian period or it is well-domesticated in Judean psalms and wisdom teaching.

In what are standardly called "apocalyptic" texts produced under the Hellenistic empires, however, heavenly powers with names and particular functions in the governance of history (or, the earth as the theater of history) suddenly become prominent, some benign and others maleficent. In Daniel 10–12, a heavenly power (Gabri-el) reveals to "Daniel" that, following battles between rival emperors and their armies, a most contemptible emperor will invade the people, violate the covenant, profane the temple, and kill the faithful sages (*maskilim*) who resist, while another heavenly power (Micha-el) defends the Judean people in the historical crisis. It has long since been recognized that this is a visionary history of the wars between the Hellenistic imperial successors of Alexander the Great for control of Syria-Palestine that led up to the military invasion of Jerusalem and profanation of the temple by Antiochus IV Epiphanes

---

36. Carr, *Writing on the Tablet of the Heart*; VanderKam, *The Book of Jubilees*; VanderKam, "The Demons in the *Book of Jubilees*"; the continuing application of terms such as "demon" and "evil" may be questionable. Horsley, *Scribes, Visionaries*, chaps. 8–9.

in 168 BCE. The sudden prominence of heavenly forces in relation to historical events is directly related to Hellenistic imperial conquest and invasion. This was the way that (at least some) Judean scribal circles dealt with their increasingly violent subjugation to Hellenistic imperial rule.

The far more elaborate portrayal of the conflict between heavenly forces in the Book of Watchers (what we know as 1 Enoch 1–36), is the first extant articulation of an understanding of Judean life that became particularly prominent in some scribal circles, as attested in subsequent "Enoch" books, the book of Jubilees, and key texts of the Qumran community.[37] In a conspiracy of rebellion against the divine governance of the world, two-hundred of "the Watchers," sons of heaven (heavenly powers), descended to earth and, with human women, fathered great giants, who begot Nephilim (1 Enoch 6). They devoured (the produce of) the labor of the people and even the people themselves. Asa-el ("maker-god"), leader of the Watchers, taught people how to make swords of iron . . . and every instrument of war and metal-working (1 Enoch 7–8). Shem-ihazah, another leader, taught people chants and medicines, Hermani taught (scribal) interpretation (of dreams, omens, portents) and wisdom, and the other Watcher-chiefs taught (the scribal) knowledge pertaining to themselves as heavenly forces (e.g., Baraq-el, "lightning-god," taught the signs of lightning; Shamsi-el, "sun-god," taught signs of the sun; 8:3). Since all of this led people to perish, they cried to heaven. Their appeal was then mediated by Micha-el, Sari-el, Rapha-el, and Gabri-el, four of the highest ranking benign heavenly powers in the governance of history (the world). The Most High then commissioned Rapha-el to bind Asa-el and to heal the earth, Gabri-el to send the giants against one another in war of destruction, and Micha-el to bind the rebel watchers and the spirits of their offspring, and to cleanse the earth from its defilement so that it would be tilled in justice (1 Enoch 9–11). The giants begotten on earth by the rebel heavenly spirits (powers), however, had become spirits on the earth that do violence, make desolation, and cause illnesses (15:8–11). What had been disempowered divine powers (of Canaanite monarchies and ancient southwest Asian imperial regimes) at the heavenly court of YHWH that helped in communication about historical affairs with prophets such as Micaiah ben Imlah have become active divine heavenly powers (note the names all ending in 'el, that is "-god") that wreak

37. The following discussion depends heavily on Nickelsburg of 1 Enoch; and my own analysis in Horsley, *Scribes, Visionaries*, chap. 8; and Horsley, *Revolt of the Scribes*, chaps. 3, 4, and 7.

violence and destruction of people in earthly historical affairs. Somewhat like certain African peoples, certain Judean scribal circles dealt with invasion of their societies by uncontrollably destructive outside powers by taking those powers into their own cultural system as the symbolization and "explanation" of their experience of invasion.

If we follow the sequence of causation in the visionary narrative of the Book of Watchers, rebel heavenly forces "father" empires, which with their weapons of war and their sophisticated knowledge of the workings of the heavenly powers (and even medicines and chants) conquer, exploit, and destroy the people. And even though the rebel heavenly powers themselves have been brought under control, their offspring, the earthly spirits, still visit violence and desolation on the people. The desolation included sickness (and death) for the people, while medicines and chants ostensibly for healing are denigrated as part of the sophisticated scribal knowledge cultivated in the imperial courts. The Book of Watchers has been dated prior to the invasion of Antiochus Epiphanes, to which Daniel 10–12 reacted with horror. It appears fairly clearly to be an attempt to (symbolize and) "explain" the violent invasions of the Hellenistic Empires, in which the Seleucid and Ptolemaic regimes had been battling back and forth for control of Palestine with their weapons of war and oppression of the people ever since the initial conquest by Alexander the Great.

This "Enoch"-scribal understanding of the world as struggling under the violent and exploitative rebel heavenly powers, their offspring of giants, and spirits let loose on the earth was further applied to the history of the Judeans (Israel) in the Animal Vision (1 Enoch 85–90). This and the parallel historical visions in Daniel 7, 8, and 10–12 anticipate a resolution to the historical crisis of destructive imperial invasion when "the Most High" would finally execute judgment on the invasive empire(s) and renew the people (pointedly without the temple-state, which was sponsored by the empires) or restore them to sovereignty.

The "Enoch" vision of a determinative struggle between rebel and faithful heavenly powers also strongly influenced the book of Jubilees. The latter is an account of "history" from the creation that inserts various laws where they fit in the "history" that was produced after the trauma of the imperial invasion. It has God create "all the spirits which minister before him" on the first day, along with the heavens and the earth and the waters (2:2). The list includes "the angels of the presence, . . . the angels of the spirit of the winds, . . . clouds, . . . hail, the angels of thunder and lightning, . . . and all of the spirits of his creatures which are in heaven and on earth." Enoch, the first to learn writing and wisdom, was taught by the angels of God everything on earth and in the heavens, including about the Watchers who mingled with the human women (4:16–22). In primordial times, these "angels of the Lord" fathered the giants, so that injustice increased on the earth, whereupon the Lord ordered them bound in the depths of the earth (5:1–11; 7:21–25), but there were now malevolent forces that were leading astray Noah's children (10:1–6). The Lord ordered that they be bound, but Mastema, chief of the spirits, successfully pleaded that a tenth of them be spared. Then one of them taught Noah "the healing of all their illnesses together with their seductions so that he might heal by means of the herbs of the earth" (10:7–14). That all of this leads to imperial conquest and oppression is finally made explicit, with fortified cities, one man raised up over the people, kingdoms going to war with weapons of battle, taking a city captive and selling the people into slavery. "Cruel spirits assisted them, . . . and the prince, Mastema, did all this . . . and sent other spirits to destroy . . ." (11:1–6). Prince Mastema continued to wreak havoc in the history of the people until the completion of the exodus, where the narrative ends.

The key passage of Jub 10:7–14 is pertinent to the understanding of and response to illnesses. In the course of the narrative it is clear that illnesses are due to people going astray and sinning. Of the myriad malign spirits that are descended from the Watchers a tenth are not sent down to judgment and evidently function as an additional explanation of illnesses. But the benign spirits who remain loyal to the Most High taught Noah how to heal their illnesses by means of herbs of the earth, lore that Noah presumably has passed down to his descendants so that at least the "Jubilees" scribes could practice herbal healing of the illnesses caused by spirit affliction.

The book of Jubilees thus offers another explanation only slightly different from the "Enoch" texts of the Judeans' continuing experience of invasion and subjugation, as due to the spirits generated by the rebel Watchers, spirits that make war on the people with their weapons of war. This is not a "cosmic dualism," but an understanding of destructive imperial invasion and exploitation (along with medicines and even some scribal knowledge) in terms of a disruption in the heavenly governance by the plethora of heavenly powers or spirits. The Watchers were rebel powers, and while they themselves have been bound, the spirits they generated in their rebellion now wreak oppressive havoc in the people's history. Mastema, in Jubilees, plays a role somewhat similar to Satan in other texts, but like Satan is not the very personification of "Evil," in an absolute cosmic opposition to God, but rather the chieftan of the maleficent (imperial) forces who can plead and bargain with God—as well as a tempter who in effect does the "dirty work" in which God acquiesces. Mastema (with all his spirits) is subordinate to God but not under the control of God. But neither Jubilees nor the Qumran Community Rule and War Rule attest a separate demonic "kingdom" of Satan against which the Most High and the benign heavenly forces are locked in a cosmic struggle.

The Community Rule of the scribal-priestly Qumran community found among the Dead Sea Scrolls, finally, expresses an understanding of history as (currently) subject to a grand struggle for control between two armies of spirits, evidently founded in the creation.

> He has appointed for him two spirits in which to walk until the time of His visitation: the spirits of truth and injustice . . . All the children of righteousness are ruled by the Prince of Light and walk in the ways of light, but all the children of injustice are ruled by the Angel of Darkness and walk in the ways of darkness. The Angel of Darkness leads all the children of righteousness astray, . . . for all his allotted spirits seek the overthrow of the sons of light. But the God of Israel and His Angel of Truth will succor all the sons of light . . . But in the mysteries of His understanding, and in His glorious wisdom, God has ordained an end for injustice, and at the time of the visitation He will destroy it for ever. (1QS 3:18–24; 4:18–19; Vermes trans.)

The War Scroll (1QM), also produced by the Qumran community, makes a direct connection between Belial and his host of hostile heavenly spirits and the Romans, for whom the code name is "Kittim," who have conquered the people. In fact, most of the text consists of an elaborate scenario in which the final battle will be conducted between the Kittim and the company of Belial, on the one side, and the sons of light aided by the heavenly forces that fight for them, on the other. Much of the War Scroll text consists of instructions for elaborate ritual drills in anticipation of the final battle, ostensibly in imitation of Israelite holy-war tradition, but clearly also influenced by the drills of the Roman legions.

These texts produced by Judean scribal circles represent a significant development of Israelite-Judean culture beyond what appears in earlier sources. "The Most High" God is seemingly remote from historical events. In the Book of Watchers, sickness, along with the violence and oppression of foreign rule are due not to the agency of God but that of heavenly forces who rebelled against the divinely ordained governance of the world and the "giants" and other powerful malevolent spirits they brought into the world. The Most High is still ultimately in control, but works through other, loyal, high-ranking heavenly forces to bind or restrain the spirits of the giants that have been generated in the historical process that is seemingly "out of control." In the grand scheme assumed and articulated in the Community Rule and the War Scroll of the priestly-scribal community at Qumran, historical affairs are determined by the struggle between the two transcendent super-human heavenly armies of spirits. Imperial rulers were operating as the historical instruments of the hostile heavenly forces directly opposed to God's will for the people. In their attempt to affirm that God was still transcendent and ultimately in control of history, the scribal circles imagined the hostile power(s) as ultimately created by God and ultimately to be defeated by God. But hostile and destructive spiritual forces were currently, during "the dominion of Belial" (1QS 1:18; 2:19), effectively controlling or working not only through "the Wicked Priest" (the incumbent high priesthood in Jerusalem) but also through "the Kittim" (the conquering Romans), as well.

The Judean scribal circles' scheme of two warring camps of spiritual forces was a *mystification* of their "real" political situation.[38] They had been invaded by the Hellenistic imperial forces and then subjected by the Romans in brutal conquests. This was utterly incomprehensible according to the earlier Judean "theology" of God as the ruler of history who would eventually gather and renew the people even though they were temporarily under foreign imperial rule. The struggle between the two camps of spirits for control of human life offered a way of comprehending, even "explaining" what was happening historically. The historical visions in Dan 7–12 and certain "Enoch" texts articulate a far more elaborate and complex understanding of the divine governance of history than was evident in earlier Judean prophetic texts. They see the hostile heavenly forces in and behind the military violence and oppressive economic demands of imperial regimes. The *mystification, however, was also protective.* The sense of a standoff between the opposing heavenly forces kept dissident Judean scribal circles—with the exception of the *Sicarioi*—from mounting or joining widespread revolts that proved to be suicidal resistance to

---

38. Somewhat similar to the Algerians' obsession with terrifying spirits, discerned Fanon, as discussed in chap. 3.

Roman rule.[39] It *even* enabled *a manner of resistance*, both insofar as they were able to maintain much of the traditional Judean social-religious way of life, including at least the facade of local rule by the priestly aristocracy, and insofar as they mounted protests against the rulers appointed by the Romans. Finally, while not a direct source for popular culture, these texts may also be helpful for understanding the far less schematic and more ad hoc understanding of spirits and spirit-possession among Judean and Galilean villagers under Roman rule that can be discerned in the Gospel stories.

The way dissident Judean scribal circles adapted Judean culture under the impact of invasive foreign powers is parallel to, yet different in form from the ways that African peoples adapted their culture under the impact of Western colonial invasion, as discussed in chapter 3. Like certain African peoples discussed in chap. 3, the Judean scribes were incorporating the "spirits" of the invading power(s) into their own culture, with significant additions and adaptations. In the "Enoch" and "Daniel" texts Judean scribes shifted their understanding and symbolization of YHWH as the sole divine ruler of history to a remote imperial heavenly ruler who ruled through many officers and was not completely in control. Somewhat as African peoples incorporated into their own panoply of spirits a whole set of new spirits that corresponded to the invading Western powers (*nasarin, maregimenti, Kashawat,* Lord Cromer, Ki-Jesu, Dona Bey), so the Judean scribes added the rebel Watchers and their offspring of "giants" to the multiple heavenly forces and their earthly effects, in opposition to the other, benevolent heavenly forces involved in the divine governance of the world. In their more systematic scheme of two opposing camps of spirits that were dominating history, however, the Judean scribes went far beyond the African peoples in the intellectual systematization of the spirits/heavenly forces.

The African peoples negotiated a combination of adjustment and resistance to the impact and domination by outside colonial powers. The Judean scribal circles, while representing their God in increasingly imperial imagery, perhaps to enhance his transcendent power eventually to deliver them from domination, rejected imperial political domination as impossible to reconcile with their traditional value of independence under the exclusive rule of their God and actively resisted or withdrew.

39. Horsley, *Jesus and Spiral,* 133–37; the more recent discussion of various scribal texts and circles in *Revolt of the Scribes*; and Fanon's insights about the Algerians, discussed in chap. 3.

Protection against Hostile Spirits

Although so-called apocalyptic texts and several texts from Qumran attest a plethora of heavenly spirits in two opposed camps engaged in intense conflict, they do not mention possession by those spirits or exorcism of spirits from people who had become possessed. The discovery and scholarly examination of the Dead Sea Scrolls also made available a whole trove of fragmentary texts that were previously unknown. Some of the specialists who examined the many fragmentary scrolls, still working with the standard construction of (Jewish) magic, suggested that certain texts focused on protection from threatening "evil" spirits or "demons" and that a few others attested possession by and exorcism of hostile spirits, as discussed in chapter 2. Closer examination of this handful of fragmentary texts, however, shows that while they offer no indications of spirit possession and exorcism, they do attest ritual practices designed for protection from hostile spirits.

In pursuing the remarkable opportunity that the Dead Sea Scrolls offer for historians to investigate a particular community or movement in late second-temple Judea, it is important to have a sense of its contours and its relation to the larger society. In the initial phase of investigation into the scrolls and who produced and/or collected them, the dominant picture was of a monastic community of priests and scribes who had withdrawn from Jerusalem into the wilderness, where they maintained little or no interaction with the rest of the society. With further investigation and discussion, a more complex picture has emerged. There was indeed a surprisingly long-lasting rigorously disciplined community in the wilderness at Qumran, but it was part of a somewhat larger movement with smaller associations of participants elsewhere. The Community Rule was apparently a handbook for the community at Qumran, while the Damascus Rule attests and was perhaps produced for a larger movement.[40] The fragmentary texts to be examined briefly here were all for performance in a (larger or smaller) community, some specifically to be recited by the "master."

According to the scheme of the two Spirits in the Qumran Community Rule, people's own life depended on whether and how intensely they were influenced or determined by the Spirit of Truth or the Spirit of Darkness. Those in the community itself were living under the guidance of the Spirit of Truth. They anticipated that the God of Israel would

---

40. Collins, *Beyond Qumran.*

soon act to resolve the extreme crisis of historical life, by terminating the rule of Belial. Meanwhile, however, they evidently felt threatened by the hostile Spirit/spirits of Darkness. They responded to such threats with ritual chants and psalms.

Among the fragmentary scrolls found at Qumran were two (dated paleographically to the late first century BCE) inscribed with a series of "songs for the *maskil* to sing" to the assembled "sons of light"/"men of the covenant" (4Q510.7; 4Q511 fr. 63, 3.5).[41] The best-preserved fragment is 4Q510.

> . . . praises. Ben[edictions for the K]ing of glory. Words of thanksgiving in psalms of . . . to the God of knowledge, the Splendour of power, the God of gods, Lord of all the holy ones. [His] dominion] is over all the powerful mighty ones and by the power of his might all shall be terrified and shall scatter and be put to flight by the splendor of the dwel[ling] of his kingly glory. And I, the master (*maskil,* sage), proclaim the majesty of his beauty to frighten and ter[rify] all the spirits of the destroying angels and the spirits of the bastards, the demons [??], Lilith, the howlers and [the yelpers . . .] they who strike suddenly to lead astray the spirit of understanding and to appall their hearts and their so[uls] during the period of the domini[on] of wickedness and the times appointed for the humiliation of the sons of lig[ht] on account of (their) guilt in the times they are afflict[ed] by iniquities—not for eternal destruction [but on]ly for the period of the humiliation of (their) sin. (4Q510.4–8)

Against the sons of light is arrayed a whole army of spirits that are more or less the same as in the Book of Watchers, that is, (the spirits of) the Watchers whose rebellion against the divine governance of the world generated such destruction, (the spirits of) their ("bastard") offspring, the giants, who brought imperial conquest and oppression, and their maleficent offspring of spirits who continued to plague people after the watchers were presumably bound by the highest-ranking heavenly forces. That the threatening (heavenly and heavenly-earthly) spirits include "the howlers and [the yelpers]" illustrates how Judean culture had changed

41. Texts, analysis, and discussion in Alexander, "Wrestling against Wickedness in High Places," esp. 319–24; and Eshel, "Genres of Magical Texts in the Dead Sea Scrolls." Their discussions are skewed by imposing the concept of magic (see chap. 2). In an ironical observation, Alexander notes (323) that "the Maskil's magical defense of his Community is conspicuous for the absence of *materia magica,* of technical magical rituals and formulae and of divine names."

since the earlier "books" of the prophets. "The howlers and yelpers" in a prophecy of Isaiah were merely images of the wild animals that would occupy the houses of Babylon after the glorious imperial city would be destroyed by the Medes in divine punishment for its violent treatment of the people of Judah (Isaiah 13, esp. 13:21–22). Another psalm or prayer (in 4Q444) appeals similarly to God for protection against this army of spirits, including the "bastards," that threaten the covenantal community.

Threatening as they are, these spirits have a certain limited function in the divine economy. They are active only for the appointed time during which people are being punished for their sins by humiliation. And the principal danger is that they would "lead astray the spirit of understanding" among the sons of light. The Song(s) of the Maskil are appeals to God for protection, by means of praise of his glory and declaration of trust in his ultimate dominion. The threatening spirits are held at bay by the *maskil*'s recitation of these songs of praise that reinforce the community's trust that the King of glory is ultimately in control of history. These protective psalms of praise, products of scribal circles, do not focus directly on sickness and spirit possession or healing and exorcism. Nor are the threatened attacks by hostile spirits an alternative to punishment for sin as an explanation of people's suffering. The hostile spirits, however, have become the active agents both of punishment for sin and of potentially leading community members astray from their highly disciplined communal regimen of rigorous adherence to the covenantal laws and regulations. In the regular performance of these protective psalms of praise the community members reaffirm their trust in God and the benign powers to defend them and bolster their own defenses.

Some other short texts on fragmentary scrolls appear to be protective chants addressed directly to threatening spirits. A collection of short "apocryphal psalms" attributed to David or Solomon (11Q11), the last of which is a version of (what we know as) Psalm 91, presuppose and refer to the same dominating conflict between opposing armies of spirits that is articulated in the Community Rule and the Songs of the Maskil. The performer is instructed to boldly declare to the spirit(s) when it/ they appear(s,) "Who are you, [who was born of] man and of the seed of the ho[ly ones]!", to aggressively identify them as "the face of delusion" and "darkness not light, injustice not justice," and finally to warn (remind) them that "the chief of the army of YHWH" will bring them down to Sheol or that YHWH will send against them a "a powerful angel/ heavenly force" who will being them down to the great abyss (11Q11 col

4.5–11; cf. 3:4–9; clearly references to the myth of the Watchers). Two of the chants appear to end with the collective expression of confidence by the assembled company, "Raphael has healed them. Amen Amen Selah"; and "(Thus) forever, all the sons of Belial. Amen Amen Selah" (11Q11 col 4.2–3; 5.2).

In two and perhaps three instances (depending on reconstruction of the text, in 11Q11 cols 1.7; 3.4; 4.1), the performer is to "adjure" the spirit(s), a term frequently used in protective incantations in Aramaic (on amulets and bowls) in the later, Byzantine period. Much has been made of another fragmentary text that refers to a number of spirits and then has the speaker "adjure" a spirit in direct address (4Q560). While difficult to make out very precisely, the text appears to have the rebellious and lawless sons/spirits entering the body and causing various sicknesses: "male shudder (spirit) and female shudder (spirit)" evidently cause "iniquity and transgression, fever and chills and heart fever [which ente]rs the tooth, male crumble (spirit) and female crumble (spirit)" (4Q560 col 1,2–5).[42] This brief text of mid-first century BCE is an early example of apotropaic (protective) texts resembling the many inscribed much later on amulets and bowls to ward off just such sicknesses that were believed to be caused by maleficent spirits. Again in this text, as in the chants of 11Q11, the spirits are not an alternative to sin as an explanation of sickness, but the agents that lead people into transgression as well as cause other suffering.

The determining factors for the absence of individual spirit possession and exorcism in texts from the community—that is if we take seriously their own expressions of their community culture—are the close relationship between the community members ("the sons of Light") and the benevolent heavenly spirits (Prince of Light/Angel of Truth, etc.) and the directly interrelated collective discipline of the community (see, e.g.,

42. Alexander, "Wrestling against Wickedness, 326, claims that texts such as 4Q560, 4Q510, 4Q511, and the "incantations" in 11Q11 address individual cases of demon-possession and "exorcism in the strict sense of the term." Eshel, "Genres of Magical Texts," 401 (building on Baumgarten, "On the Nature of the Seductress in 4Q184"), still pressing an "exorcism" interpretation, acknowledges the extreme difficulties of evaluating and interpreting (including translating) such fragmentary texts. Such "exorcism" readings result from the continuing assumption of the modern scholarly construct of magic and its uncritical appeal to isolated phrases in the Magical Papyri, specifically that "adjure" was a technical term of exorcism in the practice of magic. The sicknesses such as fever and chills and "heart fever" caused by the spirits entering the body in 4Q560 appear to be spirit afflictions, rather than symptoms usually associated with spirit possession.

1QSa). Following in the path of the learned scribes (the *maskilim* and "Enoch" scribes) who produced the visions and visionary interpretation of history in Daniel 7–12 and the Book of Watchers and the Animal Vision, (at least the leaders of) the community had regular communication and interaction with "the sons of heaven"//"angels of holiness." The principal text usually cited to attest this intimate relationship is the War Rule, in which the Qumranites express confidence that the Spirits of Light will fight alongside them against Belial and the Kittim, that is, the Romans: "the congregation of the holy ones is among us, . . . the host of His spirits is with our foot-soldiers and horsemen" (1QM 12:6–9). A more general affirmation of their intimate interaction with "the angels of holiness" (CD 15:16–17) comes in the master's long hymn of praise at the end of the Community Rule:

> God has given (knowledge of the design of history) to His chosen ones
> > as an everlasting possession,
> and has caused them to inherit
> > the lot of the holy ones.
> He has joined their assembly
> > to the sons of heaven . . . (1QS 11:7–9)

The community was thus already intensively guided (one might say collectively "possessed") by the Spirit(s) of Light/Truth. Correspondingly, the community maintained rigorous personal and collective discipline, as articulated in the ordinances of the Community Rule, reinforced by the regular (annual) covenant renewal ceremony outlined at the beginning of the text. The latter, moreover, included the covenantal blessings on the sons of light and curses on the lot of Belial pronounced by the priests and Levites.

Yet another factor in why no spirit possession and exorcism are indicated in texts from Qumran, finally, is the ritual warfare that the community evidently performed regularly. Contrary to some earlier interpretations, the War Scroll (1QM) refers not to an "eschatological war" (the end of the world) but to an anticipated historical battle that "the sons of Levi, Judah, and Benjamin" who had become exiles in the wilderness would fight against the Kittim, whom they understood as the Romans (1:4–6).[43] The exiles surely knew that active revolt would be suicidal. But

43. Among others who find the "eschatological war" in the War Rule are Schiffman, *Dead Sea Scrolls*, 380; and Collins, *Apocalypticism*, 93. Collins cites passages from several other scrolls as referring to "the final conflict" at "the end of days," but offers none from 1QM itself. Collins' earlier discussion (56–58) of the Hebrew phrase

they held drills of ritual warfare, for which the War Rule must have served as a "handbook," adapting the holy war ideology and instructions in the Judean scriptures about banners and trumpets and priestly leadership. The priests are to reassure the warriors that God and "the holy ones"/"the host of the [heavenly] messengers" will fight with them "from heaven" (11:1–2, 16–17). In the anticipated battle for which they are ritually rehearsing, however, the priests and the warriors fight against the Kittim, and God fights through them (as in 16:1–2). In the trust that God and "the holy ones" would ultimately fight for them, the exiles were taking action, *ritual* action in their rigorously disciplined renewed covenantal community.

What scholarly interpreters of all of these Qumran texts tend to miss is that they all involve performance, from the Master's recitation of psalms to protective chants or "incantations" to the formal blessings and curses pronounced by the priests and Levites in the regular covenant renewal ceremony and the highly elaborate ritual of marching around in prescribed military formations and maneuvers. The scribal and priestly community at Qumran, like other scribal circles, lived in a culture dominated by two opposing camps of benign and hostile heavenly spirits. The community's ritual warfare, along with their prayers of confession, protective songs, and chants directed at the hostile spirits left little or no social-psychological "opening" through which those spirits could invade and possess someone.

Some of the ritual practices in which the Qumran community protected themselves from hostile spirits and resisted further encroachment of invasive forces bear some resemblance to two of the measures taken by certain African peoples in response to European colonial invasion. Traditional healers among the Zulus "inoculated" people afflicted by invasive spirits with indigenous soldier-spirits to help them resist further invasion. The intimate relation and communication of the Qumran covenanters with the heavenly holy ones could be seen as a massive collective inoculation of protective spirits to hold off any incursions of the hostile spirits. The ritual warfare against the Kittim rehearsed by the wilderness exiles resembles somewhat the military drills of Africans attired in uniforms resembling those of the British army. In fact, in addition to following "holy war" instructions in Israelite tradition, the priests and soldiers at Qumran were also imitating certain features of Roman army

---

(*'aharit hayyamim*) translated "end of days," however, suggests that it refers to future time less ominous than an "eschatological" ending of time.

drills. In both cases opposition to hostile invasive forces were channeled into ritual resistance. But the covenanters at Qumran did eventually do battle with the Romans, toward the end of the great revolt of 66–70, and the cults mainly in West Africa did eventually become transformed into anti-colonial movements.

Spirit Possession among the People

The Gospel stories are evidently our only direct sources for popular culture in ancient Galilee, Judea, and nearby areas, as noted above. Spirit possession and Jesus' exorcisms portrayed in the Gospels will be discussed in chaps. 7–10. In anticipation of that discussion, the conflict between camps of heavenly spirits in Judean scribal culture strongly influenced by ancient Near Eastern scribal culture but still rooted in Israelite tradition may form a helpful backdrop of comparisons and contrast for the stories in the Gospels of spirits and conflict of spirits in popular Israelite culture.

Judging from particular episodes of possession and exorcism as well as summary passages, possession by "unclean spirits" or *daimonia* was a frequent phenomenon among villagers. As noted before, it is misleading to translate *daimonia* simply as "demons" since the latter term has connotations of the demonic, influenced by the centuries of "demonization" of (officially disapproved) other people's and ordinary people's spirits, gods, or other forces, whether maleficent, benevolent, or ambiguous with relation to people. It is surely significant that the Gospel sources do not label the spirits as "evil." That some spirits were thought of as "unclean" suggests that there were others. But the "unclean spirits" or *daimonia* were invasive, took possession of people so that they were no longer "themselves" in social interaction, and even (were thought to have) caused convulsions and severely violent behavior injurious to themselves and others.

The spirits that populate the Gospel narratives and summary passages do appear different from those represented in "apocalyptic" texts and texts from Qumran. They invade people (in cross-cultural studies called "hosts") and control their behavior. The possessed people can be extremely violent, particularly to themselves, and can be uncontrollable, except by extreme measures of restraint, such as being chained in a cemetery. When Jesus overpowers them and "casts them out" they severely wrench the person they have been possessing. But they are not rebel heavenly forces (the watchers) or the semi-divine offspring of heavenly forces. Nor do the Gospel exorcism stories and summary passages share anything resembling the grand scheme of two opposing armies of heavenly spirits, the Spirit and forces of Truth/Light versus the Spirit and forces of Darkness/Belial known from Qumran texts. That scheme is a systematized product of scribal culture that, in turn, built on many generations of reflective/speculative wisdom.

The closest that any of the episodes in the Gospels comes to opposing forces would be in the Beelzebul controversy, of which there are different but similar versions in Mark 3:22–26 and the "Q" speech parallel in Matt 12:22–30 and Luke 11:14–23. As will be discussed in chapters 7 and 8, in both Mark's version and the "Q" version in Matthew, however, it is the scribes or Pharisees who charge Jesus with casting out *daimonia* by Beelzebul, the leader of *daimonia*. Coming from scribal advisers of the Jerusalem temple-state, the name Beelzebul sounds like it is rooted in an earlier official/scribal demonization of one of the indigenous divine "lords" (*ba'al*) of the Canaanites or the country people. Like the later sixteenth- and seventeenth-century Protestant and Catholic demonologists who labeled popular healers and midwives as "witches," the scribes/Pharisees were "demonizing" Jesus as working in the power of (one of) the maleficent force(s). Jesus' response in both versions shows the absurdity of the charge, and shows that he (and/or his followers) understood the elite/official scheme of opposing camps of spirits. As will be discussed in chaps. 7 and 8, his response indicates that he and/or his followers did not share the Judean scribal understanding in which all those unclean spirits and *daimonia* were led or coordinated by a "ruler" (*archon*). Judging from the Gospel exorcism stories and summary passages, the maleficent activities of spirits were uncoordinated and much more ad hoc, striking one person here and another there.

In the exorcism story in Mark 5:1–20, the name (identity) of the unclean spirit that was causing the severely violent behavior of the demoniac turned out to be "Legion," or Roman troops. The Matthean story, which generally shortens the episodes, does not include this name. It nevertheless seems likely that, as among African peoples, their response to their invasion by powerful outside political-economic forces (conquest by the Roman legions and continuing domination by Roman imperial rule) included the appropriation of those invasive forces into their culture in the form of hostile spirits. From the only texts that offer any indirect indication, it is clear that even scribal circles that were far less directly impacted than villagers had understood and articulated the direct relationship between the hostile heavenly spirits and the imperial violence and oppression, incorporating the hostile spirits into their (Judean), indeed had done so for the previous two centuries.

In sum, in the Galilean and other villages where Jesus interacted with people, as in nearby areas into which Jesus movement spread, as among virtually any traditional agrarian people, sickness was handled in households and broader support networks in village communities. Among Galileans, Samaritans, and Judeans, sickness was understood in terms of the ancestral Mosaic covenantal culture. God (YHWH), who had liberated their ancestors from hard bondage under the Egyptians (and subsequent rulers), demanded that the people conduct their community life according to key commandments and customs that would ensure a basic livelihood for families and village communities. In the sanctions motivating observance of the commandments, God would provide blessings of livelihood and welfare (crops, family, health) if people observed the covenantal demands, but curses of dearth if they did not. As the exclusive ruler of the people, God was the ultimate agent or cause of sickness, which might well be explained as due to disobedience, and of healing, which would more likely happen in response to penance and, in Judea closer to the temple, in response to a sacrifice. In its cultural understanding as well as in its management, sickness was thus embedded in family and community that had multigenerational extension.

Interestingly in comparison with other agrarian societies, there is little or no evidence of folk-healers. On the other hand, local knowledge of the healing qualities of certain roots and herbs can surely just be assumed; such ancestral village lore would have been the source of the scribal knowledge. Yet dissident scribal circles came to see the knowledge of herbal and other healing cultivated by professional scribes in imperial regimes that had become oppressive to the Judean people as derived from heavenly powers hostile to God and the people. The rulers in Jerusalem were served by professional physicians and their medicines. But the scribe Ben Sira is careful to attribute healing ultimately to God the creator and to recommend appropriate penance and sacrifices in the temple.

There are some indications, in what might be termed a certain culture of being a conquered people, that some of the sickness that people were "suffering" or "plagued with" were the effects of imperial conquest.

This took the form of longing for a renewal of the people in which their typical injuries and malaise would be overcome (the blind see, the lame walk, the prisoner released, etc.). Longing and hope for deliverance from domination and renewal of the people was clearly resilient among the people. At both the popular and elite level, hope was clearly informed by the strong memory of the prophet Elijah, whose renewal of the people had included healings.

The obsession with hostile heavenly spirits that suddenly appears in second-century scribal texts, finally, and the upsurge of spirit possession among the people, is fairly clearly a response to the Hellenistic and Roman empires that violently conquered and then oppressed the people in a dramatic intensification of imperial rule.

Part III

Understanding and Using the Gospel
Stories Appropriately as Sources

6

The Sources

Gospel Stories in Performance

THE PRECEDING STEPS HAVE prepared the way conceptually, and established the historical context, for moving beyond the limitations of standard historical Jesus studies toward a fuller understanding of the healings and exorcisms as the principal actions in Jesus' mission. The next major step is to discern the character of the Gospel sources for the historical Jesus (-in-interaction) and how they can be used critically.

Study of the historical Jesus, a branch of New Testament studies, which is a division of Christian theology, developed an idiosyncratic understanding and use of its primary sources and a conceptual apparatus very different from those of ordinary historical inquiry. In the recent surge of "Jesus-books" interpreters simply refined the standard approach of the previous century, focusing on text-fragments, individual sayings and/or "miracle stories," as the sources for the historical Jesus. They assumed that the Gospels were mere collections of these fragments that, after certain criteria were applied, were the "data" for their constructions. They simply assumed that these fragments had been circulating independently, though there is no evidence for this in the Gospels themselves.[1]

---

1. The assumption that individual sayings and stories were originally independent appears to have been determined by the typographic fixity of the print-formatting of the Gospels and other texts in separate verses (e.g., in the KJV and the Lutherbibel) or paragraphs (e.g., NRSV; Jerusalem Bible). See esp. the incisive pioneering analysis by Werner Kelber in "Jesus and Tradition" and other essays updated in the revised versions in *Imprints, Voiceprints*.

Having dispensed with the Gospels as sustained narratives with speeches as possible indications of the meaning context of the sayings and stories they had isolated, Jesus scholars then supplied meaning contexts themselves, often from the (theological) constructs of New Testament studies, such as "Judaism" or "magic." They isolated the story of the woman who had been hemorrhaging for twelve years, for example, from the series of Jesus' "acts of power" in the Markan story. Then they heroized Jesus as having overcome the "ritual impurity" governed by the purity code of "Judaism," and found the flow of power from Jesus to the woman either as a troublesome motif of "magic" or a prime indication that Jesus was a "magician."[2]

Study of the historical Jesus, however, has remained seemingly unaware of the ways in which new and highly significant developments in other areas of New Testament studies during the last forty years were challenging its basic assumptions and procedures. Well before the revival of interest in the historical Jesus, scholars studying the Gospels had come to recognize that they were not mere collections of sayings and miracle stories, but sustained narratives interspersed with speeches, whole stories about Jesus and his mission. The cumulative effects of several new lines of research into various aspects of ancient media of communications, moreover, are indicating that the Gospel stories would have been orally performed in communities of Jesus-loyalists.

Taking the Gospels Whole
as the Sources for the Historical Jesus

One of the most basic responsibilities of historians is to assess critically the character of their sources. Literary and rhetorical analysis of sources, including of their historical social location and political agenda, is necessary to discern how they may be used for investigation of historical events, actors, and circumstances. Historians would not separate individual statements or short anecdotes from a source and then categorize them by key words or apparent subject matter.[3] Nor would they imagine

2. Meier, *Mentor, Message, and Miracles*, 708–10; Funk et al., *Acts of Jesus*, 80–81.

3. In a sharp critique of narrow focus on individual sayings, their categorization, and assessment for authenticity, Werner Kelber asks rhetorically, "is there a single modern historian who would base her or his primary evidence for the writing of the life of a historical figure on an extremely selective group of sayings attributed to that personage?" *Imprints, Voiceprints*, 113–14.

that particular anecdotes in isolation from literary and social-historical context could provide reliable attestation of actual historical incidents. If their purpose is critical understanding of a historically significant figure in historical context, however, Jesus-scholars could appropriately learn from standard methods of historical investigation, including critical assessment of sources. The problem for investigation and interpretation of Jesus-in-interaction is that we do not have the corresponding complete speeches and contemporary reports (even though we have gained a far more comprehensive and precise picture of the historical context, as sketched in chap. 4). The question is how to assess the character of the sources we do have, that is whole Gospel stories with speeches, and how they might be used as sources for Jesus-in-interaction in historical context.

Since the 1970s increasing numbers of New Testament scholars have been (re-) discovering and analyzing the "literary" integrity of the Gospels as whole stories about Jesus' mission in interactive speech and action. Most fundamental was the recognition that the Gospels are sustained complex narratives comprised of many episodes that are components of developing stories and intelligible only in the context of whole stories.[4] Far from being mere collections or containers of sayings and brief anecdotes the Gospels are stories with overall plots, in which earlier episodes and speeches and events both set up and lead to subsequent episodes and speeches and events.

The rapidly developing and diversifying literary criticism focused on the Gospels recognized that they are organized narratives with discernible "structures" or sequences of narrative ebb and flow. As noted in chapter 1, the Gospel of Mark can be discerned to proceed in a sequence of (five) narrative steps, with Jesus' speech in parables following the first and his speech about the future preceding the narrative of his arrest and crucifixion.[5] Most obvious is the organization of the Gospel of Matthew in a sequence of five narrative sections each followed by a major speech of Jesus, all preceded by a prologue of genealogy and birth-infancy narrative and climaxing in Jesus' confrontation with the rulers and crucifixion and resurrection in Jerusalem.

---

4. Influential early treatments were Kelber, *Mark's Story of Jesus*; Rhoads and Michie, *Mark as Story*; Kingsbury, *Matthew as Story*. Critical review of literary critical readings of whole Gospel stories in Moore, *Literary Criticism and the Gospels*.

5. See further Horsley, *Hearing the Whole Story*, 11–17.

In the excitement of their discovery of the Gospels as narratives many interpreters borrowed heavily from the criticism of modern narrative fiction that had become prominent in other academic circles. Particularly influential was French structuralism, in which literary texts were thought to have become independent, virtually self-contained. Once a text left the hand of its author, it took on a life of its own. Meaning and the key to finding it lay in the text itself. Literary interpreters claimed that the text should be interpreted from "the world of the text" that it articulated. "Narrative critics" read the Gospels in somewhat the same way that literary critics read modern novels or short stories, looking for implied authors, narrators, and implied readers, and expecting suspenseful plots and character development.[6] Not surprisingly, interpreters who viewed the Gospels as texts that had taken on a life of their own—including as scriptures in various branches of Christianity and focal texts in their own graduate training—found in "the world of the text" much that derived from Christian piety, theology, and the field of New Testament studies. "Miracle stories," for example, were taken as manifestations of the divine. Among the "characters" in the Gospels narrative critics tended to focus on the disciples, whom they "characterized" as "fallible followers," and found that the Gospel stories (particularly Mark) were mainly about discipleship.

Other literary interpreters of the Gospels as narratives, partly in reaction to treating the texts as autonomous objects, latched onto reader-response criticism, focused on "what does the text mean to me/us." This reading lent itself even more to the individualism that had become dominant in modern Western culture. Reader-response critics also tended to find that the Gospel stories focus on the disciples, whom they took as paradigms of discipleship that is difficult to sustain midst the temptations of modern life.[7]

These methods borrowed from modern literary criticism may well be appropriate for the Gospel narratives once they have taken on a life of their own as scriptures of Christian piety and as prime texts in theological

6. See, for example, the summary statement and exemplary practice on Mark 4–8 in Malbon, "Narrative Criticism." Insofar as structuralist interpretation sought cultural polarities, narrative critics found it, for example, in the opposition of the "Jewish" vs. the "Gentile" sides of the Sea of Galilee that Jesus repeatedly crossed in the Gospel narratives. See Malbon, "Narrative Criticism."

7. Fowler, "Reader-Response Criticism."

education.[8] The Gospels, however, originated as ancient stories in particular historical contexts. And like other ancient stories the Gospels are different from modern narrative fiction in fundamental respects. Their plots are not linear; they rather cycle or spiral back and forth in repetition of similar episodes and the narratives unfold with a complex array of foreshadowings and echoes.[9] The Gospel stories are not full of suspense, but give clear clues or explicit indications of what will happen later in the narrative. The characters in the Gospels are types, often collectives, and even stereotypes; they play important roles but do not undergo "character development." The Gospels as ancient stories are thus not comparable to modern narrative fiction.

The major and decisive way in which the Gospel stories are fundamentally unlike modern prose fiction, however, is that they purport to be historical stories, to narrate historical events.[10] They are, ostensibly at least, stories of events that took place in the recent past, first in villages of Galilee such as Capernaum that were under the political jurisdiction of Herod Antipas and then in the Jerusalem temple-state in confrontation with the high priestly rulers appointed by the Roman governor, Pontius Pilate, who ordered Jesus crucified by his soldiers as an insurrectionary leader. The Gospels of Matthew and Luke locate the story more explicitly in the wider Roman imperial context of the repressive Roman client king Herod, as well as his son Antipas in Galilee and the high priestly rulers in Jerusalem, and of the imperial rule of Caesar in which subject peoples were laid under tribute.

Moreover, not only are the Gospels sustained narratives and speeches about ostensibly historical events, but they fit into the historical context as known from other sources (as summarized in chap. 4 above). There is a chronological and geopolitical fit between the figures and events of the Gospel stories and those known, for example, from the histories of Josephus. The birth of Jesus coincides with the end of the reign of the tyrannical Herod. His mission begins in the villages of Galilee under the rule of Antipas (thus no longer under the jurisdiction of Jerusalem) and

8. Incisive summary and criticism, from viewpoint of deconstruction and postmodernism, in Moore, *Literary Criticism*.

9. Dewey was a pioneer in opening up these aspects of the Gospel of Mark, esp. in Dewey, "Mark as Interwoven Tapestry."

10. Of the growing body of literature, as steps into ever fuller consideration of historical forms and context, see Kelber, *Mark's Story of Jesus*; Myers, *Binding the Strong Man*; Wills, *Historical Gospel*; and Horsley, *Whole Story*.

comes to its climax in Jerusalem, where the high priest at the head of the temple-state was Caiaphas, who collaborated closely with the Roman governor Pontius Pilate.

Even more impressive and more to the point of the Gospels as historical stories, however, the dominant conflict in the Gospels stories is the same as the dominant political-economic-religious conflict portrayed in Josephus' histories and other sources. As discussed in chapter 4, history in Roman Palestine centered around the fundamental division between the people living in hundreds of villages and the Romans and their client rulers who repeatedly conquered them and demanded tribute, taxes, and tithes, leaving village communities disintegrating and traumatized. The resilient people, however, responded with movements of resistance and renewal led by (popularly acclaimed) kings or prophets, patterned after Israelite memories of popular kings like the young David and prophets like Moses and his successors. The always simmering tensions between the people and their rulers often erupted into the open at the Passover festival, the celebration of the people's origins in the exodus liberation. These protests and movements and their leaders, however, were suppressed by the Roman military and the Roman governors often crucified the leaders in public display as a way to further terrorize the people into submission.[11]

As ancient historical stories that fit remarkably well into the general historical situation that they portray, the Gospel stories must be read (critically) in historical context.[12] The Gospels in effect portray Jesus as yet another of the leaders of popular movements of renewal and resistance against the Romans and their client rulers in Palestine in mid-first century. With their distinctive twists and emphases, the Markan, Matthean, and Lukan stories present Jesus and his disciples healing, exorcising, and teaching in the villages of Galilee and beyond. The people, who are in distress, hunger, debt, even possessed by invasive spirits, respond eagerly and generate an expanding movement of renewal, led by Jesus in the role of a prophet like Moses and Elijah. From the outset, however, his activities are threatening to the Roman client rulers, since he is exercising power/

---

11. Discussed in chap. 4; fuller discussion in Horsley, with J. S. Hanson, *Bandits, Prophets, Messiahs*; and Horsley, *Jesus and the Spiral of Violence*, chaps. 3–4.

12. I attempted a critical reading of the Gospel of Mark in historical context, with analysis of its dominant conflict and several "sub-plots" in Horsley, *Hearing the Whole Story*. Continuing historical research and analysis and critical reading of the Gospel stories requires further refinement and adjustment of the presentation there.

authority among the people, in contrast to their own lack of authority among the people. Scribes and Pharisees "come down from Jerusalem" to plot his destruction, and Herod Antipas, ensconced in his royal palace, orders the prophet John the Baptist beheaded. Jesus announces that his destiny as a prophet will be martyrdom at the hands of the rulers in Jerusalem. Accordingly he marches into Jerusalem at the Passover festival for a direct confrontation with the high priestly heads of the temple-state. They apprehend him surreptitiously and hand him over to Pontius Pilate the governor, who orders him crucified as an insurrectionary leader.

Just as the Gospels are now being recognized as sustained stories, so the teachings of Jesus parallel in Matthew and Luke are being recognized as a series of short speeches, at least by some American scholars (discussed briefly in chap. 1; more fully in chap. 8).[13] These speeches are poetic in form, in sequences of parallel lines with frequent repetition of sounds, verbal endings, words, and whole lines, and some of the speeches take traditional Israelite prophetic forms (such as woes and a lament).[14] The main theme that holds the speeches together is "the kingdom of God" that appears prominently in most of them. It was important in chapter 1 to note that even though what is called "Q" consisted of speeches, not narrative episodes, it included references to and discussion of Jesus' healings and exorcisms. Here it is important to recognize that this series of speeches parallel in wording and sequence in Matthew and Luke appears to be a source (= *Quelle*) those Gospels used, a text (a series of Jesus-speeches) with its own distinctive form and features. Thus, insofar as they existed at some point prior to Matthew and Luke and independent of Mark, this series of speeches is evidently another early source for memory of Jesus-in-interaction and the movement(s) he generated. Only this (hypothetical) source is a series of Jesus-speeches on issues of concern to a Jesus-movement instead of a sustained narrative in a sequence of episodes.

The sources for Jesus-in-interaction-in-historical context are thus not isolated individual sayings and miracle stories, but rather the Gospels

---

13. Kloppenborg, *The Formation of Q*, took the first step, seeing Q as a composed set of "clusters." Analyzed as speeches/discourses in Horsley, "Q and Jesus." See now also Kirk, *The Composition of the Sayings Source*; Robinson, "History of Q Research," lxii–lxvi; and, for fuller statement, Horsley with Draper, *Whoever Hears You Hears Me*, 61–93.

14. Extensive analysis and presentation in Horsley with Draper, *Whoever Hears You Hears Me*, chaps. 7–14.

as whole stories, of which speeches and series of anecdotes are integral. It is with criticism of the Gospels as sustained narratives and coherent speeches that an approach to the historical Jesus in historical context can begin.[15] It is then essential to investigate the character of the Gospels as sources, working from the implications of the lines of new research that are changing how the Gospels can be understood. By bringing together some of these new lines of research and theory of performance we may be able to develop an approach to the historical Jesus in interaction more appropriate to what we are learning about the Gospel sources in the communications-context of the ancient world.

Oral Communication and the Cultivation of Texts

Recognition that the sources for investigation of the historical Jesus are the Gospels as sustained stories, however, is now being complicated as well as reinforced by other recent lines of research that are challenging standard assumptions and preparing the way for more appropriate investigation into the Gospel sources in particular and into ancient texts and history more generally.[16]

Both the precise analysis of text fragments isolated from their contexts in the Gospels and the recent recognition that the Gospels were sustained narratives, like biblical studies in general, were based on the assumptions of modern print-culture. It has simply been assumed that ancient texts that we have in writing were "written" by "authors" and then were widely "circulated" for "reading" by literate people. Biblical scholars, embedded in print-culture in which multiple copies of texts emerged from printing presses in stable standard format, also assumed that once

15. Ideally we would all have access to a good translation of the Gospels without the intrusive chapter-and-verse numbers (and especially without the often misleading editorial headings for particular anecdotes). I encourage any reader who has not done so before to read straight through one or more of the Gospels (Mark is the shortest and most lively). In order to encourage consideration of whole stories, I may often, on purpose, not give chapter-and-verse references in Mark, Matthew, and Luke. On the other hand, the only way to identify the (hypothetical) speeches in Q is by where they are used by Luke and Matthew, which will require indication of chapter-and-verse.

16. The following discussion draws heavily on my continuing attempts to bring together the implications of the several largely separate but related lines of new research as they bear on understanding of the Gospel stories and speeches, including their use as sources for the historical Jesus in historical context, most recently in "Can Study of the Historical Jesus Escape Its Typographical Captivity?"

the Gospels were "written" they provided a stable form and wording of the sayings and stories they included. Scholars of the historical Jesus or of particular Gospels trusted that their colleagues who specialized in tex criticism had "established" the "original" or at least the "earliest" (written) text from the variants in ancient manuscripts. The whole procedural apparatus of historical Jesus scholarship was thus built up on the basis of print-cultural assumptions.

Several related lines of research are now challenging the projections of modern print-cultural assumptions onto ancient social and cultural life. Most fundamental is the steadily increasing recognition that *communication in the ancient world*—indeed in all pre-modern pre-printing press societies—*was predominantly, pervasively oral*. Separate but closely related studies are showing that texts, whether from the elite or from ordinary people, were *cultivated in oral performance before groups of people*.

The Dominance of Oral Communication in the Ancient World

In the Roman empire generally literacy was limited to a tiny minority of the population located mainly in the cities (around 10%).[17] The largely localized ancient economy did not require writing. Only a few urban artisans used brief written forms. Roman aristocrats often had written contracts drawn up for major economic transactions. But the vast majority of people, urban artisans and rural peasants, conducted transactions of all kinds orally, usually face to face. Local loans, for example, were agreed upon orally, perhaps confirmed by witnesses, the transfer of symbolic objects, and/or personal oaths. Such interactions were regulated by time-honored customs and rituals. Ordinary people understood that personal witnesses and testimony were far more trustworthy than written documents that could be manipulated by the literate for their for their own advantage. Communication and culture among the at least partially literate elite in the ancient world were also largely oral. Various forms of poetry were orally performed (sung!) at festivals and in great households. Plays were performed in theaters. While they may have used writing in preparation of their speeches, orators displayed their rhetorical prowess

17. The standard work is Harris, *Ancient Literacy*, on which the following sketch depends. Harris' analysis and conclusions are confirmed by other scholars' research and analysis, such as Mary Beard et al., *Literacy in the Roman World*; and Bowman and Woolf, eds., *Literacy and Power in the Ancient World*.

orally at city festivals and before emperors. The ceremonial conduct of "political" affairs proceeded in oral communication.

More important than the rate of literacy were the uses and functions of writing in a world where communication was predominantly oral. Writing was used mainly by the political and cultural elite, mostly as an instrument of power. Administration of the Roman Empire required considerable use of writing, such as the imperial correspondence carried out by slaves in the "family of Caesar." The "census" of how much tribute could be taken from the people of a given territory (Luke 2:1) was kept in writing. The operations of the Roman military also required extensive, if less public, writing. Writing in various forms was thus used mainly to maintain or expand military, economic and/or social power. The vast majority of the people had no use for writing, indeed were often suspicious of writing as an instrument of their landlords or rulers.

The rate of literacy in Roman Palestine was much lower than in the Roman Empire generally, as low as three percent, as is now well-documented.[18] Judean and Galilean villagers and urban artisans communicated orally, with no need for writing. As in other areas of the Roman Empire, Palestinian villagers conducted transactions concerning land, loans, and marriage by oral agreement, with oaths and witnesses, judging from rabbinic references. People placed their trust in the personal presence of living witnesses. In contrast to the elite, artisans and peasants were sometimes hostile to written documents, as in records of loans drawn up by wealthy creditors. One of the first actions in the popular insurrection in Jerusalem in 66 CE, for example, was "to destroy the money-lenders' bonds and prevent the recovery of debts" (Josephus, *War* 2.426–427).

Literacy in Roman Palestine (in Hebrew, Aramaic, or Greek) was limited mainly to scribal circles in Jerusalem, the administrations of Rome's client rulers, and later the nascent rabbinic circles. In addition to written records of the loans they had made to the poor the wealthy kept records of their dealings with each other regarding land and other material concerns, as in the Babatha letters found in the Judean wilderness.[19] Texts inscribed on scrolls, some of which had become authoritative at least for the scribal elite were kept in scribal circles such as the Qumran community and perhaps also laid up in the temple. As in other societies

18. The extensive research in Hezser, *Jewish Literacy*, confirms and much more fully documents what several of us sketched earlier.

19. Documentation in Hezser, *Jewish Literacy*. See further the discussion and more recent documentation in Kirk, "Who Are the Q Scribes?," 78–84, 92–95.

where writing was rare, inscribed texts possessed special authority, with a numinous aura. For example, throughout the Empire the Romans built massive monuments inscribed with names, slogans, and accounts of the great acts of the emperor in bringing "Salvation and Security" to the subject cities and peoples (the *Res Gestae* of Augustus). Such monumental writing supposedly impressed subject peoples even though they could not read the inscriptions. Some of the written texts kept in scribal circles (and in the temple?) may similarly have been monumental writing that held (numinous) authority, and not intended as literature to be read or documents to be consulted.[20]

It is thus clear from the well-documented studies of literacy and the uses of writing in Roman Palestine that oral communication was dominant and that the use of writing was limited to the cultural elite, often as instruments of power. Insofar as texts that were (also) written were limited to and cultivated by the cultural and presumably the political-economic elite, it is clear that there was a significant difference between elite culture and the culture of ordinary people among whom communication was almost exclusively oral. From recent studies of scribal culture in Jerusalem (and earlier in the imperial courts of Mesopotamia and Egypt), however, it is evident that texts that were written on scrolls and their scribal cultivators were also embedded in a pervasive culture of oral communication. Exploration of these two key issues, how (written) texts were embedded in oral communication, and the differences between elite/scribal culture and popular culture, can lead to more appropriate understanding of the Gospels as sources for the historical Jesus(-in-interaction).

Since non-literate ordinary people almost never left written remains, we have virtually nothing from antiquity as more direct evidence for how popular texts were composed and cultivated—the Gospel stories being almost unique in antiquity as extant texts that were produced by ordinary people. We must hope that investigation of Judean scribal culture and its cultivation of texts can shed some light on how popular texts were embedded and cultivated not just in oral communication but in a wider and

20. For example, in Nehemiah 8 the (Judean-Persian) scribe Ezra, standing on a raised platform flanked by other high ranking figures, "opened the writing [large scroll?] in the sight of all the people," who then acclaimed "'Amen, Amen,' lifting up their hands," and "bowed their heads and worshipped Yahweh with their faces to the ground." This "writing of the teaching of Moses" was clearly a sacred object of great power. Inscribed on the scroll in Hebrew, it had to be "interpreted" (translated?) for the Aramaic-speaking Judeans. See further Niditch, *Oral World*; Horsley, *Scribes, Visionaries*, 98–99; and van der Toorn, *Image and the Book*, 229–56.

deeper (popular) culture, while also highlighting the differences between elite and popular traditions.

Before summarizing recent investigations of Judean scribal culture and practice, however, it is necessary to broaden our understanding of what a *text* was/is, to counter our anachronistic print-cultural assumptions. Academic discourse is so deeply embedded in the assumptions of print-culture that the term 'text' is assumed to refer to a written text. But even in a culture heavily dependent on writing, now in electronic media as well as print media, people still know and regularly recite texts whose life and function are (mainly) oral, especially in songs, hymns, prayers, and in the stories, some traditional and some personal, that we tell and retell to our children and friends.[21] Since it is difficult to think of a term adequate to designate oral texts, it seems best to attempt deliberately to broaden our usage of the term *text* to include oral and/or written. After all, the Latin term *texere,* from which the English term "text" is derived, meant "to weave," which could become a metaphor for "weaving" a tale or song or epic. At points, for clarity or emphasis, a given text can be designated as oral, or written, or oral and also written, as (we can now discern) was frequently the case in Judean scribal culture.

Oral-Memorial and Oral-Written Cultivation of Texts in Judean Scribal Circles

Related but still largely separate lines of recent research are illuminating the texts and practices of Judean scribal circles roughly contemporary with the origin of the Gospels.

The discovery of the Dead Sea Scrolls in 1947 added immeasurably to the number and variety of Judean written texts known to us. Analysis of the variety and character of these texts inscribed on scrolls are also leading to challenges to some of the most basic assumptions and concepts of biblical studies. The field had long since become entrenched in a conceptual scheme that assumed the existence of the synthetic religion "(early) Judaism," the essentials of which were articulated in the supposedly widely read Torah (Pentateuch) or "the Law and the Prophets." Interestingly, prior to the discovery of the Scrolls, the earliest manuscripts

---

21. From his close critical study of the Dead Sea Scrolls, Miller, *Dead Sea Media,* 47, reinforces the point here that it is important to break the (print-cultural) bond between text and writing.

of any of these texts in Hebrew dated from the (European) middle ages. Among the Scrolls were multiple manuscripts of most books that were later included in the Hebrew Bible, manuscripts over a thousand years older than those previously known. Based on decades of meticulous analysis of these manuscripts, leading text-critic Eugene Ulrich reached two interrelated conclusions that undermined previously standard assumptions.[22] In late second-temple times, at least in the Qumran community, there were different versions of most books later included in the Hebrew Bible. Not only that but the different versions were still undergoing development, in the same way that they had been developing in previous centuries.

That several copies of most texts were found in the cache at Qumran suggests that the five books of the Torah (Pentateuch) and books of prophets such as Isaiah were revered and authoritative, at least in scribal circles (whether those still serving the temple-state or the dissident priestly-scribal circle that had withdrawn to Qumran).[23] But evidently there was no standardized text of each "book." And of course the set of "books" that eventually comprised the Hebrew Bible was not defined until centuries later. So ironically there was no (Hebrew) Bible yet in what is often called the "biblical" world.

In a closely related but separate line of investigation, recent studies of scribal practice in the Judean temple-state have recognized the extent to which even scribal culture was still embedded in the dominant oral communication.[24] In their rigorous training for service in the Judean temple-state scribes indeed learned to read and write. But they learned texts by repeated oral recitation so that the texts became "written on the tablet of their heart" (Prov 3:3). This was not rote memorization. It was rather the scribes internalizing texts by repeated oral recitation so that

22. Ulrich, *The Dead Sea Scrolls and the Origins of the Bible*. In the last two decades other text critics focused on manuscripts from the DSS adjusted their views toward Ulrich's generalizations; see esp. Emanuel Tov, *Scribal Practices and Approaches*. For a critical summary of the puzzlement and debate about "variants" and original texts among Scroll scholars, see now Miller, "Introduction," in *Dead Sea Media*.

23. "Authoritative" seems the most appropriate term to use for these texts, rather than "scriptures/scriptural," since the latter has connotations of a later canonically-defined set of books that had become sacred and possessed more exclusive authority for religious institutions and communities.

24. The following discussion is dependent on Carr, *Writing on the Tablet of the Heart*; Jaffee, *Torah in the Mouth* ; and Horsley, *Scribes, Visionaries*, which is partly dependent on Carr and recent studies of ancient Near Eastern scribal practice.

they could recite them as called for in their service of the royal regime or temple-state, with appropriate adaptation to the circumstances. Thus texts of all kinds—whether collections of laws and ordinances, collections of the oracles of the prophets, or (sections of) the Deuteronomic history (and the archaic legends and royal annals used in its composition)—were held in the memory of well-trained scribes.[25] And scribes continued to learn texts that had already reached distinctive form (with well-defined contours and contents) through oral recitation.

Lest we imagine that the only issue is recognition that scribes learned texts by repeated oral recitation, however, it is important to note that something far deeper and more significant was happening. As recent critical investigation of scribal training and practice has emphasized, the purpose of this scribal training was character formation, that is, the formation of a certain conservative character in the scribes whose role was service of the temple-state.[26] The instructional wisdom and hymnic celebration of the temple and high priesthood articulated by the Jerusalem scribe Jesus ben Sira in the collection by his grandson provides a sense of this conservative character and commitment to the temple-state in the special culture into which their training socialized the scribes.[27] This conservative character-formation and deep socialization into Judean scribal culture helps explain the strong reaction of scribal circles when their high priestly patrons compromised or abandoned the traditional Judean (Israelite) covenantal culture of which they viewed themselves as the official cultivators and guardians. It also helps explain their role as representatives of the temple-state in Gospel stories and prophecies.

The role of the Pharisees in the Judean temple-state provides another illustration of the depth and the function of this Judean elite culture. Josephus explains that while the Sadducees viewed only the laws of Moses inscribed on scrolls as authoritative, the Pharisees also cultivated "traditions of the ancestors," rulings that they had promulgated and that might be approved or disapproved by the reigning high priest as part of the laws of the temple-state (*Ant.* 13.288, 296–297, 408–410). Josephus states repeatedly that the Pharisees had the most accurate knowledge of

25. Thus when it came time to inscribe a certain text on a new scroll, the scribes were not dependent only on a previously inscribed scroll but also on the text already "written" in their memory. This could help explain why already defined texts written on scrolls continued to be developed in different versions.

26. A principal point in Carr, *Written on the Tablet of the Heart.*

27. Horsley, *Scribes, Visionaries*, chaps. 3–5.

the laws generally (e.g., *Life* 191; *War* 1.110; note that he does not say "interpretation") and claims that affairs in the Jerusalem temple were conducted according to their rulings (*Ant.* 18.15). Like the Pharisees in the late second-temple period, the rabbinic circles in late antiquity not only continued to cultivate texts of torah and the rulings of their revered teachers by oral recitation.[28] This repeated oral recitation served the formation of a certain character socialized into the rabbinic subculture that gained increasing prestige in the centuries following the Roman destruction of the Judean temple-state.

A key passage in the Community Rule found among the Dead Sea Scrolls further illustrates how oral recitation of an authoritative text could function alongside other orally performed (and probably not also written) legal material and hymns in a tight-knit scribal-priestly community of renewal and resistance. Insofar as modern scholars have projected their own practices of study and interpretation of scripture into standard translations, the latter must be adapted to the historical realities of scribal oral-written communication. The Community Rule prescribes that at the regular evening gatherings of the community,

> the many shall watch in community for a third of every night of the year, to recite the writing [*lqrw' bspr*] and to search the justice-ruling [*ldwrs mšpt*] and to offer communal blessings [*lbrk byḥd*]. (1QS 6.6–8; Vermes trans. adapted)

All three of these activities were clearly oral performances. The "writing" is usually assumed to have been a "book" of "the Torah." But since authoritative texts had become "inscribed on the tablet of their hearts," the recitation would have been from memory even if a scroll of torah were partially unrolled in front of the reciter(s). The function of this oral performance of torah in the community at Qumran, like the learning by recitation of texts by scribes-in-training, was not external study and interpretation, but the internalization of spiritual-moral discipline, in this case communal as well as individual. The nightly communal "watch" of collectively hearing torah, group regulations, and common blessings was effecting community solidarity. And of course the recitation also reinforced the common oral-memorial knowledge of many texts

---

28. Jaffee, *Torah in the Mouth*. It is a telling indication of the dominance of oral recitation that they evidently did not commit the tractates of the Mishnah and Tosefta to writing for several generations and that the further elaboration of rabbinic rulings that were eventually codified in the Talmuds developed in oral debates for many more generations after that.

and intensified the personal and collective socialization into the deeper scribal-priestly culture in which those texts were embedded.[29]

Popular Oral Cultivation of Israelite Popular Tradition

If even the scribes, who were literate, cultivated orally their texts and the deeper scribal culture of which they were a part, then how much more would *the ordinary people have cultivated orally the Israelite popular tradition in which they were embedded.*[30]

It is difficult to imagine that Galilean and Judean villagers had direct contact with the authoritative written Judean texts that were kept and cultivated in scribal circles as well as, presumably, laid up in the temple. As noted already, literacy in Roman Palestine was limited mainly to scribal circles and the Judean scribal texts were written in Hebrew, while villagers presumably spoke dialects of Aramaic.[31] The people who lived under the rule of the Jerusalem temple-state surely knew of the existence of authoritative written scrolls of "the Law and the Prophets." But it is difficult to imagine how they might have acquired knowledge of their contents. The scribes and the Pharisees were active mainly in Jerusalem. The only source that portrays the scribes and Pharisees as active in Galilee in the first century CE is the Gospel of Mark (followed by Matthew and Luke, likely depend on Mark). It would be difficult to argue on the basis of the Markan references alone that scribes and Pharisees had been reciting or teaching the contents of scriptural texts in the villages of Galilee.

29. On this collective and individual internalization of spiritual-moral discipline resulting from the recitation of authoritative texts, see further now Shem Miller, *Dead Sea Media*. This repeated recitation provides not only the basis of but a model for how the recitation of apotropaic (protective) psalms worked to mold the group discipline that served as a protective cordon around the Qumran community in its anxiety about affliction by hostile spirits, as discussed in the previous chapter.

30. Fuller discussion in Horsley with Draper, *Whoever Hears You Hears Me*, esp. chaps. 5–6; Horsley, "Popular vs. Scribal Tradition," in *Text and Tradition*, 99–122.

31.. Critical review of the relation of the varied and limited evidence for and use of languages, spoken or written, in late second-temple Judea and Galilee in Horsley, *Galilee*, 247–50; Horsley, *Archaeology, History, and Society in Galilee*, chap. 7. On Aramaic in particular, taking into account the more extensive evidence now available, see Casey, *The Aramaic Sources of Mark*. Coverage of the expanded evidence in Smelick, "The Languages of Roman Palestine." Critical review of the evidence, considering multiple factors, in Horsley, "The Language(s) of the Kingdom," 201–7.

Their lack of contact with authoritative written texts, however, did not mean that Galilean and Judean villagers were ignorant of Israelite tradition(s). The lines of recent research summarized above show that we can no longer use written Judean scribal texts as evidence of what "the Jews" generally knew and practiced. But we do have sources that provide evidence that Galilean and Judean villagers in late second-temple times knew and acted upon Israelite traditions that they must have cultivated orally.

Josephus' accounts of popular movements in the generations before, during, and after Jesus' mission indicate that many of them took one or another of two distinctively Israelite forms (as discussed in chap. 4).[32] The movements led by the popular prophets anticipated new acts of divine deliverance patterned after those experienced by the early Israelites led by Moses or Joshua. The people who acclaimed their leaders as "kings" were following the model of the earlier Israelites who "messiahed" the young brigand chieftan David to lead them against invasion by the Philistines. Both of these distinctively Israelite types of movements indicate that formative traditions of Israel were not only cultivated among the villagers but were so vivid in the popular culture that they provided the patterns for sizeable movements led by popular prophets and messiahs.[33]

Studies of many other agrarian societies find that the people have their own version of cultural tradition (or traditional culture) that parallels but differs in emphases and implications (and sometimes in content) from the official or dominant version of the cultural tradition, which may appear partly in written texts. Anthropologists have referred to these parallel yet different versions of culture as "the little tradition" and "the great tradition."[34] Because the official/elite tradition is usually cultivated by cultural specialists, such as scribes, it is usually more unified and standardized (but not necessarily in supposedly stabilized written form). Popular tradition, which is cultivated in oral communication locally in village communities, usually has regional variations. These studies of

32. See further Horsley with J. S. Hanson, *Bandits, Prophets, and Messiahs*, chaps. 3–4.

33. In other bits of evidence, Josephus' accounts of several actions by "the Galileans" in attacking Antipas' palace in Tiberias or Herodian figures during the great revolt in 66–67 indicate that they were acting in defense of Mosaic covenantal commandments, discussed in Horsley, *Galilee*, 152–55.

34. Especially helpful is Scott, "Protest and Profanation." For application to Jesus and the Gospels, see the essays in Horsley, ed., *Hidden Transcripts*.

other societies that find "little traditions" running along "underneath" the politically-religiously dominant cultural tradition may give us confidence that Israelite popular tradition was cultivated orally in village communities, even though we do not have the direct sources from which to reconstruct its substance in any detail (except, of course, from the Gospel stories, to be discussed in chaps. 7–10).

In addition to the heroes, stories, festivals, and customs they share, there is usually regular interaction between the official or scribal tradition and the popular tradition. As noted in chapter 4, it is evident that victory songs, such as the Song of Deborah, stories of resistance, such as those about Gideon, covenantal customs such as lending at no interest, and prophecies, such as those by Amos and Micah, were taken up into the books produced by scribes that were later included in the Hebrew Bible. Particularly pertinent to the Gospels as sources for Jesus' healing are the stories of the prophet Elijah and his protege Elisha (as mentioned in chapter 5). Judging from the sudden change of style when the narrative in 1–2 Kings comes to Elijah and Elisha, these stories were evidently cultivated in popular circles before being included in the Deuteronomic history.[35] The Gospel stories attest that Elijah remained alive in the popular culture in Galilee, and it seems likely that it was the Israelite popular tradition (or social memory), not the books of Kings, that informed the connections made in the Gospel stories between Jesus and Elijah, including the healings. The cultural context in which Jesus worked and in which the Gospel/Jesus tradition developed from Jesus' interaction with people thus would have been Israelite popular tradition that continued to be cultivated orally in village communities.

Three particular aspects of Israelite popular tradition can be discerned operating through the accounts of Josephus—and in the narratives and speeches in the Gospels to be discussed in chaps. 7–10. To appreciate these it is necessary to move beyond the individualism of modern Western culture and beyond the habit in biblical studies of focusing on text fragments of individual verses and their supposed relation to other individual verses.

First, Israelite popular tradition was *collective*. While there would have been local and regional variations, Israelite popular tradition was the cultural heritage that villagers had in common. Insofar as "tradition" is a term used in different ways, it might be helpful to refer to this cultural

---

35. See the essays in Coote, ed., *Elijah and Elisha*.

heritage as it operated among the people in terms of Israelite popular *social memory*, which has received a great deal of theoretical attention and application in other fields in recent decades.[36] "The salient past, immanent in the narrative patterns in which it has become engrained in social memory, provides the very cognitive and linguistic habits by which a group perceives, orients itself, has its being in the world."[37] Thus Israelite popular tradition/social memory was not a mere transmission of particular stories and songs and laws in a popular version that paralleled the scribal versions known from extant Judean written texts. The memories, stories, incidents, and customs that are detectable from our sources were all part of a broader and deeper culture—like the broader and deeper Judean scribal culture, only more so. It was a culture in which the people were embedded, the cultural medium in which the people communicated and interacted. The popular culture was not just remembered or handed down, it was lived.[38] Foundational stories and commandments were reinforced by rituals and celebrations—as in the Passover celebration of liberation from bondage under the ancient Egyptian regime. As discussions of social memory have emphasized, *people's collective identity* was embedded in and expressed in the popular culture. And in early Roman Palestine, as noted in chap. 4, the collective identity of Galilean and Judean villagers was oppositional, not loyal, to the temple and high priesthood that functioned as representatives of the Roman imperial order.

Second, the stories and customs of Israelite popular tradition, moreover, portrayed *social relations and interactions*. The stories portrayed and remembered the people's life circumstances and the people's and God's actions in response. Customs/laws/commandments were not

36. See especially the very helpful concise summary of social memory theory, with rich references to many suggestive studies, by Kirk, "Social and Cultural Memory," in the introduction to the collection of essays in which he and Tom Thatcher introduced "social memory" into the New Testament field, *Memory, Tradition, and Text: Uses of the Past in Early Christianity*. See also Kelber, "The Words of Memory," in the same volume, which places this collection of essays in the broader context of studies of cultural/social memory.

37. Kirk, "Social and Cultural Memory," 15–16. Social memory theory has been used as an approach to particular Jesus-traditions and segments of the Gospel stories and speeches by Rodriguez, *Structuring Early Christian Memory*, in correlation with research on oral communication and oral performance (drawing on the performance theory of John Miles Foley); see also the review discussion in *JSHJ* 15 (2017) 169–259.

38. Werner Kelber has aptly used the metaphor of a biosphere for the shared culture in which people lived and derived their identity; see his essay on "Jesus and Tradition," in *Imprints, Voiceprints*, esp. 119–30.

just statements, but principles about social-economic relations in village communities or how conflicts were resolved. One of the reasons customs or principles were remembered is because they applied to people's circumstances and interactions and were practiced. Israelite popular tradition contained *patterns*, not just patterns of cultural meaning and collective identity, but paradigmatic patterns *of social interaction and collective social-political action*.[39] Scholars, focused on texts codified and printed in chapter and verse, become habituated not only to referring to such text-fragments but to thinking in terms of separate verses. They find that a particular verse, say in Luke 6, has reference to particular verses in Exod 22 or Lev 25. But their habits of reading and interpretation thus block recognition of the broader pattern of the Mosaic covenant evident in Luke 6:20–49 and Matt 5–7 and the earlier scribal working with the same pattern in Exod 20 and Josh 24.

Third, a return to the popular prophetic movements contemporary with Jesus discussed above can illustrate how stories about certain figures in Israelite popular tradition/social memory that were alive among the people were not just about a legendary figure, but about the *pattern of social interaction* represented. Recent explorations in social memory discuss how some figures can become "frame images" around which subsequent historical relations and even events can become configured.[40] Legends of deliverance led by Moses and his mediation of God's covenant with the people became such "frame images" according to which popular movements sprang to life in Roman Palestine. Stories of Elijah and Elisha would have been another key "frame-image" in Israelite social memory around which a social movement could have been catalyzed.[41]

That Galilean and Judean villagers were embedded in Israelite popular tradition, however, does not mean that they had no knowledge of the parallel Judean scribal tradition. Judean peasants, from many centuries under Jerusalem rule, and Galilean peasants, from their century under Jerusalem rule (roughly from 104 to 4 BCE), would have know that there were authoritative texts and even knew that their contents included

---

39. "Subjugated groups cultivate memories of ideal pasts characterized by freedom, memories that have the capacity to inspire resistance to oppressive conditions." Kirk, "Social and Cultural Memory," 17, with references to several studies.

40. See esp. Schwartz, "Memory as a Cultural System"; and Schwartz, "Frame Image."

41. See further the essays on popular social memory in Horsley, *Jesus in Context*, chaps. 5–7.

much parallel to what they cultivated as Israelite popular tradition. New Testament scholars embedded in print-culture standardly believe that when the term "writing" (*graphe*, usually translated "scripture") or the term "it is written" (*gegraptai*, "as it is written") it appears the "author" of the Gospel or the Epistle is "quoting" from a written text of the Jewish scripture(s); or perhaps the "author" is quoting from memory of a written text of the Jewish scripture(s). These are more likely references to the *authority* of the scribal texts that stood written in scribal circles and/or the temple and were presumably read and known by the scribes and Pharisees. This was an authority that the people also recognized, to a degree, and that Jesus-loyalists could claim for their hero-martyr and movement in resistance to the authorities.[42]

As will be discussed in the following chapters, the Gospel stories are full of references to Israelite tradition. Most of these are echoes or allusions or suggestive references. The people were deeply familiar with stories and customs. They hardly needed scrolls to recite psalms and stories or to apply covenantal commandments. When more explicit references appear, then they generally fall into three types. First, some references are general appeals that offer no specifics, but are claims that certain events in the story of Jesus happened "according to the scripture(s)" (for example, 1 Cor 15:3–5; several events in the Gospel "passion narratives"). Second, some references that include specific words or lines supposedly "quoted" are brief or are combinations of lines that either do not come from the "book" supposedly "quoted" or are "inaccurate" or different from any version known to scholars. The explanation could be that these references are to what composers not directly familiar with written texts thought was in particular written texts. Closely related to these are the "formula quotations" in the Gospel of Matthew, all of which except the first are references to "what was *spoken* by the prophet (e.g., Isaiah), saying . . ." (e.g., Matt 2:15, 17–18, 23; 3:3; 12:17–21; 13:35; etc.). Third, at several points in the Gospel of Mark, "Jesus" is throwing back in the face of the scribes and/or Pharisees that they surely have "read" in their "writing(s)" some incident or lines that the "authorities" presumably recognize or claim as authoritative (e.g., Mark 3:25–26; 7:9–13; 10:2–9).

The standard understanding of these references in the Gospel stories to what was "written" as "quotations" of particular passages from written

42. Fuller discussion in Henderson, "Didache and Orality in Synoptic Comparison"; Horsley with Draper, *Whoever Hears You*, 140–44; and Horsley, *Hearing the Whole Story*, 59–61.

copies of books of Scripture, rooted in modern print-cultural assumptions, is anachronistic. It does not accord with the realities of ancient media and cultivation of texts. But these references are evidence that ordinary Galileans and Judeans not only knew what they assumed was contained in those written texts, but knew that those texts had authority, to which they appealed in the Gospel stories.[43]

The Sources Are the Gospel Stories (and Speeches) Cultivated in Oral Performance

The implications of these and other related but heretofore separate lines of recent research are now becoming clear for how the gospel stories were cultivated. Contrary to the standard assumption of New Testament studies rooted in print culture, the Gospel stories and other texts would have been communicated and appropriated not through the writing of and reading from written texts. Rather the Gospel stories were communicated and appropriated in oral performance in communities of Jesus-loyalists. Even in circles of the literate elite in the Roman Empire, including those of Judean scribes, texts were communicated in oral recitation or performance in groups. The implication for the Gospel stories bears repeating: How much more would these stories about ordinary people evidently generated by ordinary people for communities of ordinary people have been communicated in oral performance in groups. Indeed, even after written copies existed, the Gospel stories and speeches evidently continued to be performed orally into the second and third centuries, from which most of the fragmentary evidence comes. And if they continued to be performed into the second and third centuries, then it seems clear that they were orally performed in their origins as they developed into distinctive stories.

43. This discussion also applies to ordinary Judeans in the Greek-speaking diaspora. The principal authoritative Judean "writings" had been translated into Greek. Josephus (*Ant.* 4.210; 16.43; *Apion* 2.175, 178, 204) and Philo (*Legat.* 115, 210) indicate that the Judean people, presumably in diaspora assemblies, had the law engraved on their hearts/souls (memories) from having heard it recited publicly.

The Continuing Performance of the Gospel Stories

The references to oral communication and writing in later Christian texts indicate that later communities and their intellectual leaders still valued the *living voice* of oral performance far more than writing, and were even somewhat suspicious of or reticent about writing. The fourth-century bishop Eusebius remembered that Papias, bishop of Hierapolis in the early second century, "did not suppose that things from books (*ek ton biblion*) would benefit [him] so much as things *from a living and abiding voice* (*zoes phones kai menouses*)" (Eusebius, *Hist. eccl.* 3.39.3–4). The erudite theologian Clement of Alexandria apologized for committing the teaching of the church to writing, which he knew was weak and lifeless in comparison with oral discourse.[44] He was concerned to explain the origin of the Gospel stories as well as their truth and authenticity as deriving from the authority of the disciples, particularly Peter.

As members of the educated elite Clement and later Eusebius presented the history of the texts in the terms of the Greek literature with which they were familiar.[45] Eusebius rewrites a report that Clement had "quoted" from an earlier source that people were eager to hear the unwritten (oral) teaching of Peter's divine proclamation. Thus they begged Mark, who was a follower of Peter, to give them a *hypomnema* in writing of teaching passed down orally. Pleased at their eagerness, Peter authorized Mark's "memoir" for use in the assemblies (*Hist. eccl.* 2.15). Eusebius notes further (*Hist. eccl.* 3.39.15) that Papias understood the (oral) Markan text that he knew (also) in writing as what "Mark" (Peter's "interpreter") *remembered* (*hosa emnemoneusen*) that Jesus had said and done, in a series of anecdotes or episodes (*chreiai*), although without proper "arrangement" (*taxis/syntaxis*, that is, that Eusebius and Clement were familiar with). This suggests that the oral text of "Mark" was about as close as Papias could come to the "living voice" of the anecdotes in which Peter had remembered (*apamnemoneusen*) Jesus' teaching and action. Eusebius' account also implies, as does the preface to the Lukan story, that the needed orderly "arrangement" (*taxis, syntaxis*) he found missing in "Mark's" series of anecdotes was supplied by the Matthean and Lukan stories, presumably with their anecdotes of Jesus' birth, blocks of his teaching in speeches, and anecdotes of his resurrection. As recent

44. Shiner, *Proclaiming the Gospel*, 18.

45. "A later gospel discourse that assumed more bookish modes of thinking," Larsen, *Gospels before the Book*, 97.

text criticism is finding, however, those Gospel stories were also fluid and pluriform in the early fragments and MSS, suggesting continuing oral performance of which they are "oral-derived" (written) texts.

Recent study of oral performance of texts in the Roman Empire generally and, more specifically, of the Gospels, finds that "readers" of the Gospels at gatherings of the faithful did not need to know how to read from a (virtually illegible) codex. "The performer could learn the Gospel from hearing oral performances or by hearing" others recite it.[46] According to the mid-second-century Christian apologist, Justin Martyr, at Sunday assemblies "the memoirs of the apostles or the writings of the prophets are read [i.e., recited] for as long as time permits."[47] Hippolytus says that "Scripture was read [i.e., recited] at the beginning of services by a succession of readers [lectors, reciters] until all had gathered . . ." This practice lasted at least to the time of Augustine. He comments that many people had learned to recite (large portions of) the Gospels themselves from hearing them recited in services.[48] These witnesses come from several generations after the origin of the Gospel stories, but the way in which stories and other texts were learned by hearing and retold orally in the context of a keenly interested community would have been the same in an oral communication environment.

The Pluriformity of Early Written Texts and Their Relation to Performance

It thus seems evident that cultivation of the Gospels continued in oral performance for several generations, with or (more likely) without access to written copies. Close analysis of early MSS and text-fragments by leading text-critics has even made them suspicious about the availability and stability of written texts of the Gospels.

Prior to the fourth century there are strikingly few references to copyists engaged in making written copies of Gospels and other Christian texts. This striking lack of evidence "regarding copyists involved in reproducing [written] Christian texts prior to the fourth century is itself instructive."[49] Some of the few references to the ad hoc production of

---

46. Shiner, *Proclaiming the Gospel*, 26.
47. Shiner, *Proclaiming the Gospel*, 45.
48. Shiner, *Proclaiming the Gospel*, 45, 107.
49. Haines-Eitzen, *Guardians of Letters*, 38–39.

written texts as an occasional occurrence suggest how and why written copies were made: as revered sacred objects rather than as writing to be read. For example a plea from a community leader in upper Egypt to "make and send me copies of books"[50] suggests four interrelated aspects of the active cultivation of nascent scriptural texts. First, although the existence of written copies of texts was known to (leaders of) communities, written copies were not readily available. Second, some leaders at least wanted to possess written copies of these "books" (probably for the prestige of having a numinous written text that added to their authority, and perhaps that of their possessor, as well). Third, someone in or hired by (a leader of) another community could make a copy. Fourth, the text already orally-memorially known probably played some role in the making of a new copy, especially if, as was likely, copying was done at dictation by someone who knew and could recite the text.

The new findings of recent investigations by text-critics reinforce the dawning recognition that oral recitation was the principal mode of appropriation and further cultivation of the Gospel stories in Christian communities. Not until the fourth century do manuscripts show evidence of some standardization of the written texts of the Gospels. This standardization, moreover, was evidently the result of the establishment of Christianity in the Roman Empire. The newly converted Emperor Constantine sent instructions to the learned bishop Eusebius that he should "order fifty copies of the divine scriptures . . . for the instruction of the church, to be written on well-prepared parchment by copyists most skillful in the art of accurate and beautiful writing" (Eusebius, *Vit. Const.* 4.36).[51]

By contrast, fragmentary papyrological evidence indicates extreme variation. As leading text-critic David Parker says, "the further back we go, the greater seems to be the degree of variation."[52] If anything, the variation in the written textual witnesses is greater on the most frequently cited statements of Jesus, such as on marriage and divorce.[53] As Parker

---

50. Haines-Eitzen, *Guardians of Letters*, 38–39.

51. Gamble, *Books and Readers*, 79n132.

52. Parker, *Living Text*, 188.

53. These findings of recent text critics further undermine the standard focus on individual sayings by historical Jesus scholars. Some of the key sayings that satisfy the central criterion of "multiple attestation" in supposedly stable written sources (e.g., in Mark, Q, etc.) display the greatest variation in the early papyri and fragmentary manuscripts.

lays out, the variation in the versions in manuscripts of Mark 10, Matthew 5 and 19, and Luke 16 is as much or more than that between the respective Gospel versions. The Lord's Prayer existed in six early forms, two versions of the Matthean prayer and four of the Lukan prayer. Parker concludes that the considerable differences across early manuscripts is not due simply to the way copyists copied already written copies.[54] Rather it seems to have much to do with the importance of the teaching of Jesus to people's lives, particularly on key matters of concern. As another leading text-critic, Eldon Epp explains, early manuscripts show marks of the social contextualizations of the Gospel texts. On this basis he also argues that (written-) textual *authority* was pluriform, in contrast to the previously standard print-cultural assumptions of text critics who took textual "variants" in early manuscripts as mistakes or accidents in copying or the more recent suggestions of "tampering with the text" or "misquoting Jesus."[55]

It would seem that the early fragments of written Gospel texts reflect circumstances of ongoing oral performance of the texts. Recent text-critical research is thus suggesting that the production of written texts of New Testament books that were so "fluid" and "free" happened in the course of the continuing oral performance of those books in the diverse early Christian communities. In a pioneering investigation that opened up appropriate understanding of the oral cultivation of Jesus' teachings, Werner Kelber explained that the reason why particular sayings and parables of Jesus are known to us is that they resonated with hearers in

54. Parker, *Living Text*; Parker continues to question whether ancient scribes were "necessarily textually oriented people," focused on faithfully copying or perhaps deliberately altering a previously written manuscript; as an illustration, he characterizes one manuscript (the sixth-century Rossano Gospels) as "somewhere between a text and a cartoon book." See Parker, "Variants and Variance."

55. Epp, "Multivalence of the Term 'Original Text'"; Epp, "The Oxyrhynchus New Testament Papyri," 10; in contrast to Ehrman, *Orthodox Corruption*; and Ehrman, *Misquoting Jesus*. In a very different approach, by comparative analysis of "unfinished" versions and "multiple authorized versions" of (the written texts of) the same works, Matthew Larsen, *Gospels before the Book*, reaches a similar conclusion, that early written texts of Mark were pluriform. While sharply critical of modern (print-cultural) assumptions of authorship and original texts, however, he continues to work on the assumption that ancient texts were composed in writing and that written Gospel texts were comparable to other written texts in antiquity, which were produced in elite intellectual circles. His discussion seems unaware of, or avoids, the lines of recent research on oral communication, the oral-written interface, and the importance of memory in the composition of texts in antiquity.

concrete situations (and not simply that they were transmitted from one tradent to another).[56] This observation can be extended to the Markan story as a whole (and to the other Gospel stories). Mark is known today because it resonated with groups of hearers in performance in antiquity.[57] The reason we have the Gospel stories is that they were developed and performed in communities of the movement(s), the origins of which (in Jesus' interactive mission) the stories narrate and some of the distinctive concerns and features of which the stories [at points] reflect. With emphasis on exorcism and healing, the story(ies) resonated with the people involved in the communities as the movement(s) expanded. Eventually the Gospel stories and speeches became sufficiently widely authoritative that by late antiquity they were included in the New Testament of established Christianity.

It is important, finally, to draw out a major implication of the findings of recent text criticism of the early fragmentary papyri and MSS of and quotations of Gospel texts for this investigation and assessment of the sources for the historical Jesus. In historical Jesus studies and New Testament studies generally, both embedded in the assumptions of print-culture, it was imagined that the "writing" of the Gospels by the evangelists brought stability to what had been "unstable" oral tradition. This was a principal reason (rationalization) for focusing on separate sayings and "miracle stories." As summarized just above, recent text critics are finding that the sayings and anecdotes/episodes are no more stable (in their wording, etc.) in the written witnesses than they were in the supposedly brief phrase of oral tradition. The separate sayings and anecdotes do not supply a stable base from which Jesus-scholars can sort out "data" for their constructions. Study of complex texts such as sagas and epics in other fields, however, are finding from analysis of oral performances of those texts that while particular episodes and lines vary, the overall story remains fairly consistent from performance to performance. There are not yet sufficient analyses of multiple early manuscripts of the Gospels to prove that the overall stories are relatively consistent from manuscript to manuscript. But comparative studies strongly suggest that this would be likely. This is yet another reason to conclude that the Gospels as whole stories with speeches, in oral performance in communities of Jesus-loyalists, are the sources for the historical Jesus. The related lines

56. Kelber, *Oral and Written Gospel*, chaps. 1–2.

57. Important analysis by Joanna Dewey in "Mark—a Really Good Oral Story"; see also Horsley, "Oral Performance in the Emergence of the Gospel of Mark as Scripture."

of new research just summarized indicate that the Gospel stories would, at the earliest stage of their composition and performance, have been actualized in oral performance and that the overall stories (with speeches) would have been more stable in their consistency than particular sayings or other text-fragments.

Imagining the Composition of the Gospel Stories (in Oral Performance)

The question of the composition of the Gospel stories as distinctively plotted texts and/or speeches has been avoided so far because how we imagine the composition as having happened in the oral communication context does not make a decisive difference for the main recognition here that the Gospel stories and speeches were communicated in oral performance. Recent discussion of the composition of the Gospels, however, does shed some light on their oral performance in communities of the Jesus movement(s).

In the oral communication environment of the ancient Mediterranean world, composition was not done in writing. Texts with traditional content were often the result of a long process of (repeated re-)composition over a period of time. The best known examples are surely the Iliad and the Odyssey. While we may continue to use the cipher "Homer" for their supposed composer, many classics scholars (after considerable discussion) have recognized that these poetic epics developed over centuries of repeated oral performance.[58]

Among texts that were later included in the Hebrew Bible, the book of Jeremiah offers a dramatic example of composition over a considerable period of time that involved the relationship between prophetic proclamation (and how seriously "the word of YHWH" was taken by ruling officials), complex texts held in memory, their dictation and inscription on scrolls, repeated oral performance, and repeated dictation and inscription. Jeremiah had been proclaiming prophecies of YHWH's condemnation of the Jerusalem monarchy and temple for years and continued those as well as prophecies against the conquering imperial city of Babylon. According to the narrative in Jeremiah 36, the prophet was banned from appearance in the temple and royal court by the threatened monarchy

---

58. See especially the papers of Milman Parry in Parry, *The Making of Homeric Verse*; as well as Lord, *The Singer of Tales*; and Foley, *The Theory of Oral Composition*.

(Jehoiakim, son of Josiah). Jeremiah summoned the scribe Baruch (evidently of a scribal family, Jer 32:12; 51:59), who must have sympathized, and dictated the prophecies to him, with instructions to "read" (that is, re-proclaim) the prophecies, which now had the added authority of being written. The officials of the monarchy, sensing the importance of having the king hear the threatening prophecies, reported to Jehoiakim, who had them "read" to him from the scroll, which he proceeded to cut into pieces and burn in a brazier. Jeremiah, who held the prophecies in his memory, then dictated them again to Baruch to inscribe on another scroll.

Years later Jeremiah dictated all the prophecies against Babylon to Baruch's brother Seriah, high ranking scribal official of king Zedekiah, to write on a scroll, re-proclaim them in Babylon itself, and then throw the scroll of prophecies tied to a stone into the Euphrates as an act symbolizing how Babylon itself would sink (Jer 51:59–64). Evidently Jeremiah also held these prophecies in his memory so that they could later be incorporated into the collection of his oracles with narrative episodes of his interactions. Centuries later, with much biographical and historical narrative included, the book of Jeremiah appeared in very different versions. The obvious explanation for the different versions is that composition continued in successive (different) scribal circles based on scribes' previous cultivation of the text(s) in memory.

Pliny the Younger, in fascinating accounts of his own practice (*Ep.* 9:34–36; 2.10; 3:18; 7:13, 17; 9:36), indicates how the literate elite in the Roman Empire composed their histories or other texts.[59] After awaking he composed in his head while lying in bed. Later he summoned a secretary to take dictation as he spoke his text. To disseminate his composition, however, he performed his text to a group of friends or in public. Composition of even a complex text was thus not done in writing.

Once we become aware of the various lines of recent research into oral communication in antiquity and how they mutually reinforce one another, it is difficult to imagine that the Gospels could have been composed in writing. They are clearly stories about a figure and movement among the ordinary people of Galilee in opposition to the political-religious and (literate) cultural elite. And they originated in and were addressed to communities of ordinary people living in a world of oral communication who had little use for writing and no training in writing.

---

59. Discussion of Pliny and others in composition in the ancient media context in Small, *Wax Tablets of the Mind.*

The Markan story has been the most carefully, critically, and creatively explored as an oral-aural narrative. Werner Kelber pioneered the appreciation of the healing and exorcism episodes and the parables in Mark in terms based on studies of the behavior of oral narrative, pushing decisively past the previous projection of print-cultural assumptions onto "oral tradition" by form criticism.[60] In a series of highly suggestive articles over two decades, Joanna Dewey explored the oral patterns and echoes and the oral-aural "event" detectable in the narrative.[61] In an imaginative study thoroughly informed by research into ancient performance practices of Greek texts in Hellenistic-Roman culture, Whitney Shiner suggestively explored how Mark could have been performed in its broader historical cultural context.[62]

More recently Anne Wire has skillfully crafted a persuasive step-by-step explanation of why and how Mark was composed in performance.[63] However, we have hardly begun to explore how the Markan story (or the Matthean and Lukan texts) may have been composed in repeated performance. Wire makes a suggestive case that the story pattern of contemporary popular prophets and their movements (discussed in chap. 4) was formative for the composition of the Markan story. Emboldened by her initiative, I have attempted to deepen, broaden, and thus strengthen the case by considering the development/composition of the story in community in historical context.[64]

It is important to recognize that the Markan story (likewise the Matthean and Lukan stories) is not Christian theology in story form. Some of the basic synthetic constructs of New Testament studies that developed

60. Kelber, *Oral and Written Gospel*—the groundbreaking work that opened investigation and discussion of oral communication and New Testament interpretation.

61. Dewey, "Oral Methods in Mark;"and "Mark as Interwoven Tapestry," republished with other important essays in *Oral Ethos of the Early Church*. Another groundbreaking article was Botha, "Mark's Story as Oral Traditional Literature," reprinted with other important articles in *Orality and Literacy*. See also Horsley, *Hearing the Whole Story*.

62. Shiner, *Proclaiming the Gospel*.

63. Wire, *Mark Composed in Performance*. See also Shiner, "Memory Technology and Mark;" Dewey, "Mark and Oral Hermeneutic;" and Horsley, "Oral Performance and the Gospel of Mark."

64. See the fuller discussion in Horsley, "Imagining Mark's Story Composed in Oral Performance," in *Text and Tradition in Performance and Writing*, esp. chap. 11, on which the following paragraphs are based; also pertinent are the suggestions in "Oral Performance and the Gospel of Mark."

as a branch of Christian theology, such as "(early) Judaism" and "(early) Christianity," are inappropriate to understanding the Markan story and how it may have been composed.[65] Critical historical studies from the last several decades have resulted in the expansion and increasing precision of our knowledge of the political-economic-religious structures and dynamics and historical movements and events in the historical context. These studies enable us to be fairly specific in making references and in discerning particular social forms, social relations, power relations, and political conflicts presupposed and portrayed in the Markan story (and other Gospel stories).[66]

It is inappropriate for biblical scholars rooted in the assumptions of print culture to impose the limitations of our own imagination onto composition in antiquity. Texts such as the complex arguments of Paul, the Q speeches, and the Markan and other Gospel stories themselves call for sensitivity and appreciation of how their composition, supported by memory, was embedded in oral communication, emerged from periodic oral performance, and "worked" in oral performance. Parallel to the literate Greco-Roman elite, such as Pliny, non-literate ordinary people were also capable of composing complex stories as well as songs and speeches. If a particular story proved compelling and was told repeatedly, it could take on distinctive form as an oral text in continuing performance. Among other aspects of popular composition in repeated performance, in contrast to the modern print-cultural assumption of an individual "author," we should be thinking in terms of a composition process. This would have been the emergence of a basic story from collective social memory and its interactive further development as it was repeatedly performed in community context.[67]

65. Similarly, modern (abstract) scholarly constructs such as "apocalypticism" and "eschatology" only distort the Markan story and the Israelite (popular) cultural tradition in which it was rooted.

66. Summarized in chap. 4, which relies on recent critical analyses of sources in avoidance of still standard synthetic scholarly constructs that tend to block recognition of the historical complexities in Roman Palestine.

67. Others who are also struggling to conceptualize composition of Gospel stories in the oral communication environment of antiquity think in terms of "co-authorship," "interactive authorship" or "collective authorship;" see Botha, *Orality and Literacy in Early Christianity*, 129, 199–200; Kelber, "On 'Mastering the Genre.'"

Consideration of three interrelated aspects of the Markan story may enable us to gain a clearer sense of how it developed (was composed) in a movement of Jesus' followers.[68]

First, many key features and much of the content of the basic story (in the Markan story and in the Matthean and Lukan as well) are given in the broader historical context of its origins, as laid out above. The ostensible history of Jesus' mission portrayed in Mark is derived from and fits in the history of the Galilean and Judean people under Roman rule, as known from other sources. The setting, the characters, and even much of the plot are given in the historical situation (as discussed in chap. 4). Most of Jesus' mission, his exorcisms, healings, and teaching take place in the villages of Galilee (and nearby regions), which is ruled by Herod Antipas. Like the leaders of the contemporary popular prophetic movements, Jesus acts and speaks primarily in the role of a prophet (like Moses and/or Elijah). Given the structural conflict between the people and the Romans and their client rulers in Palestine, Jesus and John the Baptist (like the other popular prophets leading movements) oppose and are opposed by the rulers. After Jerusalem had ruled Galilee for the previous century, even after Antipas had ruled Galilee for a generation, Galileans may well have viewed Jerusalem as the capital of Israel. This presumably set up Jesus' confrontation with the rulers there in accordance with his assumption of the traditional Israelite prophetic role (e.g., of a prophet like Elijah). But since the Roman governor retained the power of execution, Jesus was crucified by order of Pontius Pilate, after the high priests arrested him and turned him over in accord with their responsibility to maintain social order.

Second, it is important to have a clear sense of the basic story, the main plot (as indicated in the dominant conflict) of the Markan story (and then of the Matthean story and Lukan story as well). The discussion of the *genre* of the Gospels, as analogous to ancient "biography," is based on the assumptions of modern print-culture and their projection onto literature in Greek and Latin antiquity. Its controlling concepts, especially its focus on "Christology," and its separation of religion from political conflict, are derived from theological New Testament studies.[69] As noted

68. I explored all of these interrelated aspects in previous books and articles, especially Horsley, *Hearing the Whole Story*, and *Jesus in Context*, chaps. 4, 7, and 9; but I did not adduce a case for Mark's story as *composed* in performance until "Imagining Mark's Story Composed in Oral Performance" (2013).

69. Most prominent in recent discussion has been Burridge, *What Are the Gospels?*,

above, the basic Markan story is not so much biography as history; its main plot is the conflict between Jesus and his movement against the rulers, the high priests and their Roman patrons. In this regard, the closely contemporary popular prophetic movements offer striking parallels: as prophets like Moses or Joshua of old, Theudas and other prophets summoned their followers to experience a new (albeit fantastic) divine act of deliverance and renewal of Israel in opposition to the rulers and were killed by the Roman governor.

The basic Markan story may well have been something like the "already existing narrative tradition" or "framework" that Dewey projects behind the more elaborate Markan story as we have it.[70] But insofar as we have access to it only through the fuller Markan story, it seems more appropriate to imagine a basic story that is already fairly complex—certainly more so than a simple sequence of episodes of Jesus' mission followed by his death-and-resurrection, as in later creedal summaries. What Jesus is doing that evokes such opposition is preaching that the direct rule of God is at hand and being manifested in exorcisms of invasive spirits and healing various illnesses in the villages of Galilee and beyond, while recruiting disciples and commissioning them to extend his own program of preaching and healing to other villages. As clearly indicated in the appointment of the twelve and in his performance of (acts of) power(s) such as sea-crossings, healings, and wilderness feedings, and clinched by his appearance on the mountain with Moses and Elijah, Jesus is engaged in the renewal of the people of Israel as a prophet like Moses and Elijah. The basic story in Mark (paralleled in Matthew and Luke) is about how Jesus is generating the renewal of Israel in opposition to and by the high priests and the Romans who maintained them in power.

3rd ed. Burridge, however, largely ignores the rich explorations of the Gospels as narratives and narrative criticism as well as the various lines of research into oral communication and performance in antiquity and revisionist text criticism (still thinking in terms of "author," "authorial intent," "original meaning"). Insofar as the most obvious feature of the Gospel stories is their narrative form, it is difficult to discern how study and interpretation of those stories that virtually ignore their (plotted) narrative can contribute to our appreciation and understanding of them. On the assumption that genre determines meaning, then the thesis that the genre of the Gospels is derived from or analogous to Graeco-Roman biography means that the meaning of the Gospels is dictated by forms of Graeco-Roman culture without much attention to the Israelite culture and historical context in which the content of the Gospel stories is rooted. See esp. the recent critique by Kelber, "On 'Mastering the Genre.'"

70. Dewey, "Good Story," 496–97. For the narrative, see also Dewey, "Mark as Interwoven Tapestry"; and Dewey, "Gospel of Mark as an Oral-Aural Event."

Third, as indicated in the previous paragraph, the Markan story (history) of Jesus' mission and the historical movements that it parallels were rooted in and resonated with Israelite cultural tradition, particularly Israelite popular tradition (sometimes in opposition to the official Judean tradition) as carried in the people's social memory (as discussed above). This would have been operative in the interaction between Jesus and his followers and opponents as well as in the (Markan and other) Jesus movements that resulted from that interaction. In how the story is shaped by and resonates with tradition we are considering not just the developing "Jesus-tradition," but the much broader and deeper Israelite popular tradition in which the Jesus-tradition was itself deeply rooted.[71] In the following chapters this resonance with Israelite tradition will be explored extensively, enabling us to discern how the basic story could have been composed orally in repeated performance as it resonated with people embedded in that tradition.

While the Matthean and the Lukan Gospel are, like the Markan Gospel, stories about Jesus generating a renewal of Israel in opposition to and by the rulers, they are each distinctive. They have distinctive plotting, distinctive additional episodes, distinctive twists on common episodes, and large blocks of teaching as well as distinctive beginnings with different "infancy narratives." While they share much Jesus-teaching not in Mark, some of it remarkably similar, even verbatim, they deploy it differently. Most striking about the Matthean "story" are the five long speeches of Jesus and most striking about the Lukan "story" is the long "journey" that Jesus is taking on his way to Jerusalem during which he delivers much of the teaching in short speeches that Matthew presents in three of five long speeches.

Once the teaching of Jesus parallel in Matthew and Luke is recognized as shorter or longer speeches in poetic form, it is much easier to imagine how it could have been repeatedly orally performed while undergoing some development and variation in particular circumstances.[72] As we know from our own experience with songs, hymns, and other poetic texts, it is not surprising at all that these speeches would have been performed, some of them virtually verbatim, in repeated performance occasions. And once we appreciate how the Markan story and the series of speeches can have been orally composed and performed in the

---

71. Discussed in the articles now reprinted in Horsley, *Jesus in Context*, chaps. 5–7.

72. Horsley with Draper, *Whoever Hears You Hears Me*.

oral communication context of the ancient Mediterranean world, then it should be easier to imagine how the Gospels of Matthew and Luke, both of which combine or parallel much of the Markan story and the series of Jesus-speeches, could have been orally performed.

Finally, and of crucial importance, the basic Markan story and its elaboration, the series of speeches, the Matthean story, and the Lukan story, were all rooted in and composed from the collective memory of the movements of Jesus-loyalists whose collective identity had been formed in that memory. And as that memory developed it became elaborated and diversified, providing the basis for further development and elaboration of the Gospel stories.

How Can We Hear the Gospel Sources in Oral Performance?

Once we bring together these lines of recent research it becomes clear that the sources for the historical Jesus were not only whole stories and speeches but were also stories-in-performance-in-communities. Given its development on the basis and assumptions of print culture, however, biblical scholarship does not (yet) include competence in dealing with texts in performance, especially texts in performance in historical context. There are surely obstacles and difficulties, some already evident and some unforeseen, that probably cannot be surmounted, certainly without far more research and analysis—for example, of (pluriform) early manuscripts and of lack of (direct and fuller) information about the communities to which the Gospel stories and speeches were probably addressed. For the daunting task of understanding texts in oral performance, however, help is available from other fields in which interpreters have been learning to appreciate texts-in-performance in other cultures. With that help we can at least discern some aspects of our situation as historians and some of the steps we might take in order to move toward a more adequate understanding of the Gospel stories and speeches as texts-in-performance and how they might be used as historical sources.

As should be immediately evident, performance of texts involves integral extra-textual aspects that biblical interpreters, including Jesus-scholars, have neither discerned nor dealt with (given how deeply embedded we are in print-culture). Some of the most obvious are a performer who speaks/chants/sings with voice inflections, facial expressions, gestures, and other body-language; and an audience that interacts with the performer and the performed text in the context appropriate to the performance, probably a gathering of a community of a Jesus-movement. Communications theory and study of communication, which is always at least "two-way," is thus directly helpful for understanding oral performance. For example, there are certain "registers" of language that are "dedicated" to certain communications and performances and their contexts, such as weddings, funerals, political rallies, or academic lectures. Less obvious perhaps is that communication and particularly performance happen not so much in detailed cognitive, denotative explanation, but in what is assumed but not spoken: innuendo, allusions, and references to common experiences and knowledge that the performer and audience share.

Complex but manageable theory of performance has been developed in the last several decades. Significant insights have emerged from sociolinguistics, performance theory of folklorists, ethnopoetics, and the ethnography of performance. Pioneering theorist John Miles Foley has drawn many of these developments and insights together in several important works.[73] After considerable interaction between Foley and biblical scholars who have explored oral communication and performance of "biblical" texts, it seems that his theory can be adapted with considerable benefit in attempts to understand the Gospels in performance. The following discussion of the Gospels in performance is based on an adaptation of Foley's suggestive synthetic theoretical reflection.

Of greatest import for understanding texts in oral performance is careful attention to and analysis of three key interrelated facets of a text-in-performance and of the *function* or effect of performing the text. In order to hear the Gospel texts (and then use them as sources), it is necessary to discern the contours and contents (message) of the *text*, to determine the historical *context* of the community of the responsive hearers, and to know as much as possible the cultural *tradition* that the voiced text referenced as it resonated with the audience. Since, as Foley explains, the meaning is immanent as the text references the cultural tradition, our goal is to discern not so much the meaning of words and phrases as the *effect* that the performed text may have had on the hearers, the *work* that the performed text may have done in (the context of) the audience.

Most studies in other fields have focused on traditional poetry, epics, sagas, story-telling, etc. in traditional cultures. The texts have been

73. Foley, *Immanent Art: From Structure to Meaning in Traditional Oral Epic*; Foley, *Singer of Tales in Performance*; and Foley, *How to Read an Oral Poem*.

deeply ingrained in the cultures, having been performed for generations, learned by children from parents or by proteges from master-singers or by members of a "guild" of singer-actors, and recited with variations in "lines" and "stanzas" but with consistency in the overall oral text (epic, saga, or story) from performance to performance. The audience's context is also traditional, such as townsfolk gathered at a festival at which the text was customarily performed, or local people at a teahouse or pub expecting to hear tales of their cultural heroes, as had their ancestors before them. In these performances the cultural tradition that the text referenced was also usually deeply ingrained in the people, so that the audience readily resonated with the allusions to places, heroes, idioms, and customs that they shared with the performer in their particular cultural tradition. The effect of such a performed text, besides the important matter of entertainment, is variously to perpetuate (and adapt) the all-important cultural memory of the people, to nurture the customs and commitments of the people, and to reinforce the collective identity of the people.

In the historical context of their origins and functions, however, the Gospels were different from such traditional sagas or poetic epics, and it is necessary to adapt theory of performance for the ways in which (the interrelations of) their text, context, and tradition were distinctive. Although the Gospels were deeply rooted in Israelite (popular) tradition, they were new stories and purported to be historical stories. Indeed they were stories about and speeches from the prophet-founder (and/ or messiah-designate) who had generated a new movement of renewal and resistance. The stories were about decisive figures and events. The audiences were evidently involved in that movement that came together in response to a crisis in the people's collective lives. And the stories and speeches not only resonated with Israelite tradition but claimed that their hero and movement were the fulfillment of that tradition. In anticipation of moving to analysis of particular Gospel stories in the next chapters, therefore, it may help to focus a little further on the key aspects of texts in performance and of the distinctive aspects of the *text, context,* and *tradition* that the Gospel stories share. Since *text, context, and tradition* are all aspects of the same performance(s) they are completely interrelated and inseparable, hence analytical observations about each aspect will often necessarily touch on the others.

Text

In attempting to discern the contours of the Gospel texts, we cannot jump directly into some hypothetical oral performance. We must begin with the early manuscripts, that is, written versions of the Gospel stories and speeches, on which we are dependent. Yet it seems clear from review of the various lines of research into ancient communications, that these written texts were derived from oral performances. Foley suggested the concept "oral-derived texts," signaling that we are dependent on the written versions for our imaginative analysis of a text in oral performance. He later suggested the concept "voices from the past," for which we are dependent on extant written copies or versions. Moreover, we depend on our own educated imagination, informed by comparative material, to explore the relationship between the written text and the (repeated) oral performance(s) from which it derived. For example, were the pluriform manuscripts "transcripts" of various oral performances? From the discussion of text criticism above it should be clear that the standard Greek text of a Gospel established by years of painstaking labor of text-critics, on which our translations are based and scholarly analysis and interpretation conducted, is a modern scholarly construction. At best it points to a "mean" or "average" performance that we are imagining. Imaginative analysis of the performed *text* would take this into account. Ideally we would consult the pluriform early manuscripts directly. But that will be possible only after extensive further analysis by trained text-critics, analysis that will take many years.[74] Meanwhile we can only work with the results of recent text-critics and our analysis of texts-in-performance will be exploratory and provisional (depending heavily on the text "established" by text-critics, but fully aware of that it is a "mean" and that actual performances were pluriform).

The texts-in-performance we are considering were whole stories (or series of speeches) or sustained narratives with speeches included, somewhat analogous to whole epic narratives such as the Iliad or Odyssey or Beowulf. It may be reassuring to those particularly concerned about the stability of historical sources to repeat what studies of other long texts

74. Text-critics, however, are beginning to make some of the key early manuscripts more readily accessible, for example, in the Marc Multilingue Project that presents seven MSS printed in parallel, with French translations on opposite pages. As Wire comments (*Mark Composed,* 39–40), this makes the performances "visible" and "can prepare us to feature the gospel's oral performance and early composition more adequately."

that were performed find: that while the "lines" (cola) and "stanzas" (periods) change from performance to performance (even with the same performer), the overall story or long speech remains fairly consistent. Contrary to what was previously assumed in "the quest of the historical Jesus," the overall story of a given Gospel was more stable than the wording of sayings, parables, and episodes, particularly than the wording of widely used and applied sayings (with "multiple attestation").

The style of the Gospel stories, particularly the Markan story, is a rapid-fire sequence of episodes. The story is not linear, like modern fiction, with suspense about how it will climax or end. The basic story (perhaps even the particular Gospel story they are hearing) is already known to the audience. While the story may seem like "one thing after another," it is far more than that. In narrative sequence earlier episodes (such as exorcism or healing) set up subsequent episodes, which in turn further illuminate or extend the implications of earlier episodes. Subplots are interwoven, as when the scribes and Pharisees challenge Jesus' healing and exorcism or the disciples, having been commissioned to extend Jesus' exorcism, prove incapable of doing so. While there may be no suspense about the outcome of the story, there are steady steps of repeated conflict toward the climax.

Moving from the mere written text to a performance of Gospels would be somewhat like moving from a mere reading of the script of a play toward an experience of the drama, including the interaction among the characters and the emotional tone of their speech. The Gospel texts tell sustained stories of multiple conflicts, between Jesus and the disciples, Jesus and the unclean spirits, Jesus and the scribes and Pharisees, and especially Jesus and the Jerusalem and Roman rulers. Those conflicts become far more emotionally charged in oral performance before an audience than in private modern individual silent reading. In the Gospel of Mark, for example, in his mission of healing and exorcism as manifestation of the direct rule of God, Jesus performs one action after another in which he acts as a new Moses and/or new Elijah, including commissioning the disciples to extend his mission, somewhat as Elijah had commissioned Elisha to continue his mission. But the disciples increasingly misunderstand what he is doing in his "(acts of) power(s)" that evoke attacks by the scribes and Pharisees who have "come down from Jerusalem." Jesus is exasperated by the time "Rock" acclaims him "the messiah," while it is evident to the villagers that he is a prophet (like Elijah) in the long line of Israelite prophets. Not surprisingly when "Rock" then protests at his announcement of his impending trial and execution, Jesus rebukes him, "get behind me, Satan."

Context

In order to understand a special form of oral communication such as a wedding, funeral, or political campaign speech, it is necessary to hear it in the appropriate collective audience context: wedding, funeral, or political rally. The same is true for the performance of a long epic poem or ballad. The context of the audience determines the expectation and the appropriate hearing of the text. Traditional oral performances were always already in the appropriate context. Ancient Greek dramas were performed in a theater in Athens or other city-states at festival times. Even in the late twentieth-century United States, two long "culture texts" that became "traditional," *A Christmas Carol* and Handel's *Messiah*, were performed multiple times by different theater companies or several different musical organizations during "the Holidays" in theaters, churches, or concert halls in many urban areas.

In the case of the Gospel stories and speeches, not only were the texts new, but the audiences were communities recently renewed or catalyzed in response to the mission of Jesus to a situation of crisis for the people involved, of which the Gospels told the story. Studies of performances of traditional epics and sagas usually consider mainly the cultural context, the particular "performance arena" of the text, while more or less assuming a relatively stable traditional social context. The context of performance of the Gospel texts was far more complex and requires broader and deeper historical analysis. The audiences of Gospel performances were close chronologically and situationally to the circumstances, characters, and events that the stories recount. The hero on whom the stories focused was the prophet (and/or messiah) who had generated the movement of renewal and resistance that had spread to the communities they had formed; he had been executed as a martyr; and he had been vindicated by God and by their own commitment to and continuation of the movement. The Gospel story was also their story. It defined their collective identity. It explained, authorized, and inspired their commitment to a movement that was at least under suspicion and sometimes persecuted (Mark 8:34–38; 13:9–11; Luke/Q 12:2–12).

Gaining an adequate sense of the context(s) of the Gospel texts in performance will require, on the one hand, loosening of the restrictive formal and abstract print-cultural approach that combined tidbits of vocabulary and legends of apostles that led to hypotheses (guesses) about "authors" and "addressees." Scholars trusting the legend that "Mark" was Peter's interpreter and the tradition that Peter eventually became the first "bishop" of Rome, the Gospel of Mark was standardly believed to have been addressed to the church in Rome during or after the "Jewish Revolt."[75]

On the other hand, it will also require more thorough and precise investigation of the historical context(s) of the early Jesus movement(s) and a more appropriate sense of the process by which such stories were composed (in repeated performance) than previously standard in New Testament studies. Standard discussions of the audiences to which the Gospels were "written" has been heavily influenced by the Christian theological scheme of Christian origins. In this scheme, the resurrection and "Easter faith" inspired the formation of "the church" and the "Christian mission" led by the apostle Paul and others established "(early) Christian" churches mainly among "Gentiles" in cities of the Roman world. The communities to which the Gospels were supposedly "written" thus stood at considerable cultural as well as geographical distance from the communities of Galileans and Judeans among whom the Jesus movement(s) started. For example, on the assumption that "the first Christians" were (mainly) "urban," the large city of Antioch became a prime candidate for the location to which the Gospel of Matthew was addressed. Very little attention has yet been given to how the teaching of Jesus and the stories about his action and interaction that is so deeply embedded in village agrarian life would have resonated with urban communities.

Yet there are at least two alternative possibilities to the standard assumption that the "early Christian" movement(s) spread mainly in urban centers predominantly among "Gentiles," alternatives that are not mutually exclusive and for both of which there is some evidence. One is that movements of Jesus-loyalists spread into towns and villages, certainly near Galilee and Judea in Syria, and even beyond (see the account of rural communities of Christ-loyalists in Pontus-Bithynia in the early second century in Pliny the Younger, *Ep.* 10.96).[76] The other is that

75. Ecclesial constraints on interpreters often influence the perpetuation of such traditions.

76. See further the discussion of the context of the Markan story in chap. 7.

the movement(s) established communities in enclaves of diaspora (displaced) Judeans (or other Israelites) in cities such as Antioch or Caesarea. In both cases, for some similar and for some different reasons, people might well have resonated with stories of a movement of renewal and resistance among subject people like them.

Only recently have Gospel interpreters recognized that not only the Gospel of Matthew, but also those of Mark and John as well give no indication that the communities they address are separate from the people of Israel. In fact, they assume that these communities are the continuation and fulfillment of (the tradition/history of) Israel. While much research remains to be done, recent historical investigations have begun to provide more precise historical information and analysis that no longer perpetuate standard synthetic essentialist concepts such as "Judaism" and "apocalypticism," and "Christian." The implication of all of this rethinking (from the previous guesses about the "authors" and "addressees" of the Gospels rooted in print cultural assumptions) is that the performance context of the Gospel stories and speeches was much closer culturally and geographically to the historical crisis of the people of Roman Palestine sketched in chapters 4 and 5 above.

Tradition

A performed text resonates with the audience as they hear it in the group context. This is clearly the case in traditional texts-in-performance, such as Greek plays or, in our own experience, at weddings, funerals, the Mass, and political rallies. In performance, however, meaning happens in a way very different from private silent reading of a modern literary text. A modern novelist individually manipulates inherited or idiosyncratic materials in a new direction or from a particular perspective, thus conferring meaning on her fresh new literary creation that is read silently by an individual reader. Traditional texts in performance resonate with the hearers by referencing the cultural tradition and evoking meaning that is inherent (or immanent). The evocation is often metonymic, as a part (such as a name or cue or motif) evokes a whole cultural pattern or complex memory. Musical passages played by flutes in Bach's cantatas or the St. Matthew Passion, for example, evoke pastoral images, perhaps of tranquility and peace and/or of the birth of the Christ child. In performance of a Gospel story, the reference to Jesus going out into the wilderness for forty days evokes a broad range of traditional associations, from Israel's wilderness period after the exodus liberation to the preparation of Moses and Elijah for their respective roles of prophets of the founding and renewal of Israel.

Certain texts in performance do not simply evoke inherent meaning but *do work on/in or have a particular effect among* the group of hearers in the context. Some performances of Bach's St. Matthew Passion or Mozart's Requiem or a replaying of Martin Luther King's "I Have a Dream" speech may evoke renewed religious-ethical commitment, renewal of group identity, or inspire and give expression to collective mourning and religious devotion. This happens through especially "effective" referencing of traditional memories, patterns, and expressive forms. The cultural tradition that a performed Gospel text referenced does not refer narrowly to the "handing down" or transmission of sayings and stories of Jesus, but rather to the whole complex of collective cultural memory in which the performer and the hearers, as well as the text itself, are embedded. Tradition in the broadest sense is the culture in which a people or movement lives, makes sense of their lives, and shapes its collective identity.[77]

As with other aspects of the Gospels in performance, established New Testament studies leaves us poorly prepared to understand how the Gospel stories and speeches may have resonated with cultural tradition. Indeed, established New Testament studies leaves us unclear about just what tradition the performed texts may have been referencing. This is partly because of the assumption that "New Testament texts" were expressions of a new religion that had split off from "Judaism" and partly because of the field's orientation mainly toward the Hellenistic-Roman culture into which "Christianity" was expanding (for which scholars use elite texts of philosophy and rhetoric as the key sources).

Not surprisingly for an academic field deeply embedded in print culture, when New Testament scholarship does consider the Gospels' referencing of "Jewish" tradition, it has focused on the surface level of written texts, that is, the Gospel texts' "quotations" of "Old Testament" texts. Recently more subtle analysis shifted and widened the focus to listen for "echoes" of and allusions to particular lines or phrases in Scripture. While still focused mostly on written texts, more recent discussion of "intertextuality" recognized an even more extensive interrelationship

77. Again see especially Kelber's essay "Jesus and Tradition," in *Imprints, Voiceprints*, esp. 119–30, in which he compares tradition in the broadest sense to the invisible biosphere in which people live.

of texts. As we are learning from some of the lines of recent research sum-marized above, however, written texts were only "the tips of the icebergs" afloat in a much wider and deeper sea of Israelite tradition. As noted above, however, direct knowledge of written texts was limited mainly to Judean scribal circles and Hellenistic Jewish intellectuals (such as Philo of Alexandria), given the severely limited literacy, and even they evidently accessed texts primarily from their memory.

Insofar as the Gospels were newly composed and performed texts addressed to communities of a new movement(s), they may be thought to have been referencing two related traditions, the narrower and new one that grew out of the broader and older one (ostensibly) as its fulfillment. In the course of a few decades a tradition of Jesus' (inter)action, teaching, and other lore developed. This would have included far more than only what was included in the "Synoptic Gospels" and the Gospel of John. The latter, for example, refers to "many other signs" that Jesus had performed, including many other healings (John 20:30).[78] *The Gospel of Thomas* in-cludes (short clusters of) sayings and parables that are not included in the Markan story or the Q speeches. Although the tradition of Jesus' teaching and healing and exorcism was broader than what was included in extant texts, however, particular pieces or text-fragments cannot be understood apart from the Gospel stories and/or series of speeches of which they were components. Insofar as the tradition of Jesus' teaching and ac-tions were cultivated orally (probably in different "Jesus-movements"), the transmission of Jesus-tradition, about which historical Jesus' studies has been so preoccupied, was not an issue. The tradition was repeatedly performed, and the development/composition (in performance) of the Gospel texts was, broadly speaking, part of that tradition.[79]

78. The non-canonical Gospels, such as the *Gospel of Thomas*, include episodes, parables, and teachings not included in the canonical Gospels, many of them probably developed later.

79. Recognition of the dominance of oral communication in Roman Palestine has led to renewed exploration of the oral transmission of Jesus' teachings and traditions about Jesus, by Horsley w/Draper *Whoever Hears You*, and James Dunn, *Jesus Remem-bered* (both informed by and dependent on Kelber's pioneering exploration). Moving directly to the oral transmission of particular Jesus-tradition from written texts of the Gospels seems premature, however, once we recognize that the Gospels or the "Q" speeches behind Matthew and Luke were embedded in and permeated by oral com-munication. (See the works mentioned below in chapters 7 and 8 on Mark and Q.) In this connection, much more critical analysis remains to be done on how collective cultural memory is operative in the Gospel tradition. See the preliminary explorations in many of the essays in Kirk and Thatcher, eds., *Memory, Tradition, and Text*; and

As has become increasingly evident, moreover, the Gospel stories and speeches are full of figures, forms, motifs, and patterns from, and countless allusions to, Israelite tradition that we recognize mainly on the basis of written Judean texts (including those later included in the Hebrew Bible), but the vast majority of which are not "quotations" from them. Moreover, as recognized perhaps first about the Gospel of Matthew and, more recently about those of Mark and John, the texts give no indication of any "split" from the people of Israel and Israelite tradition,[80] and contain few allusions to any other cultural tradition.

It is becoming clear from the related lines of recent research summarized above that both the wider Jesus-tradition and the Gospel texts are rooted in, draw upon, and resonate with Israelite popular tradition. It is clear that the Gospel texts also at points refer to bits and pieces of the Judean scribal tradition ("it is written;" "have you (Pharisees) not read?"). In order to appreciate the Gospel texts in performance, however, it will be important to gain an expanded sense of the Israelite popular tradition that they reference in resonating with the communities of the Jesus movement(s). Since we have no direct sources for it, however, this will require exercise of our educated imagination informed by a sensitive awareness of when and how Judean scribal texts (including those later included in the Hebrew Bible) may have reflected or paralleled or provide windows onto Israelite popular tradition.

What We Are Listening For

As we now move far beyond well-charted study of written texts into exploration of the Gospel texts in performance, it is important to keep in mind what we are listening for. It has been standard in New Testament studies to seek the meaning of text-fragments. In study of the "historical Jesus" this has usually meant the meaning of a saying in itself, as noted above. In exploration of the Gospel texts in performance, however, while we are focusing on whole stories or a series of speeches, we are seeking to sense the "work" that the performed text did in the communities of addressees, the effect that it had on the communities. This involves far more of the dimensions of life than does analysis of a written text-fragment. It

---

Horsley, *Jesus in Context*, chaps. 3–7.

80. See, for example, Saldarini, *Matthew*; Horsley, *Hearing the Whole Story*; Horsley and Thatcher, *John, Jesus, and the Renewal of Israel*.

will also require hearing the referencing of Israelite popular tradition in concrete social and political contexts. This will require drawing on information about the historical crisis of Galilean, Judean, and nearby peoples and the changing culture in which they were responding to political-economic pressures sketched in chaps. 4 and 5 above.

It may be useful to explain how the historical recognitions and resulting procedures followed here differ from what have been standard assumptions, concepts, and procedures in studies of "the historical Jesus." Some of the leading "Jesus-scholars" seemed to be on the same cultural "wave-length" with the producers of TV documentaries on Jesus in the 1990s, only too eager as "talking heads" to answer what was often the producers' central question, "what was Jesus really like." That question and answers to it, of course, are the chimeras of modern romantic fascination with "the life of the great man." It is significant that a number of "Jesus books" bore the title or subtitle, "the life of . . . ." They were locked into what had long since become the standardized approach that focused on a smaller or larger number of sayings taken out of context in the Gospel sources. Thus the answer to "what was Jesus really like?" was that he was a talking-head who uttered precious nuggets of wisdom or revelation, that is, he was either a wisdom teacher of an unconventional individual lifestyle or an apocalyptic preacher of the end of the world.

Several of the lines of recent research summarized above are forcing us to recognize that figures become historically significant in interaction with others, followers and opponents, with whom they are embedded in social forms and institutionalized power relations. They may take on or step into roles and relations already operative in a particular society/ culture in particular times of crisis. The historical effect or work of such a figure is inseparable from those adapted roles and interaction determined by contingencies of historical crisis. In the Gospel sources Jesus was embedded in and inseparable from the interrelations with the movement that formed around him and his/their conflict with the rulers. And, in turn, those interrelations and conflicts are embedded in the Gospel stories as our sources. The *historical* Jesus was Jesus-in-interaction-in-crisis in the lives of Galileans, Judeans, and nearby peoples (under Roman conquest and rule) and our access is through the Gospel stories that were developed and performed in the communities of Jesus-loyalists in the ensuing decades.

The next four chapters will be devoted to attempts to critically imagine how Gospel texts in performance were heard in performance and resonated with communities of Jesus movements in which they were being formed. These attempts will deploy theory of complex texts in performance developed by leading theorist John Miles Foley adapted to the Gospels as ancient texts in their historical contexts. These will of course be provisional attempts to pull together the implications of the various lines of new research that have challenged our previous assumptions, procedures, concepts, and conclusions.

7

The Markan Story

CONSIDERATION OF THE SOURCES for the historical Jesus and his exorcisms and healings begins with the Markan story for several interrelated reasons. The Markan story is thought to be the earliest, which was followed and adapted by the Matthean and Lukan stories. In the first narrative steps in the Markan story exorcisms and healings are the principal actions of Jesus' mission that also open up the principal conflict of the story, between Jesus and the rulers and their representatives. The Markan story, moreover, has been the subject of most analysis and interpretation of a Gospel text in performance. Consideration of the Markan story in oral performance can thus prepare the way for consideration of the Matthean and Lukan stories in performance.

Recently developed theory of oral performance (as discussed in chap. 6) suggests that we attempt to discern the contours of the *text*, to ascertain the *context* of the audience, and to explore how the story resonated with the audience in referencing Israelite cultural *tradition*. That these three key aspects were inseparable in performance, hence are only analytically separable, means that consideration of one aspect will involve consideration of the others. The most intelligible procedure may be first to focus briefly on how the overall story unfolds and what it is about, next to discern the context of the audience, in order then to explore the Markan story more fully as it resonated with the audience in referencing Israelite tradition. Discussion here will focus on exorcism and healing, but will also consider other aspects of the story in order to gain a sense of how the Markan story presents exorcism and healing as central to the overall mission of Jesus-in-interaction.

Special Note: Let me strongly recommend that readers, before proceeding into the following discussion, read through the whole Markan story in a translation without chapter and verse markers that interfere with the continuity and dynamics of the narrative. Among other effects, this will help avoid the fragmenting reading habits of standard biblical studies that break the story up into verses and pericopes and scriptural lessons. It is important in hearing the performed text to have a sense of the narrative sequence of the component episodes. In order not to perpetuate those fragmenting reading habits, I will as much as possible avoid inserting chapter-and-verse indications in referencing particular episodes in the Markan story.[1] (I hope that this will help push us toward learning how the story unfolds in the sequence of its narrative steps and component episodes.) It is also important to keep in mind that performance of the story was pluriform and that while the overall story may have remained consistent from performance to performance, particular cola and episodes probably varied (as is sometimes indicated in "textual variants" listed in certain editions of the Greek text). Also it would be most beneficial to hear-and-watch one or more video performances of the Markan story (e.g., by David Rhoads). Also, it would lend a jolting sense of the ancient story-telling style of one brief colon after another linked by repetitive "and" to read a few episodes (in Greek or) in literal word-by-word translation with successive cola in successive separate lines. Modern English or other translations obscure this style by transforming some of these cola into relative clauses.

Text

The Markan text is most obviously a narrative: about Jesus' mission of exorcism, healing, and teaching in the villages of Galilee and beyond, the people's trusting response, and the resulting conflict with the rulers in Jerusalem and their representatives. The story's main plot is Jesus' mission in Galilee and beyond and his conflict with the rulers. But the story also has subplots, such as the ever expanding crowds in response mainly to his exorcisms and healings, the quickly escalating conflict between Jesus and the scribes and Pharisees, the growing misunderstanding of the disciples and their resistance to his impending martyrdom, and the increasing prominence of women as paradigms of trust. This is a compelling story.

---

1. Exceptions are made for brief references across episodes in the narrative and references out of narrative context.

The Markan story in its spiraling plot and its complexity of interwoven subplots, with episodes echoing forward and backward through the narrative, has become increasingly evident as a result of decades of analysis of "Mark as story" and narrative criticism.[2] Appropriation of the Markan story has thus moved well beyond the fragmentation of the text into paragraphs in standard translations for readings in churches and Bible study and the standard commentaries that focus on such fragments and their words and phrases. Appreciation of the narrative has thus moved well beyond the kind of interpretation that could discern only collections of mini-stories linked by "keywords" and "topics" and a few "bracketing stories." The story can now be read and heard as proceeding in successive narrative steps, with a speech in parables following the first and a speech about the future preceding the final step (as discussed in chap. 1). The narrative steps are marked (e.g., by the speeches' beginning and end) and/or have discernible infrastructure (two successive sequences of "acts of powers"). But the overlapping subplots proceed through several narrative steps of the whole story.

If we then attend to the main characters, the settings, as well as the plot and subplots we can discern (hear) what the story is about. The Markan narrative tells a story about Jesus of Nazareth proclaiming the direct rule of God and performing many exorcisms and healings in the villages of Galilee and nearby areas. As the people respond with trust (*pistis*) in the power(s) working through him, his fame spreads and a movement develops. Recognizing that the healings and exorcisms and the people's eager response—his growing authority/power with the people—are a threat to their authority, the scribes and Pharisees, representatives of the Rome-appointed high priestly rulers in Jerusalem, actively oppose him and plot to destroy him. Meanwhile Jesus recruits disciples and commissions the Twelve, who are representative of the people of Israel, to expand his proclamation and exorcism, and he renews mutually supportive (Mosaic) covenantal community. What Jesus says and does indicates that he is a prophet like Moses and Elijah generating a renewal of the people in opposition to and by their rulers. As the disciples increasingly misunderstand him as a king (messiah) who will set up his own kingdom, he explains three times that he must be executed in Jerusalem. The misunderstanding of the disciples becomes a foil for his renewal of the Mosaic

2. See especially the early discussions by Kelber, *Mark's Story of Jesus*; Rhoads and Michie, *Mark as Story*; and the suggestive essays of Joanna Dewey, now collected in *The Oral Ethos of the Early Church*.

covenantal guidelines for community life in the movement he is generating. In the climax of the story Jesus goes directly into the seat of political-economic-religious power, the Jerusalem temple, where he carries out a prophetic demonstration of God's judgment on the high priestly rulers. After seizing him surreptitiously the Roman-appointed high priests turn him over to the governor, who has him crucified as "the king of the Judeans" (i.e., as a leader of insurrection), while the disciples betray, deny, and abandon him. In a suggestive "open ending" to the story, however, three women who continue to trust find his tomb empty and are told that he will meet the disciples back up in Galilee—where presumably the movement will continue. A much fuller sense of what the Markan story is about and how it unfolds will emerge from considering how it resonates with the audience as it references Israelite tradition.

Context

The immediate performance-context of the Markan or other Gospel stories and speeches was evidently gatherings of communities of a Jesus-movement. Jesus' instructions at "the last supper" set up a regular covenant renewal ceremony in communities of the movement(s) remembering his martyrdom as "the breakthrough" from which the movement expanded rapidly. The Markan text offers several interrelated clues about the circumstances of the listening communities, clues that mesh with ever-expanding information about the likely historical context now available from other sources. These clues lead to conclusions that differ from some of the standard concepts and generalizations of New Testament studies.

The abrupt ending of the Markan story may be a key clue about the audience addressed.[3] At the Passover meal that Jesus transformed into a covenant renewal ceremony that his loyalists were to continue until he could "drink the cup anew in the kingdom of God," he had told them that after he was raised he would go before them (back) to Galilee. Then at the empty tomb the figure dressed in white told the three frightened women, and through them the audience of the story, that Jesus was "going ahead of you to Galilee; there you will see him." In this open ending to the story

---

3. It is standardly recognized that the longer endings of the Markan text in some MSS were influenced by the endings of the other Gospels: it needed a resurrection appearance, instruction to the disciples, even an ascension, and a rehabilitation of Peter.

the hearers are evidently being called to meet Jesus back in Galilee (or "Galilee"), where they are to continue the movement he had started. Here is a clue that the communities among whom the Markan story was performed were in villages and towns of Galilee and perhaps in a "Galilee" that included nearby areas in Syria.

This abrupt ending that points to Galilee (or "Galilee"), moreover, follows upon the conflict between Jesus and the disciples, particularly Peter, James, and John, that intensifies from midway through the story. After being commissioned to extend Jesus' mission, the disciples seriously misunderstand that mission and, in the crisis of his arrest and crucifixion, deny and abandon him. This suggests that, while the Markan story and the movement it addresses acknowledged the central role of the Twelve in the mission of Jesus, they were rejecting the leadership of Peter and other leading disciples who had become the heads of the movement based in Jerusalem (as in the beginning of the book of Acts).[4] The audience of the Markan story understood themselves as continuing the movement that Jesus had generated in Galilee and beyond in some degree of separation from the leaders of the movement that had established their base in Jerusalem.

Closely related and mutually reinforcing to the ending of the story back in Galilee are the references in the narrative to the provenance of people flocking to Jesus and to the areas beyond Galilee into which he extends his mission. In the first narrative step a summary of the people who are gathering to seek exorcism and healing from Jesus lists not only a great multitude from Galilee, but large numbers from Judea, Jerusalem, Idumea, beyond the Jordan, and the region around Tyre and Sidon as well (3:7–10). In the second and third narrative steps Jesus then extends his exorcisms and healings and preaching into villages or "countryside" or "regions" subject to (the rulers of) the cities of Tyre, Sidon, Caesarea Philippi, the Decapolis, Bethsaida, and Jerusalem.[5] These extensions of Jesus' mission to villages beyond the frontiers of Galilee appear to be the

---

4. See the analysis and discussion in Horsley, *Hearing the Whole Story*, chap. 4.

5. Mark 5:1–20; 7:24–30; 8:22–26; 8:27—9:29; 9:30–49; 10:1–52. The itinerary in mid-story that has seemed awkward to interpreters—from the regions of Tyre by way of (the area subject to) Sidon to the regions of the Decapolis to Bethsaida, and then to the villages of Caesarea Philippi, before coming back to Galilee and Capernaum—is not all that strange if one considers the short distances and the Markan portrayal that Jesus and his disciples are working in the villages/regions they visited. Cf. the closely argued analysis in Michael Flowers, "Jesus' 'Journey' in Mark 7:31."

"tracks" of the expansion of the movement, whether carried out by Jesus himself or in the following decades.

In this connection it is important to attend carefully to what is (indicated) in, and not (indicated) in, the Markan text and what we now know from recent historical investigations that has previously been obscured by synthetic constructs that had become standard in New Testament studies (such as the dichotomy between "the Jews/Judaism" and "the Gentiles"). In contrast to previous assumptions, the Markan text gives no indication that the Gospel was addressed to "Gentiles" as opposed to "Jews."[6] For example, there is no basis in the text for the theological scheme that in his journeys across the Sea of Galilee Jesus was mediating between "the Jews" who lived on the West side and "the Gentiles" on the East side. The only mention of "the Judeans" in the Markan story links them closely with the Pharisees: "the Pharisees and all the Judeans, who carefully wash their hands, thus observing the traditions of the elders" (Mark 7:1–4). The Pharisees had come from Jerusalem, in Judea, which is where the Markan story understands the Judeans to live. The Markan story is thus consistent with Josephus' histories and the Gospel of John, both of which distinguish geographically between "the Judeans" in Judea, "the Samari(t)ans" in Samaria, and "the Galileans" in Galilee. Mark portrays Jesus as working among the villagers of Galilee, with no indication whatever that they are "Judeans." Nor does the Markan story refer to the people in the villages of nearby areas across the frontier as (other) "peoples." The Markan narrative uses *he ethne* (the peoples) mainly in reference to the Romans, who killed Jesus, lord it over their subjects, and make war on other peoples (Mark 10:33, 42; 13:8).

While Jesus carries his mission beyond the villages of Galilee into nearby areas, the Markan story portrays Jesus throughout his mission as generating a renewal of the people of Israel, as indicated by the plethora of references to Israelite (popular) tradition (as will be discussed below). The text gives no indication of any sort of split between Jesus and/or his loyalists and the people of Israel. The story has Jesus move easily across the frontiers of Galilee without comment on the cultural heritage of the

6. Previous readings that Mark was addressed to "the Gentiles" (a later Christian concept, the term derived from the Latin for peoples), which appealed to passages such as the supposed "cleansing of the temple" to make it a house of prayer "for all peoples" (Mark 11:17; Isa 56:7) and "the vineyard" being given to "others" (12:9), were evidently determined by the old theological scheme of Christian origins according to which "(early) Christianity" quickly became mostly "Gentile."

villagers in the neighboring areas. In the one exception, the woman explicitly identified as a Greek of Syrophoenician origin, persuades Jesus that "the little dogs" (evidently non-Israelites) should be allowed to share in the "bread" (healing) he is bringing to "the children" (of Israel). This episode indicates that (the Markan) Jesus and/or his movement was open to participation of other peoples subject to Roman client rulers among whom his mission and movement expanded from its beginning in the villages of Galilee.[7]

While some members or even whole communities of the movement addressed by the Markan story may well have been non-Israelite, they had evidently identified with Israelite tradition, even with the Israelite people that Jesus was renewing.[8] There would have been less of a difference of culture and political-economic situation and interests between the villagers subject to Tyre or Caesarea Philippi and the Galilean villagers than between the scribes and Pharisees who "came down from Jerusalem" and the Galilean villagers.[9] As we know from other sources such as Paul's letters and the book of Acts, however, non-Israelite peoples also subject to the Roman Empire identified with and joined the movements and communities of Jesus-/Christ- loyalists from early in its expansion. The presence of non-Israelites in the movement would explain why the Markan story offers "translations" of key Aramaic words, significantly of

7. The lines of political control and economic exploitation were imposed by the rulers, most recently the Romans, and were periodically changed, as indicated by the histories of Josephus and other ancient sources. As comparative political and sociological studies have pointed out, moreover, in terms of their interests, villagers of one area (such as the Galileans) may have had more in common with those of nearby areas than with their rulers (the Herodians in Tiberias or the high priests in Jerusalem or the client rulers of Tyre and Sidon).

8. Josephus report that Agrippa II's kingdom, in areas to the East and North of Galilee, had a mixed population of Judeans and Syrians (*War* 3.56–58) suggests that Judeans and Syrians had been living side by side for some time in interaction of cultures.

9. The sources from which earlier generations of New Testament scholars and scholars of "Judaism" constructed the supposed high boundaries between "the Jews" and "the Gentiles" and/or surrounding peoples were primarily rabbinic texts from several generations after Jesus and the Gospels. New Testament scholars assumed that the Pharisees, as the supposed immediate predecessors of the rabbis, were the representatives of "Judaism." It is clear from the Markan narrative that Jesus did not share the views of the Pharisees. It should be clear from chaps. 4 and 5 above, moreover, that the cultural as well as political-economic differences between villagers and their rulers and their representatives were significant.

particular commands in performantive speech by Jesus in his healings (e.g., *talitha cum*, 5:41; *ephphatha*, 7:34).[10]

If these mutually reinforcing clues point to communities in the villages and towns of Galilee and nearby areas as the addressees, then hearers of the Markan story would have possessed considerable knowledge, perhaps direct experience, of the historical context in which the story fit—knowledge far broader and deeper than what is included in the "story world" to which recent literary critics would limit silent individual modern readers. They would have known about, perhaps even experienced, the collective trauma of villages destroyed and relatives killed or enslaved in Roman conquests. They would have known that Galilean Israelites had become subject to the rule and taxation of the Jerusalem high priesthood only a few generations before, so that Jerusalem, with its temple massively rebuilt by Herod, had become the capital from which they were ruled. And as villagers in the areas of northern Palestine they would have known that villagers in other areas were also subject to client rulers installed by the Romans, whether Herod Antipas and Agrippa I in Galilee, Herod Philip in Bethsaida and Caesarea Philippi, or the corresponding rulers in Tyre and other cities. And they would have known of and perhaps experienced the recent invasion of Roman troops sent by the emperor Gaius, that would have reopened memories of previous trauma.[11]

The Markan story also includes indications that the addressees were experiencing opposition, even persecution and repression, from local rulers and authorities. Immediately following Jesus' rebuke of Peter's protest about his own martyrdom Jesus exhorts "the crowd" that in their commitment to Jesus and the movement they must be prepared to "take up their cross," that is, become martyrs themselves, if necessary. That the exhortation also addresses the hearers of the Gospel is confirmed by its

10. These terms and the explanations of the meaning of *qorban* in 7:11 and of "the day of preparation" in 14:42 have been used in arguments for the Gospel as addressed to "Gentiles." But if non-Israelites, such as the SyroPhoenician woman, were included in communities of the movement in the villages and towns of Syria, such explanations would have been appropriate.

11. We modern readers (and now would-be hearers) living at great historical distance from this historical context can gain at least some knowledge of the historical context by reading Josephus' histories and attending to the expanding information available from recent historical studies. This has been a principal purpose of much of my research. See especially *Galilee*; *Archaeology, History, and Society in Galilee*; and, *Jesus and the Politics of Roman Palestine*.

repetition in Jesus' speech about what to expect in the future, that is, the present of the addressees (as well as by the reference to persecution in the interpretation of the parable of the sowing of the seed). Participants in the movement, probably the leaders in particular, must "watch out" for themselves, for

> you will be handed over to councils,
> and you will be beaten in assemblies,
> and you will stand before rulers and kings . . .
> (Mark 13:9, 11; see 8:34–38)[12]

As for the temporal relation of the hearers of the Markan story to the mission of Jesus that the story is about, the escalating political-economic turmoil in Roman Palestine in mid-first century[13] points to an early composition-and-performance of the Gospel. Post–70 CE "dating" of the Gospel of Mark keyed narrowly on what were taken as allusions to dramatic historical events in "the Jewish War" of 66–70 CE in what has standardly been viewed as "the little apocalypse" in Mark 13.[14] This dating was also influenced by the standard theological scheme of Christian origins, with "Mark" understood as addressed to (largely Gentile) "Christians" following the destruction of the temple as prophesied by Jesus (Mark 13:1–2; 14:58; 15:29).

A more complete reading of Josephus' histories and related sources, however, indicates that figures, incidents, movements, and events that scholars previously associated with "the Jewish War" had been happening

---

12. The councils and assemblies (*synagogai*) would likely have been city or village jurisdictions, the rulers and kings probably Roman client rulers, such as the Herodian rulers in Bethsaida and Caesarea Philippi or a "tyrant" in Chalchis, etc. Critical discussion of synagogues as village assemblies in Horsley, *Galilee*, chap. 10.

13. Laid out with extensive references, e.g., in Horsley, *Jesus and the Spiral*, chap. 4; *Galilee*, chap. 3, *Jesus and the Politics of Roman Palestine*, chap. 2.

14. Whether the speech in Mark 13:3–37 should be labeled an "apocalypse" has little or nothing to do with the context of the hearers of the story. "Apocalypticism" is a modern scholarly construct based on a somewhat literal reading of text-fragments as references to "cosmic catastrophe"; critical deconstruction of the construct in Horsley, *Prophet Jesus and the Renewal of Israel*, chaps. 1–4. In contrast to the common reading of the imagery of disturbances in the usual paths of the sun, moon, and stars in Mark 13:24–25 as cosmic collapse, such imagery had long been standard in Israelite prophecies of God's future epiphany in judgment of oppressive imperial regimes, as in Isaiah 13:10; 34:4. Further discussion in Horsley, *Scribes, Visionaries*, 158–59; and Horsley, *Revolt of the Scribes*, 52, 78.

throughout the previous decades as well.[15] The events and figures mentioned in Jesus' speech about the future (Mark 13) were only too familiar to the peoples of Roman Palestine and Syria, particularly in the lifetime of Jesus and the next generation (as discussed in chapter 4 above). "Kingdom [already had risen] against (made war on) kingdom" (Mark 13:8) in the Roman conquest and reconquest. "Wars and rumors of war" (13:7) were frequent, from the Roman reconquest in 4 BCE and the Judean refusal to pay the tribute in 6 CE to Roman governors sending out the military against prophetic movements and the Roman military expedition sent by the emperor Gaius to install his statue in the temple.[16] The "desolating sacrilege set up where it ought not to be" would most likely have been a reference to that anticipated installation of Gaius's statue.[17] Subject peoples had long since known that they "must flee to the mountains" (13:14) when the "suffering" (13:19) of the people became severe, from slaughter, destruction, and crucifixion. "False messiahs" (13:21–22) had been acclaimed by their followers in 4 BCE and "false prophets" had led large movements in the decades after Jesus' crucifixion. If the context of the composition-and-performance of Mark is to be "dated" by allusions to figures, incidents, and events referenced in Jesus' speech about the future, then it would appear to be sometime after the Roman military expedition to install Gaius' statue in the temple in 40, say in the 50s, and not necessarily only after the great revolt of 66–70, of which the Markan story gives no particular indication.

Critical review of our increasingly precise knowledge of the historical context thus suggests that the context of the early hearers of the Markan story was in fairly close proximity, both geographically and temporally, to the context of the events that the story recounts. This would help explain how the story resonated with the people, who were familiar with the fundamental conflict that the story is about and familiar with Israelite tradition which the story referenced repeatedly.

15. Fuller discussion in Horsley, *Hearing the Whole Story*, 131–35; Horsley, *Galilee*, 62–72; *Jesus and Spiral*, 43–58, 99–120.

16. Laid out in Horsley, *Jesus and the Spiral*, chap. 4.

17. See Yarbro Collins, *Mark*, ad loc.

The Story Resonating with the Hearers
as it References Israelite Tradition

We can appreciate how the Markan story of Jesus' renewal of Israel, mani-fested mainly in exorcisms and healings, resonated with communities of hearers in their life-context by attending to its references to Israelite tra-dition in which the performer(s) and audience(s) were embedded—the same tradition in which Jesus and the people with whom he interacted were embedded. As explained in chap. 6 above, tradition should be un-derstood broadly to include the recent history and contested life-context of the temple-state, Galilean and Judean and near-by areas' experience, and contemporary movements, all of which were aspects of the virtual "biosphere" in which the audiences of the Markan story lived.

Sensing how the performed story resonated by referencing the tra-dition will not be a simple endeavor. The resonance involved (further) aspects of the audience context and the complexities of a narrative in which episodes are interdependent, earlier episodes setting up later ones, and later episodes referring back to or further illuminating earlier ones. Complicating our hearing of the story from a considerable historical dis-tance, moreover, it is necessary to deliberately displace anachronistic and distorting assumptions and concepts in order to appreciate more sensi-tively how the text may have resonated with those communities.

The audience would likely have already known the overall story since it had probably developed in performance. This means that the effect (including inherent meaning) depended on narrative sequence, that what was indicated in earlier episodes unfolded in subsequent epi-sodes, and that the impact was cumulative. It is thus necessary to keep in mind the overall narrative while hearing particular episodes in narrative sequence.[18]

"Prologue"

It seems unlikely that the story began with the words "the beginning of the gospel of Jesus Christ Son of God." This was probably a title added

---

18. The following survey presupposes the discussions of particular episodes of healing and exorcism in Horsley, *Jesus and Magic*, 119–36 and 143–47, and earlier in Horsley, *Hearing the Whole Story*, 136–48 and 208–15. These episodes often appear somewhat differently when considered more carefully in the narrative sequence and context of the overall Markan story.

(much later) in some manuscripts and does not indicate a genre (discussed in chap. 6). Rather, the story begins with an explicit reference to the formative events in the history and tradition of the people of Israel: the exodus from bondage and the ensuing (Mosaic) covenant of the people with God. Appealing to the authority of what was "written" in the prophet Isaiah, "Prepare the way of the Lord" proclaims a new exodus in Jesus' mission of the renewal of Israel about to be recounted in the story. That the prophecy is not all from Isaiah (as *we* know it from Isa 40:3), but resembles alternative versions of Exodus 23:20 and Mal 3:1, suggests that it was derived from popular memory, perhaps a conflation of what may have been separate prophecies in scribal texts.

John's baptism of repentance is a ritual of renewal of the Mosaic covenant that entails repentance for having "sinned" in violation of the covenant commandments—for which the current distress of the people in subjugation to Rome and its client rulers would have been understood as their "curse" or punishment (as stated in the covenant pattern/ceremony, discussed in chap. 5). John's baptism thus sets up the covenant renewal that becomes central to Jesus' renewal of Israel in several subsequent episodes of the story: in his declaration that those who do the will of God constitute a familial covenantal community, in his renewal of covenantal commands as a charter for the movement he is catalyzing, and in his transformation of the Passover meal at the "last supper" into a covenant renewal meal that is to become the central ritual binding together the communities of the expanding movement. John's working in the wilderness and his garb and living off wilderness food marks him as a new Elijah (cf. 2 Kgs 1:8; cf. Mark 9:11–13), the great prophet of the renewal of Israel. John proclaims that an even more powerful figure is coming who will baptize with the holy spirit, soon manifested in Jesus' healings and exorcisms of the ensuing narrative.

Jesus being baptized suggests that he joined the covenant renewal movement. With allusion to the calling of Israelite prophets, the cleavage of the heavens and the spirit descending and the (heavenly) voice powerfully reveal that he was specially designated by God as the prophet who will generate the wider renewal of the people. His being driven into the wilderness for forty days was his testing (by Satan, the "adversary") for his prophetic mission, as Elijah had been tested, with the divine messengers attending him.

After John was arrested, Jesus began his mission in Galilee, *proclaiming*[19] that the direct *rule of God* was at hand and people should repent and trust[20] in the good news. The pointed statement that at the outset of his mission Jesus proclaimed the kingdom/direct rule of God signals that this is the "theme" and agenda of his mission, even though the Markan narrative does not repeat the phrase "the kingdom of God" often in the rest of the story. It becomes repeatedly evident in the course of the narrative what the direct rule of God is about: the renewal of the people of Israel, as manifested in Jesus' exorcisms and healings and his renewal of the Mosaic covenant in accordance with which the people live a cooperative life of social-economic justice. The narrative then alludes to Elijah's calling of Elisha as his protege, when Jesus immediately "calls" proteges to recruit people into the movement. Like Elisha, they left everything behind to assist in the renewal the people of Israel. The hearers moreover, would have known that Elijah's-Elisha's mission had included healing.

First Narrative Step

At noted in chap. 1, the first major narrative step in the story is a sequence of exorcism, healings, summaries of exorcisms and healings, and closely related episodes all embedded in the "life-world" of Jesus' mission among the Galilean villagers. The narrative maintains a close connection between healing/exorcism and proclamation in the sequence of episodes from the very beginning. In the first action of his mission, in Capernaum, he *taught* and immediately *cast out a possessing spirit*. Not only do proclaiming the direct rule of God and teaching and casting out spirits

19. Manuscripts differ on the wording here, some including "the gospel," others "the gospel of God," both of which seem redundant to the main statement that Jesus "proclaimed" that "the kingdom of God is at hand, repent, and trust in the gospel"— which illustrates that the manuscripts varied considerably, particularly at crucial points in the narrative.

20. The Greek *pistis/pisteuo* is standardly translated "faith/believe (in)." In modern Western culture, however, "faith/belief/believe" has a narrow meaning of religious belief or a religion that is separate from other aspects of life, particularly political-economic life. "Trust" far better conveys the more comprehensive relational meaning in the "Gospel" stories. In the Roman Empire, moreover, the Greek *pistis* and the Latin *fides* meant loyalty to the rulers and the Roman imperial order. In the letters of Paul, *pistis* should thus be translated as "loyalty" to Jesus Christ as the "Lord," instead of to Caesar. In the "Gospel" stories as well, *pistis* probably has connotations of loyalty, which is better conveyed by the translation "trust" than "faith/belief."

continue to figure prominently in subsequent episodes, but the episodes indicate a particular relationship between them. In the first episode Jesus' teaching and casting out spirits are paired. The second summary of his activities pairs proclaiming and exorcising. They are paired again when Jesus commissions the twelve disciples that he constitutes as representative of Israel (twice: in the first narrative step and again in the second) to proclaim and to have power over spirits. From the interplay of the episodes in the narrative sequence a relationship between the proclamation, teaching, and exorcism/healing begins to emerge more clearly. The proclamation refers to what is happening: the direct rule of God is at hand. Exorcism of spirits and healings are the manifestations of the direct rule of God happening among the people. The teaching further develops the people's response in trust, particularly in the renewal of the Mosaic covenant.

The same sequence of episodes indicates the life-circumstances in which the exorcisms and healings, along with the teaching, happen in the narrative. After Jesus came into Galilee proclaiming the direct rule of God, he went to Capernaum and on the sabbath entered the village assembly and taught (Mark 1:14–21). These social circumstances indicated in the first exorcism episode are those in the rest of the narrative as well.

Just as Jesus went initially into *the village of Capernaum*, so in the ensuing narrative he repeatedly taught and performed exorcisms and healings in *villages* or in *houses* in villages (referred to variously as "villages," "places" [hamlets], "towns," "[rural] regions" ruled by certain cities, and "cities").[21] Villages and households were the fundamental social forms in which people lived in Palestine, as in any traditional agrarian society (discussed in chap. 4). The site of Jesus' teaching and first exorcism was the *synagogue* in Capernaum. This is where Jesus taught and performed healings in the rest of the story as well, as indicated in summaries and subsequent episodes. In the Markan story (and the other "Gospels"), the synagogues were not ("religious") buildings, but rather the village assemblies, the gatherings of members of local communities.[22]

21. Calling a village a "city" may not be simply a projection back from cities into which the movement spread. Bethsaida, where Jesus healed a blind man (Mark 8:22–26), was a large village that Herod Philip made into one of his capitals (named for Julia, the emperor Augustus' daughter; *Ant.* 18.28, 108).

22. Archaeologists have excavated buildings in Galilean villages they identify as "synagogues." Nearly all of these are dated to late antiquity. The excavation reports and secondary literature are voluminous. It seems questionable to project back to the first century from excavated buildings dated to late antiquity.

The local assembly was the form of community cohesion as well as local governance.[23] Jesus enters the village assembly in Capernaum, as he does later in the narrative in other villages, on *the sabbath*. Although village assemblies may have gathered more often, they customarily came together at least on the sabbath.

That Jesus *taught as one with authority, and not as the scribes* indicates the dominant conflict in the overall story as well as in Jesus' principal activity of exorcism and healing. In Israelite society in Roman Palestine those who supposedly held and wielded authority were the high priests in Jerusalem and the scribes and Pharisees as their representatives. At the very outset of the narrative the people—and the audience as well—recognize that Jesus is bringing life-giving power to them. Then in several of the healing episodes, the Beelzebul controversy, and the interspersed episodes, the scribes and/or Pharisees, who have "come down from Jerusalem," accuse and even seek to destroy Jesus, evidently because his healing and exorcism are threatening to their authority over the people.

The First Exorcism Episode

In the midst of Jesus' teaching on the sabbath gathering of the assembly "a man with an unclean spirit" suddenly appears. This is a case not of spirit-affliction but of a man possessed by a spirit, as evident in the distinction between the man and the possessing spirit: an overwhelming outside spirit-force has taken control of the man, at least temporarily or periodically. As indicated in the pronouns, the spirit is one of many such spirits that might possess people. As discussed in chapter 5, invasive maleficent spirits had appeared in Israelite society under the increasingly violent and invasive Hellenistic and Roman imperial rule. While scribal circles such as the Qumran community had developed a more systematic view of opposed camps of spirits (see chap. 5), in popular circles spirit-possession was more *ad hoc*, as in this episode in the Capernaum assembly and subsequent exorcism episodes in the Markan story. In contrast with two later episodes of spirit-possession (5:1–20; 9:14–29), this episode does not identify any particular symptoms of the possession, other than the spirit's crying out against Jesus whom it recognizes as a threat: "What have you to do with us? Have you come to destroy us?" It seems that the

23. References and discussion in Horsley, *Galilee*, chap. 10; and Horsley, *Archaeology, History, and Society*, 145–53.

presence of Jesus in the assembly, a prophet who has come in from outside the community, has evoked the sudden manifestation of the spirit's possession of the man, who would presumably have been a member of the community.[24]

The encounter is between the possessing spirit and Jesus. While it is not clear whether the members of the assembly are privy to this, the hearers of the story certainly are (and already familiar with the basic story, they know that Jesus would exorcize the spirit). In this first episode of such an encounter between a spirit and Jesus, the spirit accuses him of having the power to "destroy" spirits, as "the holy one of God." This was not a "messianic title," as sometimes claimed.[25] It was rather a reference to a prophet, such as Elijah or his protege Elisha, who were called "a/ the man of God" when they healed young people in the popular cycle of Elijah-Elisha stories that had been taken up into the books of Kings (1 Kgs 17; 2 Kgs 4:9, 21–37). The implication of the spirit's identification of Jesus is that he will subdue possessing spirits generally, as confirmed in the ensuing summary passages that he "cast out many *daimonia.*"

Jesus' response to the spirit's outcry is sharp and brief in the extreme.[26] The usual translation, that Jesus "rebuked" the spirit is not strong and sharp enough to render the Greek term *epitiman* and its equivalent, *ga'ar*, in Qumran and other Judean scribal texts.[27] The translation "rebuke" may be appropriate for the prophetic vision of Satan as heavenly accuser of the high priest Joshua: "the Lord rebuke you, O Satan" (Zech 3:2). But something stronger is necessary for Abram's or God's subjection

24. In the manifestation of the possession being evoked by the presence of the exorcist this episode resembles what happened in the *zar* cult in the Sudan (discussed in chap. 3).

25. There is no indication in the written texts later included in the Hebrew Bible that this was a "messianic title": an anointed king was not expected to be a healer or exorcist.

26. This episode resists the attempts of earlier form-critics to explain the origin of the "miracle stories" as patterned after stories of miracles and magic (including exorcisms) from (largely later) Hellenistic texts: it does not use what have been claimed are the standard Hellenistic terms in exorcism, such as when the exorcist (or "magician") supposedly declares "I adjure (*horkizo*) you!" Later in the story, Mark 5:7, it is the spirit who "adjures" Jesus not to torment it. The episode also does not use the usual term for exorcism in Mark's story, "cast(ing) out" (*ekballein;* 1:34, 39; 3:15, 22; 6:13; 9:18).

27. In several psalms, for example, *ga'ar/epitiman* appears parallel to strong language, such as "blot out, root out, destroy, vanquish, trample, stun, make perish," in appeals to YHWH/God as a Warrior coming in judgment against foreign monarchies or imperial regimes who conquer Israel and take spoil (e.g., Pss 9:6; 68:31; 78:6; 80:16).

of afflicting spirits in the Genesis Apocryphon from Qumran (1QGA) and especially for a fragment of the War Rule (1QM 14:9–11, as supplemented from 4Q491):

> During all the mysteries of his [Belial's] malevolence he has not made us stray from thy covenant. You have driven his spirits [of destruction] far from [us] (*ga'ar*). You have preserved the soul of your redeemed [when . . .] of his dominion [. . .]. (Vermes translation, adapted)

While the spirit cries out in fear of being "destroyed," there is nothing in this episode or other exorcisms in the Markan story that suggests that Jesus destroyed possessing spirits. More appropriate to the term in Israelite tradition would be "subdue" or "defeat" or "overpower."[28] Jesus subdued (the spirit), saying, "Be Silent, and come out of him!" And this fits well the implication in the narrative sequence that the direct rule of God is being manifested or established in Jesus' casting out possessing spirits.

Besides being sharp, Jesus' response to the spirit is brief. Not only does he use no incantation or adjuration or special material or special technique. This episode in the Markan story presents a contrast with Eleazar's use of a ring (of Solomon) to draw the spirit out through the nose in Josephus' account that places this exorcisms directly in scribal tradition of Solomon as the fountainhead of scribal wisdom and technique (quoted in chap. 5). In their more ad hoc experience of spirit possession, with no training in scribal lore, Galilean and other peasants may not have known of figures such as Eleazar. Jesus in this episode simply utters the brief but powerful command: "Be silent, and come out!" This is performative speech, a command that effects what it commands. Because the spirit had taken possession of the man, however, and was resisting expulsion, it convulsed him; but, crying with a loud voice, it came out of him. The result of the encounter is that Jesus subdued the spirit, casting it out of the man, who was thus freed from possession. In contrast with Christian theological reading, the episode does not glorify Jesus, there is no "christology" and no mention of agency by God or the Holy Spirit.[29] Rather the focus is on Jesus' forceful verbal action, at which the assembly members are astounded. "What is this? A new teaching, with authority."

---

28. This discussion is adapted from Horsley, *Hearing the Whole Story*, 137–38, which leans heavily on Kee, "Terminology of Mark's Exorcism Stories."

29. Like other exorcisms in the Gospels, this one does not qualify as a miracle according to the modern definition, discussed in chap. 2 above.

As the people exclaim, in casting out the possessing spirit, Jesus was acting with power/authority for the people—in contrast with the scribal representatives of the temple-state. And his action is not separate from his
teaching—again rooted in Israelite tradition, in which teaching (torah)
was the articulation of the will or direct rule of God for the life of the
people.[30]

The final statement in the episode—"And his fame immediately
spread everywhere throughout the whole surrounding countryside of
Galilee"—is yet another way in which the episode exemplifies and prepares the way for the rest of the Markan story of exorcism and healing.
The hearers of the story already know that the fame of Jesus' exorcisms
and healings had spread far beyond the countryside of Capernaum. But
it all began (supposedly) with this exorcism in the Capernaum assembly.
And the fame of the exorcist and healer that began with reports and rumors is a crucial aspect of the effectiveness of Jesus in subsequent healing
and exorcism by generating the trust with which people came to Jesus in
expectation of exorcism and healing. It was thus also a crucial factor in
the generation and expansion of a movement. Implicit in this episode is
that the spread of his fame was the result of interaction between Jesus and
the members of the assembly who witnessed the exorcism. The people
were already exhibiting their excitement about and confidence in his
powers, which the story later identifies explicitly as trust (*pistis*).

First Healing and First Summaries

In the first healing episode, that of Simon' mother-in-law, the disciples
(and the audience) already know that Jesus can also perform healing:
they tell him that she is suffering with a fever, implicitly suggesting that
he heal her. In contrast with modern medicine, in which fever is often
understood as a symptom of something else, in this episode fever is understood as an intrusive agent: "the fever left her."[31] In this healing Jesus

---

30. In contrast to modern academics in which teaching is distinguished from action, as exemplified in the passing comment by Donahue and Harrington, *Gospel of
Mark*, 79, that Mark contains "little teaching and is rather a gospel of action" and, in
the programmatic procedure of the Jesus Seminar in analyzing the teaching and the
actions of Jesus in separate projects (and volumes).

31. We do not have access to the understanding of fever in popular circles. References in extant ancient medical and other literature suggest ambiguous constructions
that were not mutually exclusive: a common somatic illness, a result of spirit possession,

exhibits no technique, utters no special words, but simply takes her by the hand and raises her up (as he does again in subsequent episodes).[32]

The two summaries that follow (1:32–34, 35–39) dramatize that the word has spread widely about his healing and exorcism "with authority (power)." His fame had evoked people's trust so that "they brought him all who were sick or possessed by spirits . . . and he healed many . . . and cast out many *daimonia*."[33] The second summary has Jesus state the agenda of his mission clearly: he is headed into the neighboring towns to pursue the purpose that he "came out" to do. So "he went throughout Galilee, proclaiming the message (of the direct rule of God) in their village assemblies and casting out *daimonia* (disordering spirits that had possessed people)."

Healing the Man with Skin Lesions

Just as Jesus' exorcism empowered renewal of personal and community life for the people, in contrast to the scribes from Jerusalem, so his healing of the man with skin lesions is the first in a sequence of healings-with-community-renewal that bypassed, hence was a challenge to, the prerogatives of the temple-state.

The term *lepros/lepra* (like the Hebrew equivalent *saraʾath* in Lev 13–14) referred not to what is considered leprosy today (Hansen's disease), but to a variety of skin lesions or irregularities.[34] A person with

---

and/or divine punishment, as laid out by Cook, "In Defense of Ambiguity." With "Jesus rebuked the fever," Luke 4:38–39, suggests the fever involved spirit-affliction.

32. Wainwright, *Women Healing*, 110–11, suggests that Simon's mother-in-law "serving them" (imperfect verb of continuing action) after her healing may indicate her continuing service in the movement, and not just a return to the customary role of women.

33. It is important to counter the misleading translations of the Markan text in these summaries. As discussed in chapter 3, the terms "disease" and "cure" suggest the narrowly focused definition of many illnesses and their treatment in modern biomedicine. The Greek terms and phrases have a broader sense of "those who were sick with various illnesses." The term "demon" in Anglophone culture has ominous connotations that are simply not inherent in the Greek cognate term *daimonion*, which is a synonym for "unclean spirit" in Mark. To avoid connotations not inherent in the text, it may be best simply to transliterate *daimonion/-a* where it appears. Also, there is no equivalent in the Greek text of the English term "evil" that often creeps into translations of *daimonion* in the Markan text.

34. See Weissenrieder, *Images of Illness*, 133–38 and 165–67, respectively, for review of scholarly interpretation and for conclusions based on an extensive critical

such lesions was considered "unclean" and was excluded from normal social interaction for the duration of the illness. "Clean/cleansed/cleansing" referred to the healing of the *lepra* (Mark 1:40–42), but was also used in reference to the declaration of a priest, after inspecting the symptoms, that the person was "clean" (or still "unclean"), and to the ritual of purification and sacrifices for atonement (Mark 1:44).[35] Even though non-literate, the people likely knew that the authoritative (written) texts of the temple-state included instructions about the social quarantine of people with skin-lesions, priestly inspections, and multiple sacrifices to be brought to the priests for purification and atonement (Leviticus 13–14). The prescribed sacrifice for such purification was two unblemished male lambs and an unblemished year-old ewe lamb, plus an offering of cereal and oil, after which a priest would purify the person, while retaining possession of the meat. Few families would have possessed such economic resources. Such a sacrifice would have ruined most families economically. For the poor the reduced rate was one male lamb and two turtledoves or pigeons—still a serious burden (though we have no information about the temple-state's enforcement of these requirements).

The man with the skin lesions comes to Jesus with trust that he can heal, an important factor in this and other healings. "If you choose (to do so), you have the power to make me clean." Jesus responds immediately by reaching out with touch and in simple performative speech, "be made clean."[36] In this episode Jesus is acting in accordance with Israelite tradition, in which healing is done by a prophet, not a priest (1 Kgs 17:17–24; 2 Kgs 4:17–37; 30:7 // Isa 38:2; for skin lesions, cf. 2 Kgs 5). A few terms in the episode, however, make the motivation and action unclear to modern readers/hearers. Some manuscripts (hence performances) have Jesus acting out of "anger" instead of "compassion" (1:41; was the latter term a softening in some manuscripts/performances?). Does Jesus "groan deeply" and "expel" the man in anger (1:44) after responding to his trust that he can make him clean (1:41)? Jesus' healing the fellow clearly bypasses

---

survey of the key terms in Greek medical texts.

35. That cleansing of the *lepros/lepra* referred to the healing and cannot be reduced to a ritual is indicated in the list of what is happening in Jesus' mission in Luke (Q) 7:22, where "*leproi* are cleansed" stands parallel to other healings, such as "the lame walk, . . . the deaf hear."

36. Given the general lack of evidence for concrete practice, there is no basis for claiming that "touch was a characteristic magical technique used by Jesus," vs. Crossan, *Historical Jesus*, 323.

the priestly prerogative and appears to make moot the requirement of costly sacrifices. His commanding the man "to make the offering that Moses commanded for his cleansing" after all "as a witness to them" thus appears to be a challenge to (or a facetious comment?), rather than compliance with, the authority of the temple-state that drained away resources from the people.[37] As in subsequent episodes, the healed man disobeys Jesus and rushes out to proclaim and spread the word. He helps generate the renewal of the people that is happening in response to Jesus' healing and exorcism.

Healing the Paralytic and Forgiveness of Sin

Jesus' return to Capernaum, where many gathered around, after he went throughout Galilee proclaiming the message in their assemblies and casting out demons, signals a growing movement. The Markan story portrays Jesus not as an itinerant teacher who occasionally does a healing, but as a prophet engaged in exorcism and healing and generating a movement that quickly spreads throughout northeastern Galilee and into nearby areas from its beginning and base in Capernaum.[38] He returns "home" again toward the end of the first narrative step where the scribes accuse him of having Beelzebul. The audience, who already knew the story, would have been anticipating the next step of the narrative in which, after extending the movement of healing into the villages of the Decapolis, of Tyre, and of Caesarea Philippi, he again returned to Capernaum (9:33) before moving through Judea and up to his faceoff with the rulers in Jerusalem.

That the paralyzed man was being carried to be healed by a dedicated local support network illustrates how in many societies most illness were dealt with by family and friends. Their bold action in lowering the fellow through the roof into the presence of Jesus indicates their strong trust in the power working through him. They also indicate how Jesus' healings are not individual acts by an individual practitioner,[39] but rela-

---

37. The political conflict in the episode is discerned by Crossan, *Historical Jesus*, 323, along with many others.

38. It is often claimed, especially by interpreters who work from sayings and "miracle stories" separated from the overall Markan story, that the exorcisms and healings were merely occasional incidents in the ad hoc wanderings of Jesus. The Gospel tells a different story.

39. Thus fitting the modern construction of magic, as in Crossan, *Historical Jesus*, 324.

tional events that happen in interaction, not simply between the person seeking healing and Jesus, but also between the sick person's wider circle of supporters and Jesus. Jesus heals in response to and is enabled by their trust ("when he saw their trust," 2:5). It is pertinent to the trust of the supporters in this case that healing of "the lame'" figured prominently in prophetic visions of the future restoration or renewal of the people (Isa 35:6; Jer 31:8; Mic 4:7; Zeph 3:19; the gist of these prophecies would probably have been known by villagers, although not in the exact wording that we know from our translated Bibles.

"When he saw their trust," Jesus declared to the paralytic simply, "Son, your sins are forgiven." This is another act of "performative" speech that enacts what it pronounces, as when a judge declares someone "innocent" of charges. The declaration that the man's sins are forgiven goes straight to the heart of the understanding of illness in Israelite culture. In the course of generations of social-religious practice, what were originally rhetorical sanctions in the Covenant structure and ceremony became the basis on which sickness (as well as poverty and hunger or conquest and subjugation) was understood as divine punishment for sin, collectively and transgenerationally as well as individually (as discussed in chapter 5). This belief easily became an instrument for social control. On the premise that only God could forgive sins and send healing, the temple-state claimed exclusive or at least special access to God if people brought sin-offerings to the temple. But this was next to impossible for people who were poor and/or lived at a distance. They could only continue in their self-blame, striving not to compound their sins and sicknesses.[40] In declaring to the paralytic, "Son, your sins are forgiven," Jesus was thus addressing the direct relation between the man's paralysis and the debilitating self-blame that underlay it.[41] The passive formulation, moreover, means that Jesus was pronouncing God's forgiveness. And the meaning of the term, *apheinai* in Greek, like the *shebhaq* in Aramaic that may lie behind it, has a broader sense than the English "forgive (sins)," including "set free" and "cancel debts" (as in the Lord's prayer?).[42]

---

40. As social-psychological analysis might explain, however, the considerable psychic energy devoted to self-regulation and self-blame left little for self-healing.

41. The same self-blame and social-blame for sickness and physical disability is presupposed and addressed in the account of Jesus' healing in John 9 following the disciples question, "who sinned, this man or his parents, that he was born blind."

42. See Casey, *Jesus*, 261–62.

The presence of the scribes, portrayed in their usual teaching posture as "sitting," serves to indicate that Jesus has just challenged the authority of the temple as the institution through which people can obtain forgiveness of sins.[43] They play their role in social control by insisting on the ideology that sickness is due to sins.[44] Jesus' declaration is "blasphemy! Who can forgive sins but God alone?"—since forgiveness was conditional on the prescribed sin-offering in the temple. Blasphemy was a capital crime, punishable by stoning (Lev 24:10–16), but it is unclear how that might have been enforced in Galilee that was no longer under Jerusalem's jurisdiction. It was different of course at the climax of the story in Jerusalem (anticipated here), when the high priest declared before the high priestly court that Jesus had committed blasphemy (14:53–65).

Jesus' rhetorical question in response slams the scribes as representatives of the temple-state and the transparency of their attempt at social control. Behind the Greek term *eukopoteron* = "easier," which does not quite make sense in the context of the episode, may lie the Aramaic term *qallil* = "light" (the opposite of which would have been *homer* = "heavy"), a legal term referring to laws that were of no great significance. The answer to his rhetorical question of course was "neither"! Neither pronouncing forgiveness of sins nor (a command of) healing was insignificant![45]

The rest of his response then makes explicit the direct connection between forgiveness and healing: "Your sins are forgiven" is equivalent to saying "Stand up . . and walk." His further statement that "the son of man

43. Interpreters who are still proceeding from form criticism emphasize that this episode is a composite of a healing story and a controversy story that has been "inserted" into it. Some, such as Funk et al., *Acts of Jesus*, 64, even conclude that the controversy about the forgiveness of sins reflects "the interests of the later Christian community." Regardless of whether a controversy story and a healing story are analytically separable in the composition history of the Gospel, however, sin and sickness were not separable in the Israelite culture in which both the Gospel and Jesus were rooted.

44. Among priestly-scribal circles, the Qumranites were the most rigorous about purity regulations, certainly more so than those they accused of being "smooth interpreters," presumably the Pharisees. But the strict regulations about participation in the covenanters' renewal community makes us wonder just how sympathetic any scribal-priestly group would have been to the people with illnesses and disabilities who are healed by Jesus. Excluded from the assembly, for example, were people who were paralyzed, lame, blind, deaf, dumb, or smitten with any blemish (1QSa 2.4–10; 1QM 7:4–6). Such exclusions were rooted in the regulations protecting the holiness of the priesthood and temple, as in Lev 21:16–24.

45. Casey, *Jesus*, 259–60.

has authority/power to forgive sins" is also a declaration of independence from the temple-state. After sustained scholarly debate about the meaning of the phrase "the son of man" (*bar-nasha* in Aramaic) it has become clear that even if this is a self-reference by Jesus elsewhere in the Gospel of Mark, it is here (also) a reference to "humanity" or "people" in general. Rejecting the authority of the temple-state, Jesus is stating that people among themselves (along with Jesus himself, who is called "the son of man" later in the story) have the authority to forgive sins.[46] The last command, to the paralytic, to "stand up, . . . and go home," restores the man to his family and village community, who are now presumably empowered to forgive sins and continue the healing in the community.

The next episode, about "eating with toll-collectors and sinners," further emphasizes that Jesus directs his mission to ordinary people, while mocking the scribes' diversionary concern with purity codes, according to which they viewed the people as sinners. The "punchline" of the episode ("those who are well do not need a physician . . . I came to call . . . the sinners") reinforces the direct connection between Jesus' healing and forgiveness of sins as well as the focus of his mission on healing.

Healing on the Sabbath and the Sabbath Restoration of the People

Two episodes later the Pharisees again serve as the foil in paired episodes focused on observance of the sabbath. This is an important issue insofar as the Markan narrative has Jesus perform many of the exorcisms and healings in local assemblies on the sabbath, when whole communities would be gathered. As indicated at several points in books later included in the Hebrew Bible, the sabbath was perhaps the prime symbol of life in Israelite society, its observance commanded by one of the "ten words," principles of social-economic relations in the Mosaic covenant. Labor, of course, was necessary to produce a subsistence living. The commandment to observe rest on the seventh day protected people from the excessive exploitation of their labor by the wealthy and powerful which would diminish their life and leave them hungry. Rest from labor on the seventh day was observed partly in remembrance of the exodus liberation of the people's life from hard bondage under Pharaoh.

---

46. That this is implicit in this Markan episode is confirmed by being made explicit in the Matthean version, where the crowds "glorified God, who had given such authority/power to human beings/people."

The Pharisees challenge the disciples for plucking grain on the sabbath, which they insist is not lawful. In Israelite tradition snacking on the ripe standing grain in someone's field was allowed, but not harvesting it with a sickle, which would have been theft (cf. Deut 23:25). Almost mocking the supposedly literate Pharisees, Jesus asks them "Have you not read . . . ?" and then tells a (popular) version (different from the scribal text that we have inherited in our critically established text of 1 Sam 21:1–6; 2 Sam 15:35) of the story of the brash young bandit-chieftan David and his men when they were hungry: they ate the bread off the altar, obviously giving hunger priority over the sacredness of bread reserved for priests. Then Jesus re-declares the purpose of the sabbath commandment: "the sabbath was made for humankind (the generic *anthropos* in Greek), and not humankind for the sabbath."[47]

As if to dramatize that principle,[48] Jesus heals "a human" (*anthropos*) with a withered hand who was in the village assembly on the sabbath.[49] Again the healing is not a private individual matter, but happens midst the whole community gathered on the sabbath. In the Markan story, this healing becomes a key point in the escalating struggle between Jesus and the scribes and Pharisees (and the Jerusalem rulers whom they represent).[50] "They kept him under surveillance to see if he would heal the man on the sabbath." Rising to the bait, Jesus commands the human to "rise to the center" where he would be the focus of attention in the village assembly (the term "rise" is key in other healings). Then he mocks them and their (ostensibly) restrictive sabbath regulations: "Is it lawful to do good or to do harm on the sabbath, to save life of to kill?" The violation

47. Jesus' discourse following his healing of the sick man on the Sabbath in John 5:1–24 elaborates on the same point, so it was not idiosyncratic to the Jesus movement addressed by the Markan story.

48. Jesus' "punchline" insists that "the sabbath was made for humankind/people (*ho anthropos*), not people (*ho anthropos*) for the sabbath—which would have been the understanding of God's creation in Israelite popular tradition rooted both in the creation story and in the reason for observing the sabbath (rest from labor, esp. the "had labor" Israel had experienced in Egypt).

49. Evidently village assemblies in Galilee did not exclude people with blemishes, such as lame legs or withered hands, as did the priestly-scribal assembly at Qumran (1QSa 2:4–10; 1QM 7:4–6).

50. Christian theological interpreters such as Funk et al., *Acts of Jesus*, 69; and Meier, *Mentor, Message, and Miracles*, 682, still take the dispute about Sabbath observance as reflecting "Christian" concerns. The Markan story, however, gives no indication that either Judaism or Christianity existed yet, much less that there was a division between them.

of particular prohibitions is less the issue than the general conflict over sabbath observance articulated in Jesus' rhetorical question.

In this healing the angry Jesus then does no work (on the sabbath), not even a touch or a word of healing, but simply commands "the human" to extend his hand. His trust is implicit; no need to state it explicitly. The Pharisees were silenced. Threatened by the expanding renewal of the people in Jesus' exorcisms and healings, however, these representatives of the temple-state began to conspire with the Herodians, representatives of the ruler of Galilee, to destroy him.

The Markan story thus repeatedly presents Jesus' exorcism and healing as responding to the people's plight—invaded by hostile spirits, paralyzed literally and figuratively by their internalization of sin and guilt. In (connection with) his therapeutic acts he gives the people a new lease on life under the direct rule of God, restoring people to their community, declaring that they have authority to forgive sins and that the sabbath rest was established for the renewal of human life. Doing these life-restoring actions also involves bypassing or displacing the functions of the temple-state and rejection of the official regulations and their debilitating effects. The community(ies) hearing the story, deeply familiar with Israelite tradition, would have known—would have been experiencing—that Jesus was renewing the people.

Expansion of the Movement and Appointing the Twelve

In the ensuing summary the movement has expanded from "a great multitude" from Galilee to include "a great multitude" from Judea, Jerusalem, Idumea, beyond the Jordan, and the region around Tyre and Sidon (anticipating the expansion of the movement into areas beyond Galilee in the next major narrative step). They had heard what he was doing in healing *many* (*polloi*, suggestive of the common people looked down upon by the elite, as well as of a great number), so that those plagued by illnesses (*mastigai*, "plagues") pressed upon him to touch him, and the unclean spirits fell down before him.

In appointing the *twelve* on the *mountain* Jesus then gives more explicit social-political form to the expanding movement that was already suggested in the many references to Israelite tradition: this is the renewal of Israel that traditionally consisted of twelve tribes; and the mountain suggests Mt. Sinai, where Israel first formed into a cohesive people in the Mosaic Covenant. Jesus' sending out the twelve here to extend his own mission "to proclaim (the message of the rule of God) and to have authority/power to cast out *daimonia*" anticipates the fuller commission later in the story.

The Scribes' Charge of Beelzebul and Jesus' Refutation

The first narrative step of the Markan story of Jesus climaxes in Jesus' response to the scribes' accusation that he is possessed by Beelzebul and is casting out *daimonia* by the ruler of the *daimonia*.[51] In a narrative device typical of the Markan story, Jesus' response to the scribes' charge is framed by a related episode that sets it up and then concludes this narrative step focused on exorcism and healing. The crowd is (again) clamoring around the house he had entered, which evokes the concern "of those around him" that he is astounded (or perhaps overwhelmed).[52] Then, at the end of the double-episode and the first narrative step in the story, the appearance of Jesus' mother and brothers serve as a foil for his first declaration of the renewal of covenantal community.

In approaching the "Beelzebul" accusation and his response it is important to free ourselves of what became the standard scholarly construct of "Jewish apocalypticism" that has determined the reading not only of "the Beelzebul controversy" but often of the whole Gospel of Mark and of theological interpreters' construction of Jesus mission. In the "apocalyptic" construct of the Markan story and of Jesus' mission, God and Satan (the personified agent of evil) and his evil demons were locked in a cosmic struggle for control of people and the world. In the fuller form,

51. As noted before, *daimonia* should not be translated with the English cognate "demons." The meaning of the term, which ranges from divine beings to beneficent to ambiguous to maleficent spirits, needs to be determined from immediate and broader contexts. My provisional approach is to transliterate and work from the contexts.

52. The text at the beginning of this double episode is difficult to ascertain and understand. That "he went into the house" must refer to the house in Capernaum (as in 2:1–12; vs. his "hometown" Nazareth, in 6:1–6). The main reason translators think that "those around him" are his family is the sudden appearance of his mother and brothers, the narrative foil for his declaration about "whoever does the will of God." In the rest of the Markan narrative and in the other Gospel texts the verb *existemi* refers to people's utter astonishment at the "(acts) of power(s) that Jesus is doing. The uncertain text at this point hardly provides a basis for the translation that Jesus was "out of his mind," much less that he himself was possessed or that he was in some "alternative state of consciousness."

articulated influentially over a century ago by Albert Schweitzer, the Jews and particularly Jesus himself were convinced that the struggle would end soon in an "apocalyptic scenario" of the Great Tribulation, Last Judgment, and End of the world in "cosmic catastrophe."[53]

Ironically, Judean "apocalyptic" texts do not attest any such "apocalyptic scenario," much less the imminent End of the world.[54] Rather, as discussed in chapter 5, late second-temple Judean scribal texts such as Daniel 10–12, the "Enochic" Book of Watchers and Animal Vision, and the book of Jubilees explained imperial military invasion and economic exploitation as the results of rebel heavenly forces in the divine governance of the world. In some passages the rebel forces have a leader or "prince," although his role is not particularly prominent. The most systematic explanation of how history has run amock comes in Qumran texts in which people are caught in a struggle between two hordes of superhuman heavenly forces, the spirits of light and the spirits of darkness, headed by Belial. The construct of a cosmic struggle between God and Satan is a modern scholarly oversimplification of such texts. The imposition of this construct distorts the Markan story in general and the Beelzebul controversy in particular.

In the Markan story so far the scribes and Pharisees, representatives of the temple-state who "came down from Jerusalem," have challenged Jesus' healing of the people, accused him of blasphemy, and, after the sabbath healing, begun conspiring to destroy him. Now they bring an even more serious charge (the equivalent of the combination of apostasy and subversion by conspiring with the enemy): "He has (is possessed by) Beelzebul" and "he is casting out *daimonia* by the ruler of the *daimonia*."[55] Judging from Jesus' restatement of the (second) charge, they view "Satan" as the ruler of the *daimonia*. Neither in the preceding nor in the subsequent narrative does the Markan story give us reason to imagine that Jesus shares the viewpoint of the scribes and Pharisees. Rather the Markan Jesus repeatedly challenges their views. In order to understand how the

---

53. Summary of the classic statement of "Jewish apocalypticism" and the "apocalyptic scenario" by Albert Schweitzer and Rudolf Bultmann in Horsley, *Prophet Jesus and Renewal*, chap. 1.

54. See the deconstruction of "apocalypticism" and the "apocalyptic scenario" in Horsley, *Prophet Jesus and Renewal*, chaps. 3–4.

55. In the version of the charge that appears parallel in Matthew (12:24) and Luke (11:15), hence probably from Q, these charges are collapsed into one: "He casts out *daimonia* by Beelzebul, the ruler of the *daimonia*."

Markan story resonated with its audience, we should not imagine that Jesus shares the scribal way of thinking in which their charges are rooted.[56]

Critical probing into the derivation of the name Beelzebul finds that it preserves "the name of an old Canaanite god, meaning 'Baal, the Prince,' or 'Baal of the Exalted Abode.'"[57] It is rooted in Judean scribal polemics against *Ba'al*, "Lord Storm" (and other deities of rival regimes) as known from texts later included in the Hebrew Bible.[58] In Judean scribal theology (cosmology) Beelzebul, the cultural descendant of *Ba'al*, would have been a threatening force in opposition to "the Most High" (God), the ultimate heavenly ruler of the world. The scribes, the professional representatives of the high priestly rulers down from Jerusalem, are thus charging that Jesus himself was possessed by a rival god utterly unacceptable and rejected in the ideology of the temple-state.

It also seems clear from the dialogue in the episode that Satan as "the ruler of the *daimonia*" is the scribes' conception (as Jesus asks them, rhetorically, "How can Satan, a.k.a. the ruler of the *daimonia*, cast out Satan?"). Satan, "the adversary," appears rarely in books later included in the Hebrew Bible: as the member of the heavenly council who tests Job in the wisdom tale of Job 1–2 and as the prosecutor in the divine court in Zech 3:1; but nowhere as ruler of the spirits. Similarly Satan appears rarely in the Markan story: as the agent who tests Jesus in his wilderness preparation for his mission as a prophet, as the agent who blocks the effectiveness of the "word" sown by the sower in the explanation of the parable, and as the tempter who makes Peter misunderstand Jesus as the messiah who would avoid arrest and execution. Elsewhere in the synoptic Gospel tradition as well, Satan (like "the devil") appears seldom, mainly in the role of tempter—and is not even associated with (other, unclean) spirits. Only in the scribal charge of Beelzebul does Satan appear as the ruler of *daimonia*, which suggests that the representation of Satan in this role comes from the scribes' charge.

56. Ironically, the evidently "Christian" intellectuals who further elaborated the Judean scribal lore evident in the Book of Watchers in producing the later Testament of Solomon portray Solomon as practicing more or less what the Judean scribes accuse Jesus of doing: gaining power over the maleficent spirits/demons by Beelzebul the prince/ruler of demons (Test. Sol. 1–3). Far from using them to exorcize possessing spirits (as the scribes accuse Jesus of doing), however, "Solomon" uses them in the construction and lavish adornment of his temple.

57. Fitzmyer, *Luke*, 2.920.

58. Beelzebul was part of scribal tradition, not the popular or "little" tradition, vs. Crossan, *Historical Jesus*, 319.

Not all scribes, of course, shared the same scheme of the forces and spirits. "The ruler of (multiple) spirits" in the scribes' charge does not yet approach the more systematic dualism of two hordes of opposed spirits controlling human life in the Community Rule and War Scroll from Qumran. But the way spirits are understood to operate under the leadership of Mastema toward the beginning of the book of Jubilees is an intriguing possible parallel to what may be the scribes' conception in their charge against Jesus. In primordial times, rebel watchers/angels/spirits who generated the giants began wreaking havoc on earthly/human life (Jubilees 1–8; similar to the portrayal in the Book of Watchers, 1 Enoch 1–36). When God was ready to order all of them bound, Mastema, the chief of the spirits, persuaded him to leave a tenth to be subject to Satan on the earth, still causing illnesses as well as other destruction of life, such as the formation of empires, weapons and wars of conquest, ruling cities, and slavery (Jubilees 10–11). Thereafter in Jubilees, however, Mastema, the chief of the spirits, operates much as Satan did in books later included in the Hebrew Bible, as a tempter and provocateur, as in the testing of Abraham (Jubilees 17–18), but not as the ruler of the spirits.

If we listen to this episode in the recognition that Jesus does not share the viewpoint of the scribes, then Jesus' response clearly has two separate steps. First he refutes the charge of the scribes. Then he articulates his more ad hoc understanding of spirits and his exorcisms. In both he is speaking "in parables," that is in metaphors or comparisons. And in both cases he may well have been alluding to recent historical events that would have lingered in the hearers' memory.

In refuting the scribes' charge that he is casting out *daimonia* by Satan, the ruler of the *daimonia*, he demonstrates their faulty "logic"—or perhaps their lack of clear thinking—by drawing out the implication of their conception of Beelzebul/Satan as a ruler. By implication, a "ruler" rules a kingdom, for which (ruling) "house" was a standing synonym.[59] If a kingdom/house were divided against itself it could not stand. According to their charge, Satan was defeating his own rule. In recent memory

59. He draws on the traditional image in Israelite culture of "house," which has a range of meaning from a patriarchal household and the lineage that rules in that household to a kingdom and the dynasty that rules, for which it is a synonym here. Probably best known from earlier Israelite tradition would have been "the house of David," which rose from a local household to imperial kingship. It then became divided against itself in the rebellion led by David's son Absalom and its rule over Israel collapsed when the majority of Israelites withdrew in insurrection after the death of Solomon.

the Hasmonean "house" that had expanded its kingdom to rule over Samaria and Galilee became "divided against itself" in civil war between rival claimants and was conquered by the Romans. It is not quite clear whether Jesus is arguing that surely Satan would not be rising up against himself or is arguing, more subtly and cleverly, that on the scribes' own assumption they should not be concerned since, if Satan is risen up against himself (as they charge), his rule must be collapsing.

Jesus then shifts to his own, evidently more popular way of understanding of spirits and his own exorcism of spirits that had invaded and possessed people. He uses an extended (narrated) metaphor that cannot be subsumed into a dualistic worldview of two opposing "cosmic" forces. His casting out of invasive possessing spirits is like plundering the goods in a powerful man's house, which is possible only after first tying up the powerful man. There appears to be no basis in this extended metaphor for equating "the strong man" with "Satan," "the prince of demons." Perhaps because Jesus has declared, as the theme of the Markan story, that "the kingdom of God is at hand," scholarly interpreters tend to project a corresponding "kingdom of Satan" and then conclude that Jesus is declaring in his response to the scribes' charge that in his exorcisms Satan' kingdom is being defeated in a "cosmic" struggle.[60] In the extended metaphor of the strong man's house/goods, Jesus' response does not suggest this. Rather the exorcisms should be understood as if Jesus were plundering "vessels" from the (supposedly large, fortified) house of a powerful man. The hearers of the Markan story would very likely have remembered the popular revolts against Herodian and Roman rule in 4 BCE, when both in Sepphoris (in Galilee) and in Jericho the insurgents broke into the royal fortresses and "plundered" the goods that had been seized and taken there. Jesus' more ad hoc, popular way of thinking about spirits and exorcism is evident again in the restatement of what the scribes had

---

60. Some theological interpreters, such as Wright, *Jesus*, 451–54, taking the metaphor/parable of the binding of the strong man and plundering his goods as an allegory referring to Jesus' successful cosmic combat with (the) Satan, claim that the temptation by the devil must have been the occasion of Jesus' victory over Satan (a common interpretation). Others who assume the cosmic battle between kingdoms exercise at least some critical caution about some of its aspects: Twelftree, *Jesus the Exorcist*, 112, notes that the temptation narratives offers "little support for the notion of the defeat of Satan"; Dunn, *Jesus Remembered*, 455–61, thinks it clear that "the strong man" would have been "an image for Satan," but cautions against pressing the imagery of Mark 3:27 (binding the strong man etc.) as though it were allegorical in every detail (460n371).

charged, that "he has an unclean spirit" (which by implication is denied as scribal blasphemy).

The crowd now "sitting around him" informs Jesus that his "mother and brothers and sisters" are asking for him. He responds that "those who do the will of God," that is, those who keep the Mosaic covenantal torah that articulated God's will for Israel, are his mother and siblings, that is his renewed familial community. In a context in which family and village community (the fundamental social forms of Israelite society) were disintegrating under the pressures of conquest, taxes, debts, etc., he is generating a renewal of covenantal community in familial form—which he states more extensively and explicitly later as he completes his mission in village communities and heads toward confrontation in Jerusalem.[61]

Second Narrative Step (4:35—8:22/26)

The resumed narrative following the speech in parables includes two series of Jesus' "acts of power" (*dynameis*) that flow in more or less the same sequence of sea-crossing, exorcism, healing, (healing,) wilderness feeding (healing).[62] It is particularly striking that there are two such series that each include an episode that alludes to the stormy sea crossing in the exodus and an episode that clearly refers to the feeding in the wilderness. This suggests that at an early stage in the development of the fuller Markan story Jesus' healings and exorcisms were being presented as actions in the renewal of the people of Israel. The more fully developed Markan story, in narrative sequence as well as substance, then elaborates on how Jesus as a prophet like Moses and Elijah is generating a renewal of Israel manifested in exorcisms and healings framed by the sea-crossings and wilderness feedings of a new exodus. Hearers familiar with Israelite tradition would have sensed this in the first major narrative step. The second major narrative step makes it unmistakable.

---

61. It is pertinent to note that in many movements of renewal and resistance—e.g., the civil rights movement in the US—the participants refer to one another as "brothers" and "sisters." In his letters, Paul uses the masculine term *adelphoi* in reference to the members of the assemblies. Also in communities under attack and hardship, orphans are often taken in or otherwise supported by remaining families; the lines between households are often flexible, including in response to outside pressures.

62. In the second series the second healing comes after the wilderness feeding so that the healing of the blind man both completes the second step and begins the third step in the narrative.

While modern readers unacquainted with the circumstances of ancient village life in Galilee and nearby areas may not immediately "get it," the intervening episodes are not mere insertions, but serve to flesh out the renewal of the people happening in the "acts of power." The ineffectiveness of the prophet's acts of power in his hometown because of lack of trust (6:1–6a) forms a contrast with the preceding healings of the women enabled by people's trust. The commissioning of the twelve (6:6b–13) expands the renewal of the people in exorcism and healing. The transition to the episode of Herod's execution of John makes explicit that Jesus is operating as a prophet like Elijah, John, and others through whom healing powers were at work. Herod's beheading of John exemplifies the opposition of the rulers to such prophets of renewal and resistance; *and* the lavish royal banquet made possible by expropriation of the people's produce sets up the new Moses' wilderness feeding of the hungry people (6:17–29, 30–44). Following the second sea-crossing, Jesus' condemnation of the Pharisees' *qorban* device to siphon away to the temple the people's resources needed to support families locally, leaving the people undernourished (hence susceptible to sickness, 7:1–13), is juxtaposed with both healings and another wilderness feeding of hungry people. All of these episodes articulate and exemplify aspects of the people's sickness and renewal in healing.

The Exorcism and Healings in the First Sequence of Acts of Power

Following Jesus' speech in parables to the crowd on the shore of the sea, he and disciples crossed to the other side in a boat. When a threatening storm arose at sea, Jesus "rebuked/subdued" the wind and commanded the sea, "Quiet! Be Still." Given the announcement of "the (liberative new exodus) way of the Lord" at the beginning of the Markan story, this crossing, with a great storm on the sea (as in the age-old "Song of the Sea," Exodus 15:1–18), and Jesus calming the storm so that they reach the other side safely, represents a new exodus.[63]

63. In the "calming of the storm" some interpreters find Jesus stepping into the role of God subduing the Sea/Chaos patterned after the ancient Canaanite monarchies' myth of cosmic origins, a myth that appears in only slightly adapted form in the enthronement psalms sung to authorize the Jerusalem monarchy (e.g., Pss 24; 29; 89). But such elite culture does not fit the Markan story of the prophet like Moses and Elijah engaged in the renewal of the people.

It has been suggested that this episode of the storm at sea "virtually paraphrases"

On the other side Jesus again worked in the countryside, now the territory ruled by one of the cities of the Decapolis, the "ten-cities" area just South and East of Galilee (Gerasa, in most manuscripts, is far to the southeast; Gadara, in some manuscripts and the parallel in Matt 8:28 is closer). This is the first step in Jesus' expansion of his renewal of the people into villages in areas beyond Galilee—with no comment on cultural differences. Different from the first exorcism episode where the man's possession suddenly manifests itself in the midst of a village assembly, in this episode the man's possession had been recurrently or constantly evident for some time. The possessing spirit(s) had driven the man into extreme antisocial behavior, in violence against others as well as himself. To control the violence, others in the (village) community had bound him in shackles and chains, which he wrenched apart in his crazed strength. "Night and day among the tombs and mountains he was always howling and bruising himself with stones." The association of the uncontrollable possessed man (who is inseparable from the spirit that had possessed him) with destruction and death (the cemetery) could not be clearer. Even before the audience heard of the identity of the spirit, the shackles and chains would have been suggestive of the restraints that village communities may have used to ward off destructive violence and death by the occupying forces/spirits.

In the narrative it was Jesus' command, "Come out of the man, you unclean spirit," that made possible the recognition of the difference of the invasive spirit(s) from the possessed man. And, in contrast with some previous generalizations about ancient exorcists typically "adjuring" a divine spirit to gain power, it was not the exorcist Jesus, but the possessing spirit who "adjured" the exorcist by God, not to torment it.

Once the spirit came out, at Jesus' command, its identity could be established: "My name is Legion, for we are many." In the context of the

---

lines from Ps 107 [106 Heb]:23–32 that, in turn, reflect the Canaanite myth of Storm defeating Sea. This is highly unlikely, given the people's limited literacy and access to scrolls. Interestingly enough, however, Ps 107 as a whole refers to the very kinds of distress of the Israelite people and God's acts of deliverance that were prominent in Israelite tradition and also crop up, for example, in Mary's song (in Luke 1:46–55) and in other contemporary popular songs. Images of the restoration of Israel via a "straight way" with the hungry being filled with good things and people bowed down with hard labor having their bonds broken asunder are reminiscent of the exodus and wilderness way. And God raising a stormy wind and waves of the sea, but then making the storm be still, alludes to the storm at sea by means of which the Israelites escaped from bondage in Egypt, for example, in the early (popular, not scribal) Israelite "Song of the Sea," (Exod 15:1–18).

Roman conquest and control of Palestine and Syria, the identity of the spirit(s) that had been the cause of such violence is clear: "Roman troops." The possessing spirits were those of the Roman troops that had, in some cases repeatedly and with considerable brutality, destroyed villages, slaughtered and enslaved the people, plundered their goods, and crucified those suspected of leading resistance. That the spirits' name "Legion" is a reference to Roman troops is confirmed by "Legion's" pleading with Jesus not to send it/them out of the countryside that it/they had invaded and "possessed." Legion's possession of the man was also (representative of) its/their possession of the countryside (the people in their villages).[64] This is further indicated in the military imagery of what happened in the dramatic turn of events after "Legion" was identified.

The next step of the episode—and thus also in the overall Markan story as it is performed before the hearers—is also a dramatic revelation of what was happening in Jesus' exorcisms and his "(acts of) power(s)" generally as manifestations of the direct rule of God he was proclaiming for the people subjected to Roman rule. After subduing the spirit(s) Jesus had commanded them to reveal their true identity as the spirits of the "Roman troops," the violently invasive forces that had conquered and possessed the countryside and its people. The hearers, who had been directly or indirectly traumatized by violent Roman conquest, were then suddenly treated to a dialogue in which the spirits of the Roman troops that Jesus has just subdued suddenly addressed him as their commanding officer about to give them their orders. They entreated him earnestly not to expel them from the countryside they had conquered and were possessing. Imagining that they could remain in (continue to ravage) the countryside in a different form, they begged Jesus to command them to enter the *agele* (a military "company") of swine feeding on the hillside. But when the Roman troops entered/took possession of the large company of swine, they "charged" down the steep bank into the Sea (whence they had come) and were "drowned in the Sea (just as Pharaoh's troops had been drowned in the Sea in the archaic "Song of the Sea," Exod 15:4–5, 10).[65]

64. It would be difficult not to discern something analogous to what was happening among various African peoples in which many were possessed by spirits with names of invasive colonial forces, often military, such as *mapolic, maregimente, khawajat* (Europeans/Arabs), or *Lord Kromer* (discussed in the case studies in chap. 3).

65. The Greek terms *agele* (hardly appropriate for a herd of swine) was used for a band of military recruits, the term *epetrepsen* referred to a military command of dismissal, and the pigs' *hormesen* ("charge" down the bank) suggests military rushing into battle. Also the term *thalassa* has connotations of a large sea, like the Mediterranean.

The episode is thus rich with allusions to the foundational legend of the people. The spirits of Roman troops who had previously conquered and "possessed" the countryside had self-destructed.

The people of the area ("the city and the fields/countryside," 5:14), however, when they saw the possessed man in his right mind, were afraid and pleaded with Jesus to leave their region. He had disrupted the *modus vivendi* that they had established with the possessing spirit(s) whose identity turned out to be "Legion." It would have been threatening to recognize the real identity of the forces that had repeatedly done such violence to themselves and their countryside. Possession by the spirits the identity of which they ostensibly remained unaware had diverted their attention so that they did not strike out in resistance to Roman rule that would only have resulted in further destruction.[66] They had been able (more or less) to control the manifestation of possession of individual community members who became violent by restraining them with shackles and chains. Far from feeling liberated by the exorcism of the spirit(s), the people saw it as a threat to their delicately balanced adjustment to Roman imperial rule. Possession by Legion, the *spirits* of Roman troops, was a mystification of the people's concrete political-economic-social situation. But this mystification was also self-protective, keeping them from recognizing the concrete cause of their subjugation that might have led them to strike out and the Romans to retaliate with even greater violence. Moreover, focusing on the spirits as the cause of their subjugation kept them from blaming either their God or themselves. The exorcism was a sudden exposé of their concrete situation, frightening for what it might mean.

This episode of casting out the most violent of spirits and its identification as Legion followed by the people's reaction in fear is a fulcrum in the Gospel narrative, further exposing what was happening in Jesus mission of exorcism and healing and pointing forward to the climax of the story in Jesus' confrontation with the rulers. In his initial exorcism Jesus was subduing the spirits that possessed people. In this episode he evokes the revelation of the identity of (at least some of) the spirits that cause such violence among the people. This is frightening because it forces the

---

66. As noted by critical medical anthropologists, a subject people's own cultural representation of their circumstances under seemingly unchallengeable power—labeled as "unscientific" or "delusional" by liberal interpreters of Jesus and the Gospels—might well be understood as defensive, even self-protective: their "mystification" distracts attention from overwhelming destructive forces that have subjected them that it would be suicidal to oppose actively.

people to recognize that the spirits are those of the Romans who have conquered and subjugated them. This demystification of the situation points toward the climax of the story in which Jesus mounts a direct political confrontation with the rulers of the Roman imperial order in Judea—and their own continuation of the movement of resistance that has them vulnerable to suppression by the "authorities."

As he was leaving, Jesus commanded the man to return to his home and his people to announce what the Lord had done for him. He went to "proclaim the message" (*kerussein*)—just as Jesus and the twelve had been "proclaiming the message"—in the Decapolis region to the south and east of Galilee. At the end of the episode is yet another reminder that in the Markan narrative the "proclamation" focuses on the exorcisms and healings.

After this episode the hearers would have sensed that the political aspect of the Markan plot was "thickening," specifically in the sequence of exorcism episodes. In Jesus' first action in his mission in Galilee, his first exorcism, it was evident that he was subduing the spirits, restoring the people in pointed contrast with the scribal representatives of the Roman client rulers in Jerusalem. At the conclusion of the first narrative step the scribes who came down from Jerusalem, increasingly aware of his exorcism and healing as a threat to the temple-state, accused him of casting out spirits by Beelzebul/Satan, the rulers of the spirits, that is, of subverting the Roman imperial order in Palestine. After casting out the spirits possessing the fellow chained in the cemetery Jesus exposed the identity of those spirits as "Legion," Roman troops, who proceeded to self-destruct. This episode prepares and points the way toward the final narrative steps that focus explicitly on the political conflict between Jesus' mission of renewal and resistance and the (high priestly) rulers of the Roman imperial order in Palestine.

The first sequence of Jesus' (acts) of power(s) continues with the healings of the woman who had been hemorrhaging for twelve years and the twelve-year old woman that are interwoven in implications as well as in the narrative. The Markan story presents them both as concrete people who had severe sicknesses and were healed *and* (more obviously than previous cases) as figures whose sicknesses and healings were representative of key aspects of the people (Israel) and its renewal.[67]

---

67. Earlier interpreters suggested that the woman's bleeding, understood as menstrual discharge, "placed her outside the religious community" and that her bleeding and the ostensible death of the twelve-year-old made them a source of pollution to

Again the healings take place in a village, where one of the local assembly leaders begs Jesus to heal his "dear daughter," who is at the point of death. The father's plea for Jesus to "lay hands upon her," a phrase that occurs repeatedly in the Markan story (5:23; 6:5; 7:32; 8:23, 25; 10:16), expresses his and the people's trust in Jesus' power to heal and bring life with his touch. How different the episode of the hemorrhaging woman sounds from other healings in Mark is immediately audible. The description of the prolonged severity of the woman's illness is the most elaborate by far among the many healing episodes in the story. The series of feminine singular participial phrases that repeatedly end in an *-ousa* or *-sasa* sound, with other broad /a/ sounds (5:25–27) intensify the hearers' sense of her suffering and its economic consequences: "a woman suffering for twelve years, enduring much under many physicians and using up everything she had and becoming no better but worse . . ." While others seeking healing or their friends and relatives take initiatives, this woman is the sole initiator and takes bold, deliberate action. She knows that "if I but touch his clothes, I will be made well." And sure enough, the narrative attributes her healing not to Jesus but to her own deliberate action. Moreover, her healing is not attested by others, but by her own experience: "she knew in her body that she was healed of her plague" (*mastigos*, 5:29, again 5:34). While in other episodes, Jesus makes some gesture or statement of healing, here he is utterly passive. Aware only that power has gone forth from him, he learns why only at the woman's initiative, and then only confirms what she already knows: that it was her own trust that made her whole. Jesus' role is simply to comment on what has just happened: "Daughter, your trust has healed you/made you whole (*sesoken*). Go in peace, and be healed of your plague (*tes mastigos sou*)."

Meanwhile villagers announce that the "child" is dead, which prompts Jesus to reassure her father, leader of the village assembly, "Do not fear, only trust!"—what the hemorrhaging woman had just exemplified dramatically. In pointed contrast with the weeping and wailing of the

---

anyone who touched them. This set up Jesus as the hero who, fearlessly risking pollution, restored the women to purity and brought them into a religious community that was "whole, inclusive, and without boundaries." The temple-state's purity regulations (e.g., Lev 15:19–30), however, did not socially ostracize a menstruating woman or classify her touch as polluting. Nor does anything in these episodes suggest that impurity was at issue or that Jesus was challenging or overcoming any purity codes. See further Kraemer, "Jewish Women and Christian Origins"; D'Angelo, "Gender and Power in the Gospel of Mark": Cohen, "Menstruants and the Sacred," esp. 278; and Rosenblatt, "Gender, Ethnicity, and Legal Considerations."

mourners, Jesus insists that the child has not died but is only sleeping (an ambiguous statement, since "sleeping" was also a metaphor for having died). We need to listen to the connotations and nuances of the Greek and the Aramaic terms in narrative sequence in order to appreciate the significance of the healing. Taking the "child" by the hand, Jesus said (in Aramaic), *Talitha koum* (literally, "little lamb, arise," *talitha* being a term of affection for a child, cf. 2 Sam 12:1–6). The Markan narrative translates Jesus' command immediately into Greek: "Young woman (*korasion*, young woman of marriageable, hence child-bearing age), I say, arise!" (*egeirein*, "rise, rise up," with connotations of arise from sleep and rise from [the "sleep" of] death). The child of the leader of the village assembly who was at the point of death is now very much alive and presumably able to produce new life.[68]

Clearly these two women whose illnesses and healings are woven together in the Markan story are representative of the illness and healing of the people (Israel) generally. The woman who had been hemorrhaging for *twelve* years represented Israel, whose life-blood had been draining away. Her trust symbolized the people's trust in the power working through Jesus that was making them whole again. The *twelve* -year-old woman (daughter of the leader of the community assembly) who was at the point of death represented Israel in its present circumstances, that is, Jesus' healing of the people in general who are becoming alive again and ready to produce new life.

In the next episode, by contrast, the people of Jesus' hometown, where he was teaching and healing again on the sabbath in the assembly, represent those who were fascinated about his wisdom and acts of power but who did not "get it." They saw Jesus merely as a local boy, son and brother of a local family. Except for healing a few people by laying on of hands, he could do no acts of power among them—illustrating again the crucial role of people's trust in the relational healings.

Again affirming and symbolizing that the exorcisms and healings manifest the renewal of Israel, Jesus commissioned the (representative) *twelve*, with authority/power over the unclean spirits, to (help) expand his program of renewal in village communities. He instructed them to

---

68. Drawing on later rabbinic texts, Weisenrieder, *Images of Illness*, 258–59, suggests that the young woman was a virgin of marriageable age and able soon to produce children; Tal Ilan, *Jewish Women*, 69, cautions that although early marriage was common for girls, rabbinic texts offer no firm indication that twelve was the customary age.

THE MARKAN STORY 293

stay in local households, while they proclaimed that people should "re-orient themselves" (in renewal of the Mosaic covenant). Extending Jesus' work, they cast out many *daimonia* and anointed with oil many who were sickly (weak) and healed them. Considering that the social-economic-political form of Israelite society consisted of hundreds of semi-independent village communities (with village assemblies) under the rule of the temple-state, the twelve/disciples-in-mission were the inter-village infrastructure of the movement of the people undergoing renewal. Given the dominance of the Roman imperial order in the temple-state and the Tetrarchy of Antipas this movement infrastructure had no chance of becoming institutionalized, and it would not have been intended to have permanent trans-village authority. As noted above, the Markan story was opposed to the evident attempt by the leading disciples (Peter et al.) to claim such authority, while the Matthean story pointedly authorizes just this authority (see chap. 9).

The transition to the episode of Herod Antipas' beheading of John makes clear that Jesus was widely recognized as a prophet: as John raised from the dead, because of the powers at work through him, or as Elijah (the prophet of renewal who had opposed rulers and performed acts of power), or as a prophet like one of the (earlier) prophets. The story of Herod's arrest and execution of John dramatizes the fundamental opposition between the rulers and the people, particularly between the rulers and the prophets that led popular movements, as the political aspect of the conflict becomes ever more evident. Since the hearers know the outcome of the whole story, Antipas' execution of John ominously prefigures the Roman crucifixion of Jesus. Also, the hearers listening to the description of Herod's birthday banquet for "his great ones and military officers and the leading men of Galilee" (6:21–22; not "leaders") would have known only too well that it was a portion of their own crops seized as taxes that funded the cities, palaces, and lavish lifestyle of the Roman client rulers and their officers. The lavish banquet that climaxed with the execution of John also sets up the next episode.

The feeding of the five-thousand flows out of "all [the twelve] had done and taught" in their extension of Jesus' mission, as people from the towns in which they had been working ran ahead of them to the wilderness place. This episode is thick with allusions to exodus and wilderness traditions of the people's origins, as well as Elijah-Elisha traditions. The "wilderness" (used generally in reference to areas too rough to be cultivated) would immediately evoke memory of the newly liberated but hungry Israelites being fed on manna and given water from the rock (cf. Exod 16:1–36; 17:1–7; cf. Num 11:4–9; and numerous summaries of the exodus-wilderness events in Pss 78; 105; etc.). When Jesus ordered the disciples to organize them into groups on the grass, they sat down in groups "of hundreds and fifties," patterned after the tradition of Moses' organization of the people in the exodus (cf. Exod 18:10–24).[69] After Jesus had broken and distributed the five loaves and two fish, the food multiplied among the people, just as it had in the legends of Elijah and Elisha (see esp. the feeding of a hundred people with twenty barley loaves, 2 Kgs 4:42–44). When all the (5000) people were satisfied—which would have been an extremely rare experience for peasant villagers who are left perpetually hungry after the "surplus" from their crops are taken to support the lavish lifestyle of the rulers such as Herod Antipas—they gathered (the representative number of) *twelve* baskets full of leftover pieces. The renewal manifested in the healing of the two women as representatives of Israel thus continued in the wilderness feeding led by a prophet/a new Moses and Elijah. In direct opposition and contrast with the rulers who were taking subsistence food away from the people, Jesus and the movement of renewal were generating provision of food for the hungry people.

The Second Sequence of Acts of Power

In the sea-crossing that begins the second sequence of acts of power, the mere appearance of Jesus seems to calm the storm. The ensuing summary of his healings in Gennesaret along the west coast the Sea of Galilee again calls attention to the expansion of the movement, as people from the whole countryside brought the sick to him wherever he went, in villages, "cities," and fields, begging merely to touch his garment, and were healed (*esosonto*, "saved/made whole").

The concern about purity regulations in eating by the Pharisees and scribes[70] who suddenly appear again serves as a foil for Jesus' substantive

---

69. In their rituals of covenant renewal and of resistance to the Kittim (the Romans) the priestly- scribal community at Qumran imitated this scheme of organization in a more systematic way (1QS 2:21–22; CD 13:1; 1QM4:1--5:17).

70. The "traditions of the elders" are evidently somewhat the same as in Josephus' account in *Ant.* 13:297. Specifically pertinent to the dispute here, rules about handwashing before ordinary meals are not attested in the Pentateuch books of torah. The Mishnah (c. 200 CE) includes a tractate (Yadayim) on rules of (im)purity associated with the hands, with comments on handwashing before touching bread (2:4).

charge that their urging villagers to "devote" (*qorban*) some of the produce of their land to God was siphoning off to the temple food intended
for support of local families—thus voiding the basic commandment of
God to honor father and mother (7:1–13).[71] This condemnation of the
representatives of the Jerusalem temple-state would have been poignant
for an audience of economically marginal people, particularly in the narrative sequence relating hunger/sufficiency and sickness/healing with
economic exploitation by the rulers.[72]

Like many of the previous healing episodes, the next episode tells
of the exorcism of a particular person, while also dealing with an important issue in the expansion of the renewal of Israel into nearby areas, as Jesus went into the regions of (subject to) the cities of Tyre and
Sidon (7:24–30). Hearing about him, a woman whose little daughter was
possessed by an unclean spirit begged him to cast it out. The episode
indicates secondarily that she was "a Greek woman, a Syrophoenician by
birth." There is no reason to imagine that she was an elite Greek woman
from the city of Tyre itself. The Markan narrative clearly sets the episode
in the regions of Tyre (and Sidon) where Jesus had gone, that is, in a village in the rural area subject to Tyre.[73] That her daughter is possessed and
the woman desperate suggests that they have experienced serious trauma
in their life. In the broader narrative she is a representative figure who, in
begging Jesus to cast the *daimonion* out of her daughter, poses the issue,

71. Commentators, such as Donahue and Harrington, *Mark*, note that the next
episode (7:14–23) often taken as continuation of the same episode, involves not
only a shift in the audience but a shift in the issues, from washing before eating and
whether there will be enough to eat, to what foods people should be allowed to eat.
The new subject introduced seems intrusive into the story's narrative and its focus on
the renewal of Israel against the rulers that is happening mainly in healing, as well as
through teaching/preaching.

72. That is, the lavish banquet at Herod's court juxtaposed with the wilderness
feeding of hungry subsistence villagers in which "all ate and were filled" (new wilderness feeding) followed by a (second) sea crossing (allusion to exodus), followed by a
summary of people from the whole region bringing the sick to be healed, followed
by a condemnation of the Pharisees for siphoning off food from hungry villagers to
support the temple.

73. Some years ago Theissen, *Gospels in Context*, 79, speculated that the woman's
designation as a "Greek" suggests that she was from the upper class. His often suggestive discussion unfortunately proceeds in terms that seem to be of questionable
historical applicability to the political-economic relations in this area of ancient Syria
("borders," "the city of Tyre" vs. "the open space of Galilee"). Elites such as Lucian
(*Parliament of the Gods* in Loeb ed. vol 5.423) and Juvenal (*Sat.* 8.158–162) portrayed
Syrophoenicians as low-born foreigners.

perhaps not so much whether non-Israelites would receive the life-giving effects of the renewal of Israel, but of the sequence in which they would be included. Unclear from the sparse information given in the episode is whether her appearance suggests that many people in the rural "regions of (subject to) Tyre (and Sidon)" were also "Greek and Syrophoenician," or suggests that she and her daughter were somewhat distinctive among the villagers who otherwise were not that different from those across the frontier in Galilee.

Jesus' initial response to the woman's entreaty was hardly encouraging. Almost insultingly, he rejects her, or at least puts her off as having secondary importance. "Let the children (of Israel) eat all they want first, for it is not good to take the bread of the children and throw it to the little dogs." Jesus' statement evokes a domestic household scene at which "little dogs" or "puppies" are underfoot. The Markan narrative thus does not necessarily have Jesus insulting the woman and daughter (and other "Gentiles") as despicable "dogs."[74] In any case, the woman was not to be denied and fired right back, shifting the metaphor to the children sharing their bread: "Sir, even the little dogs under the table make a meal of the crumbs the children give them." Knowing that she had bested him in the debate, and seeming to agree with her statement, he yielded and sent her home, assuring her that the *daimonion* had left her daughter. (Unlike the other exorcism episodes in the Gospel, this episode includes no effects of the possession and no encounter between Jesus and the spirit.)

This episode has striking reminiscences of the story of Elijah (prophet of the renewal of Israel) in encounter with the widow in Zarephath, a town subjected to Sidon (north on the coast). In the story there is a multiplication of food, the woman confronts Elijah over the death of her son, and the prophet makes the simple pronouncement, "Your son lives" (1 Kgs 17:8–24). The episode also echoes a story of Elisha, in interaction with a woman of Shunem, who persistently begs the prophet to revive her dear son, and he eventually declares simply, "Take your son" (2 Kgs 4:18–37). In both stories the non-Israelite women confront the prophet and insist on what they want. The episode of the exorcism of the Syrophoenician woman's daughter would have resonated deeply with such stories in Israelite tradition of non-Israelites participating/sharing in the

---

74. This has been a standard interpretation; see the review in Cotter, *Miracle Stories*, 148–54, and see the "reassessment of dogs" in Israelite tradition in Miller, "Attitude toward Dogs."

life-giving benefits of the renewal of Israel generated by the paradigmatic prophets whose mission of renewal extended to nearby peoples as well.

The last two healings in the double series of "acts of power" communicate further the renewal of the people under the direct rule of God. They address a yearning deep-seated in Israelite tradition for God's redeeming action in healing illnesses typical of the people languishing under imperial conquest and domination. As will be discussed further in treatment of the "Q" speeches, several passages in the book of Isaiah (29:18–19; 42:6–7; 61:1) appear to be reflections of the people's longing for the healing of several typical illnesses of the people under imperial rule. Particularly pertinent here is (the tradition behind) the prophecy in Isa 35:5–6:

> Then the eyes of *the blind* will be opened
> and the ears of *the deaf* will hear.
> Then the lame man will leap like a deer
> and the tongue of the dumb will be clear.[75]

As Jesus works his way through nearby areas back to Galilee he heals a man who is hard of hearing and has a speech impediment. Again a support network (with implicit trust in the powers working through Jesus) takes the initiative in bringing the fellow and begging Jesus to lay his hand on him (7:31–37). Taking him away from the crowd, "he put his fingers in his ears, spat and touched his tongue, and looking up to heaven sighed and said (in performative speech in Aramaic), *Ephphatha!* that is, *"Be Opened."* In contrast to the frequent over- or misinterpretation of this episode as having "magical elements," Jesus' gesture of putting fingers in his ears pertained directly to the man's malaise; and saliva was commonly thought to have a therapeutic effect in the ancient world (Pliny, *Natural History* 28.4.7; Tacitus, *Histories* 4.81; Suetonius, *Vespasian* 7; John 9:6). *Ephphatha!* that is, *"Be Opened,"* moreover, was not some sort of incantation but performative speech in Aramaic, which lent it all the more authority and "authenticity." "Immediately 'his hearings' (not 'his ears') were opened and the bond of his tongue was freed." That the speech-impediment is understood as a "bond" is suggestive of the situation of the Israelite and other peoples' bondage under imperial rule. This fellow whose tongue had been bound was representative of a people who had no voice in their own fate and life-conditions. While Jesus had taken the man

---

75. Cf. the statement in Exod 4:11 that God gives speech or muteness, hearing or deafness, sight or blindness).

aside, the healing was nevertheless public and the episode concludes with a significant step in the Markan narrative. Despite Jesus' admonition not to tell anyone, the people "proclaimed" (the message about Jesus' healing in renewal of the people). In allusion to Israelite tradition, Jesus is fulfilling the prophecies of the healings of the people's suffering of deafness and blindness (etc.) under imperial rule—responding to and enabled by their longing for such healing and renewal as a people. In what is in effect the conclusion of the exorcism and healings in the second sequence of acts of power, leading directly into the second wilderness feeding, the exceedingly astounded people proclaim "Wonderfully he has done everything, even made the deaf hear and the speechless speak!"

When there was again a great crowd (gathered to experience the renewal in healing and preaching) without anything to eat (referring back to the first great feeding in the wilderness) Jesus again, in compassion for the people, mounted a mass feeding in the wilderness (8:1–10). This time it was less explicitly staged as "Israel" in its traditional formation. But as before, all were satisfied and (corresponding to the seven loaves) seven baskets full of fragments were collected. Again hunger parallels (accompanies/is connected with) illness, and provision of and no restrictions on or expropriation of food parallels (is connected with) healing.[76]

The disciples' misunderstanding about the feedings prepares the hearers for the further development of the disciples' misunderstanding in the next main narrative step, to which the healing of the blind man in Bethsaida is the transition. This episode is (formally) parallel to the preceding healing of the man who was hard of hearing and had a speech-impediment, and has Jesus healing one of the other illnesses for which the people were yearning for healing (e.g., Isa 35:5–6). In connection with this common yearning articulated in the Isaiah tradition and considering the framing of healings in the sequences of acts of power that include sea

76. The demand for a sign from heaven by the suddenly reappearing Pharisees in the next episode sounds like a desperate ploy. Some of the literate elite of scribes and Pharisees probably continued to cultivate the typical intellectual scribal lore of heavenly signs and portents, a Judean version of which can be seen in the Book of Heavenly Luminaries in 1 Enoch. By contrast, Judean and Galilean villagers and popular prophets focused instead on new acts of deliverance like those led by Moses and Joshua, or on collective refusal to plant the crops in protest of imperial arrogance, or on healings, like those of Elijah. Only in their desperate circumstances under Roman military siege and imminent slaughter did the populace in Jerusalem hear from voices fantasizing heavenly armies coming to the rescue, and this was in an account of an historian who loved to exaggerate (Josephus, *War* 6.299).

crossing and feeding in the wilderness—that is a new Moses leading a new exodus—would the people have been aware of the further image of God taking Israel by the hand, leading them out of bondage, and opening their blind eyes that we know in Isa 42:6–7? People came carrying the man in their (implicit) trust that Jesus could heal him. Jesus (unspoken) took him away from the people (village), spat on his eyes and laid hands on him. As noted, spittle was a common substance effective in healing, especially for eyes (Pliny, *Nat. Hist.* 28.37.86; b. Sabb. 108b, which forbids using saliva on the Sabbath, even on the eyes). In their trust the people clamored for the sick to touch Jesus, and his "laying hands on" the sick (twice) emphasizes his intentional agency.) As he could see only incompletely, Jesus again laid hands on his eyes, whereupon his sight was fully restored. Jesus sent him home, with instructions not to enter the village (so as not to spread the word?).

Third Narrative Step

The healing of the blind man in Bethsaida both completes the second narrative step of the Markan story and begins and frames its third narrative step. The narrative now focuses on the disciples' increasing misunderstanding of Jesus' mission that is juxtaposed with his repeated announcement that he must be arrested and executed by the rulers in Jerusalem. The narrative uses Jesus' healings of blindness at the beginning and end of this step to frame the "blindness" of the disciples.

It is crucial to attend carefully to the narrative sequence to "get" the story here (8:27—9:1). Jesus' question to the disciples is a "set up." They (like the hearers of the story) know, from all his (acts of) power(s), that Jesus is widely known as a prophet, whether by the people or by Herod Antipas, as indicated earlier in the story. But Peter, speaking for them, declared instead, "You are the messiah." This is happening as Jesus and his disciples are working in the villages of Caesarea Philippi, the capital of another Roman client ruler not only named for Caesar but identified with Roman imperial domination; the significance would not have been lost on the hearers of the story. Thus, ostensibly, Peter's enthusiastic "confession" was an attempt to articulate opposition to the Roman imperial order.[77] Jesus, however, rebuked the disciples not to tell anyone about him.

77. In one of the very few, but widely cited, Judean scribal texts attesting "the Messiah" (Psalm of Solomon 17) his task is to restore the independence of the twelve tribes

Then after Jesus taught them "in bold speech" that he must be killed by the rulers, Peter rebuked Jesus, whereupon Jesus rebuked Peter in front of the disciples, "Get behind me, Satan."[78] In having Jesus rebuke Peter for identifying him as "the messiah" and then rejecting that he would be martyred the Markan story is rejecting interpretation of Jesus as an "anointed king." More particularly, the Markan story may be rejecting the view of the movement of Jesus-loyalists in Jerusalem headed by Peter and other disciples in which, according to the speeches of Peter in the early chapters of Acts, Jesus had become designated as the "messiah" at his vindication/exaltation as a martyr.[79] This narrative sequence in Mark is *not* suddenly declaring, in Peter's "confession," Jesus' true identity as an anointed king who will lead an insurrection to establish the direct reign of God. Rather the narrative sequence presents in clear bold terms Jesus' announcement that his mission is leading to his arrest and execution, and his warning that his followers (similarly) must be prepared to persist under persecution, while clearly rebuking the disciples' misunderstanding. Jesus is the prophet leading resistance to the Roman imperial order in Galilee, Judea, and beyond, but not in a way that he and his disciples would become imperial rulers, as articulated again a few episodes later.

The following episode of the appearance of Jesus on the mountain could not be a clearer revelation of what Jesus had been doing in his acts of power as a prophet like Moses and Elijah in renewal of the people. The episode is full of references to Israelite tradition focused on Moses as founder/mediator of the covenant that constituted the people and Elijah as the paradigmatic prophet of renewal of the people. Again, the hearers of the Markan story would have known a rich array of legends and lore, some of which we also know from their inclusion and adaptation especially in Exod 24 and 34. "After six days," probably an allusion to the six days Moses spent awaiting the appearance of God on Sinai (Exod 24:15–17), Jesus took the leaders of the twelve disciples (Peter, James, and

---

of Israel by defeating arrogant rulers with "the words of his mouth."

78. Standard Christian theological interpretation has taken "Peter's confession" as rightly having identified Jesus as "the Messiah," while not yet understanding that he would be a suffering messiah. But this interpretation ignored the Markan narrative sequence and gave little attention to the overall Markan story.

79. The only people in the Markan story (other than Peter) who identify or acclaim Jesus as "king" are Pontius Pilate (and the inscription he erects over the cross), the Roman soldiers, and the high priests at the crucifixion, and these are all in mockery or derision.

John),[80] "up to a high mountain" where they were alone. The central figure in the revelation appeared in glorious radiance, evoking fear among the onlookers (Exod 34:29–30, 35), and the voice came from the cloud (Exod 24:16). The focus falls on the appearance with Jesus of Moses, on Sinai (for forty days and nights) as mediating prophet of the covenantal formation of Israel, and of Elijah, on Horeb/Sinai (for forty days and nights; 1 Kgs 19) as prophet of renewal of the people (cf. Mark 1:13). If it had not been clear before in the many allusions to Israelite tradition, it is now clear that "My beloved son" is Jesus as a prophet like Moses and Elijah.[81]

The following exorcism episode is very long and repetitious. We may suspect that in the performances that lie behind later manuscripts it continued to be expanded and developed past the point at which the Matthean and Lukan stories may have adapted it. Thus the wording of the episode that we are attempting to hear is more hypothetical in this episode than usual. If our procedural principle is to focus mainly on those aspects of the (pluriform) Markan episode that appear also in the (pluriform) Matthean story or the (pluriform) Lukan story or both,[82] then we may pay less attention to the appearance of the scribes arguing with the crowd (9:14–16), the duplication of the symptoms of the boy's possession (9:17–18, 20–24), the characterization of the spirit as "deaf and dumb"

---

80. Is this an allusion to Moses having taken (only) Aaron, Nadab, Abihu, and the seventy elders?

81. The conversation in the ensuing episode attempts to clarify what must have been confusion between the branches of the wider Jesus' movement(s) and their knowledge of what the scribes had been teaching and what the supposedly authoritative scriptures of the temple-state contained. There is little or no Judean textual evidence that scribal groups, much less even the early Jesus movements, had a clear and consistent view of resurrection of the dead in general or of Jesus in particular. Judean scribes had indeed taken up the tradition that the prophet Elijah, who had been taken up into heaven, would return to "restore the tribes of Jacob" (Sirach 48:10; Mal 4:5–6). The Markan Jesus, who otherwise always opposes the scribes and their teachings, only ostensibly agrees that Elijah is coming "to restore all things" (Israel). No, the son of man must go through much suffering, "as written" (in the scriptures in general). In fact, Elijah has come, in John the Baptist, and he (too) was martyred, "as it is written." That these events are explained as happening "as written" (in the scribal scriptures in general) suggest a somewhat puzzled and defensive conflict with "the authorities," with whom the addressees are in conflict, as indicated in the preceding episode (8:34—9:1) and again in Jesus final speech (13:9–13).

82. This is not a sudden reversion to a hypothesis of an *Urmarkus*. As discussed in chap. 6, recent text-critics' analysis of early MSS and fragments suggests that the text of all of the Gospel stories were pluriform, continuing to undergo development probably related to their functioning in oral performance.

(9:25), the boy being like a corpse after the spirit departed (9:26), and the reference to prayer (9:29) Thus also the exorcism formula (9:25), the only such elaborate declaration by Jesus in the Gospels, which does not fit the symptoms of possession just described, appears to be an elaboration in later development of the Markan text. The disciples' lack of trust (9:19), on the other hand, better fits the immediate and overall narrative context of the disciples deepening misunderstanding and the many allusions to the healings and exorcisms as associated with a new exodus.[83]

The episode would still have an elaborate description of symptoms of possession: since childhood the possessing spirit had seized the boy, dashed him down so that he foamed at the mouth, ground his teeth, and became rigid or rolled on the ground, even cast him into fire or water. As in other exorcisms and healings a father brings the boy to Jesus and the encounter with the spirit happens in public, in a crowd. As in the first exorcism the Markan narrative has Jesus subdue (stronger than "rebuke") the spirit, which convulsed the boy and "came out." Even without being greatly elaborated, the episode also functions in its narrative context to illustrate the disciples deepening misunderstanding and lack of trust.[84]

Jesus' command not to stop others from casting out *daimonia* in his name in the admonitions to the disciples following his second announcement of his impending arrest and execution indicates that the practice of exorcism continued among other branches of the movement of his followers (9:30–41/50).

The narrative sequence in the third main narrative step now parallels and repeats more explicitly the sequence in the first narrative step. At the end of the first narrative step a brief statement of the nascent familial community that was keeping the covenantal will of God followed upon performance of exorcism and healing. Now at the conclusion of the third major narrative step that is also the conclusion of Jesus' mission of renewal in exorcism and healing in Galilee and beyond comes an explicitly Mosaic covenant renewal in a series of dialogues between Jesus and the Pharisees or the disciples (Mark 10:2–45). The narrative position of these

83. Jesus' expression of frustration at their lack of trust may be an allusion to the frustration with the people recently liberated from Egypt in the Song of Moses that would presumably have been familiar in Israelite popular tradition, Deut 32, esp. 32:20.

84. Jesus' complaints about "this generation," that is, the disciples' lack of trust way well be alluding to Israelite tradition (e.g., Deut 32:20; Num 14:11); see Marcus, *Mark*, 653, 659.

dialogues, as Jesus completes his exorcism and healing in renewal of the people in Galilee and beyond, before marching up to Jerusalem where he confronts the rulers, provides a kind of "charter" for the communities of hearers of the Gospel story. Appealing to the explicitly cited covenant commandments, the series of dialogues gives renewed law-like torah/ teaching on marriage and divorce, membership in the community, non-exploitative community-minded economic relations, and leadership that serves the collective.[85]

In the final episode of the third narrative step, the healing of the blind Bartimaeus frames and juxtaposes the disciples' intensifying "blindness" as Jesus, the disciples, and a large crowd leave Jericho on their way up to Jerusalem. Hearing that it was Jesus of Nazareth, Bartimaeus begged for mercy to "Jesus, Son of David." We should not imagine that this is somehow an identification of Jesus as "the Messiah," that is, the divinely anointed king[86]—and that the Markan story is suddenly reversing Jesus' rejection of Peter's and James' and John's misunderstanding of his mission as that of a victorious king rather than a martyred prophet. In the Markan narrative, Jesus seems to ignore the address by Bartimaeus, and later argues that the scribes are wrong that the Messiah would be "Son of David" (12:33–37).[87] Only after Bartimaeus addresses Jesus as "my teacher" (rabouni) and asks to see again does Jesus heal him (implied; no word or gesture), declaring again, "your trust has saved/healed you."

85. See further Horsley, Hearing the Whole Story, chap. 6; and Horsley, Covenant Economics, 116–23.

86. Theological interpreters looking for fragments to piece together into a synthetic concept of "The Messiah" seize upon "Son of David" here as a "messianic title." While Paul draws upon a line of interpretation that claims that "Jesus Messiah" was descended from David according to the flesh (Rom 1:3–4), the only attestation of a connection between "the messiah" and "the son of David" prior to the time of Jesus is the passing reference in Psalms of Solomon 17. The concept "messianic title" has a heavy modern scholarly christological overlay that is not applicable to the Markan story. See further the critical discussions in Achtemeier, "And He followed him": and Struthers Malbon, "The Jesus of Mark and "Son of David." Le Donne, The Historiographical Jesus, offers an extensive exploration of "the son of David" in "early Christian" social memory behind the Gospel of Mark.

87. The issue in Mark 12:33–37 may not be a "title," but simply that the scribes were thought to teach that "the messiah" was from the lineage of David, somewhat similar to how the scribes, in speculative answer to Herod's (and the Magi's) question of where "the messiah" was to be born, answered "in Bethlehem" because it was the city of David's origins in Israelite tradition, whence a future ruler of Israel, presumed to be a descendant of David, would come (as in the prophecy of Mic 5:2; Matt 2:2–6).

The Climactic Narrative Steps

In its climactic narrative steps, the Markan story presents Jesus' sustained confrontation with the high priestly rulers in Jerusalem and their response in arresting him and handing him over to the Roman governor for crucifixion. Jesus' exorcism of the extremely violent spirit(s) whose identity had been exposed as "Legion," that is, Roman troops, had made unavoidably clear that his mission was in opposition to Roman imperial rule in Palestine. After completing the stage of exorcism and healing in Galilee and beyond, he is now ready for direct political confrontation with the high priesthood at the head of the temple in the capital city of Jerusalem. Since the climactic events in Jerusalem are so heavily overlaid with centuries of Christian ritual and theological concepts that obscure the Markan story in its historical context, it is all the more important to "overhear" the climactic steps of the story in the historical context of those who heard it performed.

Passover was the celebration of the origins of the people in the exodus liberation from bondage in Egypt. Passover had originally been a family celebration in the village communities that were the fundamental form of Israelite society. Perhaps already under the monarchy but certainly under the temple-state celebration of the Passover had been centralized in the pilgrimage feast of unleavened bread in Jerusalem. Under Roman rule Passover had become a highly charged time in the general structural conflict between the people and their rulers, often an occasion for mass protest (as discussed in chap. 4). To keep the Judeans' and other Israelites' celebration of their liberation from foreign bondage in check, the Roman governors brought their troops into the city and posted them atop the porticoes of the temple—which Herod had massively rebuilt in grand Hellenistic-Roman style (*Ant.* 20.106–108; *War* 2.223–225). This only exacerbated the resentment of the crowd, as illustrated in the vociferous protest over a crude gesture by one of the soldiers under the governor Cumanus. Such large-scale festivals in capital cities like Jerusalem, however, provided a certain "cover" of anonymity and protection for protest midst the festive excitement.[88] Jesus' entry into Jerusalem as represented in the Markan story would have been a highly provocative "demonstration" of opposition to Roman and high priestly rule in this already highly charged context. The Markan narrative has Jesus' "entry"

---

88. Fuller discussion in Horsley, *Jesus and the Spiral*, 90–99; Horsley, *Jesus and the Politics*, 42–43.

into Jerusalem and the temple as the introduction to the sequence of episodes in which Jesus boldly confronts the ruling institutions of temple and high priesthood.

In a whole series of confrontations with the rulers in the temple Jesus acts and speaks like earlier Israelite prophets such as Elijah or Jeremiah. He carries out a forcible demonstration that was a symbolic prophetic action of condemnation of the temple and high priests (clear from its framing by the cursing and withering away of the fig tree). The second line of his "quotation" comes from the prophet Jeremiah's famous prophecy condemning the (first) temple and its priesthood for oppressing the people in violation of the Mosaic covenant commandments and then seeking refuge in the temple as their sacred hideaway, like a band of brigands. His parable of the tenants, adapting the well-known "song of the vineyard" of Isaiah (cf. Isa 5) that indicted earlier Jerusalem rulers, announced God's impending judgment against the high priests in the temple for having hoarded the produce of the vineyard to augment their own wealth.

These prophetic pronouncements of God's judgment against the temple and high priesthood being also attacks against the Roman imperial order in Judea, "they" sent some Pharisees and Herodians to entrap him: "Is it lawful to pay the tribute to Caesar?" All present knew that it was not lawful for Israelites. Twenty-some years earlier the scribal and Pharisaic leaders of the "Fourth Philosophy" had mounted resistance to paying the tribute because it violated the first two commandments: Caesar was displacing God as their King and, as illustrated by the inscription on the coin, was honored as divine, and Israel was forbidden to "bow down and serve" other gods (with taxes and tribute). But the Romans viewed failure to yield up the tribute as tantamount to insurrection. Jesus adeptly wriggled out of the trap by avoiding a direct answer. Yet he indicated clearly that, since all things are God's, there would not be anything belonging to Caesar to be paid in tribute.

Hearers familiar with the political-economic-religious structure of the Judean temple-state, compounded by the Romans' extraction of tribute, would immediately have understood that, like the earlier prophets, Jesus was pronouncing God's judgment because of the economic exploitation that went with political-religious domination. In the last of the confrontations, similarly, Jesus condemned the scribes for "devouring widows' households" (their subsistence living). This is illustrated in narrative sequence by the poor widow giving to the temple her last copper coins (so that she was utterly destitute). Finally, in the narrative sequence, Jesus made a Jeremiah-like announcement of the destruction of the temple. Midst the other confrontations the narrative repeats, in a way that is ominous for the high priests, that Jesus is acting and speaking with power/authority for and among the people, as opposed to the utter lack of authority of the high priestly "authorities" who, like their scribal representatives, were oppressing the people.

The high priests, whom (as the hearers of the story knew well) the Romans held responsible for maintaining the imperial order in Judea, finally took action to arrest Jesus by stealth, and handed him over to the Roman governor, who had him crucified as "the king of the Judeans," as the Romans viewed a leader of insurrection. Several other key episodes in the climactic narrative of the Gospels, however, indicate that Jesus' confrontation with the rulers and his martyrdom became the breakthrough that energized the movement into its rapid expansion.

As he faced imminent arrest and execution Jesus transformed his (last) Passover meal with the disciples, representative of the movement(s), into a covenant renewal ceremony (the cup as his blood of the covenant) that he would celebrate anew in the kingdom of God. This Passover meal-become-covenant-renewal ceremony evidently became the central ritual of communities of the movement in anticipation of its celebration again with Jesus. Its narrative placement in the regularly performed story between the confrontations and the arrest and crucifixion, powerfully reinforced its connection with the earlier narrative in which covenant renewal followed the healings and exorcisms.

The Markan story is distinctive among the Gospels in lacking resurrection appearances. In the generations following its early performances the story was thought to be incomplete and endings supplied that included resurrection. Christian theological readings of the Gospels have similarly emphasized "the resurrection faith" as what led to the formation and expansion of movement(s) that quickly blossomed into "Christianity." If, on the other hand, we follow the Markan story of Jesus' renewal of the people in exorcism and healing and covenant renewal followed by his confrontation of the rulers, then this confrontation resulting in his martyrdom death appears to be the principal event that leads to the expansion of the movement. The exorcism and healing episodes that are Jesus' principal actions in the story are not just occasional individual acts of healing suffering individuals. They are the focus of the renewal of the people that has recommitted to collective renewal in village communities.

Continuing to act as a prophet like Moses and Elijah Jesus had "spoken truth to power" in his confrontation with the rulers in Jerusalem. Then he had boldly endured the torturous Roman execution of crucifixion intended to suppress resistance and intimidate people. In the Markan story, Jesus' martyr death by crucifixion became the "breakthrough" event that energized the extension of the movement he had catalyzed.[89]

Both at the end of the covenant renewal "last supper" and at the empty tomb, Jesus' disciples and the women learned that he would meet them back in Galilee where presumably they would continue the movement he had generated (as discussed above as a clue to the context of the audience). Jesus had already indicated, in his speech that followed the confrontation with the rulers and the prophecy of the destruction of the temple, that the movement would continue and expand. He reassured them that despite persecutions and political turmoil they should not be anxious but confident that the movement would result in the fulfilment of the renewal of the people already begun in his mission and continuing in performance of the Gospel story.

The effect of the Markan story on the communities in which it was performed will be discussed in chap 11.

---

89. See further the discussion in Horsley, *Jesus and the Powers*, chap. 8.

8

A Series of Jesus-Speeches
Adapted in Matthew and Luke

THE GOSPELS OF MATTHEW and Luke include a good deal of the "teachings" of Jesus in strikingly parallel versions, often verbatim in their wording, as noted in chapter 1 and again in chapter 6. At several points these "teachings" presuppose and indeed pronounce that Jesus performed many healings and exorcisms, proclaim that his healings and exorcisms manifested the (direct) rule of God, and dramatize how his exorcisms were threatening to the guardians of the Roman imperial order in Palestine. These teachings thus appear to provide an early semi-separate source for investigation of Jesus' healings and exorcisms.

The largely separate lines of recent research into communication and the cultivation of texts in antiquity, however, are undermining the basis on which these teachings were delineated, (re-)constructed, and interpreted in standard New Testament studies. These teachings of Jesus, therefore, can be used as a source for Jesus-in-movement only with the utmost critical attention to text and context.

Discerning the Orally Performed Text

In retrospect it seems that the discernment and delineation of the Sayings Source "Q" was made possible (only) on the assumptions and format of modern print culture. The Gospels, assumed to be stable written texts, were laid out visually in parallel so that both the sequence and wording of the three "Synoptic" Gospels could be closely compared. Scholars could examine how Matthew and Luke had "edited" or "redacted" Mark. They could observe the parallel sayings and other material in Matthew and Luke but not in Mark that must have been derived from a second common written source, which was conveniently labeled "Q," short for *Quelle* (German for "Source"). Since most of the "Q" material consisted of what were presumed to be separate sayings that were assumed to have been circulating independently and were later "collected" into a written source, "Q" was understood as "the Sayings Source."[1]

In the revival of interest in "the Sayings Source" in the 1980s and 1990s, moreover, "Q"-scholars still deeply rooted in the assumptions of print-culture took bold new steps in their (re)construction and interpretation of an already admittedly hypothetical written text. Leading American Q-scholars further hypothesized separate layers in the supposedly written composition of "Q" on the basis of their own (theological) classification of the supposedly separate sayings included in the hypothetical document into the categories of "sapiential" and "apocalyptic."[2] Then, evidently unaware of or unimpressed with the concurrent work of revisionist text-critics' findings that it would be utterly impossible to reconstruct reliably stable early written texts of the Gospels, an international team of Q-scholars presumed to (re)construct the wording of each separate saying in "The Critical Edition (Text) of Q."[3] Given the separate but interrelated lines of recent new research into ancient communication

1. Particularly problematic for what was included in Q was how certain passages that had some degree of verbal agreement between the Matthean and Lukan versions yet were also (partly) narrative could be fit into a "Sayings Source." Most problematic was the tripartite temptation narrative (Matt 4:1–11; Luke 4:1–13), with its distinctive dialogue between Jesus and the Devil. "Devil" and "the son of God" as a title for Jesus occur only here in the hypothesized Q. Having little or no thematic link with the rest of Q, the temptation narrative was deemed to have been a late addition to Q. But since it had no thematic link with the rest of Q and a distinctive form as well as distinctive titles, there is little reason to consider the temptation narrative as part of the instructions and prophecies of Jesus (parallel in Matthew and Luke) that seemed to be cohesive in various ways. In another example, the "peculiar story" of the healing of the centurion's servant (Luke 7:1–10; Matt 8:5–13), with distinctive issues such as "being under authority" and "faith," seems to have had little or no relation to the rest of Q.

2. Kloppenborg, *Formation of Q*. Criticism by Horsley, "Questions about Redactional Strata and the Social Relations Reflected in Q."

3. As evident in the format of Robinson, Hoffmann, and Kloppenborg, eds., *The Sayings Gospel Q in Greek and English, with Parallels from the Gospels of Mark and Thomas*. The "Introduction" to this volume by Robinson (11–72) is a definitive delineation of "the major turning points in the history of Q research."

(summarized in chap. 6), such reconstructions of hypothetical written texts appear to be chimeras of the modern print-cultural imagination.

The teachings of Jesus parallel in Matthew and Luke but not in Mark, however, are not separate sayings, but take the form of short speeches or discourses. For example, Luke 11:2–4 and its longer parallel in Matt 6:9–13 do not present separate sayings about the kingdom of God, sufficient bread, debts, and the test, respectively. They are rather a sequence of petitions constituting a short prayer, beginning with the general plea for the direct rule of God, then focusing on key concrete examples of what that would mean, and finally asking deliverance from testing (judgment). Luke 10:2–16 (partly paralleled in Matthew 10) does not list separate sayings, one about an abundant harvest, another about what not to carry on a journey, another about accepting hospitality, and yet another about cursing an unreceptive town. Here, rather, is a speech that commissions envoys to extend Jesus' own mission of preaching and healing, beginning with the importance of the mission, moving to particular instructions for working in villages, and ending with sanctions against potentially unreceptive villages. Luke 12:22–31 and the nearly verbatim parallel in Matt 6:25–33 are not a bunch of separate sayings, one about ravens, another about lilies, and another about grass. This succession of parallel lines is rather an extended admonition to poor people not to be anxious about food and clothing, using observations about God's care for ravens and lilies as encouragement, all climaxing in the insistence that single-minded pursuit of the direct rule (kingdom) of God will result in sufficient subsistence.

The teachings of Jesus parallel in Matthew and Luke should thus be reconceptualized as a series of speeches rather than a collection of individual sayings.[4] These speeches focus on particular issues or concerns of a movement of Jesus-loyalists. Many of them follow a traditional Israelite form (covenantal or prophetic) and/or have a certain rhetorical progression or logic. These speeches were orally-performed text(s), known (in memory) and re-performed by those who composed Matthew and Luke—somewhat similarly to the way in which we know and re-perform freedom songs, protest chants, poetic vignettes of heroes and heroines, or the Lord's Prayer. Consideration of the speeches in oral performance led to recognition that, whether a prayer, prophecies in traditional Israelite form, or admonitions, they were poetic in form. They feature multiple

4. Horsley with Draper, *Whoever Hears You Hears Me*; Kloppenborg, *Formation of Q*; Kirk, *Composition of the Sayings Source*.

parallel lines, most often with two or more parallel lines that repeat the same idea, or with the second line completing the idea started in the first. The multiple lines are replete with repetition of words, sounds, and parallel verb forms typical of orally-performed texts.[5]

While it would be impossible to "establish" or "reconstruct" Q as a written text, we can still know a great deal about the text of these speeches from the two different performances in Matthew and Luke (via the varying performances of them evident in ancient manuscripts).[6] Where the wording of the speeches is not verbatim or at least closely parallel in Matthew and Luke it is not possible to reconstruct the likely wording before they were incorporated into the larger Gospels. In many cases it is not possible to discern the complete contours of a speech.[7] Some of the careful work done in constructing the (supposedly written) text of the Q "sayings" is suggestive and may be helpful for consideration of the speeches in oral performance. The only way to proceed, however, is to attend closely to the respective Matthean and Lukan texts, contexts, and adaptations of what they evidently derived from these speeches.[8] (For

5. Laid out, and "illustrated" in print-presentation of the parallel lines in transliteration and translation, with indication of repetition of words, verb endings, and sounds, etc., in Horsley with Draper, *Whoever Hears You Hears Me*, chaps. 8–13.

6. There are many possible analogies. For example, in their researches Milman Parry and Albert Lord recorded different performances by the same guslar (singer) of the same epic and different performances by different guslars of the same epic song(s). On the basis of those performances they could posit that such a song (text) "existed" in the memory of the guslars and that they could know many of the "stanzas" and "lines" and "words" of the song(s), which varied from performance to performance, as well as the overall plot and sequence of "events," which remained fairly consistent from performance to performance. In a simpler example perhaps familiar to some of Anglophone Christian background, there are multiple different musical settings/performances of what we recognize as the 23rd Psalm (e.g., an Appalachian tune and "Brother James Air"). Even if we did not have the KJV translation on which they are based, we could still determine that there was a common text of the Psalm and what it was about.

7. It is not clear, for example, how sayings that Luke leaves separated (such as 14:26, 27 or 16:13 and 16:16) may have fit into a speech, or whether the two parables of the kingdom in Luke 13:18–21//Matt 13:31–33 were part of a larger speech, or just how the prophecies in Luke 13:28–29 and 13:34–35 fit into a larger prophetic speech.

8. Ideally readers of this chapter who are attempting to hear the Q speeches in historical context will have some printed approximation(s) of the text of the speeches in front of them to read. The text of individual sayings (re-)constructed by the International Q Project may be more of a hindrance than a help since it obscures the contours of the speeches and their poetic form. Compromising with, but also hoping to benefit from their project, I have adapted their hypothetical text in arranging the speeches in

this reason I will reference the "location" of the respective speeches in both Matthew and Luke, particularly when they are not closely parallel, but occasionally revert to the Q-scholars' practice of referencing only the location in Luke.)

Despite the difficulties posed for critical consideration, the parallel texts of these speeches in Matthew and Luke provide a good basis for imagining them in oral performance in historical context.[9] As noted, most of the lines in many of the speeches are verbatim or closely parallel in Matthew and Luke. Even in cases where Matthew has combined the "Q" version of the "mission speech" and the "Beelzebul controversy" with the Markan versions, the overall pattern of the Q speeches is discernible. Many of the speeches come in the same order in the two Gospels. "The kingdom/reign of God," which occurs at a crucial point in most of the speeches, is clearly the theme of the whole series and the link between them. In nearly every speech Jesus (like John) speaks and/or is identified as a prophet in the long line of Israelite prophets, providing further coherence to the speeches.

As will be elaborated further below, the adaptation of and rich references to Israelite (popular) tradition indicate what the speeches are all about: the prophet Jesus' renewal of the people of Israel under the direct rule of God in opposition to and by the Jerusalem rulers and their scribal-Pharisaic representatives. In a link between the speeches that provides coherence to the series, John the Baptist prophesies a *krisis* (judgment) in

---

poetic form both in transliteration and translation, in *Whoever Hears You Hears Me* and in an "Appendix" to *Jesus in Context*. To consider (and critically compare!) the respective versions and adaptations in the Matthean and Lukan stories and speeches, Kloppenborg's workbook *Q Parallels*, which does lay out the text in a succession of (sections of) short speeches, is very helpful despite the failure to discern the poetic form of the speeches. Because our understanding of the oral-derived text of the Q speeches is still developing, along with the developing understanding of oral communication and oral performance in antiquity, in the discussion below I will often provide further adaptations of my previous translations in verse blocked out (visually) for performance in a way that attempts to represent the repetition of words, sound, verb endings, etc.

9. Once the dominance of oral communication in antiquity is recognized, so that texts would have been orally performed, then the precise delineation of the wording of Q as parallel sayings (based on assumptions of print-culture) is not possible (see the sophisticated analysis of John Miles Foley, "The Riddle of Q"). But once it is recognized that Matthew and Luke were orally performed texts, the presence of parallel poetic speeches with closely similar or verbatim wording clearly suggests that they were adapting and re-performing the same series of speeches that had been previously performed.

traditional prophetic harvest imagery that cuts positively for the people and negatively for the rulers. The next several speeches elaborate on and specify the ways in which the prophet who is coming after him "baptizes" the people "with Spirit" and how remarkably concrete the direct rule of God is or will be: mutual economic aid and cooperation in village communities in renewal of the Mosaic covenant (6:20–49); healings of the lame and blind, etc. and preaching good news (Q/Luke 7:18–35); sending out envoys to expand the healing and preaching the kingdom (10:2–16); anticipation of sufficient bread and cancellation of debts in the prayer for the kingdom (Q/Luke 11:2–4; cf. 12:22–31); and casting out hostile spirits (11:14–26). Then the prophet "baptizes . . . with fire" as well: some of the subsequent speeches are prophetic declarations of judgment against the scribes and Pharisees and the Jerusalem ruling house. In the communication mode of speeches to communities of hearers very different from the extended story in the Gospel of Mark, the speeches parallel in Matthew and Luke thus articulate roughly the same agenda: the renewal of Israel under the direct rule of God manifested in healings and exorcisms, in opposition to and from the rulers.

The following outline lists most of the speeches that are readily discernible from the parallels in Matthew and Luke with the issue on which each focuses. Occurrences of the linking theme, the rule of God, is in parentheses.

It is significant to note that these speeches contain no suggestion that Jesus was some sort of "anointed" figure (messiah). Throughout the speeches Jesus speaks as and is assumed to have been a prophet, the most significant in the long line of Israelite prophets. And while they make no mention of a crucifixion, several of the speeches assume that Jesus was killed as a prophet by the rulers.

Adapting the synthetic theory of oral performance developed by John Miles Foley (as summarized in chap. 6), it should be possible to discern much more fully how the text in performance resonated with the audience after discerning the life-context of the audience from clues in the text just outlined.

SERIES OF SPEECHES PARALLEL IN MATTHEW AND LUKE
THAT ADDRESS JESUS-MOVEMENT ISSUES

3:7–9, 16–17	John/prophet announces the stronger one coming to baptize with Spirit and fire
6:20–49 (20)	Jesus/prophet enacts Covenant renewal as center of direct rule of God
7:18–35 (28)	Jesus claims he is the coming prophet, performing healings as direct rule of God
10:2–16 (9, 11)	Jesus/prophet sends envoys into villages to heal and declare direct rule of God
11:2–4, 9–13 (2)	prayer for direct rule of God = bread and cancellation of debts, with testing
11:14–20 (20)	Jesus/prophet declares exorcisms are manifestations of direct rule of God
11:29–32	Jesus/prophet declares something greater than Jonah or Solomon is here
11:39–52	Jesus/prophet utters woes against Pharisees, who block way to the direct rule of God
12:2–12	Jesus exhorts bold confession when hauled before authorities, with vindication
12:22–31 (31)	Jesus insists subsistence materializes from single-minded pursuit of direct rule of God
13:28–29, 34–35+14:16–24 (29)	Jesus/prophet pronounces reign of God banquet, both positive and judgmental
17:22–37	Jesus/prophet warns of the day of the son of man = judgment, positive and negative
22:28–30 (30)	Jesus/prophet charges followers to establish justice for Israel in rule of God

Context

The liberal theological construction of the "Q-people" as individuals who had abandoned home and family to become itinerant vagabonds was based on a literalistic reading of Jesus' teaching as separate individual sayings—as well as on a general projection of modern western individualism onto ancient life.[10] It was not considered, for example, that Jesus'

10. The anachronistic individual interpretation by Theissen in *The Sociology of Early Palestinian Christianity* was taken over uncritically by many Q-scholars and by

declaration that "the one who does not hate his father and mother cannot be my disciple" (Luke/Q 14:26) was hyperbole. On the assumption that Q was composed in writing and that this required authors who were at least somewhat educated, some Q-scholars hypothesized that the Sayings Source was produced by "village scribes" in Galilee.[11] They evidently did not recognize that virtually the only evidence for "village scribes" has them in Egypt, and Egyptian papyri indicate that they were uneducated (nonliterate) local representatives of the imperial administration charged with making records of fellow villagers' payment of taxes.[12] As is evident from the many studies of oral-derived texts and texts-in-performance, non-literate ordinary people are fully capable of producing poetry, prophecy, sagas, and many other forms of texts that become formative articulations of people's culture and social-economic life.

Once the prophecies and teachings of Jesus parallel in Matthew and Luke are recognized as a series of speeches it becomes evident that they contain a number of indications of the audience in their historical context. Like the people among whom Jesus evidently worked in his mission, those addressed in the speeches were evidently villagers. The envoys whom Jesus commissions to expand his mission (10:2–16) are instructed to work in villages and to share the subsistence nourishment of host households. They are to work with villagers collectively as well as individually; the speech closes with woes against whole villages that are held responsible for their response to the mission of preaching and healing. The petitions of the Lord's Prayer (Luke 11:2–4) indicate villagers who are hungry and in debt, conditions that we might expect considering their historical situation (discussed in chap. 4). The acrimonious economic and social interactions addressed in the covenant renewal speech are those of villagers who have been borrowing from one another and becoming desperate and resentful (Luke 6:27–38). The people admonished not to be concerned about food and shelter are evidently living at or below subsistence (Luke 12:22–31). These indications, moreover, are aspects of the often observed general "agrarian ethos" of Jesus' teaching.

Crossan, *Historical Jesus,* and others in the Jesus Seminar, despite the serious criticism by Horsley, *Sociology and the Jesus Movement,* chaps. 1–4.

11. Kloppenborg, "Literary Conventions"; followed by Arnal, *Village Scribes*; similarly, Bazzana, *Kingdom of Bureaucracy.*

12. Evidence and discussion in Horsley, "Introduction," in *Oral Performance.* See now the critical survey of sources and scholarly analysis by Kirk, "Who Are the Q Scribes?," 67–85.

The speeches address people who stand opposed to and by rulers, Herod Antipas in Galilee and the Jerusalem high priests and their scribal representatives. John the Baptist and other prophets are contrasted with (opposed to) "those who wear luxurious garments and live in houses of kings," evidently a reference to Herod Antipas (whom Galileans viewed as a king despite his official Roman designation as only Tetrarch over Galilee and Perea). The hearers, moreover, are contrasted with (the scribal) "sages" (Luke 10:21–22), and "Jesus" delivers a series of woes against "the scribes (lawyers) and Pharisees," who exhort people to pay the tithes and load them with heavy burdens, evidently as representatives of the Jerusalem high priesthood (Luke 11:39–52 mostly parallel in the woes in Matthew 23). Another speech is a prophetic lament over the ruling house in Jerusalem for having exploited the "children" (villages) that God wanted to protect and killed the prophets sent with warnings (Luke 13:34–35). The only geographical indication of the villages—the woes against Chorazin, Capernaum, and Bethsaida—clearly points to Galilee, particularly villages in the northeast (Luke 10:13–15). The snide comment about those arrayed in luxurious garments living in the palaces of kings, an allusion to Antipas in his palace in Tiberias, confirms the focus on Galilee.

On the other hand, the speeches were evidently already being performed in Greek when they were adapted into the Gospels of Matthew and Luke. This suggests that the movement to which they were addressed had already spread into villages of nearby areas of Syria, where the villagers were either Greek-speaking or bilingual in Greek and Aramaic.[13] This suggests hearers in situations similar to the hearers of the Markan story: in the villages of nearby areas, where conditions and relations with the rulers resembled those of villagers in Galilee to whom the speeches had been addressed earlier. In another similarity to the audience of the Markan story, the people addressed in the speeches appear to have been experiencing some serious repression by the authorities, as indicated in the speech in Luke 12:2–12 and in what appear as a supplementary blessing and curse about being persecuted in Luke 6:20–26.

---

13. See Adams and Swain, "Introduction"; and Taylor, "Bilingualism and Diglossa"; and the provisional discussion in Horsley, "The Language(s) of the Kingdom."

The Q Speeches Resonating with the Hearers in Referencing Israelite Tradition

John's Renewal of the Mosaic Covenant and Prophecy of a Stronger One Coming

In what may have been parts of a longer speech with which the series evidently began (Luke 3:7–9, 16–17), the hearers know that John has been performing a baptism of repentance as the central ritual in a renewal of the Mosaic covenant. In traditional Israelite prophetic speech, John proclaims the *krisis* (judgment) of God in connection with the renewal of Israel that cuts negatively against the (Judean) rulers. John first delivers a blistering prophetic harangue aimed at those who presume they are safe from God's judgment/wrath because of their elite lineage from their "father" Abraham (their identification in Matthew as Pharisees and Sadducees thus fits clues in these prophetic lines). But the audience also hears John prophesying that his baptism is the renewal of Israel as a covenantal society in which God is raising up children to Abraham from the stony ground from which they are struggling to eke out a subsistence living. Shifting to (traditional prophetic) harvest imagery of the judgment, gathering the grain but burning the chaff, John prophesies that *one stronger* than he is coming who will *baptize them with holy spirit and fire*. The audience knows that this *krisis* of positive and negative judgment in covenantal renewal of the people, but condemnation of their rulers, is well underway. The following speeches in Q focus on the different aspects of this *krisis,* mainly on the renewal (movement) of Israel, but also on judgment against the Jerusalem rulers and their scribal representatives.

Jesus' Renewal of Covenantal Community

Picking up where John left off, in the longest of the speeches (Luke 6:20–49, with the broader structure of the speech parallel in Matt 5–7) Jesus enacts a renewal of the Mosaic covenant in performative speech. Not only would the extensive allusions to Mosaic covenantal customs and teachings (especially in Luke 6:27–36) have resonated with hearers embedded in Israelite culture, but the transformation of the structural components of the covenant would have addressed their despair about their circumstances.[14]

14. Fuller analysis and discussion in Horsley with Draper, *Whoever Hears You,*

As a broader pattern deeply rooted in Israelite tradition, the making and renewal of the Mosaic covenant happened in three steps: the declaration of deliverance (originally the exodus liberation from bondage in Egypt); God's demands ("words," commandments, principles) that the people practice justice in their social-economic-political interaction; and sanctions of blessings if they kept the commandments and curses if they violated them (discussed briefly in chap. 5). That this broader covenantal pattern of social relations and organization was still influential in political-economic affairs is known now from the Community Rule of the Qumran community found among the Dead Sea Scrolls. Even a community of scribes and priests, who had been trained to serve the Jerusalem temple-state, patterned their protest movement into the wilderness as a new exodus and the community they established as a renewed Mosaic covenant. In forming a movement opposed to the Jerusalem establishment, however, they transformed the blessings and curses that had become a means of social control into the new declaration of deliverance (1QS 1–4).

In the Q covenant renewal speech, Jesus begins with just such a transformation, in delivering blessings to people who thought that they were hopelessly cursed by poverty and hunger because of their sins.

> Blessed are   the poor   for yours is   the kingdom of God!
> Blessed are   the hungry   for you shall be filled! . . .
> For so   they did   to the prophets.

Jesus, speaking as a new Moses, is proclaiming new deliverance for the people driven into poverty and hunger (evidently in contrast to woes on the wealthy and well-fed, whom the hearers would have assumed were blessed, as explained in chap. 5). This transformation of what had been a debilitating device of social control (their poverty and hunger taken as God's punishment for sinning) gave the hearers the enabling basis for recommitment to the covenantal demands for justice in their communities.

In reformulating the covenantal demands Jesus addresses directly the cumulative effects on their lives of Roman conquest and subsequent Roman imperial rule (through client rulers). The context and circumstances are indicated in the content of the commands and principles.

> Love   the enemies   of you(rs),
> Do good   to those who hate   you,

---

chap. 9; and Horsley, *Covenant Economics*, chap. 7.

| Bless | those who curse | you, |
| Pray for | those who abuse | you. |

| To the one who strikes you | on the cheek | turn | also the other. |
| And from the one who takes | your coat | offer | also the tunic. |

| To the one who asks from you | give. |
| And from the one who borrows | do not ask back . . . |

| But love | your enemies | and do good | and lend. |
| And your reward | will be | great. . . . |

| (You) be | merciful | as your father | is merciful. |
| And do not judge | | and you will not be judged. . . . |

For with the measure you measure it will be measured to you.

Having been forced to render up tribute, taxes, and tithes to the multiple layers of (Roman, Herodian, and high priestly) rulers, the people are poor and hungry. They have made loans to one another, but neighbor-creditors are now demanding repayment to feed their own hungry children. Not surprisingly, they have fallen into local quarreling. Having proclaimed the direct rule of God, however, Jesus restates the traditional Israelite practices and customs demanded in the commandments and principles of the Mosaic covenant, of mutual aid and cooperation among members of village communities: "love your enemies, do good, and lend," even in the face of the difficult circumstances into which they have come. These lines of the speech are virtually full of references and allusions to traditional Israelite commandments, customs, rulings, and other covenantal teachings many of which are familiar to us from the "Covenant Code" and "Holiness Code" and "Deuteronomic" torah that were later included in the Hebrew Bible.[15] At the end of the speech, replacing the ominous threats of the former curses, the double parable about the houses provides a sanctioning insistence on "doing" Jesus' "words" (the traditional term for the covenantal commandments).

That this was performative speech means that the renewal of the covenant was enacted in the village communities hearing the performance. This was not merely the teaching of Jesus but a collective reenactment of or recommitment to the cooperation and mutual support of

15. This analysis first laid out in Horsley, *Jesus and the Spiral*, chap. 9.

the members of the community that had been breaking down under the pressures from the rulers.

The teaching of the prayer for the coming of the direct rule of God ("the Lord's Prayer") in one of the following speeches (Q/Luke 11:2–4, 9–11) provides the people with a powerful reinforcement of the new possibility of life offered by the covenant renewal, all the more powerful from what must have been their regular recitation. The hungry people petition for sufficient food, for cancellation of their debts as they cancel the debts of their neighbors, and for deliverance from repression by the authorities. Another subsequent speech (Q/Luke 12:22–31) reinforces the renewal of covenantal community life by reassuring the hearers that if they single-mindedly seek the cooperative sharing of direct rule of God, the provision of sufficient food and shelter will result.

Healings: The (Direct) Rule of God in Jesus' Actions

This speech closely parallel in Luke 7:18–35 and Matt 11:2–19, clearly presupposed that Jesus had been performing healings of all sorts as well as proclaiming the good news of the direct rule of God. John's question to Jesus follows up on his prophecy of the stronger one coming who will "baptize" in Spirit and fire (in Luke 3:16–17).

> John,   sending   his disciples,   said to him:
> Are you   the coming one   or shall we expect   another?
>
> And answering he said to them:
> Go   announce to John   what you hear and see:
>
> The blind   see   and the lame   walk,
> the lepers   are cleansed   and the deaf   hear,
> the dead   are raised   and the poor   evangelized.
>
> And blessed is   whoever is not offended   by me.

Jesus' answer points John's disciples, and through them the hearers, to what they are hearing and seeing happen in his actions, the actions that were already assumed to be central to his mission and clear indications that he was indeed the prophet that John had prophesied was coming. The speech presents these in a series of parallel phrases with repetitive sounds that would have made them all the more vibrantly resonant with the deep longings of the people expressed in Israelite tradition (discussed in chap. 5). The resonance of the poetic prophetic proclamation of what is happening is important to hear in the repetitive sounds and verbal forms in Greek (here transliterated for readers whether or not they know Greek).

Tuphloi	*anablepousin*	*kai*	*choloi*	*peripatousin*
leproi	*katharizontai*	*kai*	*kophoi*	*akouousin*
kai nekroi	*egeirontai*	*kai*	*ptochoi*	*euaggelizontai*

Instead of concentrating on the immediacy of the sounds, the symmetry of the phrases, and the excitement of the message, biblical scholars deeply rooted in the assumptions of print culture and the standard theological assumptions and procedures of New Testament studies focus on how the "author" of Q is "quoting" from the written text of Isaiah. But precisely on the assumptions of print culture, it is impossible to discern which particular written "text" (fragment) in Isaiah is being "quoted," whether 35:5 or 42:6–7 or 61:1. Each of these mentions one or more of the kinds of malaise that are healed, but none of them mentions more than two or three. As discussed in chapter 6, it is highly unlikely that ordinary people had access to scrolls that were authoritative in scribal circles and that they would have known how to read what was inscribed on them. Moreover, once we recognize that there was a wide and deep Israelite cultural tradition at both the popular level and the scribal level (in interaction), both cultivated orally, then it is not difficult to surmise what is happening in these lines of the speech. The similarity of, yet difference between, the several references to images of healing in Isaiah, in the later stages of the book's development ("Deutero-Isaiah" and "Trito-Isaiah"), suggests that these references were drawing on a standard set of images that expressed the longings of the people for deliverance, as discussed in chap. 5. From the kinds of malaise mentioned in these references, the deliverance for which people yearned in the centuries after the Assyrian and Babylonian conquests was mainly from maladies suffered by the lowly as a result of their political-economic circumstances in having been subjected to a succession of empires. In this speech "Jesus" was drawing on a common cultural repertoire of images of these maladies that the composers of the later stages in the development of the book of Isaiah had drawn upon earlier.[16]

16. Fuller discussion in "Israelite Tradition and the Speeches of Jesus in Q," in *Text and Tradition*, chap. 6, esp. 142–50.

322 EMPOWERING THE PEOPLE

Thus much is packed into this series of clauses as they were performed to communities of a Jesus movement rooted in Israelite tradition. They indicated that Jesus had been performing many healings of different sicknesses. He had healed the blind, the lame, the deaf, cleansed the lepers (those with skin lesions), given new life to the dead or dying. These healings are linked in series with his having also brought good news to the poor, the same close link also articulated in the summaries of healing and preaching and in narrative sequences in Mark, and the same emphasis on the healings as the principal activity of Jesus' mission. The reference of these healings and proclamation to the widespread longings that ran deep in Israelite tradition (and surfaced in "Isaiah" prophecies) indicates that Jesus' actions constituted the deliverance that the people had been longing for. The healings, along with the proclamation (of deliverance), moreover, is framed by John's question and presented in response as the actions of the prophet he had prophesied as coming to baptize with Holy Spirit in a renewal of the people/Israel.

The sense in which the healings of Jesus are central to the people's longings and the renewal of Israel increases dramatically as the speech continues into Jesus' questions and declaration to the crowds—presumably crowds of the poor, the hungry, and the disheartened whom he had addressed in the covenant renewal speech.

He began   to say   to the crowds   concerning John:
What did you go out into the wilderness to see?
A reed   by the wind   shaken?
But what   did you go out   to see?
A man   in finery   arrayed?
Behold,
Those in finery   are in the houses   of kings.
But what   did you go out   to see?
A prophet?
Yes!   I tell you,
And more than   a prophet!

This is the one   about whom   it has been written:
Behold,
I send   my messenger before your face
Who shall prepare   your way   before you.
I tell you:
There has not arisen among those born of women
                                         anyone greater than John.
Yet the least   in the kingdom of God   is greater than he!

The repeated rhetorical questions build the anticipation and excitement of the answer. "What did you go out to see?" again referring back to John's baptism and prophecy. "A man attired in "soft" raiment?" Surely not, as the audience concerned about how they could clothe and feed themselves knew only too well (as in the speech in Luke 12:22–31). Such luxury was found only in royal palaces, that is of (the Rome-appointed) Herod Antipas (or his successor) in his recently constructed palace in Tiberias, which would have been funded by the produce of their labor that he expropriated as taxes. The speech does not just "reference" Israelite tradition but is a *continuation* of the popular tradition in which prophets prophesied hope and deliverance for the people against such rulers. "A prophet. And more than a prophet!"

In the next lines, in referring to Israelite tradition, "Jesus" does quote what "is written." If we listen (and look) carefully, however, the lines supposedly quoted, which to modern scholars means from a written text, do not correspond closely with either the Septuagint (the Judean scriptures in Greek) or the Masoretic text known from much later Hebrew manuscripts of either Mal 3:21 or Exod 23:20 (the two texts that scholars usually cite). The composer-performers of Q texts would not have been literally quoting from an expensive and inaccessible scroll. But they would have known that references to deliverance in the exodus or in the anticipated new exodus were "written" on the authoritative scrolls kept in scribal circles or laid up in the Jerusalem temple. As noted in chap. 5, in a society where writing was rare there was an aura surrounding written texts that lent them authority among the people. A village-based movement was only too happy to claim the authority of what was "written" for the prophets who had generated their movement in opposition to the authorities. Referring to John as "the messenger who will prepare your way before you" identifies him as the prophesied prophet who would fulfill the deep longings of the people for new deliverance anticipated in images of the exodus deliverance. "Your way" is the new exodus way in which God is leading the people into renewal, but now includes Jesus, whose healings and proclamation are the actions of "the stronger one" prophesied by John as the prophet of the renewal of the people.

The "I tell you" signals the decisive declaration that is coming, *the* point in this speech, replete with the hyperbole in its comparison: John is the crucial, most important figure (prophet) in history; but the humblest person in the kingdom of God is greater than he! What is being manifested in Jesus' healings is the presence of the direct rule of God, and what is happening in Jesus' actions is greater than anything (yet) in (Israelite) history.

Interpreters who believe that Q is merely a collection of separate sayings are unsure about their placement of the lines about the kingdom of God suffering violence (Matt 11:12–13//Luke 16:16). Once we recognize that these are a series of oral speeches, then it seems that we should follow the Matthean version that has those lines as the transition from the second to the third step of this speech (Matt 11:7–11, 12–13, 15–19, with 11:14 as the transition). That is, these lines are the connection between John as the greatest figure in history leading up to the direct rule of God now being manifested in Jesus' healings and the attacks on John and Jesus (a theme prominent elsewhere in the speeches, e.g., Luke 11:49–52; 13:34–35).

> The prophets   and the law   [were] until John.
> From then on   the rule of God suffers violence,
> And the violent   plunder   it.

These lines lead into the final step of the speech about how "this type/ilk," like petulant children, attack the prophets of renewal, charging that John "is possessed by a *daimonion*" and "the son of man" ("yours truly"/"the human one"/Jesus) is "a glutton and a drunkard, a friend of tax-collectors and sinners." The final line then insists that they have been vindicated, referring back to the healings (or in Luke, to the prophets John and Jesus who are being attacked): "Yet wisdom is vindicated by her works (children)!" Considering that here as in other Q speeches it is the scribes and Pharisees who oppose the prophets (including Jesus) and that the learned scribes were well-known for their cultivation of (heavenly) wisdom, this assertion may be an ironic slam at "the wise." In a subsequent speech, following the Lord's Prayer, "Jesus" praises God for pointedly not revealing these things to "the wise and learned" but to the "infants/children" (*nepioi*; 10:21–22), whom "the wise" viewed as incapable of knowing wisdom.

This speech focuses on the many healings of Jesus as his principal actions in which it is clear that he is the coming one that John had prophesied would enact the renewal of Israel. In bringing the direct rule of God manifested in the healings Jesus is surpassing the prophet John, the greatest figure of Israelite history in preparing the way of this renewal. With rich referencing to the central events and prophecies of liberation in Israelite tradition combined with rhetorical questions that build the anticipation, the speech presents the healings and the proclamation of

Jesus as the satisfaction and fulfillment of the deep longings of the people for healing and renewal.

It is significant to note that although these speeches are a different mode of communication from the Markan narrative, both present the same close relation between Jesus' healing of the people and his renewal of covenantal community. Both the sequence of speeches and the Markan narrative also closely link Jesus' healings (and exorcism) and covenant renewal with his commission of envoys to extend his mission, which is the focus of the next speech.

Commissioning Envoys to Extend the Mission of Healing and Exorcism

In the next speech (Luke 10:2–16; partly paralleled in Matt 10:2–15) Jesus commissions envoys to extend his mission into (other) villages, healing the sick and proclaiming that the direct rule of God has come upon them, while staying in receptive households and eating whatever they can provide. Some interpreters think that the three short dialogues that precede this mission speech (Q/Luke 9:57–62), with their allusions to Elijah's commissioning of Elisha as his prophetic protege, serve as a prologue to it. At the end of the speech Jesus delivers prophetic woes on (particular) villages that did not respond positively to "the (acts of) power(s)" that happened in them during this mission, suggesting that the envoys had indeed extended Jesus' healings and exorcisms in those village communities. The speech includes several significant references to Israelite tradition that enable us to hear how it would have resonated with the communities that were hearing it performed.

The opening declaration that "the harvest is great" signals that the/a great ingathering of the people (of Israel/the covenant) is at hand, with implications of deliverance and judgment. Harvest was a prominent traditional image in prophecies, as in the punitive judgment against part of Israel (Hos 6:11), but more often judgment against oppressive imperial regimes (Mic 4:11; Isa 18:3–6; Jer 51:33; Joel 3:12–13). Especially striking is a late prophecy (Isa 27:2–13) of the gathering of Israel while God "threshes" the imperial regimes. The harvest also links the mission speech with John's prophecy of the stronger one coming who will gather, with the debate about Jesus' exorcisms, where his activity is represented as "gathering," and with the prophecy about the gathering of the people from far and wide for the banquet of the kingdom.

That many more workers are needed in the great harvest suggests that in John's and Jesus' activity, the harvest has barely begun and there is much more work to be done in the gathering or renewal of the people. Harvest was always the most intense time for agrarian villagers: there were never enough workers in families who had to labor intensively when the crops were ready. The image of many workers might also have been influenced by the royal and other large estates in the Great Plain to the south with which many Galileans and other villagers would have been familiar (cf. Matt 20:1–16). "Workers" quickly became a term parallel to "those sent" ("apostles"; as in 2 Cor 11:13), as suggested in the verb "behold I send you (out)" in the next line. The emphatic "I" in Matthew's version of the declaration "Behold, *I* send you . . . ," unnecessary in Greek style, suggests that "Jesus" is speaking as a prophet in the sending. This phrase, along with the traditional prophetic form "woe to" in the closing sanction indicate that the whole commissioning is in performative speech, enacting what is spoken.

Being sent out "as sheep/lambs in the midst of wolves" was another traditional image with which the hearers would have resonated deeply. Contrary to a standard theological scheme of Christian origins, this does not suggest Christian missionaries as innocent sheep among hostile Jews. It was rather an image of the people at the mercy of their predatory rulers. The princes and other officials of the Jerusalem monarchy had been like "roaring lions" or "wolves tearing their prey, shedding blood, destroying lives to get dishonest gain" (Ezek 22:23–27; cf. Zeph 3:1–3; Prov 28:15). In its origins, Israel had been sheep oppressed by the wolves of the Egyptian imperial regime (1 Enoch 89:13–27). The people are like lambs at the mercy of the "nations of the earth" in a lament over the Roman conquest of Jerusalem that leads to a plea to "bring together the dispersed of Israel" (*Pss. Sol.* 8:23; cf. 4 Ezra 5:18). The image is one of vulnerability, but refers mainly to the potential political trouble that the envoys could run into because their mission might be threatening to Roman client rulers such as Antipas, who could take repressive measures. In other speeches in Q, specifically the beginning of the covenant renewal, the woes against the Pharisees, and the prophetic lament over the Jerusalem ruling house, Jesus, John, and the addressees themselves are represented as like the earlier prophets, persecuted and killed, and the speech in Luke 12:2–12 admonishes the hearers to bold confession when they are put on trial.

The prohibition on carrying a knapsack (or purse) or stick fit the purpose for which the envoys are sent, to work in villages, while staying in households and eating whatever the host family can offer. The instructions for envoys, balanced as to reception, indicate that the purpose is to extend Jesus' own mission, that of healing and preaching. If anything, the emphasis in the instructions about the envoys' work in the villages is on their healing and exorcism. Previous reconstruction of this speech has often not noticed that the Lukan adaptation has shortened a fuller list of what Jesus instructs them to do in Matt 10:8–9 that is not derived from the mission instruction in Mark 6:7–13. The parallel poetic clauses with repetition of sounds in Matt 10:8 (par. Luke 10:9), moreover, pick up on Jesus' reference to his own actions in response to John's question in Q/ Luke 7:22 and anticipate his casting out of *daimonia* in Q/Luke 11:19–20.

asthenountas	*therapeuete,*
nekrous	*egeirete,*
leprous	*katharizete,*
daimonia	*ekballete . . .*

The Q mission speech thus gives the envoys an extended charge of healing and exorcism that matches Jesus' own healing of many illnesses and casting out of spirits. As in the Markan story healings and exorcisms are (the) principal manifestation of what the envoys declare, that "the (direct) reign of God is at hand."

The (actual or potential) failure of a village community to "hear" them and respond positively evokes a ritual gesture and pronouncement of prophetic woes that anticipate God's judgment. Sodom had been judged and destroyed not just because of its wickedness but also because its people did not recognize God's messengers. The prophetic woes against Chorazin and Bethsaida (and Capernaum) are not only packed with images that would evoke resonance in the hearers, but with information that has all but been ignored by modern interpreters. "(Acts of) power(s)" (*dynameis*) had been done in those villages/towns, evidently by the envoys and/or perhaps by Jesus himself. Given the limited information about what their mission in the villages consisted in, the *dynameis* must refer to the healings. Not only had Jesus been performing healings of various sicknesses, but the movement of Jesus-loyalists presupposed and addressed in the mission speech had continued to perform healings.

In using Tyre and Sidon as comparisons for how bad the judgment would be for the unresponsive villages, "Jesus" was referring to the cities perhaps most resented by Galileans and nearby peoples. In Israelite tradition they were the principal carriers of trade in luxury goods for the elite of Jerusalem and Samaria, which the rulers would have paid for by taxation and other exploitation of villagers. In addition, at the time of Jesus and the Q speeches, Tyre and Sidon were the nearest, most wealthy and powerful cities that directly or indirectly drained away the resources of the villagers, hence the most hated symbols of their exploitation under the Roman imperial order.[17]

Jesus' Response to the Accusation of Casting out Spirits by Beelzebul

Jesus' response to being charged with casting out *daimonia* by Beelzebul indicates how fundamental exorcisms were to Jesus' mission in the series of speeches. The lines and their wording in Matt 12:22–30, 43–45 and Luke 11:14–26 are closely parallel or verbatim for most of the speech, but there are some noticeable differences. The episode appears to have begun with a brief (two-line) reference to Jesus casting out "a *daimonion* that was mute" and the crowd's astonishment. Judging from the sharp opposition between Jesus and the scribes and Pharisees elsewhere in the Q speeches (especially the series of woes in Luke 11:39–52, paralleled in Matt 23), it is likely that Matthew best represents the accusers in the Beel-zebul charge as Pharisees.[18] This would parallel the similar controversy in Mark where the charge is brought by the scribes (3:22–27), as well as the historical dynamics in Judea as portrayed by Josephus.

> He cast out   a *daimonion*   that was mute.
> The mute   spoke and the crowds marveled.
> The Pharisees said:
> By Beelzebul   the ruler   of the *daimonia*
>   he casts out   the *daimonia*.
>
> Knowing   their thoughts   he said   to them:
> Every kingdom divided against itself is laid waste,
> Every house   divided against itself will not stand,

17. Note the reference in Acts 12:20-23 to how Tyre and Sidon "depended on" Agrippa II's territory (including Galilee) for food; that is, they imported food grown by Galileans and then expropriated by the Rome-appointed rulers such as Antipas and Agrippa to sell in trade for luxury goods provided by sea-borne traders in Tyre and Sidon.

18. As in introducing John the Baptist's harangue (3:7-9), Luke again here appears to be mitigating the sharp opposition between the Jerusalem rulers and their represen-tatives and the prophets John and Jesus.

And if Satan   against himself is divided
how   will stand   the kingdom of him?
And if I   by Beelzebul   cast out   the *daimonia*
your sons   by whom   do they cast out?

Therefore   they   your judges   shall be.
But if by the finger of God   I cast out   the *daimonia*
then   has come upon you   the kingdom of God.

(Or how can   one enter   the house   of a strong man
   and the possessions of him   plunder
   unless he first   ties up   the strong man?
Then the house   of him   he can plunder.)

Whoever is not   with me is against me,
And whoever does not gather with me   scatters.
   (Luke 11:14–26//Matt 12:22–30, 43–45)

Modern theological interpretation of the combination of the charge
of Beelzebul and the different steps of Jesus' response has resulted in the
dualism of a cosmic battle between God (and/or Jesus) and Satan being
imposed on this speech in particular and on Jesus' exorcisms in general,
even his whole mission (as noted in chap. 7 above).[19] This scheme, however, is not *in* or *behind* or *expressed in* this charge and response. Nor is
such a "cosmic dualism" of the demonic kingdom of Satan locked in a

19. The lengthy discussion of Luke 11:20//Matt 12:28 and its "coherence with other
sayings" by Meier, *Mentor, Message, and Miracles*, 413–21, is representative of New
Testament scholarship generally in its assumption that in the apocalyptic view of Jews
in late second-temple times, human existence was understood as subject to a cosmic
combat between the rule of God and the rule of Satan. Ironically theological interpreters may have constructed the cosmic struggle between God and Satan, between the
kingdom of God, whose agent was Jesus, and Satan the ruler of the demons, from
the very Gospel texts they were attempting to interpret, particularly (the versions of)
the "Beelzebul" controversy. Further on in his discussion Meier (*Mentor, Message,
and Miracles*, 462–63n40) outlines the "demonic synthesis" that he imagines resulting from Q's "stitching together originally independent sayings" on the basis of the
systematic scribal scheme from Qumran about "the prince of light" vs. "Belial and the
whole army of his rule." Ironically—parallel to his finding "popular" belief in magic to
be so problematic (Meier, *Mentor, Message, and Miracles*, 535)—he then suggests that
"the Beelzebul complex in the Synoptics reflects ideas about the reign of Satan/Beelze-
bul over a kingdom of demons, ideas held by Jewish peasants in Palestine around the
turn of the era." Because this modern scholarly construct of an "apocalyptic cosmic
combat" is so prominent in scholarly interpretation of Jesus and the Gospels, it is important to "deconstruct" it, as in the discussion in chap. 5 above.

struggle against the divine kingdom attested in late second temple Judean texts produced by scribal circles (reviewed in chap. 5). The lines in Luke 11:14–23/26 are rather a sequence of (a) the charge that Jesus is exorcizing by Beelzebul, then (b) Jesus' refutation of the charge in comparisons and rhetorical questions, and finally (c) Jesus' statement of what is happening in the exorcisms.

If we listen carefully to Jesus' response to the "Beelzebul" charge it becomes clear that he and the audience do not share the scribal speculation about the struggle between beneficent and maleficent spirits/heavenly forces. The line that Jesus "knew their thoughts" indicates that in the ensuing comparison to "every kingdom" and "every house" and the two rhetorical questions he is responding to their way of thinking as well as to their specific accusation. The Pharisees making the accusation (like the scribes in Mark) think in terms of Beelzebul as the ruler of the spirits, and it is they who think of Satan as synonymous with Beelzebul. As explained in connection with the Markan version of this "controversy," "Beelzebul" almost certainly derived from Judean scribal culture, an incorporation of the Canaanite god, Ba'al, into Judean scribal speculation as (one of) the principal force(s) hostile to the Judean temple-state.[20] As in the Markan version, the accusation "demonizes" Jesus as subverting the Judean temple-state by collaborating with its most hostile divine enemy force.

Again as in the Markan version of the dispute, the first step in Jesus' response was to explain that the charge was absurd by drawing comparisons with ruling "houses" (dynasties) and "kingdoms" that would have evoked memories of Israelite-Judean history. Every (ruling) house or kingdom divided against itself would fall. In recent history the Hasmonean house, which had arrogated to itself the title of king/kingdom and had taken over rule of Galilee and conquered other nearby peoples, had become divided against itself and had fallen (as noted in chap. 7 above). The audience of the Q speeches living in northern Palestine (as well as the Pharisees whose predecessors became active in the division of the Hasmonean house against itself) would have remembered this recent history well. "Jesus" is arguing that it is absurd to imagine that Beelzebul/Satan, (understood by his accusers to be) the ruler of the *daimonia*, would empower Jesus to cast out *daimonia* because, thus divided against himself, his rule would collapse. The next step of his response, a

20. See Fitzmyer, *Luke*, 2:920; and the discussion of the parallel Beelzebul controversy in Mark in chap. 7 above.

rhetorical question distinctive to the Q version of the Beelzebul dispute, assumes that others, supposedly the disciples of the Pharisees, were also performing exorcisms. Jesus challenges the accusers who are "demonizing" him to be consistent in their attribution of the cause in the casting out of spirits.

Having refuted the accusation of Beelzebul, Jesus states the alternative understanding of his exorcisms, in a pronouncement addressed now pointedly to the audience. If, on the other hand, he is casting out the *daimonia* not by Beelzebul but "by the finger of God," then "the kingdom of God has come upon them." Interpreters have reached a consensus that "finger of God," not "spirit of God" as in Matthew, was the more likely phrase in the speech prior to its Matthean and Lukan performances, since the composers of Luke who are so keen on the role of the (holy) Spirit (of God) would not have changed "spirit" to "finger." Also, after decades of debate, rooted partly in a kind of modern literalism about verb tense, it seems clear that "has come upon you" is the appropriate translation (for *ephthasen*).

It may help modern hearers to discern the sense of the declaration to consider several interrelated aspects of the clearly political *basileia tou theou* in the historical context of the communities of the Jesus' movement in Galilee and surrounding areas and how Israelite tradition would have informed the hearing of Jesus' pronouncement. To modern ears, the translation "kingdom" suggests the actual exercise of political control over territory and people. People in Roman Palestine and Syria lived in and under the kingdom (rule) of Rome/Caesar, and in late first-century BCE Galilee and Judea also in and under the kingdom of Herod. Nevertheless, in Israelite tradition, particularly under the Mosaic covenant and covenantal tradition, God was the literal and exclusive king or sovereign over Israel. Thus "the kingdom of God" was an alternative to and in opposition to the kingdom of Rome or Herod. The scribes and Pharisees of the "Fourth Philosophy" based their refusal to pay the tribute demanded by Rome/Caesar on the covenantal principal that God was the exclusive lord and master of Israelites/Judeans. It may also help to remember that *basileia* also meant "rule," and that villages were semi-independent and semi-self-governing communities; to an extent they could operate their own village affairs under the direct rule (kingdom) of God, that is, according to Mosaic covenantal principles, commandments, and customs.

Land and people, however, had been devastated by Roman conquests and under the rule of Rome and its client rulers they were forced to render up their crops in tribute and taxes (in violation of the covenant). They thus lived in an acute conflict between the rule/kingdom of God and the rule/kingdom of Caesar and his client rulers. As discussed in chap. 5, the spirits/*daimonia* became both a mystification of and a self-protective buffer between subject people and their invasive rulers, keeping them from focusing directly on their rulers and taking what would have been suicidal action of rebellion. Some of the people became invaded and possessed by the spirits/*daimonia*, who controlled their behavior. The casting out of those spirits freed the possessed people, their families and communities, from that possession or rule. Thus the truth of and the impact of Jesus' declaration: "If it is by the finger of God that I cast out the *daimonia* then the (direct) rule of God has come upon you." This statement is parallel to the initial declaration in the (performative) covenant renewal speech conferring the blessing of the direct rule of God on the poor—as the basis on which Jesus then demanded the people recommit to the practice of covenantal cooperation and sharing in village communities.

There is also another dimension of the declaration as it resonated with people embedded in Israelite tradition. The phrase "the finger of God" was a direct reference to the struggle led by the founding prophet Moses against the people's bondage under Pharaoh's kingdom/rule in Egypt. "The finger of God" was a symbol for when the actions that Moses was taking finally began to move effectively toward the liberation of the people from Pharaoh's kingdom/rule in Egypt. Jesus is declaring that in the exorcisms the direct rule of God has come upon the people—with the implication that the rule of God will continue coming upon the people. As we are now learning from studies of oral performance, one of the ways this continued happening was through performances of this and other speeches in the Q series.

To pull together what the steps of Jesus' response to the charge of Beelzebul say, in contrast to the accusers way of thinking and even more to the modern theological reading of this "controversy," at no point does Jesus say that he is battling Satan/Beelzebul, the ruler of the *daimonia*. In fact, nothing in these lines suggests that Jesus and the hearers of the speech even think in terms of Satan, much less as "the ruler of the demons." It is the Pharisees, like the scribes in the Markan version, who think in those terms, as articulated in their accusation. The first step in Jesus' response argues that their charge is, on the surface of it, absurd and illogical. Separated and set up by his rhetorical question about how their own disciples do their exorcisms, Jesus' pronouncement about what is happening in the exorcisms does not include Satan. His declaration focuses on his casting out of *daimonia,* and insofar as he is doing those by "the finger of God" the exorcisms are manifestations of a new exodus liberation of the people, so that the direct rule of God has come upon them.

In what was evidently the next step in Jesus' refutation of the charge of Beelzebul he shifted to the "parable" or extended metaphor of plundering the strong man's house.[21] As in the Markan version, there is nothing to suggest that "the binding of the strong man" has reference in some way to the scribal speculation about the archaic binding of the rebel heavenly powers (1 Enoch 10:4; 21:1-10; Jubilees 10:7-9). The application of the parable/metaphor, however, suggests that Satan's rule has been checked/weakened (by God?) so that it is possible to cast out the invasive spirits.

The final two lines in Jesus' response to the accusation refers back to the reference to the others who were exorcizing in a slam against his accusers (note the rhetorical parallel with the third step in the speech in Luke 7:18-35). The sharp opposition between Jesus and those who are against him fits the sharp opposition between Jesus and the scribes and Pharisees and Jerusalem ruling house in other Q speeches. "Whoever does not gather with me scatters,"[22] moreover, closely parallels the harvest imagery of Jesus' "gathering" or renewal of the people in opposition to and by those who "lock the kingdom"/"take away the key of (covenantal) knowledge" (Luke 11:52) and those who persecute/kill the prophets (6:22-23; 11:49-51; 13:34-35).[23]

---

21. It is somewhat unclear whether this step that applies the metaphor of plundering the strong man's goods was part of the speech. The Matthean version closely parallels the Markan version of the dialogue here. On the other hand, the "parable of plundering the strong man," while very different in the Matthean and Lukan versions, does fit the same sequence of steps in the episode. The extended metaphor of combat between armed soldiers in the Lukan version at Luke 11:21-22 (different from the plundering of a strong man's house in Matthew 12:29 and Mark 3:27) may have been another influence on the scholarly scheme of two kingdoms locked in battle.

22. Casey, *Aramaic Approach to Q,* 148-49, 176-77 (and Casey, *Jesus of Nazareth,* 254), suggests that behind Greek *skorpizo,* translated "scatters," may lie the Aramaic *baddar,* that referred to a group being scattered, as in Israel as "scattered sheep" (Jer 50:17). Jesus, on the other hand, is gathering those sheep = Israel, as Matt 10:6; 18:12-14; Luke 15:4-7.

23. With the line about gathering and scattering having provided a fitting ending of the speech, it is difficult to discern how the unclean spirit's return to the person (Luke 11:24-26) concluded or even fit into the speech. The focal term is now "unclean spirit" instead of the *daimonion* cast out (11:14). These lines may well be a warning,

Prophetic Pronouncements against
the Rulers and Their Representatives

Several of the subsequent speeches are Jesus' prophetic pronouncements against the rulers and their representatives for their exploitation of the people, in traditional Israelite prophetic forms.

The next two speeches are directed against the Pharisees who (in the Matthean version) brought the charge of Beelzebul against Jesus for his exorcism (and healing) of the people. Ironically they ask him for "a sign" (interpretation of omens and divination generally were central to scribal service of rulers). In declaring that "no sign shall be given except the sign of Jonah" (Matt 12:38–42//Luke 11:16, 29–32), he draws an analogy from the legendary (in Israelite tradition) imperial city of Nineveh that refused to heed the warnings of the prophet Jonah to "this wicked generation" (the Pharisees and their patrons) who refuse to heed the manifestations of the rule of God in his preaching, healing, and exorcism. Also, in Jesus and his exorcisms and preaching of the kingdom, something greater than Solomon is here. It is impossible to tell whether the figure of Solomon here is simply the legendary great imperial king of Israel (not necessarily a positive figure in the popular social memory), or perhaps (also) the legendary monarch whose wisdom included (scribal) healing lore.

The speech behind Luke 11:39–52 appears to have been at least part of the basis of Jesus' harangue against the Pharisees and scribes in Matthew 23. Jesus pronounces a series of indictments ("Woe to you for . . . !") against them for the effects on the people of the work they were doing as representatives of the temple-state, directly in a form familiar from the prophecies of Amos, Isaiah and Micah.[24] These have been seriously misunderstood in Christian theological interpretation as a harangue against Jewish obsession with ritual legalism, especially rigorous

---

added to Jesus' response to the accusation, not to presume on the permanence of exorcism. It is surely a reminder that the exorcism of invasive spirits was not a permanent defeat (and certainly not a destruction). The hostile spirits/daimonia, like the invasive political-economic forces they represented, were still active, still invasive. The person/"house" from whom the spirit had been cast out should not remain empty or complacent, but filled with/occupied by an alternative. But here it is difficult to discern how the metaphor might have continued.

24. As in the Q speech, most such woes came in multiple sets (two, four, or more) followed by a declaration of punishment (Amos 6:1–3, 4–6 + 7; Isa 5:19–19, 20, 21, 22–23, + 24; Hab 2:9–11, 12, 15 + 16–17, 19. See the fuller analysis and discussion in Horsley, "Social Relations and Social Conflict."

observance of purity laws. But only two of the woes even mention purity (Luke 11:39–41 and 44) and then only as a rhetorical device. The series of woes (Luke 11:39–52 and par.) begin by mocking the Pharisees and the scribes for their concern for purity or tithing. But the substantive charges are for extortion, neglecting justice, imposing burdens on the people "with your fingers" (scribal pens?), and even being complicit in killing the prophets. The punishment declared fits the most serious of the crimes in the indictments: "Therefore the blood of all the prophets who were martyred will be required of "this generation" (or "this type/ilk," that is, the Pharisees and legal-experts). The whole series of woes is in performative speech, so that pronouncing them effects what they pronounce.

The speeches also include pronouncements of judgment against the Jerusalem ruling house, which we recognize as the high priests maintained in power by the Romans (Luke 13:28–29 and 13:34–35) The first makes more sense in the Matthean sequence of lines (= Luke 13:29–28): many will come from east and west into the banquet of the kingdom of God with Abraham and Isaac and Jacob; but "the (presumptive) sons of the kingdom" will be cast out, and there will be weeping and gnashing of teeth. Contrary to Christian theological interpretation, the people coming from east and west are not "Gentiles" who are replacing "the Jews" in the kingdom of God. This is rather the gathering of Israel in renewal, as anticipated in John's opening prophecy and as underway and expanded in Jesus' mission and his sending out workers to expand his mission of healing and preaching.

The gathering of Israel here, however, references Israelite popular tradition, and not elite tradition. In the many prophecies of the gathering of the dispersed Judeans (or Israelites) in texts produced in scribal circles, the ingathering was expected to focus on Jerusalem/Zion (Zech 8:7–8; Bar 5:5; *Pss Sol.* 11:2). Jesus' prophetic declaration in Q not only does not mention Jerusalem as the center of the ingathering, but "turns the tables" on the elite who presumed on their lineage from the patriarchs (referring back to John's warning to the aristocrats, 3:7–9) as "the sons of the kingdom." It is conceivable that the parable of the great banquet (Luke 14:16–24, parallel in Matt 22) belongs with Q/Luke 13:28–29 as an elaboration of the prophecy about the banquet of the kingdom of God. The wealthy elite are too busy expanding their wealth, so the *poor* and maimed and *blind* and *lame* are gathered into the banquet, in images that pick up on John's prophecy and particularly on the people Jesus has healed (with some of the same terms used).

The prophetic pronouncement (Q/Luke 13:34; that forms the ending of the speech against the Pharisees and scribes in Matthew 23) explicitly condemns the Jerusalem ruling house. The prophecy stands directly in the tradition of prophetic laments that declare God's judgment in anticipation. The parallel lines with repetition of sounds makes all the more powerful the plaintive analogy between God wanting to protect the villagers and a mother hen wanting to protect her children. Again Jesus makes the prophetic pronouncement in "performative speech" that makes it so.

Repression and Martyrdom

Not only do the Q speeches present Jesus as a prophet, indeed as the greatest in the long tradition of Israelite prophets, but as a prophet who was killed by the rulers, again in a long line of prophets that most recently had included John the Baptist. This is clearest in the pronouncement of God's judgment at the climax of the woes against the Pharisees and in the statement of the reasons for God's judgment of the Jerusalem ruling house. Although the speeches make no mention of Jesus having been crucified, the final statement in the speech about Jesus' healings as the manifestation of the direct rule of God and Jesus as the fulfillment of John's promise of the stronger one declares that both prophets are vindicated in their works, at least in the Matthean version.

As the loyalists in communities of the movement that originated in the healings, exorcisms, and proclamation of the kingdom, moreover, the people addressed in the speeches understand themselves as continuing the prophetic mission Jesus generated. As articulated at the beginning of the covenant renewal speech, they think of themselves as "blessed" when they are persecuted, as were the prophets before them (Luke 6:20–26). Then in the speech (Luke 12:2–12) that follows upon the pronouncement of woes and judgment on the scribes and Pharisees whose ancestors attacked the prophets, Jesus exhorts the hearers, when they are dragged before the authorities, to speak boldly in court about what has been happening in the movement that formed in response to Jesus' mission.

The Series of Speeches

These speeches address a crisis for the Israelite people in Roman Palestine under the rule of Herod Antipas and the Jerusalem high priests.

The people are suffering numerous illnesses evidently brought on by centuries of imperial conquest and domination. They are experiencing possession by invasive spirits. They are poor and hungry and indebted to one another and outsiders. Living in a society deeply rooted in the Mosaic covenant their ancestors made with the Force who had liberated them, they have also evidently been assuming that their sicknesses and poverty are the results of their having broken the covenant. Meanwhile, their rulers live in luxury and the scribes who could mitigate their dire circumstances continue in their customary role of pressing for payment of tithes and even aid the rulers in their persecution and killing of the prophets who protest.

John and Jesus have come forward as the climactic prophets in the long line of Israelite prophets. John has launched a renewal of the people centered in a renewal of the Mosaic covenant focused on the ceremony of baptism for remission of sins. Jesus, however, is the principal prophet of renewal of the people. In this series of speeches, as in the Markan story, his principal actions were healings and exorcisms. The healings were understood by the people as the fulfillment of the deep longings for relief from the wounds and plagues of centuries of imperial conquest and domination. The exorcisms were evidently threatening to the rulers and their scribal representatives, who accused Jesus of collusion with the Beelzebul, the latter-day rival god of the perennial Canaanite enemy peoples. Center in Jesus' renewal of the people is his performative speech in a covenant renewal ceremony that engages the people in recommitment to the covenant demands of cooperation and mutual sharing. In other aspects of his role of the prophet like Moses and Elijah who is generating a renewal of the people, Jesus in traditional Israelite prophetic forms pronounces God's condemnation of the Jerusalem rulers and their scribal representatives for attacking and killing the prophets (like himself and John). Other speeches give evidence that a renewal movement has emerged in response to Jesus' mission, a movement that sees itself as a collective prophetic community focused on its martyred prophet like Moses and Elijah. And the movement appears prepared to continue in the social renewal and opposition to the rulers despite periodic persecution.

The effect of the Jesus-speeches on the communities in which it was performed will be discussed in chap 11.

9

The Matthean Story

PREVIOUSLY STANDARD STUDY-AND-INTERPRETATION OF the Gospels has worked on the basis of modern print-cultural assumptions and the confidence that text criticism had discerned their stable early if not original written texts. On the basis of these assumptions, scholars sought to determine the relation between the ("Synoptic") Gospels. Consensus among a majority of Gospel scholars focused on the two-document hypothesis: Matthew and Luke both used Mark and Q (and their respective special materials) as their sources. "Redaction critics" then combed through the particular ways in which Matthew and Luke had changed or edited the Markan text and the Q "sayings" in order to determine Matthew's or Luke's theology (Christology, ecclesiology, etc.) and so shed light on Mark's theology as well. While the many generations of such scholarship served the use of the Christian Scripture by theology and churches, it is of questionable utility once the Gospel stories are recognized as sustained narratives with speeches. Bringing together the implications of the different lines of recent research that have demonstrated the dominance of oral communication and the instability of written texts strongly suggests that the Gospel stories were composed and cultivated in oral performance in communities/movements of Jesus-loyalists. And this recognition forces us to use our freshly informed imagination, working on more appropriate assumptions and understanding of ancient communications-media and knowledge of changing historical circumstances, to seriously rethink the relation between the different Gospel stories-and-speeches.

The relation of both the Matthean story-and-speeches and the Lukan story-and-speeches with the Jesus-speeches they both incorporated are simpler to discern than their relation to the Markan story. We hypothesize that there was a series of speeches composed and performed prior to Matthew and Luke only because much of their respective speech material is so similar, even virtually verbatim in several passages. Once we recognize the prominence of oral communication in Roman Palestine, of course, we can no longer pretend to reconstruct the wording and parameters of those common speeches with any precision. Yet it seems clear that the Matthean composers and the Lukan composers knew the same speeches already being performed in a Jesus-movement and adapted them in distinctive ways. What these speeches may have been we discern only by discerning how they are adapted, respectively, in the Matthean and Lukan stories.

Both the Matthean and the Lukan stories, once they come to John the Baptist, include and parallel the Markan episodes.[1] The Matthean text leaves out or rearranges a few of the exorcism and healing episodes in early narrative steps, but after the episode commissioning the disciples to extend his mission it follows the Markan narrative sequence with only a few additions, mainly of speech materials. The Lukan text, except for blocks of speeches and some additional episodes not in Mark, follows the Markan sequence of episodes with only a few additions. So Matthew and Luke still include what we imagine must have been the basic story behind the more developed Markan narrative and most of the Markan episodes in narrative sequence. But they are new and different stories with their own narrative sequences, different infancy episodes, and especially the addition of a great deal of teaching in shorter or longer speeches. Among other significant differences from the Markan story, the Matthean and the Lukan stories both address communities and/or movements in the significantly changed circumstances following the Roman destruction of Jerusalem (Luke 19:39–44; 21:20–22; Matt 22:1–14, discussed further under "Context").

Again adapting the synthetic comparative theory of John Miles Foley outlined in chap. 6, this chapter explores how the Matthean story-and-speeches in performance resonated with its audience as it referenced Israelite tradition, after an outline of the *text* and an analysis of whatever clues the text may offer about the historical *context* of the audience.

---

1. Counting the contents of the Markan text (whether of words, "verses," or episodes) that are included in Matthew does not reveal very much. Once we recognize that the Gospel texts were narratives (with speeches), then it is more significant to note the parallels to Mark in the sequence of episodes in the Matthean and Lukan texts.

Chap. 10 will focus on the Lukan story. Many of the observations about the complex procedure of "hearing" the Markan story, especially at the beginning of the section on referencing Israelite tradition, are also pertinent to "hearing" the Matthean story.

Text

The Matthean story of Jesus' mission proceeds in a sequence of five narrative steps each followed by a thematic speech (as noted in chap. 1).[2] The text begins with a genealogy of Jesus as son of Abraham and son of David, his birth as the Messiah, and an infancy narrative that indicates just how threatening he was to the Roman imperial order in Palestine ruled by the Roman client rulers. John's baptism prepares the way for Jesus' mission, for which he is tested in the wilderness. The Matthean story climaxes in a narrative of Jesus' arrest, Passover-covenant meal, trial, crucifixion, and resurrection. While the Matthean story seems long and complex in comparison with the Markan story, its procedure in five steps of narrative-and-speech would have facilitated its learning and performance and its hearing in communities.

The brief first narrative step, focused on his beginnings in Galilee, concludes with a programmatic summary of his mission: teaching in the village assemblies, proclaiming the good news of the kingdom, and healing every kind of sickness among the people so that his fame spread throughout all Syria and crowds from Galilee and the other areas of Israelite people followed him. This narrative leads to Jesus' extensive speech that renews the Mosaic covenant of the people with God and one another that guides their common life (Matt 5–7). The second narrative step recites particular episodes of healing and exorcism, concluding with a summary of his teaching in assemblies, proclamation, and extensive healing of every sickness similar to that of the first narrative step. This leads to a speech in which he commissions the disciples to extend his mission into (other) villages, giving them authority to cast out invasive spirits, heal every sickness and to proclaim the kingdom, even in the face of repression by rulers (Matt 10). This leads to further episodes of healing and exorcism and his refutation of the charge by the scribes and

---

2. The speeches are clearly marked at the beginning by a call and/or an appropriate setting and at the end by the same explicit statement of its conclusion ("when Jesus had finished saying these things . . .").

Pharisees that he is casting out spirits by Beelzebul, the rulers of spirits, in the third narrative step. The first three narrative steps in the Matthean story are thus devoted mainly to Jesus healings and exorcisms, his principal actions. The third speech, in parables, offers explanation of what is happening in his mission, as history comes to its climax in his movement, at the end of the age (Matt 13).

The long fourth narrative step includes further healings and exorcisms and other *dynameis* (acts of power) such as two wilderness feedings, the extension of his mission into areas beyond Galilee, further conflicts with the scribes and Pharisees, his announcement of his impending martyrdom in Jerusalem, Simon's declaration that Jesus is the Messiah, and the ominous appearance of Jesus with Moses and Elijah. In the short fourth speech Jesus gives instructions for community discipline in his movement (most of Matt 18). The fifth narrative step consists mainly of Jesus' dialogues, especially with the disciples, as he travels toward Jerusalem, that lead to torah-like declarations and prophetic statements about social-economic-political life in his movement, in effect a restatement of Mosaic covenant renewal. The narrative continues with the entry into Jerusalem and Jesus' confrontation with the Jerusalem rulers in the temple, which concludes with his prophetic indictment and condemnation of the scribes and Pharisees. That leads directly to Jesus' fifth main speech, about the future (Matt 24–25). The Matthean story climaxes in the narrative of his Passover-covenant meal, his arrest and trial by the high priestly rulers, his crucifixion by the Romans, his resurrection appearances, and his closing commission of the disciples to make disciples of all peoples.

Like the Q speeches it adapts and the Markan story, most episodes of which it parallels, the Matthean story-with-speeches is also about Jesus' renewal of Israel in opposition to and by the rulers of Israel. The theme, mentioned repeatedly throughout the story, is "the kingdom (rule) of the heavens," the Matthean circumlocution for "kingdom of God," manifested in the exorcisms and healings and in the renewal of the Mosaic covenant, all performed by Jesus as a Moses- and Elijah-like prophet. The range of Jesus tradition in the collective memory of Jesus movements that the Matthean story includes is wider than in the Markan story. And the Matthean story makes more explicit and sharpens key aspects of the renewal of Israel and the political conflict with the rulers and their representatives. The overall pattern of the programmatic first Matthean speech, a restatement and intensification of the Mosaic Covenant, is adapted from the covenant renewal speech also adapted in the programmatic covenantal speech in Luke. The so-called antitheses that are the fulfillment of the torah/law extend and sharpen the covenantal demands to the very motivation behind observation of the covenant commandments. Going beyond the many Markan allusions and references to Israelite tradition, the Matthean "formula quotations" make Jesus and his mission explicitly the fulfillment of Israelite history and prophecy. In both his actions and speeches, Jesus performs as a prophet in the long tradition of Israelite prophets, especially Moses and Elijah. But the Matthean genealogy and infancy narrative present him as the Messiah and, in contrast to the Markan story, Jesus accepts Peter's declaration that he is the Messiah. While the scribes and Pharisees do not seem to have Jesus so regularly under "surveillance" as in Mark, Jesus' declaration of God's judgment against them is sharper and more intense in Matthew. The end of the Matthean story intensifies the dramatic confrontation between Jesus and the Jerusalem rulers, elaborating on the measures taken to ensure that he is crucified—a martyr for his movement—and making his death and vindication more ominous for the divine judgment of the high priests and the temple.

Context

The composition of the Gospel of Matthew is usually dated a decade or so after Roman destruction of Jerusalem in 70 CE. Much in Jesus' speech about the future (Matthew 24–25) could refer to resistance movements and Roman military suppression in Judea and Galilee earlier than the great revolt of 66–70.[3] But the Matthean reference to "the desolating sacrilege standing in the holy place" (that is, in the temple) seems to be referring to a past event. In the parable of the wedding banquet, the enraged king sending in his troops who kill the predatory invited guests and burn their city is a clear allusion to the Roman emperor sending the legions to destroy the ruling city of Jerusalem.

Previously Matthew was widely understood as addressed mainly to "Gentile Christians," according to the standard theological scheme of Christian origins in which Christianity expanded rapidly among the "Gentiles" and superseded Judaism and "the Jews." This scheme was

3. The Romans took repressive actions against popular turmoil and resistance movements, such as those referenced in Matt 24–25 as well as Mark 13, in mid-first century as well as during the great revolt of 66–70; see the analysis and discussion in Horsley, *Hearing the Whole Story*, 129–36, and chap. 7 above.

imposed on some key passages. For example, Jesus' declaration to "the chief priests and the elders" (and the Pharisees) that "the kingdom of God will be taken away from you and given to a people that produces the fruits of the kingdom" (Matt 21:43) was read as addressed to "the Jews" generally. Similarly, the centurion in the second Matthean healing story was taken as a "Gentile" and an exemplar of faith in contrast to "Israel." And the "many coming from east and west to eat with Abraham, Isaac, and Jacob in the kingdom, while the heirs of the kingdom will be thrown out" were taken as a scenario of the supersession.

Such readings, while still influential, are not borne out by a more careful analysis of the text and a more complete and precise knowledge of the historical context of the Matthean story. The synthetic construct of (early) Judaism hides a deep division both in the historical context and in the Matthew story between the rulers of Judea and Galilee, who were clients of the Romans, and the people they ruled (discussed in chap. 4). The fundamental conflict in the Matthean narrative and speeches is between the people of Israel and the chief priests and elders in the Jerusalem temple-state and their representatives, the scribes and Pharisees. The Matthean story, composed and performed a decade or so after the Roman destruction of Jerusalem and the temple, presupposes that God's judgment against the temple and high priests prophesied by Jesus has already happened. The addressees are the second-third generation of the expanding movement that Jesus generated. They are communities of the people of Israel-in-renewal that began in opposition to and by the (client) rulers of Roman Palestine. That the temple and Jerusalem were destroyed and the high priests and their representatives removed from power while the Jesus movement was expanding ("under the radar") would have reinforced the sense that the Jesus-loyalists were the fulfillment of Israelite history.

The key passages in the Gospel mentioned just above should be read in this context. "The chief priests and the elders of the people" were the rulers of Judea who were opposed by and to Jesus and the movement he generated, while "a people producing fruits of the kingdom" were his followers, those involved in his movement.[4] The centurion was likely an

4. While the fundamental political-economic-religious divide was between the rulers and the ruled, it is important to discern who's who in narrative context in order to hear the Matthean or other Gospel story in historical context. This is particularly important for vague general terms such as "the crowd(s)" or "the people." That Jesus will "save his people from their sins" (Matt 1:21) refers to all Israel. "The (large)

officer in the military (or other administration) of Herod Antipas, which was probably comprised largely of Judeans (see further below). "The many coming from east and west" to the banquet of the kingdom refers to the Judeans and other Israelites (perhaps from the diaspora?) joining in the renewal of Israel.

This fits much better with the rest of the Matthean story. The narrative and speeches present Jesus engaged in the renewal of Israel, in healings, exorcisms, and covenant renewal speeches that manifest the direct rule of heaven. Jesus declares explicitly that "I was sent only to the lost sheep of the house of Israel" (15:24). He previously stated this programmatically in the mission speech to the disciples: "go nowhere among the (other) peoples, . . . but go rather to the lost sheep of the house of Israel" (10:5–6). Moreover, the Matthean Jesus declares pointedly that Peter is the "Rock" on which he will build his assembly (Matt 16:13–20), and, as Paul recalls (in Galatians 2), from early in the rapid expansion of communities of Jesus-loyalists, Peter was preeminent as the apostle to the circumcised, while Paul claimed to be the principal apostle to the (other) peoples. Only toward the end of the Matthean story do we hear the exalted Jesus say that "this good news of the kingdom will be proclaimed throughout the world, as a testimony to all peoples, and then the end will come" (24:14). And at the very end of the story Jesus commands the eleven disciples "to make disciples of all peoples" (28:18–19). But there

---

crowd(s)" that gather to Jesus are mainly villagers from Galilee but also from other areas (4:25, etc.). The "large crowd(s)" that come with Jesus from Jericho and acclaim him as he enters Jerusalem are evidently rural people following Jesus, who explain to the "whole city in turmoil" that Jesus is a prophet from Nazareth in Galilee (Matt 21). And these seem to be (part of) the crowd that the high priests and elders are afraid of in confrontation with Jesus (Matt 22). The narrative states explicitly that "the large crowd with swords and clubs" who seize Jesus are "from the high priests and elders" (26:47; Josephus refers to prominent high priestly figures who maintained their own "goon squads," *Ant.*20.181, 206–207). The "crowds" who call for Jesus to be crucified appear to be Jerusalemites manipulated by "the high priests and elders" (27:20). And "the whole people" who cry "his blood be on us . . ." appear to be the same Jerusalemites (27:25), and do not include the crowd of followers who entered the city with Jesus, much less the crowds of Galileans and other Israelites who had gathered to him earlier. While biblical scholars often write about "Israel" or "Judaism" or "the Jews" generally, many texts later included in the Hebrew Bible make clear distinctions between the people of Judah/Judea/Israel/the land, on the one hand, and the rulers of Jerusalem, their officers, and the people of the city, on the other. For example, Josiah called together "all the people of Judah; all the rulers [or officers, not inhabitants as in the NRSV] of Jerusalem; the priests and prophets; and all the people [of Jerusalem], both great and small," to hear the recently discovered book of the covenant (2 Kgs 23:2).

is little or nothing in the overall story that would suggest that the addressees were separate from Israel. Key passages in Matthew as well as the overall text indicate that the hearers were not only a movement of the renewal of Israel but the fulfillment of Israel's history as well as tradition.

Closely related to the view that Matthew was addressed to "Gentiles," on the assumption that "early Christianity" was largely urban, interpreters of Matthew hypothesized that it was addressed to a Christian community in Antioch. The Antioch hypothesis has continued even when interpreters discern that the story and speeches are addressed to people who are still part of Israel, indeed Israel in renewal, because there was a large and thriving Judean/Israelite population in Antioch, one of the largest cities in the Roman Empire.

A question that has hardly been asked, given the assumption that the Gospels were composed in writing and then sent to a "church" in a major city of the Empire for reading, is about the relation between the setting of the interaction and events in the story, on the one hand, and the situation of the addressees, on the other. This is an essential consideration for an attempt to appreciate how the performed story may have resonated with the community of hearers and its effect, and may be a good indicator of the historical social context of the audience.

The Matthean story portrays Jesus (and disciples sent on mission) working "throughout Galilee" teaching and healing in villages and village assemblies (as stated in key summary passages, 4:23; 9:35; cf. 2:9; 13:54). As in the Markan story, his chosen "hometown" and base of operations is Capernaum. His other interactions with people are also in rural areas such as fields and mountains and the seashore. He also works, that is, does exorcism or healing, in the district of Gadara (in the Decapolis across the Sea of Galilee) and in Judea on his way to Jerusalem. The programmatic summary of Jesus' teaching, proclamation, and healing every sickness that sets up the foundational covenant renewal speech (4:23-25) signals that the (Matthean) Jesus-movement had spread to a wider area: "his fame spread through all Syria." The list of areas from which come "the great crowds that followed him"—Galilee, the Decapolis, Jerusalem, Judea, and from beyond the Jordan—suggest that the movement had expanded mainly among peoples of Israelite heritage.

The Matthean story and its speeches, however, offer little by way of clues to the particular context of its audience. Because the Gospel is in Greek, we assume that its audience spoke Greek, although it is possible that some of them were bilingual (Greek and Aramaic or Syriac).

It is evident from the programmatic covenant renewal speech that the people the Gospel addresses were not new communities that had just been formed in the previous few years (such as the assemblies Paul and his co-workers catalyzed in Philippi, Thessalonica, and Corinth). The Gospel addresses already established communities of a movement of Jesus-loyalists in which practices such as alms-giving, prayer, and fasting (and their varying observance and abuse, 6:2–18) are standard. This suggests that the addressees were communities of Israelites that had become Jesus-loyalists in the expansion of a Jesus movement or, if they were in a large city, communities of recruits from the wider Judean/Israelite population living in the city. Unclear is just where these communities may have been located geographically and culturally.

In comparison with the Markan story, Matthew has hardly any "footprints" into the villages or towns in Syria into which a movement it addresses may have spread. Jesus goes into the districts of Tyre and Sidon and debates a "Canaanite woman" and heals her daughter while there, which is possibly a suggestion of a presence of the movement there. In contrast with the Markan story, the Matthean story makes no mention of any villages in Caesarea Philippi, which is the scene of Peter's "confession" that Jesus is "the messiah." On the other hand it is difficult to find any indication in the narrative or speeches that the people addressed live in cities. And it is difficult to discern how episodes and speeches that portray and deal with social-economic relations in agrarian communities would resonate with urban people.

It seems likely that the Gospel would have resonated most readily with village or town communities not far removed from traditional agrarian social-economic relations. Yet urban communities cannot be dismissed as possibilities if we keep in mind that both the traditions of Jesus' mission of renewal of the people and the Israelite tradition in which it was rooted articulated a village ideal of non-exploitative social-economic relations. Particularly important was to escape or resist exploitation by rulers. Thus people of Israelite heritage who lived in cities and were not themselves involved in agrarian communities would already have shared such Israelite tradition and could understandably have resonated with its renewal in Jesus' mission in village communities.

The social-economic circumstances of the audience would appear to have been modest. Like those addressed in the Markan story and Q speeches, the Matthean hearers were evidently struggling to manage a subsistence living (e.g., Matt 6:25–33). In comparison with the Lukan version of "the Lord's prayer" (Luke 11:2–4), the Matthean "Jesus" teaches the people to petition the heavenly Father for cancellation of their debts. Does this indicate that the Matthean audience were (mutually) indebted? It may just represent the pre-Matthean text, since "forgive our sins" is probably the Lukan performance. If the communities the Gospel addressed were not in Judea or Galilee, they would probably not have undergone the same devastation that Galilean and Judean village communities experienced in the Roman reconquest of 67–70. In the aftermath of the great Roman "victory" over the widespread revolt in Judea and Galilee, however, Judeans/Israelite communities in Syria and elsewhere may have come under suspicion and been subject to harassment by Roman (client) officials and loyalists (Matt 10:16–18; 24:9–13). If anything their political-economic situation would have deteriorated, probably with continuing illnesses and spirit possession, in the aftermath of the revolt and Roman reconquest.

In comparison with the Markan story and the Q speeches, the Matthew story has sharpened the conflict between Jesus and the scribes and Pharisees. It is clear from the portrayals of the scribes and Pharisees in the Markan story, in Jesus' woes against them in Q, and in Josephus' histories that they were advisers and representatives of the Jerusalem temple-state. It is not possible to construe any of these sources in such a way as to construct the Pharisees as a rival group or sect to the Jesus movement(s). Critical scholarly investigations have shown that even if (some) scribes and Pharisees who survived the Roman destruction of Jerusalem were, in effect, precursors of the small circles of rabbis that emerged in the second century in Galilee, they did not suddenly become the leaders of "Judaism" or "the synagogue(s)."[5] In episodes of conflict and Jesus' polemical woes against them, the Matthew story, like Mark and Q, portrays them as representatives of (the interests of) the high priests and temple. But Matthew gives no indication that the Pharisees (also) represent some sort of self-appointed authorities who, after the destruction of the Jerusalem temple-state, were attempting to exert influence over Judean/Israelite communities in Antioch and/or elsewhere in Syria. The episodes of the high priests and Pharisees persuading Pilate to post guards at Jesus' tomb and then the priests and elders bribing the guards to claim that the disciples had stolen his body (27:62–66; 28:11–15), however, suggest that (some) Judean authorities were speaking in opposition to the

5. Levine, "The Jewish Patriarch (Nasi) in Third-Century Palestine"; Cohen, "The Significance of Yavneh," 36–38.

movement of Jesus-loyalists, before and/or after the Roman destruction of the temple-state.

Judging from the repeated warnings and admonitions about persecutions, the people addressed, however, may well have been experiencing attacks from local "authorities" and rulers or from other communities of diaspora Judeans/Israelites. And/or persecutions may have been happening to the communities addressed earlier in the expansion of the movement. One might speculate that if the communities addressed by Matthew were an expansion of the movement of Jesus-loyalists based in Jerusalem that was headed by Peter, then the sharp polemic against the Pharisees came from an earlier stage in the development of that branch of the Jesus-movement.

Other than the Matthean story having been given distinctive form sometime after the Romans' destruction of Jerusalem in 70 CE, we are left with a fairly indeterminate sense of the audience addressed by the Matthean story and its context. They are evidently not "Gentiles," but rather of Israelite heritage or people who have identified with Israel and understand their movement and/or communities to be the fulfillment of Israelite tradition and history. The community/ies are not necessarily in a city such as Antioch. To have resonated with the Matthean story-and-speeches they would seem either to have been based in villages and small towns or, if in a large town or city, to have been deeply rooted in Israelite tradition that was in turn rooted in village covenantal community.

Text Resonating as it References Tradition

The Matthean story opens with a genealogy of Jesus as "the Messiah" descended from ("son of") Abraham and King David that sets up his mission as the fulfillment of Israelite history as well as tradition. Then the story of Jesus begins with his birth as "the Messiah" and his being named Yeshua because he will deliver his people from their sins. In Israelite tradition, in contrast with subsequent Christian soteriology, this suggests that he will deliver the people from their current subjection to imperial rule. The ensuing narrative of his birth, the quest of the Magi, and Herod's massacre of the infants indicates clearly that this deliverance from imperial rule by one born "king of the Judeans" is exactly what the Roman client King Herod is concerned to suppress from its outset.

There is very little evidence from (Judean scribal) texts close to the time of Jesus for any expectation of a/the messiah.[6] The commonly-cited *Psalm of Solomon* 17 stands virtually alone as a description of an anticipated anointed king, the son of David, who would rule over Israel, destroy unjust rulers, and drive out sinners. But the mission of Jesus in the Matthean story has no such agenda. The forgiveness of sins, extensive healings and exorcisms, and renewal of the Mosaic covenant that are featured in the Matthean story, moreover, are not what was anticipated in Psalm of Solomon 17 or in earlier prophetic texts about the anointed king, son of David (such as Isa 9:2–7; 11:1–9).

On the popular level, in contrast with the poorly attested expectation of an anointed king in scribal circles, memory of the young David "messiahed" by the people (2 Sam 2–5)—before he became an oppressive king—was alive among the people in both Galilee and Judea. As noted in chap. 4, a generation before and again a generation after Jesus, Judean and Galilean villagers acclaimed leaders as "kings" who successfully led movements of deliverance from Roman rule, according to the accounts of Josephus (as noted in chap. 4).[7] The Matthean story, however, presents Jesus *neither* as a leader of popular revolt against Roman rule *nor* as a more imperial king who lords it over his subjects, but as a martyr for his mission and movement.

Beginning with the conception of Jesus and running through the Matthean narrative, events or actions of Jesus, including his healings, and responses by the people are interpreted as fulfillments of "what was spoken by the Lord through the prophet," adding to the sense of the climactic historical significance of his mission. It is important for modern readers to note that in the oral communication context of the audience, the performer says "this happened to fulfill what was (had been) *spoken* (by God) *through* the prophet" (often Isaiah), which makes the ancient prophecy alive and present in the performance.[8]

---

6. As indicated in the critical research and analysis in de Jonge, "The Use of the Word 'Anointed'"; and in the many articles in Neusner and Green, eds., *Judaisms and their Messiahs*; and Charlesworth, ed., *The Messiah*.

7. References and analysis in Horsley, "Popular Messianic Movements."

8. This phrase is a significant reminder of the oral communication context of the composition and performance of the Gospel stories. The composer-performers and the audience who, as ordinary people, were not literate, were nevertheless well-acquainted with Israelite tradition, both their own popular tradition that was orally cultivated and the official or elite scribal tradition in which (some? most?) texts were also inscribed on scrolls. They would have known many prophecies, including, in some

The narrative of Jesus' infancy suddenly brings the hearers into the wider historical context, with the search of the Magi, famous priestly sages from the East, for the one born "king of the Judeans." This touches off the massacre of the children by the tyrannical Herod, who (the audience would have known) had been set in power as "the king of the Judeans" by the Romans. The fugitive family's escape into Egypt and return to the land of Israel recapitulated the people of Israel's descent into bondage and their liberating exodus, all in fulfillment of what was spoken by the Lord through the prophets.

The Matthean story has John the Baptist proclaim the same message that Jesus proclaims, that the rule/kingdom of the heavens[9] is at hand/ has come near, which becomes the theme and the agenda of Jesus' mission. That agenda, as spoken by the prophet Isaiah, is a new exodus of the people, led by a more powerful one who is coming and will baptize in Holy Spirit and fire. At his own baptism the Spirit of God descends upon Jesus, God's beloved son. That, led by the Spirit, he is forty days and nights fasting in the wilderness indicates that this is the new Moses and/or Elijah being tested in preparation for his mission of deliverance of Israel.

First Narrative Step and Speech

Jesus Heals All Kinds of Illnesses in All of Galilee

Following John's baptism of repentance in renewal of the Mosaic Covenant and Jesus' baptism and testing for his mission as a prophet like Moses and Elijah, the Matthean narrative sets up Jesus' long covenant renewal speech with a programmatic summary of the beginning and scope

---

cases, by which prophet (e.g., Isaiah or Jeremiah) they had been "spoken" (and were still cultivated as spoken). The term and concept "scripture," that is, sacred writing, is not appropriate for such prophecies cited as "spoken through the prophet." Ordinary people would also have known that many of those prophecies were also "written" on scrolls, hence (all the more) authoritative, particularly for the scribes and high priests (Sadducees). The Matthean narrative, like the Markan story, is a good illustration. In narrative contents where Jesus is interacting with or addressing scribes and Pharisees or the high priests, he states "it is written" to claim the fulfillment of what stands written or asks "have you not read?" to both mock them and to claim the authority of what is written.

9. As often pointed out, the Matthean story, produced in an Israelite/Judean movement concerned to observe the Mosaic commandment against "taking the name of God" in vain, spoke of "the kingdom of the *heavens*" instead of "the kingdom of God."

of his mission. He establishes a base in the village of Capernaum and begins his mission of renewal of Israel in the northernmost territories of Zebulun and Naphtali—this in fulfillment of what was spoken through the prophet Isaiah, that light would dawn for these lands that had sat in the region of darkness and the shadow of death, that is under the debilitating domination of foreign empires for centuries. After Jesus begins to recruit proteges, reminiscent of Elijah, the Matthean narrative presents his whole mission compressed into a wide-ranging summary: in the same three interrelated principal activities as in the Markan summaries, he proclaims the kingdom, teaches in the village assemblies of Galilee, and heals every sickness among the people. In the Matthean elaboration, however, the emphasis is on his extensive healing of all kinds of illnesses, with the result that his fame spreads throughout all Syria.

This extended summary passage in the first narrative step of the story offers a good illustration of short parallel clauses (cola) and repetition of sounds that indicate its origin in speech and continuation in oral performance. This can be appreciated by reciting aloud the following transliteration of the Greek.

> *Kai periegen   en hole te Galilaia,*
> *   didaskon   en tais synagogais auton,*
> *kai kerusson   to euangellion tes basileias*
> *kai therapeuon pasan noson kai pasan malakian en toi laoi.*
> *Kai apelthen   he akoe autou   eis holen ten Syrian;*
> *kai prosenegkan auto pantas tous kakos echontas*
> *   poikilias nosois kai basanois synechomenous*
> *   kai daimonizomenous*
> *   kai seleniazomenous*
> *   kai paralytikous,*
> *   kai etherapeusen autous.*

By hearing how this speech may have sounded in performance we can appreciate how the audience would have heard the rhythmic parallel clauses and the repetition of key words and sounds. Even in English translation (which follows the Greek word order as closely as possible) we can hear the repetition of key words (and synonyms) in the parallel clauses.

> And he went around   in the whole (of) Galilee,
> teaching   in their assemblies
> and preaching   the gospel of the kingdom
> and healing   every sickness and every illness among the people.

And his fame spread   into the whole (of) Syria.
and they brought to him   all those who had illness:
         those suffering various sicknesses and affliction,
         and those who were spirit-possessed,
         and those who were moon-struck,
         and those who were paralyzed.
And he healed them.

He went into the *whole* of Galilee where he was teaching in their village assemblies and healing among the people, and his fame spread to the *whole* of Syria. He was healing *every* sickness and *every* illnesses, and he healed *all* of those suffering with various sicknesses. In this summary the Matthean story, like the Markan story, indicates that from the outset of his mission, Jesus' principal activity was healing of all kinds of illnesses in all the areas of Palestine where Israelites lived.[10] Again as in the Markan story, only more programmatically, the Matthean story has Jesus performing his healings, like his preaching, "among the people" in the local assemblies of the villages (see the similar summary in 9:35; and further references in 12:9; 13:54).[11] This remarkable initial summary is a programmatic statement of Jesus' mission in which healing is his primary activity (throughout the whole of Galilee) from which his fame spreads (throughout the whole of Syria) that sets up and flows into his renewal of covenantal community in the programmatic first speech.

Programmatic Speech: Renewal of the Mosaic Covenant

The Markan narrative of Jesus' mission in Galilee and beyond had Jesus' exorcisms and healings lead to his renewal of the Mosaic covenant. The Matthean first narrative step and speech make this sequence more

10. The summary of Jesus' healings in Mark 3:8 also has crowds coming from Judea, Jerusalem, and beyond the Jordan, as well as Galilee; Mark has Idumea instead of the Decapolis; Syria in Matthew would likely include Mark's "the region around Tyre and Sidon."

11. The *synagogai* in the Gospels are village assemblies, the longstanding social form in which the coherence and governance of local community were embodied and conducted, as explained in Horsley, *Galilee*, chap. 9. Archaeological explorations have shown that villages in Galilee generally did not have buildings in which such assemblies gathered until late antiquity. If the Matthean audience were communities located in cities, they also were organized and met regularly in assemblies. *Synagoge* and *ekklesia* are synonyms and, depending on the narrative context, can refer to the local assembly or the assembly of the whole people.

programmatic and explicit. As signaled by Jesus going "up the mountain," the speech is a renewal, perhaps even more a reinstitution of the covenant of the ancestors with God on Mount Sinai mediated by the founding prophet Moses. Like the pre-Matthean covenant renewal speech (see chap. 8) that it evidently uses as an overall structure, the Matthean covenant renewal speech is entirely in performative speech: as it was performed in communities of the movement that the Gospel addresses, it enacted the renewal of the covenant. The speech proceeds according to the three traditional structural components of the Mosaic covenant, a declaration of deliverance, the demands for social-economic justice in the interaction of households in the community, and sanctions on keeping the commandments ("words"). More than the speech it has adapted with considerable elaboration, the Matthean speech transforms the covenantal pattern and intensifies the covenantal demands. The Matthean speech, moreover, is skillfully crafted with repetitive patterns and sounds that make it all the more effective in oral performance in the communities it addresses.

The opening sequence of nine blessings (not just "beatitudes") pronounces to the people that the kingdom of heaven that John and Jesus announced is at hand. The performative speech makes the blessings of the direct rule of Heaven (God) present to them. The pronouncement of the blessings also indicates that the qualities and relationships that the kingdom includes and produces are (to be) present among the hearers, who (are to) embody these qualities, such as yearning for and practicing justice, being merciful and peacemakers, and being comforted and resilient in their difficult circumstances, such as persecution. If we take narrative sequencing seriously, the story's implication is that the healings and exorcisms enabled these qualities and relations in the Jesus-movements that are now pronounced as the declaration of new divine deliverance.

In transition to his statement of the covenantal demands Jesus declares that he has come (not to abolish but) to fulfill the law (torah/teaching) and the prophets, that is, Israelite tradition. He also states explicitly what was implicit in the blessings, that the will of God was articulated in the Mosaic covenantal laws and customs and that those who were keeping the covenant law were great in the direct rule of God, implying that this was now being embodied in the community ("on earth as it is in heaven," in the words of the ensuing prayer).

In the oral performance of this and other performative speeches, the phrase "For (truly) I tell you" (5:18, 20, etc.) is a verbal cue calling special attention to Jesus' declaration of a specially important command or principle. In the transitional statement between the declaration of new deliverance (5:3–16) and the pronouncement of the covenantal demands (5:20–48), these specially cued statements of principle (5:17–19) declare that and how the renewal of the Mosaic covenant is a fulfillment of Israelite tradition.[12] To hear the second cued statement of principle more in the way that the Matthean addressees would have heard it, it is important to recognize that *dikaiosyne* meant covenantal justice. Later in the story Jesus condemns the scribes and Pharisees for undermining justice and mercy (e.g., 15:1–6; 23:4, 23) and tells the hearers "do what they teach, but not what they do" (Matt 23:2–3). Thus the declaration that the justice of the covenanted community must exceed that of the scribes and Pharisees was evidently "tongue in cheek."

The intensification of the demands of the covenant that follows (in 5:20–48) requires justice in the renewed covenant community that remarkably exceeds the justice of the scribes and Pharisees. The repetition of the same format of presentation in the pronouncement of the covenant demands, effectively opens the audience to their elaboration and exemplification. These repetitions of the format, "you have heard that it was said (to the ancient ancestors) . . . , but I say . . . ," have been referred to standardly as "antitheses." But this is a misleading term. The first two are intensifications and the next three are expansions of traditional covenantal commands. The first two focus on two of the ten commandments (that we are familiar with from Exod 20 and Deut 5), suggesting that they are focal instances of a broader intensification and/or expansion of the covenant commandments. In the first two "Jesus" intensifies the

---

12. Modern readers embedded in the assumptions of print-culture may miss just how extreme the statement, "not an iota, not a stroke (of the scribe's pen) will pass from the law" would be for an audience of ordinary people. As discussed in chap. 6, they would have known (popular) Israelite tradition, the law and the prophets, in their collective memory. While they could not read or write themselves, however, they would have known about writing and authoritative written texts that were authoritative for the temple-state and that the role of scribes and Pharisees, the literate elite, was to interpret the laws (e.g., of tithing). In Jesus' speech against the scribes and Pharisees later in the Matthean story he charges that they "tie up heavy burdens" on the people (in their written documents) and "are unwilling to lift a (scribal) finger to move them" (23:4). It seems likely that "an iota and a stroke (of a pen)" may have become a standing image (idiom) for just how rigorous and onerous the law could be in the hands of the scribes. Probably Jesus' statement in Matt 5:18 would have been heard as hyperbole, an exaggeration of how he had come to fulfill the whole of the law (and prophets), the basic concern of which was justice and mercy.

commandments to include the motives/motivation of social interaction in the covenant community. He intensifies the demand "you shall not murder" to include not even being or remaining angry and resolving conflicts so that they would not lead to murder. He intensifies the prohibition of "adultery" to the lust that might lead to adultery. In the third he extends the prohibition on swearing falsely to not swearing or taking oaths at all, but being honestly straightforward in social-economic interaction in the community. In the fourth he expands the principle of equivalency (in retaliation, of "an eye for an eye, a tooth for a tooth") to the generous sharing of scarce resources (mainly food) in what are difficult economic circumstances, with the clearly stated intention that this would defuse social tension and conflict among desperate neighbors. In the fifth, he extends the principle of love to include treatment of those outside the community as well as those inside.

The covenant renewal speech continues with particular instruction and further commands for the social-economic life of the community, in clearly organized and orally signaled steps, first in a series of "whenever you give alms . . . , pray . . . , fast . . ." (6:1–18), then in another series of "Do not's . . ." supplemented with exhortations (6:19–-7:14). For modern readers oriented mainly to individual piety and ethics, it is important to recognize that these instructions and commands address the community and community life, including mainly economic life. Alms are for the destitute in the community. The prayer for the coming of the kingdom focuses on the people's most fundamental economic concerns, for sufficient food and cancellation of debts that were driving them further into poverty. Jesus prohibits the storing up of private earthly wealth as contradictory to (the will of) serving God. He commands people not to worry about subsistence food and shelter; if they (everyone of them) give priority to the kingdom (of God), then sufficiency will result. This principle and the demand for sharing and the mutual cancellation of debts in the prayer would have been mutually reinforcing for the audience, and may be helpful in explaining to modern listeners what might seem to be utterly unrealistic commands.

The covenant renewal speech ends with a sanction on keeping the commands that replaces the traditional "blessings and curses" component of covenant-making and -renewal. The double parable of the houses built on the rock and sand gives a "down to earth" sense of the consequences of doing the covenantal commands, which are the will of God. The comment after the speech ends, that the listening crowd was amazed because Jesus taught them as one having authority/power, and not as their scribes, indicates that his renewal of the covenant stands in contrast to the teaching of the representatives of the Jerusalem rulers.

The subsequent narratives and speeches of the Gospel further elaborate and specify Jesus' healing of the people and the renewal of Mosaic covenantal community just presented so programmatically and explicitly in the first narrative step and speech.

Second Narrative Step and Speech

A Series of Healings and Exorcisms

As Jesus comes down the mountain after delivering the covenant speech the Matthean story resumes with a narrative of particular healings and exorcisms, in three sets (Matt 8–9). The narrative shortens the episodes that parallel those in the Markan story.

In a fitting sequel to the renewal of the covenantal people, the first healing is of a fellow with skin lesions, which according to the purity codes of the temple-state meant that he was (temporarily) excluded from normal social interaction (Leviticus 13). He already has trust in Jesus: "if you will you can make me clean." Jesus' response is spontaneous and immediate: "He stretched out his hand and touched him, saying, 'I do will. Be made clean.'" The healing was immediate. In touching the man Jesus went further than had Elisha in healing Naaman (2 Kgs 5:1–14). Having precluded the need for the offering that Moses had commanded, with an examination by a priest, Jesus commands him to do it anyhow, as "a testimony to them," presumably the priests.

As he returned to Capernaum, which he had earlier made his home in Galilee (4:13), a centurion appealed to him to heal his "boy" (*pais* can mean either servant or son) who was paralyzed, in terrible distress. Jesus agreed to do so. The episode has been a source of dispute partly because of what is included in the dialogue and partly because of a standard assumption that "(early) Christianity," having become mainly "Gentile," displaced "(early) Judaism." The parallel to this episode in John 4:46–54 has a "royal officer" request the healing for his child. Assuming with the Matthean narrative that he was stationed in Capernaum, a village on the frontier between the territory of Herod Antipas and that of Philip, he could well have been called a "centurion" and would likely have been a

Judean serving the Herodian administration based in Tiberias.[13] This is the only episode in the Gospels in which Jesus is "astonished," which leads to his pointed comment to those who followed him, "Truly, in no one in Israel (yet) have I found such trust." His ensuing statement that "many will come from east and west . . ." is a reference to the gathering of Israelites into the kingdom, and the displacing of the elite who presumed that they were the heirs of the kingdom (thus no suggestion of a displacement of "the Jews" by "the Gentiles").[14] Emphasis in this episode falls upon the centurion's astonishing trust as an integral factor in healing, his principal activity in the renewal of Israel, and the direct connection of Jesus' healing with the presence of the rule of heaven.

In the simplified Matthean episode of the healing of Peter's mother-in-law only Jesus entered the house and no one told him she was ill. He simply saw her "thrown aside on a sickbed with a fever." Jesus' healing is simple and immediate: "he touched her hand, and the fever left her." While in the Markan version she got up and served "them," in the Matthean episode "she served him," suggesting that she became his disciple in service. In a brief summary comes the first mention that Jesus "cast out spirits" from many who were possessed "with a word" (i.e., no elaborate chant or ritual) and healed all who were sick. This Matthean summary concludes with the distinctive fulfillment statement that Jesus' healings happened "to fulfill what was spoken through the prophet Isaiah," citing lines from one of the 'servant of the Lord' songs: "He took away our sicknesses and bore our illnesses." (Isa 53:4) This and the subsequent statement of fulfillment in another (brief) summary have the effect of including all of Jesus' healings and exorcisms in the fulfillment of "what was spoken through the prophet Isaiah."

The series of healings and exorcisms is interrupted by Jesus' admonitions, in statements of hyperbole, to a scribe and another disciple, about just how demanding it will be to follow him in his mission of healing (all the sicknesses of all the people). The episode of crossing the lake reveals how ominous the struggle will be with life-threatening forces. But Jesus

---

13. A centurion, moreover, was not a high-ranking military officer but someone who rose up through the ranks to serve perhaps as a low-level administrator or overseer of projects rather than a low-level officer of a military contingent, as explained by Meier, *Mentor, Message, and Miracles*, 721–22.

14. "Q"-scholars suggest that "Matthew" has moved this prophecy from its place in Q to this episode.

"subdues" the wind and sea (same verb as in some exorcisms), amazing his disciples, whose lack of trust had been exposed.

The forces that threaten the people's life immediately confront Jesus in the next episode, the first exorcism in Matthew. That this story is considerably shorter than the Markan version has been taken as an example of Matthew's written composition. Yet the Matthean episode has all the features of oral storytelling, such as short clauses/cola, repetition of sounds, and dramatic confrontation, as can be seen even in a translation of several lines:

> And (when) he came   to the other side,
>   into the countryside   of the Gadarenes
> [there] met him   two spirit-possessed-ones
>   coming out of the tombs,   extremely fierce,
>   so that no one   could walk along that way.
> And immediately   they cried out, saying
> "What have you [to do]   with us,   son of God?
> have you come   before the time   to torment us?"
> At some distance from them   a herd of many swine   was feeding.
> The *daimones* begged him   saying,
> "If you cast us out   send us   into the herd of the swine."
> And he said to them, "Go."
> And coming out   they went into the swine;
> and immediately   the whole herd charged
>   over the cliff   into the sea
>   and they perished   in the water.

That possessed people hung out among the tombs and were dangerously fierce indicates that the possessing spirits were associated with death, perhaps death-dealing spirits. While the Matthean version does not include the identification of the possessing spirits as "Legion," it does have the spirits ask to be sent into the herd of swine, whereupon they immediately self-destruct. And as in Mark, the people of the city (not the countryside?) beg Jesus to leave their territory.

In another shorter version of an episode also in Mark, once Jesus returns to his home town (Capernaum), the Matthean narrative (9:1–8) has a support group bring a paralytic to him. In response to their trust, he declares to the fellow, "your sins are forgiven." Knowing that some of the scribes are saying that he is blaspheming (assuming that the audience knows why, that only God can forgive sins), he asks rhetorically: which is easier, to say "Your sins are forgiven!" or "Rise and walk!" The Matthean narrative then makes explicit what is implicit in the Markan narrative: that "the human-like-one has authority on earth to forgive sins" meant that God had given authority to people to forgive sins (9:8). This episode and the next one, in which Jesus answers the Pharisees about his eating with tax collectors and sinners—that it is the sick (whom they consider sinners) who need healing—also indicate that his healing is threatening to the temple-state.

By beginning the next episode with "while he was saying these things" the Matthean narrative sets the audience up for hearing the interwoven healings of the two women, along with the subsequent healings and exorcisms, as examples of how his mission is a time of celebration (wedding) and "new wine" that cannot be put in old wineskins. The episode (9:18–26) is much shorter than in the Markan story (as we have it in the "established text"), which may well have been expanded in a secondary development of the episode during repeated performances (see chap. 7). In appealing for healing, the leader (presumably of the local assembly) states that his daughter (evidently young, since still living in her father's house) has just died (not just "near death") and that if Jesus lays his hand on her she will live. As Jesus is following him, the woman who had been hemorrhaging for twelve years came up behind him and touched the fringe of his garment, presented in a way that is parallel to the leader's interruption, "Behold . . . ."[15] While the Matthean episode does not include the description of how long and severely she has suffered and of the interaction following her immediate healing, including Jesus' sense that power has gone forth from him, she takes the initiative in her own healing, as in the Markan story. Jesus declares, "Daughter, your trust has saved you" (*sesoken*, "made you whole"). In response to the mourning underway when he arrives at the leader's house, Jesus declares that the girl is not dead but sleeping. In the brief Matthean episode, which lacks the words "little girl, arise," Jesus simply "took her by the hand and the girl arose." At the end of both this and the next episode, a report of the healings spreads throughout the area (of Galilee).

In the first episode of the Matthean special attention to the healing of the blind, two blind men follow Jesus crying out loudly "Have mercy on us, son of David!" (9:27–31). The same happens at the end of his mission in Galilee and Judea (20:29–34) in an episode that appears to be the Matthean version of the Markan story of blind Bartimaeus, who uttered

15. See further the fine discussion of this double episode in Wainwright, *Women Healing*, 146–53.

the same plea. In both Matthean episodes Jesus touches their eyes and they regain their sight. This episode stresses the instrumental role of their trust that Jesus could heal them. It is unclear how the address of Jesus as "son of David" is related to his presentation as the Messiah in the Matthean genealogy. Nothing in Israelite tradition suggests that the Davidic messiah was associated with healing, much less expected to heal.[16] As mentioned in chap. 5, Josephus' account of the exorcism by Eleazar is an illustration of the remarkable wisdom of Solomon (who was David's son) who had devised chants and roots for the healing of people.[17] In the Matthean episodes of healing of the blind, however, Jesus lacks the key aspects of a practitioner of Solomon's wisdom: he does not confront a hostile spirit, he has no secret knowledge of exorcism chants and rituals, and he lacks a seal-ring with special root.[18]

To bring the series of healings and exorcisms to a conclusion and to set up the following speech sending out envoys to expand Jesus' mission, the Matthean narrative supplies a brief exorcism and a summary that forms an inclusio with the summary that introduced the covenant renewal speech. Amazed when Jesus cast out the *daimonion* that had made a man mute so that he spoke again, the crowd exclaimed, "Never has a thing like this been seen in Israel" (9:32–34). This is in effect an exclamation about all of the healing and exorcism Jesus has been performing. The Pharisees' charge that "he casts out *daimonia* by the ruler of the *daimonia*" indicates the intensifying conflict that has developed between Jesus and the temple-state. It also anticipates the Beelzebul episode, in which a possessing spirit has rendered another fellow mute, the Pharisees repeat the charge, and Jesus responds (12:22–32).

Another lengthy summary of Jesus' actions (in 9:35–38) forms the transition to his mission speech, just as the nearly identical earlier summary in 4:23 introduced the covenant renewal speech: Jesus went about all the towns and villages (but not the ruling cities), teaching in their assemblies, and proclaiming the good news of the kingdom, and healing

16. See the good review of the critical literature in Meier, *Mentor, Message, and Miracles*, 688–70 and notes.

17. This is a different Judean tradition in conflict with the tradition of an anointed king, son of David. See the discussion by Duling, "Solomon, Exorcism, and the Son of David." The clear implication in Duling's analysis is that the title "son of David" for king Solomon as an exorcist in the Testament of Solomon was influenced by the Gospel of Matthew, not vice versa.

18. As noticed by Novakovic, *Messiah, Healer of the Sick*, 104, 187; critical discussion of "son of David" in Matthew in Duling, "Therapeutic Son of David."

every illness and sickness. What motivates the next major move in the Matthean Gospel is Jesus "seeing the crowds that were harassed and help-less, like sheep without a shepherd." This had been a prominent image in prophetic laments and charges against the rulers (kings) of the people, who as "shepherds" exploited and oppressed them, leaving them weak, sick, and injured (see esp. Ezek 34:1–6). Jesus sets up the ensuing mission speech, saying "The harvest is plentiful, but the laborers are few; there-fore ask the Lord of the harvest to send out laborers into his harvest."

Speech Commissioning the Disciples to Extend Jesus' Exorcism, Healing, and Proclamation

While Jesus has many disciples in the Matthean story, he addresses the mission speech to "his twelve disciples." He commissions them mainly to perform exorcisms and healings: "He gave them authority (power) over unclean spirits, to cast them out, and to heal every illness and sickness" (10:1) These are the primary actions in the renewal of Israel, which is the focus of their mission: "Go nowhere among (other) peoples, and do not enter a town of the Samaritans, but go rather to the lost sheep of the house of Israel."[19] The juxtaposition of the instruction to proclaim the kingdom and to perform various healings and exorcisms in successive poetic lines indicates that the healings and exorcisms are the principal manifestations of the kingdom as well as the disciples' primary purpose.

As you go	proclaim,	saying:
"The kingdom	of heaven	is at hand."
Heal	the sick.	
Raise	the dead.	
Cleanse	those with skin-lesions.	
Cast out	*daimonia*.	

Jesus instructs them to stay in households while working in villages and towns, content with whatever support the people can provide them, giv-ing blessings to those who are welcoming but curses to those who reject them.

19. The Matthean story of the renewal of Israel does not seem to break through the split and hostility between the Judeans and the Samaritans, both Israelite peoples, like the Galileans (but were the Samaritans included in the risen Jesus' charge to the eleven disciples at the end of the story?). In contrast, the Johannine Gospel story pointedly includes Jesus' interaction with the Samaritans (John 4:1–42) and the movement it addresses evidently includes some (communities of) Samaritans.

While ostensibly instructions to the twelve disciples as part of Jesus' own mission, the Matthean mission speech also clearly addressed the continuation of the mission in the expansion of (the Matthean branch of) the Jesus movement (10:16–33). The movement of renewal in resistance to the rulers evoked measures of repression. As "sheep" sent out "among wolves," a traditional image in Israelite tradition for the people facing predatory rulers (see previous chapter), the leaders of the movement would be handed over to official councils and assemblies and dragged before (Roman-appointed) governors and client kings. That they, like their master, will be accused of (doing the work of) "Beelzebul" indicates that the exorcisms were (part of what was) threatening to the established authorities. The leaders of the movement might have to stay on the move, one step ahead of rulers' efforts to suppress them. Jesus reassures them that if they remain steadfast under repression, they will be vindicated: "Whoever acknowledges me before others, I also will acknowledge before my Father in heaven." Jesus also warns that disciples' extension of his mission of preaching, healing and exorcism will result in divisions, even in splits between generations and even splits within families (10:21–22, 34–39). Loyalty to Jesus and the movement may require personal struggle with families, and even the suffering of martyrdom. The speech ends with reassurance to the envoys, who are (also) "prophets" extending the mission of a "prophet" (Jesus) and with promise of rewards to those who receive and support them.

Third Narrative Step and Speech

Further Healing and Exorcism

The focus on Jesus' healing and exorcism continues in the Matthean narrative following the mission speech, in which Jesus instructed the twelve disciples to work primarily on casting out unclean spirits and healing every sickness. The Matthean Gospel must have taken over most of the earlier speech of Jesus' answer to John's question, judging from the near verbatim agreement of Matthew 11:2–19 with the parallel episode(s) in Luke (7:18–35). In the Matthean story, Jesus' response carries the same message as the earlier speech also adapted in Luke: while John was the greatest prophet in (Israelite) history, the direct rule of God is now being manifested in the healings (and preaching) of Jesus among the people who had been longing for relief from the various forms of sickness under which they had been suffering (as discussed more fully in chap. 8).

The Matthean episode begins with John hearing about "the works of the messiah." This seems strange since the next step in Jesus' response suggests fairly clearly that the healings and preaching are works of a prophet, the one promised by John, and even greater than John. As noted already, moreover, there was no expectation in Israelite/Judean tradition that a/the messiah would perform healings. The Gospel of Matthew presents Jesus as the messiah in the genealogy and the birth-narrative, and later in the narrative Jesus accepts Peter's confession that he is "the messiah." Otherwise it is only here (Matt 11:2) and in the polemic against the Pharisees (23:10) that the Matthean Gospel refers to Jesus (indirectly but matter-of-factly) as "the messiah."[20] But the reference is puzzling here since thus far in the Matthean narrative Jesus has done no "works" that would have been identified with a/the messiah. The reference to Jesus as "the messiah" here, moreover, makes the thrust of John's question puzzling. Is he asking Jesus, "are you the messiah who is to come or should we expect another messiah"?

It is important to hear the Matthean story, as other Gospel stories, not with subsequent Christian assumptions, but with the mind-set of first-century hearers rooted in Israelite tradition who did not yet have a composite "christology" composed of multiple roles and titles. It seems most likely that the composers/performers of the Matthean story, assuming that Jesus was "the Messiah," simply felt no tension in referring to actions that had previously been presented (in Q and Mark) as those of a prophet as "the works of the messiah." The point of the episode in Matthew is the same as in the dialogue in Q: in all of the various healings (and preaching to the poor), Jesus is indeed the expected/promised one who is responding to the deep longings of the people for the healing of the various forms of their malaise that had long been articulated in Israelite tradition (as we know from various passages in Isaiah, such as 35:5–6 and 61:1; discussed in chaps. 5 and 8).

20. In the trial before the council (26:57–64), the high priest asks Jesus, "tell us if you are the Messiah, the son of God." Jesus answers, "you have said so," and refers (instead) to the human-like one coming on the clouds of heaven, which was a symbol of the imminent renewal of the whole people, judging from Dan 7. Others slap him and mock him, saying, "prophesy to us, you Messiah!" In the Barabbas episode (27:15–23), Pilate refers to him as "Jesus who is called the Messiah." Would the audience have heard the mockery by those who did not believe that Jesus was the Messiah as irony (that is, he really is/was the Messiah, despite his having just said "you have said so")?

Retaining in this episode a statement that Luke places elsewhere, the Matthean Jesus confirms what he had just said in the mission speech, that the direct rule of God is suffering violence, presumably of persecution of the leaders of the movement (the disciples). In the closing statement that offers reassurance in the face of persecution and the earlier attacks against John and Jesus, Jesus declares that "Wisdom (a synonym for God or for God's will/plan") will be vindicated by her "works," that is, by the works (healings) that Jesus has been doing in response to the deep longings of the people.

The Matthean narrative fittingly follows this statement of reassurance with woes against the towns that did not respond to all the acts of power (*dynameis*, presumably healings and exorcisms, as in the pre-Matthean speech) that had been performed in them (Matt 11:20–24). Declaring that they would fare worse in the judgment than Tyre and Sidon would have been particularly stinging, since in Israelite tradition these cities had been unusually oppressive to the (northern) Israelites and had been vilified by earlier prophets.

Jesus' following prayer of thanksgiving assumes and articulates the political-economic and cultural division between the wise (e.g., scribes who served the temple state) and the villagers among whom Jesus was performing "these things," his acts of power (11:25–27). The terms, the rhetoric of the prayer ostensibly to the "Father," but aimed at the audience of the Gospel as well as the hearers in the narrative, mocks the self image of the wise. The intellectual elite who produced wisdom texts claimed that they were "the wise and intelligent" to whom "the Lord of heaven and earth" (or "the Most High") had revealed wisdom.[21] They looked down their noses at or perhaps pitied ordinary people as "infants" who, at most, had only an elementary understanding of torah and the divine governance of the world. The Matthean narrative adds to this brief speech Jesus' summons of the weary people to find rest in him (and his movement), a call to those who are carrying heavy burdens (that he later accuses the scribes of not alleviating) to find rest for their souls—and rest from their labors and restoration of life on the sabbath, in the next episode.

The next two episodes draw out the relationship between Jesus' healings and people's wellbeing that must be sustained by food and rest. In the argument with the Pharisees Jesus insists that people's hunger

21. This was apparently a standard claim in the "wisdom tradition" behind texts such as Sirach and Wisdom of Solomon.

takes priority over law codes that supposedly protect the sanctity of the sabbath. This sets up the conflict with the Pharisees over healing on the sabbath. Again the setting is a village assembly on the sabbath, where there is a man with a withered hand. Although the Matthean version of the episode does not include the Pharisees' motivation, the hope to accuse Jesus, it seems to be implicit in their question, "is it lawful to heal on the sabbath?" The Matthean Jesus asks a counterquestion about how they would handle the case of a sheep who had fallen into a pit. The superstrict scribal-priestly community at Qumran had a ruling that forbade rescuing an animal on the sabbath (CD 11:13–14). Jesus' question seems to assume that the Pharisees were not so strict. But they were silent. He simply ordered the man to stretch out his hand, and it was restored, which led the Pharisees to conspire to destroy him.

The following brief summary that many crowds followed him and he healed all of them concludes with his ordering them not to make him known (of course they already had). "This was to fulfill" another servant song of Isaiah that emphasizes just how meek and mild he is while bringing justice to the peoples (Isa 42:1–4). Somewhat similar to Jesus' call to the weary to find rest in him since he is gentle and humble, this prepares an escalation in the conflict with the Pharisees, their charge that he is casting out *daimonia* by the ruler of the *daimonia*.

The Matthean version of the charge of Beelzebul and Jesus' response (Matt 12:22–30) is very close to the Lukan version (Luke 11:14–23), except for a brief passage (12:29) that is closer to the Markan version (Mark 3:19–30). Since it is thus likely an adaptation of the version that is adapted in both Matthew and Luke, it carries much the same message, with a few Matthean twists. The possessed man is blind as well as mute, and the Matthean version (12:22) has Jesus "heal" him (so that he saw and spoke), not cast out the spirit, as in Luke (11:14). The Matthean story that presented Jesus from the outset as "the Messiah" now has the amazed crowds wondering out loud, "can this be the son of David?" so that the ensuing charge by the Pharisees' is set over against the crowds as well as Jesus himself. That the crowd wonders whether Jesus can be "the son of David" appears to be distinctive to the Matthean Gospel, like the cry of the two blind men (9:29; 20:30–31).[22]

---

22. Again the Matthean narrative evidently just overlays "the messiah" ("the works of the messiah," 11:2) and "son of David" onto a few episodes of Jesus' healing and exorcism that otherwise appear as "works of a prophet."

As discussed in consideration of the Markan and the "Jesus-speeches" versions of the "controversy," the charge of Beelzebul comes from scribal lore, in which the name of the principal god (divine power) of earlier Canaanite monarchies became transformed into the symbol of subversion of the Jerusalem temple-state and the divine order that it represented. "The ruler of the *daimonia*/invasive hostile spirits" was also scribal lore, the closest parallel to which is the figure of "Mastema" and/or "Satan, ruler of the spirits" in the book of Jubilees (10:7–11). Given the opposition between Jesus and the scribes and Pharisees in the Matthean story and the now escalating conflict between the Pharisees and both Jesus and the crowds, it is hardly likely that the Matthean Gospel, any more than the Markan story and the pre-Matthean speeches, would imagine that Jesus shared the views (and certainly not the political-economic interests) of scribes and Pharisees.

No more than the Markan story or the Q speeches does the Matthean Gospel present Jesus as engaged in some sort of "cosmic" conflict. None of the statements in the Matthean Jesus' response to the charge suggest that he understood his casting out of spirits as a battle against Satan or the kingdom of Satan. The agency of the Spirit in the key statement by the Matthean Jesus, "if it is by the Spirit of God that I cast out demons, then the kingdom of God has come to you" (12:28), does not change this. The Matthean account of Jesus' baptism has the Spirit descend upon him, and has the Spirit lead him into the wilderness to be tested by the devil. But the devil, who comes to test him, is "the tempter" (as usual in his rare appearances in Matthew and the other Gospels), and hardly "the ruler of demons" or some cosmic force of evil. Similarly, nothing in the statement about casting out *daimonia* by the Spirit of God suggests that they are part of a (cosmic) war against Satan as ruler of the *daimonia*. It is surely significant that Jesus' casting out possessing spirits by "the Spirit of God" does not carry over into any of the particular cases of Jesus casting out spirits in the rest of the Gospel.

What the key statement in Jesus' response to the charge does do is to declare that since it is by the Spirit of God that he casts out invasive spirits his exorcisms are manifestations of the direct rule of "heaven" (God) coming upon the people. The Matthean account of Jesus' response then includes the warning that blasphemy against the Holy Spirit would be unforgiveable. Evidently in contrast to the time of Jesus' mission, when he had been sharply criticized, the expanding Jesus-movement of renewal of Israel (under the guidance of the Spirit) developed a rigorous collective discipline in which criticism was sanctioned as blasphemy.

Then, via the extended metaphor of the good and bad trees and their respective fruit, Jesus continues his polemic against the Pharisees: "You brood of vipers!" Some of the uncomprehending scribes and Pharisees, after Jesus has just performed an exorcism, ask to see a "sign" from him. Whereas in the pre-Matthean Jesus-speech also included in Luke "the sign of Jonah" was his preaching of repentance, the Matthean episode draws an analogy from Jonah in the whale to Jesus buried in the earth prior to his resurrection, which leads to the scene of future judgment of "the wicked and adulterous generation/kind," that is, the scribes and Pharisees.

The discussion of the return of the unclean spirit(s) must be a warning about what is necessary to keep the spirits, once cast out, from returning. And that is a step to what is the answer: the familial covenantal community (renewed in the long first speech) symbolized in Jesus' "mother" and "sister" and "brothers" and represented by all his disciples, that is, those who keep the will of God.

Speech in Parables/Allegories

The "parables" speech includes extended metaphors and allegories of Jesus' mission (the proclamation and practice of the direct rule of heaven). The allegories in particular function as an explanation of the response to Jesus' proclamation of the direct rule of heaven, in personal practice and in the historical social-political context, and as a sanction on the audience's response to the proclamation of the gospel (including the hearing of the Gospel of Matthew).[23] Heard in the context of the overall Matthean Gospel these allegories, along with the parable of the dragnet, pick up on the covenant renewal speech, particularly the practice of justice (*dikaiosune*) in the covenant demands and the sanctioning parables on

---

23. In order to hear the parables and particularly Jesus' explanation with the audience in historical context, it is necessary for modern readers/hearers to avoid standard translations (and interpretation) heavily influenced by Christian theology and the modern theological construction of apocalypticism. In both the allegory of the seed sown by the sower and that of the weeds and their interpretations (13:3–9, 18–23, 24–30, 36–43) the issue is the response to and practice of the word, in the practice either of justice or of injustice. The Greek term *poneros/oi* should be translated as "wicked," not "evil" (as in the NRSV, in which "the evil one" too easily suggests the later Christian reification and personification of "The Evil One").

practicing the word at the end of the speech (5:17–48; 7:21–29). Following in the story shortly after admonitions and episodes focused on negative response and opposition to Jesus' mission (10:16–42; 11:20–24; 12:1–14, 22–42), the allegory of the weeds provides an explanation of the situation of Jesus' mission and its opposition.

The Matthean story to this point consists (almost entirely) of narratives of the healings and exorcisms of Jesus that lead to (and then again continue after) his renewal of Mosaic covenant and his commissioning of the disciples to extend his program of healing and exorcism and proclamation of the kingdom in village communities. The repeated and pervasive references and allusions to Israelite tradition and the periodic explicit statements that Jesus' actions are in fulfillment of what was spoken through the prophet(s) indicate that the healings, exorcisms, and covenant renewal are a renewal of the Israel that became collectively embodied in an expanding movement.

Fourth Narrative Step and Speech

Narrative of Feedings, Exorcisms, and Other Acts of Power

The Matthean narrative resumes with references to his acts of power, including an exorcism among other episodes. As a contrast to the healings Jesus performs in response to the trust of the crowds who bring the sick to him, people in his hometown assembly, while astounded at his wisdom and acts of power, lack trust, limiting his effectiveness there (13:54–58). This again indicates that the people's trust is an integral, enabling aspect of the healings.

The Matthean account of Herod Antipas' beheading of John (14:1–12), besides prefiguring the execution of Jesus, dramatizes the escalating conflict between the people and the rulers, who are threatened by the power generated in the interaction between the people and the prophets John and Jesus. Herod had put John in prison because of his protests, but had not executed him for fear of the people, who regarded him as a prophet. That relation between people and prophet was rooted in the long Israelite tradition of prophets who had been spokespersons for the people's interests against exploitative kings and their officers. Especially prominent in people's memory was the prophet Elijah, who had also been a healer and a leaders of the people. In the introduction to the episode Herod believed that Jesus was John raised from the dead because of the powers at work in him. The relational power (among the people) generated by John's protests against Antipas' acts of injustice were related to the power operative in Jesus' relational healing of the people.

The references to Jesus' healing of the people continues in the introduction to the feeding of the 5,000, a new feeding in the wilderness led by the new Moses (14:13–21). As the symbolic number of twelve baskets of leftovers are gathered, it is evident that the people were now sufficiently nourished. Healing and sufficient food were integrally related in the renewal of the people. Jesus' blessing and breaking the loaves is an anticipation of the communities' celebration of the Lord's supper, so that the hearers of the episode would associate it with the wilderness feeding. Although the Matthean narrative does not highlight the two sequences of acts of power that we hear in Mark's story, the juxtaposition of the second crossing of the stormy sea (prefaced by Jesus going up to the mountain, like Moses) with the feeding in the wilderness is clearly suggestive of a new exodus. The summary of the healing of all the sick throughout the region of Gennesaret hoping just to touch the fringe of his garment is yet another statement that healing was the principal activity of his mission of renewal (14:34–36).

In response to another challenge by the Pharisees and scribes, Jesus shifts the focus from their concern about maintaining purity codes to their manipulating the people into supporting the temple out of their produce needed instead to sustain subsistence in their family and community (15:1–20). Speaking to and for the people, in opposition to the Pharisees, he emphasizes social interaction in opposition to rules that regulate what foods may be eaten in what way. While nothing in this episode suggests that other (non-Israelite) peoples are in mind, the next episode deals with inclusion of other peoples in the movement of the renewal of Israel.

More pointedly than in the Markan narrative, the Matthean Jesus then "went away" (or "withdrew," after his conflict with the Pharisees and scribes from Jerusalem) into the district of Tyre and Sidon. There "a Canaanite woman from that region came out and cried 'Have mercy on me, lord/sir, son of David; my daughter is severely possessed by a *daimonion*.'" In Israelite tradition, "Canaanite" is a term for non-Israelites in Palestine (the land of Canaan) in general, some of whom became Israelites at points in the history of the people. That the Matthean narrative identifies the woman as "Canaanite" suggests that she, like Galileans and Judeans and Samaritans was among the peoples who had been subjected to Hellenistic and then Roman imperial rule, in this case to the Hellenized client rulers of Tyre and Sidon.[24] Her address of Jesus as "son of David" parallels that of the two blind people in both an earlier and a later episode (9:27–31; 20:29–34; it is difficult to know what its special significance may have been in the Matthean story). Jesus rejects her and her plea for mercy: "I was sent only to the lost sheep of the house of Israel" (a repetition from the sending out of envoys). . . . "It is not fair to take the children's food and throw it to the dogs."[25] The issue is not that of Israelites having precedence in being fed, as in the Markan episode of the Syrophoenician woman's child, but whether non-Israelites would be fed at all from the "food" of the renewal of Israel. But the persistent woman fired right back, "Yes, Lord, yet even the dogs eat the crumbs that fall from their masters' table." Bested in debate, he finally yielded: "Woman, great is your trust! Let it be done..." The daughter was healed instantly. Because of the intense trust of (some) non-Israelite people the mission of Jesus was expanding beyond "the lost sheep of Israel" (despite his supposed restriction).

Yet another summary, back along the Sea of Galilee (15:29–31), recapitulates his many healings. After he went up on the mountain and sat down (as he had before to deliver the covenant renewal speech), great crowds came bringing "the lame, the maimed, the blind, the mute, and many others . . . and he healed them, so that the crowd saw "the mute speak, the maimed made whole, the lame walk, and the blind see," in phrases that remind the hearers that Jesus is fulfilling the longings of a suffering people, as he had articulated in response to John's question whether he was the coming one. The Matthean story, continuing to parallel the Markan sequence of episodes, includes the second feeding in the wilderness (with allusion to the origins of Israel),[26] Jesus' refusal of a sign

24. Depending on how aware the composers and audience of the Matthean story were of much earlier history, rulers in Jerusalem and Samaria had also subjected Canaanite peoples.

25. How strong a rejection or insult the "dogs" image indicates is not clear; see G. Miller, "Attitude toward Dogs"; and see further Wainwright, "Of Dogs and Women."

26. It is difficult to discern what all to hear in the narrative sequence of the episode of the Canaanite woman and the feeding of the four thousand, with the repeated symbol of seven (fish and baskets of left-overs). It is less clear in the Matthean narrative than in the Markan narrative that in the feeding Jesus and his disciples are still working in nearby areas beyond the frontiers of Galilee. But the symbolism in the feeding, like that in the exorcism of the Canaanite woman's daughter, might suggest inclusion of other, non-Israelite people in the renewal of Israel, who "glorify the God of Israel" in response to Jesus' many healings and are included in the second wilderness feeding, symbolic of the renewal of Israel (Matt 15:29–31, 32–39).

other than the sign of Jonah, to satisfy the Pharisees' and Sadducees' test, and Jesus' warning to the disciples about the leaven of the Pharisees and Sadducees (15:32–39; 16:1–4, 5–12). This series of episodes interweaves the healings and exorcism of Jesus as the principal activity of his mission with the people's need for food in opposition to and by the rulers and their representatives who exploit them and are threatened by the power generated in the relationship between the people and Jesus (in his acts of power).

Several principal aspects of Jesus' mission and movement reverberate backward and forward through the Matthean Gospel in the episode in Caesarea Philippi. The name given to his capital city by Herod's son Philip vividly symbolizes Roman imperial rule through their client rulers over subject peoples. In contrast to the widespread view that Jesus was John or Elijah that would have resulted from his healings (or perhaps earlier had enabled them), renewal of the Mosaic covenant, and prophecy against the rulers, Simon Peter declares, "You are the Messiah." In contrast to the Markan story, the Matthean Jesus responds by blessing him and designating him as the head of (the Matthean branch of) the movement, the "rock" on which he would build his *ekklesia*. "Assembly" was a traditional Israelite term for the whole people and the term for the people or citizen body-politic of Greek-Hellenistic cities.[27] Even though the Matthean Jesus tells the disciples not to tell anyone that he is the Messiah, this was hardly a secret to the communities among whom the Gospel was being performed. Jesus' command not to tell anyone was evidently a warning about becoming too public about their loyalty to the anointed king of a resistant subject people.

Immediately following Peter's confession and blessing, however, comes Jesus' first announcement that he must suffer under the Jerusalem rulers and be killed (and raised). Peter rebuked Jesus, who accused him of functioning as Satan (the tempter). Jesus' rebuke does not appear to rescind his designation of Peter as the head of the movement. But it puts Peter and the disciples on notice that there be no misunderstanding that he might be an imperial king. Rather, he will be killed by the Roman imperial rulers. Moreover, in the ensuing admonition, those who would be his followers must also be prepared to "take up their cross."

The appearance of Moses (the founding prophet of Israel) and Elijah (the prophet of renewal) on the mountain with the transfigured Jesus

27. The assemblies had lost most of their power to wealthy aristocratic "councils" in Hellenistic-Roman times.

confirms what has been apparent in many episodes such as renewal of the covenant, feeding in the wilderness, and the healings, that Jesus is the new Moses and Elijah engaged in the renewal of the people. The Matthean narrative presents Jesus both as the martyred messiah and as the prophet of renewal who performs covenant renewal and acts of power as acts of deliverance like those of Moses and Elijah. Here the account of the disciples' descent from the mountain makes explicit what is implied in the Markan episode, that John the Baptist was Elijah who was expected to return to prepare the way.

Following the "transfiguration," the Matthean story presents a short version of Jesus' exorcism of the moonstruck boy (17:14–21). The father tells of his son falling into the fire and often into water, and complains that the disciples were unable to heal him. With a rebuke to the disciples, Jesus subdues the *daimonion*, which "came out of [the boy], who was healed instantly." This becomes the occasion for Jesus' scolding the disciples that trust is necessary for such exorcism, with hyperbole that it can empower movement of a mountain.

Jesus' second announcement that he will be killed (and be raised) and his statement about payment of the half-shekel tax to the temple remind the hearers that Jesus' mission and movement are opposed by and to the rulers, both the Romans and their clients. That the question and Jesus' answer are addressed to Peter, just named as the rock of the movement, indicates clearly that the Matthean story is addressing the communities of Jesus-loyalists. Jesus' statement that "the sons are free," on the analogy that kings (such as the Roman emperor) take tribute from others and not from their own people, is a declaration that the people of Israel, whose king is God, do not really owe tribute (tithes, etc.) to the temple-state (or other client rulers). The following "however" statement evidently instructs the hearers not to press the issue lest they evoke more severe repression.

Speech on Reconciliation in Covenantal Community

The disciples' utter misunderstanding about rank and position in the kingdom and Jesus' admonition on humility begins the fourth of his speeches in the Gospel, about care for members of the community, especially the "little ones," and about forgiveness and reconciliation of members who may come into conflict. These admonitions, delineation of procedures of reconciliation, and the parable about the importance of forgiveness serve as reinforcements of the renewed covenantal community of people, some of whom have been healed.

Narrative of Jesus' Confrontation with Rulers in Jerusalem and Speech about the Future

Restatement of the Agenda of Jesus' Mission and Movement

As the narrative resumes following the speech on community discipline that insists on mutual forgiveness and reconciliation, the Matthean story follows the Markan sequence of episodes with some rearrangement and insertions. The series of episodes as he goes into "the region of Judea beyond the Jordan" are further statements and illustrations of the agenda of Jesus and his movement of covenantal cooperation and sharing and anticipated martyrdom. These immediately precede and provide a stark contrast with the program and practices of the rulers and representatives of the temple-state that he is about to confront when he enters Jerusalem. The renewed covenantal community under the direct rule of heaven will not include anyone who has become wealthy by exploiting others. Jesus declares explicitly that in the renewal of the people[28] the disciples' responsibility is to establish justice for the twelve tribes of Israel.[29] After the third announcement that the rulers would condemn him and hand him over to the (other) peoples (i.e., the Romans) to be crucified, he admonishes the twelve disciples that, in contrast to the rulers of the peoples (the Romans) who lord it over their subjects, their leadership is to be that of service to the people (the movement).

As Jesus leaves Jericho, headed up to Jerusalem, the Matthean narrative again has two blind men cry out, "Have mercy on us, son of David." The crowd ordered them to be quiet but they shouted all the more loudly, "Have mercy on us, son of David." When Jesus stopped and asked what

---

28. Not "of all things" (NRSV), as if this were the "cosmic" regeneration of the Stoics; see further Horsley, *Jesus and the Sprial of Violence*, 201–3. This statement by Jesus is a reminder that, while other peoples were welcome and joined the movement, the agenda of Jesus' mission in the Matthean story, as in the Markan story, is the renewal of the people of Israel.

29. "Judge," the standard translation (NRSV, etc.), is a misunderstanding of *krinein* in the context of Israelite tradition, in texts such as Pss 9; 35; 58; 82:1–4; etc., as explained in Horsley, *Jesus and the Spiral*, 201–8.

they wanted him to do for them, they replied, "Let our eyes be opened."
As in the first healing of two blind men, Jesus touched their eyes; immediately they regained their sight; and they followed him. The healing is both
concrete and symbolic, juxtaposed with the persistent misunderstanding
("blindness") of the disciples and the blind people regaining their sight
and following Jesus as he heads toward confrontation and martyrdom.

Confrontation with the Rulers in the Temple

In the immediately following episode, as Jesus enters Jerusalem from the
Mount of Olives, he and the disciples and the crowd stage a "messianic"
demonstration. He rides on a donkey/colt, in explicit fulfillment of the
prophecy of a popular king[30] coming to the city (which we know from
Zech 9:9). The crowd spreads cloaks and branches on the road, in clear
reference to (repetition of) the popular acclamation of Jehu as king after
Elisha's anointing him (2 Kgs 9:1–3), and the crowds shout "Hosanna
to the son of David." The crowd acclaims him as "son of David," placing him in the role of the popular king prophesied by Zechariah. Immediately, however, when the city asks who this is, the crowd (from the
countryside)[31] answers from how he has become known in his work of
healing and covenant renewal: "This is the prophet Jesus from Nazareth
in Galilee." Again in the Matthean narrative there is no tension between
Jesus' actions and pronouncements as a prophet in fulfillment of Israelite
tradition and his acclamation as the (prophesied) popular king.

The Matthean narrative has Jesus go directly into (the courtyard of)
the temple, where he forcibly blocked the usual business that accompanied the sacrifices. The second of the two lines he cites from two well-
known prophecies of judgment against the temple explains the purpose/
motive. Just as Jeremiah had prophesied the destruction of "Solomon's"
temple because the rulers/priests were using it as their sacred hideout
after plundering the people, like a band of brigands, so Jesus mounted a
prophetic demonstration against the temple that pronounced its impending destruction. The immediately following statement, that "the blind
and the lame came to him in the temple, and he healed them" (21:14)

---

30. Not an imperial king like Solomon or a client-king of empire like Herod.

31. It is important to note that the Matthean story distinguishes between "the great
crowd"/"the crowds" that have accompanied and acclaimed Jesus and "the whole city,"
i.e., the Jerusalemites. See further note 4 above.

is distinctive to the Matthean narrative. It serves to contrast, indeed to oppose the whole preceding story of Jesus' healing of the people to the temple(-state), God's judgment of which Jesus has just prophetically demonstrated and pronounced. And it is these amazing actions and the people's response, with children crying out "Hosanna" ("Save, oh Save!), that evoke the rulers' anger.

Even more than the Markan story, the Matthean story has Jesus on the offensive throughout his confrontation with the high priests and their representatives in Jerusalem. In prophetic parables he pronounces that the ruling aristocracy stands under God's condemnation, that the rule of God will be taken away from them and given to people who produce fruits of God's rule. But the rulers were immobilized by their fear of the crowds, by the power of the people generated in their interaction with Jesus (and John), whom they regarded as a prophet. When the Pharisees attempt to entrap him with the question whether it is lawful to pay tribute to Caesar, Jesus skillfully formulates a response that declares, in effect, that the people (Israelites) do not owe tribute to Caesar.[32] The ancient audience rooted in Israelite tradition centered in the Mosaic covenant— and aware that Caesar was honored as divine in the Roman Empire— would have understood that Jesus' declaration was a restatement of the first two commandments. The people of Israel were to have one God only, and they were not to "bow down and serve" (the visual representations of) other gods with portions of their crops taken as tribute.[33]

The confrontation is lengthened and escalated by Jesus' series of woes against the scribes and Pharisees that concludes with a declaration that God will punish them for murdering the prophets and other martyrs for justice, and concludes with the prophecy (lament) that God is about to make "desolate" the ruling house of Jerusalem.

Speech about the Future to the Disciples

That the temple will be destroyed in judgment is immediately confirmed by Jesus prophecy in transition to his speech about the persecutions to

32. Modern interpreters have anachronistically imposed their assumption of the separation of religion and politics, church and state onto this episode.

33. The audience would also have known that the group of scribal teachers and Pharisees that Josephus calls "the Fourth Philosophy" had resisted payment of the tribute to Caesar on the same basis, that God was their only "lord and master" (as in the account of Josephus, *Ant.* 18:23).

come and eventually the ingathering of the elect at "the coming of the son of man" (human-like one). The coming will also include the judgment of people according to the justice and mercy of their treatment of his brothers and sisters.

Concluding Narrative: Covenant Meal, Arrest, Trial, Crucifixion, Resurrection-Exaltation

In the Matthean as in the Markan story Jesus transforms the Passover meal into a ceremony of covenant renewal. That the cup is the blood of the covenant poured out "for the forgiveness of sins" suggests that in the Matthean communities forgiveness of sins was specially associated with the covenant meal that anticipated celebration in the kingdom rather than with baptism. This reinforces the "breakthrough" of Jesus' forgiveness of sins in the healing of the paralytic, in connection with which Jesus declared explicitly that people have the authority to forgive people.

Several issues that affected the audience's hearing (and our understanding) of the Matthean story are interwoven in the episodes of the arrest, trial(s), and crucifixion of Jesus as presented with some distinctive touches in the Gospel.

The Matthean narrative addressed the audience in the aftermath of the great revolt in 66–70 CE. As discussed above, Jesus' mission of healing and renewal of covenantal community was also resistance to the Roman imperial order in Palestine. But it was hardly revolt, even though it strengthened local communities' ability to resist. Jesus' command in the arrest scene against use of a sword appears to be an explicit statement against revolt, perhaps reinforced in retrospect following the brutal Roman destruction of people and their villages as well as Jerusalem and the temple in 70 CE.[34] Also his claim that he could have appealed to the Father to send twelve legions of angels (the "heavenly hosts" in early

---

34. The Matthean narrative has an apologetic "explanation" in the episode of Jesus' arrest as (if) a brigand/rebel. A prophet who opposed the rulers would be arrested (and killed) by the rulers, as anticipated earlier in the story in the episode of John's execution (14:1–12) and in Jesus' prophetic lament over the ruling house of Jerusalem (23:37). Now, having throughout the story presented Jesus' actions as the fulfillment of "what was spoken through the prophet," the Gospel appeals to the written texts of the prophets (*graphai*, 26:56) as the explanation. The explanation that the crucifixion and resurrection of Jesus as "according to the writings" had become a standard explanation early in other movements of Jesus- or Christ-loyalists, as in the "creed" cited by Paul in 1 Cor 15:3–5.

Israelite and prophetic tradition that continued to be cultivated in scribal circles at least) cautions that the audience should not be tempted by such fantasies (cf. the warning about false prophets and their omens in Matt 24:24).[35]

The overall Matthean story, however, may have left some ambiguity about Jesus role and agenda in presenting him as the Messiah as well as the prophet of renewal. At the outset of the story Jesus was born as "the Messiah" and in the next episode he is identified as "the king of the Judeans," at least by the Magi, leading Herod to send out his military against the threat of the movement Jesus represents. The question the Roman governor Pilate[36] asked Jesus, "Are you the king of the Judeans?" reflected the Roman view of the most serious resistance to the Roman imperial order in Judea/Palestine, as had happened in 4 BCE and again happened in the great revolt in the movement led by Simon bar Giora (discussed in chap. 4).[37] In both the trial before the high priests and the questioning by Pilate, the Matthean narrative seems to have Jesus backing away from the role of the Messiah, that is, as leader of liberation from Roman rule. When asked if he was "the Messiah," Jesus dodges the question and answers with emphasis, "*You* have said so. But . . ."—and points to God's judgment yet to come.

As exemplified in that judgment yet to come, on the other hand, the Matthean narrative sharpens the opposition between Jesus and the high priestly rulers in Jerusalem. When the high priest asked him if he were the Messiah, son of God, Jesus answered with emphasis, "*You* have said so. But from now on you will see the human-like one . . . coming with the clouds of heaven." This was a well-known symbol of the restoration of the people that would be made possible by God's judgment of the imperial rulers. This scenario of God's judgment of oppressive imperial rule and the corresponding restoration of the people first appeared (to our knowledge, anyhow) in the visions of the learned *maskilim* who attributed it to the legendary sage/prophet, Daniel (Dan 7). Along with the Aramaic idiom *bar-nasha*, translated in Greek as *huios tou anthropou*, the

---

35. Perhaps with a touch of exaggeration, Josephus mentions that prophets inspired persistent resistance with visions of heavenly armies hurtling to the defense of the besieged people in Jerusalem (*Ant.* 6.296–99).

36. In installing the high priests as their client rulers of Judea, the Romans kept the power of capital punishment in the hands of their governor.

37. By contrast, in their mockery of Jesus, the high priests, insiders to Israelite tradition, say "king of Israel".

human-like one, this visionary scenario of judgment-plus-renewal evidently became well-known in popular circles as well. The audience of the Gospel would have understood that Jesus—as an Israelite prophet like Elijah or Jeremiah—was boldly pointing to the imminent judgment of the rulers and renewal of the people. No wonder the high priests charged him with blasphemy, that is, with prophesying ominously against the high priesthood at the head of the temple as God's (as well as Caesar's) regent over Judea.

In order to avoid the previously standard supersessionist reading of the Gospel of Matthew, it is particularly important to hear the narrative of the arrest and trial of Jesus in the context of the story's audience and in the historical context of Roman Palestine before and after the great revolt. The Gospel is not about the origins of Christianity from Judaism, but about Jesus' generation of the renewal of Israel in opposition to and by the rulers of Israel, particularly the Roman-appointed high priests and their representatives. The Matthean story and its audience know that the Romans had destroyed the temple-state along with the temple. The story and the audience understood themselves as the continuation of the renewal of Israel in Jesus healings and covenant renewal. The sharpening of the conflict in the trial narrative was part of the explanation or rationalization of what had happened. Thus, as part of the utterly unhistorical Barabbas episode, the high priests had manipulated the Jerusalem crowd (*not* "the Jews" generally, as often misunderstood) into calling for Jesus' crucifixion and taking his death upon themselves (27:24–26). And in another legend that had developed—and was still told among "the Judeans" opposed to the Jesus-movement—the high priests' obtained a guard of soldiers for Jesus' tomb and then bribed the soldiers to say that the disciples had stolen away the body. The opposition continued after the crucifixion of Jesus, as the expanding movement(s) of Jesus-loyalists faced periodic persecutions. As noted in connection with the Pharisees, it is unclear what group, if any, the Romans placed in control of Judeans in Judea and beyond. Was the sharp opposition between Jesus and the Jerusalem and Roman rulers in the Matthean story mainly a reflection of the continuation of the struggle between the Matthean movement and the temple-state prior to the great revolt and the Roman devastation?

The Matthean narrative makes the death of Jesus extremely ominous, more prominent and interwoven with his resurrection/vindication. Not only is the temple veil torn in two, symbolizing the beginning of God's judgment on the temple (that Jesus had prophesied and dramatized in his prophetic demonstration). The Matthean narrative adds that in an earthquake tombs opened and saints who had "fallen asleep" arose and appeared to many in the city.[38]

Although there was no standard scenario of "the resurrection" in Israelite tradition, the hope for resurrection had arisen (in second-century BCE scribal circles) in response to imperial invasion and violent suppression of the people and was closely linked with the trust in God's judgment of imperial rulers and renewal of the people.[39] In response to Hellenistic imperial attacks, resurrection became the way in which those who had been martyred in their resistance would be vindicated by God and included in the renewal of the people (see esp. Dan 11:32–35; 12:1–3). Resurrection/vindication was thus closely associated with martyr death. The Matthean narrative portrays the martyr death of Jesus as touching off the divine judgment symbolized in the earthquake, which in turn causes the opening of tombs in anticipation of the general resurrection (understood as having begun with the raising of Jesus) as part of the renewal of the people. The Matthean account of Jesus' resurrection is almost as short as the Markan account of the empty tomb and the call to return to Galilee.[40] Then the Matthean story ends suddenly with the exalted/vindicated Jesus' commissioning the eleven disciples to make disciples of all peoples. The Matthean Gospel clearly places less emphasis on the resurrection than on the arrest-trial(s)-and-execution of Jesus as a martyred prophet who is crucified as a leader of resistance for having healed the people, renewed the covenant, and prophesied judgment against the rulers. And this is what energized the expansion of the Matthean Jesus movement once the eleven were commissioned to "make disciples of other peoples," to include them in the renewal of Israel begun in Jesus mission. The effect of the Matthean story on the communities in which it was performed will be discussed in chap 11.

38. Earthquakes and other disturbances in the created order were longstanding images of God's coming in judgment and/or deliverance; see Horsley, *Scribes, Visionaries*, 158–59, 170; and Horsley, *Revolt of Scribes*, 52, 78.

39. Revivification of deceased ancestors had become a symbol of the renewal of the people (as in Ezek 37; Isa 26).

40. The principal differences are the Matthean elaboration of the appearance of the messenger and the brief appearance of Jesus to the two Marys.

10

The Lukan Story

AT ITS OUTSET, THE Lukan (hi)story appears more sophisticated "literarily" than the other Gospel stories. Like the contemporary history of the Judean people by Josephus, it begins in good Hellenistic style with a boastful apology about its superiority to previous accounts and a dedication to an ostensible patron. The "most excellent Theophilus," of course, might be a symbolic name, "God-beloved," for the collective addressees. In any case, Hellenistic historiography such as that of Josephus focused on events among the rulers and magnates, and mentions ordinary people only when they make trouble for the wealthy and powerful elite. The Lukan story, on the other hand, whatever its pretense as history or its apologetic claim that the history it narrates is of great significance, focuses on a mission and movement among ordinary people in opposition to and by the rulers.

Text

The Gospel of Luke, like Matthew and Mark, tells a historical story about Jesus' renewal of the people of Israel through exorcisms and healings, proclamation of the direct rule of God, and renewal of covenantal community among the Galileans and Judeans under Roman rule in Palestine. While "Luke" has been thought to have been a more sophisticated "writing" than the other Gospels, little attention has been given to the story as possibly orally performed. The Markan story appears to have proceeded in narrative steps that would have made it easily learnable and performable. The Matthean Gospel is even more clearly "organized" into a beginning prologue, five narratives each followed by a major speech, all climaxing in the confrontation, arrest, trial, crucifixion, and resurrection-vindication in Jerusalem. The Lukan Gospel parallels much of the Markan sequence of episodes and presents much of the teaching of Jesus in speech material that closely parallels the Matthean speeches in sequence and in wording.[1] But it has its own distinctive narrative organization.

After the "prologue" of infancy narratives, John's mission of baptism, and the testing of Jesus, the Lukan narrative has Jesus deliver a programmatic summary of his mission, followed by a series of exorcism and healings that lead to his covenant renewal speech, followed by more healings and exorcism that lead to commissioning the disciples, the new feeding of Israel, his appearance with Moses and Elijah, and two announcements that he would suffer and be killed (4:14—9:50). The Lukan narrative then continues the episodes of Jesus' mission along the way as he had "set his face to go to Jerusalem": After commissioning seventy envoys to extend his healing and exorcism, he delivers a series of teachings to people in the movement, comes into sharp conflict with the Pharisees and lawyers, delivers prophetic condemnations of the Jerusalem rulers, insists on just economic relations in the keeping of the (Mosaic) covenant and teaching, and offers some illustrative instructional parables, with several episodes of healing or exorcism interspersed (9:51—19:28). The narrative finally has Jesus enter Jerusalem acclaimed by the multitude and engage in a series of confrontations with the high priestly rulers, then deliver a speech about the future, after which comes the climactic series of last supper, arrest, trial, crucifixion, and resurrection. While the Lukan story may seem to us (who have been socialized into print culture) more difficult to learn and perform than the Markan or Matthean story, it does have clear, if longer, narrative steps, with some of the same narrative sequences as Mark and Matthew. For example, Jesus' exorcism and healing lead directly to his Mosaic covenant renewal; more healings lead into sending the disciples on a mission of exorcism and healing.

The Lukan story, like the Markan and Matthean stories and the series of speeches adapted in Matthew and Luke, is clearly about the

---

1. The composer(s) of the Gospel of Luke know(s) of "many orderly accounts" of "the events fulfilled among us." Comparison with the other "Synoptic Gospels" indicates that the Lukan story includes most of the episodes that are in the Markan story and a great deal of speech material paralleled in the Matthean Gospel. Making comparisons with the Markan narrative and "Q" speeches, however, does not require the assumption or lead to the hypothesis that an "author" of Luke was "editing" or "redacting" a written text of Mark and "Q."

renewal of Israel in opposition to and by the rulers. The exorcisms and healings are the principal manifestations of the *power* working through Jesus that the story emphasizes. The Lukan narrative may lend less of a sense of immediacy than the Markan narrative. In both the sequence of episodes and the wording of particular episodes, however, the healings and particularly the exorcisms seem more ominous as well as central to Jesus' mission. The Lukan story adds several episodes to those that parallel the ones in the Markan story. Moreover, the story has Jesus commission the twelve, with power and authority, to cast out spirits and heal sicknesses and a few episodes later commissions seventy others to extend his mission of exorcism and healing, who perform acts of power in more villages communities. The healings and exorcisms thus gain rather than lose historical significance in the Lukan story in comparison with the others. This is (partly) because the Lukan story draws out the opposition to Roman imperial rule more than the other stories, particularly in the revolutionary songs, Jesus' designation as the messiah born to head up the restoration of Israel to independence, and the theme of the fulfillment of Israel's history in the birth narrative.

In the rest of the story Jesus acts and speaks, with the people's response, as the (Moses- and Elijah-like) prophet engaged in the healing of the people and the renewal of their covenantal communities. He declares explicitly that the confrontation with the rulers in Jerusalem is integral to the prophetic role of renewal and resistance: "it is impossible for a prophet to be killed outside of Jerusalem." After delivering a classic prophetic lament over the impending desolation of the ruling house of Jerusalem because it has killed the prophets sent by God (13:31–35), he stages a provocative demonstration of entry into Jerusalem, where he confronts the Jerusalem rulers and the Roman imperial order. He is crucified, but vindicated, so that the movement continues and expands.

Context

The Lukan text indicates clearly that it addresses a historical context well after the Roman destruction of Jerusalem. Jesus' (second) lament over God's visitation (of judgment) on the city is clearly prophecy-after-the-fact: "your enemies will surround you, . . . crush you, . . . and will not leave one stone upon another " (19:43–44). Similarly, Jesus' speech about what to expect in the future announces that Jerusalem will be "surrounded by armies, . . . desolation . . . , trampled on by the [imperial] peoples" (21:20–24). The Lukan audience, in contrast with that of Mark, were hearing the Lukan story and speeches (repeatedly) performed in the knowledge that the Romans had again devastated the Galilean and Judean people, more severely than ever, and destroyed Jerusalem and the temple, events that were of ominous historic significance for anyone associated with Israelite tradition. While not as clearly as the Matthean audience, the communities addressed by the Lukan story would already have been familiar with the basic Gospel story and speeches, perhaps also in other versions. This is indicated, for example, in the standardized forms included in the story such as the "Lord's prayer" and the formulaic ceremony of the covenant-renewal meal and the extent to which the narrative parallels the Markan narrative sequence of episodes.

With regard to the location and composition of the Lukan audience, it is important to avoid the old dichotomy between "Jews" and "Gentiles." This standard dichotomy in New Testament studies has grossly oversimplified the complex mix of peoples, cultures, and power-relations around the Eastern Mediterranean and even in Roman Palestine and distorted understanding of Luke as well as the other Gospels.

The episode of Jesus' healing of "the centurion's servant" that has been claimed as an indication that Luke is addressed to "Gentiles" provides a telling illustration. There is no reason to assume that the "centurion" was "a Gentile." The Lukan story presents Jesus' mission as focused on people in the villages of Galilee. The Judean historian Josephus refers to people of the villages of Galilee as "the Galileans." Herod had placed garrisons in strategically located fortresses in Galilee to control and extract revenues from the people. Antipas, having been appointed by the Romans to replace his father, would likely have staffed his administration in Sepphoris and Tiberias with officers of Judean provenance, judging from Josephus' accounts. Like Herod, moreover, Antipas had his own military, and the officers were probably of Judean provenance. It is surely significant that the version of this healing in the Gospel of John (4:46–65) refers not to a "centurion" but to a "royal" (officer). So it seems reasonable that those who composed the Lukan story could well have imagined that a (Herodian-Judean) military officer could have been stationed in the border town of Capernaum.[2]

---

2. See further the thorough discussion of this episode in Meier, *Mentor, Message, and Miracles*, 718–26, including the observation of a large number of Semitisms in the episode, as laid out by Wegner, *Der Hauptmann*, 409–19.

In looking for clues to the possible location(s) and composition of the audience(s) it is important to consider their historical development as communities of Jesus-loyalists. That the great multitude of people who gathered to be healed and to hear the covenant renewal speech came from the coast of Tyre and Sidon, as well as from Jerusalem and all Judea, may be footprints of the movement as it expanded. The (presumed) continuation of the Lukan story in Acts as the movement of Jesus-loyalists continued to expand may be a better indication of just how widely-spread the audience may have been as well as of its composition. Acts tells the story of the movement's spread through Syrian towns, then through Asia Minor and into cities of Greece. According to the scheme of the narrative in Acts, the movement spread first among assemblies (*synagogai*) of diaspora Judeans. Then "God-fearers" and eventually many (Greek-speaking) folks from among other "peoples" (*ethne*) joined the assemblies of Christ-loyalists. But other Judeans in those diaspora assemblies attacked Paul and his co-workers in disputes over what Judean practices would be required of Greeks and other peoples for participation in the movement.

If we can take these features of the narrative in Acts as clues, then the Lukan story was evidently addressed to Greek-speaking communities in cities and towns of Syria and/or in the province of Asia.[3] The communities would appear to have included diaspora Judeans and "God-fearers" along with other peoples. The diaspora Judeans would already have been deeply familiar with the Israelite tradition in which the Jesus-movement(s) were embedded and claimed to be fulfilling. The "God-fearers" and their children's generation would long have identified with Judean/Israelite tradition. In becoming Jesus-loyalists, those from other peoples were identifying with Israelite tradition of which Jesus' mission, crucifixion, and exaltation was being proclaimed as the fulfillment.[4] The narrative in Acts, moreover, has this happening at least by the 40s and 50s, after which these loyalists from the "Greeks" or other peoples had a generation of assimilation or (secondary) socialization into the Israelite tradition with which they had identified prior to (during the development of?) the composition of the Lukan Gospel. If some or many of the

3. Thus in their conceptualization of illnesses both the composers of the Lukan story and its hearers, insofar as they lived in cities and towns of Greek/Hellenistic culture, would have been influenced by images of illness in Greek culture, as explored in the thorough study by Annette Weisenrieder, *Images of Illness*.

4. Cf. Paul's reassurance to the Galatians that they had become the adoptive heirs of the promise to Abraham.

Jesus-loyalists in the Lukan audience were of Judean heritage, then the Lukan text may well be signaling their inclusion by having Jesus work in the villages of Judea and having many Judeans join the crowds who respond to his mission (5:17; 6:17; cf. 4:44, in which some manuscripts have "villages of Judea" while others have "villages of Galilee").

The beginning of the Lukan story may, among other things, be connecting the origin of Jesus mission and movement with its continuation following the Roman destruction of Jerusalem and the temple-state. The story begins simultaneously in an ordinary priestly family in the hill country of Judea as well as among ordinary people in a village in Galilee. Jesus' birth is juxtaposed with the beginning of the Empire that was the context of his mission and movement that started the fulfillment of the history of Israel that is now an oppositional social order to its dominance. The child was born in Bethlehem of Judea as the Messiah but also the people's "Savior," in opposition to the divine imperial "Savior."

Insofar as the Lukan story continues the basic Gospel story told in Mark, it also fits with the fundamental political-economic-religious division and dynamics in early Roman Palestine. With greater historical distance from the movement's origins in Roman Palestine, however, it is not surprising that the Lukan story exhibits a certain unfamiliarity with particular circumstances of social life and relations in Galilee and Judea as known from other sources, such as Josephus. The Lukan story and speeches share with Josephus' histories and the Markan and Matthean stories that the scribes' and Pharisees' historical function was to serve in the temple-state. But the Lukan story (at least in many manuscripts) has them come from "every village in Galilee and Judea." Does this reflect conditions in Palestine a decade or so after the Roman destruction of Jerusalem and the temple-state and a dispersion of Pharisees into villages and towns (where they would have had no economic base), or simply an unfamiliarity with social-structure and relations in Judea earlier in the first century CE? Lukan episodes portray Jesus eating with Pharisees, which seems highly unlikely given Jesus' extensive conflicts with and sharp condemnation of them in the same Lukan episodes, as well as in the Markan story and the speeches that are included in the Lukan story. And it seems odd that in Luke the Pharisees give Jesus a friendly tip-off that Herod Antipas is out to get him. The scene of Jesus' reading from a scroll sounds like a projection from the sabbath practice of diaspora congregations (cf. Acts 13:14–15; 15:21).

The Lukan story and speeches repeatedly address the hearers as ordinary people, "poor," "hungry," in debt, etc. in contrast to "the rich," the "wise," and repeatedly condemn the wealthy as well as the rulers. This suggests that the story and its speeches are addressed mainly to people living at subsistence. Just such economic circumstances are addressed specifically in the speech on not worrying about food and shelter; the necessities for subsistence would be forthcoming from "seeking first the direct rule of God." The insistence in several speeches, including the covenant renewal speech, on sharing in the community and aiding the needy point to the same circumstances of the addressees. In many of these episodes and speeches the Lukan story is adapting earlier "Jesus-tradition," the collective memory of Jesus' mission that is deeply rooted in Israelite popular tradition. Significant episodes and parables that are distinctive to the Lukan story (Luke's "special material"), moreover, also insist on mutual aid and cooperation in community social-economic life according to the Mosaic covenantal commandments and customs, according to "Moses and the prophets." The Lukan Jesus is no less adamant than the Markan Jesus that it would be impossible for a rich person to enter the kingdom of God.

As the movement(s) of Jesus-loyalists expanded, however, they evidently attracted and included people who were not living at subsistence. Judeans from diaspora communities who had evidently come to Jerusalem as pilgrims, such as Stephen, Philip, and Saul, became significant leaders in the expansion and some Pharisees in Jerusalem evidently joined the movement. The Lukan narrative mentions a few distinctive figures who became what look like benefactors of the movement, at some point in its development. The "centurion" from Capernaum whose servant Jesus healed, discussed just above, supposedly funded the construction of a synagogue building. This appears to be a projection from diaspora communities in Greek-speaking cities.[5] That he sent "elders of the Judeans" as emissaries to Jesus suggests that this may be an episode from further on in the movement's expansion among communities of Judeans, projected back into the mission of Jesus.

5. Except for the episode about the centurion (that he "built" a synagogue), *synagoge* in the Gospel narratives and in Acts usually refers to an assembly of villagers or urban Judeans, not to a building—as vividly evident in Acts 13:43, where "the synagogue broke up." Almost all of the (synagogue) buildings found in Galilean villages by archaeological digs have been dated to late antiquity, suggesting they would have been rare in the first century, discussed in Horsley, *Galilee*, chap. 10; and in Horsley, *Archaeology, History*, chap. 6.

A distinctively Lukan narrative bridge between episodes makes a link between Jesus' exorcism and healing and some women who provided for Jesus and his disciples out of their resources. That the women are mentioned by name—Mary, called Magdalene, Joanna, the wife of Herod's (Antipas) steward Chuza, and Susanna (along with "many others")—must mean that at some point in the development of the Jesus movement behind the Lukan story they had become highly significant figures. That the names are in a narrative bridge and not part of a speech also in Matthew or in an episode paralleled in Mark suggests that their traveling with Jesus and the disciples is a later projection into the mission of Jesus. It is difficult to know what to make of the implication that Joanna and Susanna were among the women who had been healed of harmful spirits or illnesses. Such would have been a powerful motive for joining the movement.[6]

The considerable extent of episodes and speeches in Luke that emphasize cooperation, mutual aid, and the sharing of resources in the portrayal of Jesus' mission indicates that this was laid out as instruction, indeed covenantal commands, to the audience communities. In the exhortation that immediately follows the reassurance to the poor that if they just single-mindedly pursue the direct rule of God, then subsistence food and shelter will be forthcoming, the Lukan Jesus demands (evidently of those who have some resources), "Sell your possessions and give alms!" In the two brief accounts of the earliest "commune" of Jesus-loyalists in Jerusalem (Acts 2:44–47; 4:32–35), it looks like even sharing of all things in common was practiced at the earliest stage in the expansion of the movement of renewal of Israel. Barnabas and Ananias and Sapphira were expected to turn over all of their (modest?) resources to the community for support of the needy (Acts 5:1–13).

In this connection, the inclusion of the Zacchaeus episode at a crucial juncture of the narrative following a series of episodes in which wealthy figures are condemned for not heeding the Mosaic covenant (and prophets) or presented as negative paradigms of greedy acquisition is perhaps a bit puzzling. On the one hand, Zacchaeus seems to be an example for anyone in communities of addressees who did have possessions to aid others who were needy. On the other hand, he relinquishes only half of his possessions following a declaration by Jesus that one must relinquish all possessions. Had there been a relaxation of the earlier demand?

6. Compare the implication in Gal 3:1–5 that acts of power were involved in the formation of communities of Christ-loyalists in Galatia.

A significant difference between the Markan and the Lukan stories and between their respective audiences is the shift of perspective that would likely have resulted from the Roman destruction of Jerusalem and the further expansion of the Jesus movements during the intervening twenty to thirty years. On the one hand, the "Lukan" generation of diaspora Judeans, God-fearers, and other Jesus-loyalists had lived through the Roman devastation of Galilean and Judean villages and its destruction of the Jerusalem temple-state. Also in the aftermath they would have experienced the suspicion of "Judeans" that Roman propaganda spread around the Empire. On the other hand, the continuing expansion and local consolidation of communities of the Jesus-movement(s), could well have confirmed their conviction that a significant new phrase of Israelite history, indeed a fulfillment of Israelite hopes for renewal and resistance to imperial domination had begun with the mission of (John and) Jesus in Galilee and Judea. For the "Lukan generation" the Jerusalem temple-state was no longer the focus and symbol of Roman imperial rule. Herod Antipas and especially the Jerusalem high priests and their representatives based in the temple had been the historical opponents of Jesus and his mission, which was still the main conflict in the Lukan story. But with Roman client rule now a memory and not the immediate source of repression, the Lukan generation, which included many diaspora Judeans whose families may have had roots in Judean villages and/or Jerusalem, could now reclaim memories of life in Judea, including life-cycle rituals, the ordinary priests who lived outside of Jerusalem, and even rituals and customs connected with the Jerusalem temple.

Finally, there may be at least some indications about sicknesses (and healing) and spirit possession (and exorcism) in the historical circumstances of the audiences of the Lukan story. Diaspora Judeans may well have had deeper memories of violent imperial conquests, including the circumstances in which they had become dislocated from Palestine. Other peoples may not have had direct experience of the trauma of conquest in Palestine, but they or their ancestors may well have experienced trauma from foreign conquest and economic exploitation. If the Lukan story should be read in connection with the narrative in Acts and the earlier mission of Paul and his coworkers, then there were sicknesses among the peoples involved. Paul and the Acts narrative both mention (acts of) power(s) prominently and Acts includes two episodes involving exorcists, including several who attempt to exorcize in the name of Jesus (Gal 3:1–5; Acts 5:12; 6:8; 8:13; 19:11–12). Also, as we know from the

Greek elite continuing to seek (and find) healing from Asclepius at well-known spas, many were involved in searches and longing for healing in the eastern Roman empire.

What clues we can pick up from the text of the Lukan story about its *context* suggest that it was addressed to communities of Jesus-loyalists in Syria and Asia a decade or so after the destruction of Jerusalem comprised of diaspora Judeans, God-fearers, and other peoples who identified with Israel/Israelite tradition and Jesus' mission as its fulfillment.

The Lukan Story Resonating with Hearers as it References Israelite Tradition

Opening Narrative

As noted about "the text," the Lukan (hi)story opens with a sharp political-economic-religious opposition between Israelite people in Galilean villages and Judean hill-country and the Roman imperial order to which they have been subjected. The story begins with the popular legends of the "birth" of the history-changing figures John and Jesus and the movement(s) they are about to lead. These are greeted with popular hymns and prophecies, all not just deeply rooted in but extensions of Israelite popular tradition as announcements of the fulfillment of the people's longings. John will restore the people's loyalty to their God and justice among the people with the spirit and power of Elijah (that is, to implement the basic agenda of the Mosaic Covenant). Jesus will fulfill Israelite history and tradition in the widest sense. Mary's song, reminiscent of Hannah's song (1 Sam 2:1–10), praises God for past deliverance and anticipates future deliverance in "bringing down the powerful (rulers) from their thrones and lifting up the lowly." Anticipated by Simeon's song, the heavenly messenger announces Jesus is born as the Messiah and the Savior (versus the imperial Savior who demanded tribute from his impoverished subjects). An audience rooted in Israelite tradition and living in cities and towns of Syria or Asia Minor where honors to the Roman Emperor had become central would readily have understood that the Lukan story is presenting Jesus as the fulfillment of Israelite history and tradition and the alternative Savior to the Emperor.

John appeared as a prophet proclaiming a renewal of the Mosaic covenant via a ceremony (of immersion?) at the Jordan River (for forgiveness of sins and recommitment), complete with warning of judgment, as the preparation of the new exodus, "the way of the Lord." Undergoing the covenant renewal ceremony in the Jordan himself, Jesus received the holy Spirit, which led him in the wilderness while being tested by the "tempter/enemy" (*diabolos*),[7] with the obvious allusions to the testing of Moses/Elijah. In the expanded testing in the Lukan story, Jesus rejected "the enemy's" offers of imperial political power and declined divine religious power.

Mission of Exorcism, Healing, and Covenant Renewal in Galilee

Jesus' "return" to Galilee and declaration in the Nazareth assembly are programmatic for the whole Lukan story. As indicated repeatedly in the birth legends and the episodes of baptism and testing, the (holy) Spirit is driving Jesus' prophetic action and teaching. Anticipating especially his exorcisms and healings, he is "filled with the *power* of the Spirit." Judging from the subsequent summaries in the story, it was because of these acts of power that his fame quickly spread throughout the countryside, as he proceeded to teach in the (village) assemblies. The Lukan story presents Jesus, at the very beginning of his mission, claiming authority explicitly from a scroll of the prophet Isaiah that the Spirit had anointed him for the mission in fulfillment of the prophecy of the Lord's restoration of Israel:

> to bring good news to the poor
>   proclaim release to the captives
>   and recovery of sight to the blind,
> to let the oppressed go free,
>   to proclaim the year of the Lord's favor.

The continuation of the sharp political opposition from the infancy narrative in the quotation of Isaiah: Jesus is announcing that the Spirit has commissioned him to bring liberation and healing to the people of Israel who are languishing in poverty under subjection to imperial rule and oppression.

The Lukan narrative enhances the authority he claims by having him "read" from the Isaiah scroll, a move directed to the audience of diaspora Judeans and those other peoples who have identified with Israel

---

7. The standard English translation "the Devil" developed connotations in Christianity over the centuries that *diabolos* did not have in the Israelite tradition behind the Lukan temptation episode. There is no "cosmic struggle" here or elsewhere in the Lukan story any more than in the Markan story.

and its authoritative prophetic texts. This is the only narrative in any of the Gospel stories in which Jesus is represented as "reading" from a written scroll[8]—in a description of what was evidently the procedure on the sabbath in a diaspora assembly that might have had a copy of an Isaiah scroll (in Greek) and a building to house it (which would have been exceedingly rare in villages of Galilee at the time of Jesus, as discussed above). His portrayal as being able to "read" from the authoritative writing enhances his previous representation, in his discussion with the teachers in the temple, as thoroughly knowledgeable in Israelite tradition that he is now fulfilling. The Lukan portrayal, however, is working from a popular knowledge of what stood "written" on the Isaiah scroll. What the narrative portrays Jesus as "reading" was (a recitation of) a composite text that articulated what the Lukan story understood to be the agenda of Jesus' (God's) renewal of Israel (a composite of phrases from a Greek text of Isaiah 61:1–2 and of 58:6). This quotation from Isaiah that authorizes the agenda of Jesus' mission also anticipated Jesus' subsequent assertion, in response to John's question, that reference other Isaian prophecies that his healings and proclamation are the fulfillment of the longings of the people for liberation.

The ensuing discussion in the Nazareth assembly indicates that Jesus' mission was focused on healing (in the reference to his widely known actions in Capernaum, and the reference to him being like a "physician"). The Lukan Jesus' escalation of the incident of the lack of trust among the people of Jesus' "hometown" that was already well-known to the audience is somewhat puzzling, considering the rest of the Lukan story. In Jesus' references to these particular actions of Elijah and Elisha, the Lukan narrative is representing Jesus as a new Elijah/Elisha, but sharply warning at least the people of Nazareth that, by analogy, the new Elijah/Elisha was sent (also? only?) to peoples other than Israel. This may be simply a rather sharp warning delivered at the beginning of the story of Jesus' mission that the deliverance will include other peoples in the renewal of

8. Even a learned scribe thoroughly familiar with the text of Isaiah would have had difficulty unrolling the scroll to just the right column and lines. There is no indication anywhere else in the Gospels except here that Jesus was literate. Reading and/or writing required intensive training. It is highly unlikely that someone from a village who interacted mainly with other villagers would have received such training. It is also unlikely that a local village assembly would have possessed a heavy unwieldy scroll, for which there was no standard version at the time (on these issues see chap. 6 above). The composers of the Lukan story must be projecting practices known from diaspora assemblies onto the situation in earlier Roman Galilee.

Israel (although in no way suggesting a rejection of Israel in favor of "the Gentiles"). But nothing in the rest of the Lukan story indicates that Jesus' mission moved (mainly) beyond Galilee to other peoples (Luke has no parallel to the episode of the Syrophoenician woman).

Having announced the program of Jesus' mission as the fulfillment of the prophecy in Isaiah, the Lukan narrative presents a sequence of an exorcism in the Capernaum assembly and healings in other villages in Galilee and summaries of many more exorcisms and healings, paralleling the Markan narrative and adding particular emphases. As in the Markan story and more explicitly in the Matthean as well, the exorcisms and many healings, which generate conflict with the scribes and Pharisees, lead to the appointment of the twelve and the renewal of mutually supportive covenantal community.

In the exorcism that sets the tone for the following sequence of healings, the Lukan narrative parallels the Markan: Jesus "subdued" the unclean spirit/*daimonion*, commanding it to "be silent and come out." The coming out is a wrenching struggle for control of the possessed fellow. The witnesses' exclamation that Jesus commands the unclean spirits "with authority *and power*" is another point at which the Lukan story emphasizes the *power* flowing through him. In the first healing, of Peter's mother-in-law, the Lukan version highlights Jesus' agency as well as the invasion of the sickness, as he "subdues" the fever. In the following summary Luke has Jesus "laying hands on" people suffering sicknesses and again "subduing" the invasive *daimonia*. In the next summary the Lukan text has Jesus state explicitly that an integral part of his healing and exorcism is "to proclaim the good news of the kingdom of God" in the other "cities."[9]

The episode that dramatizes how Simon Peter and other disciples will become "fishers of people" anticipates how Jesus will give social-political form to the nascent movement of people responding to his exorcism and healing. It points ahead in the narrative to the naming of the twelve disciples and their commissioning to extend Jesus' own agenda of exorcism and healing. Simon's worry that as a sinful man he is unworthy of a good catch of fish also points ahead more immediately in the

---

9. In the next sentence some manuscripts of Luke have Jesus proclaiming in "the assemblies of Galilee." Other manuscripts have "the assemblies of Judea." The latter wording could be part of the Lukan presentation of Jesus' mission as more actively including the villages/cities of Judea and/or the outside perspective (that originated in Hasmonean and Herodian times) that greater "Judea" included Galilee.

narrative, to Jesus' declaration of the forgiveness of sins that empowers healing. The Lukan narrative uses the episode of the healing of skin lesions to dramatize how the spreading of the word about Jesus' healings led to greater crowds gathering to hear him and be healed of their illnesses (again *not* to be "cured" of their "diseases").

The Lukan story prefaces the episode of the healing of the paralytic to dramatize the threatened Pharisees' and law-teachers' opposition to Jesus' exorcism and healing[10] and restates that "the *power* of the Lord was in(to) him for healing." The Lukan story thus here and repeatedly makes explicit what was more implicit and ad hoc in the "(acts of) power(s)" of the Markan narrative. The episode of the healing of the paralytic focuses on how (Jesus') forgiveness of sins is closely connected with and can even effect healing. If "the son of humanity" in Luke has become a title for Jesus, and not just a self-reference and/or a reference to the vision of the renewal of Israel (as in Dan 7), then Jesus' pronouncement that the people generally have the authority to forgive sins may not have carried over into this Lukan episode. An important aspect of this and other Jesus healings, however, has carried over in the group of family and/or neighbors who are supporting and caring for the paralytic (carrying him on a palet and bringing him to Jesus). The Lukan addition that "he went to his home" indicates that Jesus was restoring people to their households and villages. Another crucial aspect of Jesus' healing stated explicitly in this Lukan episode is the trust of the support group or whole community. Following the episode of eating with sinners, that confirms Jesus' role in forgiveness of sins in connection with his healing, and the dispute over what is allowed on the sabbath, Jesus pointedly heals a man with a withered hand in a local assembly on the sabbath. This leads the angry scribes and Pharisees to scheme about what to do to Jesus.

The preceding sequence of an exorcism and healings leads Jesus to adapt Israelite tradition in giving fuller social-political form to the burgeoning movement of people who have been clamoring to hear him and be healed of their illnesses. His moving up onto "the mountain" to pray is a clear allusion to Moses on Sinai. As the new Moses on the mountain he designates twelve disciples as representatives of (the twelve tribes of) Israel undergoing renewal. He then moves back to level ground to (re-)enact the Mosaic covenant in which the people were bonded with God

10. The comment that the many Pharisees and teachers of the law had come from "every village of Galilee, Judea, and Jerusalem" appears to be unaware that Galilee was not under the jurisdiction of the temple-state during the mission of Jesus.

and one another. Like the Matthean story the Lukan story prefaces Jesus' speech with an elaborate summary of his mission and nascent movement so far. All these disciples and the great multitude

> had come to hear him and to be healed of their illnesses,
>   and people troubled with unclean spirits were healed.
> And all were trying to touch him,
>   for power came out from him and healed all of them.

The Lukan story, like the Markan and Matthean, was presenting Jesus' healings and exorcisms as the focal actions that were bringing deliverance and renewal to the people, with explicit emphasis on the power flowing from Jesus.

Jesus delivers the covenant renewal in performative speech that enacts as it articulates. Hearers familiar with Israelite tradition would have recognized that Jesus is adapting the structure as well as the teachings (torah) and foundational commandments of the Mosaic covenant that had for centuries formed the core and basis of Israelite tradition (as discussed in the previous three chapters).[11] Once we are listening for the patterns embedded in Israelite tradition and in the scribal texts that draw upon them, it is clear that the major covenant-renewal speeches in Matthew and Luke have the same overall structure, particularly striking at the beginning and end (even though Matthew expands on the middle). Compared with the components of the Mosaic covenantal pattern evident in scribal texts of torah, Jesus' covenant renewal speech paralleled in Matthew and Luke has clearly transformed the pattern, and in a way that fits and reinforces the rest of the mission of Jesus.

Immediately striking to hearers familiar with Israelite tradition is Jesus' pronouncement of blessings on the poor and hungry, and then woes against the wealthy, at the very beginning of the speech (as discussed in chap. 8). Jesus is speaking directly to the effects of the original blessings and curses as they became an explanation of poverty and illness as punishment for sinning, in violation of the Mosaic covenant and the self-blame that would have resulted (discussed in chaps. 5, 7, 8 above). The most important function and effect of the (repeated) renewal of the Covenant were the cooperation, mutual aid, and communal solidarity

11. Again, see the fuller discussion begun in Horsley, *Jesus and the Spiral*, chap. 9; and further explored especially in Horsley with Draper, *Whoever Hears You Hears Me*, chap. 9; Horsley, *Hearing the Whole Story*, chap. 8; and Horsley, *Covenant Economics*, chaps. 2, 7, 8, and 10.

that would have been fostered by the reformulation of the demands on the people in response to the renewed deliverance announced in the opening blessings. The covenant renewal would have consolidated the deliverance performed in the healings and exorcisms and the trust and renewed hope and commitment of the people in response to them.

As in the Matthean story, so in the Lukan story the healings and exorcisms continue after the covenant renewal speech and lead to the commission(s) of the twelve and the seventy to expand the exorcism and healing and preaching of Jesus' mission. The Lukan story now includes somewhat longer episodes that we know only from Luke and discussion of what is happening in Jesus' mission, as well as parables and exorcisms and healings parallel to the Markan story.

In the long-distance healing, effected without a gesture or a word, the Lukan narrative appears to have Jesus and the (probably Herodian) centurion maintain a certain distance from one another by having the elders of the Judeans residing in Capernaum function as intermediaries. The emphasis in the Lukan episode is Jesus' statement, somewhat hyperbolic, that he has not found *such* trust in Israel. The contrast is not between a "Gentile" and "the Jews," as noted above, but between a Herodian officer (who is probably a Judean; and perhaps the elders of the Judeans who willingly serve as his emissaries as well) and the multitude of Galilean villagers who previously in the story have been clamoring for healing. This is the contrast that would have been striking to the hearers of the story. But the episode of a Judean who sought healing offered a link to other Judeans either in Palestine or in diaspora synagogues who had become Jesus-loyalists.

The raising of the son of the widow of Nain is paired with the healing of the centurion's servant. This Lukan episode is deeply reminiscent of the story of Elijah's raising of a widow's son (1 Kgs 17:17–24 and/or Elisha's similar healing, 2 Kgs 4:32–37). The people's response, that "a great prophet has arisen among us!" in a traditional Israelite idiom, sets up the next episode in which Jesus explains what is happening in his mission, that is, the fulfillment of Israelite history as well as Israelite tradition.

Jesus' response to John's questions is yet another programmatic statement of what is happening in his mission of the renewal of Israel. Not only is he the prophet for whose healing the people had been longing, but the manifestations of the kingdom in his healing (and preaching) is the fulfillment of (the) history (of Israel). As if the audience needed a reminder, the Lukan narrative inserts that no sooner had the Baptist's disciples asked their question than Jesus took the occasion to heal many people of illnesses, plagues, and invasive spirits,[12] and to give sight to many who were blind (alluding to his prefatory summary of the fulfillment of Isaiah's prophecy and anticipating his response to John's question in his next statements). Jesus' answer to John picks up the longstanding yearning of the people from Israelite tradition that had been articulated at multiple points in the book of Isaiah (as discussed in chap. 8 above), a yearning for healing of the illnesses brought on by imperial conquest and domination. The hearers would have known that the acts of Jesus listed here were precisely those he was performing in the story: the lame (paralyzed) walking, lepers cleansed, dead raised, and poor given good news in the previous episodes, and the blind seeing and the deaf hearing in the ensuing episodes. Jesus' statement about John first mocks Antipas, in his royal finery, ensconced in his palace as the ruler against whom John had prophesied. He then declares that John was the greatest prophet in history, yet the kingdom of God that Jesus himself is proclaiming and manifesting in his healings is incomparably greater. Finally, he takes a crack at his opponents, the Pharisees and law-teachers, insisting that he and John will be vindicated.

The long episode of the woman who was a sinner anointing Jesus while he was eating at a Pharisee's house reinforces the theme of Jesus' forgiveness of sins and trust as a key factor in the forgiveness—which in turn reinforces the importance of trust and forgiveness of sins in the healings. The following summary passage of his further proclamation of the kingdom also indicates that some of those Jesus healed became prominent in the movement he generated, most significantly Mary Magdalene, who had been intensively spirit-possessed.[13]

12. The NRSV translation of Luke 7:21 and 8:2 with "evil spirits" exemplifies and reinforces the Christian theological misinterpretation of the Gospel stories' portrayal of the mission of Jesus as an apocalyptic "cosmic struggle" between Jesus and the horde of "evil spirits" or "demons" headed by "The Evil One"/Satan/the Prince of Demons. It could be that these phrases in Luke and especially the tall-tale episode of "the sons of Sceva" in Acts 19:11–20 influenced the later Christian theological overinterpretation that resulted in the conceptualization of "magic" and the cosmic struggle of God and "the Evil One" with his horde of "evil spirits/demons."

13. Again the NRSV (mis)translation in Luke 8:1–3) leads to Christian theological overinterpretation. It is not clear how the women could have been "cured" (as in biomedicine; see chap. 3) of "evil spirits." In the Greek text they "had been healed . . . of harmful spirits (*apo pneumaton poneron*)." The passive perfect verbs suggest that the brief report is retrospective and/or is a late addition to the Lukan story. The NRSV mistranslations "miracles," "evil spirits," and "magic"—most vividly evident in

The telling of the parable of the sower and its explanation that the Lukan story has located here (and shortened) from the Markan sequence is evidently an example of Jesus' proclamation of the kingdom. His proclamation to "a great crowd" of "those who came to him in town after town" seems to "update" the teaching to the communities of hearers, as does his warning about "how you listen" at the end. "The word of God" symbolized by the seed includes the Mosaic covenantal tradition that his proclamation of the kingdom renews, which is clearly indicated by the restatement of the by then well-known declaration that his "mother and brothers" ("sisters" has disappeared) are "those who hear the word of God *and do it*."

The Lukan narrative continues with the first sequence of "acts of power" episodes that appear in the Markan story: the exorcism and healings reminiscent of Elijah, prefaced by a sea-crossing and followed by a feeding in the wilderness that reference the foundational deliverance led by Moses. In the storm at sea Jesus "subdued" the threatening wind, the same term used for his "subduing" of possessing spirits.

In the Lukan story the episode of the Gerasene/Gadarene, largely parallel to that in the Markan story, is the most elaborately described exorcism. The Lukan version has an ambiguity about the relations between people in the countryside and those in the city, perhaps not even distinguishing them[14]—which might be among the possible indications that the Lukan story was addressed to communities in cities and towns. This is clearly a case of possession: the fellow "had many *daimonia*/unclean spirits" that had "entered into him." The effects were bizarre, unusually violent behavior directed toward himself as well as others in the community. His living among the tombs associated him with death. He had been restrained with chains and shackles, but the possessing spirits had driven him to break the bonds and rush into the wilds. Jesus had commanded them to "come out of the man." It is surely significant, as in the Markan version, that it is only after the spirits came out of the man that

---

the episode of "the sons of Sceva" in Acts 19:11–20—help perpetuate the Christian misunderstanding of what is being portrayed in the Gospels and Acts. Paul was doing "(acts of) power(s)" so that "harmful spirits" came out of some possessed people; then at the end of the episode, those who practiced (certain) ritual-works and possessed "handbooks" of formulas and incantations (see chap. 2 above), impressed or frightened when the would-be exorcists' conjuration backfired, burned their books.

14. Do the terms and phrases "the countryside," "the city and the countryside," "the surrounding countryside," and "the whole city" (8:26, 34, 37, 39) all refer to the same entity?

Jesus elicits their identity, "Legion," with the explanation of "many." But it would hardly have been lost on the hearers especially after the devastating Roman suppression of the great revolt that "Legion" was a division of Roman troops that had conquered and reconquered the people of nearby areas as well as the Galileans and Judeans. These brutal reconquests had left destruction and death in their wake, which would have resulted in long-term and repeated social trauma. The Lukan version that the spirits begged not to send them back to "the abyss" suggests that the composers (if not the audience) had at least some knowledge of scribal lore.[15] The Lukan episode also retains the motifs of the local people's anxiety about Jesus having upset their modus operandi with Roman rule in the aftermath of conquest and the restoration of the man to his community, where he proclaimed what Jesus had done.

The Lukan story, continuing the Markan sequence, then narrates Jesus' (interwoven) healings of the woman hemorrhaging for twelve years and the nearly dead twelve-year-old girl, both clearly representative of the people/Israel in acute distress. As in the Markan episode, the father who begged Jesus to come heal his daughter who was dying (not "dead," as in Matthew) was one of the leaders of a local assembly (synagogue) in Galilee.[16] A woman who had been hemorrhaging for twelve years intervened and, taking the initiative as in the Markan version, touched his garment and was healed. And, as in the Markan narrative, Jesus sensed that *power* had gone forth from him, and told her that her trust had made her whole. Because of her trust and initiative, healing/saving power had flowed from him to her. Meanwhile the daughter appeared to have died. But Jesus, telling the family simply to trust and she would be made whole (same verb as with the hemorrhaging woman) and insisting that she was only sleeping, took her by the hand called out, "Child, arise." Her "spirit" (that is, life) returned and, indicating that she was embodied and needed nourishment, he ordered that she be given something to eat.

Having already narrated Jesus' conflict in the assembly in Nazareth as the occasion of a programmatic statement of his mission of fulfillment, the Lukan story here moves directly from Jesus' further exorcism and

15. Cf. the binding of the giants and their maleficent spirit-offspring by the heavenly forces most loyal to the Most High in the governance of earthly affairs in the Book of Watchers, 1 Enoch 1–36, and Jubilees 10.

16. *Not* "a ruler of the synagogue," a translation that is rooted in the misleading synthetic construct of "Judaism" and perpetuates the "Jesus vs. Judaism" reading of Luke as well as Mark and Matthew.

healing to the commission of the twelve to extend them in combination with proclamation of the kingdom. The Lukan narrative expands Jesus' empowerment of the twelve from "authority" to "power and authority" over all *daimonia* and to heal illnesses and sends them out to proclaim the kingdom and to heal everywhere among the villages, extending his own mission. The Lukan story, like that Markan and Matthean story and the commissioning in the series of speeches, repeatedly emphasizes the close link between the proclamation of the kingdom and the healing of the people.

As a counterpart, the ruler of Galilee, Herod Antipas, hears about all that is happening. While the prologue represents Jesus as "the Messiah," the Lukan story presents his mission of healing and proclamation as the work of a prophet in continuity with the people's understanding of him as a prophet, such as John redivivus or as Elijah's having come (back) or as one of the ancient prophets having arisen (again).

Following upon the empowerment of the disciples and the further exorcism and healings, comes the feeding of the five thousand that evokes memory of Moses' mediation of the manna. While the Markan and Matthean versions had Jesus and his disciples withdraw to a wilderness (unsown) place, the Lukan narrative has them withdraw into Bethsaida, a large village that Herod Philip was upgrading into one of his capitals. The Lukan narrative does retain the traditional Israelite formation of the people into "companies of about fifty each," and *twelve* baskets of leftover pieces were gathered up, symbolizing the feeding of a renewed Israel.

Although the Lukan story has been following the sequence of the Markan story, it does not include the second Markan sequence of sea-crossing, exorcism, healings, and wilderness feedings. It moves again to the question of how people understand Jesus, that is, as a prophet like John or Elijah, which sets up Peter's pronouncement that he is "the Messiah of God." This is followed by the first announcement that Jesus must suffer and be killed. But the Lukan story does not include Peter's protest and Jesus' rebuke of Peter. It does include the exhortation to followers to maintain steadfast loyalty in the face of likely persecution.

The story's inclusion of the appearance of Moses and Elijah on the mountain with Jesus then confirms all of the portrayals of Jesus' performance of healing and exorcism, covenant renewal, and proclamation of the kingdom in renewal of Israel as a prophet like Moses and Elijah. In contrast with Mark and Matthew, Luke does not include the discussion that identifies John as Elijah returned.

Again a parent seeks healing for a child in a public setting of a great crowd, with an elaborate description of the symptoms of sudden seizure by a spirit (*daimonion,* unclean spirit), such as convulsions and foaming at the mouth. When the disciples prove unable to cast out the spirit, Jesus becomes exasperated at their lack of trust. As in previous exorcisms, Jesus "subdued" the unclean spirit and "healed" the boy, and returned him to his father (family, community).

Despite being warned to listen, the disciples do not hear the implication of Jesus' second announcement of his betrayal, and argue about which of them is the greatest. And while they had been unable to cast out a spirit, they want to forbid someone who can exorcize in Jesus' name. But Jesus allows others to exorcize in his name (which suggests that this continued in the subsequent development of the Jesus-movement(s).

Healings, Prophecies, Parables, and Disputes along the Prophet's Way to Jerusalem

A second long narrative step in the Luan story begins as Jesus, clearly in the role of an Israelite prophet, sets his face toward Jerusalem (9:51–19:28). The audience knows that he is headed to the capital to confront the rulers, who will arrest and execute him. Among instructions on mission, prayer, social-economic relations, including parables and some sanctions, are four healing or exorcism episodes.

Significantly the first major instruction is the second Lukan commissioning, of seventy others that Jesus sends on ahead of him in pairs to every town and village. As the audience communities would realize, this anticipates the later expansion of Jesus' mission of healing and proclamation by the movement that Jesus had generated. The mission speech is prefaced by Jesus rebuking his messengers for wanting to call down fire from heaven in judgment against the Samaritan villagers who are rejecting him (because he was so focused on his prophetic mission in Jerusalem). Three brief dialogues introduce the speech. In them Jesus insists on the immediate and unswerving commitment necessary to "follow" him, reminiscent of Elijah's demands on Elisha for absolute commitment to the prophetic mission to which he had been commissioned. The Lukan Jesus then expands his mission beyond anything suggested in the Markan or Matthean stories, commissioning the seventy envoys to work in pairs, staying in village households and eating whatever the families could spare. In an even closer link, what Jesus instructs the envoys to declare indicates that the healings are a manifestation of the kingdom of God having become near. Different from the earlier sending of the twelve, which paralleled their charge in Mark and Matthew to extend the mission of Jesus, the commission of the seventy does not bestow power on them. Yet the sanction on villagers' response indicates that these envoys performed "acts of power" (*dynameis*), and the seventy return exclaiming that "even the *daimonia* submit to us in your name."

The Lukan Jesus' response, "I saw Satan fall like lightening from heaven" sounds like it was derived from scribal lore, a speculative vision of what was happening in the heavenly court (see again, e.g., the Book of Watchers in 1 Enoch 1–36; see chap. 5). And of course this could be a piece of scribal lore that filtered down into popular culture and/or the Lukan composers' showing off their speculative knowledge. But the Lukan as well as the Markan and Matthean stories all have Jesus warn against "seeking a sign" and mistaking particular incidents as "signs" and being misled by "false prophets" and "false messiahs." So it seems likely, following his rejection of "calling down fire from heaven" in judgment, that Jesus is here teasing or mocking the envoys—and the hearers addressed—about getting carried away. His next statements continue the warning: "Do not rejoice that I have given you authority to tread on scorpions, . . . that the spirits submit to you," but that (you will be vindicated after sustaining the work of this movement because) "your names are written in heaven," probably a metaphor derived from scribal lore.

The ensuing prayer of Jesus and his blessing on the disciples confirms that this is the way the audience would have heard this series of episodes. Jesus, who had become the "son of God" for the Gospel stories and their audiences and was empowered by and in close communication with the Spirit, thanks the Lord of heaven and earth (i.e., who rules history) for having hidden these things (what is happening in his renewal of Israel) "from the wise and revealed them to infants." The audience would have known that the intellectual elite such as the scribes and Pharisees had represented the temple-state and looked down on ordinary people as mere "babes" needing nurture and guidance. Jesus follows with a blessing on the disciples that in effect continues the blessings with which he begins the covenant renewal speech: what is happening in the movement of healing and proclamation he is generating is the fulfillment of (Israelite promises and) history that many prophets and kings had desired to witness.

Jesus' teachings in the next few episodes are set in opposition to the lawyers and Pharisees (who are "the wise"): the lawyer's testing Jesus with questions about eternal life and who is one's neighbor, the teaching of the prayer for the kingdom that includes subsistence food and forgiveness of sins, the reassurance of God's response to prayer, the charge of casting out spirits by Beelzebul, the request for a sign, and Jesus' woes against the Pharisees and lawyers.

The Beelzebul controversy is prefaced by a brief report that he cast out a *daimon* that was dumb. In response to the charge that "he casts out *daimonia* by Beelzebul the ruler of *daimonia*" in the Lukan version (derived from a speech known also by Matthew) Jesus does not accept the view of the world assumed in the charge (as discussed above in chaps. 7, 8, 9). He first demonstrates that their charge must be false, based on their own premise. Then he suggests that since their own disciples also perform exorcisms their motivation in the charge must be political. The Lukan version of the decisive declaration must have retained "the finger of God" from the pre-Lukan speech. The Lukan story that places so much emphasis on the Spirit elsewhere would presumably have retained "Spirit" if it had been in the earlier version of the dispute. The assertion that it was "by the finger of God that he was casting out spirits" suggests that his exorcisms are in effect a new exodus (see Exodus 8:19; that is, just as the Israelites were liberated from hard bondage in the exodus, so now they were liberated from spirit-possession) in which the direct rule of God had come upon the people among whom Jesus worked. Jesus' exorcisms are a manifestation of the direct rule of God. The following warning about how possession by invasive spirits might come back (almost verbatim in Luke and Matthew) indicates not only that Jesus was not destroying spirits, but was driving them out and/or subduing them. It also is a warning about the importance in the continuing healing and renewal process of supportive covenantal community, not just at the origins of the movement but in its continuation in the communities the story addresses.

In the speeches that both Matthew and Luke are adapting at this step in their narratives, Matthew has the Pharisees voice the ironic request for a sign immediately following the charge of Beelzebul that the Pharisees bring. It is difficult to judge whether the Lukan narrative simply assumes that the Pharisees and lawyers are the challenging interlocutors, continuing as the targets of his woes. In any case, his prophetic declaration that "something greater than Solomon (etc.) is here" not only again points to the historical process (not unusual signs and omens, a quest in scribal lore), but again emphasizes that the fulfillment of Israelite history as well as tradition is happening in his mission.[17] Again, as in his response to John's questions, the Lukan Jesus tells the audience that they are participating in a movement of decisive historical significance.

In the series of woes the Lukan story presents God's condemnation of the Pharisees and lawyers who represent the temple-state as the judgment-counterpart of the healing and renewal that are happening in Jesus' mission. Not simply a reference to Israelite tradition, this series of woes and accompanying pronouncement of judgment is itself a traditional Israelite form of indictment and declaration of divine judgment.[18] Jesus mocks their obsession with purity codes, the meticulous details of tithing, and building monuments of martyred prophets, while charging them with extortion, neglect of justice, and loading people with burdens of tithing and taxation.

In more general terms, he charges that they have taken away the key to knowledge, that is knowledge of (which means also obedience to) the Mosaic covenantal torah, the will of God for social-economic justice. They and their predecessors had even killed the prophets sent to warn them. Thus "this generation" (this kind/type; these people) will be accountable for the blood of all the martyred prophets.

The audience at any stage in the development of the movement, including the Lukan addressees, would have known the tradition and resonated with the performative speech. The resonance would likely have been more intense in communities more closely aware of the scribes' and Pharisees' function in the Jerusalem temple-state in the decades prior to the Roman destruction of Jerusalem (including the retainers of the temple-state). In the Lukan story itself, whose portrayal of the Pharisees has them (unhistorically) interacting directly with Jesus in Galilean villages, they function as foils in the next series of episodes. Might they

17. Might there also be a touch of irony or even sarcasm in the reference to Solomon? Ordinary people as well as educated elite priests such as Josephus would have known that Solomon was most famous for his wisdom, and only a few episodes earlier in the Lukan story Jesus had thanked the Father for hiding "these things from the wise and the intelligent . . . and kings" (Luke 10:21–24).

18. Series of prophetic woes, that is, indictments and pronouncement of God's sentence, in Amos 6:1–3, 4–6 + 7; Isa 5:18–19, 20, 21, 22–23, +24; Hab 2:9–11, 12, 15 + 16–17, 19. Fuller discussion of Jesus' series of woes in Q/Luke 11 in Horsley with Draper, *Whoever Hears You Hears Me*, 285–91; and Horsley, "Social Relations and Social Conflict in the *Epistle of Enoch*."

perhaps also be ciphers for the somewhat parallel role of retainers of local rulers in Syria and beyond?

After Jesus had pronounced God's condemnation of the scribes/lawyers and Pharisees for the effects on the people of their political-economic-religious role, it would hardly be surprising that the scribes and Pharisees began lying in wait to catch him in something for which he could be arrested. And in the following exhortation, just as the prophet was suppressed and crucified, then vindicated, as the hearers well knew, so the communities of his movement had to be prepared to face severe suppression, to remain steadfastly loyal, and would be vindicated.

The ensuing series of episodes in Jesus' long "journey toward Jerusalem" focuses on economic relations in the communities of the movement and, in negative examples (of what not to do) of the wealthy expanding their possessions at the expense of the poor, in the Roman imperial order in Palestine. The series begins with the (negative) example of the wealthy man with a large estate who built ever larger storage facilities for his burgeoning crops, only to face God's judgment. This serves to set up Jesus' speech, adapted from the series of speeches also in Matthew, exhorting his disciples not to worry about subsistence food and clothing but to single-mindedly pursue the direct rule of God and subsistence would (somehow) be forthcoming. This speech clearly presupposes the covenant renewal speech in which the covenantal communities had re-dedicated themselves to mutual economic aid and cooperation. And the Lukan extension of the speech provides further assurance and a command that implements the mutual aid: "Fear not, little flock, for it is your Father's good pleasure to give you the kingdom [cf. Blessed are you poor . . .]. Sell your possessions, and give alms."

In a sequence of episodes that includes much conflict, mainly between Jesus and the Pharisees, the Lukan narrative includes another episode of his healing in a local assembly on the sabbath. A woman had a spirit that had severely bent her over for eighteen years. Jesus declared "Woman, you are set free from your illness." And when he laid his hands on her, she immediately stood up straight. In this episode not the Pharisees but the leader of the assembly objected to his healing on the sabbath. Jesus' replies sharply: "Ought not this woman, a daughter of Abraham whom Satan bound for eighteen long years be set free from his bondage on the sabbath." The reference to the binding "spirit" as "Satan" is probably rhetorical, hyperbole in Jesus' sharp reply; "binding" would still have been within the range of Satan's (rarely mentioned) functions in

Israelite tradition (that is, there is no reason to imagine that the Lukan audience would have understood "Satan" as a personified principle of evil or thought that the woman was spirit-possessed).

The freeing of the woman from her ailment and the crowd's rejoicing at all the other wonderful actions he was doing—manifestations of the direct rule of God—lead "therefore" to Jesus pronouncements of two brief parables, of the mustard seed and the leaven. The direct rule of God is undergoing amazing expansion that provides shelter and food. And these parables lead immediately to a sustained opposition between Jesus' continuing mission of exorcism and healing in one (Galilean) town and village after another as he heads to his confrontation with the rulers and his martyrdom as a prophet in Jerusalem, on the one hand, and his prophetic pronouncement of the renewal of Israel and the condemnation of the Jerusalem ruling house, on the other. The first prophecy is yet another indication in the Gospel story that Jesus' mission of renewal of the people is the beginning of the fulfillment of Israelite (tradition and) history, in the "banquet" of the kingdom of God with Abraham, Isaac, Jacob, and all the prophets (as those who boast of their patriarchal lineage are thrown out). The Pharisees again serve as foils even as they warn Jesus that Herod Antipas wants to kill him (as he killed John), which sets up Jesus summary of his work: casting out invasive spirits and performing healings (again the main activity of his mission). He then states explicitly that he is a prophet in the line of Israelite prophets whose destiny is to be killed by the Jerusalem rulers. This sets up his second prophecy: a prophetic lament (in traditional form) that the Jerusalem ruling house that kills the prophets stands desolate, having been condemned by God's judgment. The communities of hearers, of course, know that this prophecy has been fulfilled.

It is surely significant that, juxtaposed with these prophecies of judgment, the next episode has Jesus again heal a man (who had dropsy) on the sabbath, in the face of the lawyers and Pharisees (14:1-6). This healing also serves as a narrative step toward a comparison (parable) of the renewal of the people with a banquet to which are invited "the poor, the crippled, the lame, and the blind," (14:13, 21; cf. 7:22)—the very people whom Jesus has been healing throughout his mission—as the wealthy and powerful reject the invitation to the banquet (14:7-24). The ensuing exhortations then emphasize the absolute commitment necessary in becoming Jesus' disciple and participating in the movement, such as being prepared to be crucified and relinquishing all one's goods (presumably for sharing in the renewed covenantal community).

After several longer parables, the Lukan story addresses community discipline, including repentance and forgiveness. Next "on the way to Jerusalem" comes another episode in which Jesus heals people with skin lesions. That many (ten) such were all living in a village between Galilee and Samaria suggests that they had been socially ostracized to an "in between" region.[19] The healing takes place as they were on their way to show themselves to the priests, as Jesus had instructed. But only one came back to thank Jesus, and it is pointedly stated that he was a Samaritan and is also called a "foreigner" (*allogenes*). The ensuing brief dialogue again pits the Pharisees, intellectuals who speculate about when future events would happen, against the popular prophet who is engaged in the active renewal of the people: the direct rule of God is "not coming with things that can be observed" in a particular place or time, but is "among you." That is, it is a collective relational reality that is happening in his mission and continuing in the communities of the movement.[20] The longer speech that follows (17:22–37) warns the disciples not to respond to rumors about "the days of the son of man" (in Daniel 7 a symbol of the future restoration of Israel) since it will be sudden and without warning.

Toward the completion of Jesus' long journey to Jerusalem, the Lukan story parallels some of the dialogues in the Markan covenantal speech. Overruling the disciples' strictures, he declares that it is necessary to receive the direct rule of God as a (humble, low-status) child. Then to the wealthy ruler who asks what he must do to inherit eternal life (while the poor among whom Jesus is working worry about having anything to eat), Jesus recites the covenantal commandments. Knowing that his claim to have kept them was not credible—a rich man acquired wealth by manipulating needy people into debt—Jesus tells him to "sell all that you have and give to the poor."[21] This he cannot do since he is attached to

19. The region between Samaria and Galilee was well known as an area of large (royal) estates belonging to the high priestly and/or Herodian rulers. Would some social outcasts have ended up there?

20. This statement, in the misleading individualistic translation of "within you," has been one of the most influential misunderstandings of Jesus' "sayings" about "the kingdom of God." The most carefully worked out individualistic interpretation of the kingdom based on isolated sayings is in Crossan, *Historical Jesus*, chap. 12.

21. The NRSV translation, "'all that you own" is anachronistic; it is doubtful there was a concept of "ownership" or "(private) property" in Luke or its context; the insertion of "money" (lacking in the Greek) into modern translations is inappropriate because the society was not yet "monetized."

his wealth. With this negative example of what not to do, Jesus declares another law-like covenantal principle, in effect that it is impossible for a rich person to enter the kingdom of God. The episode concludes with Jesus' assurance to Peter and the disciples (and the audience) that those who had left house and family for the sake of the kingdom would have it restored to them "in this age." As in the Markan story, the "eternal life in the age to come" appears to be an ironic (sarcastic?) "throwaway line" about something that only the wealthy would desire,[22] while the Jesus-loyalists are praying for sufficient food, mutual forgiveness, and avoidance of repression.

After Jesus' third announcement that he would be killed and rise again, which the twelve do not understand, Jesus heals the blind man who was calling to him, "Jesus, son of David," (which is not problematic in the Lukan story), affirming that his trust had saved him. The Lukan story, like the Markan, thus has Jesus performing healings right up to the entry into Jerusalem.

In the final two episodes before the entry into Jerusalem, the rich tax collector Zacchaeus repents and gives half of his possessions to the poor and makes restoration of fourfold to anyone he has defrauded (manipulated into debt).[23] The Lukan "parable" of the three servants, as introduced in narrative sequence, fits the Lukan story and agenda; it is not susceptible of misunderstanding in the way that modern interpreters often project onto the supposed parallel "parable of the talents" in Matt 25 (that is, as support for modern capitalism). As they neared Jerusalem, Jesus' listeners supposed that the kingdom of God was to appear immediately. Recalling them (and the hearers of the story) to reality, that they were still living under the Roman imperial order, Jesus tells the only somewhat disguised story of the arrogant Archelaus after his father Herod's death.[24] He had gone to Rome to receive the kingship, but leading Judeans (Jerusalemites) sent a delegation to head off the appointment, unsuccessfully, and paid the price (19:27). In standard practice, client kings and other wealthy who controlled land rewarded their servants (officers) who were effective in exploiting the peasants to gain wealth by giving them authority over more territory (villages, "cities"). The "parable"

22. The term "eternal life" appears only in this episode and the similar questions of the lawyer, 10:25.

23. Would the audience have heard this as a relaxation of Jesus' uncompromising instruction to the wealthy ruler to give all that he had to the poor?

24. Known also from Josephus, *Ant.* 17.219–228, 299–313.

about a well-known (and vengeful) client king who "reaped what he did not sown" was another vivid negative example of defrauding and exploiting the people, like that of "the rich young ruler" earlier in the story. This is what the Herodian kings and their Herodian officers and the powerful priestly families had been doing. The hearers of the story would have known this and would have known that before and after the Roman destruction of Jerusalem other client rulers of Rome were engaged in similar political-economic practices. The parable warned communities of hearers that the Jesus movements remained under conditions of Roman rule and should not indulge in unrealistic fantasies.

Confrontation with the Rulers

The Lukan story gives distinctive touches to Jesus' entry into Jerusalem. As he rides into the city on the colt, in fulfillment of the Zechariah prophecy, the multitude exults for "all the acts of power" they had experienced. In a Lukan addition to the lines from the Passover psalm, the crowd acclaims Jesus more explicitly, "Blessed is the king who comes in the name of the Lord." As he draws near the city he delivers another prophetic lament over the impending Roman destruction (that recalls his earlier prophetic lament over the Jerusalem ruling house). The audience of the Gospel would have been well aware of the Roman devastation a few decades earlier that had been widely propagandized throughout the Empire. The distinctively Lukan episode has Jesus weeping over the destruction of the city and its "children" (the Judean/Israelite people, many of whom had taken refuge there from the Roman devastation of their villages). The overall narrative of Luke-Acts has Jesus instruct the twelve disciples to remain in Jerusalem and has the movement based in and expanding from the city.

The Lukan episode of Jesus' demonstration in the temple, which is not framed by the cursing of the fig tree, seems less ominous than the Markan episode as a declaration of God's judgment. It has Jesus "teaching daily in the temple," protected from the rulers' arrest and destruction by the eagerly listening people. The rest of Jesus' dramatic confrontation of the Jerusalem rulers proceeds parallel to that in Mark, exposing their lack of "authority/power" with the people, pronouncing (God's) judgment on them, declaring that the people (Israel) do not owe tribute to (the deified)

Caesar (since everything belongs to God), and concluding with the prophecy of the destruction of the temple that was their base of power.

The ensuing Lukan Jesus' speech about what to expect in the future that includes the Roman devastation of Palestine and Jerusalem and enslavement of people, is mostly a description of the movement's historical experiences, with warnings about being misled about their significance. The Lukan adaptation of the standard prophetic theophany imagery seems to shift (from the Markan "ingathering of the elect") toward a world-historical significance of the "coming of the Son of Man" as a time of more general "redemption." The closing comment in the Lukan account of the confrontation in Jerusalem has Jesus teaching in the temple every day, in command of the situation during the daytime, while spending the nights on the Mount of Olives out of danger of apprehension by the Jerusalem and Roman rulers.

The Lukan story also adds a few distinctive touches to the narrative of the climactic events. Satan is suddenly active, entering Judas and testing Peter, but only as a tempter and not as some embodiment of evil or the cosmic force of opposition to God. The Lukan story moves what in Mark is Jesus' sharp rejection of the power of (imperial) domination to the last supper and tones it down. In contrast with the kings of the peoples (the Romans) who dominate over them, the leaders of the Jesus movement are to serve. Jesus includes the disciples in the kingdom his Father has given him, but that kingdom is the restoration or renewal of Israel, in which the disciples will sit on twelve chairs/stools effecting justice for the twelve tribes (22:24–30).[25]

The Lukan story also has some distinctive features in the arrest and trial of Jesus. In the arrest scene, Jesus heals the ear of the servant of the high priest that one of those standing near had cut off. When they take Jesus before Pilate, the high priests and scribes bring political charges against him that, except for claiming to be the messiah, fit the preceding story: "We found this man subverting our people, forbidding us to pay tribute to the emperor, and saying that he himself is the messiah, a king." The hearers of the Lukan story would recognize that from the rulers' point

---

25. The standard translation "judging the twelve tribes of Israel" is yet another projection into the text of the Christian theological scheme that has "Gentile" "Christianity" not just superseding "Judaism" but the disciples negatively "judging" or condemning it. In the Psalms, God does not "judge" but "effects justice for" the widow and orphan. See the fuller critical examination of such texts and a more appropriate translation of the Lukan and Q passage in Horsley, *Jesus and the Spiral*, 199–208.

of view these are not exaggerations. The Lukan story also includes political particulars: that since Jesus was a Galilean he came properly under the jurisdiction of Herod Antipas, and that the entourage that came with him to Jerusalem were also Galileans. The story also has Pilate find Jesus not guilty of the charges, yet eventually yield to the demands of the high priests, rulers, and people (of Jerusalem) to crucify him. The centurion confirms his innocence. The episodes of the resurrection appearances, finally, have his followers talking about Jesus as a "prophet *powerful in deed* and word before God and all the people" and how they hoped he would be the one to redeem Israel. The risen Jesus then explains that "the writings" had been fulfilled that the Messiah must suffer and rise from the dead so that repentance and forgiveness of sins be proclaimed to all peoples, beginning from Jerusalem—and instruct the eleven (disciples) to remain in Jerusalem, where the story had begun and from which it would continue, once they were clothed with power from on high. The effect of the Lukan story on the communities in which it was performed will be discussed in chap 11.

Part IV

The Effect and Significance
of Exorcisms and Healings

11

The Effects of the Gospel Stories in Performance

IN THE DISCUSSION OF how the Gospel stories and speeches are the sources for the historical Jesus in interaction in historical context in chap. 6, it seems clear that the historical Jesus in interaction is triply embedded:

- Jesus interacted with people in the villages of Galilee and beyond, and they responded in a particular political-economic context of crisis and conflict for those villagers and their rulers and the particular cultural context of Israelite popular tradition (social memory).

- Collective memory of Jesus' interaction in context took form and developed in the movements that formed in response to his mission.

- The collective memory of Jesus-in-interaction in these movements took the forms of distinctive stories and speeches that developed into the Gospel stories and speeches, some of which we know as the Markan, Matthean, and Lukan stories with speeches and the series of speeches adapted in Matthew and Luke.

In the pervasive oral communication environment at the time, all of these stories and speeches were repeatedly performed in communities of their respective movements. While the New Testament field is still ill-equipped to appreciate oral performance of texts in community context, other fields have developed appropriate theory of oral performance of long complex (orally-derived) texts in their respective contexts. The deeply informed theory of oral performance of John Miles Foley has become very suggestive for understanding the Gospel stories and speeches. Adapting Foley's theory, chapters 7–10 considered particular Gospel stories and speeches as performed in their respective contexts with special attention to how they may have resonated with their respective audiences by referencing (and adapting and continuing/perpetuating) the Israelite tradition in which Jesus-in-interaction and the movements of his loyalists were embedded. From this consideration of how the Gospel stories-with-speeches-in-performance resonated with communities of Jesus-loyalists it may be possible to discern some of their principal effects in those communities.

The Markan Story

The Markan story evidently addressed its hearers directly in the circumstances in which they lived, which were basically the same as (or similar to) those portrayed in the interaction between Jesus and the people in the story. As discussed in chap. 7, clues in the text indicate that the hearers were village and town communities in Galilee and nearby areas (of Syria) in the mid-first century CE. These communities were struggling with the often devastating long-term effects of Roman military conquest and of the intensified exploitation of subject peoples by Roman client rulers. The brutal violence of Roman conquests and rulers' demands for tribute and taxes left many villagers unable to feed their families and needing to borrow at high interest only exacerbated their poverty, leaving them hungry, hopelessly indebted, and malnourished. The story addresses people who, like those in the story itself, were plagued with various illnesses, some of them seriously debilitating for persons and their families. Evident from Judean scribal texts as well as from the Gospel stories, there had been a striking upsurge of attacks and possession by hostile alien spirits in connection with Roman conquest and imperial rule (discussed in chap. 5).

The Markan story presents Jesus coming into such villages and their community assemblies and even individual households where he cast out those spirits and healed the illnesses plaguing the people. The effect(s) on the hearers in similar situations would have been a continuation of the effects of Jesus' mission as narrated in the story. The performance of the story they were already familiar with told again of the divinely-designated prophet subduing and casting out hostile spirits and healing various illnesses directly in the midst of community and family life. The story told again of his fame spreading widely through Galilee and surrounding areas, people flocking to him for healing with trust that enabled the healing, and the movement focused on his healing and exorcism expanding into other villages in ever wider areas. One of the effects of hearing the story of Jesus' extensive healing and exorcism, the spread of his fame and people's coming to him with trust, would have been to solidify the hearers' trust in the healing power flowing through the movement. That Jesus twice extended the power to cast out hostile spirits and heal illnesses to the Twelve, who are symbolic representatives of the people (of Israel) undergoing renewal, suggests that exorcism and healing was continued in the expanding movement. The continuing healing and exorcism may have happened in a less intense atmosphere than portrayed in the story, but the performance of the story enabled the continuing healing.[1]

The exorcism and healing effected in the performance of the story, like that in the mission of Jesus portrayed in the story, was enabled by a complex of cultural and social-political supporting factors—factors that would likely be missing in the experience of most modern hearers/readers seeking medical care for their diseases at clinics or hospitals.

The longings, memories, and expectations of Israelite popular tradition in which Galilean villagers were embedded, and which nearby peoples could easily have identified with, both enabled the healings of Jesus and their continuation in the movement and provided a basis on which they were integral aspects of a broader historical breakthrough for subjected people. Galileans, Judeans, Samaritans, and nearby peoples had been subject to one empire after another for centuries, empires that had become far more intrusive into their life conditions in recent generations, especially under the Romans. Prophetic voices and scribal texts had articulated the general suffering or malaise, including destruction, captivity, blindness, lameness, and other physiological dysfunctions. But these were not the conditions intended by God. Earlier Israelite tradition and continuing popular cultivation of that tradition included legends of liberation from hard bondage in Egypt under Moses and successful struggles against oppressive foreign rulers (such as Sisera and local kings) or oppressive kings of their own (David, Solomon, Ahab), under the

---

1. Continuing exorcism and healing in the movement to which the Markan story is addressed is confirmed in the episode of the strange exorcist who casts out spirits in the name of Jesus. Continuing exorcism and healing in other Jesus-movements is attested in episodes in Acts and Paul's touting the acts of power among the Galatians (Gal 3:5).

leadership of early prophets such as (Ahijah and) Elijah and Elisha. The latter were remembered for their healing as a key aspect of their leadership of a broader struggle against Ahab and Jezebel. The contemporary movements led by prophets greeted as the new Moses or Joshua indicate that such memories were sufficiently strong as to *inform* the form of new movements seeking deliverance. The Markan story easily builds on these popular memories and expectations in presenting Jesus' healings as the manifestation and fulfillment of longings and expectations for new deliverance led by a new Elijah or other prophet, as repeatedly symbolized and explicitly stated in successive episodes. That Elijah and Elisha had reached beyond northern Israelites in the legends of their leadership would have made the Israelite popular tradition and its fulfillment in Jesus' mission all the more compelling as the (Markan) Jesus-movement expanded among peoples beyond Galilee.

It made the exorcisms and healings all the more significant and effective that they were Jesus' principal actions in a movement of the renewal of Israel in its village communities that anticipated being independent (liberated) of Roman rule and the domination of Rome's client rulers. In the first exorcism Jesus subdued the hostile alien spirit; in the second the spirit that he had cast out identified itself as the possessing spirit of Roman military and, symbolically, self-destructed. In many of the healings, Jesus was evidently challenging the Jerusalem high priests and their scribal/Pharisaic representatives and, in effect, declaring the people's independence. The story strongly reinforces this with Jesus' reference to renewed (familial) covenantal community in the (brief) concluding episode of the first narrative step of the story. Then at the transition from the narrative of the mission in Galilee and beyond to the confrontation in Jerusalem, the series of Jesus' short dialogues that constitute the renewal of the Mosaic covenant provided guidance for their social-political-religious village life that would have strengthened their ability to resist further pressures from their rulers.

The renewal of the independent communal life of the people, however, was not simply an anticipation in the performed story. The performance of the story in its successive episodes enacted in the communities of listeners a renewal of community life that in various ways reinforced and strengthened mutual commitment and cooperation. As noted in chap. 4, village communities and their constituent families, in which the family and/or wider support group usually cared for people plagued with illness, had been disintegrating under the pressures of Roman conquest and the demands of multiple levels of rulers. In the Markan story Jesus purposely entered villages and their assemblies and particular households to heal and drive out invasive spirits. There he restored people who had been suffering from leprosy, paralysis, near fatal sickness, or possession by spirits that were debilitating to their families and to their wider village communities. Some episodes even suggest that he restored people who had been suffering serious illness to active roles in their communities, in reproductive labor (the twelve-year-old) as well as productive labor (the paralytic). Hearing repeated episodes of Jesus healing the sick and restoring them to their families and community and restoring the wider covenantal community would have had the effect of reinforcing community renewal in several ways. One of the principal effects of performance of the story in communities would have been to strengthen the group's common identity, cohesion, and mutual support. That, in turn, strengthened the local familial and neighborly support groups of those suffering and recovering from illness.

Another, related way in which the Markan story does not just anticipate but asserts the independence and strengthening of local community life is the displacement and replacement of the temple-state's influence on personal and community life in the healings Jesus performs. If Jesus healed a man with skin lesions and declared him "clean," enabling him to rejoin social interaction, then it was not necessary for him make the offering in the temple declared necessary in official torah pertaining to skin lesions. Once Jesus had set the precedent of declaring "your sins are forgiven" and then declared more generally that "the human one," i.e., people, can forgive sins, then it was not necessary to take sin offerings to the priests in the temple. Illnesses were no longer occasions for the temple-state to drain away resources needed for local nourishment that would sustain people's health. Closely related are the episode in which Jesus condemns the Pharisees for pressing people to "devote" some of their produce to the temple (thus violating the covenantal commandments that require use of peasant produce to support families locally) and the later episode condemning the scribes for "devouring widow's livings" in pressing them to give to the temple. Hearing such episodes performed empowered villagers to forgive sins themselves and harbor local resources needed to nourish life and health in resistance to the demands of the Jerusalem temple-state (or, by analogy, of Roman client rulers in other areas).

As suggested in the effects just summarized, the power generated in the dynamic interrelations between the healing and exorcizing prophet Jesus and the people who responded in trust in the story carried over into the communities of the movement who heard it performed. The Markan story indicates this repeatedly. Indeed the story frames the narrative of exorcism and healing toward the beginning and again toward the end with an explicit statement about this power that continued in the movement. In response to Jesus' first exorcism, in the Capernaum village assembly, the people exclaim in amazement that this is a "new teaching with authority/power" among the people, in pointed contrast with that of the scribes in Jerusalem who, by implication, lack such authority. Following the narrative full of the trust-enabled healings of the people, after Jesus' demonstration against the temple, the high priests challenge his authority, only to be confronted with the reality of the authority/power that has been generated by the interaction of John and the people and, by implication, by the interaction of Jesus and the people. The Markan story, moreover, refers to Jesus' healings and exorcisms and wilderness feedings as *dynameis*, "(acts of) power(s)." The narrative repeatedly states explicitly that these acts are enabled by the trust of the people, such as the hemorrhaging woman and Bartimaeus. As the story was performed, it continued to generate such power among the trusting people—and to undermine the authority of ruling institutions as the people further withdrew and resisted.

All of these effects, the reinforcement of community, the fame of and trust in Jesus' "acts of power," and the power generated in the interaction of Jesus and those who responded, suggest that the performance of the story strengthened the wellness of community members hearing the Markan story. Episodes of the healings of particular illnesses in the story, which were presumably typical in the historical context, are suggestive of some of the likely effects on the audience.

To the paralytic, Jesus declares that saying "your sins are forgiven" is equivalent to saying "take up your pallet and walk," and then declares that the people themselves have authority to forgive sins. As discussed above, this addresses directly the Israelite cultural definition of sickness as divine punishment for sinning and the temple-state's laws that healing required sin-offerings/sacrifices. The effect of this understanding of sickness as caused by one's own or one's parents' sins, particularly with scribal reinforcement as a means of social control, was that people blamed themselves for sickness and expended much (social-)psychic energy in self-surveillance—a psychic and social "paralysis" that may have been a direct factor in the paralysis of a man unable to walk. Jesus' declaration of forgiveness of the paralytic's sins and extension of the authority to forgive sins to the people themselves would have evoked a release of (social-) psychic energy that became available for (self-)healing the paralytic, the witnesses, and others who heard the report. Similarly, hearing of this declaration as a key episode in a story full of healings would have evoked a release of psychic energy previously devoted to self-regulation among the hearers (and this would have been renewed in each subsequent hearing). Performance of the story featuring this episode was a new declaration of forgiveness, evoking the hearers' trust that their sins were or could be forgiven, with a corresponding release from self-blame and a freeing of potentially healing-power.

Other healing episodes are similarly suggestive that hearing the story in performance would reinforce the release or availability of life-giving energy individually and collectively, which would be reinforced by the supportive community. Declaring that the Sabbath was created for people relieved the audience from worries about the Sabbath so that life-enhancing energies could flow freely, as exemplified in Jesus' healing on the Sabbath. The healing of the hemorrhaging woman and the young woman near death, both representatives of the people as a whole, dramatized the life-giving power flowing from the renewal mission of Jesus, suggesting that life-enhancing and whole-making energy would be flowing in the community so that such draining-away of life would no longer plague people who were now in a supportive rather than a disintegrating community. The pairing of the two women, and the increasing importance of women in the Markan narrative, may well have led especially women in the communities addressed to identify with them and take leadership roles.[2]

With regard to spirit possession and exorcism in particular, there would appear to be several interrelated but distinguishable effects of performance of the Gospel on the audience community. First, repeated performance of the Markan story, particularly the episodes in which Jesus cast out possessing spirits and the summaries of how many more he had cast out, would have evoked trust in the continuing effects of his exorcisms among the people-in-renewal.

2. Rosenblatt, "Gender, Ethnicity, and Legal Considerations," 141; Horsley, *Hearing the Whole Story*, chap. 9.

Second, the supportive and cooperative community that was reinforced by performance of the story of renewal focused mainly on healings and exorcisms would have become a protective shield around its members, a protective spirit in and among its members. They would thus have been less susceptible to attack by the invasive hostile forces that had come into the society with the conquest and domination by the Romans. The far more developed and "rationalized" system of diametrically opposed spirits in the scribal-priestly community that had withdrawn to the wilderness at Qumran provides a suggestive comparison. According to its central ritual of initiation and renewal laid out in its Community Rule (1QS), the life of the community was under the control of the Spirit of Light (and all the beneficent spirits) that was locked in a (historical) struggle with the Prince of Darkness/Belial (and all the maleficent spirits). If that was meant and taken seriously, then it should not be surprising that in the extensive collection of other documents, there is no mention of spirit-possession and exorcism, but only the malevolent threat of hostile spirits and certain protective psalms and rituals to ward off potential attacks. That is, the community and its pervasive Spirit/spirits formed a cordon or shield around members that protected them from the spirits that had possessed others in the wider society (particularly the high priestly rulers in Jerusalem). Similarly, the supportive community that had formed in response to Jesus' mission and was reinforced by performance of the Markan Gospel provided a protective *esprit de corps* that left less vulnerability to the hostile spirits. Insofar as the Jesus-communities were still fully engaged in the political-economic conflicts of the society under Roman rule and their life was not so intensively determined by a pervasive Spirit of Light, however, their protective shield would not have been so all-encompassing, although repeated performance of the Gospel story would have strengthened it.

Third, the particular exposure of the identity of (some of) the spirits that had invaded and taken possession of some people as "Legion," that is the Roman army, brought a certain demystification of the power-relations that dominated the people's lives. Members of a community or movement of Jesus-loyalists could, or were forced to, recognize that it was the Roman troops that had invaded their land and lives and generated the trauma of debilitating illnesses and spirit possessions. With the performance of the story that included the casting out and exposure of Legion, the invasive/possessing spirits that were a mystifying screen that enabled a certain *modus vivendi* with Roman violence were replaced by the sobering recognition of the true cause of their social malaise. But perhaps the implication of the episode, that the invasive Roman troops would self-destruct in the sea, emboldened the Markan communities to persevere, even under repression, when they were called before the "authorities."

This is a prime example of how a contemporary listener to the story must pay close attention to the overall narrative sequence of episodes to appreciate the likely effect of the story for the ancient hearers in their political-economic-cultural performance context. The first exorcism indicates that Jesus acts with power to defeat the possessing spirits. Then the casting out of "Legion," representing the Roman troops that had invaded the people's lives with such destructive violence is followed by their implied self-destruction, exposing their identity as the Roman conquers and invaders. In the ensuing narrative sequence the way has been cleared for demystified direct recognition and confrontation with the Roman imperial order (in Syria–Palestine). Jesus announces that his opposition to the rulers will result in his martyrdom in Jerusalem, and adamantly rejects any fantasy of replacing Roman rule with himself and the disciples as the new rulers. In the very next episode he declares to the crowd (the movement) that they must be prepared to follow him in "taking up their cross." Thereafter the narrative moves into his direct confrontation with the rulers in Jerusalem.[3] And in his speech about what to expect in the future, they face the sobering scenario of being handed over to councils, beaten in assemblies, and standing trial before governors and kings." In this narrative sequence, the crucial episode in which is the exorcism of the spirits identified as "Legion" and their self-destruction, the hearers are called to recognize their now demystified situation and emboldened to persevere in their renewed supportive communities, even under repression, when they were called before the "authorities."

The Speeches Adapted in Matthew and Luke

The series of speeches that were adapted by the Matthean and Lukan Gospels were presumably performed in communities of Jesus-loyalists. The performers made present the pronouncements of what was happening among the people: of God's judgment against the rulers who were

---

3. Fuller discussion of how Jesus' exorcisms are integrally related to the struggle against Roman rule in the Markan story in *Hearing the Whole Story*, chap. 6.

exploiting them, of renewal of covenantal community, of prayer for the sufficiency and communal sharing of the community, and commission of the envoys who were continuing the healing, exorcism, and proclamation with which Jesus had generated the renewal of the people in village communities only a decade or so before. We can discern several interrelated effects that performance of these speeches would have had in communities of Jesus-loyalists who cultivated and were addressed by the speeches.

These are prophetic speeches, some of them in traditional Israelite prophetic form, as in Jesus' woes against the Pharisees and his prophetic lament over the imminent judgment of the Jerusalem ruling house. In pronouncing a renewed Mosaic covenant Jesus speaks as a new Moses, the founding prophet of Israel. In the healings that he points to as the manifestations of the direct rule of God and then in commissioning proteges to extend his mission, he channels Elijah, the great prophet of Israel's renewal. Jesus declares that John is the greatest prophet in history to highlight that "the least in the kingdom of God is greater." The speeches further include a myriad of allusions and references to, and indeed a continuation of, Israelite tradition. The performers of the speeches speak as "Jesus" and "John," the climactic figures in the prophetic role and tradition.

Israelite tradition included the yearnings and expectations of the people. These yearnings come vividly to the fore in the way the speech about John's prophecy of "the coming stronger one" and Jesus' demonstration of how he has been fulfilling those yearnings for the healing of the people's plagues and illnesses that the historical context suggests were the effects of repeated imperial conquest and exploitative rule. The speeches do not include particular healing episodes, as does the Markan story. Rather, they focus on the turning point in the history of the people: the renewal of their personal and community life that Jesus' healings have effected. His healings have responded to the deep longings of the people who have been plagued with the debilitating illnesses left in the wake of imperial invasion, destruction, and subjugation. And his casting out invasive spirits is an exodus-like liberation from their subjugation.

Most of the speeches are also in performative speech. In contrast with a story told about events in the past, performative speech not only establishes what is spoken but also has the immediacy of prophetic declarations delivered (again) "live" to the communities of hearers. The spokesperson for Jesus delivers the speeches to the current audience just as (presumably) Jesus had delivered them to Galilean villagers (in

Aramaic) a few decades previously. While these speeches are steeped in traditional prophetic rhetoric, they are not just rhetoric. In these performative speeches in the context of deep division between rulers and ruled, of struggles against increasingly adverse circumstances, the people hear that God has indicted and irrevocably condemned the predatory rulers. Because the hearers are rooted in cultural tradition that remembers that domination and exploitation has been going on for generations and that protests have been registered for generations, they have the sense of "finally!" relief and justice is happening and continues to happen when they hear the prophecies re-pronounced. "Finally" we will have enough to eat, our debts cancelled, we are relieved from blaming ourselves for our poverty, and cooperation with our neighbors is restored.

While offering hope for subsistence living and cooperative community, however, the speeches do not pull the hearers into fantasies of utopia and a denial of their own real life circumstances. Like the demands made in the covenant renewal speech, other speeches made demands of commitment and solidarity. The admonition to bold confession when hauled before the authorities, for example, faced directly the repression that the communities of the movement were experiencing. The hearers knew very well that as members of a renewal community they were involved in a resistance movement.

To the modern listener far removed from the historical situation, the speeches focused on the healings and the exorcisms may seem a step removed from the events by comparison with the Markan retelling of particular exorcisms and healings for which crowds clamored, Jesus responded, and people trusted and spread the word. These speeches presuppose that Jesus performed many healings and exorcisms and emphasize their central significance in what was happening in Jesus' mission. These speeches declare that it was precisely in the healings and exorcisms that the direct rule of God was happening. The healing of the illnesses for which the people had been longing and the casting out of invasive spirits that were plaguing the people were the fundamental acts of power at the center of the renewal of the people/Israel.

As with the hearers of the Markan story, so also with the audience of the pre-Matthean and pre-Lukan speeches the effect of hearing about the healings and exorcisms that Jesus had performed in the origins of their movement would have been continuing healing power and protective collective spirit in the continuing communities. The speech in which Jesus commissioned envoys, moreover, included instructions to continue the healings and exorcism in the expanding movement. The spirit of healing/health in the community as well as the continuing healing and exorcism would both have been reinforced by the renewal of covenantal community and would have helped empower the communities to maintain their mutual cooperation and commitment in resistance to the political-economic and spiritual powers still arrayed against them.

The Matthean Story

With its more schematic sequence of narrative steps and speeches the Matthean story seems to involve the hearers in less intense immediacy and more perspective than does the Markan story. This can be sensed from the different ways the two stories begin. After a brief account of his baptism, testing in the wilderness, and calling of disciples as he moves quickly into his mission in Galilee, the Markan story has Jesus go immediately into the assembly in Capernaum where he encounters and subdues an unclean spirit and performs one healing after another. With more historical distance and overview of his mission, following genealogy, birth-infancy legends, and temptation, the Matthean Gospel presents a grand summary of his extensive healings of people from all areas of Israel that sets up the long covenant renewal speech that constitutes (the communities of) the movement that the healings generated. The general sequence of events in the two Gospels is the same, but the Matthean presentation is more schematic. Jesus heals the various illnesses among the people, so that his fame spreads and crowds "followed" from/in all the districts of Israel leading to his renewal of the Mosaic covenant that revitalized communities (in independence of rulers and ruling institutions). The Matthean Gospel focuses more explicitly and extensively on the renewed community life, including aspects such as prayer, alms, and fasting as well as elaboration of explicit covenantal forms, before moving into narrative of particular healings and exorcisms. This fits, and reinforces, communities that are already formed and have some "staying power."

The Matthean story also leads the audience(s) through historical perspective and reflection on Jesus mission of healing and exorcism and renewal of the people that has resulted in their own movement. The genealogy and the repeated declaration of fulfillment of prophecy reassures them that their communities are the result of Jesus' fulfillment of the history and tradition of Israel. This would have been particularly important in their historical situation as a movement whose prophet/messiah leader had catalyzed a renewed people in opposition to the client rulers in Jerusalem, whose Roman patrons had recently destroyed the temple-state and devastated much of Galilee and Judea. The reassurance would have been all the more important considering that they would have been apprehensive about their own situation following the vengeful Roman retaliation against their insurrectionary fellow Israelites.

The performance of the Matthean story, like that of the Markan story, would have generated trust in the healing power of Jesus and its continuation in the movement. It would also have generated an ethos of healing in the communities of the movement. Performance of the story with which they were already familiar told again of how the prophetically promised prophet Jesus came into community assemblies (the precursors of their own) just for the purpose of casting out the spirits and healing the illnesses that were plaguing the people. Just as his fame spread in the story, so in its performance it would have spread further and become ever more deeply ingrained in the hearers. Just as Jesus' healings and exorcisms and the spread of the word about them generated trust in the crowds as well as in family members and persons seeking healing in the story, so the performance of the story would have generated and solidified trust in the hearers collectively as well as individually. And the episodes retold, the fame deepened, and the trust solidified all would have generated an ethos of people having been healed and a continuing flow of healing energy.

Performance of the story, moreover, would have generated a receptive context in the communities for the continuation of the healing and exorcism of Jesus by leaders in the movement. The communities of hearers were thus prepared for the continuation of healings that Jesus commissioned his disciples to perform in the mission speech (10:1, 8) and the exorcisms that continued to be done "in his name" (7:22). The continuing healing and exorcism may have happened in a less intense atmosphere than that portrayed in the story, but the performance of the story created a receptive context and an enabling trust.

The same memories, longings, and expectations in Israelite popular tradition that enabled the healings of Jesus narrated in the story also would have enabled the continuing therapeutic effect of the performance as well as the healings of Jesus that it narrated. The memories and longings also provided a basis on which the healings and exorcisms became integral aspects of a broader historical breakthrough for subjected people of Israelite heritage. Prophets had given voice to the sufferings of Israelite people under imperial conquest and domination, including destruction, captivity, blindness, lameness, and their longing for deliverance. These were not the conditions intended by God, who had inspired earlier prophets such as Elijah to lead renewal of the people, including healing, in resistance to oppressive rule. Other prophets such as Isaiah had prophesied God's future deliverance. Like the Markan story and the pre-Matthean series of Jesus-speeches, the Matthean narrative builds on these memories and expectations in presenting Jesus' healings as the manifestation of the direct rule of God now at hand (e.g., Matt 11:2–6). The Matthean narrative, moreover, regularly adds that Jesus' healings and exorcisms and other incidents and events were done "to fulfill what was *spoken* (by God) *through* the prophet (Isaiah)." This repeatedly makes what the prophets had spoken and its fulfillment in Jesus' actions present for the hearers.

As in the Markan story, so also in the Matthean story, Jesus' healings and exorcisms were the principal activities in the renewal of the people of Israel, for whom the Mosaic covenant constituted the fundamental guidelines of their community life. Even more in Matthew than in Mark, the healings and exorcisms and the renewal of covenantal community would have been mutually reinforcing for the hearers (just as they were interwoven in the performed narrative). The healings and exorcisms re-generated the life of the community as well as members and families. And the renewal of covenantal commitment to mutual aid and cooperation strengthened the ability of families and communities to care for their members. In the Markan story, narrative of particular exorcisms and healings led to a declaration and later a set of dialogues of covenant renewal. In Matthew, as noted above, a grand summary of Jesus' wide-reaching healing set up the elaborate covenant renewal speech. The performative speech that enacted the renewal of the covenant community then set up a receptive and reinforcing context for the ensuing narrative of particular healings and exorcisms (Matt 8–9). This was in turn followed by commissioning the twelve disciples to extend Jesus mission of exorcism, healing, and pronouncement of the kingdom in other communities (extending to the hearers themselves; Matt 10). Further narrative of particular healings and exorcisms and related episodes (Matt 11–12; 14–17) led to Jesus' teaching on further aspects of renewal of covenantal community (Matt 18; 19).

Their communal commitment having been renewed in the covenant renewal speech, the hearers' personal and community life would have been strengthened by the narrative of the many particular healings and exorcisms that had embodied the renewal of the people. The healings of various illnesses also dramatized among the hearers significant aspects of the renewal of the Israel:

- the reintegration of people such as the fellow with skin lesions;

- trust as an integral aspect of the healing;

- healings as fulfillment of prophecy;

- the exorcism of violently invasive *daimonia* that symbolized death of the people so that they self-destructed;

- healing that included the forgiveness of sins, with people empowered to forgive one another;

- healing of the hemorrhaging of the woman in response to the trust she manifested in her bold initiative and the transmission of new life to the daughter who seemed dead;

- opening the eyes of the blind; and

- restoring speech by casting out an invasive spirit that had struck a man dumb.

These were the particular cases of the healing of the people that Jesus had performed as the beginning of the renewal of the people that was continuing in the audience hearing the Gospel.

The Matthean narrative, like the Markan story, presents Jesus' healings as displacements and replacements of ways in which the temple-state impinged on personal and community life while it was still intact (prior to the Roman destruction in 70 CE). This was integrally related to the ways in which the healings effected renewal of community life, and made it more independent of temple-state influence. When Jesus healed a man with skin lesions and declared him "clean," enabling him to rejoin social interaction, then it was not necessary for him to make the offering in the temple declared necessary in official torah pertaining to skin lesions. Once Jesus had set the precedent of declaring "brother, your sins are forgiven" and then declared more generally that "the human one," i.e., people, can forgive sins, then it was not necessary to take sin offerings to the priests in the temple. Illnesses were no longer occasions for the temple-state to drain away resources needed for local nourishment that would sustain people's health. Closely related are episodes in which Jesus condemns the Pharisees for pressing people to "devote" some of their produce to the temple (thus violating the covenantal commandments that require use of peasant produce to support families locally) and the scribes for "devouring widow's livings" in pressing them to give to the temple.

Hearing such episodes performed empowered villagers and/or urban communities to forgive sins themselves and to harbor local resources needed to nourish life and health in resistance to the demands of the Jerusalem temple-state (or, by analogy, of Roman client rulers in other areas). The long sequence of prophetic woes against the scribes and Pharisees included condemnation of ways in which the retainers of the temple-state (and by implication of other Roman client rulers) attempted to siphon off resources of the people. The intensification of the Matthean Jesus' attacks on the temple-state, particularly the scribes and Pharisees, may be a reflection of how onerous its attempt at oversight and influence on the people's life had been and a certain sense of relief and vindication of the movement's assertion of independence.

Performance of the Matthean story—with all of these interrelated healings and renewal of covenantal community and condemnation of the Jerusalem rulers and their retainers—would have strongly reinforced the independence of the audience communities of (Judeans or other) Israelites in towns that had not been directly under the political jurisdiction of the Jerusalem temple-state. The temple and high priesthood had been destroyed by the Roman armies and could no longer exert even minimal influence over them. Of course they were evidently still vulnerable to suspicion and attacks in the imperial ethos of victory over the revolt by the Galilean and Judean people. The Gospel gives several indications that the hearers were experiencing harassment from the authorities.

The ideal in Israelite popular tradition, particularly the stories of early Israel, the leadership of Elijah-Elisha, and the pronouncements of prophets such as Amos, Isaiah, and Jeremiah, was for covenantal communities to be (as) independent (as possible) from the influence and exploitation of central rulers. The Matthean presentation of the mission of Jesus as the desired prophet of renewal and the fulfillment of Israelite history would have instilled a sense in the hearing communities that they were sharing in that fulfillment. The performance of the story explained that the displacement and condemnation of the Roman client rulers in Jerusalem had begun in the healings and exorcisms and prophetic pronouncements of Jesus' mission. Presented as the fulfillment of many prophets' pronouncements, moreover, it helped vindicate Jesus' mission and the communities of Jesus-loyalists in the broad sweep of history as the long-awaited renewal of the people/Israel. And that would have strengthened their collective solidarity as communities of renewal still living under local authorities of the Roman imperial order. The supportive ethos of healing and the continuing performance of healings and exorcisms were integral to the strength of those communities of renewal and resistance.

A key indicator of how performance of the Gospel would have strengthened the coherence, healing ethos, and persistence of the audience communities is how John and Jesus generate power/authority (*exousia*) in interaction with the people, which enables Jesus' and his disciples' (performance of acts of) power(s) (*dynameis*), which in turn become part of the power of John and Jesus that is threatening to the Roman client rulers. This power/empowering runs throughout the Gospel. At the close of Jesus' performative speech of covenant renewal, the Gospel comments that he taught with power/authority, in contrast with the scribes (7:29). In the second healing that follows, the centurion articulates what is obvious, that Jesus is a person of/with/under authority (8:9). As the key point of the healing of the paralytic, Jesus declares that God has given the people the authority/power to forgive sins (which effects healing; 9:6–8). Jesus' principal action in his performative commissioning of the disciples for mission is that he gives them power/authority over the unclean spirits (10:1). Thus empowered, Jesus and the disciples perform (acts of) power(s) in village communities (11:20, 21, 23). That these (acts of) power(s) are relational, power generated in interaction with the people who have trust in Jesus, is illustrated by how few (acts of) power(s) he could perform in Nazareth (13:54, 58). Herod's reluctance to execute John "because he feared the people" indicates that the power of these prophets that was generated in their teaching and healing among the people was also political power that protected both people and prophets from the rulers' power, illegitimate because they lacked authority with the people (14:1–5). Then integral to Jesus' series of confrontations with the rulers in Jerusalem is their fear of the people among whom Jesus had also generated power (21:23–27), which is also why they seize Jesus surreptitiously at night (26:3–5). The performance of this story of the generation of power among the people would have strengthened the audience's sense of empowerment to continue their renewed communities in resistance to the Roman client rulers under whom they lived.

The Lukan Story

Assuming that the Acts narrative is a continuation of the Lukan story telling of the spread of a movement of Jesus-loyalists into the towns and cities of Syria, Asia Minor and Greece, it would seem to offer clues to the location and composition of the audience of the Lukan story of Jesus' mission. The communities of Jesus-loyalists in those towns and cities were evidently comprised of diaspora Judeans and other peoples who had identified with the Israelite tradition and its fulfillment in Jesus' mission and movement(s), as discussed in chap. 10. The distinctively Lukan Gospel story indicates that the Romans had destroyed Jerusalem and its high priestly ruling house, client rulers for the Romans, some years before. Thus the high priestly heads of the temple-state that Jesus had opposed in his mission of healing and covenant renewal and that had finally handed him over for crucifixion were no longer in power in Judea itself. Roman propaganda about their glorious victory over the Judeans, however, must have cast suspicion on Judean communities and people associated with Judeans.

In these circumstances, in composing "an orderly account, after investigating everything carefully from the first," there would have been reason to tone down the opposition between Jesus' mission and the now defunct temple-state and to present the movement of Jesus-loyalists as less sharply opposed to the Roman imperial order. According to accounts in Paul's letters and Acts, as the movement of Jesus-loyalists has spread into towns and cities of Syria, Asia Minor, and Greece, some local authorities had taken repressive action (Phil 1:2–12; Acts 14:4–5; 16:19–24; 17:1–9).

In comparison with the Markan and Matthean stories, however, the Lukan story does not mitigate the conflict of Jesus' mission with the temple-state and, if anything, sharpens the conflict with the Roman imperial order. That the Jesus movement spread so quickly and broadly suggests that the people among whom it expanded were ready for some movement opposed to and offering an alternative to the Roman imperial order. The Lukan story must be addressing just such people. It has both broadened the scope and sharpened the political-economic-religious opposition of Jesus' mission and the emergent movement. The story now begins in the hill country of Judea as well as in the villages of Galilee. The songs and prophecies that greet the births of John and Jesus proclaim them as the fulfillment of the deep, long-standing yearnings of the

Israelite people for liberation from their centuries-long subjugation to imperial rule and for renewal as an independent people. The anticipated implications are empire-wide: displacement of the imperial Savior who demands tribute (and honors) juxtaposed with the birth of the popular Savior and Messiah whose liberation has implications for other peoples as well as Israel. The beginning of Acts makes the implications explicit in anticipation that the movement will expand to "the ends of the earth." As the fulfillment of Israelite longings, tradition, and history, Jesus' mission and movement are an alternative society of covenantal justice in opposition to the temple-state that is the representative of the Roman imperial order in Palestine. With the Roman destruction of the temple-state in Jerusalem, moreover, the Jesus movement(s) behind the Gospel stories may have thought that a huge obstacle to the further fulfillment of Israelite tradition had been removed.

In addition to or perhaps rather in connection with sharpening the general political-economic conflict with the rulers, moreover, the Lukan story makes the exorcisms and healings more prominent. Besides including the episodes in the Markan story (except in the second sequence of acts of power), the Lukan story adds several additional episodes. The story has Jesus commission the twelve, with power and authority, to cast out spirits and heal sicknesses and a few episodes later commissions seventy others to extend his mission of exorcism and healing, who perform acts of power in more villages communities. The Lukan emphasis on power and empowerment pertains particularly to Jesus and his envoys' exorcism and healing.

The Lukan story has a remarkably confident tone in the face of the overwhelming forces arrayed against the people. This confident tone would have lent confidence to the hearers about their own continuity with the fulfillment of history that has been running through the people of Israel in Jesus' mission and movement. Roman armies had utterly destroyed Jerusalem and devastated villages in Galilee and Judea only a decade or two before the story was being performed. In communities of the Jesus-movement that had been centered in and spread out from Jerusalem, the Roman devastation must have been a major crisis, a challenge to continuity and confidence. In that context, the boldness of the Lukan story in sharpening the opposition between Jesus' mission and movement and overwhelmingly powerful rulers would have bolstered (or restore) the communities' confidence in their connection with the origins of the movement.

Perhaps precisely because of the Roman destruction of Jerusalem and environs that was widely known around the empire (far more than what had happened a few years before in the remote area of Galilee), the Lukan story enhanced the historical continuity by including more links and interaction between Judeans and Jesus. The story's beginnings in the hill country of Judea and statement that a great multitude of people from *all Judea and Jerusalem* had come to hear Jesus and be healed of their illnesses and affliction by unclean spirits (6:17–18) surely helped diaspora Judeans and God-fearers who had become loyalists identify with the healing and covenant renewal at the center of Jesus' mission. Given the historical circumstances of the recent manifestation of invasive and possessive imperial power, the Lukan expansion of the role of invasive spirits, some of whom were identified as "Legion," and the emphasis on Jesus' having been filled with power over them would presumably have been reassuring to the audience communities.

The (general) function/effect of (repeated) performance of the Lukan story among the addressees would have been to make present to them the mission of Jesus in which the movement they had joined had begun. The story told again of his extensive healing and exorcism, his fame spreading widely through Galilee and surrounding areas, people flocking to him for healing with trust that enabled the healing, and the movement focused on his healing and exorcism expanding into other villages in ever wider areas. One of the principal effects of hearing the story of Jesus' extensive healing and exorcism, the spread of his fame and people's coming to him with trust, would have been to solidify the hearers' trust in the healing power flowing through Jesus himself. The Lukan story adds additional episodes of healing and at several points makes explicit the power to heal that was working through Jesus. The Lukan story may heroize Jesus somewhat more than the other Gospel stories, emphasizing the power with which he was endowed. But there is no less emphasis on the enabling factor of the people's trust in the healing interaction with Jesus.

The story also intensified the sense that the healing power continued operative in the communities of the movement. Jesus extended the "power and authority" over all spirits and to heal sicknesses to the Twelve, symbolic representatives of the people (of Israel), and then also commissioned seventy disciples to extend his mission of healing and exorcism to other towns, which suggests that exorcism and healing was continued in the expanding movement. The continuing healing and exorcism may have happened in a less intense atmosphere than portrayed in the story, but the (repeated) performance of the story enabled the continuing healing.

As in the effects of the Markan and Matthean stories performed in their respective movements, there would have been enabling factors in the communities of Lukan addressees. One of the most important enabling factors would have been deep familiarity with and identification with Israelite tradition and, indeed, history. The standard Christian theological scheme of how "early Christianity" had quickly become predominantly "Gentile" and the assumption in New Testament studies that "Jewish" cultural tradition had functioned through written texts, that is, Scripture, have blocked the way that diaspora Judeans and other peoples who joined these communities would have been knowledgeable in, if not imbued with Israelite tradition. Texts that have been misunderstood as references to widespread literacy and reading of Scripture are Josephus' explanation of how distinctive Judeans and their communities were in the Roman imperial world. He insists that it was a widespread practice in (diaspora) Judean communities to gather in their assemblies on the sabbath and hear recitation of texts such that those texts became engraved in the hearts of the people, that is, deeply embedded in their collective memory.

Also there was a great deal of tension, even open conflict, between diaspora Judeans and other peoples in some cities, especially in Alexandria, Antioch, and the Phoenician cities. There was thus a good deal of dissatisfaction among diaspora Judeans with the Roman imperial order. Diaspora Judean communities usually constituted a (small) minority of the population of cities of the Empire, so it was hardly likely for a serious resistance movement to emerge, (although an insurrection did occur among the large Judean population in Cyrenaica in 115 CE [*CPJ* 1.88; 2.228–40]). By the time of Jesus, however, there was considerable contact and movement back and forth between Judeans from various diaspora communities and Jerusalem. The early narratives in Acts recount how some of these opposed the movement of Jesus-loyalists and others who joined the movement and even became important leaders. They were joining a movement of opposition and resistance to the temple-state and the wider Roman imperial order. Such diaspora Judeans would have resonated with the Lukan story as it referenced and continued Israelite tradition in its political-religious resistance.

The hearers of the Lukan story, like those of the Markan and Matthean stories, deeply aware that domination and exploitation by rulers had been going on for generations, in hearing performance of the Gospel story they may have had the sense that finally relief and justice, healing and community renewal are happening and continue to happen. "Finally!" we will have enough to eat, our debts will be cancelled, we are relieved from blaming ourselves for our poverty, and cooperation with our neighbors is restored.

One of the aspects of sickness and healing that appears stronger in the Lukan story is the association with the forgiveness of sin. Luke includes the episode in which the healing of the paralytic is equated with the forgiveness of sin in opposition to the debilitating scribal exploitation of the belief that sickness was caused by one's own or one's parents sin. The episode distinctive to the Lukan story of the "sinful woman" at the house of a Pharisee then reinforces the declaration of forgiveness. For audiences that included diaspora Judeans as well as the Markan addressees, this would have had the effect of releasing for healing the psychic energy that before would have been used for self-blame and self-regulation. Declaring that the Sabbath was created for people would have had a similar effect on an audience embedded in Israelite tradition, relieving worries about how they observed the Sabbath so that life-enhancing energies could flow freely, as exemplified in Jesus' healing on the Sabbath. Again the Lukan story includes an additional healing story making the point about enhancing life rather than diminishing it.

With regard to spirit possession and exorcism, repeated performance of the Lukan story, particularly the episodes in which Jesus cast out possessing spirits and the summaries of how many more he had cast out, would have evoked trust in the effects of exorcism that continued in the movement, performed by those on whom he had bestowed the power. The Lukan story included the political implication of the sequence of Jesus' exorcisms that climaxed in the identification of many of the possessing spirits as "Legion." This presumably effected demystification of the power-relations that dominated the people's lives. Even if the communities addressed had not recently experienced Roman conquest, the demystification called for a recognition of the concrete superhuman forces that dictated the conditions of their lives. And perhaps the implication of the episode, that the invasive Roman forces would self-destruct in the sea, emboldened the communities to persevere, even under repression, when they were called before the "authorities." The hearers knew very well that as members of a renewal community they were involved in a resistance movement. The admonitions to bold confession when hauled before the authorities, for example, faces directly the repression that the communities of the movement were experiencing.

Accordingly, the Lukan story in particular warns against fantasies of utopia and not getting carried away about successful exorcisms or events as omens of imminent political transformation. The "parable" that Jesus tells when his disciples get overly excited about entering Jerusalem was a reminder from recent history: the story of Herod's son Archelaus' reception of royal power in 4 BCE and how he placed his officers to have power and to exploit the people of multiple villages was a sobering reminder of how the Roman imperial rule worked in areas such as Palestine and Syria and would remain operative—requiring wise, bold, and steadfast resistance in community solidarity.

Finally, the speeches in Luke declare explicitly what the narratives imply, that it was precisely in the healings and exorcisms that the direct rule of God was happening. The healing of the illnesses for which the people had been longing and the casting out of invasive spirits that were plaguing the people are the fundamental acts of power at the center of the renewal of the people/Israel. The speech in which Jesus commissioned seventy more envoys, moreover, included instructions to continue the healings and exorcism in the expanding movement. The healing power central to Jesus mission continued in the movement.[4] The spirit of healing/health in the community as well as the continuing healing and exorcism would both have been reinforced by the renewal of covenantal community and would have helped empower the community to maintain its mutual cooperation and commitment in resistance to the political-economic and spiritual powers still arrayed against it.

Distinctive Developments and Features in Particular Gospel Stories

Chapters 7–10 were attempts to listen carefully to the respective Gospel stories and speeches of Jesus' mission, particularly to the episodes and speeches about exorcism and healing and renewal of covenant

---

4. The narrative in Acts gives plenty of indications of spirit possession and sicknesses and memories that exorcisms in Jesus' name and healing by apostles continued among the communities of the expanding movement.

community that are central to the Gospels. Each of the Gospel stories and the series of speeches adapted in the Matthean and Lukan Gospels underwent separate development in different movements of Jesus-loyalists in somewhat different contexts, such as before and after the Roman destruction of Galilee, Judea, and Jerusalem. The next steps in a critical and comprehensive approach to Gospel stories and speeches as sources in oral performance in the respective contexts then would appear to be:

- To assess key differences in the Gospels' respective portrayals of Jesus-in-interaction, since distinctive features of those portrayals may be significant for historical analysis.

- To compare distinctive features of particular Gospels' portrayal of Jesus-in-interaction with what we know about the historical political-economic-religious contexts in order to ascertain their historical credibility. Key distinctive features of particular Gospel stories may have influenced the development of Christian theology (including New Testament studies) and its scheme(s) of Christian origins that in turn have influenced the assumptions and concepts of previous interpretations of Jesus.

These comparisons and analyses may help make it possible to discern what appears to be common collective memory of Jesus in interaction shared by different movements of Jesus-loyalists and the Gospel stories and speeches they produced.

Matthew and Luke Present More Explicit and Schematic Fulfillment of Israelite Tradition

From our provisional attempt to hear the Gospel stories and/or speeches as they (may have) resonated with their respective audiences in historical context it is clear that they all portrayed the healings and exorcisms as Jesus' principal actions in close relations to his proclamation of the direct rule of God and renewal of covenantal community. In all of these texts the healings and exorcisms and renewal of covenantal community constituted a renewal of the people of Israel in opposition to and by the rulers. Each of the Gospel texts-in-performance, of course, as they underwent different development in different movements, became distinctive in various ways.

One aspect of these differences regards the scope of the significance of Jesus' mission and movement(s). In the series of speeches adapted in Matthew and Luke, Jesus' healings, exorcisms, and prophetic pronouncements are opposed to and by the "king" in Galilee and the ruling house of Jerusalem and its scribal and Pharisaic representatives. Jesus was martyred, like other prophets, but there is no mention of a confrontation in Jerusalem or of the crucifixion. In the Markan story the scope of Jesus' mission is a good deal broader and the main conflict more specific and dramatic. Along with its portrayal of specific cases of healing and exorcism, the Markan narrative expands the renewal of Israel into areas beyond Galilee and expands his conflict with the Jerusalem temple-state and its representatives into specific condemnations and confrontations. The Markan narrative of the Gadarene exorcism and speech about the future and Jesus' declaration that the people do not owe tribute to Caesar, moreover, give dramatic and vivid indications that Jesus' mission and movement are opposed to and by the Roman imperial order in Palestine and its brutal enforcement by the Roman legions and governors. Both the series of speeches and the Markan story appear to have taken their distinctive forms prior to the Roman devastation of Galilee, Judea, and Jerusalem in suppression of the great revolt in 66–70.

The Matthean and the Lukan stories-and-speeches, on the other hand, both refer to the Roman destruction of Jerusalem and the temple, hence evidently took their distinctive forms in the wake of the Roman destruction. Partly because of the collective trauma and historical significance of those events, both the Matthean and the Lukan stories voice broader significance to Jesus' mission and a sharper political conflict between the Roman imperial order and Jesus' mission focused on healing, exorcism, and the renewal of covenant community. Both make the fulfillment of Israelite history as well as tradition more explicit, and pointedly on a wider "map" of Israelites in Roman Palestine. Both present Jesus' mission in general and in particulars as the fulfillment of Israelite prophecies. Both have the story of Jesus begin, as well as climax, in Judea, and in pointed direct opposition to and by the Roman-appointed Herodian kings and even Caesar's demand for payment of tribute. The Matthean infancy narrative weaves together the search by the paradigmatic representatives of the wisdom of the East for the newborn "king of the Judeans" who represents a new reign of justice for the people in opposition to the oppressive Roman imperial order and the desperate efforts of the family to escape the cruel slaughter of newborns to suppress the movement before it can get started—efforts that also recapitulate Israel's formative history in the exodus. The Lukan Gospel has the story begin among ordinary people in the Judean hill country as well as in the villages of Galilee in a narrative that includes new legends, songs, and prophecies in keen longing for, and evidently inspired by, the agent of liberation from imperial subjugation.

Both Gospels make more explicit the form and intensify the implications of Jesus' renewal of the Mosaic covenant. Both Gospels, through the unfolding of the story and particularly in its climax, sharpen the conflict between Jesus' actions and speeches and the scribes and Pharisees in the temple-state/Jerusalem rulers. In accord with the expanded context and implication, both the Matthean and the Lukan stories make the healing and exorcism more programmatic (and the renewal of covenant more explicit) at the outset of Jesus mission.

All of these distinctive developments of the Matthean and Lukan stories and speeches claim wider significance of and voice intensification of the basic story and agenda of Jesus also articulated in the Mark story and the common speeches adapted in Matthew and Luke. But they do not conflict with or change what was evidently the shared common memory of Jesus mission in the different movements that developed from it. They all present the mission of Jesus focused on healing and exorcism and renewal of covenantal community.

Jesus as the Messiah in Matthew and Luke

In terms of its lasting effect on developing Christian faith and doctrine, the most important distinctive development of the Matthean and Lukan stories was the representation of Jesus as "the Messiah." In the last generation or so it has been increasingly recognized that in the diversity of movements of Jesus-loyalists and the texts they produced Jesus was understood and presented basically in two different roles, both rooted in Israelite tradition.[5] As noted in chap. 8, the series of speeches incorporated by both Matthew and Luke knows nothing of Jesus as "the

5. The following discussion focuses only on roles that are attested in Judean texts near contemporary with Jesus. As is increasingly recognized, "Son of man" was a complex development in Jesus' movements themselves. Supposed roles such as "eschatological/apocalyptic prophet," "sign prophet," "(Jewish Cynic) sage," and "Jewish rabbi" are modern scholarly interpretive concepts of New Testament scholars and Jewish historians.

Messiah." He is rather a prophet in the long tradition of Israelite prophets, the greatest of whom is John, before Jesus proclaimed the kingdom of God. It seemed clear in chap. 7 that the Markan story is criticizing, perhaps even rejecting the understanding of Jesus as the Messiah or a king. Most telling is Jesus' response to Peter's acclamation "you are the messiah," in close narrative sequence: "Get behind me Satan." The Roman soldiers mock him as "king of the Judeans" and the high priests' and scribes' mock him as "the Messiah, the king of Israel." But the Markan story and the collective memory of Jesus' mission on which he draws know Jesus in the role of a prophet like Moses and Elijah.

On the other hand, both the Lukan and Matthean stories that parallel the Markan narrative of Jesus as a prophet in his healing and teaching begin with infancy narratives in which Jesus is born as the Messiah—in pointed juxtaposition, either to Caesar as the "Savior" who decrees that all peoples shall pay tribute, or to Herod whom the Romans had appointed "King of the Judeans." In contrast with the Markan story, both the Lukan and Matthean narratives accept Peter's declaration that Jesus is the Messiah. Curiously, then, in the climactic episodes of the trial and the high priests' charges before Pilate (22:66–71; 23:1–2) the Lukan narrative has Jesus cagily avoiding identification as the Messiah, indicating that this is a (false) charge brought against him and saying, "You say so." Not until the Emmaus road meeting does the risen Jesus explain to his disciples (Luke 24:26, 44–49) that it was necessary for the Messiah to be martyred and finally rise (in fulfillment of "the writings"). The Matthean story refers to "the Messiah" in passing as the disciples' one teacher in the indictment of the scribes and Pharisees (23:10). But then the Matthean story, like the Lukan story, seems to have Jesus ward off identification as the Messiah at his trials and presents it as mockery (26:63, 68; of course the mockery could be irony). The principal association of the Messiah with healing in any of the Gospels comes in the Matthean adaptation at the outset of the speech about whether he is the coming one where the list of healings are referred to as "the works of the Messiah" (11:2).

As discussed in chap. 5, there was very little "expectation" (in elite circles) of a royal "Messiah," either in collections of prophecies such as from Isaiah or in Judean scribal texts closer to the time of Jesus and the Gospels. The role of the Messiah ("their king, the son of David") with scribal traits in Psalms of Solomon 17 will be to establish justice for the restored Israel with "the words of his mouth." The role of the two messiahs, of Aaron and of Israel, in the Qumran community's anticipation of the future will be to lead the ceremonial banquet of the restored people (1QSa 2:11–23). There was thus little in elite Israelite tradition that would have prepared the way for Jesus to be understood as "the Messiah" and nothing that would have set up his healings as "the works of the Messiah."

While elite Judean texts offer little or no evidence for a "Jewish expectation" that Jesus supposedly fulfilled, Israelite people mounted several revolts led by figures whom they acclaimed as "kings." As discussed in chap. 4, this was the other distinctively Israelite paradigm of popular leadership around the time of Jesus and the movement(s) that formed in response to his mission. These movements were evidently informed by the stories of Israelite people having "messiahed" the young David to lead them in gaining independence from the Philistine cities whose soldiers had invaded them. It is at least conceivable that some "followers" of Jesus responded to him according to this scenario in Israelite popular tradition. This role of a popular "king," however, does not appear to be what Jesus is reacting against in response to the misunderstanding of his impending martyrdom by Peter and James and John. Jesus' objection to their misunderstanding refers rather more to an imperial king who lords it over his subjects, as the kings of "the nations" do (i.e., the Romans; Mark 10:42–45). Moreover, no more than the few Judean scribal texts that refer to messiah-figures do Josephus' accounts of the popular kings give any suggestion that they might engage in healing.

So how can it be explained that the Matthean and Lukan stories that consist principally of narratives of exorcism and healings by a prophetic figure and of prophetic speeches that know nothing of a messiah nevertheless begin with Jesus born as the Messiah who would deliver or restore Israel?

Judging from the diversity of understandings of Jesus in early texts later included in the New Testament, there were different movements of Jesus- or Christ-loyalists. Although the apostle Paul claims to have spent fifteen days with Cephas in Jerusalem three years after the vision in which he received his "gospel" (Gal 1:18–19), he evidently knew little about Jesus' mission. His gospel focuses on the crucifixion, resurrection, and parousia of Jesus Christ. In the letters of the apostle Paul, "Messiah/ Christ" seems to be part of the name "Jesus Christ"; "Lord" (*Kyrios*), not "Messiah," is his title. From text-fragments such as the "creed" in 1 Cor 15:3–5 it is clear that the movement from which Paul spun off his own mission had identified Jesus as Christ/Messiah. In a more complex picture, the narrative of Acts, which claims to present the history of the

movement that began in Jerusalem following the crucifixion and resurrection, includes several speeches, supposedly delivered by Cephas/Peter
(in Acts 2:22–36; 3:12–26; 5:29–32; 10:34–43). These speeches present
Jesus as the latest *prophet* (performing acts of power) in the history of
Israel who was crucified by the high priestly rulers but then vindicated
by God in exaltation as *the Messiah*-designate or as the one whom God
would send (back) as the Messiah in "the restoration of all" (Israel) announced by the prophets.[6] Evidently the understanding of Jesus as the
Messiah in addition to having been the prophet who had performed
great acts was rooted in the conviction that he had been exalted (to the
right hand of God) and would return. The movement led by Cephas and
others of the Twelve from which Paul spun off his mission became convinced that Jesus had been exalted and designated as the Messiah.[7] The
genealogies and the "infancy narratives" and beginning of the Matthean
and Lukan stories appear to be further developments of this understanding in movements related to the speeches in Acts. That is, birth legends,
prophecies, and psalms that emerged among Jesus' loyalists retrojected
his designation as the messiah who would liberate the people and were
adapted into the Gospel stories of Matthew and Luke.

The Matthean and Lukan prefacing the story of Jesus' mission with
legends and prophetic hymns of his birth as the Messiah destined to lead
the liberation of the people from the Roman imperial order—juxtaposed
with the imperial Savior's decree of tribute and Herod as the client "King
of the Judeans"—certainly added a political edge to the story. In the aftermath of the vindictive Roman destruction of Jerusalem and the temple-
state, it only expanded some Jesus-loyalists' sense of the implications of
Jesus' mission of healing and exorcism and covenant renewal that began
in the villages of Galilee and near-by areas and climaxed in confrontation
and martyrdom in Jerusalem.

As for the Messiah performing healings, with no precedent in elite
Judean texts or in Israelite popular tradition of a "therapeutic messiah,"
this would appear to be distinctive to the Matthean Gospel story and

---

6. The NRSV (mis)translation, "the restoration of all things" sounds like Stoic philosophy or a Christian theological concept of a new world that follows "the End of the
world" in the modern scholarly construct of "Jewish apocalypticism."

7. Might Pilate's labeling Jesus as "the king of the Judeans," which was likely influenced by the popular "messianic" movements headed by "kings" fresh in the memory
of the Romans, have influenced the disciples in Jerusalem in their visions of the ex-
alted/vindicated martyr Jesus as "the messiah" designate?

its development.[8] As noted in chap. 9, however, the Matthean story indicates no tension between Jesus the prophet performing healings and exorcisms and Jesus as messiah; the story refers to healings as "the works of the messiah" right in the midst of continuing narrative of Jesus the prophet performing healings and exorcisms. Neither the portrayal of Jesus as the Messiah, mainly in the infancy narratives of Matthew and Luke, nor the Matthean juxtaposition of Jesus as messiah and Jesus as prophet performing healings, alters the common collective memory of Jesus-in-interaction presented in all of the Gospel sources as a popular prophet whose principal actions were healings and exorcisms.

Do Aspects of Gospels' Stories of Jesus' Mission Conflict with the Historical Context?

Healings and Exorcisms in the Conflict of Jesus-in-Movement with the Temple-State

In the Markan, Matthean, and Lukan stories and the speeches adapted in Matthew and Luke, the dominant conflict was between Jesus and the rulers. Jesus was generating a renewal of Israel in opposition to and by the Jerusalem temple-state headed by the high priestly aristocracy as representatives of the Roman imperial order. The stories climax in Jesus' aggressive confrontation with the high priests in the temple, who finally seize him surreptitiously and hand him over to the Roman governor, Pontius Pilate, who orders him crucified. Unless we want to believe that Jesus' crucifixion was just one of the many incidents of Roman terrorization of people they had subjected, the shared collective memory embedded in the "Gospel" stories provide a highly credible explanation for why it happened. The opposition of Jesus and his movement to the Roman imperial order in Palestine and the client rulers who headed it fits the general pattern of popular renewal and resistance movements led by prophets or local kings, all (eventually) killed by the Romans (discussed in chap. 4).

Jesus' condemnation of the scribes and Pharisees for the ways their role in the temple-state in key passages in the Gospel sources, moreover,

---

8. The Matthean references to "son of David" in healing episodes (Matt 9:27; 12:22; 22:41–45) would appear to have been a development based on the Bartimaeus episode (Mark 10:46–52), as argued by Le Donne, *Historigraphical Jesus*. It remains unclear what the relationship of "son of David" may have been to "the messiah" in Israelite tradition prior to the Matthean story.

also fit the representation of the Pharisees role in non-Gospel sources. In his historical accounts Josephus describes the Pharisees as high-ranking servants of the temple-state whose "traditions of the ancestors" were included in state law (depending on their being in or out of favor with the high priestly "head-of-state," *Ant.* 13.288–298,[9] 405–409). Key episodes in the Markan story as well as the speech of woes adapted by Matthew and Luke Jesus' condemnation of the scribes and Pharisees focuses on their functions as representatives and advocates of the interests of the temple-state in ways that exploit the people (Mark 7:1–13; 12:38–44; Luke 11:37–52).

As noted in chaps. 7, 9 and 10 above, however, the Gospel stories represent the scribes and Pharisees as involved in direct conflict with Jesus during his mission in Galilee. The scribes and/or Pharisees "come down from Jerusalem" to challenge Jesus' healing and exorcism in the villages of Galilee. Early in the Markan and Matthean narratives the Pharisees (in collaboration with the Herodians) plot how to destroy him, immediately following his pointed healing of a "human being" (*anthropos*) on the sabbath in a village assembly. A few episodes later, the scribes who had come down from Jerusalem charge him with "having Beelzebul" and "casting out daimonia by the ruler of the daimonia." The Lukan narrative (as we have it in the established text) embellishes the episode of the healing of the paralytic with the seemingly parenthetic note that the Pharisees and teachers of the law sitting near "had come from every village of Galilee and Judea" as well as from Jerusalem (Luke 5:17). The Lukan narrative also stages some of the conflictual encounters between Jesus and the Pharisees at their "houses," evidently imagined as in the villages and towns that Jesus passes through (e.g., Luke 7:36–49; 14:1–6).

That the scribes and Pharisees "came down from Jerusalem" to the village assemblies in Galilee to keep Jesus under surveillance, however, does not square with what we know about them from other sources. The Gospel stories, Mark followed by Matthew and Luke, are the only contemporary sources that have the scribes and Pharisees active in

9. A lack of more critical sociological analysis behind translation of Josephus' accounts has led to a misunderstanding of the Pharisees and their role in the temple-state. In this passage (as in general), Josephus is focusing on public affairs in the temple-state in Jerusalem. In *Ant.* 13.288–98 and other accounts, the term *demos/demotikos*, which is paralleled by *to plethos*, evidently refers to the populace of Jerusalem who have confidence in (the "party" of) the Pharisees, in contrast to the wealthy and well-born (presumably the priestly aristocracy and other wealthy priests, etc.). Judean villagers do not appear to figure in this account.

Galilee. The other principal contemporary sources, the histories of Josephus, locate the Pharisees and other scribal groups in Jerusalem as the intellectual-legal retainers of the temple-state. Nothing in Josephus' accounts suggests that they were active in Judean villages, much less in the villages of Galilee after the Jerusalem high priests took control of the territory in 104 BCE. After the widespread revolts in 4 BCE, a century later, moreover, the Romans placed Galilee under Herod Antipas, ending Jerusalem jurisdiction in the territory. The only time Josephus ever portrays the Pharisees as active outside Jerusalem is as envoys of the provisional (high priestly) government in Jerusalem sent to try to hold the lid on the Galileans' resistance in 66–67, including to displace Josephus himself in that role. Without corroboration from other sources, it seems unlikely that the scribes and Pharisees would ever have been an active presence in the villages of Galilee during the time of Jesus' mission. Hence it is highly unlikely that they conducted active surveillance on Jesus' activities in the villages of Galilee and plotted with the Herodians to destroy Jesus, as portrayed in Gospel episodes. That Jesus is eating with the Pharisees in their houses (in Galilean villages) is narrative "stage-setting" to bring them into direct conflict, imaginary projection onto the historical context of Jesus' mission.

It thus seems unlikely that the heads and representatives of the temple-state in Jerusalem would have viewed Jesus' healings and exorcisms as a threat. Ancient rulers paid little attention to villages and villagers, except for collection of tithes, taxes, and tribute from the heaps of grain on threshing floors at harvest time—and of course rapid suppression of popular protests and of outbursts of social banditry, often a barometer of economic distress.[10] According to Josephus, Herod Antipas viewed the prophet John as a threat because of the widespread support his prophecies against Antipas had evoked (*Ant.* 18.116–119). But the Gospel stories make little of Jesus' opposition to Antipas, other than his mocking him as wearing fine garments and living in a "king's house" and

10. In the history of the Herodian rule in Palestine there were evidently two "exceptions that prove the rule," both the result of the rulers' oppression or provocative repression. Herod recognized that the extreme drought and famine had exacerbated his heavy taxation of his subjects so that his peasant tax-base was in danger of dying—and imported grain from Egypt to keep them alive. When the emperor Gaius ordered Roman troops to march through Galilee and Judea to install his image in the temple and numbers of Galilean peasants refused to plant their crops, Herodian officers attempted to cajole the villagers while consulting with Petronius, the Legate of Syria, about the threat to the Roman tribute.

perhaps calling him a "fox." During the lifetime of Jesus, of course, the high priests in Jerusalem did not have jurisdiction over the villages of Galilee, so probably paid little or no attention to local stirrings in Galilee. It seems unlikely that Jesus' mission would have drawn much attention from the temple-state, until Jesus and his entourage caused some sort of disruption in Jerusalem, however minor its scope. Then the movement of Jesus-loyalists that expanded in and beyond Jerusalem led by Peter and other disciples following the crucifixion of Jesus, however, would have drawn the attention of the high priests. It seems highly likely that the temple-state took measures to suppress this movement, as portrayed toward the beginning of the narrative in Acts. Paul claims to have played a role in this, motivated by his zeal for *ioudaismos* as a counter to the dominant imperial culture of Hellenism.[11]

On the other hand, from the perspective of Galilean villagers during the preceding generations, the Jerusalem temple-state and then Herod's rule were major causes of/factors in their poverty, hunger, and indebtedness. As noted in chap. 4 above, a century before the lifetime of Jesus the high priesthood had subjected the Galileans to "the laws of the Judeans," according to Josephus' account (*Ant.* 13.318). During those generations Galileans would have become at least partially habituated to, but also presumably resentful of the Jerusalem temple-state as the political-economic-religious capital from which they were ruled and taxed. After the initial Roman conquest in 63 BCE, the high priests were charged with the collection of the tribute, which added to the people's economic burden. Even though they probably did not appear in the villages, the scribes and Pharisees would have been known to the people as the officials who promulgated and cultivated the laws about matters such as tithes and offerings, sacrifices at festivals in the temple, sin-offerings, and observance of the sabbath. The scribes and Pharisees continued to play an active role as agents of the temple state during the early development of the Jesus-tradition as Jesus-movements continued the healing and community renewal in resistance to Jerusalem and other rule. Also, it is conceivable that, after the Romans had placed Galilee under the jurisdiction of Antipas instead of Jerusalem, the temple-state was trying to find ways to continue to tap resources from Galilean peasants, e.g., through

---

11. Why were the Jerusalem authorities trying to suppress (a) Jesus-movement(s)? Perhaps because it might bring the Roman military down on the whole people, as they fear in John's Gospel.

the *qorban* mechanism that was evidently included in the Pharisees' "tradition of the elders" (Mark 7:1–13).

We have good reason to doubt that the scribes and Pharisees actually "came down from Jerusalem" to keep Jesus under surveillance. Even less does the Lukan portrayal of Jesus eating with Pharisees in their houses fit the historical context known from other sources. But Jesus' healings and exorcisms and declaration that people could forgive one another's sins and his renewal of local covenantal community would have been assertions of independence of the influence (and already diminishing power) of the temple-state over village life. Thus it is understandable that the scribes and Pharisees who served as the legal retainers of the temple-state, would have become the foils for the episodes about forgiveness of sins and observance of the sabbath as these issues were addressed in the development of episodes in Gospel stories.

By the time the Matthean and Lukan stories were developed, of course, the temple-state had been destroyed by the Romans. They nevertheless include these episodes that dramatize the conflict between Jesus' mission of healing and exorcism and the official functions of the temple and priesthood according to official torah.

Critical examination of distinctive developments in Matthew and Luke and ways in which they conflict with what we know about the context of Jesus' mission in Galilee shows that they do not alter or change the common memory of Jesus-in-interaction as portrayed in all of the Gospel stories and speeches. All of these Gospel sources portray Jesus as an Israelite prophet like Moses and Elijah performing exorcisms and healings and enacting a renewal of the Mosaic covenantal community, that is, a renewal of the people in opposition to and by the rulers. The Matthean and Lukan stories, produced following the Roman devastation of the land and destruction of Jerusalem and the temple, make more explicit and systematic the fulfillment of Israelite tradition in Jesus exorcism, healing, and covenant renewal. With the historical retrospect provided by the Roman destruction of Galilee, Judea, and Jerusalem, they sharpen the political-religious conflict, discerning and articulating a wider historical significance to the interactive mission of Jesus.

The Empowerment of
Jesus' Exorcisms and Healings

STUDY AND INTERPRETATION OF the Gospels led to the recognition in New Testament studies that they were not mere collections of separate sayings and anecdotes but sustained narratives in a succession of inter-related episodes and speeches. Further analysis of the Gospel stories and speeches led to the recognition that they fit the historical context of the mission of Jesus in Galilee and beyond and its climax in Jerusalem that they portray in somewhat differing ways. The clear implications are that the Gospels as sustained stories and speeches—and not text-fragments that modern scholars extracted from those stories and speeches—are the historical sources for the historical Jesus-in-interaction (as explained in chap. 6 above).

Analysis of the implications of recent lines of research into the predominance and interrelated aspects of oral communication in antiquity leads to a more critical historical recognition of the character of the Gospel stories that are the primary sources for Jesus' mission (also surveyed in chap. 6). Given the oral communications context in the ancient world, we can no longer treat the Gospel stories as if they were archival documents, under the standard modern print-cultural assumptions that they were stable, completed written texts. The texts of the Gospels that have been "established" by generations of text critics from diverse ancient manuscripts never existed in antiquity. As leading text critics have recently indicated, the earliest manuscripts and written fragments of the Gospel stories are highly diverse, displaying what were apparently different versions of the stories. In the dominant oral communications environment of the ancient world those pluriform early manuscripts were "oral-derived" texts, that is, written copies based on continuing oral performance of the Gospel texts that had been developed (composed in performance) in Jesus-movements. While as yet we have no choice but to rely on the "average" or "mean" texts that have been established by text critics, it is important to be aware that these are approximations of texts that were developed in oral performance from the collective memory of the communities of Jesus-loyalists in which they played a significant role.

Yet it is possible, as we learn about performance of oral-derived texts from other fields, to discern the distinctive contours and features of each of these Gospel stories and set of speeches. Recognition that the Gospel stories and speeches in their early development were performed in communities forces us to recognize, in turn, that Jesus-in-interaction is embedded in those stories and speeches and in the Jesus-movements in which they were developed. What we are after is the interaction and communication of Jesus with people that resonated with them so that they were remembered in ever-developing stories and speeches. But we cannot pretend to separate the interaction and the memory of the interaction and development of the memory in the Gospel stories and speeches.

It was thus only appropriate to investigate and appreciate the Gospel stories and speeches knowledgably, sensitively, and critically by adapting performance theory developed from analysis of oral performance of complex texts in other fields (as in the provisional attempts in chaps. 7–10 above, adapting the work of theorist John Miles Foley). Then it was possible to compare the Gospel stories and speeches as they assumed and referenced the historical context with that context as known from other sources. On the basis of these double comparisons it was possible to discern what aspects of Jesus-in-interaction they have in common, how aspects of those portrayals may fit or not fit the historical context as known from other sources, and what appears to be idiosyncratic to particular Gospel stories and may not fit the historical context (chap. 11). In this approach it is possible to discern some of central aspects of the common collective social memory of Jesus-in-interaction as they are embedded in different Jesus-movements and developed into particular Gospel stories and speeches, and to distinguish them from developments of that social memory that are distinctive to particular Gospel stories and the movements in which they emerged.

In what appears to have been the common collective memory of Jesus-in-interaction shared by the different Gospel stories and speeches, the principal actions of Jesus, that were manifestations of the direct rule of God, were exorcisms and healings in the village communities of Galilee and beyond. As presented in the Gospel stories, the exorcisms and healings led to a renewal of Mosaic covenantal community, which in turn led to more exorcisms and healings, as the fame of Jesus spread and people came seeking healing.

According to the portrayal in all of the Gospel sources, in interactive acts of power Jesus was generating collective power among the people in a movement of the renewal of the people of Israel in opposition to and by the rulers in Roman Palestine. By building on the steps of new research and critical analysis outlined in earlier chapters it is possible to construct a more comprehensive multifaceted understanding of the exorcisms and healings of Jesus in his interactive mission in historical context. Recent studies of sickness and healing by critical medical anthropologists and others lead to consideration of personal, social, and political-economic factors that may well have been involved in the sickness and healing and in the spirit-possession and exorcism (chap. 3). Moving underneath the standard synthetic modern constructs of New Testament studies makes it possible to discern the complex and conflict-filled historical situation in Roman Palestine (chap. 4). Recognition that the Gospel sources for Jesus-in-interaction are the sustained Gospel narratives and speeches facilitates the recognition of social forms, social relations, and political-economic conflicts that simply did not appear in analysis of isolated text fragments—and/or were hidden by the synthetic constructs of "(early) Judaism" and "(early) Christianity" (chaps. 6–10).[1]

General and Particular Conditions of the People

The sicknesses experienced by people are directly related to the conditions in which they live, as medical anthropologists have explained. The conditions in which villagers in Galilee, Judea, and nearby areas were

1. In composing this concluding chapter I purposely did not consult my earlier discussion in *Jesus and Magic*, chaps. 8–10. I wanted this concluding chapter to arise from the complex sequence of steps taken in the preceding chapters. While there is considerable continuity in my analysis and discussion from seven years ago, this chapter aims at a more comprehensive analysis, understanding, and "explanation" of Jesus' interactive exorcism and healing in his renewal of Israel.

living has been summarized in chap. 4, mainly on the basis of references in extra-Gospel sources. The Gospel stories confirm and extend those indications. As examination of memory of Jesus' mission (in the development of oral tradition among Jesus-loyalists) have indicated, the teaching and actions of Jesus-in-interaction were remembered as they resonated with the people (and were not just transmitted or "handed-down" from one individual to another). The combination of evidence from different sources indicates that the general condition of the people, with particular variations according to location, was subsistence living that had become threatened by the devastation of repeated Roman conquests and the demands for tribute, taxes, and tithes from multiple layers of rulers.

The assumption in Gospel narratives and speeches is that the people are poor, hungry, seriously in debt, and anxious about sufficient food and shelter. Most poignant are the people's petitions in the Lord's Prayer for subsistence food and cancellation of debts. The prophetic pronouncement at the beginning of the covenant renewal speeches that the direct rule of God will mean relief of poverty and hunger is a further indication of the addressees' poverty, hunger, and discouragement. Jesus' condemnation of the scribes and Pharisees in all of the Gospel stories and speeches indicates how the chronic conditions of poverty among the people are directly related to the demands of their rulers and their representatives. Episodes in the Markan narrative have Jesus condemn the Pharisees for siphoning off to the temple people's resources needed to feed their families. He later warns that the scribes' encouraging support of the temple has the effect of "devouring widows' living." As "heard" in the previous four chapters, the Gospel stories recount several episodes of negative examples of rulers and/or other wealthy expanding their wealth at the expense of needy people, leaving them further in debt and hunger, which inevitably meant undernourished. The effects of such conditions on people are by now well-known.

The Cultural Understanding of Sicknesses and Possession in the Gospel Stories

Medical anthropologists' insistence that sickness and healing are culturally defined suggests that it is important to examine the (Greek) terms and phrases used with reference to the sicknesses of the people who were coming or being brought to Jesus for healing. The point is to discern the connotations of the terms in the context of the Gospel stories and their historical context—and not rely on standard translations that often lessen the seriousness of the sicknesses and/or distort them as "diseases" that can be miraculously "cured."

Sicknesses

As medical anthropologists emphasize, it is important to attend to the personal and social aspects of sickness, even the political-economic or colonial aspects in the process of the "social production" of illness and the social "manufacture" of madness as the people adjust to outside forces (discussed in chap. 3 above). Critical medical anthropologists go so far as to speak of a "political-economy of brutality," and as recent historical studies have shown, the systematic brutality of Roman conquest and reconquest of subject peoples—slaughter, enslavement, destruction, and crucifixion—was a vivid historical example.[2] As medical anthropologists explain, moreover, the impact of the historical political-economic forces that produce sickness also affect subject peoples' cultural understanding of sickness. What might seem like separate incidents of sickness or a small-scale local malaise have a much broader context in large-scale political-economic structures and historical events. The following survey seeks to be aware that sicknesses to which Jesus responds in the Gospel stories were not just "somatic," and were certainly not "diseases" that he "cured" (vs. recent mistranslations).[3] They were at least "psychosomatic" and even "social-psycho-somatic," with the "social" dimension understood broadly as possibly including political-economic factors.

2. For example, Mattern, *Rome and the Enemy*; application to Roman Palestine (and, for example, the historical accounts of Josephus) in Horsley, *Jesus and Empire*, chap. 2; and chap. 4 above.

3. In a series of articles collected in *Healing in the New Testament*, 13, 25, 59–60, 93, that offer several (helpfully) simplified summaries of Arthur Kleinman's cultural medical anthropological theory (in *Patients and Healers*) and applies them to the Gospels, John Pilch notes that the illnesses Jesus healed cannot be understood in terms of biomedicine. Crossan, *Jesus: A Revolutionary Biography*, 80–82, argues that people in the Gospel stories were suffering from both diseases and illnesses, an anachronistic distinction resulting from the modern development of biomedicine. Sharp criticism of both Pilch and Crossan in Craffert, "Medical Anthropology as an Antidote," 8–11. The earlier application of cultural medical anthropological theory to the healings of Jesus in the Gospel stories does not appear to have taken into account the more recent work of critical medical anthropologists (discussed in chap. 3 above).

The summaries in the Gospel stories offer what appear to have been standard phrases in reference to the various kinds of sickness. The summaries in the Markan story (1:32, 34) speak of "those having [something that affects them] badly," evidently sicknesses with varying degrees of suffering. Matthean summaries have Jesus and the disciples healing *pasan noson kai pasan malakian* (4:23; 9:35; 10:1) among the people, which seems appropriately translated as "every sickness and every illness." These *nosoi* could vary in severity, so that the connotations might be suffering, distress, anguish, plague, or madness.

These terms for various sicknesses that Jesus heals are paired in the summaries with possession by *daimonia* or unclean spirits that he casts out, associating the sicknesses with seemingly far more serious problems. Moreover, the Gospel stories use other terms that make the sicknesses sound more ominous. As mentioned at the outset of chap. 3, they are characterized as *mastix/mastigai*, a term that referred widely to the whipping, flogging, beating, or scourging of horses, slaves, soldiers, prisoners, those being examined under torture, or those the Romans condemned to crucifixion, a gruesome slow torturous form of public execution (as in Mark 10:34; Matt 10:17; 23:34; Josephus, *War* 2.306). Jesus was flogged and then crucified, the envoys he commissioned would be flogged, as the prophets had been flogged and killed before them (Mark 10:34; Matt 10:17; 20:19; 23:34; Luke 18:33). *Mastix* thus compares the torment of sickness to being beaten by the political authorities, suggesting extreme suffering under some plague or scourge (such as the woman who had been hemorrhaging for twelve years, Mark 5:29; cf. Mark 3:10; Luke 7:21). Another term used was *basanos*, which commonly referred to torture, torment, or serious pain. The sense can be discerned in the exorcism episodes in which the spirits that have possessed people cry out to Jesus not to torment them (Mark 5:6–7; Matt 4:24). The grand summary in the first narrative step of the Matthean story gives a sense of the range of sicknesses that Jesus healed: those coming to Jesus "brought with them all those who were afflicted with sicknesses (*vosoi*) and torments (*basanoi*) of all kinds, along with those who were spirit-possessed and those who were suffering seizures and paralysis."[4]

4. An important first step toward fuller appreciation of the seriousness of the sicknesses that Jesus healed, as presented in the Gospel stories, would thus be deliberately to avoid the standard recent reductionist and misleading translations of terms such as *nosoi*, *basanoi*, and *mastigoi* as "diseases" (e.g., in the NRSV)—and to substitute more appropriate translations, such as "sicknesses, plagues, and torments."

As discussed in chap. 3, among the points made by critical medical anthropologists was that the effects of indigenous and/or outside rulers on sickness and how it is understood may be as important as the (prior) indigenous understanding.[5] It would be too simple (monocausal) to suggest that Roman and/or Herodian violence in brutalizing the subjected people was the only and direct cause of such sicknesses. But the use of terms that were also used for flogging or torture by the authorities or military do suggest that (some of) their sicknesses were experienced as related to their violent subjugation in which their neighbors, parents, or grandparents or people in nearby villages had been killed or enslaved or maimed and their villages destroyed and crops seized. The excruciating and prolonged torture of trouble-makers by public crucifixion that inflicted torture on the social body as well was designed as a way of terrorizing subject peoples into submission. The traumas experienced would have had lasting effects on the people. Just as political-economic forces left their traces on recent southern Italian peasant women,[6] it seems likely they would also have made an impact on the personal and social body of recently conquered and reconquered Galileans (and peoples of Syria nearby).

The particular episodes of healing in the Markan story, many of which also appear in the Matthean and Lukan stories, are of a man with skin lesions (*lepra*), a paralytic, a fellow with a withered hand, a dying young woman, a woman with prolonged hemorrhaging, a deaf-mute, the blind man of Bethsaida, and blind Bartimaeus. Matthew and Luke have the centurion's servant who is crippled, Matthew has other blind people, and Luke has other people who are paralyzed or afflicted with skin lesions. There is a fairly close correspondence between these "sicknesses" and those that appear in Jesus' answer to John the Baptist's question about the coming one: "the blind see, the lame walk, the lepers are cleansed, the deaf hear, the dead are raised, and the poor have good news brought to them." Blindness, deafness, skin-lesions, and short life-expectancy may

---

5. As if the "indigenous" understanding of sickness had ever been independent of outside forces. In earlier generations anthropologists often proceeded on the assumption that the peoples/cultures they studied were independent of outside influences. That assumption appears (in retrospect on Western academic studies) to have been historically naive. While the impact of outside forces would not always have been as severe as under European colonialism and then the "globalization" of capitalist industries, "indigenous" peoples had not been somehow immune from indirect or direct outside forces.

6. As indicated in a recent study by Pandolfi, "Boundaries Inside the Body." 255.

well be (have been) problems in any agrarian society in which people live near subsistence, at best, and are often malnourished. But agrarian people are almost always subject to rulers who control them and make demands on their produce. That Jesus' response to John references the longings of the Israelite people who had been subject to one empire after another for healing of just these kinds of malaise, moreover, suggests that the people experienced them as the typical sufferings or plagues of being subjugated by imperial domination. That the healing of the blind, deaf, and lame are linked with release of captives (prisoners) and with proclamation of good news to the poor in the longings of the people (Isa 35:5–6; 42:6–7; 61:1–2) and in Jesus' reference to his actions adds to the impression that the people understood just these kinds of malaise and suffering as related to their subjugation by imperial rulers. Paralysis could have been an effective self-control of the impulse to strike out in resentment, at a considerable cost to one's life. It is also conceivable that, as critical medical anthropologists suggest, paralysis or lameness or a withered hand might be a form of resistance to the demands of rulers, at a considerable cost to oneself and one's family.

Finally, in surveying the understanding of sicknesses in the Gospel stories and speeches, it should be noted that they do not separate different aspects of personal and communal life. There is no separation of religion from the rest of life, or no separation of sickness from hunger. This is illustrated in the sequence of episodes in the Markan story of observance of the sabbath and ensuing healing on the sabbath. Blindness, for example, was related to malnutrition. That sickness was understood in Israelite culture as due to sinning, in not observing the commandments, may well have resulted in people expending their life-energy in self-blame rather than in supporting their own health.

Spirit-Possession

In both the narrative sequences and the summary statements of Jesus' actions in the Gospel stories Jesus' healings of severe sicknesses are paired with his exorcisms of *daimonia* that had possessed some of the people.[7]

---

7. As noted in chap. 5, it became standard in Christian theology and New Testament studies to translate and conceptualize these spirits as "demons," even as "evil demons." The terms *daimonia/daimones* in Greek and Hellenistic culture, however, referred to a class of semi-divine beings that were trans-human and superhuman, and could exert benign and/or malign influence on people, depending on the context and

For a sense of how spirits and spirit-possession were experienced and understood among the ordinary people in the villages of Galilee, Judea, and nearby areas, we are dependent primarily on the Gospel representations themselves. Yet, as mentioned in chap. 6, we may also be able to derive some impressions indirectly by comparison with Judean scribal texts that suddenly focus on malign and benign heavenly forces/spirits in late second-temple times.[8]

Spirits and spirit possession appear in an *ad hoc* way in the Gospel stories and exorcism episodes, in contrast with the elaborate schematic and systematic portrayal in Judean scribal texts of the late second temple period of the two opposing hordes of heavenly forces engaged in a struggle for control of historical life (discussed in chap. 5). Texts such as the Book of Watchers (1 Enoch 1–36) and the Animal Vision (1 Enoch 85–95) presented visionary versions of a fundamental conflict in the divine governance of history in which rebel heavenly forces had generated a race of giants who launched violent military invasion and economic exploitation. The book of Jubilees had the maleficent forces headed by Mastema (10:7–8). In the most schematic worldview, the Community Rule and the War Rule of the Qumran community understood their life and history subject to the on-going struggle between two camps of spirits, the forces of Light and those of Darkness headed by Belial. Community members were subject to temptation and affliction by the malign spirits, but evidently not to individual possession. Adherence to the community and its discipline and rituals provided protection.

The Gospel stories present spirits in an unschematic way. There is no dualism of warring camps of heavenly forces. In the more popular sense of spirits in the Gospel sources they are rather described in terms

---

circumstances. In the Gospel stories they have afflicted and invaded/possessed people. But "demons" (and especially "evil demon") is too strong and "demonizing" a term. It thus seems only appropriate, as noted previously, to use the transliteration of the Greek term *daimonia* instead of "demons" in our attempt to understand the Gospels' representations.

8. In the late-twentieth century some interpreters (such as Stephan Davies, *Jesus the Healer*; Crossan, *Jesus: A Revolutionary Biography*) applied concepts and diagnoses previously current in psychological/psychiatric circles, such as "multiple personality" or "transference." Those diagnoses/constructs projected the integrated personality that had become normative in recent generations of Western culture onto people in antiquity. Heeding the insistence of medical anthropologists that sickness is culturally defined, however, it should be taken seriously that both Gospel episodes and texts from Judean scribal circles understand spirit possession in terms of invasion by outside superhuman forces.

of individual and community experiences. While scribal texts mention spirit affliction, Gospel episodes speak of spirit possession, in which superhuman spirits invade and control the behavior of people. Although there are few episodes of particular appearance and exorcism, spirits and possession are represented as frequent and nearly ubiquitous in the villages that Jesus and his envoys visited. In some of the narrative summaries and in the episodes of commissioning the disciples to extend Jesus' mission, spirit-possession and power over them seem to have relatively more importance than healing.

Spirits are many. Spirits that enter into a person have both an individual and a collective aspect, even in the same episode, as in the village assembly in Capernaum and in the village community among the Gerasenes/Gadarenes. The symptoms of possession could be ad hoc or chronic. In the case in the Capernaum assembly it seems that it was the presence of the outside prophet-exorcist that evoked the sudden manifestation of bizarre behavior of the possessed person; yet the symptoms had been evident to the community before. The spirits were experienced as superhuman in strength so that they overpowered the human host they possessed. They caused a variety of symptoms that were at least debilitating for the possessed person, who might become violently self-destructive, as in the case of the son who throws himself into the fire. In the most extreme case, that of "Legion," the spirit(s) drove the possessed fellow not only to self-destructive violence but to violence against the wider community that bound him in chains among the tombs to control his violent behavior.

Although the spirits are many and their possession of people is one of the principal factors that must be overcome in bringing about the direct rule of God in the Gospel narratives and speeches, they do not appear to be coordinated or to have a leader. That Satan was the ruler of the spirits/*daimonia* was evidently a scribal view, part of the accusation that the scribes/Pharisees brought against Jesus, as evident from the critical "hearing" of the Beelzebul controversy in Mark and Q in chaps. 7 and 8. It has been a Christian theological reading of these episodes that has identified "the strong man" as Satan and "his goods/vessels" as the *daimonia*. In his rare appearances in the Gospel stories, as in his rare appearances in texts later included in the Hebrew Bible, Satan is principally the tempter/tester (as discussed in chap. 7). The Lukan story includes an episode about a woman with a spirit that had crippled her for eighteen years that Jesus interprets as or compares to Satan having bound her (Luke 13:10–17). At most, however, that episode has Satan acting as a spirit, not as the ruler of the spirits. The closest any of the Gospel stories comes to linking Satan with the (other) spirits is the Lukan narrative sequence in which, when the seventy envoys report back to Jesus that "even the *daimonia* submit to us in your name," he replies "I watched Satan fall from heaven like a flash of lightning" (Luke 10:1–16, 17–20). This unique "flash" of scribal lore in the Lukan story, however, is hardly a sufficient basis for claiming that among the people with whom Jesus worked or in the movements that produced the Gospel stories, Satan was understood as "the ruler of the *daimonia*."

While the popular experience of spirit-possession evident in the Gospel stories offers no parallel to the schematic understanding of an all controlling conflict between hordes of heavenly forces in some scribal circles, a significant parallel to the scribal understanding appears in the episode of spirit-possession among the Gerasenes/Gadarenes. The War Scroll and other texts from the Qumran community were explicit in their understanding: the "Kittim," the community's code name for the Romans, were being controlled and driven by the spirits of Darkness headed by Belial in their conquest and control of the people of Israel.[9] In the Markan and Lukan story the identity of the possessing spirit(s) who drives the possessed fellow to such violence against himself and the community turns out to be "Legion," that is Roman troops. After the spirits beg not to be thrown out of the country they had invaded/possessed, moreover, they are portrayed in military terms, as a "division/company" that, under "orders from a commander," "charged" down the bank.

That Judean scribal circles, for more than two centuries, had made a direct link between the conquest of the people by the Hellenistic and then especially the Roman imperial armies and maleficent spirits makes it difficult not to take seriously the identity of the spirit(s) in this episode. Starting with the Roman conquest of the eastern Mediterranean in 63 BCE, the peoples living in Syria and especially Palestine experienced repeated (re-)conquests of great brutality, in destruction of villages and slaughter and enslavement of villagers (as discussed in chap. 4). The Markan and Lukan accounts of violent possession suggest that Palestinian villagers also identified some of the forces that had invaded and

9. As discussed in chap. 6, the War Scroll describes how the Qumran community itself, in its control by and intimate interrelation with the spirits of light, engaged in ritual drills for how they would participate with the spirits of light in the eventual determinative battle against the spirits of Darkness and the Kittim/Romans.

possessed them as the spirits of the Roman troops—just as peoples in East Africa and further south identified their invasive spirits as the *khawajat* (light-skinned spirits of Europeans invaders) or the *maregimente* and the *mapolic*.

Certain features of the "Legion" episode suggest that the spirits were possessing not just the fellow exhibiting the bizarre violence but the whole people (and that the exorcism of the spirits from the fellow had serious implications for the whole people). That the spirits beg Jesus not to "send them out of the country" indicates that they had invaded and had been possessing the people in general. That the people of the surrounding country ask Jesus to leave suggests that exorcism and exposure of what the spirits represented (Roman troops) had upset the *modus vivendi* that had been established in the possession by spirits that had been focused on a few people.

Earlier generations of New Testament scholars dismissed or denigrated belief in spirits and "demons" as delusional and unscientific, something that scientific-minded people knew were utterly unreal. Critical medical anthropologists—and before them Frantz Fanon—discerned that fear of and possession by spirits, while a mystification of their concrete situation, was also some colonized peoples' defense against their subjugation, an alternative to an aggressive reaction that would only have led to their destruction by the colonial/imperial rulers.[10] As attested in Josephus' historical accounts, Galilean and Judean villagers would have been all too familiar with how, in suppressing revolt, the Roman Empire sent in the legions to slaughter or enslave villagers, destroy villages, and crucify fugitives they suspected as agitators. They also saw how the Roman governors sent out their military to kill bands of brigands and even the (unarmed) movements anticipating new divine deliverance. Focusing their fear and anxiety on *daimonia* instead of on Roman military retaliation was self-protective. A social-psycho-somatic analysis of this episode would suggest also that their possession by the spirits "Legion" was the way the community achieved a certain *modus vivendi* with their situation under Roman rule. The fellow possessed by Legion embodied and enacted the violence of their subjection by the Romans. The community's

10. Fanon, *Wretched of the Earth*; see the section "On Violence." Critical medical anthropologists suggest that in some cases spirit possession or hysteria is a form of resistance to the invasive outside forces, as when the young women factory workers in Malasia, in effect, refused to work in the intolerable conditions of their labor (discussed in chap. 3).

restraints of the man's violence also represented their restraint of whatever impulses they had to strike out against their own subjugation. The people's mystification ("misrepresentation") of the cause of their subjugation also enabled them to continue in their traditional way of life, albeit seriously altered by spirit possession and fear of sprits.

Speculation That Jesus Himself Was Possessed

It has been argued that Jesus himself was spirit-possessed, largely on the basis of studies of spirit-possession in other cultures, often by social scientists who construct a pattern that they claim occurs in many cultures.[11] Drawing on text-fragments or episodes from here and there in the different Gospel stories, the thesis of Jesus' possession depends on some of the same passages as the "apocalyptic" reading of Jesus defeating Satan as "the strong man" and ruler of the demons in a "cosmic" battle. Jesus' forty days in the wilderness (Mark 1:12–13) and his fasting (Luke 4// Matt 4) are taken as a way of inducing an "altered state of consciousness" (trance/vision experience/soul journey). The ("bodily") descent of the Holy Spirit upon Jesus at his baptism and his being filled with the Spirit in the wilderness and in his return to Galilee (Luke 4:1, 14) is taken as a reference to his own personal experience of being taken over by the Spirit. That "those around him" think he had "gone out of his mind" (the NRSV translation of Mark 3:21) is taken as being possessed by some sort of spirit, giving the scribes the opportunity of charging that he "has Beelzebul." One suspects, however, that the "model" (of "altered state of consciousness," or of "shamanism") derived from cross-cultural studies is what controls these readings of various passages.[12]

11. For a recent presentation of this thesis, see Craffert, *The Life of a Galilean Shaman*, chap. 8. Having taken into account the cultural medical anthropologists' point about possession being culturally defined (that is, by the particular culture in which it occurs), Craffert includes examination of Israelite religious traditions (204–8); but he constructs his "Social-Type Model" (based in an "alternative state of consciousness" pattern) from earlier cross-cultural studies and earlier synthetic discussion of "shamanism." Criticism of Craffert's construction and of the earlier studies he relies on in Strecker, "The Duty of Discontent."

12. The Jewish philosopher Philo of Alexandria, heavily influenced by (and a principal source for the continuing development of Platonic philosophy in) Hellenistic intellectual circles, describes a certain mania-ecstasy in which a higher spirit drives out the (rational) mind. This mania-ecstasy discussed in elite intellectual circles, however, should not be projected onto the Gospel stories—in the way that Philo projects such

Taken rather as components in the narrative of the different Gospels these episodes contribute to a story of Jesus' mission rooted in distinctively Israelite tradition and social-cultural context. The descent of the Spirit symbolizes and signals the divine designation of Jesus for his mission. The Lukan narrative gives special emphasis to his empowerment by the Spirit as he enters the temptation and launches his mission in Galilee. His forty days in the wilderness suggest that he was tested in preparation for his mission just as Elijah had been. Both the Matthean and the Lukan narratives indicate that his fasting left him "famished" and vulnerable to the *temptations* of the devil. In the Markan narrative he is besieged by the crowds clamoring for him to heal and especially to cast out spirits so that he is "out of his mind" in the sense of "astounded" or "astonished," using the same term as for the people's astonishment in previous and subsequent episodes (of healing, 2:12; 5:42). This is the most intense that the pressure from the crowds has become, following earlier episodes or summaries in which he must be extricated from the situation (Mark 1:35; 3:7–10; cf. 2:2). Of course Jesus may well have experienced some sort of empowerment by the Spirit. But it seems doubtful that an experience of seizure is what the Gospel narratives are about or to which they provide access.

The Inseparable Dimensions of
Jesus' Healings and Exorcisms

Were we interested only in the portrayals of Jesus' exorcisms and healings in the Gospel stories and speeches, this project could have concluded with chapters 7–10. Those chapters will hopefully be helpful for appreciation of the Gospel stories and speeches as they were performed in and affected the communities of the respective Jesus movements in which they were developed. Now we may be able to use the Gospel stories in performance in those communities as sources through which to discern and understand the exorcisms and healings of Jesus in interaction (as central to his renewal of Israel). Contrary to the assumption and procedure standard in many studies of "the historical Jesus," however, Jesus' mission is not accessible by stripping away the Gospel narratives in order to expose sayings and elements in "miracle stories" that seem to "go back to" Jesus. The mission of Jesus rather is doubly embedded. It is embedded

---

mania-ecstasy onto figures such as Abraham or Moses in authoritative Jewish texts.

in the social memory of the movements that developed in response to Jesus' interaction with people, and that social memory in turn is embedded in the Gospel stories and speeches as they were developed and performed in particular Jesus movements.

An appropriate way to proceed would seem to be to analyze some of the aspects or dimensions of the healings and exorcisms that we discern in the Gospel narratives and speeches. These aspects are not separable in the Gospel narratives and also would not have been separable in the interaction of Jesus with others in historical context as it was remembered in Jesus-movements and the Gospel texts in performance. Nor is one dimension of the healings and exorcisms logically or chronologically prior to another. But distinguishing and focusing on these interrelated aspects may help us more fully appreciate and understand the healings and exorcisms as central to Jesus' interactive mission.

Sickness and Healing, Possession and Exorcism in Supportive Networks and Community

The most clearly distinguishable dimensions of Jesus' healings and exorcisms in the Gospel stories is that they *happened in supportive communities or networks of people and affected whole communities.* They were most definitely not the individual actions by Jesus and not actions simply on individuals. Modern interpreters' projection of modern individualism is quite inappropriate, as is the further heroization and even divinization of Jesus beyond what has already happened in the Gospel portrayals.

Sickness and spirit possession involved far more than individuals.[13] Portrayals in the Gospel stories resemble what medical anthropologists found in their studies: *sicknesses* were experienced and *dealt with primarily in the family and/or network of friends and neighbors.* This is evident repeatedly in both the healing episodes and the exorcism episodes in the Markan story, most of them paralleled in the Matthean and/or Lukan stories.[14]

13. Scholarly investigation (esp. in form-criticism) of healing and exorcism stories is that the standard form they follow involves only two characters, Jesus and the individual afflicted. This is misleading about many of the episodes. It is simply wrong about the healings and exorcisms in narrative context and understood in the historical context presupposed in the episodes.

14. As discussed in chap. 3 and mentioned again in chap. 5, it would be anachronistic to imagine that there was a "health-care system" with different sectors in Roman

The illnesses involve families, support networks, and village communities, who are concerned and struggling to care for their family or community members. The Markan narrative mentions this in most episodes. Peter's mother-in-law's fever has Peter and other disciples concerned. Most obvious is the episode of the paralytic, in which the group of friends carrying the fellow on a pallet were evidently a local network that had been struggling to care for the fellow. That the deaf man and the (first) blind man in the Markan story are brought by other people suggest that local networks had taken on the burden of their care. The twelve-year-old woman has a father and family and community concerned that she is near death.

In the Matthean story, the centurion and his household have been caring for the son/servant. The Matthean narrative usually includes the support group, as in the episodes of the paralytic, the twelve-year-old young woman, and the blind and mute fellow in introduction to the Beelzebul charge (9:2–8; 9:18–26; 12:22). In the healing episodes that appear only in the Lukan story, as well, both the woman with infirmity and the man with dropsy were long-lasting cases well-known to their respective communities. Summaries in the Gospel stories, moreover, assume or make explicit the same situation, with concerned and care-giving family and/or neighbors bringing those who are sick to Jesus and begging for healing (see esp. Mark 6:54–56, and the programmatic first summary in Matthew 4:23–25; 8:16; 14:34–36). Family and friends were affected by the sicknesses, were involved in care, and active in seeking healing.

Spirit possession also affected and *involved* not just individuals but *families and communities.* The first spirit-possession and exorcism episode in the Markan story happens in the midst of the gathering of the local Capernaum village assembly on the Sabbath. Although the episode does not indicate how often the spirit possession was manifest in unusual or bizarre behavior, it assumes that such possession was common, the unclean spirit indicates that there were many spirits, and the subsequent narrative indicates repeatedly that spirit possession was common. That spirit possession affects whole communities could not be more dramatic than in the episode of the demoniac in a village of the Gerasenes/ Gadarenes. The possessing spirit had driven the fellow to severe violence against others and against himself. In this case, however, the villagers were not taking care of the possessed fellow, but protecting themselves

---

Palestine.

(and him, in a way) from his violent behavior. They had repeatedly put him in restraints that he had burst with uncanny strength. He appeared from out of the tombs where his neighbors had attempted to keep him in chains. By contrast, the mother of the spirit-possessed girl in the region of Tyre and Sidon had become desperate for help while attempting to care for her daughter. The boy who is convulsed by a spirit not only makes his father desperate for relief, but family and community and the "whole crowd" also must struggle with the bizarre behavior of the "moon-struck" boy.

A part of or a continuation of a healing, moreover, is that *Jesus restores the healed person to the family and the village.*[15] As would have been known by hearers familiar with Israelite culture, a result of being "made clean" would have been to enable the fellow with skin lesions to rejoin social interaction in his community. The healing of the paralytic not only enables him to again become active in household and village, but results in renewal of the local community now empowered with permission to forgive one another's sins. Jesus instructs the family and friends of the twelve-your-old woman near death to give her some nourishment as she rejoins the family and community. Even when Jesus takes a deaf and/or blind fellow aside for the healing gesture, the healed fellow now hearing or seeing returns to social interaction in the family or community. Only in episodes used to make certain other narrative points, such as that of Bar-Timaeus, does the healed person "follow him on the way." The commission of the twelve is to cast out the possessing spirits and heal the sicknesses of the whole communities as they exorcise and heal particular people. Some of the healed become active in the movement as it expands. Peter's mother-in-law's arising to 'serve them' suggests a role in the wider movement. The fellow made "clean" of skin lesions and the fellow freed from possession by "Legion" both become active carriers of the message of renewal.

As portrayed in the Gospel stories and speeches, moreover, Jesus' exorcisms and healings had restorative effects on families and communities, the fundamental social-economic forms of the people's life that were disintegrating under the impact of Roman conquest and economic

---

15. Both Pilch (*Healing in the New Testament*, 13, 25, 59–60, 93) and Crossan, (*Jesus: A Revolutionary Biography*, 80–82) recognize that in the Gospel portrayals Jesus reintegrated the healed into "society." It is not clear how this fits with Crossan's construction of healings and exorcisms as individual acts of magic or with his main thesis that Jesus' authentic sayings summon individuals to an individual itinerant life-style.

pressures. Again and again in the Markan story, and in the other Gospels as well, the narrative states that Jesus' mission of healing and exorcism was in villages, often in the village assemblies, and often in the sabbath gatherings of those assemblies. Just as illnesses and spirit possession affected and involved families and networks of neighbors, so also the healings and exorcisms affected them, sometimes dramatically, and usually (though not always) the effect was restorative of community well-being.

Several episodes indicate or suggest a variety of *restorative effects*. The first exorcism, in Capernaum, performed in the village assembly, frees the village community from the effects of the spirit(s) that had possessed one of its members. The villagers exclaim that Jesus is exercising power for the good of the people, acting with authority/power for them, in contrast to the scribal representatives of the temple-state, who do not. In several healing episodes the healed return, or Jesus returns them, to their families and communities. In some episodes, after families and/or other villagers seeking healing for their loved ones, they then welcome their restoration to the family and community. In the Capernaum community, which is probably meant to be representative, the people witness and also receive the authority to forgive sins, making it possible to share in the offering of new life in the wider community. The Markan version suggests this clearly in the 'son of man' idiom; the Matthean version makes this explicit.[16]

The Gospel narratives that Jesus' exorcisms and healings that were liberating and healing for village communities were *also restorative and renewing for the people of Israel*. This is explicit in Jesus commissioning the Twelve and/or seventy disciples to extend his healing and exorcism into other villages. But it is also indicated symbolically in some of the healing episodes. Anthropologists and others have long since recognized that the individual body can be representative of the social body as a whole, and such symbolism is evident in the Gospel healing episodes in which the sickness is typical of what people were experiencing in Galilee and nearby areas under Roman rule. It is particularly clear in the interwoven narrative of the sickness and healing of the woman who has been

16. As explained in chap. 7, the Aramaic idiom behind *ho huios tou anthropou* in Greek referred to "humanity" or "people" and could be used as a self-reference (in the "third person," like "one" in English, or "yours truly"). This is how it could come to be used as a visionary/dream image for "the people of the saints of the Most High," as in Daniel 7. In the Gospels it comes to be a self-reference of Jesus, at points of the exalted Jesus. In the Markan episodes of the paralytic and of observance of the sabbath it refers to both "people/humanity" and (exalted) Jesus.

hemorrhaging for twelve years and the twelve-year-old woman who is near death. The symbolism of *twelve* signals that they are representative of Israel as a whole, that traditionally consisted (at least symbolically) of twelve tribes. The woman who had been hemorrhaging for twelve years symbolizes a whole people that had been "hemorrhaging" its life blood in subjugation and the expropriation of its crops by multiple layers of rulers. But by her trust and the trust of the people in the power flowing through Jesus she and they were enabled to be made whole again (to be "saved," *sozo*). The twelve-year-old woman, daughter of a leader of the local assembly, who is near death, making it difficult for her family and the community to trust that she is not simply dead, is symbolic of a whole people that is near death. Lest we miss another aspect of the symbolism of the twelve-year-old, that is, about the age of puberty, her restoration to life (and being given something to eat) symbolized new life for the people, who would now be able to reproduce in their renewal. The episode of the wilderness feeding that follows upon the interwoven healings of the women confirms that their sickness and healing were symbolic of the whole people. After the people, perpetually hungry, suddenly have sufficient nourishment, twelve baskets of pieces are gathered, suggesting continuing sufficiency for the people.

While the exorcisms and healings are liberating and healing for whole communities, however, they are *also potentially disturbing*. The exorcism of the possessed fellow in the countryside of the Gerasenes/Gadarenes dramatizes the potential problem for the people still subject to the Roman imperial order in Palestine. One can imagine that the local village community, who had been suffering violence from the possessed fellow and struggled to control his manic behavior, would be relieved to have the invasive spirit(s) cast out. But the exorcism also involves the identification of the spirit(s) as "Legion," (the spirits of) the invasive Roman troops who had repeatedly devastated their villages and killed or enslaved the people. This demystification or exposure of the causes of the malaise and dysfunction in the village communities or towns threatened to disrupt the *modus vivendi* that the people had reached with Roman rule that allowed them to maintain some community life, albeit with the violence now embodied in neighbor against neighbors. The people asked Jesus to leave, not yet having come to the trust in Jesus' exorcism and able to "hear" or trust (the story) that "Legion" would somehow self-destruct by its own violent behavior (the "battalion" of swine "charging" down the hill into "the Sea" whence it had come to "occupy" the country). In addition to that sobering episode, the episodes of Jesus sending out envoys to exorcise and heal indicate that some villages were not receptive to the mission. The woes in the mission discourse adapted in both Luke and Matthew connect this with the "(acts of) power(s). And, that the problem villages named include Capernaum along with nearby villages suggest that whole communities were involved in positive or negative reception of Jesus' and his disciples' mission—and that a positive response might later turn negative.

Jesus' Healings and Exorcisms were Relational and Interactive

Nearly all the episodes of healing and exorcism are interactive. Throughout the Gospel stories Jesus is represented as the agent of healing and exorcism—and then after he has empowered his disciples to cast out spirits and heal, they also are the agents. Jesus' healings and exorcisms, however, are not simply matters of his action, in word and/or gesture. They involve interaction or even an interactive process, at least with the person seeking healing or the possessing spirit, and often with others as well.

Jesus is the Agent of the Healings and Exorcisms

Contrary to the modern construction of "miracle" that has been projected onto the exorcism and healing episodes in the Gospel stories, Jesus and not God or the Holy Spirit or some "supernatural" force is the agent of the exorcism and healings. As indicated in the survey of the Gospel narratives and speeches in chap. 1, these were the principal actions in which Jesus was engaged in his renewal of the people. The Gospel stories, especially Luke, have Jesus empowered to heal and exorcise by the Spirit. Thus empowered, however, he is represented as the agent. Some Christian theological readings of the Gospel stories claim that the Holy Spirit descending on Jesus and the heavenly voice naming him "son" (of God) means that the divine indwelt him and that the Holy Spirit was active in all his teaching and deeds. In the Matthean version of Jesus' response to the charge of Beelzebul he declares that it is "by the Spirit of God" that he casts out spirits (whereas the Lukan version has "the finger of God," suggesting that the exorcisms are a new exodus). The Lukan narrative has him "filled with the Spirit" (4:14) as Jesus launches his mission in the villages of Galilee. Yet in the Matthean and Lukan stories, like the

Markan, the Spirit is not active in particular healings or exorcisms. Rather, throughout the Gospel stories Jesus is the agent who commands the unclean spirits with "authority and power" and heals the sick, as power comes forth from him. In the Johannine Gospel story as well Jesus' healings and presumably the other "signs" are not some supernatural "acts of God" or the Spirit, but are "the works that the Father had given (him) to complete" (John 5:36).

In episode after episode, Jesus confronts the spirits that have taken possession of a person, gives a simple (but sometimes stern) command, or reaches out and raises up a sick person. The people know that he is the agent who is healing and casting out invasive spirits and come or bring their sick to (touch) him. The Syrophoenician woman and the royal officer who plead with him are assured that the healing or exorcism has happened, even at a distance.

The Healings and Exorcisms were Interactional

While Jesus is the agent of the exorcisms and healings, they are interactional: with the spirit-possessed, the sick, and often their parent or support group and/or the onlookers. Perhaps most striking is that, while healings and exorcisms are his principal actions in the Gospel stories, Jesus does not take the initiative. In the healings, either the person seeking healing or a parent or support group takes the initiative. The disciples tell Jesus of Peter's mother-in-law having a fever. The man with skin lesions pleads to be made clean. The paralytic's supporters take extreme measures to bring him into the presence of Jesus. A head of a local assembly takes the initiative about his daughter, the Syrophoenician woman about her little daughter, and the father about his possessed son. In the summaries as well as in other episodes, family and friends take the initiative to seek healing for their loved ones.

The most dramatic case is the hemorrhaging woman, who boldly takes the initiative to reach out and touch his garment, while Jesus remains unaware and inactive until after she is healed. Similarly the summary in Mark 6:53–56 has the trusting people from the whole region bringing the sick, who take the initiative, and all who reached out and "touched his cloak were healed." One of the few episodes in which Jesus takes the initiative to heal is the Lukan story (13:10–17) of when he saw a crippled woman in a village assembly on the sabbath. Otherwise

Jesus appears to take the initiative only to make a demonstration to the scribes or Pharisees, as with the man with the withered hand in the local assembly on the sabbath (Mark 3:1–6) and the man with dropsy (Luke 14:1–6). In the Matthean story Jesus "has compassion on the people" and heals in the mission speech (Matt 10) and in a feeding story (14:13); but otherwise he does not take the initiative, either in healing and exorcism stories themselves or in summaries such as 15:29–31.

Some cases involve a negotiation or even a confrontation: the father of the possessed boy has to press and plead his case, the man with the skin lesions "negotiates" with Jesus, and the Syrophoenician mother confronts Jesus and bests him in debate. As in these cases, the supporting parent or the support network or people are often enabling factors in the healing. The exorcisms involve confrontation, indeed a power-struggle, between Jesus and the possessing spirit(s), in which Jesus defeats or overcomes the spirit(s).

The relational aspect of Jesus' healings and exorcisms comes through all the more clearly because the episodes have little or no embellishment of the particular actions, no complex formulas pronounced and minimal ritual gestures, just simple commands or touch or gesture. In the healings he makes simple commands, such as "be made clean" or "little girl, get up." With no particular ritual action, he simply takes the girl or Peter's mother-in-law by the hand. He makes simple gestures appropriate to particular sicknesses in laying hands on blind eyes or inserting fingers in deaf ears. In the latter case, he lifts his eyes to heaven, presumably a gesture of prayer, but utters no formulaic phrases. Similarly in casting out spirits, Jesus declares simple commands such as "come out" or "come out of him and never enter again"—or says nothing as the exorcism happens at home at a distance from him. He does explain to the disciples who have failed to cast out a spirit that "this kind can only be cast out through prayer," but offers no formulaic phrases. He uses no *pharmaka* that were commonly mixed in peasant communities[17] (much less any *materia magica* imagined by some modern scholars); just a bit of spittle which, as noted in chap. 5, was a common healing substance. In his exorcisms he used no particular substance or chant, such as those used by the Judean exorcist in Josephus' account, or burning a fish's gall, as Tobit did to drive away the spirit afflicting the bridal chamber.

17. Jesus can thus not be classified as a "folk-healer" in a larger "health-care system."

People's Trust: The Crucial Enabling Factor

The Gospels repeatedly indicate that the *people's trust was the crucial enabling factor* in the interactive process of the healing and exorcism. As discussed briefly before, the standard translation of *pistis/fides* and the corresponding verbal forms with "faith" or "believe in" have become inadequate and even misleading. This is primarily because in their usage in modern (Anglophone) society these terms reference mere religious belief and/or a particular religious belief and practice that is separate from political-economic life and have little or no implication for concrete social-political-economic life. By contrast, *pistis/fides* in the Roman imperial world referred to loyalty, with the implication of (excusive) loyalty to a ruler and/or a political-economic-religious order. "Loyalty" is the primary meaning in the Gospel of John where Judeans as well as Galileans and Samaritans "become loyal to" Jesus, in opposition to the high priests and Pharisees as heads of the Judean temple-state (representatives of the Roman imperial order in Palestine). The term has this connotation also in the Markan, Matthean, and Lukan stories. But with regard to Jesus' healing and exorcism in these Gospel stories, the primary meaning is individual and collective *trust* in Jesus and the powers flowing through him and the (acts) of power(s) he performs.

Several episodes in the Markan story and the parallel Matthean and Lukan versions make this explicit. The trust of the people who lower the paralytic into the presence of Jesus evokes Jesus' declaration that his sins are forgiven, tantamount to saying "take up your palet and walk." Jesus declares to both the woman with the long-term hemorrhage and the blind Bar-timaeus that "your trust has healed/saved you." In the Lukan narrative, Jesus repeats that declaration to the lone "Samaritan" whose skin lesions are healed. In the brief Matthean episode of the healing of two blind men, Jesus declares their healing "according to" their trust. In the Matthean episode of the "Canaanite" woman, Jesus declares that the insistent woman's "great trust" is instrumental to her daughter's "healing." In the healing of the centurion's "boy" in both the Matthean and the Lukan stories, Jesus declares that he had not found such trust (before) in Israel. The most dramatic case is the woman who had been hemorrhaging for twelve years. She boldly takes the initiative to approach him and touch his garment, and is healed; the unaware Jesus takes no action, but feels power go forth from him. As Jesus declares: "daughter your trust has healed you."

Even though not mentioned explicitly the people's trust is clearly implicit in most other episodes of healing. The first four disciples trust that Jesus can and will heal Peter's mother-in-law. The man with skin lesions approaches Jesus out of such trust. The head of the local assembly whose daughter is near death approaches Jesus out of trust, and Jesus reassures him not to fear but to trust that his daughter will be healed. The Syrophoenician woman trusts that Jesus can cast the spirit out of her daughter. The father of the possessed boy trusts but asks Jesus to deepen his trust, and the crowd's implicit trust also plays a role in the successful exorcism. The blind Bartimaeus cries out to Jesus from his trust that he can heal, before Jesus declares this after the healing. In all of the summary passages in the Gospels the people's trust is implicit as they bring their sick to Jesus for healing.

That Jesus had only limited success in his "hometown" of Nazareth demonstrates the importance of the trust of the people in the healings and exorcisms. This suggests that trust was necessary, essential for the healing process that was relational and interactive. The power(s) working through Jesus could be effective only if people were coming to him and responding with trust that he could and would heal them and/or cast out invasive spirits.

Jesus' Spreading Fame

The Gospel stories present Jesus as healing, casting out spirits, and proclaiming the direct rule of God, restoring and strengthening families and village communities. Both particular episodes and summaries then emphasize the ensuing results. In Mark, no sooner has Jesus cast out the spirit in the Capernaum village assembly than "his fame immediately began to spread throughout the surrounding countryside of Galilee." After he had healed Peter's mother-in-law, people from the area brought to him all who were sick or possessed by spirits, and he healed many with various illnesses and cast out many spirits. The man with skin lesions, once cleansed, began to spread the word, and people came to Jesus from everywhere. Repeatedly in the Gospel stories, when people hear of what Jesus has been doing, crowds of people from other villages, near and far, come to find him, bringing their sick to be healed.[18] Jesus' spreading reputation

18. Even before the episodes of particular healings, Matthew presents a summary of the effects of Jesus' spreading fame at the very beginning of the narrative of Jesus mission.

and growing fame thus intensified the people's trust in the (relational, interactive) power working through him. As the result of Jesus' expanding fame, a movement that was generating collective power spread through Galilean villages and beyond.

The embellished summary accounts of great crowds flocking to Jesus from wide areas of Palestine and Syria (e.g., in Mark 3:7–8; and the programmatic summary in Matt 4:23–25) reflect the spread of Jesus-movements in the immediate decades following his mission focused in Galilee. But the spread of Jesus' fame would have been integral from the outset to the relational generation or flow of power and the development of a movement that resulted from and then enabled Jesus' interaction with trusting people in the healings and exorcisms. Rumor has played an integral role in the emergence of many popular movements.[19] One of the better known historically may be the "Great Fear" (*La Grande Peur*) that spread among French villagers at the outbreak of the French Revolution. Rumor spread rapidly in the countryside that now all people would be equal, with no more bishops and lords, peasants were free from tithes and feudal dues.[20] We can imagine how rumor would quickly have spread among the villagers in mid-first-century Judea to leave all behind and join the prophet Theudas or the prophet (returned) from Egypt who were promising new acts of divine deliverance like those led by Moses and Joshua (as discussed in chap. 4). Similarly with Jesus, rumor of his healing and exorcism spreading from village to village would have extended his fame, inspiring trust that he could provide relief from the illnesses that had long plagued the people.[21] It would have been a spiraling effect: people's trust enables Jesus' (acts of) power(s) that led to his fame spreading that in turn led to extended trust among the people.

19. See esp. Scott, *Domination and the Arts of Resistance*, 145–148. Application to the mission of Jesus and other popular movements in Roman Palestine in Horsley, "The Politics of Disguise," 68–70.

20. The classic study is Lafebvre, *The Great Fear of 1789*.

21. Dube, *Jesus the Best Capernaum Folk-Healer*, draws parallels between the spreading of Jesus' fame as a healer and the spreading of healers' fame via "praise-giving" in Zimbabwe.

The Israelite Social Form of a Prophet
Leading the People in a Renewal Movement[22]

What held together the other aspects of Jesus' interactive mission focused on healing and exorcism was the prominent paradigm derived from Israelite tradition of a popular prophet leading a movement of renewal and resistance among the people. This was evident repeatedly in the exploration ("hearing") of how the Gospel stories would have resonated with their audiences in referencing Israelite tradition in chaps. 7–10.[23]

Leader Role and Movement Response
in Historical Context and Cultural Tradition

The concept of "charisma/charismatic," borrowed from sociology has been used periodically in interpretation of Jesus. The development and use of this (cross-cultural) concept, however, have not adequately analyzed and theorized the dynamics of the interrelationship of role and response and both political-economic context and cultural context. Charisma continues to be popularly misunderstood as a personal quality. As developed by Max Weber and others charisma was a relational concept.[24] It referred not to a personal quality, but to a social-political-religious relationship between a leader and followers who resonated with his (or her) message.

The conception of this two- or three-dimensional relationship, however, paid insufficient attention to the problematic situation in which the leader resonated with the followers. Even more limiting and disabling, the concept virtually ignored the cultural tradition of social

22. In one of the now standard interpretations of Jesus, he is presented as an "eschatological prophet" or an "apocalyptic prophet." This (mis)interpretation, however, not only focuses narrowly on selected separate sayings of Jesus but also projects the modern scholarly construction of "the apocalyptic scenario" from the end of the nineteenth century onto "Jewish expectations" and Jesus. See the "deconstruction" of the construct in chap. 5 above.

23. This was missed by the fragmenting approach standard in historical Jesus studies that focused narrowly on individual sayings. And it was hidden by the standard theological scheme of Christian origins that emphasized the discontinuity of Jesus' teaching with "Judaism" and paid little or no attention to the distinctively Israelite popular movements of renewal and resistance that were happening in the historical context of Roman Palestine contemporary with Jesus' mission and with the development of the Gospel stories.

24. See especially the restatement of the concept as relational by Peter Worsley in his introduction to *The Trumpet Shall Sound* in the Schocken edition.

forms and roles that informed the interaction and collective action of particular leaders-and-movements. For example, the concept would supply a superficial sense of the US civil rights movement and its leaders such as Martin Luther King. Deeper understanding of the movement and its leaders would require knowing the historical background of slavery and segregation, and the social form of the Black churches and role of the African-American preachers that were adapted by King and other leaders in interaction with the movement. To understand the civil rights movement it is necessary to have a sense of the slavery, beatings, lynchings, and daily indignities that African Americans had suffered for generations and the ways those experiences and the yearning for freedom had been influenced and shaped by biblical stories of bondage in and then exodus from slavery in Egypt led by Moses that had been articulated for generations by preachers in the churches at the center of segregated communities, as well as in spirituals, hymns, and funerals.

To put the main point another way, the social forms that leadership in interaction with followers and movements take is, like sickness and healing, culturally defined. *To understand and appreciate how leaders emerge in interaction with followers and movements develop it is essential to discern those social forms of leadership and movements given in the cultural tradition in which the interaction happens and the movement(s) emerge.*

Interpretation of Jesus, like New Testament scholarship in general, has long relied on the generalization that Jesus (as portrayed in Gospel traditions) was "fulfilling Jewish expectations" (for example, of "the Messiah" in certain prophecies in the book of Isaiah). The concept of "expectations," however, reduces historical realities to a cognitive cultural dimension and makes the people passive, denies them agency. It reduces them to mere belief, with no inquiry into what difference it made in their collective life. However, it is possible to understand the development of the Gospel stories and, behind them, the interactive mission of Jesus in a more engaged and dynamic (profound) way by including in the investigation the Israelite (popular) tradition in which both Jesus and the people were embedded.

As evident in the Gospel stories, Jesus, his mission, and his movement(s) originated among a people who were embedded in the long and deep Israelite tradition of stories of liberation and renewal in situations of subjugation and exploitation. That this cultural tradition or social memory was very much alive among the Galilean, Samaritan, and

Judean villagers is indicated by the distinctively Israelite movements of resistance and renewal led, respectively, by popularly acclaimed "kings" and popular prophets, as discussed in chapter 4. The widespread revolts in 4 BCE and again in the great revolt of 66–70 CE took the form of regional movements in Galilee, Judea, and the TransJordan, each led by a prominent figure whom the people acclaimed as "king." This distinctively Israelite social form-and-leadership-role were evidently patterned after memories (stories) of earlier Israelites having "messiahed" the young bandit-chieftan David as "king." Closer to the time of Jesus' mission leaders presented themselves, and were followed by large numbers of people, as prophets who promised new divine acts of deliverance, patterned after the formative acts of deliverance led by Moses and/or Joshua.[25]

These movements indicate not only that stories of deliverance led by the young David or by Moses and/or Joshua were (deeply) familiar to villagers, but also that such stories served as formative paradigms for new movements of deliverance and the renewal of Israel. It is important but too limiting to note that these popular movements provide evidence of distinctively Israelite "roles" of popular leadership in early Roman Palestine. It is significant for a more comprehensive analysis to discern that these dynamic formative paradigms are relational and multidimensional. The repeated telling of stories in Israelite popular tradition had shaped the prophets' or the "messiahs'" and their followers' experience of domination under the Romans and high priests. The repeated telling of such stories had shaped not just an "expectation" but a yearning for liberation and renewal according to the model of their ancestors' deliverance led by Moses and/or Joshua or of their ancestors' struggle against the Philistines led by David. The visionary promise of the prophet or the leadership of the newly acclaimed "king" and the response in trust of the remembering and yearning people led to an interactive collective action to realize the new deliverance according to the pattern etched in their social memory.

In the cases of the popular prophetic movements in mid-first-century Palestine it is evident that Israelite tradition of the people's formative deliverance led by Moses and Joshua shaped the multiple dimensions of

---

25. As noted above in chap. 4, to label these as "signs prophets" relies on Josephus' generalization in summary passages, not on his description of particular prophets in which the jargon of "signs" is missing. To categorize these prophets as "apocalyptic" or "millennial" (Crossan, *Historical Jesus*, 158–67) imposes a modern scholarly construct of not attested in ancient Judean texts. So also the dichotomy of "apocalyptic" and "sapiential" (in Crossan's and others' work) is not attested in ancient Judean texts.

those movements: the collective experience of intolerable circumstances; the collective desire for deliverance; the role of a prophet who announced and led collective action patterned after (stories of) one of the great acts of deliverance led by Moses or Joshua; and the response by followers who trusted the announcement or action. The popular prophet Theudas, for example, tapped into such tradition in promising that a new act of divine deliverance was about to happen, in a reenactment of the formative events of Israel. Even if he did not go village to village pronouncing his promise, rumor of the new deliverance he was preaching would have spread into many villages, resonating with the yearning for new liberation rooted in Israelite popular tradition.

The images and stories of activities associated with the prophet role in interaction with the people, however, included far more than the leading of liberation in early Israel. In the legendary Israelite tradition, Moses, the paradigmatic prophet of Israel's origins, also mediated the Covenant of the people with God and one another and taught covenantal torah. The stories of Elijah performing multiple healings of people and restoration of the covenanted twelve tribes while confronting oppressive rulers would have been particularly prominent in Israelite popular tradition— and especially in the north (where Elijah had been active), as discussed in chap. 5. Those memories of Elijah, moreover, informed (not just an "expectation" but) a yearning for a new or returning Elijah who would restore the people. Also associated with the prophet role in relation with the people was the yearning for a prophetic agent of healing of the sicknesses of imperial conquest and rule, such as healing the blind and lame.

The Gospel Stories and Speeches Present Jesus Primarily in the Popular Prophet Role

As repeatedly evident in chapters 7–10, the Gospel stories and speeches present Jesus primarily as a prophet engaged in the renewal of the people Israel. After presenting Jesus briefly as messiah in their "prologues," the Gospels of Matthew and Luke like the Gospel of Mark, present most of his actions and his teaching/speeches as those of a prophet. Jesus is prepared for his mission by a (forty-day) testing in the wilderness, as were Elijah and also Moses before him, according to Israelite tradition. In the climactic events of the Gospel stories, Jesus engaged in a sustained confrontation of the high priestly rulers in the temple in a prophetic demonstration and prophetic pronouncements of God's condemnation of their exploitation of the people (Moses and Elijah had both confronted the rulers, Pharaoh and Ahab, and pronounced God's condemnation of their exploitation of the people). In the series of speeches adapted in both Matthew and Luke, the longest is an enactment of covenant renewal by Jesus as the new Moses. This becomes the first and programmatic speech in both the Gospels of Matthew and Luke. In the whole series of speeches adapted in Matthew and Luke, Jesus speaks and acts as a prophet (these speeches have not even a hint of another "role" such as a "messiah"/"king"). In a way that becomes cumulative, the Markan narrative presents Jesus as the new Moses and Elijah who carries out sea crossings, wilderness feedings, healings, and a series of dialogues that constitute a covenantal charter for the movement.

The most dramatic representation of Jesus as a prophet like Moses, the founding prophet of the people, and Elijah the great prophet of the renewal of the people, comes in the episode on the mountain in which Moses and Elijah appear with Jesus to the leading disciples. Both the Markan and Matthean narratives immediately have Jesus clarify that while he is an Elijah-like figure (as in the vision), the Elijah whom the scribes taught would to return to restore the people had already appeared as/in John. Nevertheless, in Matthew, where this identification of John as the returning Elijah is explicit, as well as in the Mark story, Jesus acts repeatedly as a new Elijah.

Among the many references to Jesus as a prophet generating a renewal of Israel in the Gospel stories and speeches are several identifying Jesus in his performance of healings and exorcisms. And these same references present Jesus as the fulfillment of the people's deep need and longing for healing and a/the prophet who would finally carry out those healings. In the second of the series of Jesus-speeches that was previously labeled "Q," as set up by John's question whether Jesus is the "coming one," he answers that the healings and preaching he is doing are the fulfillment of that deep longing of the people for a prophetic figure who would heal the people's sicknesses. Jesus' response to John's question climaxes in the statement that John is the greatest prophet in (Israel's) history that has now reached final fulfillment in the direct rule of God proclaimed by the (even greater!) prophet, Jesus. In the elaborate and complex Lukan story Jesus inaugurates his mission focused on healing and exorcism by identifying himself as acting in the fulfillment of a prophecy from the book of Isaiah of a prophetic figure being anointed to bring sight to the blind and freedom to the oppressed. The extended episode then compares Jesus' healing interaction with the people with that of Elijah and Elisha. In the Markan and Lukan episode of the exorcism of Legion and in the Lukan Jesus' declaration of what is happening in his exorcisms in response to the accusation of Beelzebul, Jesus casting out *daimonia* is presented as a new exodus, which of course had been led by the founding prophet Moses.

In the second main narrative step in the Markan story, Jesus' (acts of) power(s) in exorcisms and healings are narrated in sequences with episodes in which Jesus leading the crossings of the sea and wilderness feedings allude to Moses' leading the exodus sea crossing and the feeding in the wilderness. In these sequences it seems evident that the healings are prophetic (acts of) power(s), like the healings performed by Elijah. These sequences of episodes in the second narrative step in the Markan story are suggestive for the way in which the exorcisms and healings were understood and narrated at an earlier stage in the development of the Jesus-tradition that resulted in the more complete Markan story. The two sequences of (acts) of power(s) are the underlying structure of this overall narrative step into which related episodes are woven. This suggests that some of Jesus' exorcisms and healings were remembered and narrated as components of sequences of his (acts of) power(s) in renewal of the people by a prophet like Moses and Elijah at an earlier stage in the development toward the more complete Markan story.

The Gospel stories and speeches thus portray Jesus in the healings and exorcisms as resulting from the people's interaction with Jesus as the prophet whom they were longing for to heal the forms of malaise and plagues they were suffering in the cumulative conditions under Roman rule.

In the Gospel stories and speeches, Jesus' interaction with people in village communities was experienced on the basis of Israelite stories of how prophets, especially Moses and Elijah, had liberated, healed, and more generally renewed the people. Recognition of this is the basis for appreciating how the healings and exorcisms *worked* in the interaction of Jesus mission in the collective memory of Jesus movements. The people's trust enabled the healing power flowing through Jesus to heal and as the fame of Jesus' healing spread among the people it deepened and strengthened their trust in the healing power that flowed into a movement focused on Jesus. But that interaction was *informed* and shaped by collective memory of Elijah and other prophets' renewal of the people, including healings.

The people were not just trusting that Jesus could heal, but were trusting in Jesus as the prophet for whom they had been longing to heal and renew the people. Stated more relationally, the interaction of Jesus and the villagers was *informed* by and a creative development of the Israelite tradition of a prophet healing the people as central to a renewal of the people. As in Jesus' reply to the question of John the Baptist, his healings (and preaching) were the manifestations that he was indeed the "coming one," the longed for prophet who would perform the renewal.[26] How all the dimensions of Jesus' exorcism and healing are held together—or not—by the role of the longed for prophet who would lead renewal of the people is illustrated in the negative example of what happened in his visit to Nazareth. Few (acts of) power(s) happened in his "hometown" where his relatives and neighbors knew him as just Jesus, their relative and neighbor.[27] That was "in the way." They could not respond like people in the rest of the Gospel narratives who understood Jesus not as an ordinary Galilean from Nazareth but as a prophet of renewal, like "Elijah" or "one of the prophets of old." If heard and probed in its function in the overall Gospel narrative this episode serves as a negative example in the continuing theme of trust. But this is not just trust in the abstract or trust that he could heal. If that is what we imagine we miss what holds together all the other aspects of Jesus' interactive mission focused on healing and exorcism: trust that Jesus is *the prophet for whom the people have longed* to heal their malaise and renew their common life.

26. In Jesus' answer to John's question whether he is the "coming one," neither the Matthean nor the Lukan story adapt Jesus' response with explicit reference to a particular "written" passage (in Isaiah). Jesus' speech that they cite virtually verbatim must be referencing a popular Israelite tradition of the people's longing for healing and good news to the poor (as discussed in chap. 5) that Jesus is now fulfilling in his mission of healing and proclamation of the direct rule of God.

27. This discussion as illustrated by the negative example of this episode provides an illustration of how Jesus interpreters—and producers of documentaries for television—are projecting a reductionist modern individualist quest in seeking to discover "what was Jesus *really like*" or "what did Jesus *really say*." What I/we are after in this project is how and why Jesus became a historically significant and influential figure in interaction with people in historical context.

The Extension of Jesus' Prophetic Mission
in the Empowerment of Envoys

Jesus' recruitment of disciples and commissioning them to extend his prophetic mission of proclamation of the rule of God and healing was part and parcel of his role as the prophet that the people longed for. Like the other popular prophets who emerged in the following decades, he was generating and leading a movement of renewal and resistance among the people. And like those other popular prophets he and his movement were informed by central stories in Israelite tradition.[28] Just as the narrative of Jesus' testing in the wilderness in preparation for his mission alludes to Elijah's testing for forty days in the wilderness, so his calling of disciples in narrative sequence alludes to Elijah's recruitment of Elisha. Similarly the introduction of the commissioning of the seventy in the Lukan story by three successive brief dialogues with followers are allusions to Elijah's calling of Elisha.

All of the Gospel stories and speeches present, in narrative sequence, Jesus appointing the Twelve as representative of Israel in renewal and his empowering them (and their expansion to seventy in Luke) to exorcise, heal, and proclaim in the expansion of his mission and movement(s).[29] Jesus as (healing) prophet had already evoked trust and generated power in previous exorcisms and healings, and could now endow his envoys. It is significant that the commissioning is in the mode of performative speech that bestows the power on them as it sends them out.

28. Understandably, given the several "books" of collections of prophecies of individual prophets, the standard conception is of an individual prophet who pronounces God's judgment. These, however, come relatively late in Israelite tradition. Prominent in earlier tradition were figures (called prophets) such as Deborah, Samuel, and Elijah-Elisha who led the Israelite people (in) movements. In second-temple Judea the narrative "books" that include their actions and movements were included in "the Prophets."

29. That the Markan story that is so severely critical of the twelve/disciples, especially Peter, James, and John, includes this episode of their empowerment to exorcise, heal, and proclaim indicates that this was an integral component of the memory of Jesus' mission as the prophet of renewal. A comparison with the instructions given in the *Didache* 11–13 about traveling apostles and prophets suggests that the Matthean and Lukan stories are drawing on memory of an earlier time. The *Didache*, an (orally derived) "handbook" for communities of Jesus-loyalists produced probably more or less the same time as the Matthean and Lukan stories, addresses a situation in which traveling prophets have become a potential problem for communities of people living at the subsistence level. The length of their stay must be limited to a few days.

Renewal of Covenant Community Reinforced
Personal and Community Renewal in Exorcisms and Healings

In many of the healing episodes of the Markan and other Gospel stories the people healed were restored to their families, support networks and communities. The restoration of personal wellbeing and of community in the healings and exorcisms was then strongly reinforced by Jesus' renewal of the Mosaic covenant that renewed the solidarity of the community and its support of those who had been sick or possessed. It seemed evident in the beginning of the Markan narrative of Jesus' interactive mission that there was a close interrelationship between his proclamation of the kingdom of God, his healing, and his teaching (as discussed in chap. 7). The direct rule of God had two closely related manifestation: Jesus' exorcism and healing, and his teaching, which consisted of Mosaic covenantal commandments and principles. Indeed, whether in the sequence of narrative steps or in the overall narrative sequence of the story, the exorcisms and healings led into renewal of covenantal community.

The most vivid example is in the first narrative step and programmatic speech of the Matthean story (discussed in chap. 9). Jesus begins his proclamation of the kingdom, moving throughout Galilee into the village assemblies. The first narrative step is condensed into an astounding summary of how Jesus healed every sickness, including spirit possession, attracting great crowds from all areas of the Israelite people. This leads to his going up to "the mountain" and delivering the programmatic renewal of the Mosaic covenant, with further instructions for on-going community life. The renewal of covenantal community is in performative speech that enacts what it declares. This is not just teaching in the academic sense, but interactive collective action, that moves into the very motivation of interaction in the covenantal community. The enactment of covenant renewal, moreover, leads into a sequence of particular healings and exorcisms in the next narrative step, which in turn lead to the commission of the disciples to extend Jesus' mission into other villages that empowers them, in turn, to proclaim the kingdom and enact its twin manifestations in healing/exorcism and teaching (torah). The Lukan narrative follows the same sequence, with an exorcism and several healing episodes leading to the enactment of Mosaic covenant renewal in performative speech.

Although less striking, the Markan narrative of Jesus' interactive mission in Galilee begins with the proclamation of the kingdom of God manifested in two modes of action, teaching (torah) and exorcisms and healings. In the first narrative step the exorcism and healings lead into a short declaration of familial community renewal of "those who do the will of God" (an allusion to the Mosaic covenant; as discussed in chap. 7).Then the first three narrative steps of Jesus' exorcisms and healings and other "(acts of) power(s)" in villages of Galilee and beyond lead to a renewal of Mosaic covenant community, more explicitly articulated in a series of dialogues that recite the covenantal commandments and declare renewed covenantal principles (again as discussed in chap. 7). Once we begin hearing or reading the whole Markan story then it is striking how in his words over the cup, Jesus transforms the Passover meal with the disciples into a ceremony of Mosaic covenant renewal that became the regular communal ritual meal that remembered the "breakthrough" of Jesus' martyrdom that empowered the expansion of the movement.[30]

Power and Resistance

In His Interaction with the People as a Healing Prophet Jesus was Generating Power

Not only do the Gospels refer to Jesus' exorcisms and healings as "(acts of) power(s)," but *in those interactions with the people as a prophet Jesus was generating power.* The Markan narrative indicates this in the beginning, in the middle, and in the climax of the story. The narrative indicates this in his very first action, casting out the spirit who was possessing the fellow in the assembly in Capernaum, even prefacing and concluding the episode with the same response by the people. They were astounded and kept saying to one another, "What is this, a new teaching, with authority! and not as the scribes. He commands even the unclean spirits and they obey him!" "Authority" is a good translation of *exousia* here since the term refers to power that has legitimacy, the approval of the people. Jesus is acting with power that benefits the people, in contrast with the scribes, the representatives of the temple-state. How the generation of such power was threatening to the rulers is evident in the narrative set-up of Herod Antipas beheading the prophet John. Jesus' spreading fame had become known to Herod, and Jesus too had become widely known as a prophet, evidently based on the "(acts of) power(s) he was performing.

30. Explored in Horsley, *Jesus and the Powers*, esp. chaps. 7–8.

How was this to be explained? All of the options were that he was a prophet familiar from Israelite tradition: first, most readily accounting for the "(acts of) power(s)" working through him, as the dead prophet John the Baptist come back to life; second, as Elijah (returned); or third as "a prophet like one of the prophets of old." The third explicit indication in the Markan story that Jesus had generated power in his interaction with the people is the episode following his prophetic demonstration against the temple in which the high priests, scribes, and elders challenge him: "By what authority (*exousia*) are you doing these things? Who gave you this authority?" Jesus responds with a counterquestion: "Was John's authority from heaven (God) or from humans?" The rulers and their representatives refused to answer. Why? Because they feared the people, who viewed John as a prophet and evidently Jesus as well—because of their preaching and acting on behalf of and for the benefit (renewal) of the people and in resistance to their rulers.

The Matthean story redeploys the people's astonishment at the teaching of Jesus with authority, unlike the scribes, to the close of the long covenant renewal speech, after having Jesus' fame from his healing and exorcism spread throughout Israelite areas and into Syria just prior to the speech. The Matthean narrative then presents a brief version of how Jesus is identified as a prophet, as John redivivus by Herod, that explains how the "(acts of) power(s) are working through him. The Matthean portrayal of the confrontation in the temple then completes the portrait of Jesus generating power as a prophet in interaction with the people in an episode that parallels that in the Markan story. The Lukan narrative has Jesus already "filled with the power of the Spirit as he launches his mission in Galilee, seeming to locate the power in Jesus. The rest of the Lukan narrative, however, parallels the Markan story in presenting the "authority and power" (*exousia kai dynamis*) generated by the interaction of Jesus as prophet with the people.

Luke includes this at the beginning and end. Immediately following Jesus' giving the twelve "power and authority over the *daimonia* and to heal sicknesses" the Lukan story has Herod perplexed because some of the people say that Jesus is John, others Elijah, and yet others one of the prophets of old. Then in the climactic confrontation in the temple, the rulers, again threatened by the power that the prophet is generating in interaction with the people, challenge him "by what authority are you doing these things." And again the rulers cannot answer Jesus' counter-question because they know that the people are loyal to Jesus—as they were to John—as a prophet acting in their interest and renewal.

These strategically placed episodes in the Gospels, however, are just the more explicit narratives in longer stories in which episode after episode flesh out portrayals of the expanding fame of Jesus as a prophet performing exorcisms and healings and generating power in the expanding movement through his interaction with the people. In direct contrast to the rulers and their representatives, who were disempowering the people, Jesus was empowering them and, in the process, generating prophet-and-people-power in resistance to them.

Collective Political Resistance Generated by Jesus' Acts of Power and Covenantal Renewal

The Gospel stories and speeches represent Jesus' mission of exorcism, healing, and renewal of covenant community as opposed to and by the Jerusalem temple-state (that had been re-imposed as the ruling institution of Judea by the Romans in 6 CE). In Jesus' exorcisms he was teaching with "authority/power" for (the renewal of) the people. In his healings he was empowering the people to forgive their (own and one another's) sins. Jesus' expanding interactive exorcism and healing and his widening fame evoked widespread response from the people who greeted him as the prophet for whom they had been longing, and brought their sick and possessed for healing. In the climax of the story, after completing his mission of exorcism and healing in Galilee and beyond, in accordance with the traditional "script" of a prophet of renewal and resistance, Jesus journeyed to Jerusalem where he engaged in sustained confrontation with the high priestly rulers. They were afraid to move against him publicly because they knew that he, like John, had generated considerable authority/power among the people (which the "authorities" knew that they utterly lacked). Jesus' *dynameis* (acts of power) had generated increasing *power* among the people in a movement of restored persons, families, and renewed covenantal communities. Those village communities became stronger in their semi-independent community life, less vulnerable to disintegration, with mutual aid and solidarity, in the renewal of covenantal community.

The mission of Jesus would appear to be a (previously unrecognized) historical case of how imperial/colonial rulers' conquests and exploitation of peoples became major factors in the generation of sicknesses and spirit possession and of how (the mission of) an indigenous prophet responded to the crisis with healing, exorcism, and measures to renew the people's mutual aid and community solidarity. Studies by critical medical anthropologists and others analyze many modern cases of the "production" of sicknesses and/or spirit possession by colonial invasion and domination of indigenous peoples and their responses in measures that are often mystifying but also self-protective. Those studies prompted some of the questions and issues about what was happening among the people in Roman Palestine that are discussed in chapters 4–5. Consideration of the Gospel stories and speeches in chapters 7–11 suggest that in his exorcism and healing Jesus was responding to just such conditions and situations, but also that Jesus and his movement were engaged in de-mystification of the invasion and exploitation by the rulers. Assuming that we take seriously the narrative sequence in the Markan story (and by implication at least in the Lukan story as well), Jesus exorcism of the spirit(s) whose identity is revealed as Legion (Roman troops) exposes the concrete cause of the people's subjugation and possession. This episode is a fulcrum in the narrative that leads to its climax in Jesus' direct confrontation of the rulers of the Roman imperial order in Judea. This de-mystification leads, indeed forces, the people into deliberate opposition to the Roman imperial order, following Jesus' lead and example of direct confrontation of the rulers. Other episodes in the stories indicate that, following Jesus' example, the communities of the movements he catalyzed resisted their domination and at times had to face rulers' suppression.[31] They were acknowledging and resisting the concrete political-economic-religious forces arrayed against them that had helped generate the sicknesses and spirit possession. The demystication that accompanied Jesus' exorcism led the renewed covenantal communities to deliberate resistance of the Roman imperial order (but not revolt) that evoked repression, persecution, arrests, and trials.

In recognizing the concrete forces that were disabling their families and communities, Jesus and his movement were among many popular movements in Roman Palestine at the time. The popular messianic movements mounted active revolt and temporary independence of village communities in different areas and the popular prophetic movements pulled people away from their villages in pursuit of fantasies of God's new

---

31. This "reading" of Mark, following the implications of the narrative sequence in the story, was laid out in *Hearing the Whole Story*, chap. 6.

acts of deliverance. By contrast, however, Jesus and his envoys/disciples focused his mission on the people's village communities. The healings and exorcisms restored suffering people to their families and communities. Enactment of covenant renewal in performative speech evoked renewed commitment to the mutual aid and cooperation that provided supportive community and strengthened the ability of the villagers to resist further encroachment on their subsistence nutrition.

The prominence both of Jesus' confrontation with the rulers in Jerusalem and of his martyrdom at the hands of the high priests and the Romans suggests that these were the "breakthrough" that energized the rapid expansion of the movement(s) generated by his mission. Healings and exorcisms continued, along with renewed community cooperation and solidarity, as evident from the mission speeches empowering his envoys and the early narratives in Acts. Jesus' speeches (had) warned of official attempts to suppress the movement(s) and called for loyalty and solidarity. Disciples and apostles were bold to proclaim, heal, and recruit in the face of opposition by the temple-state and its agents. They continued to expand the mission Jesus had begun as the movement(s) gained momentum and staying power. This was continuing popular opposition to the Roman imperial order and its rulers. But it was neither revolt nor pursuit of fantasies of divine acts of deliverance. It was continuing acts of power that healed the people and revitalization of supportive community in villages and in Jerusalem itself, as movements of Jesus-loyalists spread rapidly into villages and towns in nearby areas.

Bibliography

Aberle, David F. "Religio-Magical Phenomena and Power, Prediction, and Control." *Southwestern Journal of Anthropology* 22 (1966) 221–30.

Achtemeier, Paul J. "And He Followed Him: Miracles and Discipleship in Mark 10:46–52." *Semeia* 11 (1978) 115–45.

———. "Toward the Isolation of Pre-Markan Miracle Catenae." *JBL* 89 (1970) 265–91.

———. "The Origin and Function of the Pre-Markan Miracle Catenae." *JBL* 91 (1972) 198–221.

———. *Jesus and the Miracle Tradition*. Eugene, OR: Cascade Books, 2008.

Adams, J. N., and Simon Swain. "Introduction." In *Bilingualism in Ancient Society*, edited by J. N. Adams et al., 1–20. Oxford: Oxford University Press, 2002.

Alexander, Philip S. "Incantations and Books of Magic." In *The History of the Jewish People in the Age of Jesus Christ*, by Emil Schürer, edited by Geza Vermes et al., III.1:342–80; Edinburgh: T. & T. Clark, 1986.

———. "'Wrestling with Wickedness in High Places': Magic in the Worldview of the Qumran Community." In *The Scrolls and the Scriptures: Qumran Fifty Years After*, edited by Stanley E. Porter and Craig A. Evans, 318–37. Journal for the Study of the Pseudepigrapha Supplements 26. Sheffield: Sheffield Academic, 1997.

———. "*Sepher ha-Razim* and the Problem of Black Magic in Early Judaism." In *Magic in the Biblical World*, edited by Todd E. Klutz, 170–90. London: T. & T. Clark, 2003.

Alkier, Stefan, and Annette Weissenrieder, eds. *Miracles Revisited: New Testament Miracle Stories and Their Concepts of Reality*. SBIR 2. Berlin: deGruyter, 2013.

Alkier, Stefan. "'For Nothing Will Be Impossible with God' (Luke 1:37) : The Reality of "The Feeding the Five Thousand" (Luke 9:10-17) in the Universe of Discourse of Luke's Gospel ." In *Miracles Revisited: New Testament Miracle Stories and Their Concepts of Reality*, edited by Stefan Alkier and Annette Weissenrieder, 5–22. SBIR2. Berlin: deGruyter, 2013.

Arnal, William. *Jesus and the Village Scribes: Galilean Conflicts and the Setting of Q*. Minneapolis: Fortress, 2001.

Attridge, Harold W. *The Interpretation of Biblical History in the* Antiquitates Judaicae *of Flavius Josephus*. HDR 7. Missoula, MT: Scholars, 1976.

Aune, David. "Magic in Early Christianity." *ANRW* 2.23.2 (1980) 1507–57.

Avalos, Hector. *Health Care and the Rise of Christianity*. Peabody: Hendrickson, 1999.

Baer, Hans A., Merrill Singer, and Ida Susser. *Medical Anthropology and the World System*. London: Bergin & Garvey, 1992.

Baltzer, Klaus. *The Covenant Formulary: In Old Testament, Jewish, and Early Christian Writings.* Translated by David E. Green. Minneapolis: Fortress Press, 1971.

Barnett, P. W. "The Jewish Sign Prophets—A.D. 40–70." *NTS* 27 (1980–81) 679–97.

Baumgarten, Joseph M. "On the Nature of the Seductress in 4Q184." *Revue de Qumran* 15 (1991) 135–36.

Beard, Mary, et al. *Literacy in the Roman World.* JRASup 3. Ann Arbor: Journal of Roman Archaeology, 1991.

Becker, Michael. "*Magoi*—Astrologers, Ecstatics, Deceitful Prophets." In *A Kind of Magic: The Art of Transforming,* edited by Michael LaBahn and Bert Jan Lietaertn Peerbolte, 87–106. LNTS 306. London: T. & T. Clark, 2007.

———. *Wunder und* Wundertäter *im frührabbinischen Judentum: Studien zum Phänomen und seiner Überlieferung im Horizont von Magie und Dämonismus.* WUNT 2/144. Tübingen: Mohr/Siebeck, 2002.

Behrend, Heike, and Ute Luig, eds. *Spirit Possession, Modernity and Power in Africa.* Madison: University of Wisconsin Press, 1999.

Betz, Hans Dieter. "The Formation of Authoritative Tradition in the Greek Magical Papyri." In *Self-Definition in the Greco-Roman World,* edited by Ben F. Meyers and E. P. Sanders, 3:161–70. Philadelphia: Fortress, 1982.

———, ed. *The Greek Magical Papyri in Translation, Including the Demotic Spells.* Chicago: University of Chicago Press, 1986.

———. "Introduction." *The Greek Magical Papyri in Translation, Including the Demotic Spells.* Edited by Hans-Dieter Betz. Chicago: University of Chicago Press, 1986.

Betz, Otto. "Das Problem des Wunders bei Flavius Josephus im Vergleich zum Wunderproblem bei den Rabbinen und im Johannesevangelium." In *Josephus-Studien: Untersuchungen zu Josephus, dem antiken Judentum, und dem Neuen Testament, Festschrift Otto Michel,* edited by Otto Betz et al., 23–44. Göttingen: Vandenhoeck & Ruprecht, 1974.

Blackburn, B. L. "The Miracles of Jesus." In *Studying the Historical Jesus: Evaluations of the State of Current Research,* edited by Bruce Chilton and Craig A. Evans, 353–94. New Testament Tools and Studies 19. Leiden: Brill, 1994.

Blacking, John. *The Anthropology of the Body.* New York: Academic Press, 1977.

Blau, Ludwig. *Das Altjüdische Zauberwesen.* 2nd ed. Berlin: Lamm, 1914.

Bloomquist, L. Gregory. "The Role of Argumentation in the Miracle Stories of Luke–Acts: Toward a Fuller Identification of Miracle Discourse for Use in Sociorhetorical Interpretation." In *Miracle Discourse in the New Testament,* edited by Duane F. Watson, 85–124. Atlanta: Society of Biblical Literature, 2012.

Boddy, Janice. *Wombs and Alien Spirits: Women, Men, and the Zar Cult in Northern Sudan.* Madison: University of Wisconsin Press, 1989.

Bokser, Baruch M. "Wonder-Working and the Rabbinic Tradition: The Case of Hanina ben Dosa." *JSJ* 16 (1985) 42–92.

Bonner, Campbell. "The Technique of Exorcism." *HTR* 36 (1943) 39–49.

Boring, M. Eugene. *Mark: A Commentary.* New Testament Library. Louisville: Westminster John Knox. 2006.

Bornkamm, Günther. *Jesus of Nazareth.* Foreword by Helmut Koester. Translated by Irene and Fraser McLuskey with James M. Robinson. Philadelphia: Fortress, 1995.

Botha, Pieter J. J. "Mark's Story as Oral Traditional Literature: Rethinking the Transmission of Some Traditions about Jesus." *HTS Teologiese Studies / Theological Studies* 47/2 (1991) 304–31.

————. *Orality and Literacy in Early Christianity*. BPCS 5. Eugene, OR: Cascade Books, 2012.

Bowman, Alan K, and Greg Woolf, eds. *Literacy and Power in the Ancient World*. Cambridge: Cambridge University Press, 1994.

Brashear, W. "The Greek Magical Papyri: An Introduction and Survey; Annotated Bibliography (1928–1994)." *ANRW* II.18.5. 3380–684.

Brooke, George J. "Deuteronomy 18:9–14 in the Qumran Scrolls." In *Magic in the Biblical World: From the Rod of Aaron to the Ring of Solomon*, edited by Todd E. Klutz, 66–84. Journal for the Study of the New Testament Supplements 245. London: T. & T. Clark, 2003.

Brock, Rita Nakashima. *Journeys by Heart: A Christology of Erotic Power*. New York: Crossroad, 1986.

Brown, Peter J., Marcia C. Inhorn, and Daniel J. Smith. "Disease, Ecology, and Human Behavior." In *Medical Anthropology: Contemporary Theory and Method*, edited by Carolyn F. Sargent and Thomas M. Johnson, 183–218. Rev. ed. New York: Praeger, 1990.

Broshi, Magen. "The Role of the Temple in the Herodian Economy." *JJS* 38 (1987) 31–37.

Bultmann, Rudolf. *The History of the Synoptic Tradition*. Oxford: Blackwell, 1963.

————. *Jesus and the Word*. New York: Scribners, 1958.

————. "New Testament and Mythology." In *Kerygma and Myth*, edited by Hans Werner Bartsch. London: SPCK, 1957.

Burke, Peter. *History and Social Theory*. Cambridge, UK: Polity, 1992.

Burkert, Walter. *Ancient Mystery Cults*. Carl Newell Jackson Lectures. Cambridge: Harvard University Press, 1987.

————. *Greek Religion: Archaic and Classical*. Translated by John Raffan. Cambridge: Harvard University Press, 1985.

Burridge, Kenelm. Review of Wilson, *Magic and the Millennium*. *History of Religions* 14 (1975) 228–30.

Burridge, Richard A. *What Are the Gospels? A Comparison with Graeco-Roman Biography*. 3rd ed. Waco, TX: Baylor University Press, 2018.

Cadbury, Henry J. *The Peril of Modernizing Jesus*. New York: Macmillan, 1937.

Carr, David M. *Writing on the Tablet of the Heart: Origins of Scripture and Literature*. Oxford: Oxford University Press, 2005.

Casey, Maurice. *Jesus of Nazareth: An Independent Historian's Account of His Life and Teaching*. London: T. & T. Clark, 2010.

————. *Aramaic Sources of Mark's Gospel*. Society for New Testament Studies Monograph Series 102. Cambridge: Cambridge University Press, 1999.

Carter, Charles. *The Emergence of Yehud in the Persian Period: A Social and Demographic Study*. Journal for the Study of the Old Testament Supplements 294. Sheffield: Sheffield Academic, 1999.

Charlesworth, James H., ed. *The Messiah: Developments in Earliest Judaism and Christianity*. Minneapolis: Fortress, 1992.

Clark, Elizabeth A. *History, Theory, Text: Historians and the Linguistic Turn*. Cambridge: Harvard University Press, 2004.

Cohen, Shaye J. D. "Menstruants and the Sacred." In *Women's History and Ancient History*. Edited by Sarah Pomeroy, 271–99. Chapel Hill: University of North Carolina Press, 1991.

————. "The Significance of Yavneh: Pharisees, Rabbis, and the End of Jewish Sectarianism." *Hebrew Union College Annual* 55 (1984) 27–53.

Collins, Adela Yarbro. *Mark: A Commentary*. Hermeneia. Minneapolis: Fortress, 2007.

Collins, John J. *Apocalypticism in the Dead Sea Scrolls*. London: Routledge, 1997.

————. *Beyond the Qumran Community: The Sectarian Movement of the Dead Sea Scrolls*. Grand Rapids: Eerdmans, 2009.

————. *The Scepter and the Star: Messianism in Light of the Dead Sea Scrolls*. Anchor Bible Reference Library. New Haven: Yale University Press, 1995.

Comaroff, Jean. *Body of Power, Spirit of Resistance: The Culture and History of a South African People*. Chicago: University of Chicago Press, 1985.

Cook, John Granger. "In Defense of Ambiguity." *NTS* 43 (1997) 184–208.

Coote, Robert B., ed. *Elijah and Elisha in Socioliterary Perspective*. SemeiaSt. Society of Biblical Literature, 2003.

Cotter, Wendy, CSJ. *Miracles in Greco-Roman Antiquity: A Sourcebook*. Context of Early Christianity. London: Routledge, 1999.

————. *The Christ of the Miracle Stories*. Grand Rapids: Baker, 2010.

Craffert, Pieter F. *The Life of a Galilean Shaman: Jesus of Nazareth in Anthropological-Historical Perspective*. Matrix 3. Eugene, OR: Cascade Books, 2008.

————. "Medical Anthropology as an Antidote for Ethnocentrism in Jesus Research? Putting the Illness–Disease Distinction into Perspective." *HTS Teologiese Studies / Theological Studies* 67 (2011) 1–14. https://hts.org.za/index.php/hts/article/view/970/1549.

Craig, William L. "The Problem of Miracles: Historical and Philosophical Perspective." In *The The Miracles of Jesus*, edited by David Wenham and Craig Blomberg, 19–23. Gospel Perspectives 6. Sheffield: JSOT Press, 1986.

Crapanzano, Victor. "Introduction." In *Case Studies in Spirit Possession*, edited by Victor Crapanzano and Vivian Garrison. Contemporary Religious Movements. New York: Wiley, 1977.

Crossan, John Dominic. *The Historical Jesus: The Life of a Mediterranean Jewish Peasant*. San Francisco: HarperSanFrancisco, 1991.

————. *Jesus: A Revolutionary Biography*. San Francisco: HarperSanFrancisco, 1994.

Csordas, T. J., and Arthur Kleinman. "The Therapeutic Process." In *Medical Anthropology: Contemporary Theory and Method*, edited by Thomas M. Johnson and Carolyn F. Sargent. New York: Praeger, 1990.

Czachesz, Istvan. "Explaining Magic: Earliest Christianity as a Test Case." In *Past Minds: Studies in Cognitive Historiography*, edited by Luther H. Martin and Jesper Sorenson, 141–65. Religion, Cognition, and Culture. London: Equinox, 2011.

Czachesz, Istvan, and Risto Uro, eds. *Mind, Morality, and Magic: Cognitive Science Approaches in Biblical Studies*. Bible World. London: Routledge, 2013.

D'Angelo, Mary Rose. "(Re)Presentation of Women in the Gospels: John and Mark." In *Women and Christian Origins*, edited by Ross Shepard Kraemer and Mary Rose D'Angelo, 137–45. Oxford: Oxford University Press, 1999.

Davies, Stevan L. *Jesus the Healer: Possession, Trance, and the Origins of Christianity*. New York: Continuum, 1995.

Deissmann, Adolf. *Light from the Ancient East: The New Testament Illustrated by Recently Discovered Texts*. Translated by Lionel R. M. Strachan 1927. Reprinted, Eugene, OR: Wipf & Stock, 2004.

Delling, Gerhard. "Josephus und das Wunderbare." *NovT* 2 (1958) 291–309.

Dewey, Joanna. "The Gospel of Mark as an Oral–Aural Event: Implications for Interpretation." In *The New Literary Criticism and the New Testament*, edited by Elizabeth Struthers Malbon and Edgar V. McKnight, 248–57. Sheffield: Sheffield Academic Press, 1994. Reprinted in *The Oral Ethos of the Early Church: Speaking and Writing, and the Gospel of Mark*. BPCS 8. Eugene, OR: Cascade Books, 2013.

———. "Mark as Interwoven Tapestry." In *The Oral Ethos of the Early Church: Speaking and Writing, and the Gospel of Mark*. BPCS 8. Eugene, OR: Cascade Books, 2013.

———. "Mark—a Really Good Oral Story." *JBL* 123 (2004) 495–507. Reprinted in *Oral Ethos of the Early Church: Speaking and Writing, and the Gospel of Mark*, 157–69. BPCS 8. Eugene, OR: Cascade Books, 2013.

———. *The Oral Ethos of the Early Church: Speaking and Writing, and the Gospel of Mark*. BPCS 8. Eugene, OR: Cascade Books, 2013.

Dickie, Matthew W. *Magic and Magicians in the Greco-Roman World*. London and New York: Oxford University Press, 2001.

———. "Magic in the Roman Historians." In *Magical Practices in the Latin West*, edited by Richard L. Gordon and Francisco Marco Simon, 78–97. RGRW 68. Leiden: Brill, 2010.

Doble, Peter, and Jeffrey Kloha, eds. *Texts and Traditions: Essays in Honor of J. Keith Elliott*. Leiden. Brill 2014.

Donahue, John R., and Daniel J. Harrington. *The Gospel of Mark*. Sacra Pagina 2. Collegeville, MN: Liturgical, 2002.

Douglas, Mary. *Purity and Danger*. Routledge and Keegan Paul, 1966.

Dube, Zorodzai. *Jesus, the Best Capernaum Folk-Healer Mark's Aretalogy of Jesus in the Healing Stories*. Eugene, OR: Pickwick Publications, 2020.

Duling, Dennis C. "The Eleazar Miracle and Solomon's Magical Wisdom in Flavius Josephus's *Antiquitates Judaicae* 8.42–49." *HTR* 78 (1985) 1–25.

———. "Matthew's Son of David in Social-Scientific Perspective: Kinship, Kingship, Magic, and Miracle." *Biblical Theology Bulletin* 22 (1992) 99–116. Reprinted in *A Marginal Scribe: Studies of the Gospel of Matthew in Social-Scientific Perspective*, 91–119. Matrix 7. Eugene, OR: Cascade Books, 2012.

———. "Solomon, Exorcism, and the Son of David." *HTR* 68 (1975) 235–52.

Dunn, James D. G. "Altering the Default Setting: Re-Envisaging the Early Transmission of the Jesus Tradition." *NTS* 49 (2003) 139–75.

———. *Jesus Remembered*. Christianity in the Making 1. Grand Rapids: Eerdmans, 2003.

Edelstein, Ludvig, and Emma Edelstein. *Asclepios: A Collection and Interpretation of the Testimonies*. 2 vols. 1945. Reprint, Baltimore: Johns Hopkins University Press, 1998.

Ehrman, Bart. *Misquoting Jesus: The Story behind Who Changed the Bible and Why*. San Francisco: HarperSanFrancisco, 2005.

———. *The Orthodox Corruption of Scripture: The Effect of Early Christological Controversies on the Text of the New Testament*. Oxford: Oxford University Press, 2011.

Eisenberg, Leon. "Disease and Illness: Distinctions between Professional and Popular Ideas of Sickness." *Culture, Medicine, and Psychiatry* 1 (1977) 9–23.

Eliade, Mircea. *Shamanism: Archaic Techniques of Ecstasy*. Bollingen Series 76. Princeton: Princeton University Press, 1964.

Elliott, John H. "Social-Scientific Criticism of the New Testament and Its Social World." *Semeia* 35 (1986) 1–33.

Epp, Eldon Jay. "The Multivalence of the Term 'Original Text' in New Testament Textual Criticism." *HTR* 92 (1999) 245–81.

———. "The Oxyrhynchus New Testament Papyri: 'Not without Honor Except in Their Hometown'?" *JBL* 123 (2004) 5–55.

Ernst, E. "Towards a Scientific Understanding of Placebo Effects." In *Understanding the Placebo Effect in Contemporary Medicine: Theory, Practice, and Research*, edited by D. Peters, 17–29. New York: Churchill Livingstone, 2001.

Eshel, Esther. "Genres of Magical Texts in the Dead Sea Scrolls." In *Demonology of Israelite-Jewish and Early Christian Literature in Context of Their Environment*, edited by Armin Lange et al., 395–413. Tübingen: Mohr/Siebeck, 2003.

Eve, Eric. *The Jewish Context of Jesus' Miracles.* Journal for the Study of the New Testament Supplements 231. Sheffield: Sheffield Academic Press, 2002.

———. *The Healer from Nazareth: Jesus' Miracles in Historical Context.* London: SPCK, 2009.

Fanon, Frantz. *The Wretched of the Earth.* Translated by Constance Farrington. New York: Grove, 1963.

Faraone, Christopher A., and Dirk Obbink. "Preface." In *Magika Hiera: Ancient Greek Magic and Religion*, edited by Christopher A. Faraone and Dirk Obbink, v–vii. Oxford: Oxford University Press, 1991.

Fay, Brian et al., eds. *History and Theory: Contemporary Readings.* Malden, MA: Blackwell, 1998.

Fitzhugh, Michael L., and William H. J. Leckie. "Agency, Postmodernism, and the Causes of Change." In *History and Theory* 40 (2001) 59–81.

Fitzmyer, Joseph A. *The Gospel according to Luke.* 2 vols. AB 28–28A. Garden City, NY: Doubleday, 1981–85.

Flowers, Michael. "Jesus' Journey in Mark 7:31: Interpretation and Historical Implications for Markan Authorship and Both the Scope and Impact of Jesus' Ministry." *JSHJ* 14 (2016) 158–85.

Foley, John Miles. *The Theory of Oral Composition: History and Methodology.* Bloomington: Indiana University Press, 1988.

———. *Immanent Art: From Structure to Meaning in Traditional Oral Epic.* Bloomington: Indiana University Press, 1991.

———. *Singer of Tales in Performance.* Bloomington: Indiana University Press, 1995.

———. *How to Read an Oral Poem.* Illinois University Press, 2002.

———. "The Riddle of Q." in *Oral Performance, Popular Tradition, and Hidden Transcript in Q*, edited by Richard A. Horsley, 123–40. SemeiaSt 60. Atlanta: Society of Biblical Literature, 2006.

Foucault, Michel. *The Birth of the Clinic: An Archaeology of Medical Perception.* New York: Pantheon, 1973.

———. *The History of Sexuality.* Vol. 1, *An Introduction.* Translated by Robert Hurley. New York: Pantheon, 1978.

Frankfurter, David. ed. *Guide to the Study of Ancient Magic.* RGRW 189. Leiden: Brill, 2019.

———. "Ritual Expertise in Roman Egypt and the Problem of the Category 'Magician.'" In *Envisioning Magic: A Princeton Seminar and Symposium*, edited by Peter Schäfer and Hans Kippenberg, 115–35. Studies in the History of Religions 75. Leiden: Brill, 1997.

————. *Religion in Roman Egypt: Assimilation and Resistance*. Princeton: Princeton University Press, 1998.

Frazer, James G. *The Golden Bough: A Study in Magic and Religion*. New York: Macmillan, 1922.

Fredriksen, Paula. *Jesus of Nazareth, King of the Jews: A Jewish Life and the Emergence of Christianity*. New York: Vintage, 2000.

Funk, Robert W., and the Jesus Seminar. *The Acts of Jesus: The Search for the Authentic Deeds of Jesus*. San Francisco: HarperSanFrancisco, 1998.

Gager, John G., ed. *Curse Tablets and Binding Spells from the Ancient World*. Oxford: Oxford University Press, 1992.

————. "Introduction." *Curse Tablets and Binding Spells from the Ancient World*, edited by John G. Gager. Oxford: Oxford University Press, 1992.

Gallagher, Eugene V. *Divine Man or Magician? Celsus and Origen on Jesus*. Society of Biblical Literature Dissertation Series 64. Chico, CA: Scholars, 1982.

Gamble, Harry Y. *Books and Readers in the Early Church: A History of Early Christian Texts*. New Haven: Yale University Press, 1995.

Geertz, Clifford. "From the Native's Point of View: On the Nature of Anthropological Understanding." In *Culture Theory*, ed Richard Schweder and Robert LeVine, 123–36. Cambridge: Cambridge University Press, 1984.

Good, Byron J. *Medicine, Rationality, and Experience: An Anthropological Perspective*. Cambridge: Cambridge University Press, 1994.

Good, Byron, and Mary-Jo Good. "The Semantics of Medical Discourse." In *Sciences and Cultures: Anthropological and Historical Studies of the Sciences*, edited by Everett Mendelsohn and Yehuda Elkana, 177–212. Sociology of the Sciences 5. Dordrecht: Reidel, 1981.

Good, Mary-Jo DelVecchio et al., eds. *Pain as Human Experience: An Anthropological Perspective*. Comparative Studies of Health Systems and Medical Care 31. Berkeley: University of California Press, 1992.

Goodman, Felicitas D. *How About Demons? Possession and Exorcism in the Modern World*. Bloomington: Indiana University Press, 1988.

Goodman, Martin. "The First Jewish Revolt: Social Conflict and the Problem of Debt." *JJS* 33 (1982) 422–34.

————. *The Ruling Class of Judaea: The Origins of the Jewish Revolt against Rome, A.D. 66–70*. Cambridge: Cambridge University Press, 1987.

Gordon, Richard L. "Religion in the Roman Empire: The Civic Compromise and Its Limits." In *Pagan Priests: Religion and Power in the Ancient World*, edited by Mary Beard and John North, 235–53. Ithaca, NY: Cornell University Press, 1990.

————. "Reporting the Marvelous: Private Divination in the Greek Magical Papyri." In *Envisioning Magic: A Princeton Seminar and Symposium*, edited by Peter Schaefer and Hans Kippenberg, 65–92. Studies in the History of Religion 75. Leiden: Brill, 1997.

Gordon, Richard L., and Francisco Marco Simon. "Introduction." In *Magical Practices in the Latin West*, edited by Richard L. Gordon and Francisco Marco Simon, 1–49. RGRW 68. Leiden: Brill, 2010.

Graf, Fritz. *Magic in the Ancient World*. Revealing Antiquity 10. Cambridge: Harvard University Press, 1997.

Gray, Rebecca. *Prophetic Figures in Late Second Temple Jewish Palestine: The Evidence from Josephus*. Oxford: Oxford University Press, 1993.

Green, William Scott. "Palestinian Holy Men: Charismatic Leadership and Rabbinic Tradition." *ANRW* II.19 (1979) 619–47.

Gregory, B. S. "The Other Confessional History: On Secular Bias in the Study of Religion." *History and Theory* 45 (2006) 132–49.

Guelich, Robert A. *Mark 1—8:26*. Word Biblical Commentary 34A. Dallas: Word, 1989.

Guijarro, Santiago. "The Politics of Exorcism: Jesus' Reaction to Negative Labels in the Beelzebul Controversy." In *The Social Setting of Jesus and the Gospels*, edited by Wolfgang Stegemann, Bruce Malina, and Gerd Theissen, 159–74. Minneapolis: Fortress. 2002.

Hadas, Moses, and Morton Smith. *Heroes and Gods: Spiritual Biographies in Antiquity*. Religious Perspectives 13. New York: Harper & Row, 1965.

Hahn, Robert A. *Sickness and Healing: An Anthropological Perspective*. New Haven: Yale University Press, 1995.

Haines-Eitzen, Kim. *Guardians of Letters: Literacy, Power, and the Transmitters of Early Christian Literature*. Oxford: Oxford University Press, 2000.

Harris, William V. *Ancient Literacy*. Cambridge: Harvard University Press, 1989.

Hartigan, Karelisa. "Drama and Healing." In *Health in Antiquity*, edited by Helen King, 162–79. London: Routledge, 2005.

Heinrichs, A., ed. *Papyri Graecae Magicae: Die Griechischen Zauberpapyri*. 2nd ed. Stuttgart: Teubner, 1973–1974.

Henderson, Ian. "Didache and Orality in Synoptic Comparison." *JBL* 111 (1992) 283–306.

Hengel, Martin. *The Charismatic Leader and His Followers*. Translated by James Greig. Edinburgh: T. & T. Clark, 1981.

Hezser, Catherine. *Jewish Literacy in Roman Palestine*. Texte und Studien zum antiken Judentum 81. Tubingen: Mohr/Siebeck, 2001.

Hillers, Delbert. *Covenant: The History of a Biblical Idea*. Seminars in the History of Ideas. Baltimore: Johns Hopkins University Press, 1969.

Hollenbach, Paul W. "Jesus, Demoniacs, and Public Authorities: A Socio-Historical Study." *Journal of the American Academy of Religion* 49 (1981) 567–88.

Hopfner, Theodor. *Griechisch-ägyptischer Offenbarungszauber*. 2 vols. 1921–24. Reprint, Studien zur Palaeographie und Papyruskunde 21. Amsterdam: Hakkert, 1974.

Horsley, G. H. R. *New Documents Illustrating Early Christianity*. North Ryde, Aus: Macquarie University Press, 1981.

Horsley, Kathryn J. "From Neurons to King County Neighborhoods." *American Journal of Public Health* 95 (2005) 562–66.

Horsley, Richard A. *Archaeology, History, and Society in Galilee The Social Context of Jesus and the Rabbis*. Harrisburg, PA: Trinity, 1996.

———. "Can Study of the Historical Jesus Escape Its Typographical Captivity?" *JSHJ* 19 (2021) 265–329. https://doi.org/10.1163/17455197-19030001.

———. "Contesting Authority: Popular vs. Scribal Tradition in Continuing Performance." In *Text and Tradition in Performance and Writing*, 99–122. BPCS 9. Eugene, OR: Cascade Books, 2013.

———. *Covenant Economics: A Biblical Vision of Justice for All*. Louisville: Westminster John Knox, 2009.

———. "Further Reflections on Witchcraft and European Folk Religion." *History of Religion* 19 (1979) 71–95.

————. *Galilee: History, Politics, People.* Valley Forge: Trinity, 1995.

————. *Hearing the Whole Story: The Politics of Plot in Mark's Gospel.* Louisville: Westminster John Knox, 2001.

————, ed. *Hidden Transcripts and The Arts Of Resistance: Applying the Work of James C. Scott to Jesus and Paul.* SemeiaSt 48. Atlanta: Society of Biblical Literature, 2004.

————. "High Priests and the Politics of Roman Palestine: A Contextual Analysis of the Evidence in Josephus." *JSJ* 17 (1986) 23–55.

————. "Imagining Mark's Story Composed in Oral Performance." In *Text and Tradition in Performance and Writing,* 246–78. BPCS 9. Eugene, OR: Cascade Books, 2013.

————. "Introduction." In *Oral Performance, Popular Tradition, and Hidden Transcript in Q,* edited by Richard A. Horsley, 1–22. SemeiaSt 60. Atlanta: Society of Biblical Literature, 2006.

————. *Jesus and Magic: Freeing the Gospel Stories from Modern Misconceptions* . Eugene, OR: Cascade Books, 2014.

————. *Jesus and the Politics of Roman Palestine.* 2nd ed. Eugene, OR: Cascade Books, 2021.

————. *Jesus and the Spiral of Violence: Popular Jewish Resistance in Roman Palestine.* San Francisco: Harper & Row, 1987.

————. *Jesus and Empire: The Kingdom of God and the New World Disorder.* Minneapolis: Fortress, 2002.

————. *Jesus in Context: Power, People, and Performance.* Minneapolis: Fortress, 2008.

————. *Jesus the Prophet and the Renewal of Israel.* Grand Rapids: Eerdmans, 2012.

————. "The Language(s) of the Kingdom: From Aramaic to Greek and Galilee to Syria." In *Text and Tradition in Performance and Writing,* 198–219. BPCS 9. Eugene, OR: Cascade Books, 2013.

————. "'Like One of the Prophets of Old': Two Types of Popular Prophets at the Time of Jesus." *Catholic Biblical Quarterly* 47 (1985) 435–63.

————. "Oral Communication, Oral Performance, and New Testament Interpretation." In *Text and Tradition in Performance and Writing,* 1–30. BPCS 9. Eugene, OR: Cascade Books, 2013.

————. "Oral Composition-and-Performance of the Instructional Speeches in Ben Sira." In *Text and Tradition in Performance and Writing,* 73–98. BPCS 9. Eugene, OR: Cascade Books, 2013.

————. "Oral Performance and the Gospel of Mark: The Oral and Written Gospel, Twenty-Five Years Later." In *Text and Tradition in Performance and Writing,* 220–45. BPCS 9. Eugene, OR: Cascade Books, 2013.

————. "Oral Performance in the Emergence of the Gospel of Mark as Scripture." In *Text and Tradition in Performance and Writing,* 279–302. BPCS 9. Eugene, OR: Cascade Books Books, 2013.

————. ed. *Oral Performance, Popular Tradition, and Hidden Transcript in Q.* SemeiaSt 60. Atlanta: Society of Biblical Literature, 2006.

————. "Oral Tradition in New Testament Studies." *Oral Tradition* 18 (2003) 34–36.

————. "The Politics of Disguise and Public Declaration of the Hidden Transcript." In *Hidden Transcripts and the Arts of Resistance,* edited by Richard A. Horsley, 61–80. SemeiaSt 48. Atlanta: Society of Biblical Literature, 2004.

————. "Popular Messianic Movements Around the Time of Jesus." *Catholic Biblical Quarterly* 46 (1984) 471–93.

————. "Popular Prophetic Movements at the Time of Jesus: Their Principal Features and Social Origins." *JSNT* 26 (1986) 3–27.

————. "Q and Jesus: Assumptions, Approaches, and Analyses." *Semeia* 55 (1991) 175–212.

————. "Questions about Redactional Strata and the Social Relations Reflected in Q." In *Society of Biblical Literature 1989 Seminar Papers*, edited by David Lull, 186–203. Chico, CA: Scholars, 1989.

————. *Revolt of the Scribes: Resistance and Apocalyptic Origins*. Minneapolis: Fortress, 2010.

————. *Scribes, Visionaries, and the Politics of Second Temple Judea*. Louisville: Westminster John Knox, 2007.

————. "The Sicarii: Ancient Jewish Terrorists." *JR* 59 (1979) 435–58.

————. "Social Relations and Social Conflict in the Epistle of Enoch." In *For a Later Generation*, edited by Randall Argall et al., 100–115. Harrisburg, PA: Trinity, 2000.

————. *Sociology and the Jesus Movement*. New York: Crossroad, 1989.

————. *Text and Tradition in Performance and Writing*, 73–98. BPCS 9. Eugene, OR: Cascade Books, 2013.

————. "Who Were the Witches? The Social Role of the Accused in the European Witch Trials." *Journal of Interdisciplinary History* 9 (1979) 689–715.

Horsley, Richard A., with Jonathan Draper. *Whoever Hears You Hears Me: Prophecy, Performance, and Tradition in Q*. Harrisburg, PA: Trinity, 1999.

Horsley, Richard A., with John S. Hanson. *Bandits, Prophets, and Messiahs: Popular Movements at the Time of Jesus*. 1985. Reprint, Harrisburg, PA: Trinity, 1999.

Horsley, Richard, and Tom Thatcher. *John, Jesus, and the Renewal of Israel*. Grand Rapids: Eerdmans, 2013.

Hull, John M. *Hellenistic Magic and the Synoptic Tradition*. Studies in Biblical Theology 2/28. Naperville, IL: Allenson, 1974.

Ilan, Tal. "In the Footsteps of Jesus: Jewish Women in a Jewish Movement." In *Transformative Encounters: Jesus and Women Re-viewed*, edited by Ingrid Rosa Kitzberger, 115–36. BibIntSer 43. Leiden: Brill, 2000.

Jackson, Ralph. *Doctors and Diseases in the Roman Empire*. Norman: University of Oklahoma Press, 1988.

Jaffee, Martin S. *Torah in the Mouth: Writing and Oral Tradition in Palestinian Judaism, 200 BCE–400 CE*. Oxford: Oxford University Press, 2001.

Janowicz, Naomi. *Magic in the Roman World: Pagans, Jews, and Christians*. Religion in the First Christian Centuries. London: Routledge, 2001.

Janzen, John. "The Comparative Study of Medical Systems as Changing Social Systems." *Social Science and Medicine* 12 (1978) 121–29.

Jensen, Morten Hørning. "Herod Antipas in Galilee: Friend or Foe of the Historical Jesus?" *JSHJ* 5/1 (2007) 7–32. https://www.academia.edu/6542935/Herod_Antipas_in_Galilee_Friend_or_Foe_of_the_Historical_Jesus

————. *Herod Antipas in Galilee*. WUNT 2/215. Tübingen: Mohr/Siebeck, 2010.

Jonge, Marianus de. "The Use of the Term 'Anointed' in the Time of Jesus." *NovT* 8 (1966) 132–48.

Johnson, Thomas M., and Carolyn F. Sargent, eds. *Medical Anthropology: Contemporary Theory and Method*. New York: Praeger, 1990.

Kapferer, Bruce. *A Celebration of Demons: Exorcism and the Aesthetics of Healing in Sri Lanka*. Bloomington: Indiana University Press, 1983.

Kautsky, John. *The Politics of Aristocratic Empires*. 1982. Reprint, New Brunswick, NJ: Transaction, 1997.

Kazmierski, Carl R. "Evangelist and Leper: A Socio-Cultural Study of Mark 1:40–45." *NTS* 38 (2003) 37–50.

Kee, Howard Clark. "Medicine and Healing." In *Anchor Bible Dictionary*, edited by David Noel Freedman, 4:659–64. New York: Doubleday, 1992.

———. *Medicine, Miracle, and Magic in New Testament Times*. Society for New Testament Studies Monograph Series 55. Cambridge: Cambridge University Press, 1986.

———. *Miracle in the Early Christian World: A Study in Sociohistorical Method*. New Haven: Yale University Press, 1983.

———. "The Terminology of Mark's Exorcism Stories." *NTS* 14 (1968) 232–46.

Keener, Craig S. *Miracles: The Credibility of the New Testament Accounts*. 2 vols. Grand Rapids: Baker, 2011.

Keesing, Roger. M. "Anthropology as Interpretive Quest." *Current Anthropology* 28/2 (1987) 161–62.

———. "Models, 'Folk' and 'Cultural': Paradigms Regained?" In *Cultural Models in Language and Thought*, edited by Dorothy Holland and Naomi Quinn, 369–93. Cambridge: Cambridge University Press, 1987.

Kelber, Werner H. *Imprints, Voiceprints and Footprints of Memory: The Collected Essays of Werner H. Kelber*. SBL Resources for Biblical Study 74. Atlanta: Society of Biblical Literature, 2013.

———. "Jesus and Tradition: Words in Time, Words in Space." *Semeia* 65 (1994) 139–67.

———. *Mark's Story of Jesus*. Philadelphia: Fortress, 1979.

———. "On 'Mastering the Genre.'" In *Modern and Ancient Literary Criticism of the Gospels: Continuing the Debate on Gospel Genre(s)*, edited by Robert Calhoun et al., 57–76. WUNT 451. Tübingen: Mohr/Siebeck, 2020.

———. *The Oral and the Written Gospel: The Hermeneutics of Speaking and Writing in the Synoptic Tradition, Mark, Paul, and Q*. Bloomington: Indiana University Press, 1997.

———. "The Words of Memory: Christian Origins as MnemoHistory—a Response." In *Memory, Tradition, and Text: Uses of the Past in Early Christianity*, edited by Alan Kirk and Tom Thatcher, 221–48. SemeiaSt 52. Atlanta: Society of Biblical Literature, 2005.

King, Helen, ed. *Health in Antiquity*. London: Routledge, 2005.

Kingsbury, Jack Dean. *Matthew as Story*. Philadelphia: Fortress, 1984.

Kirk, Alan. *The Composition of the Sayings Source: Genre, Synchrony, and Wisdom Redaction in Q*. NovTSup 91. Leiden: Brill, 1998.

———. "Social and Cultural Memory." In *Memory, Tradition, and Text: Uses of the Past in Early Christianity*, edited by Alan Kirk and Tom Thatcher, 1–24. SemeiaSt 52. Atlanta: Society of Biblical Literature, 2005.

———. "Who Are the Q Scribes? Questioning the Village Scribes Hypothesis." In *Bridges in New Testament Interpretation: Interdisciplinary Advances*, edited by Neil Elliott and Werner H. Kelber, 67–95. Lanham, MD: Fortress Academic, 2018.

Kirk, Alan, and Tom Thatcher, eds. *Memory, Tradition, and Text: Uses of the Past in Early Christianity*. SemeiaSt 52. Atlanta: Society of Biblical Literature, 2005.

Kleinman, Arthur. "Concepts and a Model for the Comparison of Medical Systems as Cultural Systems." In *Concepts of Health, Illness, and Disease: A Comparative Perspective*, edited by Caroline Currer and Meg Stacey, 29–47. New York: Berg, 1986.

―――. "Depression and the Translation of Emotional Worlds." In *Culture and Depression: Studies in the Anthropology and Cross-Cultural Psychiatry of Affect and Disorder*, edited by Arthur Kleinman and Byron Good, 63–100. Comparative Studies of Health Systems and Medical Care. Berkeley: University of California Press, 1985.

―――. "Medicine's Symbolic Reality: On the Central Problem in the Philosophy of Medicine." *Inquiry* 16 (1973), 206–13.

―――. *Patients and Healers in the Context of Culture: An Exploration of the Borderland between Anthropology, Medicine, and Psychiatry*. Comparative Studies of Health Systems and Medical Care 3. Berkeley: University of California Press, 1980.

Kleinman, Arthur, and Byron Good, eds. *Culture and Depression: Studies in the Anthropology and Cross-Cultural Psychiatry of Affect and Disorder*. Comparative Studies of Health Systems and Medical Care. Berkeley: University of California Press, 1985.

Kleinman, Arthur et al. "Pain as Human Experience: An Introduction." In *Pain as Human Experience: An Anthropological Perspective*, edited by Mary-Jo DelVecchio Good et al., 1–28. Comparative Studies of Health Systems and Medical Care 31. Berkeley: University of California Press, 1992.

Kloppenborg, John S. *The Formation of Q: Trajectories in Ancient Wisdom Collections*. Studies in Antiquity and Christianity. Philadelphia: Fortress, 1987.

―――. "Literary Convention, Self-Evidence, and the Social History of the Q People." *Semeia* 55 (1991) 77–102.

Klutz, Todd. *The Exorcism Stories in Luke-Acts*. Society for New Testament Studies Monograph Series 129. Cambridge: Cambridge University Press, 2004.

Knight, Douglas. *Law, Power, and Justice in Ancient Israel*. Library of Ancient Israel. Louisville: Westminster John Knox, 2011.

Koester, Helmut. "One Jesus and Four Primitive Gospels." In James M. Robinson and Helmut Koester, *Trajectories through Early Christianity*, 158–204. 1971. Reprint, Eugene, OR: Wipf & Stock, 2006.

Koskenniemi, Erkki. "The Function of the Miracle Stories in Philostratus's *Vita Apollonii Tyaenensis*." In *Wonders Never Cease: The Purpose of Narrating Miracle Stories in the New Testament and Its Environment*, edited by Michael Labahn and Bert Jan Lietaert Peerbolte, 70–83. LNTS 288. London: T. & T. Clark, 2006.

Kotansky, Roy. "Incantations and Prayers for Salvation on Inscribed Greek Amulets." In *Magika Hiera: Ancient Greek Magic and Religion*, edited by Christopher A. Faraone and Dirk Obbink, 107–36. Oxford: Oxford University Press, 1991.

Kraemer, Ross S. "Jewish Women and Women's Judaism(s) at the Beginning of Christianity." In *Women and Christian Origins*, edited by Ross S. Kraemer and Mary Rose D'Angelo. Oxford: Oxford University Press, 1999.

Kramer, Fritz W. *The Red Fez: Art and Spirit Possession in Africa*. New York: Verso, 1993.

Labahn, Michael, and Bert Jan Lietaert Peerbolte. *Wonders Never Cease: The Purpose of Narrating Miracle Stories in the New Testament and its Religious Environment*. LNTS 288. London: T. & T. Clark, 2006.

Lange, Armin. "The Essene Position on Magic and Divination." In *Legal Texts and Legal Issues: Proceedings of the Second Meeting of the International Organization for Qumran Studies, Cambridge 1995. In Honour of Joseph M. Baumgarten*, edited by Moshe Bernstein et al., 377–435. Studies on the Texts of the Desert of Judah 23. Leiden: Brill, 1997.

Larsen, Matthew. *Gospels before the Book*. New York: Oxford University Press, 2018.

Le Donne, Anthony. *The Historiographical Jesus: Memory, Typology, and the Son of David*. Waco: Baylor University Press, 2009.

Lefebvre, Georges. *The Great Fear of 1789: Rural Panic in Revolutionary France*. Translated by Joan White. Princeton: Princeton University Press, 1973.

Leppin, Hartmut. "Imperial Miracles and Elitist Discourses." In *Miracles Revisited: New Testament Miracle Stories and Their Concepts of Reality*, edited by Stefan Alkier and Annette Weissenrieder, 233–48. SBIR 2. Berlin: deGruyter, 2013.

Levine, Lee I. "The Jewish Patriarch (Nasi) in Third-Century Palestine." *ANRW* II.19.2 (1979) 649–88.

Levine, Amy-Jill. "Discharging Responsibility: Matthean Jesus, Biblical Law, and Hemorrhaging Woman." In *Treasures Old and New: Recent Contributions in Matthean Studies*, edited by David Bauer and Mark Powell, 379–97. SBL Symposium Series. Atlanta: Scholars, 1996.

Lewis, I. M. *Ecstatic Religion: An Anthropological Study of Spirit Possession and Shamanism*. Harmandsworth, UK: Penguin, 1971.

Liew, Tat-siong Benny. *Politics of Parousia: Reading Mark Inter(con)textually*. BibIntSer 42. Leiden: Brill, 1999.

———. "Postcolonial Criticism: Echoes of a Subalterns Contribution and Exclusion." In *Mark and Method: New Approaches in Bible Studies*, edited by Janice Capel Anderson and Stephen D. Moore, 211–31. 2nd ed. Minneapolis: Fortress, 2008.

Lock, Margaret. "On Being Ethnic: The Politics of Identity Breaking and Making in Canada, or *Nevra* on Sunday." *Culture, Medicine, and Psychiatry* 14 (1990) 237–54.

Lock, Margaret, and Nancy Scheper-Hughes. "A Critical-Interpretive Approach in Medical Anthropology: Rituals and Routines of Discipline and Dissent." In *Medical Anthropology: Contemporary Theory and Method*, edited by Thomas M. Johnson and Carolyn F. Sargent, 41–72. New York: Praeger, 1990.

Lord, Albert. *The Singer of Tales*. Cambridge: Harvard University Press, 1960.

Lorenz, C. "Can Histories Be True? Narrativism, Positivism, and the 'Metaphorical Turn.'" *History and Theory* 37 (1998) 309–29.

Luig, Ute. "Constructing Local Worlds: Spirit Possession in the Gwembe Valley, Zambia." In *Spirit Possession, Modernity, and Power in Africa*, edited by Heike Behrend and Uta Luig, 124–41. Madison: University of Wisconsin Press, 1999.

Luke, Trevor Stacy. "A Healing Touch for Empire: Vespasian's Wonders in Domitianic Rome." *Greece & Rome* 57 (2010) 77–106.

Lutz, Catherine. "The Domain of Emotion Words on Ifaluk." *American Ethnologist* 9 (1982) 113–28.

MacRae, George. "Miracle in the Antiquities of Josephus." In *Miracles: Cambridge Studies in Their Philosophy and History*, edited by C. F. D. Moule, 129–47. London: Mowbray, 1965.

Malbon, Elizabeth Struthers. "The Jesus of Mark and 'Son of David.'" In *Between Author and Audience in Mark: Narration, Characterization, Interpretation*, edited by

Elizabeth Struthers Malbon, 162–85. New Testament Monographs 23. Sheffield: Sheffield Phoenix, 2009.

————. "Narrative Criticism: How Does the Story Mean?" In *Mark and Method: New Approaches in Bible Studies*, edited by Janice Capel Anderson and Stephen D. Moore, 29–58. 2nd ed. Minneapolis: Fortress, 2008.

Malina, Bruce J. "Social-Scientific Methods in Historical Jesus Research." In *The Social Setting of Jesus and the Gospels*, edited by Wolfgang Stegemann et al., 3–26. Minneapolis: Fortress, 2002.

Margalioth, Mordechai. *Sepher Ha-Razim: The Book of Mysteries*. Translated by Michael Morgan. SBL Texts and Tools 25. Chico, CA: Scholars, 1983.

Marcus, Joel. "The Jewish War and the *Sitz im Leben* of Mark." *JBL* 111 (1992) 441–62.

————. *Mark 1–8: A New Translation with Introduction and Commentary*. AB 27. New York: Doubleday, 2002.

————. *Mark 9–16. A New Translation with Introduction and Commentary*. AB 28. New York: Doubleday, 2009.

Martin, Dale B. *Inventing Superstition: From the Hippocratics to the Christians*. Cambridge: Harvard University Press, 2004.

————. *The Corinthian Body*. New Haven: Yale University Press, 1999.

Masquelier, Adeline. "The Invention of Anti-Tradition: Dodo Spirits in Southern Niger." In *Spirit Possession, Modernity, and Power in Africa*, edited by Heike Behrend and Uta Luig, 34–50. Madison: University of Wisconsin Press, 1999.

Mattern, Susan P. *Rome and the Enemy: Imperial Strategy in the Principate*. Berkeley: University of California Press, 1999.

McCullagh, C. B. "What Do Historians Argue About?" *History and Theory* 43 (2004) 18–38.

McKinlay, John B. "The Case for Focusing Upstream: The Political Economy of Illness." In *The Sociology of Health and Illness: Critical Perspectives*, edited by Peter Conrad and Rochelle Kern, 9–25. 2nd ed. New York: St. Martin's, 1986.

McNeill, William H. *Plagues and Peoples*. Garden City, NY: Anchor, 1976.

Meier, John P. *A Marginal Jew: Rethinking the Historical Jesus*. Vol. 1: *The Roots of the Problem and the Person*. New York: Doubleday, 1991.

————. *A Marginal Jew: Rethinking the Historical Jesus*. Vol. 2: *Mentor, Message, and Miracles*. New York: Doubleday, 1994.

Mendenhall, George E. "Covenant." In *Interpreters Dictionary of the Bible*, edited by George Arthur Buttrick, 1:714–23. Nashville: Abingdon, 1962.

Miller, Geoffrey. "Attitude toward Dogs in Ancient Israel: A Reassessment." *Journal for the Study of the Old Testament* 32 (2008) 487–500.

Miller, Patricia Cox. "In Praise of Nonsense." In *Classical Mediterranean Spirituality: Egyptian, Greek, Roman*, edited by A. H. Armstrong, 481–505. World Spirituality 15. New York: Crossroad, 1986.

Miller, Shem. *Dead Sea Media: Orality, Textuality, and Memory in the Scrolls from the Judean Desert*. Studies on the Texts of the Desert of Judah 129. Leiden: Brill, 2018.

Moore, Stephen D. *Literary Criticism and the Gospels: The Theoretical Challenge*. New Haven: Yale University Press, 1989.

————. "Mark and Empire: 'Zealot' and 'Postcolonial' Readings." In *The Postcolonial Biblical Reader*, edited by R. S. Sugirtharajah, 193–205. Malden, MA: Blackwell, 2006.

Morgan, Lynn M. "Dependency Theory in the Political Economy of Health: An Anthropological Critique." *Medical Anthropology Quarterly* n.s. 1 (1987) 131–54.

Morgan, M. Gwyn. *The Year of Four Emperors.* Oxford: Oxford University Press, 2006.

Morsy, Soheir. "The Missing Link in Medical Anthropology: The Political Economy of Health." *Reviews in Anthropology* 6 (1979) 349–63.

―――. "Political Economy in Medical Anthropology." In *Medical Anthropology*, edited by Carolyn F. Sargent and Thomas M. Johnson, 21–40. Rev. ed. London: Praeger, 1996.

―――. "Sex Roles, Power, and Illness in an Egyptian Village." *American Ethnologist* 4 (1978) 137–50.

Moyer, Ian. "Thessalos of Tralles and Cultural Exchange." In *Prayer, Magic, and the Stars in the Ancient and Late Antique World*, edited by Scott Noegel et al., 39–56. Magic in History. University Park: Pennsylvania State University Press, 2003.

Myers, Ched. *Binding the Strong Man: A Political Reading of Mark's Story of Jesus.* Maryknoll, NY: Orbis, 2008.

Navarro, Vicente. *Medicine under Capitalism.* New York: Prodist, 1976.

Naveh, Joseph, and Shaul Shaked. *Amulets and Magical Bowls: Aramaic Incantations of Late Antiquity.* Jerusalem: Magnes, 1985.

Neusner, Jacob. *A History of the Jews in Babylonia.* Vol. 4: *The Age of Shapur II.* Studia post-Biblica 14. 1969. Reprint, Eugene, OR: Wipf & Stock, 2008.

―――. *A History of the Jews in Babylonia.* Vol. 5: *Later Sasanian Times.* Studia post-Biblica 14. 1970. Reprint, Eugene, OR: Wipf & Stock, 2008.

―――. *The Wonder-Working Lawyers of Talmudic Babylonia: The Theory and Practice of Judaism in Its Formative Age.* Studies in Judaism. Lanham, MD: University Press of America, 1987.

Neusner, Jacob et al., eds. *Judaisms and Their Messiahs at the Turn of the Christian Era.* Cambridge: Cambridge University Press, 1987.

Neville, David J. "Moral Vision and Eschatology in Mark." *JBL* 127 (2008) 359–84.

Newheart, Michael Willett. *"My Name is Legion." The Story and Soul of the Gerasene Demoniac.* Interfaces. Collegeville: Liturgical, 2004.

Nickelsburg, George W. E. *Jewish Literature between the Bible and the Mishnah.* Philadelphia: Fortress, 1981.

Nickelsburg, George W. E., and James C. VanderKam. *1 Enoch: The Hermeneia Translation.* Minneapolis: Fortress, 2012.

Nock, Arthur Darby. "Paul and the *Magos*." In *Essays on Religion in the Ancient World*, edited by Zeph Stewart, 1:308–10. Cambridge: Harvard University Press, 1972.

―――. "The Greek Magical Papyri." In *Essays on Religion in the Ancient World*, edited by Zeph Stewart, 1:176–94. Cambridge: Harvard University Press, 1972.

Novakovic, Lidija. *Messiah, the Healer of the Sick: A Study of Jesus as the Son of David in the Gospel of Matthew.* WUNT 2/170; Tübingen: Mohr/Siebeck, 2003.

Oakman, Douglas E. "Rulers' Houses, Thieves, and Usurpers: The Beelzebul Pericope." *Forum* 4/3 (1988) 109–23. Reprinted in Oakman, *Jesus and the Peasants*, 118–31. Matrix 4. Eugene, OR: Cascade Books, 2008.

Ogden, Daniel. *Greek and Roman Necromancy.* Princeton: Princeton University Press, 2001.

Ong, Aihwa. "The Production of Possession: Spirits and the Multinational Corporation in Malaysia." *American Ethnologist* 15 (1988), 28–42.

————. *Spirits of Resistance and Capitalist Discipline: Factory Women in Malaysia*. Albany: State University of New York Press, 1987.

Onoge, Omafume. "Capitalism and Public Health: A Neglected Theme in the Medical Anthropology of Africa." In *Topias and Utopias in Health: Policy Studies*, edited by Stanley R. Ingram and Anthony E. Thomas eds., 219–32. World Anthropology. The Hague: Mouton, 1975.

Owusu, Daniel A. "Jesus, the African Healer." Master thesis in Contextual Theology, Faculty of Theology, University of Oslo, 2001.

Pandolfi, Mariella. "Boundaries Inside the Body: Women's Sufferings in Southern Peasant Italy." *Culture, Medicine and Psychiatry* 14 (1990) 255–73.

Parker, D. C. *The Living Text of the Gospels*. Cambridge: Cambridge University Press, 1997.

————. "Variants and Variance." In *Texts and Traditions: Essays in Honor of J. Keith Elliott*, edited by Peter Doble and Jeffrey Kloha, 25–34. Leiden: Brill, 2014.

Parry, Milman. *The Making of Homeric Verse: The Collected Papers of Milman Parry*. Oxford: Oxford University Press, 1987.

Peel, J. D. Y. "An Africanist Revisits *Magic and the Millennium*." In *Secularization, Rationalism, and Sectarianism: Essays in Honour of Bryan R. Wilson*, edited by Eileen Barker et al., 81–100. Oxford: Clarendon, 1993.

Penner, Hans H. "Rationality, Ritual, and Science." In *Religion, Science, and Magic: In Concert and in Conflict*, edited by Jacob Neusner et al., 11–24. Oxford: Oxford University Press, 1989.

Penny, Douglas L., and Michael O. Wise. "'By the Power of Beelzebub': An Aramaic Incantation Formula from Qumran (4Q560)." *JBL* 113 (1994) 627–50.

Perkins, Pheme. "The Gospel of Mark." In *New Interpreter's Bible*, edited by Leander E. Keck, 8:509–733. Nashville: Abingdon, 1995.

Perrin, Norman. *Rediscovering the Teaching of Jesus*. New York: Harper, 1967.

Philostratus. *The Life of Apollonius of Tyana; the Epistles of Apollonius and the Treatise of Eusebius*. Translated by F. C. Conybeare. Loeb Classical Library. Cambridge: Harvard University Press, 1960.

Pilch, John J. *Healing in the New Testament: Insights from Medical and Mediterranean Anthropology*. Minneapolis: Fortress, 2000.

Portier-Young, Anathea. *Apocalypse against Empire: Theologies of Resistance in Early Judaism*. Grand Rapids: Eerdmans, 2011.

Preisendanz, Karl, ed. *Papyri Graecae Magicae: Die Griechischen Zauberpapyri*. Stuttgart: Teubner, 1928–1931. Revised and republished, A. Heinrichs. Stuttgart: Teubner, 1973–1974.

Price, Simon. *Rituals and Power: The Roman Imperial Cult in Asia Minor*. Cambridge: Cambridge University Press, 1984.

Rea, John. "A New Version of P. Yale Inv 299." *Zeitschrift für Papyrologie und Epigraphik* 27 (1977) 1511–56.

Reddy, W. M. "The Logic of Action: Indeterminacy, Emotion, and Historical Narrative." *History and Theory* 40 (2001) 10–33.

Remus, Harold. "Miracle, New Testament." In *Anchor Dictionary of the Bible*, edited by David Noel Freedman, 4:856–69. New York: Doubleday, 1992

————. *Pagan-Christian Conflict over Miracle in the Second Century*. Patristic Monograph Series 10. Cambridge, MA: Philadelphia Patristic Society, 1983.

Rhoads, David. *Reading Mark: Engaging the Gospel*. Minneapolis: Fortress, 2004.

Rhoads, David, and Donald Michie. *Mark as Story: An Introduction to the Narrative of a Gospel.* 1st ed. Philadelphia: Fortress, 1982.

Richardson, Peter. *Herod: King of the Jews and Friend of the Romans.* 1996. Reprint, Minneapolis: Fortress, 2001.

Ricks, Stephen D. "The Magician as Outsider in the Hebrew Bible and the New Testament." In *Ancient Magic and Ritual Power,* edited by Marvin Meyer and Paul Mirecki, 131–44. RGRW 129. Leiden: Brill, 1995.

Ritner, Robert K. *The Mechanics of Ancient Egyptian Magical Practice.* Chicago: Oriental Institute, 1993.

———. "The Religious, Social, and Legal Parameters of Traditional Egyptian Magic." In *Ancient Magic and Ritual Power,* edited by Marvin Meyer and Paul Mirecki, 43–60. RGRW 129. Leiden: Brill, 1995.

Rives, James B. "Magic in Roman Law: The Reconstruction of a Crime." *Classical Antiquity* 22 (2003) 313–39.

———. "*Magus* and its Cognates in Classical Latin." In *Magical Practices in the Latin West,* edited by Richard L. Gordon and Francisco Marco Simon, 53–77. RGRW 68. Leiden: Brill, 2010.

Robbins, Vernon K. "The Beelzebul Controversy in Mark and Luke: A Rhetorical and Social Analysis." *Forum* 7 (1991) 261–77.

———. "Sociorhetorical Interpretation in the Miracle Stories in the Synoptic Gospels." In *Miracle Discourse in the New Testament,* edited by Duane F. Watson, 17–84. Atlanta: Society of Biblical Literature, 2012.

Robinson, James M. "History of Q Research." In *The Critical Edition of Q,* edited by James M. Robinson et al., xix–lxxi. Hermeneia Supplements. Minneapolis: Fortress, 2000.

Robinson, James M. et al., eds. *The Critical Edition of Q: Synopsis Including the Gospels of Matthew and Luke, Mark and Thomas with English, German, and French translations of Q and Thomas.* Hermeneia. Minneapolis: Fortress, 2000.

———, eds. *The Sayings Gospel Q in Greek and English, with Parallels from the Gospels of Mark and Thomas.* Minneapolis: Fortress, 2002.

Rodriguez, Rafael. *Structuring Early Christian Memory: Jesus in Tradition, Performance, and Text.* LNTS 407. London: T. & T. Clark, 2010.

Rosaldo, Michele Zimbalist. *Knowledge and Passion: Ilongot Notions of Self and Social Life.* Cambridge Studies in Cultural Systems 4. Cambridge: Cambridge University Press, 1980.

Rosenblatt, Marie-Eloise. "Gender, Ethnicity, and Legal Considerations in the Haemorrhaging Woman's Story. Mark 5:25–34." In *Transformative Encounters: Jesus and Women Reviewed,* edited by Ingrid R. Kitzberger, 137–61. BibIntSer 43. Leiden: Brill 2000.

Said, Edward W. *Orientalism.* New York: Pantheon, 1978.

Saldarini, Anthony J. *Matthew's Christian-Jewish Community.* Chicago Studies in the History of Judaism. Chicago: University of Chicago Press, 1994.

———. *Pharisees, Scribes and Sadducees in Palestinian Society: A Sociological Approach.* Wilmington; Glazier, 1988.

Sanders, E. P. *Jesus and Judaism.* Philadelphia: Fortress, 1985.

———. *The Historical Figure of Jesus.* London: Penguin, 1993.

Scarborough, John. *Roman Medicine.* Aspects of Greek and Roman Life. Ithaca, NY: Cornell University Press, 1969.

Scheper-Hughes, Nancy. "The Madness of Hunger: Sickness, Delirium, and Human Needs." *Culture, Medicine, and Psychiatry* 12 (1988) 189–97.

Scheper-Hughes, Nancy, and Margaret M. Lock. "The Mindful Body: A Prolegomenon to Future Work in Medical Anthropology." *Medical Anthropology Quarterly* 1 (1987) 6–41.

Schiffman, Lawrence H., and Michael D. Swartz. *Hebrew and Aramaic Incantation Texts from the Cairo Genizah: Selected Texts from Taylor-Schechter Box K1.* Semitic Texts and Studies 1. Sheffield: JSOT Press, 1992.

Schwartz, Barry. "Frame Image: Towards a Semioticsa of Collective Memory." *Semiotica* 121 (1998) 1–38.

———. "Memory as a Cultural System: Abraham Lincoln in World War II." *American Sociological Review* 61 (1996) 908–27.

Scott, James C. *Domination and the Arts of Resistance: Hidden Transcripts.* New Haven: Yale University Press, 1990.

———. "Protest and Profanation: Agrarian Revolt and the Little Tradition." *Theory and Society* 4/1 and 2 (1977) 1–38, 211–46.

———. *Weapons of the Weak: Everyday Forms of Peasant Resistance.* New Haven: Yale University Press, 1985.

Sharp, Lesley A. "The Power of Possession in NW Madagascar: Contesting Colonial and National Hegemonies." In *Spirit Possession, Modernity, and Power in Africa,* edited by Heike Behrend and Uta Luig, 3–19. Madison: University of Wisconsin Press, 1999.

Shiner, Whitney. *Proclaiming the Gospel: First-Century Performance of Mark.* Harrisburg, PA: Trinity, 2003.

Singer, Merrill. "Reinventing Medical Anthropology: Towards a Critical Realignment." *Social Science and Medicine* 30 (1990) 179–87.

Small, Jocelyn Penny. *Wax Tablets of the Mind: Cognitive Studies of Memory and Literacy in Classical Antiquity.* London: Routledge, 1997.

Smelick, Willem. "The Languages of Roman Palestine." In *The Oxford Handbook of Jewish Daily Life in Roman Palestine,* edited by Catherine Hezser, 122–41. Oxford: Oxford University Press, 2010.

Smith, Jonathan Z. "The Temple and the Magician." In *Map Is not Territory: Studies in the History of Religions,* 172–89. Studies in Judaism in Late Antiquity 23. Leiden: Brill, 1978.

———. "Towards Interpreting Demonic Powers in Hellenistic and Roman Antiquity." In *ANRW* II.1.16 (1978) 425–39.

———. "Trading Places." In *Ancient Magic and Ritual Power,* edited by Marvin Meyer and Paul Mirecki, 3–27. RGRW 129. Leiden: Brill, 1995.

Smith, Morton. *Jesus the Magician.* San Francisco: Harper & Row, 1978.

Sorenson, Eric. *Possession and Exorcism in the New Testament and Early Christianity.* WUNT 2/157. Tübingen: Mohr/Siebeck, 2002.

Stafford, Emma. "'Without You No One Is Happy': The Cult of Health in Ancient Greece." In *Health in Antiquity,* edited by Helen King, 120–35. London: Routledge, 2005.

Stark, Rodney. "Reconceptualizing Religion, Magic, and Science." *Review of Religious Research* 43 (2001) 101–20.

Stratton, Kimberley B. *Naming the Witch: Ideology and Stereotype in the Ancient World.* Gender, Theory, and Religion. New York: Columbia University Press, 2007.

Strecker, Christian. "'The Duty of Discontent': Some Remarks on Pieter Craffert's *The Life of a Galilean Shaman: Jesus of Nazareth in Anthropological-Historical Perspective.*" *JSHJ* 11 (2013) 251–80.

———. "Jesus and the Demoniacs." In *The Social Setting of Jesus and the Gospels*, edited by Wolfgang Stegemann et al., 117–33. Minneapolis: Fortress. 2002.

Sundkler, Bengt G. M. *Bantu Prophets in South Africa.* 1948. Reprint, Oxford: Oxford University Press, 1961.

Sussman, Max. "Sickness and Disease." In *Anchor Bible Dictionary*, edited by David Noel Freedman, 6:6–15. New York: Doubleday, 1992.

Swartz, Michael D. "Magical Piety in Ancient and Medieval Judaism." In *Ancient Magic and Ritual Power*, edited by Marvin Meyer and Paul Mirecki, 167–83. RGRW 129. Leiden: Brill, 1995.

Tambiah, Stanley J. *Magic, Science, Religion and the Scope of Rationality.* Lewis Henry Morgan Lectures 1984. Cambridge: Cambridge University Press, 1990.

———. "The Magical Power of Words." *Man* n.s. 3 (1968) 175–208.

Taussig, Michael. "Reification and the Consciousness of the Patient." *Social Science and Medicine* 14B (1980) 3–13.

Taylor, David G. K. 2002. "Bilingualism and Diglossa in Late Antique Syria and Mesopotamia." In *Bilingualism in Ancient Society: Language Contact and the Written Text*, edited by J. N. Adams et al. 298–331. Oxford: Oxford University Press, 2002.

Tcherikover, Vicator A., ed. *Corpus Papyrorum Judaicarum.* 3 vols. Brepols: Turnhout, 1957–1964.

Theissen, Gerd. *The Gospels in Context: Social and Political History in the Synoptic Tradition.* Translated by Linda M. Maloney. Minneapolis: Fortress, 1991.

———. *The Miracle Stories of the Early Christian Tradition.* Translated by Francis McDonagh. Edited by John Riches. Philadelphia: Fortress, 1983.

———. *The Sociology of Early Palestinian Christianity.* Translated by John Bowden. Philadelphia: Fortress, 1978.

Tieleman, Tuen. "Miracle and Natural Cause in Galen." In *Miracles Revisited: New Testament Miracle Stories and Their Concepts of Reality*, edited by Stefan Alkier and Annette Weissenrieder, 101–3. SBIR 2. Berlin: de Gruyter, 2013.

Toner, J. P. *Homer's Turk: How Classics Shaped Ideas of the East.* Cambridge: Harvard University Press, 2012.

Toorn, Karel van der, ed. *The Image and the Book: Iconic Cults, Aniconism, and the Rise of Book Religion in Israel and the Ancient Near East.* Contributions to Biblical Exegesis and Theology 21. Leuven: Peeters, 1997.

Tov, Emanuel. *Scribal Practices and Approaches Reflected in the Texts Found in the Judean Desert.* STDJ 54. Leiden: Brill, 2004.

Trachtenberg, Joshua. *Jewish Magic and Superstition.* 1939. Reprint, New York: Behrman, 1972.

Trocmé, Étienne. *La formation de l'Evangile selon Marc.* Paris: Presses Universitaires de France, 1963.

———. *The Formation of the Gospel of Mark.* Translated by Pamela Gaughan. Philadelphia: Westminster, 1975.

Tuckett, Christopher, ed. *The Messianic Secret.* Issues in Religion and Theology. Philadelphia: Fortress, 1983.

Twelftree, Graham H. *Jesus the Exorcist: A Contribution to the Study of the Historical Jesus.* WUNT 2/54. Tübingen: Mohr/Siebeck, 1993.

————. *Jesus the Exorcist: A Contribution to the Study of the Historical Jesus*. Peabody: Hendrickson, 1993.

Tylor, Edward B. *Primitive Culture: Researches into the Development of Mythology, Philosophy, Religion, Art, and Custom*. London: Murray, 1871.

Udoh, Fabian E. *To Caesar What Is Caesar's: Tribute, Taxes, and Imperial Administration in Early Roman Palestine (63 B.C.E.—70 C.E.)*. Brown Judaic Studies 343. Providence: Brown University Press, 2005.

VanderKam, James C. *The Book of Jubilees: A Critical Text*. 2 vols. Corpus scriptorium Christianorum Orientalium 510, 511. Leuven: Peters, 1989.

————. "The Demons in the *Book of Jubilees*." In *Demonology of Israelite-Jewish and Early Christian Literature in Context of Their Environment*, edited by Armin Lange et al., 339–65. Tübingen: Mohr/Siebeck, 2003.

————. *Enoch and the Growth of an Apocalyptic Tradition*. Catholic Biblical Quarterly Monograph Series 16. Washington, DC: Catholic Biblical Association, 1984.

Veltri, Giuseppe. *Magie und Halakha: Ansätze zu einem empirischen Wissenschaftsbegriff im spätantiken und frühmittelalterlichen Judentum*. Texte und Studien zum antiken Judentum 62. Tübingen: Mohr/Siebeck, 1997.

Vermes, Geza. *Jesus the Jew: A Historian's Reading of the Gospels*. 1973. Reprint, Philadelphia: Fortress, 1981.

Vlahogiannis, Nicholas. "'Curing' Disability." In *Health in Antiquity*, edited by Helen King, 180–91. London: Routledge, 2005.

Wallis, R. T. "The Spiritual Importance of Not Knowing." In *Classical Mediterranean Spirituality, Egyptian, Greek, Roman*, edited by A. H. Armstrong, 460–80. World Spirituality 15. New York: Crossroad, 1986.

Wainwright, Elaine. "Of Dogs and Women." In *Miracles Revisited: New Testament Miracle Stories and Their Concepts of Reality*, edited by Stefan Alkier and Annette Weissenrieder, 55–69. SBIR 2. Berlin: de Gruyter, 2013.

————. *Women Healing/Healing Women: The Genderisation of Healing in Early Christianity*. Bible World. London: Equinox, 2006.

Watson, Duane F., ed. *Miracle Discourse in the New Testament*. Atlanta: Society of Biblical Literature, 2012.

————. "Miracle Discourse in the Pauline Epistles: The Role of Resurrection and Rhetoric." In *Miracle Discourse in the New Testament*, edited by Duane F. Watson, 189–96. Atlanta: Society of Biblical Literature, 2012.

Wax, Murray, and Rosalie Wax. "The Notion of Magic." *Current Anthropology* 4 (1963) 495–518.

Webb, Robert L. "John the Baptist and His Relationship to Jesus." In *Studying the Historical Jesus: Evaluations of the State of Current Research*, edited by Bruce Chilton and Craig A. Evans, 179–229. New Testament Tools and Studies 19. Leiden: Brill, 1994.

————. *John the Baptizer and Prophet: A Socio-historical Study*. Sheffield: Sheffield Academic Press, 1991.

Wegner, Uwe. *Der Hauptmann von Kafarnaum: (MT 7,28a; 8,5–10.13 par LK 7,1–10): Ein Beitrag zur Q-Forschung*. WUNT 2/14. Tübingen: Mohr/Siebeck, 1985.

Weissenrieder, Annette. *Images of Illness in the Gospel of Luke: Insights of Ancient Medical Texts*. WUNT 2/164. Tübingen: Mohr/Siebeck, 2003.

Wills, Lawrence. *The Quest of the Historical Gospel: Mark, John and the Origins of the Gospel Genre*. London: Routledge, 1997.

Wilson, Bryan. *Magic and the Millennium: A Sociological Study of Religious Movements of Protest among Tribal and Third-World Peoples*. New York: Harper & Row, 1973.

————. *Religious Sects*. London: Weidenfeld & Nicolson, 1971.

————. *Sects and Society: A Sociological Study of Three Religious Groups in Britain*. London: Heinemann, 1961.

Wire, Antoinette Clark. *The Case for Mark Composed in Oral Performance*. BPCS 3. Eugene, OR: Cascade Books, 2011.

Wolf, Eric R. *Peasants*. Foundations of Modern Anthropology Series. Englewood Cliffs, NJ: Prentice-Hall, 1966.

Worsley, Peter. "Non-Western Medical Systems." *Annual Review of Anthropology* 11 (1982) 315–48.

————. *The Trumpet Shall Sound: A Study of "Cargo" Cults in Melanesia*. 1958. Reprint, New York: Schocken, 1987.

Wrede, William. *The Messianic Secret*. Translated by J. C. G. Greig. Library of Theological Translations. Cambridge: James Clarke, 1971.

————. *Das Messiasgeheimnis in den Evangelien*. Göttingen: Vandenhoeck & Ruprecht, 1901.

Wright, N. T. *Jesus and the Victory of God*. Christian Origins and the Question of God 2. Minneapolis: Fortress, 1997.

Yalman, Nur. "Magic." In *International Encyclopedia of the Social Sciences*, edited by David L. Sills, 9:521–27. New York: Macmillan, 1968.

Young, Allan. "The Anthropology of Illness and Sickness." *Annual Review of Anthropology* 11 (1982) 257–85.

Zachman, Randall C. "The Meaning of Biblical Miracles in Light of the Modern Quest for Truth." In *Miracles in Jewish and Christian Antiquity: Imagining Truth*, edited by John C. Cavadini, 1–18. Notre Dame: University of Notre Dame Press, 1999.

Zanker, Paul. *The Power of Images in the Age of Augustus*. Ann Arbor: University of Michigan Press, 1988.

Index

African peoples, spirit possession among, 110–17, 194, 200–203
approach to illness and healing more comprehensive, holistic, 97–98, 102–7, 447–49
"apocalypticism" (modern scholarly construct), 3, 9, 142–43, 183, 186–87, 280–81
Asclepios (god of healing), 166–68
assemblies, village. *See* village assemblies (=synagogues)

Beelzebul, charge and refutation, 280–85, 328–33, 365–67, 402
Bible translations, 12, 82–85, 158, 183, 256
  distort portrayals of Jesus' healings, 7, 45, 82–85, 158, 183, 450–51
blessings and curses (in Mosaic covenant), 171–75
Bultmann, Rudolf, 17, 37, 394–95

"Christianity," as a synthetic concept, 236–37, 249, 342–43, 356, 433
Clement of Alexandria, 54, 76, 229
collective memory, 12, 241, 341–42, 386, 448–49. *See also* Israelite tradition/social memory

common memory of Jesus-in-interaction, 12, 386, 436, 446, 448–49
communications media (ancient) lines of new research on, 214–28, 447–49
confrontation in the temple, 304–6, 374–75, 408–9
conquest(s), 125
  effects of, 8, 126, 133–35, 398, 414, 450, 457, 483
  and illnesses, 126, 483
covenant, Mosaic, 9, 130, 171–75, 265, 318
covenant renewal, 1–2, 265, 302–3, 306, 317–20, 352–56, 373, 389–90, 394–95, 406
  declaration of deliverance in transformation of, 318, 353, 394–95
  demands, commandments in, 130, 144, 318–19, 353–55
  reenacted in performative speech, 319–20, 353–56
covenantal community, 1–2, 265, 285, 317–20, 352–56, 416–17, 426, 435
  sense of independence, 428–29
Crossan, John Dominic, 22, 64–69, 71, 73, 273–74, 282, 315, 406, 451, 455, 463, 474
culture
  elite, 10
  Hellenistic–Roman, 41–43
  Judean, 38–41

in Matthew, 27–30
in Luke, 30–31
in the "Source" of teachings,
31–32
missing in John, 32–33
rare in elite Judean sources, 182
story of Eleazar, 184–85
relational/ interactive, 466–68
as renewal of community,
479–81
trust, the enabling factor,
469–70
exorcism episodes, 268–71, 287–90,
295–97, 301–2, 369–70, 372,
392, 397–98, 400

families, 4, 8, 104, 122, 124, 129–30,
135–37, 203, 159, 416–17,
461–66, 481–83
disintegration of, 139, 147, 416
Fanon, Frantz, 101–2, 104–6, 140,
186, 193, 458
Foley, John Miles, 11, 225
adapting Foley's theory of
performance, 242–54, 312–
13, 339–40, 413–14, 448
"Fourth (Judean) Philosophy," 145–
46, 150, 154, 305, 331, 375
Funk, Robert, and Jesus Seminar,
20–22, 208, 276, 278

Gaius (Caligula, Roman emperor)
seeking divine honors, 148–50,
261, 263, 444
Galileans
distinguished from Judeans, 259
"laws of the Judeans" imposed
on, 132
no longer under Jerusalem rule,
137–38
peasant strike, 148–50
ruled by Herod Antipas, 137–38,
409–10
ruled by Jerusalem, 132–33,
445–46
under separate imperial
jurisdiction for centuries,
127–28

Galileans and Judeans, 123–30,
140–42, 146–56, 223
historical crisis for, 157
resistance to rulers, 146–56
Gospels
extreme variation in early
manuscripts, 231–32
related to performances,
232–23
as mere collections, 20
as products of "Easter faith," 18
rare references to written copies
of, 230
as sustained stories with
speeches, 208–9
(thought) unreliable as sources,
18
Gospel stories, 6
addressed to ordinary people,
235
as ancient stories, 211
composition of, 234–41
continuing performances of,
229–30
pluriformity in, 230–34
cultivated in oral performance,
228–30
fit their historical contexts,
211–12
as historical stories, 211
narrative criticism of, 209–10
overall stories more consistent
than sayings/anecdotes, 233
rooted in collective social
memory, 241
as sources (for Jesus' mission), 3,
10, 33–34, 208–14
summary of, 212–13
Gospel stories in performance
as sources for Jesus' mission,
228–41, 447–49
hearing the stories in
performance, 241–53, 254,
310–12, 351–56
effects of stories in communities,
413–14